Scotland

HOTELS & GUEST HOUSES

Published by the Scottish Tourist Board
P.O. Box 705, Edinburgh EH4 3EU

CHAIRMAN'S WELCOME

This guide is intended to help you take the first steps on what I know will be an unforgettable journey — a holiday in Scotland.

This guide to Hotel and Guest House accommodation will assist you in getting the most from this magnificent country. It is not my purpose here to tell you about the history, the heritage, the scenery, the people, the places and the activities. They are yours to discover.

I believe that whether you are a first time visitor or one of the many who return again and again, you will enjoy an experience that is incomparable anywhere in the world.

We have 172 Tourist Information Centres, where you can find people who will introduce you to the secrets and attractions of their area.

In the following pages I would like to highlight the range and quality of accommodation available to you during your visit to Scotland.

I would particularly commend to you the establishments in this guide which have been inspected and "graded" by the Scottish Tourist Board. They are colour coded in blue to draw to your attention the quality and level of facilities on offer.

I hope that your visit leaves you and your companions with memories that will bring you back to Scotland. If you do, you can always be sure that a warm welcome awaits you.

Ian Grant
Chairman

ABOUT THIS BOOK

For more than thirty years **Where to Stay** has been the Scottish Tourist Board's official guide to holiday accommodation in Scotland. It is recognised as the most comprehensive of its kind and is revised annually. Hotels, guest houses and university accommodation in all parts of Scotland are listed here in alphabetical order under the name of the place where they are situated, or, in the case of isolated countryside locations, under the nearest town or village.

If you are looking for accommodation in a particular area, the map section on pages xxv to xxx will enable you to identify locations.

Telephone numbers. The telephone number, exchange name and dialling code (in brackets) are given immediately below the address. The dialling code applies to calls made anywhere in the UK except for local calls. If in doubt, call the operator by dialling 100.

Telephone Dialling Codes. There are several changes to telephone dialling codes throughout Scotland this year. Where possible we have printed the most up-to-date codes, but some may have changed since going to print.

If you are having difficulty contacting an establishment, phone British Telecom directory enquiries on 192 and they will be happy to advise you of the correct number.

Map References. These are given against each place name listed in the guide. The first figure refers to the map number, the latter two figures give the grid reference.

DISABLED VISITORS

Many places listed in this book welcome disabled visitors. Those which have been inspected under the Scottish Tourist Board's Grading and Classification Scheme have their access facilities shown thus:

&   Access for wheelchair users without assistance
&A   Access for wheelchair users with assistance
&P   Access for ambulant disabled
&R   Access for residents only

It is always advisable to telephone the establishment in advance for further information.

Details of the criteria used for these symbols are shown on page 380. Further details from STB.

The undernoted organisations are also able to provide further information and advice:–
Disability Scotland
Information Dept
Princes House
5 Shandwick Place
EDINBURGH EH2 4RG
Tel: 031-229 8632

Holiday Care Service
2 Old Bank Chambers
Station Road
HORLEY
Surrey RH6 9HW
Tel: Horley (02934) 74535

BOOKING

It is always advisable to book accommodation in advance. This applies particularly during Easter and July and August.

Your travel agent will always be delighted to help you and to take care of your travel arrangements.

For those visitors who have not booked their accommodation in advance, Tourist Information Centres across Scotland provide a very useful accommodation booking service. For more details see page xiv.

There are about 173 Tourist Information Centres in Scotland, a list of which is given on pages xv to xxiv. All operate the Book a Bed Ahead scheme and local accommodation booking, while many operate an advance reservations service in addition. Tourist Information Centres are always glad to help with any accommodation problems.

RESERVATIONS

Accommodation should be booked directly through the hotel or guest house, through a travel agent or through a Tourist Information Centre. While the Scottish Tourist Board can give advice and information about any aspect of holidays in Scotland, it is *not* in a position to arrange accommodation or to make reservations.

ABOUT THIS BOOK

Accepting accommodation by telephone or in writing means you have entered into a legally binding contract with the proprietor of the establishment. A deposit is usually requested in order to secure your booking. This deposit does not necessarily represent compensation for the loss of a booking, and should you cancel or fail to take up the accommodation, for whatever reason, the proprietor may request further compensation. You should always check cancellation terms in advance and, if you must cancel a booking, advise the management immediately. We strongly advise taking out a holiday insurance policy to cover any such eventuality.

COMPLAINTS

Any complaints or criticisms about individual establishments should be taken up immediately with the management. In most cases the problems can be dealt with satisfactorily, thus avoiding any prolonged unhappiness during your stay.

If this procedure fails to remedy the grievance to your satisfaction, and particularly where serious complaints are concerned, please write giving full details to the local Area Tourist Board (see pages xv-xxv) or to the Customer Liaison Department at the Scottish Tourist Board where appropriate.

VALUE ADDED TAX (VAT)

Please note that VAT is calculated by establishments for this publication at a rate of $17^{1}/_{2}\%$. Any subsequent changes in this rate will affect the price you will be charged.

PRICES

The prices of accommodation, services and facilities stated in this guide are based on information received from the relevant advertisers. To the best of the Board's knowledge the information received was correct at the time of going to press. The Board can accept no responsibility for any errors or omissions.

To make this guide available at the earliest possible and practical time for 1994, the information received has had to be submitted well in advance of the 1994 holiday season. The prices stated are therefore not guaranteed to be the prices that will be charged throughout the holiday season. The prices are estimates at the time of going to press of the prices that establishments expect to apply but are subject to change without further notice. As there may have been amendments to prices, you should check with the establishment before making a booking or otherwise relying on the information.

Subject to the proviso that they are estimates and subject to change as stated above, the prices quoted in this guide are per person and normally represent the minimum (low season) and/or the maximum (high season) charges expected to apply to the majority of rooms in the establishment and include service charges, if any, and Value Added Tax as applicable. In addition, prices often vary according to season and are usually lower outside the peak holiday weeks. In a few cases where breakfast is normally charged separately, the rates quoted include this charge; it is normally for full breakfast, but as some establishments only provide Continental breakfast, this should be checked at the time of booking. In many cases, double/twin bedded rooms can accommodate families; the availability of these and of family rooms is shown, along with other details.

There is a statutory requirement for establishments to display overnight accommodation charges. When you arrive at the place you are going to stay it is in your interests to check prices.

September 1993

Your key to a

When you're choosing your holiday from home, quality and comfort are too important to leave to chance.

That's why, since 1985, STB has been annually inspecting hotels, guest houses and bed & breakfasts, defining the standards that our visitors expect and helping owners and operators meet those standards. Serviced accommodation all over the country – from the simplest to the most sophisticated is GRADED for quality and CLASSIFIED for its facilities.

Here's how it works
Look out for the blue oval plaques displayed by members of the GRADING and CLASSIFICATION Scheme.

The centre panel of the plaque tells you whether the establishment is APPROVED (an acceptable standard), COMMENDED (offering a good standard), HIGHLY COMMENDED (offering a very good standard) or DELUXE (offering an excellent standard).

The GRADES are awarded by the STB inspectors once they have checked all the important factors that contribute to quality in an establishment. Just as you would, they look for clean, comfortable surroundings, well furnished and heated. They sample meals, sleep in the beds and talk to staff. Like you, they appreciate atmosphere and a friendly smile of welcome.

great holiday!

The lower section of the plaque displays the CROWN Classification, denoting the range of facilities and services on offer. From a basic LISTED, up to 5 CROWNS can be added. The criteria are cumulative and must be provided in full up to the level of the CROWNS displayed.

The following table gives an indication of some of the facilities to be expected at each level. For a full list of all CROWN Classification criteria, contact:
STB, 23 Ravelston Terrace, Edinburgh EH4 3EU.
Tel: 031 332 2423.

	Listed	1	2	3	4	5
Clean, comfortable accommodation	•	•	•	•	•	•
Adequate heating at no extra charge	•	•	•	•	•	•
Breakfast	•	•	•	•	•	•
Wash basin in bedroom or in private bathroom		•	•	•	•	•
Bedroom key provided		•	•	•	•	•
Shared lounge area available		•	•	•	•	•
Colour TV in bedrooms or in guests' lounge			•	•	•	•
20% of bedrooms with private facilities			•	•	•	•
Early morning tea/coffee available			•	•	•	•
Hot evening meal until 7.00pm				•	•	•
50% of bedrooms ensuite				•	•	•
24-hour access available to registered guests				•	•	•
Radio, colour TV and telephone in all bedrooms					•	•
Room service of drinks and snacks between 7.00am-11.00pm					•	•
All bedrooms ensuite with bath and shower						•
At least 1 suite and range of room services						•
Restaurant open for breakfast, lunch and dinner						•

In 1993 STB introduced a Lodge Classification. Here you will find 100% ensuite bedrooms, dining facilities on site or nearby but restricted ancillary services.

Over 3,300 serviced establishments, 38,000 bedrooms, are members of the Grading and Classification Scheme and they are to be found in all parts of Scotland.

BOOKING DIRECT? BOOKING THROUGH THE TOURIST INFORMATION CENTRE? REMEMBER ALWAYS CHECK THE GRADING AND CROWN CLASSIFICATION OF YOUR CHOSEN ESTABLISHMENT.

FRANÇAIS

OÙ SE LOGER EN ECOSSE

Bienvenue en Ecosse!

Voici le guide touristique officiel, publié par l'Office écossais du tourisme Revu chaque année, ce guide est reconnu depuis trente ans comme le plus complet en son genre. Des hôtels, pensions de famille et résidences universitaires de toutes les régions de l'Ecosse y sont classés selon l'ordre alphabétique des localités. Sauf indication contraire, l'indicatif téléphonique est celui de la localité.

Au moment de mettre sous presse, il ne nous est pas possible de donner des prix définitifs; il est vivement conseillé aux visiteurs de demander confirmation des prix lorsqu'ils effectuent la réservation.

Nous avons signalé à l'attention des gourmets les hôtels qui offrent les spécialités de la cuisine écossaise (recettes écossaises traditionnelles à base de produits écossais de haute qualité).

NB. L'Office écossais du tourisme (Scottish Tourist Board) décline toute responsabilité en cas d'erruers ou d'omissions.

AVERTISSEMENT: CHIENS ETC.

Il est rappelé aux visiteurs étrangers que l'introduction d'animaux domestiques en Grande-Bretagne est soumise à une réglementation très stricte, qui prévoit une longue période de quarantaine. Etant donné le danger de propagation du virus rabique, des peines très sévères sont prévues pour toute infraction aux réglements.

SUR LES ROUTES D'ECOSSE

Veillez à attacher votre ceinture de sécurité, si votre voiture en est munie. Le port de la ceinture est obligatoire en Grande Bretagne.

La légende des symboles se trouve au volet de la couverture, qui fait aussi office de signet.

Logez a l'enseigne de l'hospitalité Ecossaise voir page 382.

DEUTSCH

WO ÜBERNACHTET MAN IN SCHOTTLAND

Willkommen in Schottland!

Dieses Buch ist der offizielle Führer des Schottischen Touristenbüros. Seit dreißig Jahren wird dieses Buch als das umfassendste seiner Art anerkannt. Es wird jedes Jahr auf den neuesten Stand gebracht. Hotels, Gasthäuser und Unterbringung in den Universitäten in allen Teilen Schottlands sind hier nach Ortsnamen in alphabetischer Reihenfolge aufgeführt. Die jeweilige Vorwahlnummer ist unter dem Ortsnamen zu finden, außer, wenn sie extra angegeben ist.

Zu Beginn der Drucklegung dieses Buches ist es noch nicht möglich, feste Preise anzugeben, und Besuchern wird daher geraten, sich nach den Tarifen zu erkundigen, wenn sie Buchungen vornehmen.

Das Schottische Touristenbüro (Scottish Tourist Board) kann keine Verantwortung für eventuelle Fehler oder Auslassung von Preisen und Einrichtungen übernehmen.

Als weitere Hilfe haben wir die echte Privatpensionen gekennzeichnet, die echte schottische Küche – Taste of Scotland – anbieten. Das bedeutet, daß hier traditionell schottische Rezepte verwandt werden unter Benutzung schottischer Produkte von hoher Qualität.

HUNDE

Das Mitbringen von Tieren jeder Art aus dem Ausland ist wegen Tollwutgefahr strengstens untersagt. Die Übertretung dieses Gesetzes wird mit hohen Strafen belegt.

AUTOFAHREN IN SCHOTTLAND

Schnallen Sie sich immer an! Es wird nun zur Pflicht. (Vorausgesetzt, Ihr Auto ist mit Sicherheitsgurt ausgestattet.)

Die Zeichenerklärungen befinden sich im eingeklebten Faltblatt am Ende des Buches.

Übernachten sie dort, wo sie das Zeichen für echt Schottische Gastlichkeit Sehen Seihe Seite 384.

YOUR HOLIDAY IN SCOTLAND

USEFUL INFORMATION ABOUT SCOTLAND

TRAVEL

Bookings for rail, sea and air travel to Scotland and within Scotland should be made through your travel agent, or directly to British Rail, airlines and ferry companies. The Scottish Tourist Board will be glad to give you information but cannot make your bookings for you.

Seats may be booked in advance on the main long-distance coaches, aircraft and for berths and cabins in the steamers to the islands. Sleeping berths on trains should always be booked well in advance. It is necessary to book seats for 'extended' coach tours and also for day coach outings operated from most holiday and touring centres.

Car hire bookings should also be made in advance wherever possible, especially for July and August. Taxis are readily available in Edinburgh, Glasgow, and other major centres at controlled charges. Taxis are generally available in most communities, but in smaller, less populous areas charges may vary considerably.

DRIVING

The 'Rules of the Road' are the same in Scotland as in the rest of the U.K. While there is limited motorway mileage in Scotland, the roads are uniformly good.

DRIVING ON SINGLE-TRACK ROADS

A few stretches of road are still single track, mainly in the north-west and on some of the islands. They demand a careful technique. When two vehicles approach from opposite directions, the car which first reaches a passing place should pull in or stop opposite the passing place to allow safe passage. Passing places are also used to let another vehicle overtake. It is an offence to hold up a following vehicle and not give way. It could, for example, be the local doctor on his or her way to an accident. At all times consideration should be shown for other road users. Finally, please note that passing places should never be used as parking places.

When touring in the far north and west particularly, remember that petrol stations are comparatively few, and distances between them may be considerable. This is particularly true if your car uses unleaded petrol. Some petrol stations close on Sundays. Fill your tank in good time, and keep it as full as possible.

Remember, it is now law that the driver and front passenger must wear seat belts, and in the back where they are fitted.

PUBLIC HOLIDAYS

The Bank Holidays which are also general holidays in England do not apply in Scotland. Most Bank Holidays apply to banks and to some professional and commercial offices only, although Christmas Day and New Year's Day are usually taken as holidays by everyone. Scottish banks are closed in 1994 on 1 and 4 January, 1 April, 2 and 30 May, 1 August and 27 and 28 December. In place of the general holidays, Scottish cities and towns normally have a Spring Holiday and an Autumn Holiday. The dates of these holidays vary from place to place, but they are almost invariably on a Monday.

MONEY

Currency, coinage and postal rates in Scotland are the same as in the rest of the U.K. Scotland differs from England in that Scottish banks issue their own notes. These are acceptable in England, at face value, as are Bank of England notes in Scotland. Main banks are open during the following hours:
Monday-Friday 0915/0930 -1600/1645 (depending on bank). Most banks are open later on a Thursday evening (until 1730). In smaller towns and villages branches may close over the lunchtime period, usually from 1230 -1330.

Some city centre banks are open daily 0930 -1530 and on Saturdays. In rural areas, banks post their hours clearly outside and travelling banks call regularly.

USEFUL INFORMATION ABOUT SCOTLAND

SHOPPING

The normal shopping hours in Scotland are 0900-1730, although bakeries, dairies and newsagents open earlier. Many shops have an early closing day (1300) each week, but the actual day varies from place to place and in cities from district to district.

Many city centre shops also stay open late on one evening each week.

A TASTE OF SCOTLAND

Guides are indispensable tools in planning a holiday or even a meal or overnight stop. There are thousands of eating establishments and nobody on the move has time to try out a large selection until a suitable one is found. In Scotland, therefore, it is natural to turn to the Taste of Scotland Guide for help. Within it are listed a wide range of highly recommended hotels and restaurants, ranging from five star hotels to farmhouses. All have been inspected and selected because they meet the exacting requirements of the Taste of Scotland Scheme. And the choice is wide so that there will be something for everyone at whatever price level they seek. The prime concern of the Scheme is to concentrate on aspects of hospitality and welcome, but particularly to ensure that food is of the highest possible standard compatible with the prices charged. To this end there is strong emphasis on the use of the fresh local produce for which Scotland is famed. Food prepared from the pick of the crop and presented with panache.

For convenience, however, the Scottish Tourist Board's classification and grading assessments are also listed, where applicable. Many establishments feature regularly or occasionally some of the mouth-watering regional specialities which are of particular interest to the visitor. The 1994 edition of the **Taste of Scotland Guide** lists many new members, and has dropped several which have failed to maintain standards or have changed ownership. The Guide may be obtained direct from Taste of Scotland, 33 Melville Street, Edinburgh EH3 7JF. (£4.50 including post and packing). Also available from Scottish Tourist Board in London, and from many Tourist Information Centres and bookshops and through the British Travel Centre in London. Use it to help plan your travels – and maximise your enjoyment.

LICENSING LAWS

Currently in Scotland, the hours that public houses and hotel bars are open to serve drinks are the same all over the country. 'Pubs' are open from 1100 to 1430 and from 1700 to about 2300 hours, Monday to Saturday inclusive and most are now licensed to open on Sundays. In addition, some establishments may have obtained extended licences for afternoon or late night opening.

Hotel bars have the same hours as 'pubs', and are open on Sundays from 1230 to 1430 and 1830 to 2300. Residents in licensed hotels may have drinks served at any time. Some restaurants and hotels have extended licences allowing them to serve drinks with meals until 0100 in the morning. Persons under the age of 18 are not allowed to drink in licensed premises.

CHURCHES

The established Church of Scotland is Presbyterian, but the Roman Catholic and other denominations have very considerable numbers of adherents. The Episcopal Church of Scotland is in full communion with the Church of England, and uses a similar form of worship. In the far north and west of Scotland, particularly in the islands, many people belong to the Free Church of Scotland and appreciate it when their views on the Sabbath as a day when there should be no recreational or other unnecessary activity are respected by visitors.

Times of services of the various denominations are usually intimated on hotel notice boards, as well as outside the churches and, of course, visitors are always welcome.

USEFUL INFORMATION ABOUT SCOTLAND

COMING FROM OVERSEAS?

Visitors to Scotland from overseas require to observe the same regulations as for other parts of the U.K. As a general rule they must have a valid passport, and, in certain cases, visas issued by British Consular authorities overseas: check with a local Travel Agent, or where appropriate, the overseas offices of the British Tourist Authority.

Currency: Overseas visitors who require information about the import and export of currency, cars, or other goods, on personal purchases and belongings, shopping concessions, etc., should consult a Travel Agent or Bank or the overseas offices of the B.T.A.

Driving: Motorists coming from overseas who are members of a motoring organisation in their own country may obtain from them full details of the regulations for importing cars, motor cycles, etc. for holiday and touring purposes into the U.K. They can drive in Britain on a current Driving Licence from their own country, or with an international Driving Permit, for a maximum period of 12 months. Otherwise, a British Driving Licence must be obtained: until the Driving Test is passed it is essential to be accompanied by a driver with a British Licence.

Seat belts: Drivers and front seat passengers must wear safety belts while driving in Britain, by law. Rear seat passengers must also wear seat belts, where fitted.

VAT: Value Added Tax, currently charged at 17.5% on many goods, can sometimes be reclaimed by overseas visitors who buy items for export. Visitors should ask the shopkeeper about the retail export schemes before making a purchase, and will be required to fill in special forms.

SCOTTISH YOUTH HOSTELS

There are over 80 youth hostels in Scotland offering simple, low-cost self catering accommodation to all people, but especially the young, Youth Hostels may be in a castle or in a mansion, or a timber building way out in the wild. All have dormitories, washrooms, common room and kitchen. Some hostels also offer accommodation for families with children under five. Telephone: (0786) 451181.

There are also over 35 hostels in Scotland for backpackers and independent travellers, telephone: (04562) 807.

PETS

Where pets are permitted, owners are asked to take responsibility for pets' behaviour. In particular, please keep dogs under control in the presence of farm animals. To identify those establishments which may accept pets, look out for the 🐾 symbol within the establishment entry. Please confirm the acceptance of your pet when making your booking.

RABIES

Britain is very concerned to prevent the spread of rabies. Strict quarantine regulations apply to animals brought into Britain from abroad and severe penalties are enforced if they are broken or ignored. Dogs and cats are subject to 6 months quarantine in an approved quarantine centre. Full details from the Department of Agriculture and Fisheries for Scotland, Chesser House, 500 Gorgie Road, Edinburgh EH1 3AW. The restrictions do not apply to animals from Eire, Northern Ireland, the Isle of Man or the Channel Islands.

SCOTLAND'S TOURIST AREAS

1. **THE LOWLANDS AND SOUTHERN UPLANDS**
2. **THE CENTRAL HIGHLANDS**
3. **THE NORTHERN HIGHLANDS AND ISLANDS**

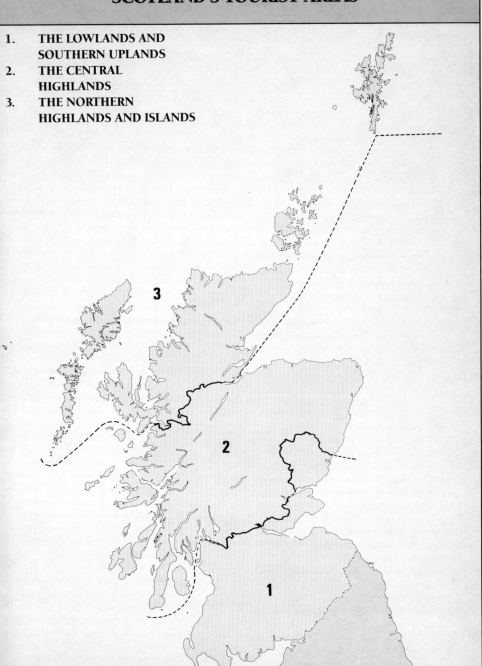

TOURIST INFORMATION CENTRES

Where you see the information [i] you are guaranteed a welcome by people who really know their country. Information Centres form a linked network which can guide you all around Scotland.

Among the wide range of services now available are:

- [i] Free information and advice on the local area, and on the whole of Scotland – events, routes, things to see and places to visit.

- [i] Accommodation booking – whether locally, or in any other part of Scotland. A small fee will be charged for national reservations and may be charged for local bookings. Ask for Scottish Tourist Board Graded accommodation for a guarantee of high quality and a warm welcome.

- [i] Maps and books – guide books, reference books, and often a wide range of Scottish literature for your holiday reading.

- [i] Tickets for events and activities, both local and national – season tickets for a wide range of attractions, including Historic Scotland and National Trust for Scotland properties.

- [i] Local excursions, tours and travel tickets.

- [i] Many major Information Centres now offer a bureau de change service.

- [i] Films, souvenirs and local craft items.

- ✉ This symbol indicates those information centres which will respond to written enquiries.

WHERE TO FIND OUT MORE ABOUT SCOTLAND

Scottish Tourist Board, Central Information.
Tel: 031-332 2433

Also, from August 1993:
24-hr Scottish Tourist Board Information Line.
Tel: 0891 666465.
(Calls are charged at 36p a minute cheap rate, 48p a minute at all other times)

In England, the following centres provide full information on Scotland:

Scottish Tourist Board London Office
19 Cockspur Street, Trafalgar Square
London SW1Y 5BL
Tel: (071) 930 8661

Southwaite Tourist Information Centre
M6 Service Area (North Bound)
Southwaite, by Carlisle CA4 0NS
Tel: (069) 747 3445

Tyne Commission Quay
Tourist Information Centre
Ferry Terminal, North Shields
by Newcastle upon Tyne NE29 6EN
Tel: (091) 257 9800

Gretna Gateway to Scotland
M74 Service Area
CA6 5HQ
Tel: (0461) 38500

1. THE LOWLANDS AND SOUTHERN UPLANDS

Angus Tourist Board

ARBROATH
Market Place
Arbroath
Angus DD11 1HR
Tel: (0241) 72609
Jan-Dec

BRECHIN
St Ninians Place
Brechin
Angus
Tel: (0356) 623050
Apr-early Oct

CARNOUSTIE
The Library
High Street
Carnoustie
Tel: (0241) 52258
Apr-early Oct

FORFAR
The Library
West High Street
Forfar
Tel: (0307) 467876
Apr-early Oct

KIRRIEMUIR
17 High Street
Kirriemuir
Forfar
Tel: (0575) 74097
Apr-early Oct

MONTROSE
The Library
High Street
Montrose
Tel: (0674) 72000
Apr-early Oct

Ayrshire Tourist Board

ARDROSSAN &
Ferry Terminal Building
The Harbour, Ardrossan
Ayrshire
Tel: (0294) 601063
Apr-Oct

AYR ✉
39 Sandgate
Ayr KA7 1BG
Tel: (0292) 284196
Jan-Dec

GIRVAN
Bridge Street, Girvan
Ayrshire
Tel: (0465) 4950
Apr-Oct

KILMARNOCK ✉
62 Bank Street
Kilmarnock
Ayrshire
Tel: (0563) 39090
Jan-Dec

LARGS ✉
Promenade, Largs
Ayrshire KA30 8BG
Tel: (0475) 673765
Jan-Dec

MAUCHLINE
National Burns Memorial Tower
Kilmarnock Road, Mauchline
Ayrshire
Tel: (0290) 51916
Jan-Dec

MILLPORT &
Stuart Street, Millport
Isle of Cumbrie
Tel: (0475) 530753
Easter-Sept

PRESTWICK
Boydfield Gardens
Prestwick
Ayrshire
Tel: (0292) 79946
June-Sept

TROON
Municipal Buildings
South Beach
Troon
Ayrshire
Tel: (0292) 317696
Easter-Sept

City of Dundee Tourist Board

DUNDEE ✉ &
4 City Square
Dundee DD1 3BA
Tel: (0382) 27723
Jan-Dec

When you visit a Tourist Information Centre you are guaranteed a welcome by people who really know their country.

For information, maps, holiday reading, accommodation bookings and much more, look for the information *i*

Clyde Valley Tourist Board

ABINGTON
Welcome Break Service Area
Junction 13, M74
Abington
Tel: (08642) 436
Easter-Oct

BIGGAR &
155 High Street
Biggar
Lanarkshire
Tel: (0899) 21066
Easter-Oct

HAMILTON &
Road Chef Services
M74 Northbound
Hamilton
Tel: (0698)285590
Jan-Dec

LANARK ✉ &
Horsemarket
Ladyacre Road
Lanark ML11 7LQ
Tel: (0555) 661661
Jan-Dec

COATBRIDGE
The Time Capsule
Buchanan Street
Coatbridge
Tel: (0236) 431133
Apr-Oct

MOTHERWELL ✉
Motherwell Library
Hamilton Road
Motherwell
Tel: (0698) 251311
Jan-Dec

STRATHAVEN &
Town Mill Arts Centre
Stonehouse Road
Strathaven
Tel: (0357) 29650
Apr-Oct

Dumfries and Galloway Tourist Board

CASTLE DOUGLAS ✉
Markethill
Castle Douglas
Tel: (0556) 2611
Easter-Oct

DALBEATTIE ✉
Town Hall
Dalbeattie
Tel: (0556) 610117
Easter-early Oct

DUMFRIES ✉
Whitesands
Dumfries
Tel: (0387) 53862
Jan-Dec

GATEHOUSE OF FLEET ✉
Car Park
Gatehouse of Fleet
Tel: (0557) 814212
Easter-Oct

GRETNA GREEN ✉ &
Old Blacksmith's Shop
Gretna Green
Tel: (0461) 37834
Easter-Oct

GRETNA – Gateway to Scotland
M74 Service Area
CA6 5HQ
Tel: (0461) 38500
Jan-Dec

KIRKCUDBRIGHT ✉ &
Harbour Square
Kirkcudbright
Tel: (0557) 30494
Easter-Oct

LANGHOLM ✉
High Street
Langholm
Tel: (03873) 80976
Easter-early Oct

MOFFAT ✉ &
Churchgate
Moffat
Tel: (0683) 20620
Easter-Oct

NEWTON STEWART ✉
Dashwood Square
Newton Stewart
Tel: (0671) 2431
Easter-Oct

SANQUHAR ✉ &
Tolbooth, High Street
Sanquhar
Tel: (0659) 50185
Easter-early Oct

STRANRAER ✉ &
Port Rodie Car Park
Stranraer
Tel: (0776) 2595
Easter-Oct

East Lothian Tourist Board

DUNBAR ✉ &
143 High Street
Dunbar
Tel: (0368) 63353
Jan-Dec

MUSSELBURGH ✉ &
Brunton Hall
Musselburgh
East Lothian
Tel: (031) 665 6597
June-end Sept

NORTH BERWICK ✉ &
Quality Street
North Berwick
Tel: (0620) 2197
Jan-Dec

OLDCRAIGHALL ✉ &
Granada Service Area
Oldcraighall
Musselburgh
Tel: (031) 653 6172
Jan-Dec

PENCRAIG ✉
A1
By East Linton
East Lothian
Tel: (0620) 860063
Apr-end Sept

Edinburgh Tourist Board

EDINBURGH AND SCOTLAND
INFORMATION CENTRE &
3 Princes Street
Edinburgh EH2 2QP
Tel: (031) 557 1700
Jan-Dec

EDINBURGH AIRPORT &
Tourist Information Desk
Edinburgh Airport
Edinburgh EH12 9DN
Tel: (031) 333 2167
Jan-Dec

Forth Valley Tourist Board

BO'NESS ✉
Hamilton's Cottage, by Bo'ness
Station
Union Road
Bo'ness
Tel: (0506) 826626
May-Sept

FORTH ROAD BRIDGE ✉
Queensferry Lodge Hotel
St Margarets Head
North Queensferry
Tel: (0383) 417759
Jan-Dec

DUNFERMLINE ✉
Abbot House
Maygate
Dunfermline
Tel: (0383) 720999
Easter-Sept

KINCARDINE BRIDGE ✉
Pine 'N' Oak Lay-by
Airth
By Falkirk
Tel: (0324) 417759
Easter-Sept

FALKIRK ✉
The Steeple
High Street
Falkirk
Tel: (0324) 20244
Jan-Dec

LINLITHGOW ✉
Burgh Halls
The Cross
Linlithgow
Tel: (0506) 844600
Jan-Dec

Greater Glasgow Tourist Board

GLASGOW ✉
35 St Vincent Place
Glasgow G1 2ER
Tel: (041) 204 4400
Jan-Dec

GOUROCK
Pierhead
Gourock
Tel: (0475) 39467
Mar-Oct

GLASGOW AIRPORT
Tourist Information Desk
Glasgow Airport
Paisley PA3 2ST
Tel: (041) 848 4440
Jan-Dec

PAISLEY
Town Hall
Abbey Close
Paisley PA1 1JS
Tel: (041) 889 0711
Jan-Dec

Kirkcaldy District Council

BURNTISLAND ✉
4 Kirkgate
Burntisland
Tel: (0592) 872667
Jan-Dec

KIRKCALDY ✉
19 Whytescauseway
Tel: (0592) 267775
Jan-Dec

GLENROTHES
Lyon Square
Kingdom Centre
Glenrothes, Fife
Tel: (0592) 610784
Jan-Dec

LEVEN ✉
South Street
Leven
Tel: (0333) 429464
Jan-Dec

Midlothian Tourism Association

BONNYRIGG ♿
Polton Street
Bonnyrigg
Midlothian
Tel: (031) 660 6814
Jan-Dec

PENICUIK
The Library
3 Bellman's Road
Penicuik
Midlothian
Tel: (0968) 673286/672340
Jan-Dec

DALKEITH ♿
The Library
White Hart Street
Dalkeith
Midlothian
Tel: (031) 660 6818
Jan-Dec

St Andrews and North East Fife Tourist Board

ANSTRUTHER
Scottish Fisheries Museum
Anstruther KY10
Tel: (0333) 311073
Easter, May-Sept

CUPAR ♿
Fluthers Car Park
Cupar
Fife KY15
Tel: (0334) 52874

CRAIL
Museum & Heritage Centre
Marketgate
Crail KY10
Tel: (0333) 50869
June-Sept

ST ANDREWS ✉
78 South Street
St Andrews KY16 9JX
Tel: (0334) 72021
Jan-Dec

Scottish Borders Tourist Board

COLDSTREAM ✉ ♿
Henderson Park
Coldstream
Tel: (0890) 882607
Apr-Oct

HAWICK ✉
Common Haugh
Hawick TD9
Tel: (0450) 72547
Apr-Oct

MELROSE ✉ ♿
Priorwood Gardens
Melrose
Kelso TD6
Tel: (089682) 2555
Apr-Oct

EYEMOUTH ✉ ♿
Auld Kirk
Manse Road
Eyemouth TD14
Tel: (08907) 50678
Apr-Oct

JEDBURGH ✉ ♿
Murrays Green
Jedburgh TD8 6BE
Tel: (0835) 863435
Jan-Dec

PEEBLES ✉ ♿
High Street, Peebles
Kelso
Tel: (0721) 720138
Apr-Oct

GALASHIELS ✉ ♿
Bank Street
Galashiels TD1
Tel: (0896) 55551
Apr-Oct

KELSO ✉ ♿
Turret House
Abbey Court
Kelso TD5 7AX
Tel: (0573) 223464
Apr-Oct

SELKIRK ✉ ♿
Halliwells House
Selkirk TD7
Tel: (0750) 20054
Apr-Oct

2. THE CENTRAL HIGHLANDS

Aviemore and Spey Valley Tourist Board

AVIEMORE ✉ ♿
Grampian Road
Aviemore
Inverness-shire
Tel: (0479) 810363
Jan-Dec

GRANTOWN-ON-SPEY ✉ ♿
High Street
Grantown-on-Spey
Morayshire
Tel: (0479) 2773
April-Oct

RALIA ✉ ♿
A9, Nr Newtonmore
Inverness-shire
Tel: (0540) 673253
Apr-Oct

CARRBRIDGE ✉
Main Street
Carrbridge
Inverness-shire
Tel: (0479) 84630
May-Sept

KINGUSSIE ✉
King Street
Kingussie
Tel: (0540) 661 297
May-Sept

Banff and Buchan Tourist Board

ADEN
Aden Country Park
Mintlaw AB4 8LD
Tel: (0771) 23037
Apr-Oct

FRASERBURGH
Saltoun Square
Fraserburgh AB4 5DA
Tel: (0346) 518315
Apr-Oct

TURRIFF
Swimming Pool Car Park
Queens Road
Turriff
Tel: (0888) 63001
Apr-Oct

BANFF ✉
Collie Lodge
Banff AB45 1AU
Tel: (0261) 812419
Apr-Oct

PETERHEAD
54 Broad Street
Peterhead AB4 6BX
Tel: (0779) 71904
Apr-Oct

City of Aberdeen Tourist Board

ABERDEEN
St Nicholas House
Broad Street
Aberdeen AB9 1DE
Tel: (0224) 632727
Jan-Dec

Bute and Cowal Tourist Board

DUNOON
7 Alexandra Parade
Dunoon PA23 8AB
Tel: (0369) 3785
Jan-Dec

Fort William and Lochaber Tourist Board

BALLACHULISH
Ballachulish
Argyll
Tel: (08552) 296
Apr-Oct

FORT WILLIAM
Cameron Square
Fort William
Tel: (0397) 703781
Jan-Dec

KILCHOAN
Argyll
Tel: (09723) 222
Apr-Sept

MALLAIG
Mallaig
Inverness-shire
Tel: (0687) 2170
Apr-Sept

SPEAN BRIDGE
Spean Bridge
Inverness-shire
Tel: (0397) 81576
Apr-Oct

STRONTIAN
Strontian
Argyll
Tel: (0967) 2131
May-Sept

Gordon District Tourist Board

ALFORD
Railway Museum
Station Yard
Alford AB3 8AD
Tel: (09755) 62052
Mid Apr-Oct

ELLON
Maket Street Car Park
Ellon AB4 8JD
Tel: (0358) 20730
Late March-Oct

HUNTLY
7A The Square
Huntly AB5 5AE
Tel: (0466) 792255
Mid Apr-Oct

INVERURIE
Town Hall
Market Place
Inverurie AB5 9SN
Tel: (0467) 20600
Mid Apr-Oct

Inverness, Loch Ness and Nairn Tourist Board

DAVIOT WOOD
A9
By Inverness
Tel: (0463) 772203
Apr-Oct

INVERNESS
Castle Wynd
Inverness IV1 1EZ
Tel: (0463) 234353
Jan-Dec

FORT AUGUSTUS
The Car Park
Fort Augustus
Tel: (0320) 6367
Apr-Oct

NAIRN
62 King Street
Nairn
Tel: (0667) 52753
Apr-Oct

Isle of Arran Tourist Board

BRODICK
The Pier
Brodick
Isle of Arran
Tel: (0770) 2140/2401
Jan-Dec

LOCHRANZA
The Pier
Lochranza
Isle of Arran
Tel: (0770) 83320
May-Oct

Kincardine and Deeside Tourist Board

ABOYNE
Ballater Road Car Park
Aboyne
Tel: (03398) 86060
Easter-Sept

BANCHORY
Bellfield Car Park
Banchory
Tel: (0330) 822000
Easter-end Oct

CRATHIE
Car Park
Crathie
Tel: (03397) 42414
May-Sept

BALLATER
Station Square
Ballater
Tel: (03397) 55306
Easter-end Oct

BRAEMAR
The Mews
Mar Road
Braemar
Tel: (03397) 41600
March-Nov
weekends in ski season

STONEHAVEN
66 Allardice Street
Stonehaven
Tel: (0569) 62806
Easter-Oct

Loch Lomond, Stirling and Trossachs Tourist Board

ABERFOYLE
Main Street
Aberfoyle
Perthshire FK8 3TH
Tel: (08772) 352
Apr-Oct

BALLOCH ✉ &
Balloch Road
Balloch
Dumbartonshire G83
Tel: (0389) 53533
March-Nov

CALLANDER ✉ &
Rob Roy & Trossachs Visitor Centre
Ancaster Square
Callander
Perthshire
Tel: (0877) 30342
March-Dec

DRYMEN
The Square
Tel: (0360) 60068
Jan-Dec

DUMBARTON ✉
A82 Northbound
Milton
Dumbarton
Tel: (0389) 42306
Apr-Oct

DUNBLANE ✉ &
Stirling Road
Dunblane
Stirlingshire FK15
Tel: (0786) 824428
May-Sept

HELENSBURGH ✉ &
The Clock Tower
Helensburgh
Dumbartonshire
Tel: (0436) 72642
Apr-Oct

KILLIN ✉ &
Main Street
Killin
Perthshire
Tel: (05672) 820254
Apr-Oct

STIRLING ✉ &
Dumbarton Road
Stirling FK8 2QQ
Tel: (0786) 75019
Jan-Dec

STIRLING – Pirnhall ✉ &
Pirnhall
By Stirling
Tel: (0786) 814111
March-Nov

TARBET – Loch Lomond ✉
Main Street
Tarbet
Dumbartonshire
Tel: (03012) 260
Apr-Oct

TILLICOULTRY ✉ &
Clock Mill
Upper Mill Street
Tillicoultry
FK13 6AX
Tel: (0259) 752176
Apr-Oct

TYNDRUM ✉ &
Main Street
Tyndrum
Perthshire FK20 8RY
Tel: (08384) 246
Apr-Oct

Moray Tourist Board

BUCKIE
Cluny Square
Buckie AB56 1AG
Tel: (0542) 34853
Mid May-Sept

CULLEN
20 Seafield Street
Cullen AB56 2SH
Tel: (0542) 40757
Mid May-Sept

DUFFTOWN
Clock Tower
The Square
Dufftown AB55 4AD
Tel: (0340) 20501
Easter-Oct

ELGIN ✉
17 High Street
Elgin IV30 1EG
Tel: (0343) 542666/543388
Jan-Dec

FORRES
Falconer Museum
Tolbooth Street
Forres IV36 0PH
Tel: (0309) 672938
Mid May-Oct

KEITH
Church Road
Keith AB55 3BR
Tel: (05422) 2634
Mid May-Sept

LOSSIEMOUTH
Station Park
Pitgaveny Street
Lossiemouth IV31 6NT
Tel: (034381) 814804
Mid May-mid Sept

TOMINTOUL
The Square
Tomintoul AB37 9ET
Tel: (08074) 580285
Easter-Oct

When you visit a Tourist Information Centre you are guaranteed a welcome by people who really know their country.

For information, maps, holiday reading, accommodation bookings and much more, look for the information *i*

Perthshire Tourist Board

ABERFELDY
The Square
Aberfeldy PH15 2DA
Tel: (0887) 820276
Jan-Dec

AUCHTERARDER
90 High Street
Auchterarder PH3 1BJ
Tel: (0764) 663450
Jan-Dec

BLAIRGOWRIE
26 Wellmeadow
Blairgowrie
Perthshire PH10 6AS
Tel: (0250) 872960/873701
from Nov 91

CRIEFF
Town Hall
High Street
Crieff PH7 3HU
Tel: (0764) 652578
Jan-Dec

DUNKELD
The Cross
Dunkeld
Perthshire PH8 0AN
Tel: (0350) 727688
from mid 92
March-Oct

KINROSS
Service Area Junction 6
M90
Kinross
Tel: (0577) 863680
Jan-Dec

PERTH
45 High Street
Perth PH1 5TJ
Tel: (0738) 38353
Jan-Dec

PERTH – Inveralmond
Inveralmond
A9 Western City By-pass
Perth
Tel: (0738) 38481
Easter-Oct

PITLOCHRY
22 Atholl Road
Pitlochry
Perthshire PH16 5BX
Tel: (0796) 472215/472751
Jan-Dec

West Highlands, and Islands of Argyll Tourist Board

BOWMORE
The Square
Bowmore
Isle of Islay
Tel: (049681) 254
Jan-Dec

CAMPBELTOWN
Mackinnon House
The Pier
Campbeltown
Tel: (0586) 552056
Jan-Dec

CRAIGNURE
The Pierhead
Craignure
Isle of Mull
Tel: (06802) 377
April-Oct

INVERARAY
Front Street
Inveraray
Argyll
Tel: (0499) 2063
Jan-Dec

LOCHGILPHEAD
Lochnell Street
Lochgilphead
Argyll
Tel: (0546) 602344
April-Oct

TARBERT
Harbour Street
Tarbert
Argyll
Tel: (0880) 820429
April-Oct

OBAN
Boswell House
Argyll Square
Oban
Tel: (0631) 63122
Jan-Dec

TOBERMORY
Main Street
Tobermory
Isle of Mull
Tel: (0688) 2182
Jan-Dec

3. THE NORTHERN HIGHLANDS AND ISLANDS

Caithness Tourist Board

JOHN O'GROATS
County Road
John O'Groats
Tel: (0955) 81373
Apr-Oct

THURSO
Riverside
Thurso
Tel: (0847) 62371
Apr-Oct

WICK
Whitechapel Road
Wick
Tel: (0955) 2596
Jan-Dec

Isle of Skye and South West Ross

BROADFORD
Car Park
Broadford
Isle of Skye
Tel: (0471822) 361
Apr-Oct

KYLE OF LOCHALSH
Car Park
Kyle of Lochalsh
Ross-shire
Tel: (0599) 4276
Apr-Oct

GLENSHIEL
Glenshiel
Kyle of Lochalsh
Ross-shire
Tel: (059981) 264
Apr-Sept

PORTREE
Meall House
Portree
Isle of Skye IV51 9BZ
Tel: (0478) 2137
Jan-Dec

Orkney Tourist Board

KIRKWALL
6 Broad Street
Kirkwall
Orkney
Tel: (0856) 872856
Jan-Dec

STROMNESS
Ferry Terminal Building
Stromness
Orkney
Tel: (0856) 850716
Jan-Dec

Ross and Cromarty Tourist Board

GAIRLOCH  ♿
Auchtercairn
Gairloch
Ross-shire
Tel: (0445) 2130
Jan-Dec

LOCHCARRON ♿
Main Street
Lochcarron
Ross-shire
Tel: (05202) 357
April-Oct

NORTH KESSOCK ✉ ♿
North Kessock
Ross-shire
Tel: (0463) 73505
Jan-Dec

STRATHPEFFER ♿
The Square
Strathpeffer
Ross-shire
Tel: (0997) 421415
Easter-Nov

ULLAPOOL
Shore Street
Ullapool
Tel: (0854) 612135
Easter-Nov

Shetland Islands Tourism

LERWICK
Market Cross
Lerwick
Shetland ZE1 0LU
Tel: (0595) 3434
Jan-Dec

Sutherland Tourist Board

BETTYHILL &
Clachan
Bettyhill
Sutherland
Tel: (06412) 342
Apr-Sept

DORNOCH
The Square
Dornoch
Sutherland IV25 3SD
Tel: (0862) 810400
Jan-Dec

HELMSDALE &
Coupar Park
Helmsdale
Sutherland
Tel: (04312) 640
Late Mar-Sept

BONAR BRIDGE ✉ &
Bonar Bridge
Sutherland
Tel: (08632) 333
Apr-Sept

DURNESS &
Sango
Durness
Sutherland
Tel: (0971) 511259
Late Mar-Oct

LOCHINVER &
Main Street
Lochinver
Sutherland
Tel: (05714) 330
Late Mar-Oct

Western Isles Tourist Board

CASTLEBAY
Main Street
Castlebay
Isle of Barra
Tel: (08714) 336
Easter-Oct

TARBERT
Pier Road
Tarbert
Isle of Harris
Tel: (0859) 2011

LOCHMADDY
Pier Road
Lochmaddy
Isle of North Uist
Tel: (08763) 321
Easter-Oct

STORNOWAY ✉
4 South Beach Street
Stornoway
Isle of Lewis PA87 2XY
Tel: (0851) 703088
Jan-Dec

LOCHBOISDALE
Pier Road
Lochboisdale
Isle of South Uist
Tel: (08784) 286
Easter-Oct

MAPS

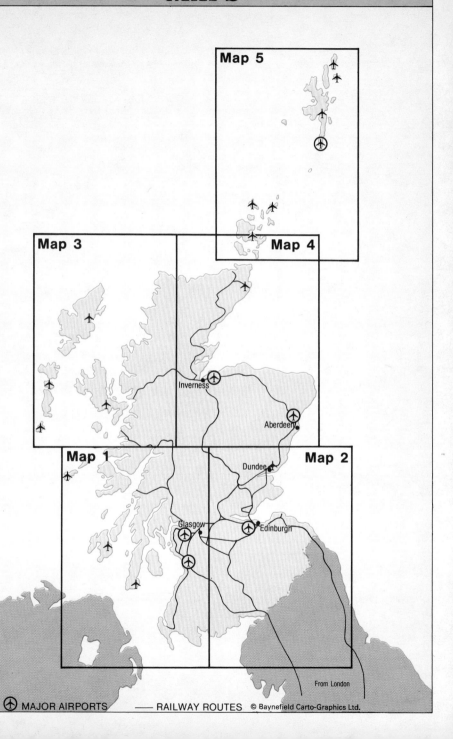

Map 5

Map 3

Map 4

Inverness

Aberdeen

Map 1

Dundee

Map 2

Glasgow

Edinburgh

From London

⊕ MAJOR AIRPORTS   —— RAILWAY ROUTES   © Baynefield Carto-Graphics Ltd.

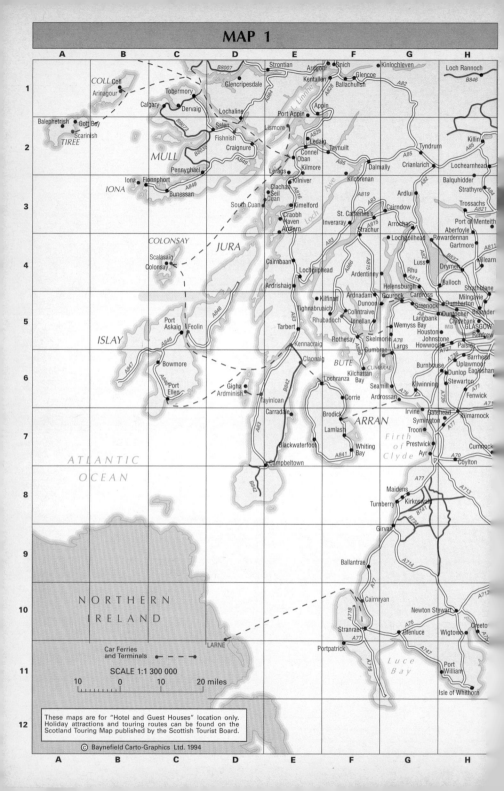

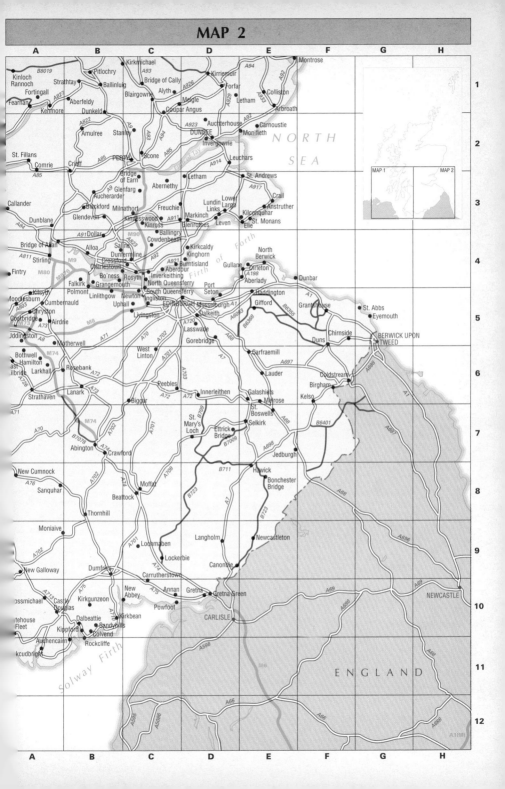

MAP 4

ORKNEY

Stornness
To Faroes (Summer only)
B9047
Longhope
Pentland Firth

MAP 3 MAP 4

Mey John o'Groats
Scrabster Dunnet A836
Thurso Castletown
Melvich Keiss A9
Bettyhill A836 Halkirk A882
Tongue A838
Wick

Forsinard A897 A895 A9

Altnaharra A836
Lybster

Dunbeath

A9 Helmsdale

Rogart Brora
Golspie
Dornoch Firth
Ardgay A949 Dornoch
A837 A836 Tain Portmahomack
B9165
Moray Firth
Alness A9 Invergordon Lossiemouth Cullen
Cromarty Burghead Hopeman Spey Bay Buckie Portsoy Banff Macduff Fraserburgh
Dingwall A832 Rosemarkie Nairn A96 Forres Elgin St. Combs
Strathpeffer Fortrose Auldearn A941 A98 A96 Turriff A950 Peterhead
Contin Munlochy A96 Dallas Rothes Keith B9170 Old Deer
Beauly Muir of Ord North Kessock Craigellachie Archiestown A95 A952
Kirkhill A862 INVERNESS A939 Aberlour A96 Huntly A947 B9005
Moy Ballindalloch Glenlivet Rhynie Old Rayne Old Meldrum B999
Flichity Grantown Cromdale A941 Inverurie To Lerwick
Drumnadrochit Tomatin on Spey A97 Insch Kemnay
Foyers Loch Ness A938 Dulnain Bridge Kildrummy Alford A944 Blairs ABERDEEN
Invermoriston Carrbridge B985 Nethy Bridge Tomintoul A944 Kincardine O'Neil A980 Banchory
Whitebridge Boat of Garten A939 A97 Aboyne A93
Aviemore A944 Dinnet A957 Stonehaven
Kincraig Crathie Ballater
Newtonmore B970 Kingussie Braemar
A86 A9 A93
Dalwhinnie
Glenshee B966 Edzell
A9 A924 B951 Glenshee A94 A92
Blair Atholl Killiecrankie Brechin

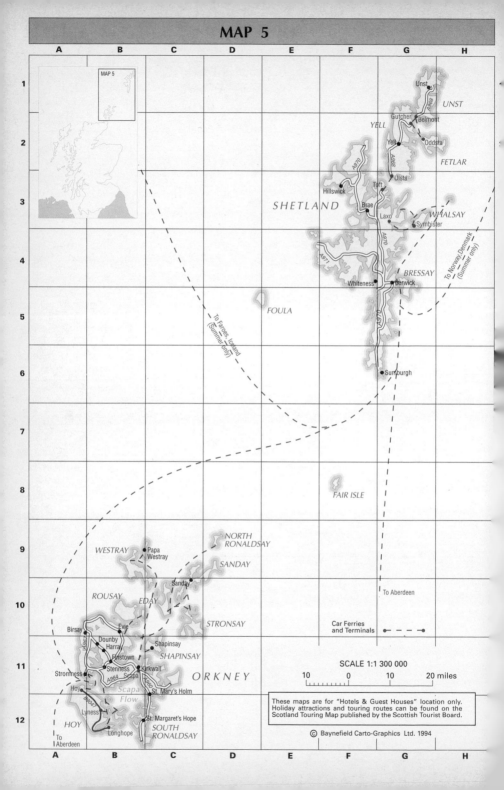

Wherever you're staying –

PICK UP A GUIDE
TO WHAT'S BEST IN THE AREA

From all leading
Tourist Information Centres
or with the compliments of
participating hotels & guest houses

ALPHABETICAL INDEX OF SCOTTISH ISLANDS

Many visitors to Scotland are keen to stay on islands in this guide, the locations on small islands are listed under the names of the islands: Isle of Eigg etc. On the larger islands, locations are listed under the name of the nearest town or village. If you want to stay on Arran, for instance, this index will show you the locations to check in the guide: Blackwaterfoot, Kildonan and so on. The number beside each place-name refers to the Maps on pages XXV-XXX., eg.5B10=Map 5, grid reference B10.

ISLE OF ARRAN
1E7   Blackwaterfoot
1F7   Brodick
1F6   Corrie
1F7   Lamlash
1E6   Lochranza
1F7   Whiting Bay

ISLE OF BARRA
3A11 Castlebay

ISLE OF BENBECULA
3A9   Liniclate

ISLE OF BUTE
1F6   Kilchattan Bay
1F5   Rothesay

1B1   **Isle of Coll**

1C4   **Isle of Colonsay**

ISLE OF CUMBRAE
1G6   Millport

1D6   **Isle of Gigha**

ISLE OF HARRIS
3C6   Leacklee
3B7   Lickisto
3B7   Strond
3C6   Tarbert

1B3   **Isle of Iona**

ISLE OF ISLAY
1C6   Bowmore
1C5   Port Askaig
1C6   Port Ellen

ISLE OF LEWIS
3C4   Breascleit
3C5   Callanish
3C4   Carloway
3C5   Keose Glebe
3D3   South Galson
3D4   Stornoway

ISLE OF MULL
1C3   Bunessan
1C1   Calgary
1D2   Craignure
1C1   Dervaig
1B3   Fionnphort
1C2   Pennyghael
1D2   Salen, Aros
1C1   Tobermory

ISLE OF NORTH UIST
3A8   Locheport
3A8   Lochmaddy

ISLES OF ORKNEY
5A10 Birsay
5B11 Dounby
5B10 Evie
5B11 Finstown
5B11 Harray
5B11 Kirkwall
5B9   Papa Westray
5B12 St Margaret's Hope
5B11 St Mary's Holm
5C10 Sanday

5C11 Shapinsay
5B11 Stenness
5A11 Stromness

ISLE OF SEIL
1E3   Clachan Seil

ISLES OF SHETLAND
5F3   Brae, North Mainland
5F3   Hillswick, North
      Mainland
5G4   Lerwick
5G6   Sumburgh
5G1   Unst
5G3   Whalsay
5F4   Whiteness
5G2   Yell

ISLE OF SKYE
3E11 Ardvasar, Sleat
3E10 Broadford
3D7   Duntulm
3C9   Dunvegan
3E10 Isleornsay
3E10 Kyleakin
3D9   Portree
3D9   Sconser
3D9   Skeabost
3E11 Sleat
3D8   Staffin
3D10 Strathaird, by
      Broadford
3C9   Struan
3D8   Uig

ISLE OF SOUTH UIST
3A10 Daliburgh
3A10 Lochboisdale
3A9   Lochcarnan

ISLE OF TIREE
1A2   Balephetrish
1A2   Gott Bay
1A2   Scarinish

Scotland

HOTELS &
GUEST HOUSES

1994

ABERDEEN	Map 4 G1					

Aberdeen Airport Hotel,
Skean Dhu
Argyll Road, Dyce
Aberdeen
AB2 0DU
Tel:(Aberdeen) 0224 725252
Tlx:739239
Fax:0224 723745

COMMENDED
♛♛♛ ♛♛

99 Twin   148 En Suite fac
49 Family

B&B per person
£91.50-£101.50 Single
£55.00-£61.00 Double

Open Jan-Dec
Dinner 1730-2200
B&B + Eve.Meal
£90.00-£100.00

Modern and conveniently located for airport; free courtesy coach.
Banqueting and conference facilities for 500 persons. Swimming pool.

Aberdeen Marriott
Riverview Dr, Farburn, Dyce
Aberdeen
AB2 0AZ
Tel:(Aberdeen) 0224 770011
Tlx:739651
Fax:0224 722347

HIGHLY
COMMENDED
♛♛♛ ♛♛

68 Twin   154 En Suite fac
86 Double

B&B per person
£62.00-£125.00 Single
£47.00-£75.00 Double

Open Jan-Dec
Dinner 1830-2230

Modern hotel with leisure facilities.
Conveniently situated for airport and Aberdeen town centre.

Aberdeen Quality Hotel
Aberdeen Exhibition &
Conference Centre
Bridge of Don, Aberdeen
AB23 8BL
Tel:(Aberdeen) 0224 706707

Award
Pending

33 Twin   123 En Suite fac
88 Double
2 Family
Suites avail.

B&B per person
£60.00-£87.50 Single
£33.75-£47.50 Double

Open Jan-Dec
Dinner 1800-2300
B&B + Eve.Meal
£46.25-£100.00

Altens Skean Dhu Hotel
Souter Head Road, Altens
Aberdeen
AB1 4LF
Tel:(Aberdeen) 0224 877000
Tlx:739631
Fax:0224 896964

COMMENDED
♛♛♛ ♛♛

150 Twin   221 En Suite fac
71 Family

B&B per person
£54.50-£103.00 Single
£36.50-£61.00 Double

Open Jan-Dec
Dinner 1700-2300
B&B + Eve.Meal
£45.00-£78.50

Sited on edge of city with easy access from A92. Bedrooms thoughtfully
designed for your comfort. A la carte restaurant. Outdoor swimming pool.

ATHOLL HOTEL

54 Kings Gate, Aberdeen AB9 2YN
Tel: 0224 323505 Fax: 0224 321555

*The Atholl Hotel situated in Aberdeen's residential west end has retained
a relaxed and friendly atmosphere. All 35 bedrooms have private
bathrooms and have been extensively refurbished to the highest
standard. The hotel, under personal ownership, enjoys a reputation for
fine cuisine and excellent friendly service.*

Atholl Hotel
54 Kings Gate
Aberdeen
AB9 2YN
Tel:(Aberdeen) 0224 323505
Fax:0224 321555

HIGHLY
COMMENDED
♛♛♛ ♛

11 Single   35 En Suite fac
16 Twin
7 Double
1 Family

B&B per person
£48.00-£80.00 Single
£28.00-£45.00 Double

Open Jan-Dec
Dinner 1800-2200

Privately owned Victorian hotel, to the west of the city.
Recent major refurbishment. Function facilities available.

Beeches Private Hotel
193 Great Western Road
Aberdeen
AB1 6PS
Tel:(Aberdeen) 0224 586413
Fax:0224 596919

COMMENDED
♛♛

2 Single   3 En Suite fac
2 Twin   2 Pub.Bath/Show
2 Double
1 Family

B&B per person
£20.00-£28.00 Single
£15.00-£20.00 Double

Open Jan-Dec

Victorian detached granite house in residential area close to city centre.
Private car parking.

ABERDEEN continued	Map 4 G1						
Belhaven Private Hotel 152 Bon-Accord Street Aberdeen AB1 2TX Tel:(Aberdeen) 0224 588384 Fax:0224 588384	COMMENDED ♛ ♛	3 Single 1 Twin 3 Double 1 Family	3 En Suite fac 3 Pub.Bath/Show	B&B per person £20.00-£30.00 Single £16.00-£22.00 Double	Open Jan-Dec	
		Late Victorian semi-detached granite house in residential area close to city centre. Sauna, jacuzzi and mini-gym.				
Brentwood Hotel 101 Crown Street Aberdeen AB1 2HH Tel:(Aberdeen) 0224 595440 Fax:0224 571593	COMMENDED ♛ ♛ ♛ ♛	23 Single 5 Twin 36 Double 1 Family	65 En Suite fac	B&B per person £32.00-£65.00 Single £22.00-£38.00 Double	Open Jan-Dec Dinner 1800-2200	
		Centrally situated personally run hotel, recently refurbished and within minutes of city centre. "Carriages" Brasserie and Bar. A la carte menu.				
Broomfield Hotel 15 Balmoral Place Aberdeen AB1 6HR Tel:(Aberdeen) 0224 588758 Fax:0224 574424	COMMENDED ♛	2 Single 4 Twin 2 Double	4 Pub.Bath/Show	B&B per person £17.50-£20.00 Single £10.00-£14.00 Double	Open Jan-Dec Dinner 1800-2000 B&B + Eve.Meal £23.00-£25.00	
		Family run hotel situated in quiet residential area on south side of city centre. In own grounds with private parking. Convenient local bus routes.				
Caledonian Thistle Hotel Union Terrace Aberdeen AB9 1HE Tel:(Aberdeen) 0224 640233 Tlx:73758 Fax:0224 641627	COMMENDED ♛ ♛ ♛ ♛ ♛	30 Single 23 Twin 25 Double 2 Family	80 En Suite fac	B&B per person from £102.00 Single from £65.00 Double	Open Jan-Dec Dinner 1830-2200	
		Recently refurbished city centre hotel in traditional style offering a choice of bars and restaurants.				
Cedars Private Hotel 339 Great Western Road Aberdeen AB1 6NW Tel:(Aberdeen) 0224 583225 Fax:0224 583225	COMMENDED ♛ ♛	5 Single 3 Twin 3 Double 2 Family	8 En Suite fac 5 Limited ensuite 2 Pub.Bath/Show	B&B per person £38.00-£45.00 Single £26.00-£27.00 Double	Open Jan-Dec	
		Family run private hotel with pool table. Car parking and good local bus service to the city centre and local amenities.				
Central Hotel 93-95 Crown Street Aberdeen AB1 2HH Tel:(Aberdeen) 0224 583685		3 Single 11 Twin 4 Double 12 Family	30 En Suite fac 1 Pub.Bath/Show	B&B per person £27.50-£45.50 Single £19.50-£26.00 Double	Open Jan-Dec Dinner 1700-2200	
Clover Leaf Hotel Kepplehills Road, Bucksburn Aberdeen AB2 9DG Tel:(Aberdeen) 0224 714294 Fax:0224 712404	APPROVED ♛ ♛ ♛	1 Single 8 Twin 6 Family	15 En Suite fac	B&B per person £41.00-£45.00 Single £32.50-£35.00 Double	Open Jan-Dec Dinner 1830-2030 B&B + Eve.Meal £53.00-£57.00	
		Modern single storey building on outskirts of city, close to airport. Onbus route to city centre. Function suite.				

ABERDEEN continued	Map 4 G1					

The Copthorne Aberdeen
122 Huntly Street
Aberdeen
AB1 1SU
Tel:(Aberdeen) 0224 630404
Tlx:739707
Fax:0224 640573

COMMENDED

11 Twin 89 En Suite fac
78 Double

B&B per person
£40.00-£110.00 Single
£30.00-£63.00 Double

Open Jan-Dec
Dinner 1900-2200
B&B + Eve.Meal
£45.00-£120.00

Traditional granite built city centre hotel with tastefully modernised interior.

Corner House Hotel
385 Great Western Road
Aberdeen
AB1 6NY
Tel:(Aberdeen) 0224 313063
Fax:0224 313063

COMMENDED

6 Single 17 En Suite fac
3 Twin
6 Double
2 Family

B&B per person
£38.00-£48.00 Single
£23.00-£28.00 Double

Open Jan-Dec
Dinner 1830-2030
B&B + Eve.Meal
£33.00-£58.00

Family run turreted hotel, 1 mile (2kms) from the city centre on the road to Royal Deeside.

Craighaar Hotel
Waterton Road, Buscksburn
Aberdeen
AB2 9HS
Tel:(Aberdeen) 0224 712275
Fax:0224 716362

HIGHLY COMMENDED

2 Single 53 En Suite fac
6 Twin
43 Double
2 Family
Suites avail.

B&B per person
from £58.50 Single
£37.25-£40.45 Double

Open Jan-Dec
Dinner 1900-2200

Newly refurbished hotel on outskirts of city, 1 mile (2 kms) from airport. Taste of Scotland approved.

Craiglynn Hotel
36 Fonthill Road
Aberdeen
AB1 2UJ
Tel:(Aberdeen) 0224 584050
Fax:0224 584050

COMMENDED

5 Single 7 En Suite fac
1 Twin 2 Pub.Bath/Show
2 Double
1 Family

B&B per person
£32.00-£43.00 Single
£29.50 Double

Open Jan-Dec
Dinner at 1900
B&B + Eve.Meal
from £44.00

Victorian elegance with modern comforts. Ideally situated for business or leisure. Taste of Scotland member. Car park. Residential licence.

Cults Hotel
Cults
Aberdeen
AB1 9SB
Tel:(Aberdeen) 0224 867632

COMMENDED

1 Twin 3 En Suite fac
5 Double 2 Pub.Bath/Show

B&B per person
£30.00-£50.00 Single
£30.00-£50.00 Double

Open Jan-Dec
Dinner 1800-2130
B&B + Eve.Meal
£40.00-£65.00

One of Aberdeen's oldest hotels recently refurbished to a high standard. Warm relaxing atmosphere with emphasis on fine foods.

Douglas Hotel
Market Street
Aberdeen
AB9 2EL
Tel:(Aberdeen) 0224 582255
Tlx:57643 PRIN HG
Fax:0224 582966

COMMENDED

36 Single 98 En Suite fac
15 Twin
40 Double
7 Family

B&B per person
£35.00-£90.00 Single
£30.00-£60.00 Double

Open Jan-Dec
Dinner 1800-2230
B&B + Eve.Meal
£45.00-£75.00

Aberdeen's oldest hotel situated in city centre close to harbour an railway station. Recently refurbished with all day brasserie.

Dunavon House Hotel
60 Victoria Street, Dyce
Aberdeen
AB2 0EE
Tel:(Aberdeen) 0224 722483
Fax:0224 772721

COMMENDED

9 Single 9 En Suite fac
2 Twin 3 Pub.Bath/Show
3 Double
2 Family

B&B per person
£26.50-£34.50 Single
£20.00-£23.50 Double

Open Jan-Dec
Dinner 1800-2100

Family run hotel, close to railway station and airport. Regular bus service to city centre. Award winning gardens.

ABERDEEN continued	Map 4 G1					
Ferndale Private Hotel 62 Bon-Accord Street Aberdeen AB1 2EL Tel:(Aberdeen) 0224 584835/580913 Fax:0224 584724		APPROVED Listed	10 Single 5 Twin 5 Double 4 Family	6 Limited ensuite 6 Pub.Bath/Show	B&B per person £25.00-£35.00 Single £20.00-£25.00 Double	Open Jan-Dec Dinner 1730-1900 B&B + Eve.Meal £35.00-£45.00
			Privately owned hotel in city centre close to all amenities, railway and bus stations.			
Gordon Hotel Wellington Road, Nigg Aberdeen AB1 3JA Tel:(Aberdeen) 0224 873012 Fax:0224 899195		COMMENDED 👑 👑 👑	16 Single 4 Twin 5 Double	25 En Suite fac	B&B per person from £50.00 Single from £36.00 Double	Open Jan-Dec Dinner 1830-2130
			Modern single storey bungalow hotel, on main road to the south side of the city centre, on Altens Estate.			
Imperial Hotel Stirling Street Aberdeen AB9 2JY Tel:(Aberdeen) 0224 589101 Fax:0224 574288		Award Pending	47 Single 46 Twin 17 Double	104 En Suite fac 4 Pub.Bath/Show	B&B per person £50.00-£95.00 Single £32.00-£50.00 Double	Open Jan-Dec Dinner 1900-2130 B&B + Eve.Meal £44.00-£107.00
Malacca Hotel 349 Great Western Road Aberdeen AB1 6NW Tel:(Aberdeen) 0224 588901 Fax:0224 571621		COMMENDED 👑 👑 👑	3 Single 8 Twin 10 Double	21 En Suite fac	B&B per person £65.00-£75.00 Single	Open Jan-Dec Dinner 1800-2200
			Friendly modern hotel with a la carte restaurant in West End of Aberdeen. Five minutes from city centre. Some annexe accommodation.			
Mannofield Hotel 447 Great Western Road Aberdeen AB1 6NL Tel:(Aberdeen) 0224 315888 Fax:0224 208971		Award Pending	4 Single 1 Twin 2 Double 2 Family	6 En Suite fac 2 Pub.Bath/Show	B&B per person £36.00-£44.00 Single £24.50-£27.50 Double	Open Jan-Dec Dinner 1830-1900 B&B + Eve.Meal £36.50-£59.00
Marcliffe at Pitfodels North Deeside Road, Cults Aberdeen Tel:(Aberdeen) 0224 861000 Fax:0224 868860			2 Single 29 Twin 12 Double 2 Family Suites avail.	45 En Suite fac	B&B per person £60.00-£125.00 Single £35.00-£80.00 Double	Open Jan-Dec Dinner 1800-2200 B&B + Eve.Meal £80.00-£140.00
Palm Court Hotel 81 Seafield Road Aberdeen AB1 7YU Tel:(Aberdeen) 0224 310351		Award Pending	4 Single 2 Twin 17 Double 1 Family	24 En Suite fac	B&B per person £40.00-£60.00 Single £24.00-£37.50 Double	Open Jan-Dec Dinner 1800-2130

ABERDEEN

Prince Regent Hotel
20 Waverley Place
Aberdeen
AB1 1XP
Tel:(Aberdeen) 0224 645071
Fax:0224 648157

COMMENDED ☸ ☸ ☸

9 Single 21 En Suite fac
7 Twin   1 Pub.Bath/Show
4 Double
1 Family

B&B per person
£30.00-£60.00 Single
£22.50-£34.00 Double

Open Jan-Dec
Dinner 1700-2200

Recently refurbished traditional hotel situated in Aberdeen's West End, with easy access to city centre. Ample on site parking.

Roselea Private Hotel
12 Springbank Terrace
Aberdeen
AB1 2LS
Tel:(Aberdeen) 0224 583060

APPROVED ☸

2 Twin   1 Limited ensuite
1 Double 2 Pub.Bath/Show
2 Family

B&B per person
£19.00-£21.00 Single
£14.00-£16.00 Double

Open Jan-Dec

Family run house with south facing garden in central location close to railway and bus station.

Russell Private Hotel
50 St Swithin Street
Aberdeen
AB1 6XJ
Tel:(Aberdeen) 0224 323555

COMMENDED ☸ ☸

10 Single 3 En Suite fac
1 Family   2 Pub.Bath/Show

B&B per person
£26.00-£41.00 Single
from £31.00 Double

Open Jan-Dec

Victorian granite house in the residential West End area.10 minutes walk from city centre, and close to bus routes.

St Magnus Court Hotel
22 Guild Street
Aberdeen
AB1 2NF
Tel:(Aberdeen) 0224 589411

4 Single   14 En Suite fac
10 Twin   2 Pub.Bath/Show
2 Double
3 Family

B&B per person
from £40.00 Single
from £25.00 Double

Open Jan-Dec
Dinner 1800-2400
B&B + Eve.Meal
from £49.00

Speedbird Inns Ltd
Argyll Road
Dyce, Aberdeen
AB2 0AF
Tel:(Aberdeen) 0224 772884
Fax:0224 772560

48 Twin   100 En Suite fac
50 Double
2 Family

B&B per person
£36.50-£46.50 Single
£18.25-£23.25 Double

Open Jan-Dec
Dinner 1800-2100
B&B + Eve.Meal
£46.50-£56.50

Stakis Aberdeen Tree Tops Hotel
Springfield Road
Aberdeen
AB9 2QH
Tel:(Aberdeen) 0224 313377
Fax:0224 312028

COMMENDED ☸ ☸ ☸ ☸ ☸

14 Single 110 En Suite fac
36 Twin
30 Double
30 Family
Suite avail.

B&B per person
£35.00-£130.00 Single
£35.00-£90.00 Double

Open Jan-Dec
Dinner 1900-2200
B&B + Eve.Meal
£45.00-£140.00

Modern and comfortable hotel in quiet residential area of the city. Choiceof restaurants, one of which has an Italian theme.

Water Wheel Inn
203 North Deeside Rd,
Bieldside
Aberdeen
AB1 9EQ
Tel:(Aberdeen) 0224 861659
Fax:0224 861515

Award Pending

21 Double 21 En Suite fac

B&B per person
£60.00-£70.00 Single
£60.00-£70.00 Double

Open Jan-Dec
Dinner 1700-2200
B&B + Eve.Meal
£65.00-£75.00

Abenjean Guest House
85 Constitution Street
Aberdeen
AB2 1ET
Tel:(Aberdeen) 0224 640171

APPROVED ☸

2 Single   2 Pub.Bath/Show
2 Twin

B&B per person
£16.00-£21.00 Single
£14.00-£15.00 Double

Open Jan-Dec

Family run granite terraced house within walking distance of town centre and beach.

VAT is shown at 17.5%: changes in this rate may affect prices. Prices shown are for guidance only. Please send SAE with each enquiry

ABERDEEN continued	Map 4 G1					

Aberdeen Guest House
218 Great Western Road
Aberdeen
AB1 6PD
Tel:(Aberdeen) 0224 211733

APPROVED Listed

1 Twin 7 En Suite fac B&B per person Open Jan-Dec
3 Double £20.00-£30.00 Single
3 Family £20.00-£30.00 Double

Granite townhouse in residential area, completely refurbished, centrally situated. Continental breakfast only.

Albert & Victoria Guest House
1-2 Albert Terrace
Aberdeen
AB1 1XY
Tel:(Aberdeen) 0224 641717

COMMENDED Listed

1 Single 2 Pub.Bath/Show B&B per person Open Jan-Dec
2 Twin £20.00-£24.00 Single
2 Double £15.00-£17.50 Double
2 Family

Victorian terraced house in quiet residential area, yet only a few minutes walk from the town centre and local amenities.

Allan Guest House
56 Polmuir Road
Aberdeen
AB1 2RT
Tel:(Aberdeen) 0224 584484

COMMENDED Listed

2 Single 1 Limited ensuite B&B per person Open Jan-Dec
1 Twin 2 Pub.Bath/Show £17.00-£19.00 Single Dinner 1800-1830
2 Double £15.00-£17.00 Double B&B + Eve.Meal
2 Family £22.00-£26.00

Victorian terraced house on bus route to city centre and close to Duthie Park and Winter Gardens. Home cooking and wide choice at breakfast.

The Angel Islington Guest House
191 Bon-Accord Street
Aberdeen
AB1 2UA
Tel:(Aberdeen) 0224 587043

COMMENDED Listed

2 Single 1 En Suite fac B&B per person Open Jan-Dec
1 Twin 3 Pub.Bath/Show £18.00-£25.00 Single
2 Double £14.00-£18.00 Double
1 Family

Semi-detached granite built Victorian house in residential area on south side of city. Shops, railway station and Duthie Park within 1 mile (2kms).

Arden Guest House
61 Dee Street
Aberdeen
AB1 2EE
Tel:(Aberdeen) 0224 580700

APPROVED

5 Single 2 En Suite fac B&B per person Open Jan-Dec
3 Twin 3 Pub.Bath/Show £18.50-£19.50 Single
2 Double £16.00-£20.00 Double
1 Family

Privately owned granite built terraced house in city centre. Close to bus and railway stations.

Arkaig Guest House
43 Powis Terrace
Aberdeen
AB2 3PP
Tel:(Aberdeen) 0224 638872

COMMENDED

4 Single 7 En Suite fac B&B per person Open Jan-Dec
2 Twin 1 Pub.Bath/Show £17.50-£23.50 Single Dinner 1700-1830
2 Double £17.50-£19.00 Double B&B + Eve.Meal
1 Family £24.00-£27.50

Traditional granite house; city centre 1/2 mile (1km). Convenient to places of interest, station, harbour, airport, both universities and hospital.

Ashgrove Guest House
34 Ashgrove Road
Aberdeen
AB2 5AD
Tel:(Aberdeen) 0224 484861

APPROVED Listed

3 Single 1 En Suite fac B&B per person Open Jan-Dec
2 Family 1 Limited ensuite from £16.00 Single
1 Pub.Bath/Show from £15.00 Double

Conveniently located for airport and local hospitals, with easy access to city centre. Television in all bedrooms.

ABERDEEN continued	Map 4 G1					
Bimini 69 Constitution Street Aberdeen AB2 1ET Tel:(Aberdeen) 0224 646912	COMMENDED ♕	1 Single 4 Twin 1 Double 1 Family	2 Pub.Bath/Show	B&B per person £16.00-£20.00 Single £15.00-£17.00 Double	Open Jan-Dec	
		Personally run guest house. In residential area close to centre and all local amenities. Car park to rear.				
Crynoch Guest House 164 Bon-Accord Street Aberdeen AB1 2TX Tel:(Aberdeen) 0224 582743	COMMENDED Listed	4 Single 2 Twin 2 Double	4 Pub.Bath/Show	B&B per person £18.00-£20.00 Single £14.00-£16.00 Double	Open Jan-Dec	
		Family run Victorian guest house in quiet residential street close to city centre, shops and all amenities.				
Denmore Guest House 166 Bon-Accord Street Aberdeen AB1 2TX Tel:(Aberdeen) 0224 587751 Fax:0224 587751	COMMENDED ♕	3 Single 2 Twin 2 Double 2 Family	3 Pub.Bath/Show	B&B per person £18.00-£25.00 Single £15.00-£16.00 Double	Open Jan-Dec	
		Victorian semi-detached house in quiet tree-lined residential street. Close to city centre, railway station and ferry terminal.				
Fourways Guest House 435 Great Western Road Aberdeen AB1 6NJ Tel:(Aberdeen) 0224 310218	COMMENDED ♕ ♕	2 Twin 3 Double 2 Family	6 En Suite fac 1 Pub.Bath/Show	B&B per person from £20.00 Single £17.00-£18.00 Double	Open Jan-Dec	
		Centrally situated in residential area of city. On main tourist route for Royal Deeside. Evening meals available.				
Furain Guest House 92 North Deeside Road, Peterculter Aberdeen AB1 0QN Tel:(Aberdeen) 0224 732189	COMMENDED ♕ ♕	1 Single 3 Twin 2 Double 2 Family	8 En Suite fac 1 Pub.Bath/Show	B&B per person £25.00-£27.00 Single £18.00-£19.50 Double	Open Jan-Dec Dinner 1900-2100 B&B + Eve.Meal £26.00-£38.00	
		Late Victorian house built of red granite. Family run, convenient for town, Royal Deeside and the Castle Trail. Private car parking.				
Greyholme 35 Springbank Terrace Aberdeen AB1 2LR Tel:(Aberdeen) 0224 587081 Fax:0224 587081	COMMENDED Listed	2 Single 1 Twin 2 Double	2 Pub.Bath/Show	B&B per person £18.00-£22.00 Single £15.00-£16.00 Double	Open Jan-Dec	
		Personally run guest house close to city centre and all amenities. Near to main bus routes.				
Gushetneuk Guest House 3 Belvidere Street Aberdeen AB2 4QS Tel:(Aberdeen) 0224 636435	COMMENDED Listed	2 Single 2 Twin 1 Double 1 Family	1 Pub.Bath/Show	B&B per person from £22.00 Single from £17.00 Double	Open Jan-Dec	
		Terraced granite house in residential area close to local public parks. Convenient for Aberdeen Royal Infirmary and bus routes to city centre.				
The Jays Guest House 422 King Street Aberdeen AB2 3BR Tel:(Aberdeen) 0224 638295	COMMENDED ♕	1 Single 4 Twin 1 Double	1 En Suite fac 1 Pub.Bath/Show	B&B per person £18.00-£25.00 Single £16.00-£20.00 Double	Open Jan-Dec	
		Traditional detached granite house close to Beach Leisure Complex, both universities and Conference Centre. Private parking and hairdressing.				

ABERDEEN continued	Map 4 G1						
Klibreck Guest House 410 Great Western Road Aberdeen AB1 6NR Tel:(Aberdeen) 0224 316115	COMMENDED ♛	1 Single 3 Twin 1 Double 1 Family	2 Pub.Bath/Show	B&B per person from £18.00 Single from £14.50 Double	Open Jan-Dec	🛏 🅲 ♦ ♨ 🍵 ℡ 📺 ▥ 📶 🅿 📠 ✕
Granite building, corner site in residential area in city's West End. On main bus route to city centre and Royal Deeside. Off road parking.							
Lillian Cottage 442 King Street Aberdeen AB2 3BS Tel:(Aberdeen) 0224 636947	COMMENDED ♛	1 Single 2 Twin 3 Double	1 En Suite fac 2 Pub.Bath/Show	B&B per person £18.00-£24.00 Single £15.00-£18.00 Double	Open Jan-Dec	🛏 🆅 🅲 ♦ ☐ ♨ 📺 ▥ 🔥 🅿 📠 ♠
Family run guest house, on main bus route to city centre. Close to beach, golf links, University and Exhibition Centre.							
Mount Pleasant Guest House 28 Abbotswell Crescent Aberdeen AB1 5AR Tel:(Aberdeen) 0224 871788	COMMENDED Listed	4 Single 3 Twin 4 Double 1 Family	1 En Suite fac 4 Pub.Bath/Show	B&B per person £17.50-£22.50 Single £14.00-£17.50 Double	Open Jan-Dec Dinner at 1830 B&B + Eve.Meal £25.50-£30.50	🛏 ♨ 🅲 ▥ ♦ ▥ ✕ 🔥 🅿 📠
Recently modernised bungalow with garden. Close to industrial estate and only 1.5 miles (2.5kms) from city centre.							
Salisbury Guest House 12 Salisbury Terrace Aberdeen AB1 6QH Tel:(Aberdeen) 0224 590447	COMMENDED ♛ ♛	1 Single 1 Twin 1 Double 1 Family	3 Pub.Bath/Show	B&B per person from £16.00 Single from £15.00 Double	Open Jan-Dec Dinner from 1700 B&B + Eve.Meal £21.00-£22.00	🛏 🆅 🅲 ▥ ♦ 🔥 ☐ 🍵 ♨ ♨ 📺 ▥ ✿ 📠 🐕
Family run guest house in quiet street near to city centre and to main busroutes. Home cooking.							
Springview Guest House 49 Springbank Terrace Aberdeen AB1 2LR Tel:(Aberdeen) 0224 587547	Award Pending	2 Twin 1 Family	2 Pub.Bath/Show	B&B per person £18.00-£20.00 Single £14.00-£15.00 Double	Open Jan-Dec	🛏 🆅 🅲 ♦ ☐ ♨ 🍵 ♨ ▥ ✕ 🐕 ✿ 🅿 ✕ 🐕
Stewart Lodge Guest House 89 Bon-Accord Street Aberdeen AB1 2ED Tel:(Aberdeen) 0224 573823	APPROVED ♛	3 Single 3 Twin 1 Family	1 Limited ensuite 2 Pub.Bath/Show	B&B per person £18.50-£22.00 Single £16.00-£19.00 Double	Open Jan-Dec	🛏 🆅 🆂 🅲 ▥ ♦ ☐ ♨ 📺 ▥ ♨ 🅿 📠 🐕 🍵
Granite mid-terrace house convenient for city centre and all amenities. Car parking.							
Strathboyne Guest House 26 Abergeldie Terrace Aberdeen AB1 6EE Tel:(Aberdeen) 0224 593400	COMMENDED ♛ ♛	4 Single 1 Twin 1 Double 1 Family	2 En Suite fac 2 Pub.Bath/Show	B&B per person £17.00-£23.00 Single £15.00-£16.00 Double	Open Jan-Dec Dinner 1750-1800 B&B + Eve.Meal from £24.00	🛏 🅲 ▥ ♦ ☐ ♨ 📺 ▥ ✕ 🐕 ✿ 📠 ✕ 🐕 🆃
Semi-detached house in residential area, close to local park. Breakfast menu and evening tea. Near bus route and 10 minutes walk to city centre.							

ABERDEEN continued	Map 4 G1					
Strathisla Guest House 408 Great Western Road Aberdeen AB1 6NR Tel:(Aberdeen) 0224 321026	COMMENDED Listed	2 Single 1 Twin 1 Double 1 Family	5 En Suite fac	B&B per person £25.00-£30.00 Single £20.00-£22.00 Double	Open Jan-Dec	
		Personally run guest house in west end of Aberdeen. Totally smoke-free enviroment.				

MARYCULTER HOUSE HOTEL

South Deeside Road, Aberdeen AB1 0BB
Tel: 0224 732 124   Fax: 0224 733 510

Maryculter House nestling on the River Dee just 15 minutes from the city. The house dated from 1227 has 23 individually appointed ensuite bedrooms. Relax and unwind whilst enjoying panoramic views of Deeside. Indulge in imaginative cuisine and fine wines. *Prices from £58 B&B.*

BY ABERDEEN	Map 4 G1					
Maryculter House Hotel Maryculter Aberdeenshire AB1 0BB Tel:(Aberdeen) 0224 732124 Fax:0224 733510	COMMENDED	1 Single 16 Twin 5 Double 1 Family	22 En Suite fac 1 Pub.Bath/Show	B&B per person £55.00-£105.00 Single £55.00-£105.00 Double	Open Jan-Dec Dinner 1730-2030 B&B + Eve.Meal £80.00-£125.00	
		Dating from 13th century. On the south bank of the River Dee. 7 miles (11kms) from Aberdeen. Banqueting and conference facilities.				
Old Mill Inn South Deeside Road Maryculter, by Aberdeen AB1 0AX Tel:(Aberdeen) 0224 733212 Fax:0224 732884	COMMENDED ♛ ♛ ♛	1 Single 3 Twin 3 Double 1 Family	8 En Suite fac	B&B per person £30.00-£40.00 Single £22.00-£25.00 Double	Open Jan-Dec Dinner 1730-2200	
		Delightful, family run, country inn, 5 miles (8kms) from Aberdeen on the edge of the river Dee. All bedrooms with ensuite facilities.				

WESTHILL HOTEL

WESTHILL. ABERDEEN. AB32 6TT TEL: (0224) 740388

Situated on the A944 in pleasant suburban surroundings. Only 6 miles from central Aberdeen and Aberdeen Airport, it is an excellent location for touring Royal Deeside, Castle and Whisky Trails. Many excellent local golf courses. Dine in "Castles" Restaurant or enjoy a superb supper in the "Tam O'Shanter" Lounge.
WESTHILL HOTEL - for business or pleasure.

Westhill Hotel Westhill, Aberdeen Aberdeenshire AB32 6TT Tel:(Aberdeen) 0224 740388 Fax:0224 744354	COMMENDED	8 Single 37 Twin 7 Double	52 En Suite fac	B&B per person £56.50-£70.00 Single £37.00-£45.00 Double	Open Jan-Dec Dinner 1900-2200	
		Modern style hotel in suburbs of Aberdeen, 7 miles (11kms) from city centre. Banqueting and conference facilities; live entertainment at weekends.				

ABERDOUR
Fife — Map 2 C4

Aberdour Hotel High Street Aberdour Fife KY3 0SW Tel:(Aberdour) 0383 860325 Fax:0383 860808	COMMENDED ⚘ ⚘ ⚘	3 Twin 7 Double 1 Family	11 En Suite fac	B&B per person £32.50-£35.00 Single £22.50-£26.00 Double	Open Jan-Dec Dinner 1800-2130 B&B + Eve.Meal £40.50-£50.00

Personally run hotel on Fife coast 6 miles (10kms) from Forth Bridges. Convenient for touring and golf.

Forth View Hotel Hawkcraig Point Aberdour Fife KY3 0TZ Tel:(Aberdour) 0383 860402		1 Single 2 Twin 1 Double 1 Family	3 En Suite fac 2 Pub.Bath/Show	B&B per person £16.00-£25.00 Single £18.50-£20.00 Double	Open Apr-Oct Dinner from 1900

THE
WOODSIDE HOTEL
HIGH STREET, ABERDOUR, FIFE KY3 0SW

Come and visit us for fine food in pleasant surroundings. The CLIPPER LOUNGE must count as one of the sights in the area. It was taken from a passenger liner. We are within walking distance of Aberdour Station - Britain's Prettiest Station - and that's official! Aberdour Castle and the picturesque harbour are also nearby.

Each of our rooms is named after a clan, and features the clan tartan and a history of the clan.

Our function room can provide a fine venue for your wedding or other function up to 80 people.

Free Golf. Dogs welcome!

For reservations/enquiries:
Tel: (0383) 860328 Fax: (0383) 860920

The Woodside Hotel High Street Aberdour Fife KY3 0SW Tel:(Aberdour) 0383 860328 Fax:0383 860920		1 Single 2 Twin 18 Double Suite avail.	21 En Suite fac	B&B per person £53.00 Single £26.50-£29.75 Double	Open Jan-Dec Dinner 1900-2130 B&B + Eve.Meal from £42.50

ABERFELDY
Perthshire — Map 2 B1

Crown Hotel Bank Street Aberfeldy Perthshire PH15 2BB Tel:(Aberfeldy) 0887 820448	APPROVED ⚘ ⚘ ⚘	2 Single 8 Twin 5 Double 2 Family	10 En Suite fac 2 Pub.Bath/Show	B&B per person £15.00-£20.00 Single £15.00-£20.00 Double	Open Jan-Dec Dinner 1700-2100 B&B + Eve.Meal £27.00-£32.00

Family run Inn-style hotel, built of local stone and situated in the town centre. Choice of bars and function room available.

Guinach House By The Birks Aberfeldy Perthshire PH15 2ET Tel:(Aberfeldy) 0887 820251	HIGHLY COMMENDED ⚘ ⚘ ⚘	1 Single 2 Twin 4 Double	6 En Suite fac 1 Priv.NOT ensuite	B&B per person from £25.00 Single from £25.00 Double	Open Jan-Dec Dinner 1900-2130 B&B + Eve.Meal from £43.50

1900 private country house with large garden. Warm friendly relaxed atmosphere with emphasis on good food and comfort. Owner well known Master Chef.

ABERFELDY continued	Map 2 B1	

Moness House Hotel
MONESS ESTATE, CRIEFF ROAD, ABERFELDY PH15 2DY
Telephone: (0887) 820446
Overlooking the picturesque town of Aberfeldy, Moness House boasts a blend of traditional hospitality and fine food with every modern amenity, including a luxury Leisure Club. A host of leisure pursuits and places of interest locally makes Moness the perfect location for a short break or centre-based holiday.

Moness House Hotel Crieff Road Aberfeldy Perthshire PH15 2DY Tel:(Aberfeldy) 0887 820446 Fax:0887 820062	COMMENDED ♨ ♨ ♨	3 Twin 8 Double 1 Family	12 En Suite fac	B&B per person £25.00-£37.00 Double	Open Jan-Dec Dinner 1830-2130 B&B + Eve.Meal £30.00-£45.00

Former hunting lodge dating from 1758, situated in thirty five acres, on the south side of Aberfeldy. Shared ownership cottages and leisure centre.

Balnearn Guest House Crieff Road Aberfeldy Perthshire PH15 2BJ Tel:(Aberfeldy) 0887 820431		3 Single 3 Twin 4 Double 1 Family	3 En Suite fac 2 Pub.Bath/Show	B&B per person £13.00-£16.00 Single £13.00-£16.00 Double	Open Apr-Oct
Dunolly House Taybridge Drive Aberfeldy Perthshire PH15 2BP Tel:(Aberfeldy) 0887 820298	Award Pending	1 Single 2 Twin 5 Double 8 Family	5 En Suite fac 1 Limited ensuite 6 Pub.Bath/Show	B&B per person £15.00 Single £14.00-£18.50 Double	Open Jan-Dec Dinner 1900-2030 B&B + Eve.Meal £22.50-£26.50
Fernbank House Kenmore Street Aberfeldy Perthshire PH15 2BL Tel:(Aberfeldy) 0887 820345	Award Pending	1 Single 1 Twin 3 Double 2 Family	7 En Suite fac	B&B per person from £19.50 Single £19.50-£22.50 Double	Open Jan-Dec
Tigh'n Eilean Guest House Taybridge Drive Aberfeldy Perthshire PH15 2BP Tel:(Aberfeldy) 0887 820109	HIGHLY COMMENDED ♨ ♨	1 Twin 2 Double	2 En Suite fac 1 Priv.NOT ensuite	B&B per person £16.00-£19.00 Single £16.00-£19.00 Double	Open Jan-Dec Dinner 1800-1900 B&B + Eve.Meal £25.00-£29.00

Elegant Victorian house overlooking the river. Warm and comfortable; homecooking. One room with jacuzzi.

BY ABERFELDY Perthshire Coshieville Hotel Coshieville Aberfeldy Perthshire PH15 2NE Tel:(Kenmore) 0887 830319/830301	Map 2 B1		2 Twin 2 Double 2 Family	6 En Suite fac	B&B per person £25.00-£32.50 Single £20.00-£25.00 Double	Open Jan-Dec Dinner 1900-2130	
Farleyer House Hotel Aberfeldy Perthshire PH15 2JE Tel:(Aberfeldy) 0887 820332 Fax:0887 829430	DELUXE ⬧ ⬧ ⬧		1 Single 3 Twin 5 Double 2 Family	9 En Suite fac 2 Priv.NOT ensuite	B&B per person £40.00-£60.00 Single £30.00-£45.00 Double	Open Feb-Oct Dinner 1830-2115 B&B + Eve.Meal £53.00-£68.00	

Farleyer House Hotel: **Sympathetically and lovingly restored, a former dower house dating back to the 16c, overlooking the Tay Valley.**

"The Weem"
by Aberfeldy Perthshire PH15 2LD
Tel: 0887 820381   Fax: 0887 820187

With its mix of self catering apartments and guest bedrooms, "The Weem" is ideally situated in the heart of glorious Breadalbane.
Not only will guests find excellent golf, fishing, walking and shooting close at hand, but also be surrounded by some of the best scenery in the world!!
This lovely old 17th century inn has been fully refurbished whilst still retaining its historic features. Wine and dine in style in its relaxing and happy atmosphere – imbibe freely of the local amber liquid before dropping contentedly into peaceful sleep.
"The Weem" is just the place to be!!

| Weem Hotel
Weem
Aberfeldy
Perthshire
PH15 2LD
Tel:(Aberfeldy) 0887 820381
Fax:0887 820187 | | | 3 Single
2 Twin
3 Double
2 Family | 10 En Suite fac | B&B per person
£26.00-£36.00 Single
£24.00-£34.00 Double | Open Jan-Dec
Dinner 1700-2030
B&B + Eve.Meal
£33.00-£46.00 | |

SPECIAL INTEREST HOLIDAYS
Write for your free brochure on Short Breaks,
Activity Holidays, Skiing, to:
Scottish Tourist Board, PO Box 15, Edinburgh EH1 1VY.

ABERFOYLE Perthshire	Map 1 H3		

COVENANTERS INN HOTEL
ABERFOYLE · PERTHSHIRE FK8 3XD
Telephone: (0877) 382347   Fax: (0877) 382785
In the foothills of the Trossachs, set in woodlands overlooking the River Forth and Aberfoyle village. Renowned for its old-worlde charm and hospitality – log fires, oak beams, cosy small lounges – and the warm welcome coupled with traditional Scottish menus awaiting you will make your visit memorable.
All rooms with private facilities, colour TV, etc.
Contact the Manager at the above address.

Covenanters Inn Aberfoyle Perthshire FK8 3XD Tel:(Aberfoyle) 0877 382347 Fax:0877 382785		5 Single 23 Twin 15 Double 4 Family	47 En Suite fac	B&B per person from £30.00 Double	Open Jan-Dec Dinner 1900-2100
The Forth Inn Main Street Aberfoyle Perthshire FK8 3UQ Tel:(Aberfoyle) 0877 382372		2 Twin 2 Double 2 Family	6 En Suite fac	B&B per person from £21.00 Double	Open Jan-Dec Dinner 1600-2030
ABERLADY East Lothian Golf Hotel Main Street Aberlady East Lothian EH32 0RF Tel:(Aberlady) 08757 503	Map 2 E4	1 Single 2 Twin 2 Double 4 Family	8 En Suite fac 1 Pub.Bath/Show	B&B per person £30.00-£35.00 Single £25.00-£27.50 Double	Open Jan-Dec Dinner 1800-2130 B&B + Eve.Meal £35.00-£40.00
Kilspindie House Hotel Main Street Aberlady East Lothian EH32 0RE Tel:(Aberlady) 08757 682/870682 Fax:08757 504/870504	**COMMENDED** 👑👑👑 👑	5 Single 17 Twin 4 Double	26 En Suite fac	B&B per person £36.00-£45.00 Single £25.00-£35.00 Double	Open Jan-Dec Dinner 1700-2100 B&B + Eve.Meal £37.00-£48.00
		Family run hotel in coastal village of Aberlady, within easy reach of 14 local golf courses.			
ABERLOUR Banffshire Aberlour Hotel High Street Aberlour Banffshire AB38 9QB Tel:(Aberlour) 0340 871287	Map 4 D9 **COMMENDED** 👑👑👑	8 Single 6 Twin 5 Double	15 En Suite fac 2 Priv.NOT ensuite 4 Pub.Bath/Show	B&B per person £30.00-£35.00 Single £25.50 Double	Open Jan-Dec Dinner 1845-2100 B&B + Eve.Meal £39.70-£49.70
		Warm personally run hotel in town centre. Ideally situated for touring Speyside, Whisky and Castle Trails. Limited fishing available.			

| **ABERNETHY** **Perthshire** Abernethy Hotel Back Dykes Abernethy Perthshire PH2 9JN Tel:(Abernethy) 073885 220 | **Map 2** C3 | | 2 Twin 3 Double 1 Family | 3 Pub.Bath/Show | B&B per person £20.00-£23.00 Single £35.00-£38.00 Double | Open Jan-Dec Dinner 1630-2200 | 🛏️ 📺 📶 🅿️ 🐕 ⬛ |

The Abington Hotel

ABINGTON, by BIGGAR, LANARKSHIRE ML12 6SD
Tel: 08642 467/223 Fax: 08642 223

Friendly family run hotel situated in the picturesque
village of Abington. Being just under a mile from the
M74 (Junction 13), the hotel is easy to find and makes
for both a good overnight stop and excellent touring
base to visit Central Scotland and Borders. Parking is
easy and free. The hotel has full central heating, and
each room has its own satellite colour television, tea
making facilities, and all are en-suite. A full menu is
available in the restaurant and suppers are also
available in the lounge bar.

For full details contact: D.J. MacBride, Proprietor.

RAC★★

| **ABINGTON** **Lanarkshire** Abington Hotel Carlisle Road Abington Lanarkshire ML12 6SD Tel:(Crawford) 08642 467 Fax:08642 223 | **Map 2** B7 | APPROVED ♔ ♔ ♔ | 5 Single 9 Twin 6 Double 5 Family | 25 En Suite fac | B&B per person £31.95-£39.50 Single £19.75-£24.75 Double | Open Jan-Dec Dinner 1900-2100 | 🛏️ 📺 🅿️ |
| | | | **Personally run hotel situated in centre of village. Good touring base for central Scotland. Easy to find, M74, Junction 13.** | | | | |

ABOYNE **Aberdeenshire** Arbor Lodge Ballater Road Aboyne Aberdeenshire AB34 5HY Tel:(Aboyne) 03398 86951	**Map 4** F1	DELUXE ♔ ♔	3 Twin	3 En Suite fac	B&B per person £25.00 Single £20.00 Double	Open Mar-Oct Dinner 1830-1930 B&B + Eve.Meal £35.00	🛏️ 📺 🅿️
			A newly built spacious house of character with large garden and wooded area. Near centre of village. All bedrooms ensuite.				
Chesterton House Formaston Park Aboyne Aberdeenshire AB34 5HF Tel:(Aboyne) 03398 86740			3 Twin	1 En Suite fac 1 Pub.Bath/Show	B&B per person £18.00-£20.00 Single £16.00-£18.00 Double	Open Jan-Dec Dinner 1800-2000 B&B + Eve.Meal £26.00-£30.00	🛏️ 📺 🅿️

ABOYNE continued

Map 4 F1

Hazlehurst Lodge
Ballater Road
Aboyne
Aberdeenshire
AB34 5HY
Tel:(Aboyne) 03398 86921

DELUXE

1 Twin	3 En Suite fac	B&B per person	Open Jan-Dec
2 Double		£28.00-£56.00 Single	Dinner 1930-2130
		£28.00-£30.00 Double	B&B + Eve.Meal
			from £38.00

Former Coachman's Lodge to Aboyne Castle with small restaurant and large garden. Ideal for touring Royal Deeside.

Struan Hall
Ballater Road
Aboyne
Aberdeenshire
AB34 5HY
Tel:(Aboyne) 03398 87241

DELUXE

2 Twin	3 En Suite fac	B&B per person	Open Feb-Nov
1 Double		£22.00-£27.00 Single	
		to £22.00 Double	

Stone built house c1870, situated near centre of village, recently refurbished to a high standard, with a warm and friendly welcome.

ACHARACLE
Ardnamurchan, Argyll

Map 3 E1

Ardshealach Lodge
Acharacle, Ardnamurchan
Argyll
PH36 4JL
Tel:(Salen) 096785 301

COMMENDED

1 Single	4 En Suite fac	B&B per person	Open Jan-Dec
2 Twin	2 Pub.Bath/Show	£18.00-£20.00 Single	Dinner 1900-2000
3 Double		£18.00-£24.00 Double	B&B + Eve.Meal
1 Family			£34.00-£40.00

Victorian former shooting lodge on working croft. Proprietor a keen cook, using local produce when available. Tuition in fly fishing and archery.

ACHILTIBUIE
Ross-shire

Map 3 G6

Summer Isles Hotel
Achiltibuie
Ross-shire
IV26 2YQ
Tel:(Achiltibuie) 085482 282
Fax:085482 251

Award Pending

7 Twin	12 En Suite fac	B&B per person	Open Apr-Oct
6 Double	1 Pub.Bath/Show	£41.00 Single	Dinner from 2000
		£31.00-£45.00 Double	B&B + Eve.Meal
			£63.00-£77.00

ACHNASHEEN
Ross-shire

Map 3 G8

Ledgowan Lodge Hotel
Ledgowan
Achnasheen
Ross-shire
IV22 2EJ
Tel:(Achnasheen)
044588 252
Tlx:75431 PREFACE "LED"
Fax:044588 240

COMMENDED

3 Single	12 En Suite fac	B&B per person	Open Apr-Oct
4 Twin		£39.50-£47.50 Single	Dinner 1930-2100
3 Double		£31.00-£49.50 Double	B&B + Eve.Meal
2 Family			£50.00-£74.00

A personally run former hunting lodge, c1904, retaining much of its original charm and character. All bedrooms have private facilities.

AIRDRIE
Lanarkshire

Map 2 A5

Tudor Hotel
39 Alexander Street
Airdrie
Lanarkshire
ML6 0BD
Tel:(Airdrie) 0236
764144/763295
Fax:0236 747589

APPROVED

12 Single	17 En Suite fac	B&B per person	Open Jan-Dec
7 Double	1 Pub.Bath/Show	£39.50-£50.00 Single	Dinner 1800-2130
		£29.75-£35.00 Double	

Modern hotel on the edge of the town centre and within easy reach of both Glasgow and Edinburgh. Most rooms en-suite.

	Map 2 A5						
AIRDRIE continued Rosslee Guest House 107 Forest Street Airdrie Lanarkshire ML6 7AR Tel:(Airdrie) 0236 765865		COMMENDED 👑 👑 👑	1 Single 3 Twin 1 Double 1 Family	3 En Suite fac 2 Pub.Bath/Show	B&B per person £17.00-£21.00 Single £17.00-£21.00 Double	Open Jan-Dec Dinner 1730-1830 B&B + Eve.Meal £24.00-£28.00	
			Former church manse, now family run guest house with comfortable rooms. Central situation for Edinburgh or Glasgow.				

	Map 4 F1						
BY ALFORD **Aberdeenshire** Forbes Arms Bridge of Alford Aberdeenshire AB33 8QJ Tel:(Alford) 09755 62108		COMMENDED 👑 👑 👑	3 Single 1 Twin 3 Double 1 Family	8 En Suite fac	B&B per person £30.00-£32.00 Single £25.00-£26.00 Double	Open Jan-Dec Dinner 1700-2000 B&B + Eve.Meal £38.95-£45.95	
			On banks of River Don, 1 mile (2kms) outside village of Alford. Own fishing and easy access to Lecht ski centre. 26 miles (42kms) from Aberdeen.				

	Map 2 B4						
ALLOA **Clackmannanshire** Gean House Restaurant and Country House Hotel Tullibody Road Alloa Clackmannanshire FK10 2HS Tel:(Alloa) 0259 219275 Fax:0259 213827		DELUXE 👑 👑 👑 👑	4 Twin 4 Double 2 Family Suites avail.	10 En Suite fac	B&B per person from £70.00 Single £60.00-£70.00 Double	Open Jan-Dec Dinner 1900-2130 B&B + Eve.Meal £89.00-£99.00	
			Haute cuisine in unique 'A' listed mansion set in its own gardens. Equidistant and convenient for both Glasgow and Edinburgh.				

	Map 4 A7						
ALNESS **Ross-shire** Morven House Hotel 70 Novar Road Alness Ross-shire IV17 0RG Tel:(Alness) 0349 882323			2 Single 2 Twin 1 Family	2 En Suite fac 1 Limited ensuite 2 Pub.Bath/Show	B&B per person £16.00-£20.00 Single £19.00-£24.00 Double	Open Jan-Dec Dinner 1800-1930 B&B + Eve.Meal £20.00-£30.00	

	Map 4 A4						
ALTNAHARRA **by Lairg, Sutherland** Altnaharra Hotel Altnaharra, Lairg Sutherland IV27 4UE Tel:(Altnaharra) 054981 222 Fax:054981 222			4 Single 13 Twin 3 Double	20 En Suite fac	B&B per person £33.00-£42.00 Single £33.00-£42.00 Double	Open Mar-Oct Dinner 1930-2030 B&B + Eve.Meal £50.00-£59.00	

	Map 2 C1						
ALYTH **Perthshire** Alyth Hotel Alyth Perthshire PH11 8AF Tel:(Alyth) 08283 2447 Fax:08283 2447		Award Pending	7 Twin 1 Double 2 Family	10 En Suite fac	B&B per person £17.50-£35.00 Double	Open Jan-Dec Dinner 1700-2200 B&B + Eve.Meal £27.50-£45.00	

ALYTH continued — Map 2 C1

Drumnacree House Hotel
St Ninians Road
Alyth
Perthshire
PH11 8AP
Tel:(Alyth) 08283 2194

HIGHLY COMMENDED

1 Single · 4 En Suite fac
2 Twin · 1 Priv.NOT ensuite
2 Double

B&B per person
£30.00-£35.00 Single
£30.00-£45.00 Double

Open Mar-Dec
Dinner 1900-2200
B&B + Eve.Meal
£46.50-£48.50

Family run country house hotel, 5 miles (8 kms) from Blairgowrie. Emphasis on comfort and food, using seasonal garden produce.

Lands of Loyal Hotel
Loyal Road
Alyth
Perthshire
PH11 8JQ
Tel:(Alyth) 08283 3151
Fax:08283 3313

9 Twin · 14 En Suite fac
5 Double

B&B per person
to £40.00 Single
to £32.50 Double

Open Jan-Dec
Dinner 1700-2200
B&B + Eve.Meal
to £55.00

Losset Inn
Losset Road
Alyth
Perthshire
PH11 8BT
Tel:(Alyth) 08283 2393

COMMENDED

3 Twin · 3 En Suite fac

B&B per person
£20.00-£25.00 Single
from £20.00 Double

Open Jan-Dec
Dinner 1900-2100
B&B + Eve.Meal
from £30.00

17C inn situated in centre of town on the edge of the beautiful Strathmore Valley. Relaxed bar atmosphere.

AMULREE, by Aberfeldy Perthshire — Map 2 B2

Amulree Hotel
Amulree,by Dunkeld
Perthshire
PH8 0EF
Tel:(Amulree) 0350 725218
Fax:0350 725218

1 Single · 8 En Suite fac
4 Twin · 2 Pub.Bath/Show
6 Double
1 Family

B&B per person
£19.50-£22.50 Single
£19.50-£22.50 Double

Open Jan-Dec
Dinner 1800-2230
B&B + Eve.Meal
£29.50-£32.50

ANNAN Dumfriesshire — Map 2 C1

Corner House Hotel
78 High Street
Annan
Dumfriesshire
DG12 6DL
Tel:(Annan) 0461 202754

APPROVED

1 Single · 4 Pub.Bath/Show
16 Twin
11 Double
3 Family

B&B per person
from £22.00 Single
from £19.50 Double

Open Jan-Dec
Dinner 1830-2100

Traditional hotel in the centre of the small town of Annan. Ideal for golfing, fishing and walking holidays.

Queensberry Arms Hotel
47 High Street
Annan
Dumfriesshire
DG12 6AD
Tel:(Annan) 0461 202024
Fax:0461 205998

COMMENDED

10 Twin · 24 En Suite fac
11 Double
3 Family

B&B per person
to £40.00 Single
to £27.50 Double

Open Jan-Dec
Dinner 1730-2130

Refurbished early 19C former coaching inn in town centre. Conference facilities available.

ANNAN Dumfriesshire	Map 2 C1	

WARMANBIE HOTEL & RESTAURANT
ANNAN, DUMFRIESSHIRE DG12 5LL
Telephone: 0461 204015

Country house hotel set in 40 acres secluded woodland grounds overlooking the river Annan, where you can relax and unwind, enjoying friendly service, creative cooking, huge breakfasts and superb bedrooms. Honeymoons are our speciality. Free fishing, ideal walking/touring. Golf nearby. Also holiday cottage. Special rates weekends, midweek, Christmas and New Year.

Warmanbie Hotel & Restaurant Annan Dumfriesshire DG12 5LL Tel:(Annan) 0461 204015	**COMMENDED** 👑 👑 👑	1 Single 7 En Suite fac 2 Twin 3 Double 1 Family	B&B per person £49.00-£53.00 Single £35.25-£38.75 Double	Open Jan-Dec Dinner 1900-2130 B&B + Eve.Meal £49.50-£54.50

Personally run Georgian country house in wooded grounds overlooking River Annan. Own Salmon and trout fishing. Excellent breakfast selection.

BY ANNAN Dumfriesshire	Map 2 C1			
Kirkland Country House Hotel Ruthwell Dumfriesshire DG1 4NP Tel:(Clarencefield) 038787 284	**COMMENDED** 👑 👑 👑	3 Twin 5 En Suite fac 1 Double 1 Family	B&B per person £23.00-£26.00 Single £20.00-£23.00 Double	Open Jan-Dec Dinner 1800-2100 B&B + Eve.Meal £30.00-£33.00

Former manse converted to a small hotel situated close to famous Ruthwell Cross. On Solway Heritage Trail.

ANSTRUTHER Fife	Map 2 E3			
The Hermitage Ladywalk Anstruther Fife KY10 3EX Tel:(Anstruther) 0333 310909	**Award Pending**	1 Twin 2 Pub.Bath/Show 3 Double	B&B per person £22.00-£26.00 Double	Open Mar-Dec Dinner from 1900 B&B + Eve.Meal £32.00-£38.00
The Spindrift Pittenweem Road Anstruther Fife KY10 3DT Tel:(Anstruther) 0333 310573	**HIGHLY COMMENDED** 👑 👑 👑	2 Twin 8 En Suite fac 3 Double 3 Family	B&B per person £25.00-£30.00 Double	Open Jan-Dec Dinner 1800-1930 B&B + Eve.Meal £35.00-£40.00

Stone built Victorian house with wealth of original features, set in fishing village. Short walk from town centre. Ideal touring base. Non smoking.

Scottish Tourist Board
COMMENDED
Facilities
👑 👑 👑

FOR QUALITY GO GRADED

APPIN Argyll	Map 1 E1

INVERCRERAN
Country House Hotel
GLEN CRERAN, APPIN, ARGYLL PA38 4BJ
Tel: (063 173) 414   **Fax: (063 173) 532**

Invercreran enjoys a location of idyllic beauty, set within a magnificent Highland glen. Beyond the delightful seclusion of the grounds you overlook stunning Glen Creran with its majestic mountain scenery. You have the opportunity to enjoy master bedrooms of unashamed luxury; our reception and lounges are excellent, all with facilities you would expect from an accredited country house hotel. A homely relaxed atmosphere, exquisite rosette awarded cuisine, excellent service and customer care has given the Kersley family country house hotel a reputation of meeting very high standards, our endeavours are exclusively to make sure that all guests have an enjoyable stay.
Contact: Mr. T. Kersley

Invercreran Country House Hotel Glen Creran Appin Argyll PA38 4BJ Tel:(Appin) 063173 414/456 Fax:063173 532	**DELUXE** 	1 Single 2 Twin 2 Double 2 Family Suite avail.	7 En Suite fac	B&B per person £50.00-£60.00 Single £48.00-£69.00 Double	Open Mar-Nov Dinner 1900-2000 B&B + Eve.Meal £74.00-£95.00

Unique country house in 25 acres of grounds. Family run; log fires and mountain views. Reputation for good food using only fresh produce.

ARBROATH **Angus** Hotel Seaforth Dundee Road Arbroath Angus DD11 1QF Tel:(Arbroath) 0241 72232 Fax:0241 77473	Map 2 E1				
		3 Single 9 Twin 6 Double 3 Family	19 En Suite fac 2 Pub.Bath/Show	B&B per person £32.50-£39.50 Single £26.00-£28.00 Double	Open Jan-Dec Dinner 1900-2130
The Kepties Christian Hotel 61 Keptie Street Arbroath Angus DD11 3AN Tel:(Arbroath) 0241 72424		2 Single 2 Twin 4 Double 2 Family	1 Pub.Bath/Show	B&B per person £17.00-£20.00 Single £17.00-£20.00 Double	Open Jan-Dec Dinner from 1800 B&B + Eve.Meal £24.00-£29.00
Rosely Country House Hotel Forfar Road Arbroath Angus DD11 3RB Tel:(Arbroath) 0241 76828		4 Single 4 Twin 3 Double 3 Family	13 En Suite fac 1 Pub.Bath/Show	B&B per person £25.00 Single £38.00 Double	Open Jan-Dec Dinner 1800-2100 B&B + Eve.Meal £33.00

ARBROATH continued — Map 2 E1

Kingsley Guest House
29-31 Marketgate
Arbroath
Angus
DD11 1AU
Tel:(Arbroath) 0241 73933

APPROVED

3 Single | 5 Pub.Bath/Show | B&B per person | Open Jan-Dec
3 Twin | | £14.00-£15.00 Single | Dinner 1730-1900
4 Double | | £12.00-£12.50 Double | B&B + Eve.Meal
4 Family | | | £17.00-£20.00

Family run guest house, in town centre, close to fishing harbour and beach. Games room. Minibus trips available to surrounding districts free of charge.

Sandhutton Guest House
16 Addison Place
Arbroath
Angus
DD11 2AX
Tel:(Arbroath) 0241 72007

HIGHLY COMMENDED

2 Twin | 1 Priv.NOT ensuite | B&B per person | Open Apr-Oct
1 Double | 2 Pub.Bath/Show | from £16.00 Single
| | from £14.00 Double

Victorian villa offering a warm welcome and comfortable non-smoking accommodation with modern facilities. Centrally located for amenities.

Scurdy Guest House
33 Marketgate
Arbroath
Angus
DD11 1AU
Tel:(Arbroath) 0241 72417

COMMENDED

2 Twin | 2 En Suite fac | B&B per person | Open Jan-Dec
4 Double | 2 Pub.Bath/Show | £13.50-£18.00 Double | Dinner 1700-1800
1 Family | | | B&B + Eve.Meal
| | | £20.00-£24.50

Family run licensed guest House. Close to harbour and town centre. Restaurant and coffee shop. A warm welcome awaits you.

ARDELVE, by Dornie
Ross-shire — Map 3 F9
Conchra House
Ardelve,by Kyle
Ross-shire
Tel:(Dornie) 059985 233

COMMENDED

1 Single | 3 En Suite fac | B&B per person | Open Jan-Dec
4 Twin | 1 Priv.NOT ensuite | £20.00-£30.00 Single | Dinner 1830-2030
3 Double | 3 Pub.Bath/Show | £18.00-£28.00 Double | B&B + Eve.Meal
| | | £30.00-£44.00

Former McRae family house dating from 1760. In secluded and tranquil lochside setting. Warm West Highland hospitality.

ARDENTINNY
by Dunoon, Argyll — Map 1 G4
Ardentinny Hotel
Ardentinny,by Dunoon
Argyll
PA23 8TR
Tel:(Ardentinny) 036981 209
Fax:036981 345

COMMENDED

2 Single | 11 En Suite fac | B&B per person | Open Mar-Nov
4 Twin | | £25.00-£45.00 Single | Dinner 1830-2130
3 Double | | £22.00-£42.00 Double | B&B + Eve.Meal
2 Family | | | £39.00-£65.00

18C whitewashed inn on the shores of Loch Long and set in the Argyll National Park. Own gardens and yacht moorings.

ARDFERN
Argyll — Map 1 E3
Galley of Lorne Inn
Ardfern,by Lochgilphead
Argyll
PA31 8QN
Tel:(Barbreck) 08525 284/668

3 Twin | 2 En Suite fac | B&B per person | Open Jan-Dec
6 Double | 2 Pub.Bath/Show | £22.00-£35.00 Single | Dinner 1830-2115
| | £22.00-£35.00 Double

ARDGAY
Sutherland — Map 4 A6
Ardgay House
Ardgay
Sutherland
IV24 3DH
Tel:(Ardgay) 08632 345

HIGHLY COMMENDED

2 Twin | 4 En Suite fac | B&B per person | Open Jan-Dec
2 Double | 1 Pub.Bath/Show | £15.00-£20.00 Double | Dinner 1700-1900
2 Family

Family run guest house on main A9. 1 mile (2kms) from Bonar Bridge with splendid views over Dornoch Firth.

Details of Grading and Classification are on page vi.

Key to symbols is on back flap.

ARDGOUR by Fort William Inverness-shire	Map 1 F1

Ardgour Hotel

Ardgour, by Fort William, Inverness-shire, PH33 7AA.
Tel: (08555) 225 Fax: (08555) 214

Cosy licensed family run West Highland Hotel on shores of Loch Linnhe. Panoramic views.
Ideal for Glencoe, Glenfinnan, Fort William, Ardnamurchan and Mull. Welcome walkers,
climbers, fishermen, yachtsmen, stalkers to wild unspoilt countryside. Abundant wildlife,
tranquil setting. Diving, watersports, salmon and sea trout fishing.
Yacht charter, stalking available.

Ardgour Hotel Ardgour,by Fort William Inverness-shire PH33 7AA Tel:(Ardgour) 08555 225 Fax:08555 214	APPROVED ♛ ♛	3 Single 2 Twin 2 Double 2 Family	4 Pub.Bath/Show	B&B per person £25.00-£30.00 Single £22.50-£30.00 Double	Open Jan-Dec Dinner 1800-2100 B&B + Eve.Meal £30.00-£50.00

Cosy West Highland, licensed, family run hotel on West shore of Loch Linnhe by
the Corran ferry. Hotel has own boats. Fishing and deer stalking.

ARDLUI Dunbartonshire	Map 1 G3

ARDLUI HOTEL

LOCH LOMOND, By ARROCHAR
DUNBARTONSHIRE G83 7EB
Telephone: 030 14-243 Fax: 030 14-268

Nestling in the midst of magnificent scenery at the head of Loch Lomond, the Ardlui Hotel stands on the shore commanding a superb panoramic view of this most famous of Scottish Lochs.

This small Country Hotel offers comfort in relaxed and friendly atmosphere, comprises 11 bedrooms, centrally heated and double glazed, all with colour TV and tea/coffee makers, with en-suite facilities available.

Fully licensed with two lounge bars serving an extensive bar meals menu, which as in our restaurant features house specialities such as fresh Loch Lomond salmon, sea trout and local venison.

Ardlui is an ideal centre for touring, water ski-ing, fishing, hill walking and mountaineering.

Boat hire, boat slip, moorings, sheltered marina, shop, petrol station and laundry. **Brochure on request.**

Ardlui Hotel Ardlui Dunbartonshire G83 7EB Tel:(Inveruglas) 03014 243 Fax:03014 268	APPROVED ♛ ♛ ♛	3 Twin 6 Double 2 Family	7 En Suite fac 1 Pub.Bath/Show	B&B per person £32.95-£42.06 Single £28.49-£35.83 Double	Open Jan-Dec Dinner 1900-2045

Former shooting lodge on A82 and on the banks of Loch Lomond with private
gardens to shore. Caravan site adjacent.

ARDNADAM by Dunoon, Argyll Anchorage Guest House Shore Road, Ardnadam by Dunoon Argyll PA23 8QD Tel:(Dunoon) 0369 5108	Map 1 F5		2 Double 1 Family	3 En Suite fac	B&B per person £24.00-£32.00 Single £14.00-£22.00 Double	Open Jan-Dec Dinner 1900-2100 B&B + Eve.Meal £26.00-£44.00

ARDNAMURCHAN **Argyll** Clan Morrison Hotel Glenborrodale, by Ardnamurchan Argyll PH36 4JP Tel:(Glenborrodale) 09724 232	**Map 3** D1	COMMENDED ♛ ♛ ♛	3 Twin 2 Double Small family run hotel on shores of Loch Sunart, with magnificent views across the Loch.	5 En Suite fac	B&B per person from £22.68 Double	Open Mar-Oct Dinner 1900-2030	
Sonachan Hotel Kilchoan, Ardnamurchan Argyll PH36 4LN Tel:(Kilchoan) 09723 211			3 Twin 2 Family	1 Limited ensuite 2 Pub.Bath/Show	B&B per person £18.50-£22.00 Double	Open Apr-Oct Dinner 1800-2000	
ARDRISHAIG, **by Lochgilphead** **Argyll** Auchendarroch Hotel Tarbert Road Ardrishaig, by Lochgilphead Argyll PA30 8EP Tel:(Lochgilphead) 0546 602275	**Map 1** E4		1 Twin 2 Double	3 En Suite fac	B&B per person from £19.00 Double	Open Apr-Oct Dinner from 1900 B&B + Eve.Meal from £27.00	
ARDROSSAN **Ayrshire** Lauriston Hotel 15 South Crescent Ardrossan Ayrshire KA22 8EA Tel:(Ardrossan) 0294 463771	**Map 1** G6		2 Twin 2 Double 1 Family	3 En Suite fac 1 Pub.Bath/Show	B&B per person £18.00-£25.00 Single £18.00-£25.00 Double	Open Jan-Dec Dinner 1700-2100 B&B + Eve.Meal from £25.00	
ARDVASAR, Sleat **Isle of Skye,** **Inverness-shire** Ardvasar Hotel Ardvasar, Sleat Isle of Skye, Inverness-shire IV45 Tel:(Ardvasar) 04714 223	**Map 3** E1		1 Single 5 Twin 2 Double 3 Family	11 En Suite fac	B&B per person £32.00-£35.00 Single	Open Mar-Dec Dinner 1930-2030 B&B + Eve.Meal £40.00-£45.00	

ARISAIG
Inverness-shire

Map 3
E1

The Arisaig Hotel
Arisaig
Inverness-shire
PH39 4NH
Tel:(Arisaig) 06875 210
Fax:06875 310

2 Single — 6 En Suite fac
7 Twin — 4 Pub.Bath/Show
2 Double
4 Family

B&B per person
£30.00-£40.00 Single
£30.00-£40.00 Double

Open Mar-Nov
Dinner 1930-2030
B&B + Eve.Meal
£42.00-£55.00

Cnoc-na-Faire Hotel
Back-of-Keppoch
Arisaig
Inverness-shire
PH39 4NS
Tel:(Arisaig) 06875 249

APPROVED

2 Single — 2 En Suite fac
2 Twin — 1 Pub.Bath/Show
3 Double

B&B per person
£17.00-£22.00 Single
£17.00-£25.00 Double

Open Jan-Dec
Dinner from 1830
B&B + Eve.Meal
£29.00-£37.00

Family run hotel in quiet location with panoramic views to Skye, Eigg and
Rhum and sandy beaches of Arisaig.

Kinloid Farm Guest House
Kinloid, Kilmartin
Arisaig
Inverness-shire
PH39 4NS
Tel:(Arisaig) 06875 366

COMMENDED

1 Twin — 3 En Suite fac
2 Double — 1 Pub.Bath/Show

B&B per person
from £20.00 Single
from £20.00 Double

Open Apr-Oct
Dinner at 1830
B&B + Eve.Meal
from £32.00

Bungalow style farmhouse on working farm about 0.5 miles (1km) from the
village. Magnificent sea and mountain views.

**Old Library Lodge &
Restaurant**
Arisaig
Inverness-shire
PH39
Tel:(Arisaig) 06875 651

COMMENDED

1 Twin — 6 En Suite fac
5 Double

B&B per person
£35.00-£40.00 Single
£30.00 Double

Open Apr-Nov
Dinner 1830-2130
B&B + Eve.Meal
£50.00

Personally run restaurant with rooms, specialising in fresh local produce,
vegetarian meals and home made bread. Magnificent views to Inner Hebrides.

ARROCHAR
Dunbartonshire

Map 1
G3

Greenbank Guest House
Greenbank
Arrochar
Dunbartonshire
G83 7AA
Tel:(Arrochar)
03012 305/513

1 Single — 3 En Suite fac
1 Twin — 1 Limited ensuite
1 Double — 1 Pub.Bath/Show
1 Family

B&B per person
£15.00-£17.50 Single
£15.00-£17.50 Double

Open Jan-Dec
Dinner 1700-2200

Lochside Guest House
Arrochar
Dunbartonshire
G83 7AA
Tel:(Arrochar) 03012 467

APPROVED

1 Single — 3 En Suite fac
1 Twin — 1 Priv.NOT ensuite
3 Double — 3 Pub.Bath/Show
2 Family

B&B per person
£15.00-£16.00 Single
£15.00-£18.00 Double

Open Jan-Dec
Dinner 1800-1930
B&B + Eve.Meal
£24.00-£28.00

Friendly atmosphere in this guest house on the shore of Loch Long with view
across the Loch to the Cobbler.

Mansefield Country House
Arrochar
Dunbartonshire
G83 7AG
Tel:(Arrochar) 03012 282

COMMENDED

2 Twin — 1 En Suite fac
1 Double — 2 Limited ensuite
2 Family — 1 Pub.Bath/Show

B&B per person
£16.00-£17.00 Double

Open Jan-Dec
Dinner 1900-2145
B&B + Eve.Meal
£26.00-£27.00

Sandstone villa in lawned grounds overlooking Loch Long and The Cobbler.
Friendly, personal attention, home cooking mainly using fresh produce.

ARROCHAR continued
Map 1 G3

Rossmay Guest House
Arrochar
Dunbartonshire
G83 7AH
Tel:(Arrochar) 03012 250

COMMENDED

1 Single
1 Twin
2 Double
1 Family

4 En Suite fac
1 Priv.NOT ensuite

B&B per person
£18.00-£22.00 Single
£16.00-£18.00 Double

Open Feb-Nov
Dinner from 1900
B&B + Eve.Meal
£24.00-£26.00

Small, friendly guest house tranquilly situated on shores of Loch Long with panoramic views across the Loch. Home cooking and a warm welcome.

AUCHENCAIRN
by Castle Douglas
Kirkcudbrightshire
Map 2 B1

Balcary Bay Hotel
Auchencairn,
by Castle Douglas
Kirkcudbrightshire
DG7 1QZ
Tel:(Auchencairn)
055664 217/311
Fax:055664 272

HIGHLY COMMENDED

3 Single
7 Twin
6 Double
1 Family

17 En Suite fac

B&B per person
£40.00-£48.00 Single
£40.00-£48.00 Double

Open Mar-Nov
Dinner 1900-2100
B&B + Eve.Meal
£45.00-£65.00

Family run country house hotel, situated on edge of Balcary Bay, affording splendid views over Solway Firth. A la carte menu. Taste of Scotland.

Collin House
Auchencairn,
by Castle Douglas
Kirkcudbrightshire
DG7 1QN
Tel:(Auchencairn)
055664 292
Fax:055664 292

DELUXE

2 Twin
3 Double
1 Family

6 En Suite fac

B&B per person
£48.00 Single
£33.00-£37.00 Double

Open Mar-Dec,
Xmas/New Year
Dinner 1915-2045
B&B + Eve.Meal
£55.00-£63.00

Elegant country house in 20 acres with outstanding views over Auchencairn Bay. Creative cuisine using fresh local produce.

Solwayside House Hotel
Auchencairn,
by Castle Douglas
Kirkcudbrightshire
DG7 1QU
Tel:(Auchencairn)
055664 280
Fax:055664 283

COMMENDED

2 Twin
1 Double
5 Family

8 En Suite fac

B&B per person
£19.50-£22.00 Single
£19.50-£23.00 Double

Open Jan-Dec
Dinner 1900-2030
B&B + Eve.Meal
£32.00-£34.50

Personally run, situated in centre of small village. Table d'hote and a la carte restaurant: fresh produce a speciality. Ideal for touring.

AUCHTERARDER
Perthshire
Map 2 B3

Auchterarder House
Auchterarder
Perthshire
PH3 1DZ
Tel:(Auchterarder)
0764 663646/663647
Fax:0764 662939

13 Twin
2 Double
Suites avail.

15 En Suite fac

B&B per person
£85.00-£110.00 Single
£65.00-£100.00 Double

Open Jan-Dec
Dinner 1800-2230

Cairn Lodge Hotel
Orchil Road
Auchterarder
Perthshire
PH3 1LX
Tel:(Auchterarder)
0764 662634

HIGHLY COMMENDED

1 Single
3 Twin
1 Family

5 En Suite fac

B&B per person
£40.00 Single
£37.50 Double

Open Jan-Dec
Dinner 1900-2100

Personally run country house hotel, with own large garden and putting green, on outskirts of Auchterarder. Steak and Platter restaurant.

Details of Grading and Classification are on page vi.

Key to symbols is on back flap.

AUCHTERARDER continued	Map 2 B3			

COLLEARN HOUSE HOTEL
Auchterarder Perthshire PH3 1DF
Tel:0764 663553 Fax: 0764 662376

Built in 1870 this privately owned Victorian House has been restored to its original splendour. Encompassed by six acre grounds Collearn House Hotel is an ideal venue for quiet breaks yet close to all the local amenities. All eight en-suite bedrooms are spacious and offer a variety of facilities including DD telephone, trouser press, colour TV and tea and coffee making. In the intimate dining room the constantly changing menu offers a variety of traditional Scottish and European cuisine. The comfortable lounge bar also offers a large selection of hot and cold meals and snacks.

Double £80 B&B Single £50 B&B.

The Collearn Hotel High Street Auchterarder Perthshire PH3 1DF Tel:(Auchterarder) 0764 663553 Fax:0764 662376	HIGHLY COMMENDED ♔ ♔ ♔ ♔	3 Single 2 Twin 3 Double 1 Family	9 En Suite fac	B&B per person £55.00-£60.00 Single £55.00-£75.00 Double	Open Jan-Dec Dinner 1800-2200 B&B + Eve.Meal £62.50-£67.50
		Family run country house hotel in extensive gardens, spacious bedrooms, magnificent panelling, stained glass windows. Bar suppers; a la carte menu			
Morven Hotel 196 High Street Auchterarder Perthshire PH3 1AP Tel:(Auchterarder) 0764 662578		5 Twin 3 Double 1 Family	9 En Suite fac	B&B per person from £29.38 Single from £23.50 Double	Open Jan-Dec
BY AUCHTERARDER Perthshire Duchally Hotel Duchally Auchterarder Perthshire PH3 1PN Tel:(Auchterarder) 0764 663071/663072 Fax:0764 662464	Map 2 B3	COMMENDED ♔ ♔ ♔ ♔	9 Twin 4 Double	13 En Suite fac	B&B per person £45.00-£70.00 Single £35.00-£50.00 Double	Open Jan-Dec Dinner 1800-2130
		Large country house set in 27 acres of parkland. Wide choice of golf courses; range of outdoor activities in area. Accent on comfort and good food.			
The Gleneagles Hotel Auchterarder Perthshire PH3 1NF Tel:(Auchterarder) 0764 662231 Tlx:76105 Fax:0764 662134		29 Single 59 Twin 130 Double Suites avail.	236 En Suite fac	B&B per person £115.00-£150.00 Single £82.50-£145.00 Double	Open Jan-Dec Dinner 1930-2200

AUCHTERHOUSE **Angus** The Old Mansion House Hotel Auchterhouse, by Dundee Angus DD3 0QN Tel:(Auchterhouse) 082626 366/367/368 Fax:082626 400	Map 2 D2	**HIGHLY COMMENDED** 👑 👑 👑 👑	2 Twin 2 Double 2 Family	6 En Suite fac	B&B per person £70.00-£75.00 Single £45.00-£55.00 Double	Open Jan-Dec Dinner 1900-2130	

16C baronial house, retaining original plasterwork and vaulted entrance hall.
In 10 acres of grounds. Outdoor swimming pool, croquet and tennis.

AULDEARN, by Nairn **Nairn** Covenanters' Inn Auldearn Nairn IV12 5TG Tel:(Nairn) 0667 452456 Fax:0667 453583	Map 4 C8	**COMMENDED** 👑 👑 👑	1 Twin 5 Double 2 Family	8 En Suite fac	B&B per person £38.00-£45.00 Single £19.50-£34.00 Double	Open Jan-Dec Dinner 1700-2130 B&B + Eve.Meal £31.00-£45.50	

Converted 17C mill in historic village 2 miles (3kms) east of Nairn on A96
18 miles (29kms) from Inverness. Seafood a speciality.

AULTBEA **Ross-shire**	Map 3 F7

Aultbea Hotel
AULTBEA · ROSS-SHIRE IV22 2HX
Tel: (0445) 731201   Fax: (0445) 731214

"On the shores of Loch Ewe" with magnificent views of the Torridon Mountains, this family-run hotel, with 8 superb en-suite bedrooms equipped with colour TV's., Direct Dial Phones, Hairdryers and Tea/Coffee Makers, offers a relaxed and friendly atmosphere. Excellent table d'hôte and à la carte menus (including local seafood, venison and home baking). Extensive Bistro and Bar menus available 9am to 9pm. Lounge and Public Bars with All Day Licence.

Hill Walking, Sea Angling and Trout and Salmon Fishing arranged. Inverewe Gardens 5 miles.

Aultbea Hotel Aultbea Ross-shire IV22 2HX Tel:(Aultbea) 0445 731201 Fax:0445 731214	**COMMENDED** 👑 👑 👑 👑	1 Single 2 Twin 4 Double 1 Family	8 En Suite fac	B&B per person £21.50-£34.00 Single £21.50-£39.00 Double £39.00-£58.50	Open Jan-Dec Dinner 1700-2130 B&B + Eve.Meal	

Family run hotel right on the loch shore with magnificent views. Fishing
available. On Naval History Trail. Inverewe gardens, 6 miles (10kms).

Drumchork Lodge Hotel Aultbea Ross-shire IV22 2HU Tel:(Aultbea) 0445 731242		4 Twin 4 Double 1 Family	9 En Suite fac	B&B per person £35.00-£38.00 Single £30.00-£33.00 Double	Open Mar-Oct Dinner 1900-2000 B&B + Eve.Meal £41.00-£46.00	

Details of Grading and Classification are on page vi.

Key to symbols is on back flap.

	Map 3 F7						
AULTBEA continued Mellondale Guest House 47 Mellon Charles Aultbea Ross-shire IV22 2JL Tel:(Aultbea) 0445 731326		**HIGHLY COMMENDED** 🦢🦢🦢	2 Twin 3 Double	4 En Suite fac 1 Limited ensuite 2 Pub.Bath/Show	B&B per person from £15.00 Single from £15.00 Double	Open Feb-Nov Dinner from 1830 B&B + Eve.Meal from £23.00	

Modern family guest house set in 4 acres with views of Loch Ewe. 9 miles (14.4 Km) from Inverewe Gardens (ideal walking centre).

	Map 3 H7						
AULTGUISH, by Garve **Ross-shire** Aultguish Inn Aultguish, by Garve Ross-shire IV23 2PQ Tel:(Aultguish) 09975 254			2 Single 7 Twin 3 Double 2 Family	13 En Suite fac 1 Priv.NOT ensuite	B&B per person £15.00-£25.00 Single £15.00-£25.00 Double	Open Jan-Dec Dinner 1700-2100 B&B + Eve.Meal £25.00-£35.00	

	Map 4 C1						
AVIEMORE **Inverness-shire** Aviemore Highlands Hotel Aviemore Centre Aviemore Inverness-shire PH22 1PJ Tel:(Aviemore) 0479 810771 Fax:0479 811473		**Award Pending**	4 Single 57 Twin 34 Double 8 Family	103 En Suite fac	B&B per person £35.00-£40.00 Single £30.00-£35.00 Double	Open Jan-Dec Dinner 1900-2130 B&B + Eve.Meal £43.00-£48.00	

Balavoulin Hotel Grampian Road Aviemore Inverness-shire PH22 1RL Tel:(Aviemore) 0479 810672 Fax:0479 811575		**COMMENDED** 🦢🦢🦢	3 Twin 5 Double	8 En Suite fac	B&B per person £18.00-£22.50 Double	Open Jan-Dec Dinner 1830-2030 B&B + Eve.Meal £30.00-£35.00	

Traditional, stone building with fully modernised interior. Close to attractions of village centre and all amenities.

Cairngorm Hotel (Lovat Hotels Ltd) Grampian Road Aviemore Inverness-shire Tel:(Aviemore) 0479 810233 Fax:0479 810791		**COMMENDED** 🦢🦢🦢 🦢	6 Single 16 Twin 6 Double 2 Family	30 En Suite fac	B&B per person £39.00-£45.00 Single £29.00-£34.00 Double	Open Jan-Dec Dinner 1900-2130 B&B + Eve.Meal £45.00-£56.00	

Traditional stone-built hotel at centre of this busy all year round holiday town.

Scotland for Golf...

Find out more about golf in Scotland. There's more to it than just the championship courses so get in touch with us now for information on the hidden gems of Scotland.

Write to: **Information Unit, Scottish Tourist Board, 23 Ravelston Terrace, Edinburgh EH4 3EU or call: 031-332 2433.**

AVIEMORE continued	Map 4 C1		

CORROUR HOUSE HOTEL

INVERDRUIE, AVIEMORE PH22 1QH TEL: (0479) 810220 Fax: (0479) 811500

A lovely Country House, full of charm and character, set in 4 acres of garden and woodland. Quietly situated, ¹/₂ mile from Aviemore, with spectacular views of the Cairngorm Mountains, in an area of outstanding natural beauty. Renowned for excellent cuisine and the hospitality of hosts David and Sheana Catto.

- Recommended by leading Hotel Guides -

Corrour House Hotel
Inverdruie
Aviemore
Inverness-shire
PH22 1QH
Tel:(Aviemore) 0479 810220
Fax:0479 811500

HIGHLY COMMENDED

1 Single 8 En Suite fac
2 Twin
3 Double
2 Family

B&B per person
£26.00-£32.00 Single
£24.00-£30.00 Double

Open Dec-Oct
Dinner 1900-2000
B&B + Eve.Meal
£40.00-£48.00

Friendly family run, country house hotel, standing in four acres of garden and woodland, with views of Rothiemurchus and Cairngorm mountains.

Mercury Hotel
Aviemore Centre
Aviemore
Inverness-shire
PH22 1PF
Tel:(Aviemore) 0479 810781
Fax:0479 811167

11 Double 94 En Suite fac
83 Family

B&B per person
£25.00-£50.00 Single
£25.00-£42.00 Double

Open Jan-Dec
Dinner 1800-2030
B&B + Eve.Meal
£35.00-£60.00

A'Anside Guest House
off Grampian Road
Aviemore
Inverness-shire
PH22 1QD
Tel:(Aviemore) 0479 810871

COMMENDED

1 Twin 5 En Suite fac
3 Double
1 Family

B&B per person
£16.00-£20.00 Single
£16.00-£18.00 Double

Open Jan-Dec

Modern bungalow sitting above the town. Stunning views over the town to the Cairngorm Mountains. Most rooms ensuite facilities.

Ardlogie Guest House
Dalfaber Road
Aviemore
Inverness-shire
PH22 1PU
Tel:(Aviemore) 0479 810747

COMMENDED Listed

1 Twin 3 En Suite fac
4 Double 2 Pub.Bath/Show

B&B per person
£14.00-£17.00 Double

Open Jan-Dec

Semi-detached house in quiet road, 5 minutes walk from centre with its many facilities. Ideal for skiing, walking and touring.

Cairngorm Guest House
Grampian Road
Aviemore
Inverness-shire
PH22 1RP
Tel:(Aviemore) 0479 810630

COMMENDED

3 Twin 9 En Suite fac
5 Double
1 Family

B&B per person
£15.00-£18.00 Double

Open Jan-Dec

Detached stone villa within 5 minutes walk of the centre and 10 minutes from bus and rail stations.

Craiglea Guest House
Grampian Road
Aviemore
Inverness-shire
PH22 1RH
Tel:(Aviemore) 0479 810210

1 Single 1 En Suite fac
3 Twin 3 Pub.Bath/Show
3 Double
4 Family

B&B per person
£14.00-£16.00 Single
£14.00-£16.00 Double

Open Jan-Dec

Details of Grading and Classification are on page vi.

Key to symbols is on back flap.

AVIEMORE continued

Map 4 C1

Kinapol Guest House Dalfaber Road Aviemore Inverness-shire PH22 1PY Tel:(Aviemore) 0479 810513	COMMENDED ♕	1 Twin 3 Double 1 Family	2 Pub.Bath/Show	B&B per person £13.00-£20.00 Single £13.00-£14.00 Double	Open Jan-Dec

Friendly welcome at modern house in large garden with views of Cairngorms. Quiet location but only 5 minutes walk to the town centre.

Lynwilg House Aviemore Inverness-shire PH22 1PZ Tel:(Aviemore) 0479 811685	Award Pending	1 Single 1 Twin 1 Double 1 Family	3 En Suite fac 1 Priv.NOT ensuite 1 Pub.Bath/Show	B&B per person £16.00-£20.00 Single £18.00-£22.00 Double	Open Jan-Nov Dinner 1900-2000 B&B + Eve.Meal £28.00-£32.00

Ravenscraig Guest House Aviemore Inverness-shire PH22 1RP Tel:(Aviemore) 0479 810278	COMMENDED ♕ ♕	1 Single 4 Twin 5 Double 2 Family	12 En Suite fac	B&B per person £16.00-£19.00 Single £16.00-£19.00 Double	Open Jan-Dec

Situated on edge of village, within a few minutes walk of Aviemore centre. All rooms en suite. Some ground floor annexe accommodation.

Ver Mont Guest House Grampian Road Aviemore Inverness-shire PH22 1RP Tel:(Aviemore) 0479 810470		1 Twin 1 Double 1 Family	3 En Suite fac	B&B per person £14.00-£18.00 Double	Open Jan-Dec

AYR

Map 1 G7

Abbotsford Hotel 14 Corsehill Road Ayr KA7 2ST Tel:(Ayr) 0292 261506 Fax:0292 261506		2 Single 6 Twin 1 Double 3 Family	12 En Suite fac	B&B per person from £35.00 Single from £32.00 Double	Open Jan-Dec Dinner 1700-2200 B&B + Eve.Meal from £42.00

Aftongrange Hotel 37 Carrick Road Ayr KA7 2RD Tel:(Ayr) 0292 265679	APPROVED ♕ ♕	1 Single 3 Twin 2 Double 2 Family	5 En Suite fac 1 Pub.Bath/Show	B&B per person £17.50-£30.00 Single £17.50-£25.00 Double	Open Jan-Dec Dinner 1700-2100 B&B + Eve.Meal £25.00-£30.00

Small family run hotel centrally situated and within walking distance of all facilities.

Annfield Hotel 49 Maybole Road Ayr KA7 4SF Tel:(Alloway) 0292 441986 Fax:0292 442368	COMMENDED ♕ ♕ ♕	2 Single 3 Twin 2 Double 1 Family	8 En Suite fac	B&B per person from £35.00 Single from £30.00 Double	Open Jan-Dec Dinner 1700-2145 B&B + Eve.Meal £35.00-£50.00

Privately owned hotel, recently refurbished, situated 1 mile (2kms) from town centre. Full range of meals available.

AYR continued	Map 1 G7					
Ayrshire & Galloway Hotel 1 Killoch Place Ayr KA7 2EA Tel:(Ayr) 0292 262626			10 Single 8 Twin 3 Double 3 Family	8 En Suite fac 4 Pub.Bath/Show	B&B per person £17.50-£30.00 Single £17.50-£25.00 Double	Open Jan-Dec Dinner 1700-2030
Belmont Private Hotel 15 Park Circus Ayr KA7 2DJ Tel:(Ayr) 0292 265588			1 Single 1 Twin 1 Double 2 Family	2 Pub.Bath/Show	B&B per person £15.00-£16.00 Single £15.00-£16.00 Double	Open Jan-Dec
Burns Monument Hotel Alloway Ayrshire KA7 4PQ Tel:(Alloway) 0292 42466 Fax:0292 43174		COMMENDED 👑 👑 👑	1 Single 4 Twin 2 Double 2 Family	8 En Suite fac 1 Pub.Bath/Show	B&B per person £30.00-£45.00 Single £25.00-£40.00 Double	Open Jan-Dec Dinner 1700-2145 B&B + Eve.Meal £40.00-£60.00

Privately owned hotel; 19C building overlooking River Doon, next to Burns Monument, Old Brig of Doon and Alloway Kirk. Riverside garden.

CALEDONIAN HOTEL
DALBLAIR ROAD, AYR KA7 1UG Tel: 0292 269331

This Jarvis hotel situated in the town centre with its own car park is only ¹/₂ mile from the station and a 5 minute walk to Ayr's sandy beach. Enjoy a meal in Hudsons Bar and Grill which is renowned for its good food and warm welcome. After visiting the many places of interest nearby, relax in our mediterranean-style pool. 22 golf courses in a 20 mile radius.

| Caledonian Hotel Dalblair Road Ayr KA7 1UG Tel:(Ayr) 0292 269331 Tlx:776611 Fax:0292 610722 | | COMMENDED 👑 👑 👑 👑 👑 | 40 Single 56 Twin 6 Double 12 Family | 114 Fn Suite fac | B&B per person to £83.50 Single to £58.00 Double | Open Jan-Dec Dinner 1830-2200 B&B + Eve.Meal to £74.00 |

Modern town centre hotel facing sea, recently refurbished with swimming pool and leisure club. Conference and business centre.

| The Chestnuts Hotel 52 Racecourse Road Ayr KA7 2UZ Tel:(Ayr) 0292 264393 Fax:0292 264393 | | COMMENDED 👑 👑 👑 👑 | 7 Single 1 Twin 4 Double 2 Family | 11 En Suite fac 1 Limited ensuite 2 Pub.Bath/Show | B&B per person £34.00-£35.00 Single £33.00-£34.00 Double | Open Jan-Dec Dinner 1800-2000 B&B + Eve.Meal £43.50-£44.50 |

Attractive Listed building on south side of town a few minutes from the sea. Personally run.

AYR continued

Map 1 G7

Elms Court Hotel
21 Miller Road
Ayr
KA7 2AX
Tel:(Ayr) 0292
264191/282332
Fax:0292 610254

COMMENDED
👑👑👑 👑

4 Single	20 En Suite fac	B&B per person	Open Jan-Dec
6 Twin		from £32.00 Single	Dinner 1700-2130
6 Double		from £31.00 Double	
4 Family			

Comfortable family run hotel convenient for all facilities. A la carte restaurant.

Horizon Hotel
THE ESPLANADE, AYR. TELEPHONE: AYR (0292) 264384

The hotel is on the sea front, with its dining room overlooking the heads of Ayr and the Isle of Arran. Several golf courses are within easy reach and for those of you who aren't golfers there is sea fishing in the harbour, a sandy beach nearby and a children's play area. All rooms have tea/coffee making facilities, central heating and colour TV's, with special rates for parties of 10 or more.

Under the personal supervision of Mr & Mrs Meikle and family.

Horizon Hotel
The Esplanade
Ayr
KA7 1DT
Tel:(Ayr) 0292 264384

1 Single	8 En Suite fac	B&B per person	Open Jan-Dec
6 Twin	1 Priv.NOT ensuite	from £20.00 Single	Dinner from 1900
2 Double	5 Pub.Bath/Show	from £25.00 Double	
6 Family			

Kingsley Hotel
10 Alloway Place
Ayr
KA7 2AA
Tel:(Ayr) 0292 262853

2 Single	2 Pub.Bath/Show	B&B per person	Open Jan-Dec
1 Double		£17.00-£19.00 Single	Dinner 1700-2200
3 Family		£15.00-£17.50 Double	B&B + Eve.Meal
			£25.00-£27.00

Kylestrome Hotel
11 Miller Road
Ayr
KA7 2AX
Tel:(Ayr) 0292 262474
Fax:0292 260863

1 Single	12 En Suite fac	B&B per person	Open Jan-Dec
7 Twin		£42.00-£47.00 Single	Dinner 1830-2200
3 Double		£45.00-£74.00 Double	
1 Family			

Lochinver Private Hotel
32 Park Circus
Ayr
KA7 2DL
Tel:(Ayr) 0292 265086

COMMENDED
👑👑

1 Twin	3 En Suite fac	B&B per person	Open Jan-Dec
2 Double	2 Pub.Bath/Show	£16.00-£22.00 Single	Dinner from 1730
3 Family		£14.00-£20.00 Double	B&B + Eve.Meal
			£24.00-£30.00

Small, family-run, private hotel in Victorian house. In quiet, leafy residential street. Close to town centre, easy street parking.

Northpark House Hotel
Alloway
Ayr
KA7 4NL
Tel:(Ayr) 0292
442336/442337
Fax:0292 445572

HIGHLY COMMENDED
👑👑👑 👑

3 Twin	5 En Suite fac	B&B per person	Open Jan-Dec
1 Double		£55.00-£75.00 Single	Dinner 1800-2200
1 Family		£37.50-£47.50 Double	B&B + Eve.Meal
			£67.50-£95.00

Fully restored country house C. 1720 in peaceful location 5 minutes from town. Ideally suited to small executive conferences.

AYR continued	Map 1 G7						

Pickwick Hotel
19 Racecourse Road
Ayr
KA7 2TD
Tel:(Ayr) 0292 260111
Fax:0292 285348

COMMENDED
👑 👑 👑

2 Single
6 Twin
4 Double
3 Family

15 En Suite fac

B&B per person
£40.00-£50.00 Single
£35.00-£45.00 Double

Open Jan-Dec
Dinner 1900-2145
B&B + Eve.Meal
£50.00-£65.00

Stone built house with period character situated in its own grounds. In residential area within 0.5 miles (1km) of town centre and beach.

Richmond Private Hotel
38 Park Circus
Ayr
KA7 2DL
Tel:(Ayr) 0292 265153

COMMENDED
👑 👑

2 Double
4 Family

5 En Suite fac
1 Priv.NOT ensuite

B&B per person
£22.00-£25.00 Single
£16.50-£20.00 Double

Open Jan-Dec

Traditional stone built town house with many period features. Easy walking distance of town centre and sea front.

The Roblin Hotel
9-11 Barns Street
Ayr
KA7 1XB
Tel:(Ayr) 0292 267595

1 Single
4 Twin
7 Double
6 Family

2 En Suite fac
5 Pub.Bath/Show

B&B per person
£19.39-£21.74 Single
£16.45-£18.80 Double

Open Jan-Dec
Dinner 1730-1800
B&B + Eve.Meal
£22.33-£24.68

Savoy Park Hotel
16 Racecourse Road
Ayr
KA7 2UT
Tel:(Ayr) 0292 266112
Fax:0292 611488

COMMENDED
👑 👑 👑
👑

1 Single
9 Twin
3 Double
4 Family

17 En Suite fac

B&B per person
£35.00-£55.00 Single
£25.00-£37.50 Double

Open Jan-Dec
Dinner 1700-2100
B&B + Eve.Meal
£40.00-£50.00

Traditional family-run hotel in its own grounds, short distance from town centre, beach and all amenities.

Windsor Hotel
6 Alloway Place
Ayr
KA7 2AA
Tel:(Ayr) 0292 264689

COMMENDED
👑 👑 👑

2 Single
1 Twin
3 Double
4 Family

7 En Suite fac
1 Priv.NOT ensuite
2 Pub.Bath/Show

B&B per person
from £20.00 Single
from £22.00 Double

Open Jan-Dec
Dinner from 1800
B&B + Eve.Meal
from £31.00

Victorian house near centre of Ayr and the promenade with its long sandy beach.

Armadale Guest House
3 Bellevue Crescent
Ayr
KA7 2DP
Tel:(Ayr) 0292 264320/282404

COMMENDED
Listed

1 Twin
1 Double
1 Family

2 Limited ensuite
1 Pub.Bath/Show

B&B per person
from £15.00 Double

Open Jan-Dec

Personally run Edwardian terraced house in quiet residential area yet convenient for beach, town centre and railway station.

Croomage Guest House
6 Eglinton Terrace
Ayr
KA7 1JJ
Tel:(Ayr) 0292 266019

2 Twin
1 Double

1 Pub.Bath/Show

B&B per person
£15.00-£16.00 Single
£14.00 Double

Open Jan-Dec
Dinner from 1800
B&B + Eve.Meal
from £19.70

Craggallan Guest House
8 Queen's Terrace
Ayr
KA7 1DU
Tel:(Ayr) 0292 264998

COMMENDED
👑 👑

3 Single
1 Twin
1 Double
2 Family

2 Pub.Bath/Show

B&B per person
£15.00-£16.00 Single
£15.00-£17.00 Double

Open Jan-Dec
Dinner 1730-1800
B&B + Eve.Meal
£22.00-£23.00

Small family guest house close to sea front, shops, harbour and public swimming pool.

AYR continued

Map 1
G7

Craig Court Guest House 22 Eglinton Terrace Ayr KA7 1JJ Tel:(Ayr) 0292 261028	COMMENDED ≋ ≋	1 Twin 1 Double 2 Family	2 En Suite fac 2 Pub.Bath/Show	B&B per person from £16.00 Single from £15.00 Double	Open Jan-Dec

Quiet Victorian terraced house, overlooking public tennis courts. Only a few minutes from the sea, yet convenient for town centre. Families welcome.

Dargil Guest House 7 Queen's Terrace Ayr KA7 1DU Tel:(Ayr) 0292 261955	COMMENDED ≋ ≋	1 Twin 2 Double 1 Family	1 En Suite fac 2 Pub.Bath/Show	B&B per person from £16.00 Single from £14.00 Double	Open Jan-Dec Dinner 1700-1730 B&B + Eve.Meal from £19.00

Small, friendly guest house with sea front location. Only a few minutes walk from the town centre.

Daviot Guest House 12 Queen's Terrace Ayr KA7 1DU Tel:(Ayr) 0292 269678	COMMENDED ≋ ≋	1 Single 1 Twin 1 Double 1 Family	1 En Suite fac 2 Pub.Bath/Show	B&B per person £18.00-£20.00 Single £15.00-£16.00 Double	Open Jan-Dec Dinner from 1700 B&B + Eve.Meal £21.00-£22.00

Friendly welcome at this quietly situated terrace house only minutes walk from the seafront and town centre.

Eglinton Guest House 23 Eglinton Terrace Ayr KA7 1JJ Tel:(Ayr) 0292 264623		3 Single 2 Twin 1 Double 2 Family	1 Pub.Bath/Show	B&B per person £14.00-£20.00 Single £13.00-£20.00 Double	Open Jan-Dec Dinner from 1800 B&B + Eve.Meal £18.00-£25.00

Glenmore Guest House 35 Bellevue Crescent Ayr Ayrshire KA7 2DP Tel:(Ayr) 0292 269830	Award Pending	1 Single 2 Double 2 Family	4 En Suite fac 1 Pub.Bath/Show	B&B per person £18.00-£22.00 Single £18.00-£22.00 Double	Open Jan-Dec Dinner 1700-1830 B&B + Eve.Meal £26.00-£30.00

Langley Bank Guest House 39 Carrick Road Ayr KA7 2RD Tel:(Ayr) 0292 264246	HIGHLY COMMENDED Listed	1 Single 2 Twin 2 Double 1 Family	4 En Suite fac 2 Pub.Bath/Show	B&B per person £15.00-£30.00 Single £15.00-£25.00 Double	Open Jan-Dec

Elegantly refurbished Victorian house close to all amenities. Most rooms have private facilities and telephones. Good base for touring Ayrshire.

Queen's Guest House 10 Queen's Terrace Ayr KA7 1DU Tel:(Ayr) 0292 265618	COMMENDED ≋	1 Twin 2 Double 1 Family	2 Pub.Bath/Show	B&B per person £15.00-£17.00 Single £14.00-£15.00 Double	Open Jan-Dec Dinner from 1700 B&B + Eve.Meal from £21.00

Terraced house in quiet location only a few minutes walk from the seafront. Convenient for the town centre.

AYR continued	Map 1 G7	

The Scottish Agricultural College Wilson Hall, Auchincruive Ayr KA6 5HW Tel:(Ayr) 0292 520331 Tlx:777400 Fax:0292 521119		90 Single 10 Twin	15 Pub.Bath/Show	B&B per person £14.00 Single £14.00 Double	Open Easter, Jul-Sep, Xmas Dinner 1700-1830 B&B + Eve.Meal £19.50
BADACHRO **Ross-shire** Badachro Inn Badachro Gairloch Ross-shire IV21 2AA Tel:(Badachro) 044583 255	Map 3 E7	1 Single 1 Twin	1 Priv.NOT ensuite 1 Pub.Bath/Show	B&B per person £15.00-£18.00 Single £15.00-£18.00 Double	Open Jan-Dec Dinner 1700-2200
BALEPHETRISH **Isle of Tiree, Argyll** Balephetrish Guest House Balephetrish Isle of Tiree, Argyll PA77 6UY Tel:(Scarinish) 08792 549	Map 1 A2	1 Single 2 Twin 1 Family	1 Pub.Bath/Show	B&B per person £15.00 Single £15.00 Double	Open Jan-Dec Dinner at 1800 B&B + Eve.Meal £20.00

ails of Grading and Classification are on page vi. | Key to symbols is on back flap. | 35

VAT is shown at 17.5%: changes in this rate may affect prices. Prices shown are for guidance only. Please send SAE with each enqui

BALLACHULISH Argyll	Map 1 F1						
Ballachulish Hotel Ballachulish Argyll PA39 4JY Tel:(Ballachulish) 08552 606 Fax:08552 629		HIGHLY COMMENDED ♨ ♨ ♨ ♨	3 Single 15 Twin 10 Double 2 Family	30 En Suite fac	B&B per person £45.50-£55.50 Single £34.00-£46.75 Double	Open Jan-Dec Dinner 1900-2200 B&B + Eve.Meal £49.50-£66.25	
			Recently refurbished Highland hotel of baronial style beside A828. Imposingly situated with panoramic views over Loch Linnhe to the mountains.				
Isles of Glencoe Hotel & Leisure Centre Ballachulish Argyll PA39 4HL Tel:(Ballachulish) 08552 603 Tlx:94013696 Fax:08552 629		COMMENDED ♨ ♨ ♨ ♨	7 Single 21 Twin 7 Double 4 Family	39 En Suite fac	B&B per person £32.50-£42.50 Single £32.50-£42.50 Double	Open Jan-Dec Dinner 1900-2200 B&B + Eve.Meal £39.50-£57.50	
			Newly-built modern hotel and leisure centre on shores of Loch Linnhe with excellent views.				
Ballachulish House Ballachulish Argyll PA39 4JX Tel:(Ballachulish) 08552 266		HIGHLY COMMENDED ♨ ♨ ♨	2 Twin 2 Double	4 En Suite fac	B&B per person £32.50-£50.00 Single £25.00-£38.50 Double	Open Jan-Dec Dinner from 1930 B&B + Eve.Meal £40.00-£58.50	
			18C Historic country house elegantly furnished. All rooms en-suite. Specialising in local produce. Warm, informal atmosphere.				

Craiglinnhe Guest House

BALLACHULISH, ARGYLL PA39 4JX   Tel: (08552) 270

Craiglinnhe, situated close to the water's edge amidst magnificent scenery, provides an excellent touring base for the Western Highlands. Set in beautiful gardens, this small, personally managed guest house offers traditional Scottish hospitality in extremely well-appointed accommodation. An ideal setting in which to relax and unwind.

Brochure on request.   ♨ ♨ ♨ *Commended*

Craiglinnhe Guest House Ballachulish Argyll PA39 4JX Tel:(Ballachulish) 08552 270	COMMENDED ♨ ♨ ♨	4 Twin 2 Double	6 En Suite fac	B&B per person from £18.00 Double	Open Dec-Oct Dinner from 1900 B&B + Eve.Meal from £27.00	
		Family run guest house overlooking Loch Linnhe and the mountains beyond. Hill walking and mountaineering in the area. Good centre for touring.				
Fern Villa Guest House Ballachulish Argyll PA39 4JE Tel:(Ballachulish) 08552 393	COMMENDED ♨ ♨ ♨	2 Twin 3 Double	5 En Suite fac	B&B per person from £15.50 Double	Open Jan-Dec Dinner from 1900 B&B + Eve.Meal from £25.00	
		Non-smoking. Traditional granite built house in this typical West Highland village on Loch Leven by Glencoe. Fort William 15 miles (24 kms).				

Key to symbols is on back flap.

| BALLACHULISH
Argyll | Map 1
F1 | | | | | |

LYN-LEVEN GUEST HOUSE
WEST LAROCH, BALLACHULISH, ARGYLL PA39 4JP
Telephone: 085-52 392

A VERY WARM HIGHLAND WELCOME AWAITS YOU at Lyn-Leven, only 1 mile from lovely GLENCOE. The house is family run, with good home cooking. We are situated with attractive well cared for gardens overlooking Loch Leven in the heart of Scotland's most spectacular scenery.
PRIVATE CAR PARKING.
AA Listed, RAC Acclaimed. 😊😊😊 **Commended**

| Lyn-Leven Guest House
Ballachulish
Argyll
PA39 4JP
Tel:(Ballachulish) 08552 392 | **COMMENDED**
😊 😊 😊 | 4 Twin
3 Double
1 Family | 8 En Suite fac
1 Pub.Bath/Show | B&B per person
£16.00-£22.00 Single
£16.00-£18.50 Double | Open Jan-Dec
Dinner from 1830
B&B + Eve.Meal
£24.00-£27.50 | |

Small, modern, family run guest house located in Ballachulish village and overlooking Loch Leven. All home cooking.

| BALLANTRAE
Ayrshire
Balkissock Lodge
Ballantrae
Ayrshire
KA26 0LP
Tel:(Ballantrae) 046583 537
Fax:0465 83537 | Map 1
F9

**Award
Pending** | 1 Twin
1 Double
1 Family | 3 En Suite fac | B&B per person
£25.00-£30.00 Double | Open Jan-Dec
Dinner 1900-2100
B&B + Eve.Meal
£35.00-£55.00 | |

COSSES
BALLANTRAE TEL: (046 583) 363

Cosses, a former shooting lodge, is in a secluded valley. The kitchen garden supplementing local produce for 'Taste of Scotland' menus. Castles Gardens, Walking, Golfing, Biking, River and Loch Fishing. Irish ferry terminals 30 minutes drive. B/B £26 –£30 per person. Dinner £18. Contact Susan Crosthwaite, Cosses, Ballantrae, Ayrshire. KA26 0LR Tel: (046 583) 363, Fax: (046 583) 598. **Deluxe** 😊😊😊

| Cosses
Ballantrae
Ayrshire
KA26 0LR
Tel:(Ballantrae) 0465 83363
Fax:046583 598 | **DELUXE**
😊 😊 😊 | 1 Double
1 Family | 2 En Suite fac | B&B per person
£31.00-£35.00 Single
£26.00-£30.00 Double | Open Jan-Dec, except Xmas/New Year
Dinner 1900-2100
B&B + Eve.Meal
£44.00-£48.00 | |

Former shooting lodge in secluded valley in 12 acres of gardens and woodland. Garden supplements Taste of Scotland cuisine. 1/2 hour to Irish ferry.

BALLATER Aberdeenshire	Map 4 E1

ALEXANDRA HOTEL

Listed hotel newly refurbished to a high standard. All bedrooms with private facilities. Situated only 7 miles from Balmoral and many places of interest in the heart of Ballater. Convenient for golf, fishing, walking, Distillery, Visitors' Centre and Castle Trail.

Excellent cuisine in our restaurant or bar.

AA ★★   Michelin Guide   Les Routiers   RAC   Logis of Great Britain

Contact: Mr Tabuteau, Alexandra Hotel, 12 Bridge Square, Ballater, Aberdeenshire AB35 5QJ.   Tel: (03397) 55376 Fax: (03397) 55466

♨ ♨ ♨ **Commended**

Alexandra Hotel Bridge Square Ballater Aberdeenshire AB35 5QJ Tel:(Ballater) 03397 55376 Fax:03397 55466	COMMENDED ♨ ♨ ♨	1 Single 7 En Suite fac 2 Twin 3 Double 1 Family	B&B per person £24.00-£30.00 Single £24.00-£28.00 Double	Open Jan-Dec Dinner 1800-2100 B&B + Eve.Meal £38.00-£44.00	
		Family run hotel in Deeside village. 7 miles (11kms) from Balmoral and 30 minutes drive from Glenshee ski slopes. Scottish and French cuisine.			
Aspen Hotel Braemar Road Ballater Aberdeenshire AB35 5RQ Tel:(Ballater) 03397 55486	APPROVED ♨ ♨	3 Single 3 En Suite fac 2 Twin 3 Pub.Bath/Show 5 Double 1 Family	B&B per person from £17.00 Single from £17.00 Double	Open Jan-Dec Dinner 1900-2100	
		Friendly family run hotel offering good food, using fresh local produce. In quiet residential area, convenient to all amenities.			
Auld Kirk Hotel Braemar Road Ballater Aberdeenshire AB35 5RQ Tel:(Ballater) 03397 55762 Fax:03397 55707	COMMENDED ♨ ♨ ♨	3 Twin 6 En Suite fac 3 Double	B&B per person £25.00-£36.00 Single £20.00-£22.00 Double	Open Jan-Dec Dinner 1830-2100	
		Hotel converted from old church, still retaining many original features. Located in scenic splendour and easy walking distance from Ballater.			

HERE'S THE DIFFERENCE

STB's scheme has two distinct elements, grading and classification.

GRADING:

measures the quality and condition of the facilities and services offered, eg, the warmth of welcome, quality of food and its presentation, condition of decor and furnishings, appearance of buildings, tidiness of grounds and gardens, condition of lighting and heating and so on.

Grading awards are: **Approved, Commended, Highly Commended, Deluxe.**

CLASSIFICATION:

measures the range of physical facilities and services offered, eg, rooms with private bath, heating, reception, lounges, telephones and so on.

Classification awards are: **Listed or from one to five crowns.**

BALLATER continued	Map 4 E1

BALGONIE
Country House

BALLATER . ROYAL DEESIDE
ABERDEENSHIRE AB35 5RQ
Tel: (03397) 55482 Fax; (03397) 55482

This charming Edwardian Country House in Royal Deeside is set in 4 acres of mature gardens, enjoying truly superb views over Ballater Golf Course towards the hills beyond. Our dining room is at the heart of Balgonie, offering fine Scottish cuisine reflecting the wealth and choice of local produce ranging from Salmon to Aberdeen Angus Beef and Scotch Lamb, Game to Seafood fresh from the East Coast. Idyllic base for Golf, Walking, Touring nearby Castle and Malt Whisky Trails or simply relaxing. Our personal attention to each guest ensures that your stay will be both relaxing and enjoyable.

Balgonie Country House Ballater Aberdeenshire AB35 5RQ Tel:(Ballater) 03397 55482	DELUXE ♛ ♛ ♛	3 Twin 6 Double	9 En Suite fac	B&B per person £50.00-£60.00 Single £40.00-£50.00 Double	Open Jan-Dec Dinner 1915-2130 B&B + Eve.Meal £65.00-£85.00	
		In heart of Royal Deeside, secluded Edwardian country house set in 4 acres overlooking golf course. Fine Scottish cuisine and attentive service.				
The Ballater Hotel & Bruno's Ristorante 34 Victoria Road Ballater Aberdeenshire AB35 5QX Tel:(Ballater) 03397 55346 Fax:03397 55346	COMMENDED ♛ ♛ ♛	4 Twin 4 Double 1 Family	4 En Suite fac 3 Pub.Bath/Show	B&B per person £20.00-£30.00 Single £22.50-£25.00 Double	Open Jan-Dec Dinner 1900-2300	
		Continental influenced style hotel with Italian restaurant. Quietly situated near golf course. Free use of health and country club.				
The Coach House Netherley Place Ballater Aberdeenshire AB35 5QE Tel:(Ballater) 03397 55462 Fax:03397 55462	COMMENDED ♛ ♛ ♛	3 Twin 3 Double	4 En Suite fac 2 Priv.NOT ensuite 2 Pub.Bath/Show	B&B per person £30.00-£32.00 Single £24.00-£26.00 Double	Open Jan-Dec Dinner 1700-2100 B&B + Eve.Meal from £28.25	
		Overlooking village green in centre of Ballater and offering a warm welcome all year. Our restaurant serves the best of fresh local produce.				
The Coyles Hotel 43 Golf Road Ballater Aberdeenshire AB35 5RS Tel:(Ballater) 03397 55064	HIGHLY COMMENDED ♛ ♛ ♛	1 Single 2 Twin 2 Double	5 En Suite fac 1 Pub.Bath/Show	B&B per person £22.00-£28.00 Single £20.00-£26.00 Double	Open Jan-Dec Dinner from 1900 B&B + Eve.Meal £30.00-£36.00	
		Recently refurbished, Victorian stone built villa with sun lounge, in quiet residential area of village. Home cooking and baking.				

BALLATER continued	Map 4 E1							
Craigendarroch Hotel & Country Club Braemar Road Ballater Aberdeenshire AB35 5XA Tel:(Ballater) 03397 55858 Fax:03397 55447	HIGHLY COMMENDED ♛♛♛ ♛♛	24 Twin 20 Double 6 Family	50 En Suite fac	B&B per person from £99.00 Double	Open Jan-Dec Dinner 1800-2230 B&B + Eve.Meal from £109.00			
		Country house elegance in an unparalleled setting, with a relaxing leisure club and timeshare lodges. Restaurant enjoys a fine reputation.						

Darroch Learg Hotel
BRAEMAR ROAD, BALLATER
GRAMPIAN AB35 5UX
Tel: (03397) 55443

The DARROCH LEARG stands in a commanding position above Ballater with superb views over the golf course and River Dee to the Grampian Mountains.

The hotel is family owned and has a relaxing country house atmosphere. Its 20 bedrooms are individually furnished and equipped to a high standard. The conservatory dining room offers diners a wonderful outlook, fine Scottish beef, lamb and fish, and interesting wines.

Ballater is eight miles from Balmoral and in the midst of Royal Deeside; an area renowned for its outstanding scenery, fine walks, outdoor sports and places of interest.

| Darroch Learg Hotel Braemar Road Ballater Aberdeenshire AB35 5UX Tel:(Ballater) 03397 55443 Fax:03397 55443 | HIGHLY COMMENDED ♛♛♛ ♛ | 2 Single 9 Twin 9 Double | 20 En Suite fac | B&B per person £34.00-£40.00 Single £29.00-£45.00 Double | Open Feb-Dec Dinner 1900-2030 B&B + Eve.Meal £41.00-£64.75 | | | |
| | | Traditional country hotel in 5 acres of wooded grounds. Fine vantage point. Panoramic views over Dee Valley and Grampian Moutains. | | | | | | |

The Deeside Hotel
BRAEMAR ROAD · BALLATER AB35 5RQ Tel: 03397 55420

A small, comfortable, family owned and run hotel situated in a quiet location. In the evening we offer a choice of freshly prepared dishes, at reasonable prices, served in our informal Bar/Restaurant. 2 ground floor bedrooms available.
Proprietors: Donald and Alison Brooker.

| Deeside Hotel Braemar Road Ballater Aberdeenshire AB35 5RQ Tel:(Ballater) 03397 55420 | COMMENDED ♛♛♛ | 4 Twin 3 Double 1 Family | 8 En Suite fac | B&B per person £17.00-£26.00 Single £17.00-£22.00 Double | Open Feb-Nov Dinner 1800-2100 B&B + Eve.Meal £29.00-£34.00 | | | |
| | | Family run hotel in quiet location, specialising in informal bar style meals. | | | | | | |

BALLATER continued	Map 4 E1					

Glen Lui Hotel
Invercauld Road
Ballater
Aberdeenshire
AB35 5RP
Tel:(Ballater) 03397 55402
Fax:03397 55545

HIGHLY COMMENDED

2 Single
9 Twin
5 Double
2 Family

18 En Suite fac

B&B per person
£30.00-£40.00 Single
£30.00-£40.00 Double

Open Mar-Nov
Dinner 1830-2130
B&B + Eve.Meal
£40.00-£60.00

Personally run hotel with friendly atmosphere, quietly situated by golf course. All rooms with private separate pine terrace accommodation.

The Green Inn
9 Victoria Road
Ballater
Aberdeenshire
AB35 5QQ
Tel:(Ballater) 03397 55701

COMMENDED

2 Twin
1 Double

3 En Suite fac

B&B per person
£20.00 Double

Open Jan-Dec
Dinner 1900-2130
B&B + Eve.Meal
£40.00

'A Restaurant with room' overlooking village green. The Inn has a "Taste of Scotland" menu specialising in freshly prepared local produce.

Loirston Hotel
Victoria Road
Ballater
Aberdeenshire
AB35 5RA
Tel:(Ballater) 03397 55413
Fax:03397 55027

COMMENDED

12 Single
32 Twin
12 Double
2 Family

58 En Suite fac
17 Pub.Bath/Show

B&B per person
£25.00-£50.00 Single
£25.00-£50.00 Double

Open Mar-Oct
Dinner 1830-2000
B&B + Eve.Meal
£38.00-£63.00

Recently refurbished hotel situated in the centre of Ballater. Close to all amenities and ideal for touring Royal Deeside.

MONALTRIE HOTEL

BALLATER · ABERDEENSHIRE · AB35 5QJ   Tel: (03397) 55417

Stay at the MONALTRIE HOTEL in Ballater and enjoy the wonders of Royal Deeside. The hotel overlooks the River Dee and has 25 comfortable bedrooms – all with private bathroom. Situated close to Balmoral Castle, Braemar, Aberdeen and the Whisky Trail.

Colour brochure and tariff available on request.

Monaltrie Hotel
5 Bridge Square
Ballater
Aberdeenshire
AB35 5QJ
Tel:(Ballater) 03397 55417
Fax:03397 55180

COMMENDED

6 Single
8 Twin
7 Double
4 Family

23 En Suite fac
2 Priv.NOT ensuite

B&B per person
£22.50-£45.00 Single
£22.50-£27.50 Double

Open Jan-Dec
Dinner 1730-2130
B&B + Eve.Meal
£35.00-£40.00

19C coaching inn overlooking the River Dee. On the eastern outskirts of Ballater with riverside gardens.

Craig Gowan
53 Golf Road
Ballater
Aberdeenshire
AB35 5RU
Tel:(Ballater) 03397 55008

COMMENDED

1 Single
3 Twin
2 Double

3 En Suite fac
2 Pub.Bath/Show

B&B per person
£17.00-£20.00 Single
£17.00-£20.00 Double

Open Jan-Dec
Dinner from 1900
B&B + Eve.Meal
£26.00-£29.00

Victorian villa in quiet residential area, two minutes walk from golf course, bowling green, tennis courts and shops. Personally run.

Gairnshiel Lodge
Glengairn
Ballater
Aberdeenshire
AB35 5UQ
Tel:(Ballater) 03397 55582

COMMENDED

1 Single
4 Twin
2 Double
4 Family

6 En Suite fac
2 Pub.Bath/Show

B&B per person
£15.50-£19.50 Single
£15.50-£19.50 Double

Open Jan-Dec
Dinner 1900-2000
B&B + Eve.Meal
£26.00-£30.00

Traditional, stone built, former hunting lodge 4.5 acres of ground, 6 miles (10kms) from Ballater and Balmoral. Home cooking.

BALLATER continued	Map 4 E1						
Glenbardie Guest House Braemar Road Ballater Aberdeenshire AB35 5RQ Tel:(Ballater) 03397 55537		2 Twin 1 Double 2 Family	2 En Suite fac 2 Pub.Bath/Show	B&B per person £18.00-£22.00 Single £15.00-£18.00 Double	Open May-Oct	

| Highland Guest House
Invercauld Road
Ballater
Aberdeenshire
AB35 5RP
Tel:(Ballater) 03397 55468 | COMMENDED ♛ ♛ | 1 Single
1 Twin
2 Double
2 Family | 3 En Suite fac
1 Pub.Bath/Show | B&B per person
£17.00-£19.00 Single
£17.00-£20.00 Double | Open Jan-Dec | |
| | | Fine Victorian house set in one acre of gardens. For the benefit of all our guests, this is a non-smoking establishment. | | | | |

| Moorside Guest House
Braemar Road
Ballater
Aberdeenshire
AB35 5RL
Tel:(Ballater) 03397 55492
Fax:03397 55492 | COMMENDED ♛ ♛ | 4 Twin
2 Double
3 Family | 9 En Suite fac | B&B per person
£27.00-£30.00 Single
£18.00-£20.00 Double | Open Mar-Nov | |
| | | Friendly family run guest House offers all rooms with en suite facilities, TVs and courtesy trays. Large garden and car park. | | | | |

| Netherley Guest House
2 Netherley Place
Ballater
Aberdeenshire
AB35 5QE
Tel:(Ballater) 03397 55792 | COMMENDED ♛ ♛ | 2 Single
2 Twin
2 Double
3 Family | 4 En Suite fac
2 Pub.Bath/Show | B&B per person
£17.00-£19.00 Single
£15.00-£20.00 Double | Open Feb-Oct | |
| | | Family run guest house in a quiet location in the centre of a renowned village. Close to shops and amenities. | | | | |

BALLINDALLOCH Banffshire	Map 4 D9					
Delnashaugh Inn Ballindalloch Banffshire AB37 9AS Tel:(Ballindalloch) 0807 500255 Fax:0807 500389	HIGHLY COMMENDED ♛ ♛ ♛ ♛	8 Twin 1 Double	9 En Suite fac	B&B per person £35.00-£50.00 Single £35.00-£50.00 Double	Open Feb-Nov Dinner 1900-2100 B&B + Eve.Meal £50.00-£65.00	
		Personally run and elegantly furnished former drovers inn overlooking River Avon. 15 miles (24kms) north of Grantown on Spey on A95.				

BALLINGRY by Loch Leven, Fife	Map 2 C4					
Navitie House Ballingry,by Loch Leven Fife KY5 8LR Tel:(Ballingry) 0592 860295	APPROVED ♛ ♛ ♛	1 Single 2 Twin 3 Double 3 Family	7 En Suite fac 1 Pub.Bath/Show	B&B per person £20.00 Single £18.00 Double	Open Jan-Dec Dinner 1900-2100 B&B + Eve.Meal £25.00	
		Detached house in its own grounds overlooking Ballingry village. Only 4miles (6kms) from the Edinburgh to Perth motorway.				

BALLINLUIG Perthshire	Map 2 B1		

LOGIERAIT HOTEL
By PITLOCHRY, PERTHSHIRE PH9 0LH
Telephone: 0796 482423
Famous old Sporting Inn ideally situated on the banks of the River Tay, one mile off the main A9, on the A827 to Aberfeldy. 7 bedrooms (3 en-suite) fully licensed, central heating and direct dial telephones.
Bar meals with a host of local produce.

Logierait Hotel Logierait Ballinluig Perthshire PH9 0LH Tel:(Ballinluig) 0796 482423		2 Twin 3 Double 2 Family	3 En Suite fac 1 Pub.Bath/Show	B&B per person £20.50-£25.00 Single £15.50-£20.50 Double	Open Jan-Dec Dinner 1900-2130 B&B + Eve.Meal £23.50-£28.50	

BALLOCH Dunbartonshire Balloch Hotel Balloch Dunbartonshire G83 8LQ Tel:(Alexandria) 0389 52579 Fax:0389 55604	Map 1 H4	COMMENDED ♕ ♕ ♕ ♕	5 Single 1 Twin 6 Double 2 Family	14 En Suite fac	B&B per person from £42.00 Single from £31.50 Double	Open Jan-Dec Dinner 1800-2130	

Situated at the south end of Loch Lomond, 25 minutes drive from Glasgow. Quality bar food from midday - 9.00 pm. Outside drinking area.

Anchorage Guest House Balloch Road Balloch Dunbartonshire G83 8SS Tel:(Alexandria) 0389 53336		2 Twin 4 Double 1 Family	4 En Suite fac 2 Pub.Bath/Show	B&B per person £15.00-£17.00 Double	Open Jan-Dec	

Gowanlea Guest House Drymen Road Balloch Dunbartonshire G83 8HS Tel:(Alexandria) 0389 52456		HIGHLY COMMENDED ♕ ♕	1 Twin 2 Double	3 En Suite fac	B&B per person £18.00-£25.00 Single £18.00-£22.00 Double	Open Jan-Dec	

Situated in residential area of Balloch, close to world famous Loch Lomond. Friendly welcome, all rooms en suite.

TELEPHONE DIALLING CODES

Many telephone dialling codes have changed this year. If you experience difficulty in connecting a call, please call Directory Enquiries – **192** – where someone will issue the correct number. Please note: a charge will be placed for this service when using a private telephone

| BALQUHIDDER | Map 1 |
| Perthshire | H3 |

Kings House
Hotel
proprietors: Bill, Rena & Graeme Courtney

This family run hotel offers friendly personal service, an excellent restaurant with good home cooking; including venison, salmon, trout and Scotch beef from local suppliers.

The hotel was built in 1747 and stands on the site of the Stuart Kings Hunting Lodge. Stag and Rough shooting together with fishing for salmon and trout is just minutes away, and, the hotel has its own fishing rights on Loch Lubnaig.

The hotel sits on the A84 trunk road at the Balquhidder road junction overlooking the majestic Braes O'Balquhidder.

Some fine walks offering spectacular scenery are near to the hotel; and there are several Munros the more energetic can climb but a few miles away.

There are several golf courses nearby and a full range of water sports is available at Lochearnhead some 3 miles away.

Over the past 2½ years the hotel has been renovated to a very high standard providing en-suite facilities in all bedrooms, but still preserving a Country Inn atmosphere. Come and visit the Balquhidder Glen – arguably one of Scotland's most picturesque spots – the home and final resting place of Rob Roy, Scotland's famous outlaw.

The Kings House is ideally situated in Central Scotland as a base to visit a large number of our tourist attractions. Standing, as it does, on the main trunk road to the Western Isles, you are only an hour or so to Glasgow, Edinburgh, Perth, Oban, Fort William, Loch Lomond and several other places of interest.

TARIFF

Bed and Breakfast	£21.00 per person
Dinner, Bed and Breakfast	£31.00 per person
Single Occupancy Supplement	£3.00 per night

COMMENDED

BALQUHIDDER, PERTHSHIRE, FK19 8NY.
Telephone: Strathyre (08774) 646 From Jan (0877) 384646

King's House Hotel	COMMENDED	1 Twin	7 En Suite fac	B&B per person	Open Jan-Dec
Balquhidder		4 Double		from £21.00 Double	Dinner 1830-2100
Perthshire		2 Family			B&B + Eve.Meal
FK19 8NY					from £31.00
Tel:(Strathyre) 0877 384646					

Family run hotel, formerly a hunting lodge situated in the heart of Rob Roy country. Ideal base for touring the Trossachs and west central Scotland.

Auchtubhmor House
Balquihidder Perthshire FK19 8NZ Tel: 0877 384632

Superbly positioned on its own elevated grounds where herds of wild deer are frequent visitors. An ideal base for touring, walking, fishing, golf, etc. All bedrooms en-suite. Partake of good food and wines after which retreat to a log fire where exchange of the days pleasantries brings your day to a successful conclusion.

Auchtubhmor House	COMMENDED	1 Twin	4 En Suite fac	B&B per person	Open Apr-Oct
Balquhidder		2 Double		£20.00-£22.00 Single	
Perthshire		1 Family		£17.00-£20.00 Double	
FK19 8NZ					
Tel:(Strathyre) 0877 384632					

Built for an ancestor of Rob Roy approx 250 years ago. A delightful house with magnificent views of the Trossachs, and surrounding countryside.

BALQUHIDDER continued Monachyle Mhor Hotel/ Farmhouse Balquhidder, by Lochearnhead Perthshire FK19 8PQ Tel:(Strathyre) 08774 622 Fax:08774 305	**Map 1 H3**	COMMENDED ♕ ♕ ♕	1 Twin 5 En Suite fac 4 Double	B&B per person £23.00-£25.00 Double	Open Jan-Dec Dinner 1930-2200 B&B + Eve.Meal £37.00-£45.00	

18C farmhouse in own 2000 acres. Magnificent situation overlooking Lochs Voil and Doine. Stalking and fishing available. Taste of Scotland

BANCHORY Kincardineshire Banchory Lodge Hotel Banchory Kincardineshire AB31 3HS Tel:(Banchory) 03302 2625 Fax:03302 5019	**Map 4 F1**	HIGHLY COMMENDED ♕ ♕ ♕ ♕	5 Twin 22 En Suite fac 8 Double 9 Family	B&B per person from £65.00 Single from £45.00 Double	Open Feb-Dec Dinner from 1900	

Privately owned Georgian country house hotel, set amidst Highland scenery with River Dee running through its extensive grounds.

Raemoir House Hotel Banchory Kincardineshire AB31 4ED Tel:(Banchory) 03302 4884 Fax:03302 2171		HIGHLY COMMENDED ♕ ♕ ♕ ♕	5 Single 21 En Suite fac 14 Double 2 Family	B&B per person £52.50-£79.00 Single £57.50-£63.00 Double	Open Jan-Dec Dinner 1930-2100 B&B + Eve.Meal £77.00-£87.50	

17/18C country house on a 3,500 acre estate. We offer salmon fishing, tennis, shooting and 9 hole mini-golf. Self catering apartments available.

Tor-Na-Coille Hotel
INCHMARLO ROAD, BANCHORY AB31 4AB
Telephone: (0330) 822242 Fax: (0330) 824012

Privately owned Victorian Country House Hotel in magnificent wooded surroundings overlooking Banchory golf course. 25 en-suite bedrooms, each individually furnished in period style. Excellent Scottish cuisine and fine wines. Families welcome. Weddings, Conferences catered for. Squash courts, croquet, log fires, lift.

Tor-Na-Coille Hotel Inchmarlo Road Banchory Kincardineshire AB31 4AB Tel:(Banchory) 0330 822242 Fax:0330 824012		COMMENDED ♕ ♕ ♕ ♕	1 Single 24 En Suite fac 11 Twin 10 Double 2 Family	B&B per person £55.00-£82.50 Single £35.75-£50.00 Double	Open Jan-Dec Dinner 1900-2200 B&B + Eve.Meal £77.00-£104.00	

Privately owned country house hotel, close to Banchory town centre with recreational facilities. Conference and private dining facilities.

Village Guest House 83 High Street Banchory Kincardineshire AB31 3TJ Tel:(Banchory) 0330 823307		HIGHLY COMMENDED Listed	2 Twin 2 Pub.Bath/Show 2 Double Suites avail.	B&B per person £18.00-£20.00 Single from £20.00 Double	Open Jan-Dec	

Charming Victorian house in centre of Royal Deeside village. Fountain patio. Warm Scottish welcome.

BY BANCHORY **Kincardineshire** Potarch Hotel Potarch Banchory Kincardineshire AB31 4BD Tel:(Kincardine O'Neil) 03398 84339	Map 4 F1	COMMENDED 👑 👑 👑	3 Twin 2 Double 1 Family	6 En Suite fac	B&B per person £25.00-£35.00 Single from £25.00 Double	Open Jan-Dec Dinner 1800-2100
			Friendly comfortable hotel. Emphasis on good food. Ideal for fishing.			
BANFF Banff Links Hotel Swordanes Banff AB45 2JJ Tel:(Banff) 0261 812414 Fax:02612 2463	Map 4 F7	COMMENDED 👑 👑 👑	2 Single 2 Twin 4 Double 1 Family	9 En Suite fac 1 Pub.Bath/Show	B&B per person £29.50-£35.00 Single £22.00-£30.00 Double	Open Jan-Dec Dinner 1700-2230 B&B + Eve.Meal £33.95-£46.95
			Family run on Links with sandy beach and all rooms en suite with sea views Ideal for fishing, golfing and outdoor activities.			
Banff Springs Hotel Golden Knowes Road Banff AB45 2JE Tel:(Banff) 0261 812881 Fax:0261 815546		COMMENDED 👑 👑 👑 👑	5 Single 10 Twin 11 Double 4 Family	30 En Suite fac	B&B per person £40.50-£44.50 Single	Open Jan-Dec Dinner 1830-2100
			Modern hotel on town outskirts with fine views of Moray Firth. Duff House golf course 1 mile (2kms). 17 others within 17 miles (27kms).			
Carmelite House Private Hotel Low Street Banff AB45 1AY Tel:(Banff) 0261 812152		COMMENDED 👑 👑	3 Single 2 Twin 3 Double 2 Family	3 En Suite fac 3 Pub.Bath/Show	B&B per person from £18.50 Single £17.50-£20.00 Double	Open Jan-Dec Dinner 1800-1900 B&B + Eve.Meal £26.00-£28.50
			Family run Georgian town house in central location. Convenient for golf course and all amenities. Evening meals available.			
Royal Oak Hotel Bridge Street Banff AB45 1HB Tel:(Banff) 0261 812494		Award Pending	1 Single 2 Twin 1 Double 1 Family	2 Limited ensuite 1 Pub.Bath/Show	B&B per person from £15.00 Single £13.00-£16.00 Double	Open Jan-Dec Dinner 1800-2200 B&B + Eve.Meal from £20.50
BY BANFF Eden House Eden, by Banff AB45 3NT Tel:(Eden) 02616 282	Map 4 F7		2 Twin 2 Double	3 En Suite fac 1 Priv.NOT ensuite	B&B per person £30.00-£32.00 Double	Open Jan-Dec Dinner 1900-2100 B&B + Eve.Meal £48.00-£50.00
BARRHEAD **Renfrewshire** Dalmeny Park Country House Hotel Lochlibo Road Barrhead, Glasgow Renfrewshire G78 1LG Tel:041 881 9211 Fax:041 881 9214	Map 1 H6	COMMENDED 👑 👑 👑 👑	20 Double 2 Pub.Bath/Show	15 En Suite fac	B&B per person £48.00-£62.00 Single £33.00-£43.00 Double	Open Jan-Dec Dinner 1900-2130 B&B + Eve.Meal £61.00-£73.00
			19C house in five acres of well maintained gardens. Within easy travelling distance of Glasgow Airport and main motorway routes.			

BEARSDEN **Dunbartonshire** Kilmardinny Guest House Kilmardinny Farm, Milngavie Road Bearsden, Glasgow Dunbartonshire G61 3DH Tel:041 943 1310	Map 1 H5		5 Single 1 Twin 2 Double	2 Pub.Bath/Show	B&B per person £16.00-£18.00 Single £16.00-£18.00 Double	Open Jan-Dec
St Andrews College Duntocher Road Bearsden, Glasgow Dunbartonshire G61 4QA Tel:041 943 1424 Fax:041 943 0106			203 Single 105 Twin	65 Pub.Bath/Show	B&B per person £19.50 Single £19.50 Double	Open Easter, Jun-Sep Dinner 1730-1830 B&B + Eve.Meal £27.50
BEATTOCK **Dumfriesshire**	Map 2 C8					

AUCHEN CASTLE HOTEL & RESTAURANT

Beattock, Moffat, Dumfries & Galloway DG10 9SH
Tel: 06833 407   Fax: 06833 667

Listed country house c1849 with modern wing in 50 glorious
acres. Ideal for an overnight break or a get-away few days in the
Borders. Egon Ronay, Good Hotel Guide 1994.
Taste of Scotland Recommended.

A Scotland's Commended Hotel. B&B from £26. DB&B from £37.

Auchen Castle Hotel & Restaurant Beattock Dumfriesshire DG10 9SH Tel:(Beattock) 06833 407 Fax:06833 667	COMMENDED 👑 👑 👑 👑		3 Single 12 Twin 9 Double 1 Family	25 En Suite fac	B&B per person £47.00 Single £26.00-£35.00 Double	Open Jan-Dec Dinner 1900-2100 B&B + Eve.Meal £37.00-£52.00

19C country house retaining original features with modern annexe in 50 acres
of private grounds. Trout loch; interesting tree and shrub collection.

Beattock House Hotel Beattock Dumfriesshire DG10 9QB Tel:(Beattock) 06833 403	COMMENDED 👑 👑		1 Single 4 Twin 1 Double 1 Family	3 En Suite fac 2 Pub.Bath/Show	B&B per person from £30.00 Single from £35.00 Double	Open Jan-Dec Dinner 1830-2130 B&B + Eve.Meal from £45.00

Unique country house standing in own grounds of lawns and mature trees.
Adjacent to A74 Glasgow-Carlisle road. Shooting, fishing, stalking arranged.

WELCOME

Whenever you are in Scotland, you can be sure of a warm welcome at your
nearest Tourist Information Centre.

For guide books, maps, souvenirs, our Centres provide a service second to
none – many now offer bureau-de-change facilities. And, of course, Tourist
Information Centres offer free, expert advice on what to see and do, route-
planning and accommodation for everyone – visitors and residents alike!

BEAULY Inverness-shire	Map 4 A8	

Caledonian Hotel
Beauly, Inverness-shire IV4 7BY. Tel: (0463) 782278

'Highland Hospitality with a fishy flavour.' Old coach house in same family
for 40 years in 'Britain in Bloom' square. Offers trout fishing, boats, etc. on
choice of lochs, birdwatching trip on Beauly estuary, en-suite D.B.B.
£295 p.p.p.w. Beer garden/cycle lock-up.
Ask for B&B only terms. All welcome.

Caledonian Hotel The Square Beauly Inverness-shire IV4 7BY Tel:(Beauly) 0463 782278	APPROVED ♛ ♛	2 Single 2 Twin 2 Double 4 Family Suite avail.	6 En Suite fac 1 Limited ensuite 3 Pub.Bath/Show	B&B per person £20.00-£30.00 Single £19.00-£25.00 Double	Open Jan-Dec Dinner 1900-2100 B&B + Eve.Meal £28.00-£38.00

Small, personally run hotel in town square 12 miles (19kms) from Inverness.
Convenient for touring the Black Isle and Loch Ness. Open fire in bar.

CHRIALDON HOTEL
Station Road, Beauly, Inverness-shire IV4 7EH.
Tel: (0463) 782336

*Whether fishing, touring, simply relaxing or walking the Glens Affric, Strathfarrar
and Cannich, Chrialdon provides the ideal base. A charming turreted house where
a warm atmosphere, open log fires, a true "Taste of Scotland" menu, and our
personal attention at all times assure a memorable stay.*
RAC and AA acclaimed.

Chrialdon Hotel Station Road Beauly Inverness-shire IV4 7EH Tel:(Beauly) 0463 782336	COMMENDED ♛ ♛ ♛	1 Single 2 Twin 4 Double 1 Family	6 En Suite fac 1 Pub.Bath/Show	B&B per person £20.00-£27.00 Single £20.00-£27.00 Double	Open Jan-Dec Dinner 1900-2100 B&B + Eve.Meal £32.00-£40.00

Attractive stone built Scottish house with ample parking. Good food using local
produce. Taste of Scotland menu.

Lovat Arms Hotel Beauly Inverness-shire IV4 7BS Tel:(Beauly) 0463 782313 Fax:0463 782862	COMMENDED ♛ ♛ ♛ ♛	1 Single 13 Twin 5 Double 3 Family	22 En Suite fac	B&B per person £40.00-£80.00 Single £35.00-£45.00 Double	Open Jan-Dec Dinner 1700-2100 B&B + Eve.Meal £50.00-£90.00

Victorian stone built hotel c1874, recently completely refurbished, in centre of
picturesque Highland village, 11 miles (18kms) from Inverness.

Priory Hotel The Square Beauly Inverness-shire IV4 7BX Tel:(Beauly) 0463 782309 Fax:0463 782531	HIGHLY COMMENDED ♛ ♛ ♛ ♛	2 Single 12 Twin 5 Double 2 Family	21 En Suite fac	B&B per person £34.75-£39.50 Single £29.75-£34.75 Double	Open Jan-Dec Dinner 1730-2100

Privately owned hotel with a la carte restaurant in attractive village square,
close to Priory ruins.

BEAULY continued Arkton Guest House West End Beauly Inverness-shire IV4 7BT Tel:(Beauly) 0463 782388	Map 4 A8	APPROVED 👑	1 Single 4 Twin 1 Double 2 Family	2 Pub.Bath/Show	B&B per person £16.00-£20.00 Single £16.00-£20.00 Double	Open Jan-Dec Dinner 1900-2000 B&B + Eve.Meal £23.00-£27.00

Personnally run hotel situated at the south end of the village square. Ideal for touring Loch Ness and Glen Affric. 12 miles (19 kms) from Inverness.

BETTYHILL **Sutherland** Tigh Na Sgoil Guest House Kirtomy Bettyhill Sutherland Tel:(Bettyhill) 06412 455 Fax:06412 457	Map 4 B3		5 Twin	5 En Suite fac	B&B per person to £26.50 Double	Open Jan-Dec Dinner 1800-2100 B&B + Eve.Meal to £37.50

BIGGAR
Lanarkshire — Map 2 C6

Shieldhill Hotel
Quothquan, Biggar, Lanarkshire ML12 6NA.
Tel: 0899 20035. Fax: 0899 21092

Historic castle like hotel, situated in the countryside. 45minutes from Edinburgh and Glasgow. Eleven luxurious en-suite guest rooms. Some with 4-poster, Jacuzzis and fireplaces. Award winning Scottish cuisine by chef's Keith and Nicola Braidwood. Golf, Tennis, and country walks located near Hotel. Six acres of woodland gardens.

Shieldhill Hotel Quothquan Biggar Lanarkshire ML12 6NA Tel:(Biggar) 0899 20035 Fax:0899 21092		HIGHLY COMMENDED 👑 👑 👑 👑	2 Single 9 Double	11 En Suite fac	B&B per person £88.00-£155.00 Single £49.00-£82.50 Double	Open Jan-Dec Dinner 1900-2130

Historic manor house dating from 1199 situated in the rolling hills and farmland of the Clyde Valley.

BIRSAY **Orkney** Barony Hotel Birsay Orkney KW17 2LS Tel:(Birsay) 085672 327 Fax:085672 302	Map 5 A1	COMMENDED 👑 👑 👑	4 Single 3 Twin 2 Double 1 Family	8 En Suite fac 1 Pub.Bath/Show	B&B per person £22.00-£28.00 Single £21.00-£24.00 Double	Open May-Sep Dinner 1900-2000 B&B + Eve.Meal £35.00-£41.00

Orkney's oldest fishing hotel, under local ownership, on Loch Boardhouse. Refurbished lounge bar and dining room. Extensive use of local produce.

BLACKFORD **Perthshire** Blackford Hotel Moray Street Blackford Perthshire PH4 1QF Tel:(Blackford) 0764 682497/682246	Map 2 B3	APPROVED 👑 👑	1 Twin 1 Double 2 Family	4 En Suite fac	B&B per person £30.00 Single £22.50 Double	Open Jan-Dec Dinner 1800-2100

Family run old coaching inn. Open all year. Numerous golf courses and good fishing nearby. Dunblane 10 miles (16kms), Perth 18 miles (29kms).

BLACKFORD continued	Map 2 B3					
Glenmuir Guest House Moray Street Blackford Perthshire PH4 1PY Tel:(Blackford) 0764 682348		2 Single 1 Twin 1 Double 3 Family	2 Pub.Bath/Show	B&B per person £15.00-£19.00 Single £15.00-£19.00 Double	Open Jan-Dec Dinner 1800-1930 B&B + Eve.Meal £22.00-£26.00	

BLACKWATERFOOT Isle of Arran	Map 1 E7					

KINLOCH HOTEL
BLACKWATERFOOT · ISLE OF ARRAN · KA27 8ET
Telephone: (0770) 860444 Fax: (0770) 860447

Enjoy the beauty of Arran from the comfort of the Kinloch Hotel, with 49 rooms with private bathroom, colour TV, and tea-making facilities. Facilities include a heated indoor swimming pool, sauna, solarium, full-size snooker table, multi-gym and squash court. Central heating throughout for those "off season" breaks, as well.

| Kinloch Hotel
Blackwaterfoot
Isle of Arran
KA27 8ET
Tel:(Shiskine) 0770 860444
Fax:0770 860447 | APPROVED | 10 Single
34 Twin
3 Double | 47 En Suite fac | B&B per person
£38.00-£42.00 Single
£38.00-£42.00 Double | Open Jan-Dec
Dinner 1900-2030
B&B + Eve.Meal
£51.00-£55.00 | |

On the sea front with views of the Mull of Kintyre. Extensive leisure facilities, indoor pool; ideal for families and open to non-residents.

BLAIR ATHOLL Perthshire	Map 4 C1					
Tilt Hotel Bridge of Tilt Blair Atholl Perthshire PH18 5SU Tel:(Blair Atholl) 0796 481333 Fax:0796 481335		3 Single 13 Twin 4 Double 8 Family	28 En Suite fac	B&B per person £24.50-£29.50 Single £26.50-£39.50 Double	Open Jan-Dec Dinner 1800-2100 B&B + Eve.Meal £39.50-£55.50	

| Dalgreine
off St Andrew's Crescent
Blair Atholl
Perthshire
PH18 5SX
Tel:(Blair Atholl) 0796 481276 | | 2 Twin
3 Double | 1 Pub.Bath/Show | B&B per person
£14.50-£16.50 Double | Open Jan-Dec
Dinner 1830-1930
B&B + Eve.Meal
£22.50-£24.50 | |

| The Firs
St Andrews Crescent
Blair Atholl
Perthshire
PH18 5TA
Tel:(Blair Atholl) 0796 481256 | COMMENDED | 1 Twin
1 Double
2 Family | 4 En Suite fac | B&B per person
£17.50-£18.00 Double | Open Easter-Oct
Dinner from 1930
B&B + Eve.Meal
£27.50-£28.00 | |

Friendly family home with half an acre of garden, in a tranquil setting. Fine touring centre, close to Blair Castle.

BLAIR ATHOLL continued Invergarry Guest House The Terrace, Bridge of Tilt Blair Atholl Perthshire PH18 5SZ Tel:(Blair Atholl) 0796 481255	Map 4 C1		1 Twin 4 Double	1 Pub. Bath/Show	B&B per person £15.50-£17.00 Double	Open Apr-Oct

BLAIRGOWRIE Perthshire Altamount House Hotel Coupar Angus Road Blairgowrie Perthshire PH10 6JN Tel:(Blairgowrie) 0250 873512	Map 2 C1	COMMENDED ☻ ☻ ☻ ☻	2 Single 2 Twin 1 Double 2 Family	7 En Suite fac	B&B per person from £37.50 Single from £35.00 Double	Open Feb-Dec Dinner 1930-2100 B&B + Eve.Meal from £55.00

Elegant Georgian country house in 6 acres of well cared for grounds and garden. Close to Rosemount golf course. Many historic Castles nearby.

Angus Hotel 46 Wellmeadow Blairgowrie Perthshire PH10 6NH Tel:(Blairgowrie) 0250 872455 Tlx: 76526 Fax: 0250 875289		APPROVED ☻ ☻ ☻ ☻	18 Single 40 Twin 21 Double 7 Family	86 En Suite fac	B&B per person £30.00-£40.00 Single £25.00-£40.00 Double	Open Jan-Dec Dinner 1700-2030 B&B + Eve.Meal £40.00-£50.00

Privately owned, in centre of town. Facilities include swimming pool, sauna and solarium. Golf and skiing packages. Entertainment in season

Dalmore Hotel Rosemount, Perth Road Blairgowrie Perthshire PH10 6QB Tel:(Blairgowrie) 0250 872150			2 Twin 2 Double 1 Family	5 En Suite fac	B&B per person £18.00-£20.00 Single £18.00-£20.00 Double	Open Jan-Dec Dinner 1900-2200 B&B + Eve.Meal £20.00-£28.00

Kintrae House Hotel Balmoral Road, Rattray Blairgowrie Perthshire PH10 7AH Tel:(Blairgowrie) 0250 872106		COMMENDED ☻ ☻ ☻	1 Single 1 Twin 1 Double 2 Family	5 En Suite fac	B&B per person £27.00-£30.00 Single £22.00-£25.00 Double	Open Jan-Dec Dinner 1830-2100 B&B + Eve.Meal £34.00-£36.00

Quietly situated in own gardens with extensive parking. On route to Glenshee and Balmoral. Fishing, skiing and golf packages available. Real Ale.

The Rosemount Golf Hotel Golf Course Road, Rosemount Blairgowrie Perthshire PH10 6LJ Tel:(Blairgowrie) 0250 872604 Fax:0250 874496		COMMENDED ☻ ☻ ☻	10 Twin 1 Family	11 En Suite fac	B&B per person £36.00-£39.00 Single £27.00-£29.00 Double	Open Jan-Dec Dinner 1700-2145 B&B + Eve.Meal to £41.50

Personally run hotel set in extensive gardens. Ideal for touring, skiing and golfing holidays. Some annexe accommodation. Restaurant and bar meals.

Royal Hotel 53 Allan Street Blairgowrie Perthshire PH10 6AB Tel:(Blairgowrie) 0250 872226 Fax:0250 875905			12 Single 27 Twin 12 Double 3 Family	25 En Suite fac 7 Pub.Bath/Show	B&B per person £19.00-£25.00 Single £21.00-£23.00 Double	Open Jan-Dec Dinner 1830-1945 B&B + Eve.Meal £27.50-£29.50

	Map 2 C1						
BLAIRGOWRIE continued							
Victoria Hotel Lower Mill Street Blairgowrie Perthshire PH10 6NG Tel:(Blairgowrie) 0250 874555		COMMENDED ♛ ♛ ♛	1 Single 1 Twin 3 Double	5 En Suite fac	B&B per person £20.00-£25.00 Single £20.00-£25.00 Double	Open Jan-Dec Dinner 1800-2200	(symbols)
			Small family run hotel, close to several golf courses and Glenshee. Good Food. Steak bar.				
Duan Villa Perth Road Blairgowrie Perthshire PH10 6EQ Tel:(Blairgowrie) 0250 873053			3 Double 2 Family	1 Pub.Bath/Show	B&B per person £16.50-£17.50 Double	Open Jan-Dec Dinner 1830-1930 B&B + Eve.Meal £25.50-£26.50	(symbols)

GLENSHIELING HOUSE

Hatton Road, Blairgowrie, Perthshire PH10 7HZ
Tel: 0250 874605

Quietly located – little traffic noise. Central heating, private facilities, colour TV's, etc. Very competitive rates, especially for 3 nights or longer. Excellent dinner available, if desired. Privately owned and run.
Please do telephone for full colour brochure etc.
B&B from £16.00.

Glenshieling House Hatton Road, Rattray Blairgowrie Perthshire PH10 7HZ Tel:(Blairgowrie) 0250 874605		COMMENDED ♛ ♛ ♛	1 Single 2 Twin 2 Double 2 Family	4 En Suite fac 2 Pub.Bath/Show	B&B per person £19.00-£22.50 Single £17.00-£25.00 Double	Open Jan-Dec Dinner 1800-2030 B&B + Eve.Meal £27.00-£41.00	(symbols)
			Lovely Victorian house tranquilly set in 2 acres of garden and woodland near Blairgowrie. Chef/Proprietor and wife preside.				
The Laurels Guest House Golf Course Road, Rosemount Blairgowrie Perthshire PH10 6LH Tel:(Blairgowrie) 0250 874920		HIGHLY COMMENDED ♛ ♛ ♛	1 Single 3 Twin 2 Double	4 En Suite fac 1 Pub.Bath/Show	B&B per person £16.00-£17.00 Single £15.00-£17.00 Double	Open Jan-Nov Dinner 1830-1900 B&B + Eve.Meal £22.50-£25.00	(symbols)
			Originally a farmhouse dating from 1873, set back from main road, on outskirts of Blairgowrie with own large garden and ample parking.				
The Old Bank House Brown Street Blairgowrie Perthshire PH10 6EX Tel:(Blairgowrie) 0250 872902		HIGHLY COMMENDED ♛ ♛ ♛	4 Twin 2 Double	6 En Suite fac	B&B per person £25.00-£30.00 Single £22.50-£27.50 Double	Open Jan-Dec Dinner 1900-2000 B&B + Eve.Meal £35.00-£40.00	(symbols)
			Former bank dating from 1837 in quiet location, 5 minutes walk from the town centre. Imaginative home cooking. Golf, fishing and shooting packages.				

BE SURE TO CHOOSE THE SCOTTISH TOURIST BOARD'S SIGN OF QUALITY

BLAIRGOWRIE continued	Map 2 C1		

ROSEBANK HOUSE
BALMORAL ROAD · BLAIRGOWRIE
PERTHSHIRE PH10 7AF · (0250) 872912
Absorb the tranquil atmosphere of this lovely Georgian House in spacious gardens. Guests return year after year, never tiring of the natural beauty surrounding Blairgowrie and of Rosebank's own enchanting charm and fine food. 7 Nights DB&B from £192.
Selected by AA and RAC for special Highly Recommended awards.
Licensed. Private facilities.

| Rosebank Guest House Balmoral Road Blairgowrie Perthshire PH10 7AF Tel:(Blairgowrie) 0250 872912 | | | 1 Single 1 Twin 3 Double 2 Family | 5 En Suite fac 2 Pub.Bath/Show | B&B per person £19.50-£21.00 Single £21.00-£22.50 Double | Open Jan-Oct Dinner from 1900 B&B + Eve.Meal £31.50-£33.50 |

| Westwood Lodge Carsie, Perth Road Blairgowrie Perthshire PH10 6QW Tel:(Blairgowrie) 0250 872768 | | | 1 Twin 1 Double 1 Family | 1 Pub.Bath/Show | B&B per person £15.00-£18.00 Single £15.00-£18.00 Double | Open Jan-Dec Dinner 1800-2000 B&B + Eve.Meal £22.00-£25.00 |

| BY BLAIRGOWRIE Perthshire Kinloch House Hotel Kinloch Blairgowrie Perthshire PH10 6SG Tel:(Essendy) 0250 884237 Fax:0250 884333 | Map 2 C1 | HIGHLY COMMENDED ♛ ♛ ♛ ♛ | 5 Single 7 Twin 8 Double 1 Family Suites avail. | 21 En Suite fac 1 Pub.Bath/Show | | Open Jan-Dec Dinner 1900-2115 B&B + Eve.Meal to £72.45 |

An elegant Scottish country home with galleried hall in beautiful Perthshire Countryside. Ideal for golfing, fishing and shooting.

| Moorfield House Hotel Myrerigg s Road Coupar Angus, by Blairgowrie Perthshire PH13 9HS Tel:(Coupar Angus) 0828 27303 Fax:0828 27339 | | HIGHLY COMMENDED ♛ ♛ ♛ ♛ | 2 Single 5 Twin 5 Double | 12 En Suite fac | B&B per person to £35.00 Single to £34.00 Double | Open Jan-Dec Dinner 1800-2200 B&B + Eve.Meal to £42.00 |

Magnificent country house in 3.5 acres, refurbished in 1989/90. The fine menu includes many dishes using fresh local produce.

| BLAIRS, Aberdeen Aberdeenshire Ardoe House Blairs, South Deeside Road Aberdeen AB1 5YP Tel:(Aberdeen) 0224 867355 Tlx:739413 Fax:0224 861283 | Map 4 G1 | HIGHLY COMMENDED ♛ ♛ ♛ ♛ ♛ | 4 Single 18 Twin 46 Double 3 Family | 71 En Suite fac | B&B per person £63.50-£148.50 Single £36.00-£78.50 Double | Open Jan-Dec Dinner 1830-2200 B&B + Eve.Meal £70.00-£176.00 |

Baronial style, Victorian country house in 12 acres of grounds overlooking the Dee. Wooded walks, petanque and croquet. 3 miles (5kms) from Aberdeen

BOAT OF GARTEN
Inverness-shire

Map 4
C1

The Boat Hotel Boat of Garten Inverness-shire PH24 3BH Tel:(Boat of Garten) 047983 258 Fax:047983 414	**COMMENDED** 👑 👑 👑 👑	4 Single 32 En Suite fac 19 Twin 8 Double 1 Family Country house atmosphere with modern amenities, overlooks golf course. Interesting collection of paintings and prints. Near Strathspey steam railway	B&B per person £35.00-£45.00 Single £35.00-£45.00 Double	Open Dec-Oct Dinner 1900-2100 B&B + Eve.Meal £55.00-£60.00

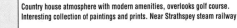

CRAIGARD HOTEL

KINCHURDY ROAD, BOAT OF GARTEN
INVERNESS-SHIRE PH24 3BP   Tel: 047 983 206

Located in peaceful setting yet close to all activities.
Overlooking golf course and Cairngorm mountains. Ideally placed
for golf, salmon and trout fishing, riding, walking and birdwatching.
All rooms en-suite, tea/coffee makers, colour TVs.
Write or phone for colour brochure.

Craigard Hotel Kinchurdy Road Boat of Garten Inverness-shire PH24 3BP Tel:(Boat of Garten) 047983 206		6 Single 20 En Suite fac 7 Twin 6 Double 1 Family Suites avail.	B&B per person £25.00-£32.00 Single £25.00-£32.00 Double	Open Jan-Dec Dinner 1900-2045 B&B + Eve.Meal £42.00-£49.00

Glenavon House Kinchurdy Road Boat of Garten Inverness-shire PH24 3PB Tel:(Boat of Garten) 047983 213 Fax:0479 83213	**Award Pending**	2 Single 6 En Suite fac 4 Twin	B&B per person £18.00-£25.00 Single £18.00-£25.00 Double	Open Jan-Dec Dinner 1930-2100 B&B + Eve.Meal £34.00-£42.00

Moorfield House Deshar Road Boat of Garten Inverness-shire PH24 3BN Tel:(Boat of Garten) 047983 646	**COMMENDED** 👑 👑 👑	1 Single 3 En Suite fac 1 Twin 1 Priv.NOT ensuite 1 Double 1 Family Personally run hotel in centre of peaceful Highland village. Ideally situated for walking, golfing, fishing, etc. Home cooking.	B&B per person £19.00-£21.00 Single £18.00 Double	Open Jan-Dec Dinner 1830-1900 B&B + Eve.Meal £27.00

Avingormack Guest House Boat of Garten Inverness-shire PH24 3BT Tel:(Boat of Garten) 047983 614	**HIGHLY COMMENDED** 👑 👑 👑	1 Twin 2 En Suite fac 2 Double 2 Pub.Bath/Show 1 Family Former croft recently redecorated and refurbished, enjoying panoramic views of Cairngorms. Trad and Veg cuisine. Mountain bike hire. No smoking.	B&B per person from £15.00 Double	Open Jan-Dec Dinner 1900-2000 B&B + Eve.Meal from £25.00

BOAT OF GARTEN continued
Map 4 C1

Granlea Guest House
Boat of Garten
Inverness-shire
PH24 3BN
Tel:(Boat of Garten)
047983 601

COMMENDED
⚜ ⚜ ⚜

1 Twin	2 En Suite fac	B&B per person
2 Double	1 Pub.Bath/Show	£15.00-£17.00 Single
1 Family		£15.00-£17.00 Double

Open Jan-Dec
Dinner 1830-2000
B&B + Eve.Meal
£23.00

Stone built Edwardian house, in village centre, close to Osprey reserve. Aviemore 6 miles (10 kms). Ski slopes 12 miles (19 kms).

Heathbank -
The Victorian House
Boat of Garten
Inverness-shire
PH24 3BD
Tel:(Boat of Garten)
047983 234

HIGHLY COMMENDED
⚜ ⚜ ⚜

2 Twin	6 En Suite fac	B&B per person
3 Double	1 Priv.NOT ensuite	£18.00-£22.00 Single
2 Family	1 Pub.Bath/Show	£18.00-£30.00 Double

Open Dec-Oct
Dinner from 1900
B&B + Eve.Meal
£32.00-£44.00

Victorian stone built house; chef/proprietor committed to fresh produce. Rooms decorated imaginatively; full of old lace, flowers, pictures, books.

Ryvoan Guest House
Kinchurdy Road
Boat of Garten
Inverness-shire
PH24 3BP
Tel:(Boat of Garten)
047983 654

COMMENDED
⚜

1 Twin	1 En Suite fac	B&B per person
2 Double	2 Pub.Bath/Show	from £15.00 Double

Open Jan-Dec
Dinner at 1900
B&B + Eve.Meal
from £25.00

Victorian house set in mature woodland with period accommodation and modern facilities. Near RSPB reserve, golf club and Cairngorms.

BONCHESTER BRIDGE Roxburghshire
Map 2 E8

Hobsburn House
Bonchester Bridge
Roxburghshire
TD9 8JW
Tel:(Bonchester Bridge)
045086 642
Fax:045086 330

1 Single	1 Priv.NOT ensuite	B&B per person
2 Twin	2 Pub.Bath/Show	to £22.00 Single
2 Double		to £22.00 Double
1 Family		

Open Jan-Dec
Dinner 2000-2130
B&B + Eve.Meal
to £40.00

BO'NESS West Lothian
Map 2 B4

Richmond Park Hotel
26 Linlithgow Road
Bo'ness
West Lothian
EH51 0DN
Tel:(Bo'ness) 0506 823213
Fax:0506 822717

COMMENDED
⚜ ⚜ ⚜
⚜

1 Single	19 En Suite fac	B&B per person
11 Twin		£49.00-£66.00 Single
10 Double		£34.00-£42.00 Double
2 Family		

Open Jan-Dec
Dinner 1700-2230
B&B + Eve.Meal
£59.00-£68.50

Family run hotel situated in elevated position overlooking the Firth of Forth. Close to centre of Bo'ness; 14 miles (22kms) to Edinburgh Airport.

Hollywood House
25 Grahamsdyke Road
Bo'ness
West Lothian
EH59 1ED
Tel:(Bo'ness) 0506 823260

1 Single	1 En Suite fac	B&B per person
1 Double	2 Pub.Bath/Show	£18.00-£25.00 Single
1 Family		£18.00-£25.00 Double

Open Jan-Dec
Dinner 1730-2000
B&B + Eve.Meal
£26.00-£33.00

BOTHWELL
Lanarkshire
Bothwell Bridge Hotel
89 Main Street
Bothwell
Lanarkshire
G71 8EU
Tel:(Bothwell) 0698 852246
Tlx:776838
Fax:0698 854686

Map 2
A6

COMMENDED

2 Single	76 En Suite fac	B&B per person	Open Jan-Dec
34 Twin		£34.00-£55.00 Single	Dinner 1800-2245
33 Double		£22.00-£33.00 Double	B&B + Eve.Meal
7 Family			£34.00-£45.00

Family run hotel, 9 miles (14kms) from Glasgow city centre and convenient for motorway. Some annexe accommodation. Business meeting room.

BOWMORE
Isle of Islay, Argyll
Lochside Hotel
Shore Street
Bowmore
Isle of Islay, Argyll
PA43 7LB
Tel:(Bowmore) 049681 244

Map 1
C6

APPROVED

2 Single	4 En Suite fac	B&B per person	Open Jan-Dec
2 Twin	3 Limited ensuite	£15.00-£32.00 Single	Dinner 1730-2100
3 Double	2 Pub.Bath/Show	£15.00-£29.00 Double	B&B + Eve.Meal
1 Family			£20.00-£49.00

Personally run, on main street of the village with views over Loch Indaal from the bar and dining room. Ideal base for touring Islay.

Marine Hotel
Bowmore
Isle of Islay, Argyll
PA43
Tel:(Bowmore) 049681 324
Fax:049681 764

3 Twin	5 En Suite fac	B&B per person	Open Jan-Dec
2 Family		£25.00-£32.50 Single	Dinner 1800-2200
		£25.00-£32.50 Double	B&B + Eve.Meal
			£35.00-£40.00

Lambeth House
Jamieson Street
Bowmore
Isle of Islay, Argyll
PA43 7HL
Tel:(Bowmore) 049681 597

2 Twin	2 Pub.Bath/Show	B&B per person	Open Jan-Dec
1 Double		from £12.50 Single	Dinner 1730-1830
1 Family		from £15.00 Double	B&B + Eve.Meal
			from £18.00

BRAE, North Mainland
Shetland
Busta House Hotel
Busta, North Mainland
Shetland
ZE2 9QN
Tel:(Brae) 080622 506
Tlx:9312100218
Fax:080622 588

Map 5
F3

COMMENDED

2 Single	18 En Suite fac	B&B per person	Open Jan-Dec
8 Twin		from £60.00 Single	Dinner 1900-2100
6 Double		£40.00-£52.50 Double	B&B + Eve.Meal
2 Family			£61.50-£74.00

Dating from 1588, formerly the residence of the Lairds of Busta; now a country house hotel. Private harbour and slipway.

BRAEMAR
Aberdeenshire
Braemar Lodge Hotel
& Restaurant
Glenshee Road
Braemar
Aberdeenshire
AB35 5YQ
Tel:(Braemar) 03397 41627
Fax:03397 41440

Map 4
D1

COMMENDED

1 Single	5 En Suite fac	B&B per person	Open Apr-Oct
2 Twin	1 Pub.Bath/Show	£34.00-£40.00 Single	Dinner 1900-2100
2 Double		£34.00 Double	B&B + Eve.Meal
			£49.50-£53.50

Former hunting lodge with 2 acre garden; log fires in public rooms. Taste of Scotland. 9 miles (14kms) from Balmoral and Glenshee ski area.

BRAEMAR continued — Map 4 D1

The Invercauld Arms Hotel
Braemar
Aberdeenshire
AB35 5YR
Tel:(Braemar) 03397 41605
Fax:03397 41428

Award Pending

5 Single
40 Twin
12 Double
11 Family

68 En Suite fac

B&B per person
£30.00-£60.00 Single
£25.00-£45.00 Double

Open Jan-Dec
Dinner 1900-2045
B&B + Eve.Meal
£45.00-£75.00

Clunie Lodge
Clunie Bank Road
Braemar
Aberdeenshire
AB35 5YP
Tel:(Braemar) 03397 41330

COMMENDED

1 Twin
2 Double
2 Family

3 En Suite fac
1 Priv.NOT ensuite
1 Pub.Bath/Show

B&B per person
£14.00-£16.00 Double

Open Dec-Oct
Dinner 1800-2000
B&B + Eve.Meal
£24.00-£26.00

Family run, Victorian, former manse in the centre of Braemar. Home cooking
5 day midweek break; ideal for skiing.

Cranford Guest House
15 Glenshee Road
Braemar
Aberdeenshire
AB35 5YQ
Tel:(Braemar) 03397 41675

COMMENDED

2 Twin
3 Double
1 Family

5 En Suite fac
1 Priv.NOT ensuite
1 Pub.Bath/Show

B&B per person
£15.00-£16.00 Double

Open Jan-Dec
Dinner 1830-1900
B&B + Eve.Meal
£25.00-£26.00

Personally run guest house situated near village centre, only 8 miles (13kms)
from Glenshee ski run.

Schiehallion Guest House
Glenshee Road
Braemar
Aberdeenshire
AB35 5YQ
Tel:(Braemar) 03397 41679

COMMENDED

1 Single
4 Twin
4 Double
2 Family

7 En Suite fac
1 Pub.Bath/Show

B&B per person
£15.50 Single
£14.50-£16.50 Double

Open Jan-Dec
Dinner from 1900
B&B + Eve.Meal
£25.00-£27.00

Comfortable, tastefully decorated, Victorian house at gateway to Royal Deeside
offering personal sevice, home cooking, log fires.

Braemar Outdoor Centre
Mar Road
Braemar
Aberdeenshire
AB35 5YL
Tel:(Braemar) 03397 41242
Fax:03397 41496

1 Twin
3 Family

3 Pub.Bath/Show

B&B per person
£6.75-£7.75 Double

Open Jan-Dec

BREASCLEIT
Lewis, Western Isles — Map 3 C4

Corran View Guest House
22a Breascleit
Breascleit
Lewis, Western Isles
PA86 9EF
Tel:(Callanish) 0851 621300

HIGHLY COMMENDED

1 Twin
3 Double
1 Family

3 En Suite fac
1 Pub.Bath/Show

B&B per person
£20.00 Single
£20.00 Double

Open Jan-Dec
Dinner 1800-1900
B&B + Eve.Meal
£35.00

Comfortable modern house overlooking sea loch, within easy reach of ferry and
airport. Ideal for touring, walking, sailing and beaches.

BRECHIN
Angus — Map 4 F1

Northern Hotel
2 Clerk Street
Brechin
Angus
DD9 6AE
Tel:(Brechin) 0356
622156/625505
Fax:03562 2714

APPROVED

4 Single
9 Twin
7 Double

17 En Suite fac
2 Pub.Bath/Show

B&B per person
£15.00-£28.00 Single
£15.00-£22.00 Double

Open Jan-Dec
Dinner 1700-2100
B&B + Eve.Meal
£19.00-£31.00

Former coaching inn and listed building, in town centre. Fax facilities and
Sky TV available. Convenient for fishing, golf courses and Angus glens.

BRIDGE OF ALLAN **Stirlingshire** Bridge Inn 2 Inverallan Road Bridge of Allan Stirlingshire FK9 4JA Tel:(Bridge of Allan) 0786 833335	Map 2 A4		2 Twin 2 Double	4 En Suite fac	B&B per person £20.00-£22.00	Open Jan-Dec Dinner from 1830 B&B + Eve.Meal £26.00-£28.00	
Walmer Hotel 90 Henderson Street Bridge of Allan Stirlingshire FK9 4HD Tel:(Bridge of Allan) 0786 832967			7 Twin 2 Double 2 Family	8 En Suite fac 3 Pub.Bath/Show	B&B per person £15.00-£29.00 Single £18.00-£20.00 Double	Open Jan-Dec Dinner 1800-2100 B&B + Eve.Meal £25.00-£39.00	
BRIDGE OF CALLY **Perthshire** Ballintuim Hotel Ballintuim Bridge of Cally, Blairgowrie Perthshire PH10 7NH Tel:(Bridge of Cally) 0250 886276	Map 2 C1		1 Twin 2 Double 3 Family	2 Limited ensuite 2 Priv.NOT ensuite 2 Pub.Bath/Show	B&B per person £18.00-£21.00 Single £19.00-£22.00 Double	Open Jan-Dec Dinner 1800-2100 B&B + Eve.Meal £30.00-£34.00	
BRIDGE OF EARN **Perthshire** Rockdale Guest House Dunning Street Bridge of Earn Perthshire PH2 9AA Tel:(Bridge of Earn) 0738 812281	Map 2 C3		2 Single 3 Twin 1 Double 1 Family	1 En Suite fac 2 Pub.Bath/Show	B&B per person £14.50-£17.50 Double	Open 11 Jan-25 Dec Dinner 1730-1900 B&B + Eve.Meal £23.50-£25.50	
BROADFORD **Isle of Skye** **Inverness-shire** Dunollie Hotel Broadford Isle of Skye, Inverness-shire 1V49 9AE Tel:(Broadford) 0471 822253	Map 3 E1	COMMENDED ♒ ♒ ♒	21 Single 44 Twin 19 Double	16 Pub.Bath/Show	B&B per person £42.00-£50.00 Single £38.00-£46.00 Double	Open Apr-Oct Dinner 1830-2000 B&B + Eve.Meal £48.00-£58.50	
			8 miles (13kms) from Skye ferry. All rooms ensuite. Friendly, willing staff create excellent base for relaxing stay, overlooking Broadford Bay.				
BRODICK **Isle of Arran** Anchor Hotel Brodick Isle of Arran KA27 Tel:(Brodick) 0770 302229/302429	Map 1 F7		1 Single 5 Twin 5 Double 3 Family	6 En Suite fac 3 Pub.Bath/Show	B&B per person £15.00-£30.00 Single £13.00-£25.00 Double	Open Jan-Dec Dinner 1800-2100 B&B + Eve.Meal £25.00-£40.00	

BRODICK

BRODICK continued	Map 1 F7						
The Arran Hotel Brodick Isle of Arran KA27 8AJ Tel:(Brodick) 0770 302265 Fax:0770 302265	COMMENDED ♨ ♨ ♨	2 Single 5 Twin 6 Double 3 Family	16 En Suite fac	B&B per person £29.50-£32.50 Single £29.50-£32.50 Double	Open Jan-Dec Dinner 1730-2030	
		Family run hotel, recently refurbished on seafront at Brodick with fine views of Arran hills and Firth of Clyde. Swimming pool; leisure facilities.					
Glenartney Hotel Brodick Isle of Arran KA27 8BX Tel:(Brodick) 0770 302220	APPROVED ♨ ♨ ♨	2 Single 6 Twin 4 Double 1 Family	7 En Suite fac 3 Pub.Bath/Show	B&B per person £19.00-£25.00 Single £19.00-£25.00 Double	Open Mar-Oct Dinner 1830-1900 B&B + Eve.Meal £30.00-£36.00	
		Family run hotel, in quiet residential area of Brodick, ideally situated for access to ferry and for touring the island.					
Hotel Ormidale Brodick Isle of Arran KA27 8BY Tel:(Brodick) 0770 302293		4 Single 2 Twin 2 Double 1 Family	2 Pub.Bath/Show	B&B per person £19.00 Single £19.00 Double	Open Mar-Oct Dinner 1800-2000 B&B + Eve.Meal £26.00	
Invercloy Hotel Brodick Isle of Arran KA27 8AJ Tel:(Brodick) 0770 302225	COMMENDED ♨ ♨ ♨	3 Single 1 Twin 1 Double 3 Family	8 En Suite fac	B&B per person £22.50-£25.00 Single £22.50-£25.00 Double	Open Mar-Oct Dinner 1830-1900 B&B + Eve.Meal £32.00-£34.50	
		Family owned hotel in the heart of the town and opposite a safe, sandy beach.					
Kilmichael Country House Hotel Brodick Isle of Arran KA27 8BY Tel:(Brodick) 0770 302219	DELUXE ♨ ♨ ♨	1 Twin 6 Double Suite avail.	7 En Suite fac	B&B per person £40.00-£45.00 Single £30.00-£40.00 Double	Open Dec-Oct Dinner 1930-2030 B&B + Eve.Meal £48.50-£58.50	
		A small historic mansion house, set in acres of beautiful wooded ground in peaceful Glen Cloy.					
Kingsley Hotel Brodick Isle of Arran KA27 8AJ Tel:(Brodick) 0770 2226/302226		7 Single 11 Twin 5 Double 4 Family	27 En Suite fac	B&B per person £22.00-£24.00 Single £22.00-£24.00 Double	Open Mar-Oct Dinner 1830-1930 B&B + Eve.Meal £35.00-£37.00	
Allandale Guest House Brodick Isle of Arran KA27 8BJ Tel:(Brodick) 0770 2278/302278	COMMENDED ♨ ♨ ♨	1 Single 2 Twin 1 Double 2 Family	5 En Suite fac 1 Priv.NOT ensuite 1 Pub.Bath/Show	B&B per person £16.00-£20.00 Single £16.00-£20.00 Double	Open Jan-Oct Dinner 1900-1930 B&B + Eve.Meal £25.00-£30.00	
		Comfortable guest house in south-facing postion on the edge of Brodick, only a few minutes walk from the ferry. Some annexe accommodation.					

BRODICK continued	Map 1 F7		

Glencloy Farmhouse

BRODICK, ISLE OF ARRAN KA27 8DA (0770) 302351

Our farmhouse is a beautiful, century-old sandstone house, situated in a peaceful glen just outside Brodick. We offer cosy rooms, log fires, and excellent food prepared by chef proprietor. We bake our own bread and our vegetables come from our kitchen garden. We are close to golf, castle and mountains.

Glencloy Farm House Brodick Isle of Arran KA27 8DA Tel:(Brodick) 0770 2351/302351	COMMENDED 👑 👑	1 Single 2 Twin 2 Double	2 En Suite fac 1 Pub.Bath/Show	B&B per person £19.00-£25.00 Single £19.00-£25.00 Double	Open Mar-Nov Dinner 1900-1930 B&B + Eve.Meal £29.00-£35.00

Farmhouse, set in peaceful glen with views of hills and sea. Within easy reach of Brodick ferry. Chef/proprietor: fresh, homegrown produce.

Rosa Burn Lodge Brodick Isle of Arran KA27 8DP Tel:(Brodick) 0770 2383/302383		2 Twin 1 Double	3 En Suite fac	B&B per person £27.50-£30.00 Single £17.50-£20.00 Double	Open Jan-Dec

Miss A Smith Tighnamara Brodick Isle of Arran KA27 8AN Tel:(Brodick) 0770 2538/302538		2 Twin 3 Double 2 Family	2 En Suite fac 3 Pub.Bath/Show	B&B per person from £15.00 Single from £15.00 Double	Open Apr-Oct

Tuathair House Brodick Isle of Arran KA27 8AJ Tel:(Brodick) 0770 2214/302214	COMMENDED 👑 👑 👑	1 Twin 2 Double 1 Family	4 En Suite fac	B&B per person £17.00-£22.00 Single £17.00-£22.00 Double	Open Jan-Dec Dinner from 1800 B&B + Eve.Meal £27.00-£32.00

Family run guest house on sea front, open views across Brodick Bay to Goat Fell. Non-smoking establishment.

BRORA **Sutherland** Links Hotel Golf Road Brora Sutherland KW9 6QS Tel:(Brora) 0408 621225 Fax:0408 621383	Map 4 C6	4 Single 9 Twin 6 Double 2 Family Suite avail.	21 En Suite fac	B&B per person £40.00 Single £35.00-£40.00 Double	Open Mar-Oct Dinner 1900-2100 B&B + Eve.Meal £50.00-£55.00

BRORA continued	Map 4 C6						
Royal Marine Hotel Brora Sutherland KW9 6QS Tel:(Brora) 0408 621252 Fax:0408 621181		COMMENDED ♛ ♛ ♛ ♛	7 Twin 3 Double 1 Family	11 En Suite fac	B&B per person £50.00-£60.00 Single £40.00-£50.00 Double	Open Jan-Dec Dinner 1900-2100 B&B + Eve.Meal £55.00-£65.00	

Traditional country house hotel, offering excellent facilities and access to golfing, fishing and countryside. Curling rink and heated indoor pool.

BUCKIE Banffshire	Map 4 E7						
Cluny Hotel 2 High Street Buckie Banffshire AB56 1AL Tel:(Buckie) 0542 32922		APPROVED ♛ ♛ ♛	1 Single 3 Twin 1 Double 3 Family	7 En Suite fac 1 Priv.NOT ensuite	B&B per person £22.00-£26.00 Single £19.00-£22.00 Double	Open Jan-Dec Dinner 1700-2000 B&B + Eve.Meal £28.00	

Victorian building conveniently situated in town centre. Free golf at sister hotel 7 miles (11kms) away.

Marine Hotel

Marine Place, Buckie AB56 1UT, Tel: (0542) 32249. Fax: (0542) 34949

Situated on Morays scenic coast, now recently refurbished, our luxuriously appointed accommodation, fine dining in Jasmines Restaurant, friendly and helpful staff, all combine to provide the holiday experience. Relax in the sauna and jacuzzi. Work out in the multi-gym. Full size snooker-table in Dodgers Sports Bar. Pets welcome. - Lift - Disabled facilities. Golf, fishing, etc, nearby.
B&B from £35.50.

Marine Hotel Marine Place Buckie Banffshire AB56 1UT Tel:(Buckie) 0542 32249		COMMENDED ♛ ♛ ♛	4 Single 4 Double 2 Family	10 En Suite fac	B&B per person £26.28-£47.50 Single £21.00-£39.00 Double	Open Jan-Dec Dinner 1600-2130 B&B + Eve.Meal £38.28-£59.50	

A modern hotel on the harbour front of this busy coastal town. Snooker sauna, jacuzzi and fitness room add to the many facilities available.

St Andrews Hotel St Andrew Square Buckie Banffshire AB56 1BT Tel:(Buckie) 0542 31227 Fax:0542 34513		APPROVED ♛ ♛	4 Single 6 Twin 4 Double 1 Family	6 En Suite fac 3 Pub.Bath/Show	B&B per person £18.00-£25.00 Single £16.00-£21.00 Double	Open Jan-Dec Dinner 1730-2030 B&B + Eve.Meal £23.00-£30.00	

Recently refurbished, late Victorian, family run hotel, close to town cente. Golfing packages available. On coastal tourist route.

SCOTTISH TOURIST BOARD
QUALITY COMMENDATIONS ARE:

Deluxe – *An EXCELLENT quality standard*
Highly Commended – *A VERY GOOD quality standard*
Commended – *A GOOD quality standard*
Approved – *An ADEQUATE quality standard*

BY BUCKIE Banffshire	Map 4 E7		

Mill House Hotel

TYNET, By BUCKIE, BANFFSHIRE AB56 2HJ
Telephone: (0542) 850233

A converted, 18th-century water mill, situated in scenic countryside offering all sport and sightseeing activities. This hospitable, family run establishment provides a relaxing atmosphere and is renowned for its excellent food and value. All 15 bedrooms are en-suite with full modern facilities. Open all year. B&B per person £40 single, £30 double/twin.

For further details, pelase contact: Gill & Philip Silver, Resident Proprietors.

Mill House Hotel Tynet Buckie Banffshire AB56 2HJ Tel:(Clochan) 0542 850233 Fax:0542 850331	COMMENDED ♛ ♛ ♛ ♛	7 Single 5 Twin 2 Double 1 Family	15 En Suite fac	B&B per person £33.00-£37.00 Single £26.00-£28.50 Double	Open Jan-Dec Dinner 1700-2100 B&B + Eve.Meal £44.00-£48.00

Modernised and extended 19C water-mill in rural setting, set back from A98and central for all local attractions. Friendly personal service.

BUNESSAN Isle of Mull, Argyll	Map 1 C3				
Ardfenaig House Bunessan Isle of Mull, Argyll PA67 6DX Tel:(Fionnphort) 06817 210 Fax:06817 210	HIGHLY COMMENDED ♛ ♛ ♛	1 Single 2 Twin 2 Double	4 En Suite fac 1 Priv.NOT ensuite	B&B per person	Open Apr-Oct Dinner 1930-2200 B&B + Eve.Meal £65.00-£78.00

A converted shooting lodge set between sea and moorland amongst lawns and woodlands. A perfect retreat to enjoy good food and fine wines.

Assapol Country House Hotel Assapol House Bunessan Isle of Mull, Argyll PA67 6DW Tel:(Fionnphort) 06817 258 Fax:06817 445	COMMENDED ♛ ♛ ♛	2 Single 2 Twin 2 Double 1 Family	6 En Suite fac 1 Priv.NOT ensuite	B&B per person £24.00-£28.00 Single £24.00-£28.00 Double	Open Easter-Oct Dinner at 1900 B&B + Eve.Meal £37.50-£41.50

Modernised 17 C former manse; all rooms have private facilities. Overlooks Loch Assapol on Ross of Mull. Salmon and brown trout fishing; shooting.

BURGHEAD Moray	Map 4 D7				
Commercial Hotel 6 Young Street Burghead, Elgin Moray IV30 2UB Tel:(Burghead) 0343 835628	Award Pending	1 Single 1 Twin 3 Double 1 Family	2 Pub.Bath/Show	B&B per person £18.00-£24.00 Single £18.00-£24.00 Double	Open Jan-Dec Dinner 1800-1900

BURNHOUSE, by Beith Ayrshire	Map 1 H6

Manor Farm Hotel
BURNHOUSE, BEITH, AYRSHIRE KA15 1LJ Tel: (0560) 484006

Family-run hotel with en-suite and farmhouse accommodation, bar and restaurant within farmhouse surroundings. Standing in own grounds, yet easy access to all main routes on the West Coast. Ideal base for touring Ayrshire Coast & Loch Lomond. Many golf courses nearby. Situated on Glasgow/Irvine road A736.

B&B £15/22 per person.

Manor Farm Hotel Burnhouse, by Beith Ayrshire KA15 1LJ Tel:(Stewarton) 0560 484006	Award Pending	1 Single 3 Twin 3 Double 2 Family	7 En Suite fac 2 Pub.Bath/Show	B&B per person £15.00-£22.50 Single £14.00-£20.00 Double	Open Jan-Dec Dinner 1700-2000 B&B + Eve.Meal £24.00-£34.00

BURNTISLAND Fife	Map 2 C4	COMMENDED ♕ ♕ ♕ ♕				
Inchview Hotel 69 Kinghorn Road Burntisland Fife KY3 9EB Tel:(Kirkcaldy) 0592 872239 Fax:0592 874866			2 Single 2 Twin 5 Double 3 Family	12 En Suite fac	B&B per person to £42.50 Single to £31.75 Double	Open Jan-Dec Dinner 1900-2145 B&B + Eve.Meal to £48.50

Family run, Georgian building overlooking links and sandy bays of Pettycur. Large fun fair through summer. Sailing, riding, golf, tennis available.

BY BURNTISLAND Fife	Map 2 C4	COMMENDED ♕ ♕ ♕ ♕				
Kingswood Hotel Kinghorn Road Burntisland Fife KY3 9LL Tel:(Burntisland) 0592 872329 Fax:0592 873123			5 Twin 4 Double 1 Family	9 En Suite fac 1 Priv.NOT ensuite	B&B per person to £48.00 Single to £35.00 Double	Open Jan-Dec Dinner 1800-2200 B&B + Eve.Meal £47.00-£60.00

Privately owned, set in 2 acre grounds with fine views across the Forth. Recently refurbished bedrooms and function facilites (up to 120 people).

CAIRNBAAN Argyll	Map 1 E4	COMMENDED ♕ ♕ ♕				
Cairnbaan Hotel Cairnbaan, by Lochgilphead Argyll PA31 8SJ Tel:(Lochgilphead) 0546 603668			1 Single 3 Twin 3 Double	7 En Suite fac	B&B per person £35.00 Single £30.00-£45.00 Double	Open Jan-Dec Dinner 1800-2100 B&B + Eve.Meal £40.00-£55.00

Privately owned, family run hotel in tranquil surroundings overlooking theCrinan Canal at Lock 5. Local seafood a speciality.

CAIRNDOW Argyll	Map 1 G3	APPROVED ♕ ♕				
Cairndow Stagecoach Inn Cairndow Argyll PA26 8BN Tel:(Cairndow) 04996 286/252 Fax:04996 220			4 Twin 5 Double 2 Family	11 En Suite fac	B&B per person £25.00-£36.00 Single £22.00-£26.00 Double	Open Jan-Dec Dinner 1900-2100 B&B + Eve.Meal £28.00-£44.00

Traditional coaching inn situated just off A83, on upper reaches of Loch Fyne. Ideal centre for a touring holiday.

CALGARY Isle of Mull, Argyll	Map 1 C1					
Calgary Farmhouse Hotel Dervaig Isle of Mull, Argyll PA75 6QQ Tel:(Dervaig) 06884 256		COMMENDED 🏅 🏅 🏅	1 Single 2 Twin 4 Double 2 Family	9 En Suite fac	B&B per person from £31.00 Single from £28.50 Double	Open Apr-Oct Dinner 1800-2100 B&B + Eve.Meal from £41.50
			Converted farmhouse and steading, close to the beautiful white sands of Calgary Beach. Local shellfish a speciality. Art gallery and tea room.			

CALLANDER Perthshire	Map 2 A3					
Bridgend House Hotel Bridgend Callander Perthshire FK17 8AH Tel:(Callander) 0877 330130 Fax:0877 331512		COMMENDED 🏅 🏅 🏅	1 Twin 5 Double	5 En Suite fac 1 Pub.Bath/Show	B&B per person £29.50-£35.00 Single £27.50-£32.50 Double	Open Jan-Dec Dinner 1800-2100 B&B + Eve.Meal £35.00-£48.00
			Small family run 18C hotel of character, offering a la carte dinner and bar meals. Children and pets welcome.			
Coppice Hotel Leny Road Callander Perthshire FK17 8AL Tel:(Callander) 0877 30188		COMMENDED 🏅 🏅 🏅	1 Twin 3 Double 1 Family	5 En Suite fac 5 Pub.Bath/Show	B&B per person £20.00-£24.00 Double	Open Jan-Dec Dinner from 1830 B&B + Eve.Meal £32.00-£35.00
			Personally run hotel with emphasis on cuisine using fresh produce when available.			
Dreadnought Hotel Station Road Callander Tel:(Callander) 0877 30184 Fax:0877 30228		COMMENDED 🏅 🏅 🏅	14 Single 32 Twin 11 Double 5 Family	62 En Suite fac	B&B per person £42.00-£50.00 Single £38.00-£46.00 Double	Open Jan-Dec Dinner 1830-2100 B&B + Eve.Meal £48.00-£58.50
			Traditional coach-party hotel in "Doctor Finlay's" village. Ideal centre for touring the Trossachs and Perthshire.			
Highland House Hotel South Church Street Callander Perthshire FK17 8BN Tel:(Callander) 0877 330269		COMMENDED 🏅 🏅 🏅	2 Single 2 Twin 4 Double 1 Family	7 En Suite fac 1 Priv.NOT ensuite 2 Pub.Bath/Show	B&B per person £18.00-£31.00 Single £18.00-£22.50 Double	Open Mar-Nov Dinner 1900-2000 B&B + Eve.Meal £29.00-£45.00
			Personally run, with friendly welcome, situated close to town centre. Taste of Scotland recommended. Most rooms ensuite facilities, all with TV.			
Lade Inn Kilmahog Callander Perthshire FK17 8HD Tel:(Callander) 0877 30152		COMMENDED 🏅 🏅 🏅	1 Twin 2 Double	3 En Suite fac	B&B per person £22.00-£30.00 Double	Open Jan-Dec Dinner 1800-2130 B&B + Eve.Meal £32.00-£45.00
			Traditional country inn. Comfortable accommodation with emphasis on good food and real ales. Ideal base for touring the Highlands.			
Roman Camp Hotel Callander Perthshire FK17 8BG Tel:(Callander) 0877 330003 Fax:0877 331533		HIGHLY COMMENDED 🏅 🏅 🏅 🏅	8 Twin 3 Double 3 Family	14 En Suite fac	B&B per person £65.00-£95.00 Single £40.00-£75.00 Double	Open Jan-Dec Dinner 1900-2100 B&B + Eve.Meal £70.00-£105.00
			Dating from 1625 and reminiscent of a miniature chateau with 20 acres of beautiful gardens bordering the River Teith.			

CALLANDER continued	Map 2 A3					
Royal Hotel Main Street Callander Perthshire FK17 Tel:(Callander) 0877 30651		1 Single 2 Double 2 Family	1 Pub.Bath/Show	B&B per person from £25.00 Single from £16.00 Double	Open Jan-Dec Dinner from 1700	
Abbotsford Lodge Stirling Road Callander Perthshire FK17 8DA Tel:(Callander) 0877 330066	COMMENDED 👑 👑 👑	1 Single 4 Twin 5 Double 8 Family	9 En Suite fac 4 Pub.Bath/Show	B&B per person from £24.50 Single from £19.50 Double	Open Jan-Dec Dinner from 1900 B&B + Eve.Meal from £30.50	
		Family run Victorian house in its own grounds with private parking, close to town centre. Home cooking and baking.				
Annfield Guest House North Church Street Callander Perthshire FK17 8EG Tel:(Callander) 0877 330204	COMMENDED 👑 👑	1 Single 2 Twin 4 Double 1 Family	2 En Suite fac 2 Pub.Bath/Show	B&B per person £15.00 Single £15.00 Double	Open Jan-Dec	
		Centrally situated in a quiet area of the town in close proximity to shops and restaurants. Stepping stone to the Highlands.				

ARDEN HOUSE
BRACKLINN ROAD, CALLANDER, PERTHSHIRE.
FK17 8EQ
Jim and Dorothy Mcgregor
Tel: 0877 330235

Peacefully situated in its own attractive gardens with marvellous views of the hills and countryside.
Arden House offers delicious home cooking, six comfortable rooms, all en-suite, tea/coffee making facilities and central heating. Two lounges, one with colour TV, and a warm, friendly and relaxed atmosphere. Reduced off-season terms. Generous reductions for children and weekly holidays. Ample car-parking space. Small putting green.
The TV home of BBC's "Dr Finlay's Casebook".
AA QQQQ Select/RAC Highly Acclaimed

Arden House Guest House Bracklinn Road Callander Perthshire FK17 8EQ Tel:(Callander) 0877 30235/330235	COMMENDED 👑 👑 👑	1 Single 2 Twin 2 Double 1 Family	6 En Suite fac	B&B per person £16.00-£18.00 Single £16.00-£18.00 Double	Open Mar-Nov Dinner from 1900 B&B + Eve.Meal £26.00-£28.00	
		Family run, peacefully situated in its own grounds. Superb panoramic views to Ben Ledi and the Trossachs. A non-smoking house.				
Arran Lodge Leny Road Callander Perthshire FK17 8AJ Tel:(Callander) 0877 30976/330976	DELUXE 👑 👑 👑	1 Twin 2 Double 1 Family	3 En Suite fac 1 Priv.NOT ensuite	B&B per person £35.20-£48.80 Single £23.50-£30.50 Double	Open Feb-Dec Dinner at 1930 B&B + Eve.Meal £35.50-£45.00	
		Delightful bungalow on A84 with tranquil riverside garden. Friendly welcome, quality cuisine and private parking.				
Ben Aan Guest House 158 Main Street Callander Perthshire FK17 8BG Tel:(Callander) 0877 30317	COMMENDED Listed	1 Single 1 Twin 2 Double 1 Family	1 Pub.Bath/Show	B&B per person from £14.50 Double	Open Jan-Dec Dinner 1830-1930	
		Family run guest house with bright comfortable bedrooms, TV lounge and dining room. Non smoking in bedrooms.				

CALLANDER continued	Map 2 A3					
Brook Linn Country House Callander Perthshire FK17 8AU Tel:(Callander) 0877 330103	HIGHLY COMMENDED ♕ ♕ ♕	1 Single 1 Twin 3 Double 2 Family	5 En Suite fac 2 Priv.NOT ensuite	B&B per person to £19.00 Single £22.00-£24.00 Double	Open Mar-Nov Dinner at 1900 B&B + Eve.Meal £30.00-£35.00	
		Comfortable, quiet family run Victorian house set in two acres of gardens with magnificent views. Short distance from town centre and all facilities				
Campfield Cottage 138 Main Street Callander Perthshire FK17 8BG Tel:(Callander) 0877 330599	COMMENDED Listed	1 Twin 2 Double	1 Pub.Bath/Show	B&B per person £15.00-£17.00 Double	Open Jan-Dec Dinner 1830-1900 B&B + Eve.Meal £24.00-£26.00	
		Dating from 1759, family cottage off main street with private parking. Evening meals available, children welcome; pets by special arrangement.				
Craig Villa, Leny Road Callander Perthshire FK17 8AW Tel:(Callander) 0877 30871	COMMENDED ♕ ♕	4 Double	4 En Suite fac	B&B per person £18.00-£19.00 Double	Open Apr-Nov	
		Stone built villa in main street, 5 minutes walk from shops and Rob Roy Centre. Own car park with easy access to ground floor bedroom.				
Dunmar Guest House Ancaster Road Callander Perthshire FK17 8EL Tel:(Callander) 0877 31199	COMMENDED ♕ ♕	1 Twin 2 Double 2 Family	2 En Suite fac 2 Pub.Bath/Show	B&B per person £13.50-£17.00 Double	Open Feb-Dec Dinner 1800-2000 B&B + Eve.Meal £22.50-£26.00	
		On quiet back road of popular village with accommodation on one level. Evening meals available: home cooking. Good walking locally in scenic area.				
East Mains House Bridgend Callander FK17 8AG Tel:(Callander) 0877 30535	Award Pending	1 Single 1 Twin 2 Double 1 Family	3 En Suite fac 1 Limited ensuite 1 Pub.Bath/Show	B&B per person £14.00-£25.00 Single £14.00-£18.00 Double	Open Jan-Dec, except Xmas Dinner 1900-2000 B&B + Eve.Meal £24.00-£28.00	
Edina Guest House 111 Main Street Callander Perthshire FK17 8BQ Tel:(Callander) 0877 30004	COMMENDED ♕ ♕	3 Single 1 Twin 5 Double 2 Family	6 En Suite fac 2 Pub.Bath/Show	B&B per person £14.00 Single £14.00-£16.00 Double	Open Feb-Oct	
		Personally run, situated in the centre of the town, an ideal base for touring. Own car park to rear. Some annexe bedrooms.				

Welcome Hosts provide a warm welcome, good service and information about their area. Look out for the people wearing the Welcome Host badge.

CALLANDER continued	Map 2 A3	

Invertrossachs Country House

INVERTROSSACHS, BY CALLANDER, PERTHSHIRE FK17 8HG
Telephone: (0877) 31126 changing to 331126
Fax: (0877) 31229 changing to 331229 ✹✹✹ **Highly Commended**

Stressed up?? Escape the pressures of everyday living at this memorable location. Our elegantly appointed lochside Edwardian mansion stands amidst 28 acres and offers unique B&B accommodations.

Enjoy breathtaking views from our en-suite Loch Room or larger Victoria Suite. High specification 5 crown apartments/Cottage also available.

Resident Proprietor: Iain H. Aitchison. Please quote Dept.EGH on enquiry.

Invertrossachs Country House Invertrossachs, by Callander Perthshire FK17 8HG Tel:(Callander) 0877 31126 Fax:0877 31229	**HIGHLY COMMENDED** ✹✹✹	1 Twin 2 Double Suite avail.	3 En Suite fac 1 Pub.Bath/Show	B&B per person £35.00-£60.00 Single £29.50-£45.00 Double	Open Jan-Dec	

Edwardian mansion in its own 28 acres of mature woodlands overlooking Loch Venachar. Quiet rural setting 4 miles (6kms) up a private drive.

Kinnell House 24 Main Street Callander Perthshire FK17 8BB Tel:(Callander) 0877 30181	**COMMENDED** ✹✹✹	1 Twin 2 Double	3 En Suite fac 2 Pub.Bath/Show	B&B per person £16.00-£22.00 Double	Open Jan-Dec Dinner 1900-2100 B&B + Eve.Meal £23.50-£29.50	

In centre of town and on main tourist route to the West Highlands. Near Trossachs and an ideal touring centre. High teas and dinner available.

The Knowe Ancaster Road Callander Perthshire FK17 8EL Tel:(Callander) 0877 30076	**COMMENDED** ✹✹✹	1 Twin 3 Double 1 Family	5 En Suite fac	B&B per person £18.00-£25.00 Single £17.00-£18.00 Double	Open Jan-Dec Dinner from 1830 B&B + Eve.Meal £27.00-£28.00	

Family run with a friendly welcome and good cooking. Quietly situated off the main road with magnificent views. Ideal for a peaceful holiday.

RIVERVIEW HOUSE

LENY ROAD, CALLANDER FK17 8AL
Tel: 0877 30635/330635

Detached Victorian house set in its own grounds near parklands yet close to shops and other venues. Private facilities in all rooms including colour TV and tea making. Good home cooking with choice on menu.
Ample parking in own grounds.

Riverview House Leny Road Callander Perthshire FK17 8AL Tel:(Callander) 0877 30635/ 330635	**COMMENDED** ✹✹✹	1 Single 1 Twin 3 Double	4 En Suite fac 1 Limited ensuite 1 Pub.Bath/Show	B&B per person £17.50 Single £17.50 Double	Open Apr-Oct Dinner 1900-1915 B&B + Eve.Meal £28.50	

19C house situated back from the main route north out of Callander. All meals with choice of menu, using fresh produce in season.

CALLANDER continued Tulipan Lodge Guest House Tulipan Crescent Callander Perthshire FK17 8AR Tel:(Callander) 0877 330572	Map 2 A3	COMMENDED ♨ ♨ ♨	2 Twin 3 Double	5 En Suite fac	B&B per person from £25.00 Single £16.00-£17.00 Double	Open Apr-Oct Dinner 1830-1900 B&B + Eve.Meal £25.50-£34.50	
			Substantial stone villa on edge of village with level walking to shops and all amenities. Evening meals available.				
CALLANISH **Lewis, Western Isles** Creag Bhan Guest House Callanish Lewis, Western Isles PA86 9DY Tel:(Callanish) 085172 341	Map 3 C5	HIGHLY COMMENDED ♨ ♨ ♨	1 Twin 2 Double	3 En Suite fac	B&B per person £17.00-£20.00 Double	Open May-Sep Dinner 1830-1900 B&B + Eve.Meal £27.00-£30.00	
			Modern bungalow on the edge of Callanish village, situated under 1 mile (2kms) from Callanish Standing Stones. Loch fishing available.				
Eshcol Guest House 21 Breascleit Callanish Lewis, Western Isles PA86 9ED Tel:(Callanish) 085172 357		HIGHLY COMMENDED ♨ ♨ ♨	2 Twin 1 Double	2 En Suite fac 1 Priv.NOT ensuite	B&B per person from £20.00 Single from £20.00 Double	Open Mar-Oct Dinner 1700-1900 B&B + Eve.Meal £29.00-£34.00	
			Modern detached house with fine views south over Loch Roag. Near to Callanish Standing Stones and Carloway Broch. En suite facilites.				
CAMPBELTOWN **Argyll** Ardshiel Hotel Kilkerran Road Campbeltown Argyll PA28 6JL Tel:(Campbeltown) 0586 552133	Map 1 E7		1 Single 5 Twin 2 Double 2 Family	4 En Suite fac 1 Pub.Bath/Show	B&B per person £25.00-£30.00 Single £25.00-£30.00 Double	Open Jan-Dec Dinner 1730-2100 B&B + Eve.Meal £30.00-£45.00	
Argyll Arms Hotel Main Street Campbeltown Argyll PA28 6AB Tel:(Campbeltown) 0586 553431		COMMENDED ♨ ♨ ♨	15 Twin 8 Double 3 Family	12 En Suite fac 1 Priv.NOT ensuite 5 Pub.Bath/Show	B&B per person £25.00-£31.00 Single £24.00-£26.00 Double	Open Jan-Dec Dinner 1700-2100 B&B + Eve.Meal from £31.00	
			Family owned and run hotel offering traditional Scottish hospitality in town centre location.				
Seafield Hotel Kilkerran Road Campbeltown Argyll PA28 6JL Tel:(Campbeltown) 0586 554385/552741		COMMENDED ♨ ♨ ♨	2 Twin 7 Double	9 En Suite fac 1 Pub.Bath/Show	B&B per person £32.95-£38.00 Single £32.95-£38.00 Double	Open Jan-Dec Dinner 1730-2130	
			On seafront overlooking Campbeltown Loch and within walking distance of town centre. Family run. Some annexe accommodation.				
Ballegreggan House Ballegreggan Road Campbeltown Argyll PA28 6NN Tel:(Campbeltown) 0586 552062		COMMENDED ♨ ♨ ♨	3 Twin 2 Double 1 Family	4 En Suite fac 2 Priv.NOT ensuite 2 Pub.Bath/Show	B&B per person from £18.00 Single from £18.00 Double	Open Jan-Dec Dinner 1800-2000 B&B + Eve.Meal from £28.00	
			Detached country house standing in its own grounds in a quiet rural area overlooking Campbeltown Loch, about 1.5 miles (2.5kms) from town.				

Key to symbols is on back flap.

69

	Map 1 E7						
CAMPBELTOWN continued		APPROVED 👑 👑	1 Single 1 Twin 5 Double	2 En Suite fac 2 Pub.Bath/Show	B&B per person from £16.00 Single from £16.00 Double	Open Jan-Dec	
Westbank Guest House Dell Road Campbeltown Argyll PA28 6JG Tel:(Campbeltown) 0586 553660							

Mid Victorian, detached, stone built house in quiet residential area close to town centre.

	Map 2 D9						
CANONBIE, by Langholm Dumfriesshire			1 Single 5 Twin 3 Double 1 Family	6 En Suite fac 2 Pub.Bath/Show	B&B per person £18.50-£22.50 Single £29.00-£38.00 Double	Open Jan-Dec Dinner 1800-2100	
Cross Keys Hotel Canonbie Dumfriesshire DG14 0SY Tel:(Canonbie) 03873 71205/71382							

	Map 1 G5
CARDROSS Dunbartonshire	

KIRKTON HOUSE CARDROSS, G82 5EZ.
COUNTRY HOUSE GUEST ACCOMMODATION

Glasgow Airport 14 miles, Dumbarton & Helensburgh each 4 miles

OLD WORLD CHARMS WITH MODERN AMENITIES

18/19th century converted farmhouse with superb Clyde views. Tranquil rural setting. Informal guest lounge and dining rooms with original stone walls & fireplaces. Drinks licence. Convivial, home cooked dinners by oil lamplight. Real open fire in the guest lounge. **Tel: 0389 841951. Fax: 0389 841868.**

Kirkton House Darleith Road Cardross Dunbartonshire G82 5EZ Tel:(Cardross) 0389 841951 Fax:0389 841868	HIGHLY COMMENDED 👑 👑 👑	2 Twin 4 Family	6 En Suite fac	B&B per person £31.00-£36.00 Single £22.00-£27.50 Double	Open Jan-Dec Dinner 1930-2030 B&B + Eve.Meal £37.50-£51.50

Built around central courtyard in a quiet, elevated rural position commanding magnificent views of the River Clyde.

	Map 2 E6						
CARFRAEMILL by Lauder, Berwickshire		APPROVED 👑 👑	1 Single 3 Twin 6 Double 2 Family Suite avail.	6 En Suite fac 3 Pub.Bath/Show	B&B per person £27.50-£32.50 Single £17.50-£30.00 Double	Open Jan-Dec Dinner 1830-2130 B&B + Eve.Meal £27.50-£45.00	
Carfraemill Hotel Carfraemill by Lauder Berwickshire TD2 6RA Tel:(Oxton) 0578 750200 Fax:0578 750640							

A former coaching inn offering friendly hospitality and bar/restaurant meals, situated in rural Lauderdale at the junction of the A697/A68.

	Map 3 C4					
CARLOWAY Lewis, Western Isles		3 Single 3 Twin 2 Double	3 Pub.Bath/Show	B&B per person £20.00-£25.00 Single £18.00-£35.00 Double	Open Jan-Dec Dinner 1900-2050 B&B + Eve.Meal £34.00-£40.00	
Doune Braes Carloway Lewis, Western Isles PA86 9AA Tel:(Stornoway) 0851 73252						

CARNOUSTIE **Angus** Carlogie House Hotel Carlogie Road Carnoustie Angus DD7 6LD Tel:(Carnoustie) 0241 53185 Fax:0241 56528	Map 2 E2	COMMENDED 🏆 🏆 🏆	3 Single 2 Twin 6 Double 1 Family	12 En Suite fac 3 Pub.Bath/Show	B&B per person to £45.00 Single to £35.00 Double	Open Jan-Dec Dinner 1700-2130 B&B + Eve.Meal £55.00-£62.50	
			Georgian House in secluded grounds, 1 mile (2kms) from beach and golf courses. Children welcome. 10 miles (16kms) north of Dundee.				
Glencoe Hotel 8 Links Parade Carnoustie Angus DD7 7JF Tel:(Carnoustie) 0241 53273		APPROVED 🏆 🏆 🏆	3 Single 6 Twin 2 Family	8 En Suite fac 3 Pub.Bath/Show	B&B per person £19.50-£22.00 Single £27.00-£30.00 Double	Open Jan-Dec Dinner 1930-2100 B&B + Eve.Meal £39.00-£40.00	
			Privately owned. Overlooks first tee of Carnoustie Championship Golf Course and the sea.				
Kinloch Arms Hotel 27 High Street Carnoustie Angus DD7 6AN Tel:(Carnoustie) 0241 53127			7 Twin	7 En Suite fac	B&B per person £25.00 Single £20.00 Double	Open Jan-Dec Dinner 1830-2130 B&B + Eve.Meal £34.50-£40.00	
Morven Hotel 28 West Path Carnoustie Angus DD7 7SN Tel:(Carnoustie) 0241 52385 Fax:0241 52385		COMMENDED 🏆 🏆 🏆	1 Single 3 Twin 2 Double 1 Family	5 En Suite fac 1 Pub.Bath/Show	B&B per person £19.50-£30.00 Single £18.50-£24.00 Double	Open Jan-Dec Dinner 1900-2100 B&B + Eve.Meal £29.50-£40.00	
			A family run hotel commanding superb views and offering fine food and cask conditioned ales. Access to golf and coastline.				
Station Hotel Station Road Carnoustie Angus DD7 6AR Tel:(Carnoustie) 0241 52447		COMMENDED 🏆 🏆 🏆	3 Single 5 Twin 1 Double	6 En Suite fac 2 Pub.Bath/Show	B&B per person £16.00-£23.00 Single £20.00-£25.00 Double	Open Jan-Dec Dinner 1900-2200	
			Long established family-run hotel close to railway station and bus routes. Conveniently situated for the beach and golf courses.				
CARRADALE **Argyll** Ashbank Hotel Carradale Argyll PA28 6RY Tel:(Carradale) 05833 650	Map 1 E7	COMMENDED 🏆 🏆 🏆	1 Single 2 Twin 1 Double 1 Family	3 En Suite fac 1 Pub.Bath/Show	B&B per person from £17.50 Single from £17.50 Double	Open Jan-Dec Dinner from 1900 B&B + Eve.Meal from £27.50	
			Family hotel with compact rooms in small village with views from the rear across the Kilbrannan Sound to Arran and Ailsa Craig.				
Carradale Hotel Carradale Argyll PA28 6RY Tel:(Carradale) 05833 223			7 Twin 7 Double 3 Family	16 En Suite fac 1 Limited ensuite 4 Pub.Bath/Show	B&B per person £33.00-£43.00 Single £33.00 Double	Open Apr-Oct Dinner 1900-2100 B&B + Eve.Meal £49.00-£59.00	

CARNOUSTIE continued

Dunvalanree Guest House
Portrigh Bay
Carradale
Argyll
PA28 6SE
Tel:(Carradale) 05833 226
Fax:05833 339

Map 2 E2

COMMENDED

2 Single	3 Pub.Bath/Show	B&B per person	Open Easter-Oct
2 Twin		£16.50 Single	Dinner from 1800
5 Double		£16.50 Double	B&B + Eve.Meal
3 Family			£25.00

Purpose built, set in peaceful location. Large garden with superb outlook to front over Portrigh Bay to Arran hills and Carradale Bay to the rear.

Kiloran Guest House
Carradale
Argyll
Tel:(Carradale) 05833 795

Award Pending

2 Twin	2 En Suite fac	B&B per person	Open Jan-Dec
2 Double	2 Pub.Bath/Show	£15.00-£16.00 Single	Dinner 1830-1900
1 Family		£16.00 Double	B&B + Eve.Meal
			£21.00

CARRBRIDGE Inverness-shire

Cairn Hotel
Main Road
Carrbridge
Inverness-shire
PH23 3AS
Tel:(Carrbridge) 047984 212

Map 4 C1

COMMENDED

2 Single	4 En Suite fac	B&B per person	Open Jan-Dec
2 Double	1 Pub.Bath/Show	£16.00-£21.00 Single	Dinner 1800-2100
3 Family		£16.00-£21.00 Double	

Family run hotel with cosy bar and friendly atmosphere, situated in the centre of small Highland village. A good base for touring and skiing.

Dalrachney Lodge Hotel
CARRBRIDGE · INVERNESS-SHIRE · PH23 3AT
Telephone: (0479) 841252   Fax: (0479) 841252   RAC ★ ★ ★

Situated in its own 16-acre grounds, this former Hunting Lodge makes the ideal base for touring the Highlands, hill-walking, fishing, pony-trekking, golfing, cycling and birdwatching. A skilful blend of old and new, Dalrachney offers spacious, comfortable rooms. Emphasis on good food, complemented by a fine selection of wines, malts and liqueurs.

Dalrachney Lodge Hotel
Carrbridge
Inverness-shire
PH23 3AT
Tel:(Carrbridge) 0479 841252
Fax:0479 841252

HIGHLY COMMENDED

1 Single	9 En Suite fac	B&B per person	Open Jan-Dec
3 Twin	2 Priv.NOT ensuite	£25.00-£35.00 Single	Dinner 1900-2130
4 Double		£23.00-£35.00 Double	B&B + Eve.Meal
3 Family			£41.00-£53.00

Victorian former hunting lodge, with many antique and period furnishings, set in 14 acres of peaceful surroundings. Cuisine using local produce.

Fairwinds Hotel
Carrbridge
Inverness-shire
PH23 3AA
Tel:(Carrbridge) 047984 240
Fax:047984 240

HIGHLY COMMENDED

1 Single	5 En Suite fac	B&B per person	Open Dec-Oct
2 Twin		£21.00-£24.00 Single	Dinner 1830-1900
2 Double		£20.00-£25.00 Double	B&B + Eve.Meal
			£32.00-£37.00

Traditional stone built former manse surrounded by mature pinewoods, in 6 acres of parkland. Near centre of village. Self-catering also available.

Feith Mhor Country House
Station Road
Carrbridge
Inverness-shire
PH23 3AP
Tel:(Carrbridge) 047984 1621

COMMENDED

3 Twin	6 En Suite fac	B&B per person	Open Dec-Nov
3 Double		£20.00-£22.00 Single	Dinner from 1900
		£20.00-£22.00 Double	B&B + Eve.Meal
			£30.00-£32.00

Elegant 19C house set in beautiful open countryside. Family run with accent on local fresh produce. 1 mile (2 kms) from Carrbridge.

CARRBRIDGE **continued** Ard-na-Coille Guest House Station Road Carrbridge Inverness-shire PH23 3AN Tel:(Carrbridge) 047984 239	**Map 4** **C1**	Award Pending	1 Twin 1 Double 1 Family	3 En Suite fac	B&B per person £15.00-£16.00 Double	Open Jan-Dec Dinner 1830-1900 B&B + Eve.Meal £23.00-£24.00

Symbols

Craigellachie House Main Street Carrbridge Inverness-shire PH23 3AS Tel:(Carrbridge) 047984 641		COMMENDED 🏆	1 Single 2 Twin 3 Double 2 Family	2 Pub.Bath/Show	B&B per person £13.00-£14.00 Single £13.00-£14.00 Double	Open Jan-Dec Dinner 1900-2000 B&B + Eve.Meal £22.00-£23.00

Warm comfortable hospitality assured. Proprietor a keen cook. Ample parking.
Centre of village. Ideal base for holiday activities.

Crannich Guest House & Lodges Carrbridge Inverness-shire PH23 3AA Tel:(Carrbridge) 047984 620			1 Single 1 Twin 2 Double 1 Family	3 Pub.Bath/Show	B&B per person £13.00-£14.00 Single £13.00-£14.00 Double	Open Jan-Dec Dinner 1800-1930 B&B + Eve.Meal £20.00-£21.00

Kinchyle Guest House Carrbridge Inverness-shire PH23 3AA Tel:(Carrbridge) 047984 243			1 Single 1 Twin 1 Double	1 Pub.Bath/Show	B&B per person £13.50-£14.50 Single £13.00-£14.00 Double	Open Jan-Dec

The Mariner Guest House Station Road Carrbridge Inverness-shire PH23 3AN Tel:(Carrbridge) 047984 331		COMMENDED 🏆 🏆 🏆	2 Twin 2 Double 1 Family	5 En Suite fac 1 Pub.Bath/Show	B&B per person £19.00-£25.00 Single £17.00-£19.00 Double	Open Dec-Oct Dinner at 1900 B&B + Eve.Meal £25.00-£27.00

A modern, purpose built house in residential area 800m from main street.
All ensuite facilities. Ideally situated for touring and skiing.

CARRUTHERSTOWN **Dumfriesshire** Carrutherstown Hotel Carrutherstown Dumfriesshire DG1 4LD Tel:(Carrutherstown) 038784 268	**Map 2** **C1**		5 Twin 1 Double 2 Family	2 Pub.Bath/Show	B&B per person £15.00-£20.00 Single £15.00-£20.00 Double	Open Jan-Dec Dinner 1800-2130 B&B + Eve.Meal £18.00-£23.00

CASTLEBAY **Barra, Western Isles** Castlebay Hotel Castlebay Barra, Western Isles PA80 5XD Tel:(Castlebay) 08714 223 Fax:08714 385	**Map 3** **A1**	COMMENDED 🏆 🏆 🏆 🏆	2 Single 6 Twin 2 Double 2 Family	12 En Suite fac 4 Pub.Bath/Show	B&B per person £28.00-£30.00 Single £25.00-£30.00 Double	Open Jan-Dec Dinner from 1730 B&B + Eve.Meal £40.00-£45.00

Elevated position, overlooking bay, pier and Kisimul Castle. Central location,
easy access to ferry terminal.

CASTLEBAY continued — Map 3 A1

Isle of Barra Hotel
Tangusdale Beach
Castlebay
Barra, Western Isles
PA80 5XW
Tel:(Castlebay) 08714 383
Fax:08714 385

COMMENDED

27 Twin	30 En Suite fac	B&B per person	Open Apr-Oct
3 Double	1 Pub.Bath/Show	£35.00-£40.00 Single	Dinner from 1800
		£32.00-£35.00 Double	B&B + Eve.Meal
			£45.00-£50.00

Modern, family run, set in splendid isolation overlooking sandy beach. 2 miles (3 kms) from Castlebay.

CASTLE DOUGLAS Kirkcudbrightshire — Map 2 A1

Douglas Arms
King Street
Castle Douglas
Kirkcudbrightshire
DG7
Tel:(Castle Douglas)
0556 502231
Fax:0556 504000

COMMENDED

7 Single	15 En Suite fac	B&B per person	Open Jan-Dec
8 Twin	3 Pub.Bath/Show	from £24.00 Single	Dinner 1900-2100
8 Double		from £26.00 Double	
2 Family			

Privately owned hotel in centre of market town. Secure undercover parking. Private fishing for hotel residents.

Imperial Hotel
King Street
Castle Douglas
Kirkcudbrightshire
DG7 1AA
Tel:(Castle Douglas) 0556
502086/503009
Fax:0556 503009

COMMENDED

2 Single	12 En Suite fac	B&B per person	Open Jan-Dec
2 Twin	1 Pub.Bath/Show	£28.50-£31.00 Single	Dinner 1730-2030
7 Double		£23.00-£27.00 Double	B&B + Eve.Meal
1 Family			£35.00-£40.00

Privately owned hotel in market town close to local leisure facilities. Ideal base for touring Galloway. Golfing holidays.

Longacre Manor
Ernespie Road
Castle Douglas
Kirkcudbrightshire
DG7 1LE
Tel:(Castle Douglas) 0556
503576/503886

HIGHLY COMMENDED

3 Twin	4 En Suite fac	B&B per person	Open Jan-Dec
1 Family		£30.00 Single	Dinner 1930-2100
		£25.00 Double	B&B + Eve.Meal
			£37.00-£42.00

Comfortable country house, featuring fully panelled lounge and hallway, in its own extensive private grounds on the edge of the town.

Station Hotel
1 Queen Street
Castle Douglas
Kirkcudbrightshire
DG7 1HX
Tel:(Castle Douglas) 0556
502152

1 Single	2 En Suite fac	B&B per person	Open Jan-Dec
2 Twin	2 Pub.Bath/Show	£16.00-£19.00 Single	Dinner 1700-2100
3 Double		£16.00-£19.00 Double	B&B + Eve.Meal
1 Family			£22.00-£25.00

Rose Cottage Guest House
Gelston, by Castle Douglas
Kirkcudbrightshire
DG7 1SH
Tel:(Castle Douglas) 0556
502513

COMMENDED

3 Twin	3 En Suite fac	B&B per person	Open Jan-Dec
2 Double	1 Priv.NOT ensuite	£15.00-£17.50 Double	Dinner at 1830
	1 Pub.Bath/Show		B&B + Eve.Meal
			£23.00-£25.50

Friendly welcome in personally run guest house situated in quiet village. Ideal for walkers and birdwatchers. Some accommodation in annexe.

CHARLESTOWN by Dunfermline, Fife
Map 2
C4

Elgin Hotel
Charlestown,by Dunfermline
Fife
KY11 3EE
Tel:(Limekilns) 0383 872257

9 Twin
2 Double
3 Family

14 En Suite fac

B&B per person
£47.00-£49.00 Single
£32.00-£34.00 Double

Open Jan-Dec
Dinner 1800-2130

CHIRNSIDE, by Duns Berwickshire
Map 2
F5

COMMENDED

Chirnside Hall Country
House Hotel
Chirnside, by Duns
Berwickshire
TD11 3LD
Tel:(Chirnside) 089081
219/0890 818219

1 Single
4 Twin
3 Double
2 Family

6 En Suite fac
2 Pub.Bath/Show

B&B per person
£30.00-£40.00 Single
£22.50-£27.50 Double

Open Jan-Dec
Dinner 1915-2100
B&B + Eve.Meal
£43.50-£53.50

19C country mansion set in 18 acres of ground with views of the Cheviots.
7 miles (11kms) from Berwick on A6105.

CHRYSTON, by Glasgow Lanarkshire
Map 2
A5

COMMENDED

Crow Wood House Hotel
Cumbernauld Road
Muirhead, Chryston
Glasgow
G69 9BS
Tel:041 779 3861
Fax:041 779 2987

4 Single
10 Twin
4 Double

18 En Suite fac

B&B per person
£55.00-£65.00 Single
£30.00-£35.00 Double

Open Jan-Dec
Dinner 1700-2200

Modernised and refurbished hotel conveniently situated on main A80. 5
miles (8kms) from Glasgow centre.

CLACHAN SEIL, by Oban Isle of Seil, Argyll
Map 1
E3

COMMENDED

Willowburn Hotel
Clachan Seil,by Oban
Argyll
PA34 4TJ
Tel:(Balvicar) 08523 276

1 Single
3 Twin
2 Double

6 En Suite fac

B&B per person
£29.00-£33.00 Single
£29.00-£33.00 Double

Open Mar-Dec
Dinner 1900-2030
B&B + Eve.Meal
£40.00-£46.00

Family run hotel in 2 acres of garden across the famous Atlantic Bridge. Lovely
views over Seil Sound. Good use of West Coast's excellent seafood.

CLYDEBANK, Glasgow Dunbartonshire
Map 1
H5

HIGHLY COMMENDED

The Patio Hotel
Clydebank Business Park
Clydebank, Glasgow
G81 2RW
Tel:041 951 1133
Fax:041 952 3713

8 Single
30 Twin
42 Double
Suites avail.

80 En Suite fac

B&B per person
to £66.00 Single
to £42.50 Double

Open Jan-Dec
Dinner 1900-2200
B&B + Eve.Meal
to £81.00

Constructed around a central atrium, this brand new hotel enjoys good access to
Glasgow, SECC, Airport and West Coast.

West Highway Hotel
Great Western Road
Duntocher, Glasgow
Dunbartonshire
G81
Tel:(Duntocher) 0389 72333
Fax:0389 78599

4 Single
11 Twin
2 Double

11 En Suite fac
1 Pub.Bath/Show

B&B per person
£32.00-£39.00 Single
£25.00-£30.00 Double

Open Jan-Dec
Dinner 1730-2130

COATBRIDGE **Lanarkshire** Georgian Hotel 26 Lefroy Street Coatbridge Lanarkshire ML5 1LZ Tel:(Coatbridge) 0236 421888/422621	Map 2 A5		6 Twin 2 Double	6 En Suite fac 1 Pub.Bath/Show	B&B per person from £30.00 Single from £22.50 Double	Open Jan-Dec Dinner 1830-2100
BY COLDSTREAM **Berwickshire** Homebank House Nr Birgham Village Coldstream Berwickshire TD12 4ND Tel:(Birgham) 0890 830285	Map 2 F6	**Award Pending**	1 Twin 1 Double	2 Pub.Bath/Show	B&B per person from £17.50 Double	Open May-Sep Dinner 1800-2000 B&B + Eve.Meal from £30.00
COLINTRAIVE **Argyll** Colintraive Hotel Colintraive Argyll PA22 3AS Tel:(Colintraive) 070084 207 Fax:070084 207	Map 1 F5	**COMMENDED** 👑 👑 👑	2 Twin 1 Double 1 Family	4 En Suite fac	B&B per person £14.00-£22.00 Single £14.00-£22.00 Double	Open Jan-Dec Dinner 1900-2100 B&B + Eve.Meal £17.00-£37.00
			Family run former hunting lodge close to ferry terminal for Bute. Magnificent views across Kyles of Bute to hills beyond.			
COLL, Isle of **Argyll** Coll Hotel Isle of Coll Argyll PA78 6SZ Tel:(Coll) 08793 334	Map 1 B1	**COMMENDED** 👑 👑 👑	1 Single 1 Twin 2 Double 2 Family	3 En Suite fac 3 Pub.Bath/Show	B&B per person £25.00-£30.00 Single £20.00-£25.00 Double	Open Jan-Dec Dinner 1800-2100 B&B + Eve.Meal £35.00-£40.00
			17c building overlooking the sea at Arinagour and under 1 mile (2kms) from the ferry terminal.			
COLLISTON **Angus** Letham Grange Hotel & Golf Courses Colliston by Arbroath Angus DD11 4RL Tel:(Gowanbank) 024189 373 Fax:024189 414	Map 2 E1	**COMMENDED** 👑 👑 👑 👑	13 Twin 7 Double	16 En Suite fac 4 Priv.NOT ensuite 1 Pub.Bath/Show	B&B per person £73.00-£93.00 Single £58.00-£72.50 Double	Open Jan-Dec Dinner 1900-2130 B&B + Eve.Meal £92.00-£112.00
			Victorian country house of character, tastefully and caringly refurbished. Set in private estate of 350 acres, curling rink and 18 hole golf course.			
COLONSAY, Isle of **Argyll** Isle of Colonsay Hotel Isle of Colonsay Argyll PA61 7YP Tel:(Colonsay) 09512 316 Fax:09512 353	Map 1 C4	**COMMENDED** 👑 👑 👑	3 Single 4 Twin 2 Double 2 Family	8 En Suite fac 2 Pub.Bath/Show	B&B per person	Open Mar-Oct Dinner from 1930 B&B + Eve.Meal £45.00-£70.00
			Charming island hotel blending a rich mixture of wildlife, outdoor pursuits, and total relaxation with comfort, good food, and warm hospitality.			

COLVEND **Kirkcudbrightshire** Clonyard House Hotel Colvend, by Dalbeattie Kirkcudbrightshire DG5 4QW Tel:(Rockcliffe) 055663 372 Fax:055663 422	Map 2 B1	COMMENDED 👑 👑 👑 👑	9 Twin 4 Double 2 Family Suite avail.	15 En Suite fac	B&B per person £30.00-£35.00 Single £27.50-£30.00 Double	Open Jan-Dec Dinner 1900-2100 B&B + Eve.Meal £35.00-£44.00

Family run hotel in wooded grounds 2 miles (3kms) from the coast. Range of spacious rooms, modern or traditional. Local produce and game in season.

COMRIE **Perthshire** Comrie Hotel Drummond Street Comrie Perthshire PH6 2DY Tel:(Comrie) 0764 670239	Map 2 A2	COMMENDED 👑 👑 👑	3 Single 5 Twin 4 Double	12 En Suite fac	B&B per person £23.00-£27.00 Single £23.00-£27.00 Double	Open Mar-Oct Dinner 1830-2100 B&B + Eve.Meal £33.00-£40.00

Friendly, traditional hotel with modern comforts, ideally situated for touring and many famous golf courses within easy reach.

Mossgiel Guest House Burrell Street Comrie Perthshire PH6 2JP Tel:(Comrie) 0764 670567		APPROVED 👑	2 Twin 3 Double 1 Family	2 Pub.Bath/Show	B&B per person £15.00-£18.00 Single £13.50-£15.00 Double	Open Jan-Dec Dinner 1830-1930 B&B + Eve.Meal £21.00-£22.50

Traditional stone built house with modern wing on the main road in the village. Near to all amenities. Choice of home cooked dishes.

CONNEL **Argyll**	Map 1 E2					

THE FALLS OF LORA HOTEL
Commended
👑 👑 👑

CONNEL FERRY, by OBAN, ARGYLL PA37 1PB
Tel: 0631 71 483 Fax: 0631 71 694
Ashley Courtenay Recommended

Overlooking Loch Etive, only 5 miles from Oban – "Gateway to the Highlands and Islands." An ideal centre for touring, walking, sailing and fishing holiday or just relaxing in a friendly atmosphere. Super Cocktail Bar with open log fire – over 100 brands of whisky to tempt you and an extensive Bar/Bistro Menu. 2½-3 hours drive north-west of Glasgow or Edinburgh.

OPEN ALL YEAR   Out-of-season mini breaks

RAC & AA
RSAC★★

Falls of Lora Hotel Connel, by Oban Argyll PA37 1PB Tel:(Connel) 063171 483 Fax:063171 694		COMMENDED 👑 👑 👑	6 Single 9 Twin 11 Double 4 Family	30 En Suite fac 2 Pub.Bath/Show	B&B per person £29.50-£49.50 Single £19.50-£49.50 Double	Open Jan-Dec Dinner 1900-2000 B&B + Eve.Meal £32.50-£61.50

Victorian house with modern wing; wide range of accommodation from cheerful family rooms to en suite jacuzzis. Weekly Scottish banquet.

Ronebhal Guest House Connel Argyll PA37 1PJ Tel:(Connel) 063171 310		HIGHLY COMMENDED 👑 👑	1 Single 4 Double 1 Family	3 En Suite fac 1 Limited ensuite 2 Priv.NOT ensuite 1 Pub.Bath/Show	B&B per person £15.00-£30.00 Single £16.50-£26.00 Double	Open Apr-Oct

Large stone built house, set back from the road, with private parking. Magnificent views of Loch Etive and mountains beyond. Oban 5 miles (8kms).

BY CONON BRIDGE Ross-shire Kinkell House Easter Kinkell by Conon Bridge Ross-shire Tel:(Dingwall) 0349 61270	Map 4 A8 **HIGHLY COMMENDED** 👑 👑 👑	1 Twin 1 Double 1 Family	3 En Suite fac	B&B per person £30.00-£35.00 Single £27.00-£32.00 Double	Open Jan-Dec Dinner 1900-2100 B&B + Eve.Meal £45.00-£50.00	

Secluded, restored farmhouse with excellent views over Cromarty Firth.
Superior rooms, quality food and wine.

CONTIN Ross-shire	Map 4 A8					

ACHILTY HOTEL

CONTIN BY STRATHPEFFER, ROSS-SHIRE IV14 9EG
Tel: 0997 421355

Ideally situated on A835 Ullapool Road only 20 mins from Inverness.
Former Coaching Inn combines old-world charm with modern amenities.
Excellent reputation for good food. 12 rooms with en-suite. Families
welcome. Open all year. Private fishing. B&B, from £17.50.
Special 3 nights and weekly rates.

Achilty Hotel Contin,by Strathpeffer Ross-shire IV14 9EG Tel:(Strathpeffer) 0997 421355	**Award Pending**	5 Twin 4 Double 3 Family	12 En Suite fac	B&B per person £24.50-£29.50 Single £17.50-£24.50 Double	Open Jan-Dec Dinner 1730-2130 B&B + Eve.Meal £30.00-£37.00	

Coul House Hotel
by STRATHPEFFER, ROSS-SHIRE
Telephone: 0997 421487 Fax: 0997 421945

Our views are breathtaking. The ancient "Mackenzies of
Coul" picked a wonderful situation for their lovely home.
Today, Ann and Martyn will give you a warm Highland
welcome. You'll enjoy the "Taste of Scotland" food of Chef
Bentley, log fires, summer evening piper and "Skye" and
"Raasay", the hotel's loveable labradors. Why not use our
"Highland Passport" to cruise on Loch Ness, visit Cawdor
Castle, sail to the Summer Isles .. or follow our "Highland
Heritage" trail to Glenfiddich Distillery, the Wildlife Park,
Culloden Battlefield ... for golfers, there's a 5-course holiday
including championship Royal Dornoch ... for anglers, we
have our own salmon and trout fishing ... there's pony
trekking too.

Ring or write for our colour brochure.

Coul House Hotel Contin,by Strathpeffer Ross-shire IV14 9EY Tel:(Strathpeffer) 0997 421487 Fax:0997 421945	**HIGHLY COMMENDED** 👑 👑 👑 👑	4 Single 7 Twin 7 Double 3 Family	21 En Suite fac	B&B per person £38.00-£54.00 Single £32.00-£43.00 Double	Open Jan-Dec Dinner 1900-2130 B&B + Eve.Meal £49.00-£66.50	

Personally run, secluded country house with friendly atmosphere. Fine views
over surrounding countryside. Taste of Scotland restaurant.

CONTIN continued

Map 4 A8

Craigdarroch Lodge Hotel
Craigdarroch Drive
Contin, by Strathpeffer
Ross-shire
IV14 9EH
Tel:(Strathpeffer) 0997
421265

6 Twin | 12 En Suite fac | B&B per person | Open Mar-Dec
6 Double | 1 Pub.Bath/Show | £28.00-£53.00 Single | Dinner 1900-2030
2 Family | | £28.00-£43.00 Double | B&B + Eve.Meal
| | | £35.00-£60.00

Contin House
Contin, by Strathpeffer
Ross-shire
IV14 9EB
Tel:(Strathpeffer) 0997
421920
Fax:0997 421841

DELUXE

3 Twin | 5 En Suite fac | B&B per person | Open Mar-Nov
2 Double | | £30.50-£41.00 Double | Dinner 1900-2400
| | | B&B + Eve.Meal
| | | £54.50-£65.00

Lovingly restored Georgian manse (c1794) with the atmosphere of a private house. Imaginative cuisine with emphasis on fresh local produce.

CORRIE
Isle of Arran

Map 1 F6

Blackrock Guest House
Corrie
Isle of Arran
KA27 8JP
Tel:(Corrie) 0770 810282

2 Single | 2 Pub.Bath/Show | B&B per person | Open Mar-Oct
1 Twin | | from £17.00 Single | Dinner from 1830
1 Double | | from £17.00 Double | B&B + Eve.Meal
4 Family | | | from £28.00

COUPAR ANGUS
Perthshire

Map 2 C1

COMMENDED

Enverdale Hotel
Pleasance Road
Coupar Angus
Perthshire
PH13 9JB
Tel:(Coupar Angus) 0828
27606

2 Single | 2 En Suite fac | B&B per person | Open Jan-Dec
2 Twin | 1 Pub.Bath/Show | £22.00-£32.00 Single | Dinner 1900-2115
1 Double | | £19.50-£26.00 Double | B&B + Eve.Meal
| | | £29.50-£36.00

Personally run hotel near the centre of Coupar Angus, offering a wide range of bar meals. Taste of Scotland award.

Royal Hotel
The Cross
Coupar Angus
Perthshire
PH13 9DA
Tel:(Coupar Angus) 0828
27549

1 Single | 4 Limited ensuite | B&B per person | Open Jan-Dec
3 Twin | 2 Pub.Bath/Show | to £15.00 Single | Dinner 1800-2100
2 Double | | to £15.00 Double | B&B + Eve.Meal
1 Family | | | to £22.00

COWDENBEATH
Fife

Map 2 C4

COMMENDED

Struan Bank Hotel
74 Perth Road
Cowdenbeath
Fife
KY4 9BG
Tel:(Cowdenbeath) 0383
511057

3 Single | 2 Pub.Bath/Show | B&B per person | Open Jan-Dec
3 Twin | | from £17.50 Single | Dinner 1900-2100
2 Double | | from £15.50 Double | B&B + Eve.Meal
1 Family | | | from £24.00

Family run hotel situated in the town centre and convenient for the railway station. Ideal centre for touring.

Details of Grading and Classification are on page vi.

| Key to symbols is on back flap. |

COYLTON, by Ayr Ayrshire The Cherry Tree Hotel 40 Main Street Coylton Ayrshire KA6 6JW Tel:(Ayr) 0292 570312	Map 1 H7		2 Twin 2 Family	2 En Suite fac 1 Pub.Bath/Show	B&B per person £29.00-£36.00 Double	Open Jan-Dec Dinner 1700-2100 B&B + Eve.Meal £39.00-£46.00	

Finlayson Arms Hotel

COYLTON · AYR · KA6 6JT
Tel: (0292) 570298

Country Inn with unrivalled facilities. Nine newly added fully appointed bedrooms with en-suite shower rooms and toilets. TV, teamaker, direct-dialling telephone, excellent food. Full Scottish Breakfast. À la carte evening meals. Egon Ronay Recommended. Explore Burns Country. Golf Holidays our speciality. Tee-off times arranged at no extra charge. Visit Castles, Country Parks, etc.

B&B FROM £26.00

Finlayson Arms Hotel Coylton, Ayr Ayrshire KA6 6JT Tel:(Joppa) 0292 570298	COMMENDED ☙ ☙ ☙	8 Twin 1 Double	9 En Suite fac	B&B per person £35.00 Single £26.00-£28.00 Double	Open Jan-Dec Dinner 1900-2100 B&B + Eve.Meal £42.00-£51.00	

Friendly village pub, offering quiet accommodation and good food. Ideally situated for Ayr Races, beaches and Robert Burns enthusiasts.

HERE'S THE DIFFERENCE

STB's scheme has two distinct elements, grading and classification.

GRADING:
measures the quality and condition of the facilities and services offered, eg, the warmth of welcome, quality of food and its presentation, condition of decor and furnishings, appearance of buildings, tidiness of grounds and gardens, condition of lighting and heating and so on.
Grading awards are: **Approved, Commended, Highly Commended, Deluxe.**

CLASSIFICATION:
measures the range of physical facilities and services offered, eg, rooms with private bath, heating, reception, lounges, telephones and so on.
Classification awards are: **Listed or from one to five crowns.**

CRAIGELLACHIE	Map 4
Banffshire	D8

CRAIGELLACHIE HOTEL

**CRAIGELLACHIE, SPEYSIDE,
BANFFSHIRE AB38 9SR
Tel: 0340 881204 Fax: 0340 881253**

Tastefully refurbished into a delightful Scottish Country House. The public rooms - with blazing log fires in the hall and lounges - encompass sauna, exercise room, solarium, billiards, library, drawing room and rod room. Enjoy the ambience of the Quaich (Cruach in the original Gaelic) cocktail bar. The Ben Aigan Restaurant sets exemplary standards of excellence for service and Scottish cuisine. Located in the heart of the Whisky and Castle Trails, the Craigellachie is your ideal base for visiting and enjoying the Highlands and sampling true Scottish hospitality.

Craigellachie Hotel
Victoria Street
Craigellachie, Aberlour
Banffshire
AB38 9SR
Tel:(Aberlour) 0340 881204
Fax:0340 881253

DELUXE

5 Single 30 En Suite fac
11 Twin
12 Double
2 Family

B&B per person
£54.50-£78.50 Single
£45.50-£56.50 Double

Open Jan-Dec
Dinner 1930-2130
B&B + Eve.Meal
£71.00-£82.00

Elegant Victorian hotel now lovingly refurbished offering a warm welcome, comfort and good food in picturesque Speyside.

CRAIGNURE	Map 1
Isle of Mull, Argyll	D2

Isle of Mull Hotel
Craignure
Isle of Mull, Argyll
PA65 6BB
Tel:(Craignure) 06802 351
Tlx:778215
Fax:06802 462

COMMENDED

10 Single 60 En Suite fac
42 Twin
8 Family

B&B per person
£42.00-£50.00 Single
£38.00-£46.00 Double

Open Apr-Oct
Dinner 1900-2030
B&B + Eve.Meal
£48.00-£58.50

Modern hotel on sea shore. Every room with view across the Sound of Mull to Oban. 1/2 mile (1 km) from ferry terminal.

Pennygate Lodge
Craignure
Isle of Mull, Argyll
PA65 6AY
Tel:(Craignure) 06802 333

COMMENDED

2 Twin 4 En Suite fac
3 Double 2 Pub.Bath/Show
2 Family
Suites avail.

B&B per person
£15.00-£28.00 Double

Open Jan-Dec
Dinner 1830-2000

Former Georgian manse set in 4.5 acres with magnificent views of the Sound of Mull. Ideal base for touring, near main bus route and ferry terminal.

Redburn
Redburn, Lochdon
Craignure
Isle of Mull, Argyll
PA64 6AP
Tel:(Craignure) 06802 370

COMMENDED

1 Twin 3 En Suite fac
2 Double

B&B per person
£16.50-£18.00 Double

Open Jan-Dec
Dinner at 1800
B&B + Eve.Meal
£26.00-£28.00

Converted croft house in quiet location on lochside. 3 miles (4.8 Km) Craignure Ferry. Area for natural history enthusiasts. Home cooking.

CRAIL – CRAOBH HAVEN, by Lochgilphead

CRAIL **Fife** Croma Hotel 33-35 Nethergate Crail Fife KY10 3TU Tel:(Crail) 0333 50239	Map 2 E3		4 Twin 3 Double 2 Family	5 En Suite fac 4 Pub.Bath/Show	B&B per person £15.00-£25.00 Single £12.50-£20.00 Double	Open Feb-Nov Dinner 1900-2200 B&B + Eve.Meal £25.00-£35.00	
Golf Hotel 4 High Street Crail Fife KY10 3TD Tel:(Crail) 0333 50206		COMMENDED ♕ ♕ ♕	5 Twin	5 En Suite fac 1 Pub.Bath/Show	B&B per person £27.00-£30.00 Single	Open Jan-Dec Dinner 1800-2100 B&B + Eve.Meal £38.00-£40.00	
			Family run hotel dating from 1763, in famous fishing village. Convenient for golf, fishing and touring East Neuk of Fife.				
Marine Hotel 54 Nethergate Crail Fife KY10 3TZ Tel:(Crail) 0333 50207		COMMENDED ♕ ♕ ♕	5 Twin 2 Double 1 Family	8 En Suite fac	B&B per person £28.50-£30.00 Single £23.50-£26.00 Double	Open Jan-Dec Dinner 1900-2100 B&B + Eve.Meal £35.50-£38.00	
			Privately owned hotel situated on shore with fine view over Firth of Forth. South facing garden with croquet lawn.				
Hazelton Guest House 29 Marketgate Crail Fife KY10 3TH Tel:(Crail) 0333 50250		COMMENDED Listed	1 Single 2 Twin 2 Double 2 Family	2 Pub.Bath/Show	B&B per person £15.00-£17.00 Single £15.00-£17.00 Double	Open Jan-Dec Dinner 1900-1930 B&B + Eve.Meal £28.00-£30.00	
			In the heart of small fishing town, a friendly guest house personally run by the owners. Fresh local produce used whenever possible.				
The Honey Pot Guest House & Tearoom 6 High Street Crail Fife KY10 3TD Tel:(Crail) 0333 50935			1 Single 3 Twin 1 Double 1 Family	1 En Suite fac 2 Pub.Bath/Show	B&B per person £14.00-£16.00 Single £14.00-£16.00 Double	Open Jan-Dec Dinner at 1830 B&B + Eve.Meal £24.00-£26.00	
Selcraig Guest House 47 Nethergate Crail Fife KY10 3TX Tel:(Crail) 0333 50697		COMMENDED ♕	2 Twin 1 Double 2 Family	2 Pub.Bath/Show	B&B per person £15.00-£17.00 Double	Open Jan-Dec Dinner 1800-1900 B&B + Eve.Meal £27.00-£29.00	
			200 year old listed house in quiet street close to sea shore. Convenient for touring the East Neuk of Fife.				
CRAOBH HAVEN **by Lochgilphead,** **Argyll** Buidhe Lodge Eilean Buidhe Craobh Haven Argyll PA31 8UA Tel:(Barbreck) 08525 291	Map 1 E3		6 Twin	6 En Suite fac	B&B per person £26.00-£31.00 Single £20.00-£25.00 Double	Open Jan-Dec Dinner 1930-2100 B&B + Eve.Meal £30.00-£35.00	

VAT is shown at 17.5%: changes in this rate may affect prices. Prices shown are for guidance only. Please send SAE with each enquiry

CRATHIE **Aberdeenshire** Inver Hotel Crathie,by Ballater Aberdeenshire AB35 5UL Tel:(Crathie) 03397 42345	Map 4 D1	COMMENDED 🏆 🏆 🏆	1 Single 2 Twin 2 Double 4 Family	9 En Suite fac	B&B per person £23.50-£25.00 Single £23.50-£25.00 Double	Open Jan-Dec Dinner 1800-2000 B&B + Eve.Meal £35.00-£37.00	

200 year old hotel, completely renovated. The nearest hostelry to Balmoral Castle on Royal Deeside. 1.5 miles (3kms) west of Crathie.

CRAWFORD **Lanarkshire** Field End Guest House The Loaning Crawford Lanarkshire ML12 6TN Tel:(Crawford) 08642 276	Map 2 B7	APPROVED 🏆 🏆	1 Single 1 Twin 1 Double 1 Family	2 En Suite fac 1 Limited ensuite 2 Pub.Bath/Show	B&B per person £14.00-£18.00 Single £18.00-£20.00 Double	Dinner 1830-1930 B&B + Eve.Meal £20.00-£24.00	

Stone villa overlooking fields, located up the hill opposite the church. Ideal half-way house and touring centre. No smoking or pets.

CREETOWN **by Newton Stewart,** **Wigtownshire** Ellangowan Hotel Creetown,by Newton Stewart Wigtownshire DG8 7JF Tel:(Creetown) 067182 201	Map 1 H1	COMMENDED 🏆 🏆 🏆	1 Single 2 Twin 3 Double 2 Family	6 En Suite fac 2 Pub.Bath/Show	B&B per person £22.50-£25.50 Single £22.50-£25.50 Double	Open Jan-Dec Dinner 1900-2200 B&B + Eve.Meal £32.50-£35.50	

Impressive granite built hotel on the edge of the village square. Family run, with emphasis on cuisine using fresh local produce.

Marclaysean Guest House 51 St John's Street Creetown Wigtownshire DG8 7JB Tel:(Creetown) 067182 319		COMMENDED Listed	1 Twin 1 Double	1 En Suite fac	B&B per person £14.00-£16.00 Double	Open Apr-Oct Dinner from 1900 B&B + Eve.Meal £21.50-£23.50	

Guest house with an en suite bedroom, conveniently situated in centre of village near to Gem Rock museum.

SPECIAL INTEREST HOLIDAYS

Write for your free brochure on Short Breaks,
Activity Holidays, Skiing, to:

Scottish Tourist Board, PO Box 15, Edinburgh EH1 1VY.

| CRIANLARICH
Perthshire | Map 1
G2 | |

Allt-Chaorain Country House

Crianlarich FK20 8RU
Tel: 0838 300283 Fax: 0838 300238
"Welcome to my home"

Allt-Chaorain, is a compact and comfortable house noted for the warmth of its welcome and hospitality. Set high, it has level gardens and outstanding views of the surrounding mountains. Guests enjoy a "house party" atmosphere, helping themselves from the honesty bar and dining together in the evening.

The table d'hote menu changes daily, usually offering a choice of dishes for the main course. The accent is on good home cooking with generous helpings and plenty of fresh vegetables. After enjoying dinner it is pleasant to sit in the sunroom and watch the evening light on the mountains, or, if the evening is chill to enjoy the log fire burning in the lounge.

Allt-Chaorain Country House Crianlarich Perthshire FK20 8RU Tel:(Crianlarich) 0838 300283 Fax:0838 300238	COMMENDED 🏠 🏠 🏠	4 Twin 4 Double	8 En Suite fac 2 Pub.Bath/Show	B&B per person £27.00-£43.00 Single £27.00-£33.00 Double	Open Mar-Oct Dinner 1900-2000 B&B + Eve.Meal £42.00-£48.00

Privately owned country house in elevated position overlooking Ben More and Strathfillan. South facing garden, 9 acres of grounds. Taste of Scotland

The Ben More Lodge Hotel

Crianlarich, Perthshire FK20 8QS
Telephone: 0838 300210

Set in spectacular scenery, our family run Lodge Hotel offers full private facilities and colour TV in all the rooms. Superb wining and dining in the adjoining Bar and Restaurant.

An ideal centre for touring, walking, skiing or simply relaxing.

B&B from £25. DB&B from £38.

Ben More Lodge Hotel Crianlarich Perthshire FK20 8QS Tel:(Crianlarich) 0838 300210	COMMENDED 🏠 🏠 🏠	6 Double 2 Family	8 En Suite fac	B&B per person £30.00-£35.00 Single £25.00-£26.00 Double	Open Jan-Dec Dinner 1730-2100 B&B + Eve.Meal £38.00-£40.00

Pine lodges of a high standard with public bar and restaurant adjacent. Ideal base for touring, hillwalking and fishing.

CRIANLARICH continued	Map 1 G2						
Suie Lodge Hotel Glendochart Crianlarich Perthshire FK20 8QT Tel:(Killin) 0567 820417			1 Single 4 Twin 4 Double 2 Family	7 En Suite fac 1 Pub.Bath/Show	B&B per person £16.00-£16.50 Single £16.00-£19.00 Double	Open Jan-Dec Dinner 1900-2100 B&B + Eve.Meal £26.00-£29.00	
Craigbank Guest House Crianlarich Perthshire FK20 8QS Tel:(Crianlarich) 08383 279			2 Twin 1 Double 2 Family	1 En Suite fac 1 Pub.Bath/Show	B&B per person from £15.00 Double	Open Jan-Dec Dinner from 1900	
Glenardran Guest House Crianlarich Perthshire FK20 8QS Tel:(Crianlarich) 08383 236		COMMENDED Listed	1 Single 2 Twin 3 Double	1 En Suite fac 1 Pub.Bath/Show	B&B per person from £19.00 Single from £17.00 Double	Open Jan-Dec Dinner 1915-2000	

Friendly welcome at recently refurbished house on A84, collection from station available. Excellent base for touring, walking or climbing.

The Lodge House Crianlarich Perthshire FK20 8RU Tel:(Crianlarich) 08383 276		COMMENDED ✹✹✹	2 Twin 4 Double	6 En Suite fac	B&B per person £24.00-£30.00 Single £24.00-£30.00 Double	Open Mar-Oct Dinner 1830-2000 B&B + Eve.Meal £37.00-£42.00	

In elevated position with panoramic views of river, mountains and glens. Ideal base for walking and day trips. Home cooking. One annexe bedroom.

CRIEFF Perthshire	Map 2 B2						
Arduthie Hotel Perth Road Crieff Perthshire PH7 3EQ Tel:(Crieff) 0764 653113			1 Twin 2 Double 2 Family	5 En Suite fac	B&B per person £25.00-£27.00 Single £22.50-£26.00 Double	Open Jan-Dec Dinner 1700-2100	
The Crieff Hotel 45-47 East High Street Crieff Perthshire PH7 3JA Tel:(Crieff) 0764 652632 Fax:0764 655019		COMMENDED ✹✹✹ ✹	4 Single 3 Double 2 Family	9 En Suite fac	B&B per person £28.00-£32.00 Single £24.50-£27.00 Double	Open Jan-Dec Dinner 1800-2130 B&B + Eve.Meal £35.00-£39.50	

Family owned hotel in town centre with leisure area, hairdressing salon and full function facilities. Fishing, shooting and golfing packages.

CRIEFF

CRIEFF continued	Map 2 B2						

Crieff Hydro
Crieff
Perthshire
PH7 3LQ
Tel:(Crieff) 0764 655555
Fax:0764 653087

COMMENDED
≜ ≜ ≜
≜

50 Single   192 En Suite fac
57 Twin
19 Double
66 Family

B&B per person
£36.50-£46.00 Single
£36.50-£46.00 Double

Open Jan-Dec
Dinner 1900-2030
B&B + Eve.Meal
£39.50-£52.00

Modernised, Victorian Hydro Hotel on hillside overlooking town. Views of Ochils and Strathearn. Extensive leisure and conference facilities.

Gwydyr House Hotel
Comrie Road
Crieff
Perthshire
PH7 4BP
Tel:(Crieff) 0764 653277

APPROVED
≜

2 Single   3 Pub.Bath/Show
3 Twin
1 Double
4 Family

B&B per person
£15.50-£18.50 Single
£15.50-£18.50 Double

Open Apr-Oct
Dinner 1900-2000
B&B + Eve.Meal
£26.00-£29.00

A small, well appointed, family hotel standing in its own grounds and in the centre of a good touring area.

Keppoch House Hotel
Perth Road
Crieff
Perthshire
PH7 3EQ
Tel:(Crieff) 0764 654341
Fax:0764 655435

APPROVED
≜ ≜ ≜

1 Single   5 En Suite fac
4 Twin   1 Pub.Bath/Show
1 Family

B&B per person
£13.00-£20.00 Single
£20.00-£35.00 Double

Open Jan-Dec
Dinner 1800-2130
B&B + Eve.Meal
£31.00-£46.00

Personally run hotel situated within walking distance of town centre with views over the Perthshire hills.

Kingarth Hotel
Perth Road
Crieff
Perthshire
PH7 3EQ
Tel:(Crieff) 0764 652060
Fax:0764 652060

COMMENDED
≜ ≜ ≜

3 Single   12 En Suite fac
5 Twin   1 Pub.Bath/Show
2 Double
3 Family

Suite avail.

B&B per person
£20.00-£32.00 Single
£20.00-£32.00 Double

Open Mar-Oct
Dinner 1900-2030
B&B + Eve.Meal
£32.00-£44.00

A Victorian family run house with well kept gardens, overlooking Strathearn to Ochil Hills. Own parking facilities. 5 ground floor rooms.

Leven House Hotel
Comrie Road
Crieff
Perthshire
PH7 4BA
Tel:(Crieff) 0764 652529

COMMENDED
≜ ≜

1 Single   5 En Suite fac
3 Twin   2 Pub.Bath/Show
3 Double
3 Family

B&B per person
£15.00-£18.00 Single
£15.00-£18.00 Double

Open Jan-Dec
Dinner 1630-1930
B&B + Eve.Meal
£21.00-£24.00

Small family run hotel near town centre serving dinners and Scottish high teas. Ideally situated for touring and golf. Spacious car park.

Lockes Acre Hotel
Comrie Road
Crieff
Perthshire
PH7 4BP
Tel:(Crieff) 0764 652526

COMMENDED
≜ ≜ ≜

1 Twin   4 En Suite fac
4 Double   2 Pub.Bath/Show
2 Family

B&B per person
£25.00-£30.00 Single
£21.50-£24.00 Double

Open Jan-Dec
Dinner 1900-2045
B&B + Eve.Meal
£33.00-£35.00

Large Victorian house set in an acre of garden with magnificent views, in the centre of a fine touring area. Modern standards of comfort and service

---

Meadow Inn Hotel
Burrell Street
Crieff
Perthshire
PH7 4DT
Tel:(Crieff) 0764 653261

1 Single   5 En Suite fac
6 Twin   2 Pub.Bath/Show
3 Double

B&B per person
£19.50-£25.00 Single
£19.50-£25.00 Double

Open Jan-Dec
Dinner 1800-2130
B&B + Eve.Meal
£27.00-£32.50

CRIEFF continued	Map 2 B2						
Murraypark Hotel Connaught Terrace Crieff Perthshire PH7 3DJ Tel:(Crieff) 0764 653731 Fax:0764 655311		COMMENDED ♕ ♕ ♕ ♕	13 Twin 6 Double 2 Family	21 En Suite fac	B&B per person £45.00-£47.00 Single £32.00-£35.00 Double	Open Jan-Dec Dinner 1930-2130 B&B + Eve.Meal £52.00-£60.00	
			Charming pink stone Victorian house, modernised but retaining original character. Taste of Scotland restaurant.				
Strathearn Hotel 57 King Street Crieff Perthshire PH7 3HB Tel:(Crieff) 0764 652089			3 Single 11 Twin 7 Double 4 Family	10 En Suite fac 5 Pub.Bath/Show	B&B per person £22.00-£28.00 Single £22.00-£26.00 Double	Open Jan-Dec Dinner 1900-2050 B&B + Eve.Meal from £34.00	
The Tower Hotel East High Street Crieff Perthshire PH7 3JA Tel:(Crieff) 0764 652678			1 Single 1 Twin 2 Double 3 Family	3 En Suite fac 4 Pub.Bath/Show	B&B per person £14.00-£18.00 Single £14.00-£22.00 Double	Open Jan-Dec Dinner 1700-2130	
The Comely Bank Guest House 32 Burrell Street Crieff Perthshire PH7 4DT Tel:(Crieff) 0764 653409		COMMENDED ♕ ♕	1 Single 1 Twin 2 Double 1 Family	2 En Suite fac 2 Pub.Bath/Show	B&B per person £14.00-£15.00 Single £14.00-£17.00 Double	Open Jan-Dec Dinner 1800-2000 B&B + Eve.Meal £22.00-£25.00	
			Personal attention and a friendly welcome. The French chef/proprietor prepares all meals and the premises are licensed.				
Galvelbeg House Perth Road Crieff Perthshire PH7 3EQ Tel:(Crieff) 0764 655061		COMMENDED ♕ ♕	1 Single 2 Twin 1 Double 1 Family	4 En Suite fac 1 Limited ensuite	B&B per person £18.00-£20.00 Single £18.00-£20.00 Double	Open Jan-Dec	
			Situated 500 yards from Crieff town centre and Crieff Golf Club. A good central base for touring and sightseeing.				
Heatherville Guest House 31 Burrell Street Crieff Perthshire PH7 4DT Tel:(Crieff) 0764 652825		COMMENDED ♕ ♕	1 Single 1 Twin 1 Double 2 Family	1 En Suite fac 2 Pub.Bath/Show	B&B per person £14.00-£15.00 Single £14.00-£15.00 Double	Open Feb-Nov Dinner from 1830 B&B + Eve.Meal £22.00-£23.00	
			Friendly welcome, private parking and 5 minutes walk from town centre. One room with en suite facilities.				
MacKenzie Lodge Broich Terrace Crieff Perthshire PH7 3BD Tel:(Crieff) 0764 653721		COMMENDED ♕ ♕	2 Twin 2 Double 1 Family	2 En Suite fac 2 Pub.Bath/Show	B&B per person £18.00-£24.00 Single £14.00-£20.00 Double	Open Jan-Dec	
			Elegant Victorian home retaining many original features. Winner of "Warmest Welcome in Perthshire 1991". Private parking.				

BY CRIEFF **Perthshire** Foulford Inn Sma'Glen Crieff Perthshire PH7 3LN Tel:(Crieff) 0764 652407	Map 2 B2	COMMENDED ≋ ≋	3 Single 4 Twin 3 Double	3 En Suite fac 3 Pub.Bath/Show	B&B per person £16.00 Single £16.00-£19.00 Double	Open Mar-Jan Dinner 1700-2130 B&B + Eve.Meal £22.00-£34.00		

Comfortable, modern accommodation ideally situated on tourist route.
Some rooms private facilities. Games room, bowling green, 9 hole Golf Course.

CROMARTY **Ross-shire** Royal Hotel Marine Terrace Cromarty Ross-shire IV11 8YN Tel:(Cromarty) 03817 217/0381 600217 Fax:03817 217/0381 600217	Map 4 B7	COMMENDED ≋ ≋ ≋	2 Single 2 Twin 4 Double 2 Family	10 En Suite fac	B&B per person £27.00-£30.00 Single £26.00-£28.00 Double	Open Jan-Dec Dinner 1800-2100		

Family run hotel overlooking harbour and beach with fine views over Cromarty
Firth. Specialising in food using good local produce.

CROMDALE **by Grantown-on-Spey** **Moray** The Haugh Hotel & Restaurant Cromdale, by Grantown-on-Spey Moray PH26 3LW Tel:(Grantown-on-Spey) 0479 2583 0479 2583	Map 4 C9		2 Single 2 Twin 1 Double 3 Family	4 En Suite fac 1 Pub.Bath/Show	B&B per person £18.00-£20.00 Single £18.00-£20.00 Double	Open Jan-Dec Dinner 1900-2100 B&B + Eve.Meal £30.00-£32.00		

CROSSFORD **by Dunfermline, Fife** Keavil House Hotel Crossford,by Dunfermline Fife KY12 8QW Tel:(Dunfermline) 0383 736258 Tlx:728227 Fax:0383 621600	Map 2 C4	COMMENDED ≋ ≋ ≋ ≋	3 Single 14 Twin 14 Double 1 Family	32 En Suite fac	B&B per person £40.00-£60.00 Single £63.00-£68.00 Double	Open Jan-Dec Dinner 1800-2200 B&B + Eve.Meal £75.00-£80.00		

Country house in its own grounds. Extensive conference and leisure facilities.
1.5 miles (3 kms) west of Dunfermline.

Pitfirrane Arms Hotel Main Street Crossford,by Dunfermline Fife KY12 8NJ Tel:(Dunfermline) 0383 736132 Fax:0383 621760			10 Single 15 Twin 12 Double 1 Family	38 En Suite fac	B&B per person £25.00-£53.00 Single £17.50-£64.00 Double	Open Jan-Dec Dinner 1900-2115 B&B + Eve.Meal £35.00-£63.00		

CROSSMICHAEL **by Castle Douglas** **Kirkcudbrightshire** Culgruff House Hotel Crossmichael, by Castle Douglas Kirkcudbrightshire DG7 3BB Tel:(Crossmichael) 055667 230/227	Map 2 A1		4 Single 5 Twin 4 Double 4 Family	4 En Suite fac 1 Limited ensuite 4 Pub.Bath/Show	B&B per person £16.00-£18.00 Single £13.50-£17.75 Double	Open Jan-Dec Dinner 1700-2200 B&B + Eve.Meal £19.75-£31.75	

CULLEN **Banffshire** Bayview Hotel & Restaurant Seafield Street Cullen, Buckie Banffshire AB56 2SU Tel:(Cullen) 0542 41031	Map 4 E7	COMMENDED 👑 👑 👑 👑	1 Single 2 Twin 3 Double	6 En Suite fac	B&B per person £35.00 Single £27.50-£30.00 Double	Open Jan-Dec Dinner 1830-2100	

Personally run hotel with intimate and cosy atmosphere and magnificent views. Overlooking harbour, golf course, sandy beaches and Moray Firth.

CULLEN BAY HOTEL
CULLEN, BUCKIE, BANFFSHIRE AB56 2XA
Telephone: 0542 840432 Fax: 0542 840900

The hotel has two restaurants, a lounge bar with patio and garden. Rooms are all newly refurbished to a high standard. Good food, friendly atmosphere and views overlooking Cullen Bay and golf course add up to an unforgettable holiday.

B&B from £200 per guest per week (June to September).

Cullen Bay Hotel Cullen, Buckie Banffshire AB56 2XA Tel:(Cullen) 0542 840432 Fax:0542 840900		COMMENDED 👑 👑 👑 👑	1 Single 6 Twin 5 Double 2 Family	14 En Suite fac	B&B per person £32.50-£40.00 Single £32.50-£40.00 Double	Open Jan-Dec Dinner 1900-2145	

Personally run hotel about 1 mile (2kms) from town. Magnificent view over golf course and Cullen Bay's sandy beach.

Seafield Arms Hotel 19 Seafield Street Cullen, Buckie Banffshire AB56 2SG Tel:(Cullen) 0542 40791		Award Pending	7 Single 9 Twin 8 Double 1 Family	21 En Suite fac 1 Limited ensuite 2 Pub.Bath/Show	B&B per person £26.00 Single £20.00-£23.00 Double	Open Jan-Dec Dinner 1800-2130 B&B + Eve.Meal £36.00-£42.00	

Scottish Tourist Board
COMMENDED
Facilities
👑 👑 👑

FOR QUALITY
GO GRADED

| **CUMBERNAULD**
Dunbartonshire
The Dovecote Travel Inn
4 South Muirhead Road
Cumbernauld
Dunbartonshire
G67 1AX
Tel:(Cumbernauld) 0236
725339
Fax:0236 736380 | Map 2
A5 | 19 Single
18 Family | 37 En Suite fac | Price per room
£32.50 | Open Jan-Dec
Dinner 1700-2230 | |

WESTERWOOD HOTEL
ST ANDREWS DRIVE, CUMBERNAULD G68 0EW
Telephone: (0236) 457171   Fax: (0236) 738478

Westerwood Hotel, Golf and Country Club is located 13 miles from Glasgow in Cumbernauld. The 47-bedroomed hotel offers a range of accommodation, many with views over the hotel's own 18-hole golf course designed by Seve Ballesteros and Dave Thomas. Indoor golf schools available. There is also a Country Club with a range of leisure activities including a swimming pool, jacuzzi, gym, tennis, snooker and bowls. Dining at Westerwood gives you the choice of an informal meal or an à la carte selection in the award-winning Old Masters Restaurant.
Various packages are on offer.

| Westerwood Hotel, Golf
& Country Club
1 St Andrews Drive
Cumbernauld
Dunbartonshire
G68 0EW
Tel:(Kilsyth) 0236 457171
Fax:0236 738478 | **HIGHLY**
COMMENDED
👑 👑 👑
👑 👑 | 49 Twin
Suites avail. | 49 En Suite fac | B&B per person
£82.50-£97.50 Single
£48.75-£58.75 Double | Open Jan-Dec
Dinner 1900-2200 | |
| | | **Modern hotel nestling on edge of Kilsyth Hills. Own championship golf course and leisure complex. Clubhouse and Old Masters restaurant.** | | | | |

| **CUMNOCK**
Ayrshire
Dumfries Arms Hotel
54 Glaisnock Street
Cumnock
Ayrshire
KA18 1BY
Tel:(Cumnock) 0290 20282
Fax:0290 22400 | Map 1
H7 | 3 Twin
2 Double
2 Family | 7 En Suite fac
2 Pub.Bath/Show | B&B per person
£26.00-£30.00 Single
£18.00-£22.00 Double | Open Jan-Dec
Dinner 1730-2130
B&B + Eve.Meal
£25.00-£29.00 | |

| Royal Hotel
1 Glaisnock Street
Cumnock
Ayrshire
KA18 1BP
Tel:(Cumnock) 0290 20822
Fax:0290 25988 | **COMMENDED**
👑 👑 | 1 Single
6 Twin
3 Double
1 Family | 5 En Suite fac
2 Pub.Bath/Show | B&B per person
£23.00-£36.00 Single
£23.00-£27.00 Double | Open Jan-Dec
Dinner 1700-2100
B&B + Eve.Meal
£32.00-£42.00 | |
| | | **In town centre on main A76 road. Small private car park. 16 miles (26kms) from Kilmarnock, 38 miles (61kms) from Glasgow.** | | | | |

DALBEATTIE Kirkcudbrightshire Burnside Hotel John Street Dalbeattie Kirkcudbrightshire DG5 4JJ Tel:(Dalbeattie) 0556 610219	Map 2 B1	COMMENDED 👑 👑 👑	2 Twin 4 Double 1 Family	5 En Suite fac 2 Pub.Bath/Show	B&B per person £30.00-£32.00 Single £22.50-£25.00 Double	Open Jan-Dec Dinner 1830-2100 B&B + Eve.Meal £32.00-£35.00	
			Family hotel with enclosed garden situated beside the Barr burn and town park. Short walk from town centre.				
The Pheasant Hotel Maxwell Street Dalbeattie Kirkcudbrightshire DG5 4AH Tel:(Dalbeattie) 0556 610345		APPROVED 👑 👑 👑	1 Single 3 Twin 3 Family	6 En Suite fac 1 Pub.Bath/Show	B&B per person £14.00-£19.50 Single £12.50-£19.50 Double	Open Jan-Dec Dinner 1800-2100 B&B + Eve.Meal £19.00-£24.50	
			Family run Inn with carvery restaurant in the heart of the town, close to burn leading to the River Urr.				

Auchenskeoch Lodge

By Dalbeattie, Kirkcudbrightshire DG5 4PG.
Tel. 038 778 277 or 0387 780 277
Traditionally furnished Victorian shooting lodge set in 20 acres of woodland and formal gardens. Personally run by the proprietors, offering every comfort in a country house atmosphere. All bedrooms en suite. Good food utilising much home grown produce. Fishing on own loch, billiard room.
Croquet lawn, turf and gravel maze.

Auchenskeoch Lodge by Dalbeattie Kirkcudbrightshire DG5 4PG Tel:(Southwick) 038778 277	COMMENDED 👑 👑 👑	3 Twin 2 Double	5 En Suite fac	B&B per person £30.00-£32.00 Single £22.00-£26.00 Double	Open Mar-Oct Dinner 1930-2000 B&B + Eve.Meal £34.00-£39.00	
		Former shooting lodge, in 20 acres of secluded ground with loch. "Taste of Scotland". Billiard room, croquet lawn and Turf Maze.				

BRIARDALE HOUSE

17 Haugh Road, Dalbeattie, Kirkcudbrightshire DG5 4AR
Tel: 0556 611468 Mobile: 0850 267251

John and Verna Woodworth invite you to relax in their elegant Deluxe - 3 Crown Victorian house, furnished with antiques yet providing modern facilities and comfort at a very reasonable price. John is a professional chef producing excellent food with choice on the menu, which changes daily. Bedrooms are large with ensuite bath and shower. An ideal base to explore our beautiful and peaceful Galloway. Car parking; large walled garden. Complimentary bikes available.

Mini-breaks: Jan-March.

Briardale House Haugh Road Dalbeattie Kirkcudbrightshire DG5 4AR Tel:(Dalbeattie) 0556 611468/0850 267251 (mobile)	DELUXE 👑 👑 👑	2 Double	3 En Suite fac	B&B per person £19.00 Double	Open Jan-Oct Dinner 1800-1900 B&B + Eve.Meal £30.00	
		Detached Victorian villa retaining many original features in residential area on the outskirts of town. Excellent food; no licence, no corkage.				

DALIBURGH
South Uist
Western Isles

Borrodale Hotel	Map 3
Daliburgh	A1
South Uist, Western Isles	
PA81 5SS	
Tel:(Lochboisdale) 08784 444	
Fax:08784 611	

APPROVED
≋ ≋ ≋

3 Single	12 En Suite fac	B&B per person	Open Jan-Dec
4 Twin	2 Limited ensuite	£30.00-£32.00 Single	Dinner 1900-2100
6 Double	2 Pub.Bath/Show	£32.00-£34.00 Double	B&B + Eve.Meal
1 Family		£40.00-£50.00	

Family run hotel in village of Daliburgh. Only 3 miles (5kms) from Lochboisdale ferry terminal.

DALKEITH
Midlothian

Barley Bree Motel	Map 2
3 Easthouses Road	D5
Dalkeith	
Midlothian	
EH22 4DH	
Tel:031 663 3105	

APPROVED
≋ ≋ ≋

2 Twin	5 En Suite fac	B&B per person	Open Jan-Dec
2 Double		from £25.00 Single	Dinner 1200-2400
1 Family		from £25.00 Double	B&B + Eve.Meal
			from £35.00

Family hotel on south side of town centre. Bus route to Edinburgh (10 miles). Function suite. Indian restaurant.

The County Hotel	
152 High Street	
Dalkeith	
Midlothian	
EH22 1AY	
Tel:031 663 3495	

COMMENDED
≋ ≋ ≋

4 Single	29 En Suite fac	B&B per person	Open Jan-Dec
16 Twin	3 Pub.Bath/Show	£40.00-£48.00 Single	Dinner 1800-2200
5 Double		£28.00-£32.00 Double	B&B + Eve.Meal
4 Family			£48.00-£56.00

Small, family run hotel modernised to a high standard in the centre of this historic town. Edinburgh city centre 7 miles (11kms).

DALLAS
Moray

Dallas Hotel	Map 4
Main Street	D8
Dallas, Forres	
Moray	
IV36 0SA	
Tel:(Dallas) 034389 323	

APPROVED
Listed

2 Twin	1 En Suite fac	B&B per person	Open Jan-Dec
1 Double	1 Pub.Bath/Show	£13.00-£22.00 Single	Dinner from 1800
2 Family		£13.00-£22.00 Double	B&B + Eve.Meal
			£20.00-£29.00

Family run village inn with one room en-suite. Ideal for exploring Highlands, fishing, trekking, sailing, walking, skiing; golf available locally.

DALMALLY
Argyll

Glenorchy Lodge Hotel	Map 1
Dalmally	F2
Argyll	
PA33 1AA	
Tel:(Dalmally) 08382 312	

Award Pending

1 Twin	5 En Suite fac	B&B per person	Open Jan-Dec
1 Double		from £28.50 Single	Dinner 1700-2100
3 Family		from £22.50 Double	

Craig Villa Guest House	
Dalmally	
Argyll	
PA33 1AX	
Tel:(Dalmally) 08382	
255/0838 200255	

COMMENDED
≋ ≋ ≋

2 Twin	5 En Suite fac	B&B per person	Open Apr-Oct
2 Double	1 Priv.NOT ensuite	£18.00-£22.00 Double	Dinner from 1900
2 Family			B&B + Eve.Meal
			£29.00-£34.00

Personally run guest house in own grounds amidst breathtaking scenery. Good touring base. Home cooking.

DALMALLY continued Map 1 F2

Orchy Bank Guest House
Dalmally
Argyll
PA33 1AS
Tel:(Dalmally) 08382 370

COMMENDED
Listed

2 Single　2 Pub.Bath/Show
2 Twin
2 Double
2 Family

B&B per person
£16.00-£17.00 Single
£16.00-£17.00 Double

Open Jan-Dec
Dinner 1900-2000
B&B + Eve.Meal
£25.00

Personally-run Victorian former village shop on banks of the River Orchy.
24 miles (38 kms) to Oban, 16 miles (26 kms) to Inveraray. Near Glencoe.

DALWHINNIE
Inverness-shire Map 4 A1

Loch Ericht Hotel
Dalwhinnie
Inverness-shire
PH19 1AE
Tel:(Dalwhinnie) 05282 257
Fax:0463 782531

APPROVED
☗ ☗ ☗

24 Twin　27 En Suite fac
3 Family

B&B per person
£27.50-£32.50 Single
£19.50-£24.75 Double

Open Apr-Oct
Dinner 1730-2100
B&B + Eve.Meal
£27.50-£39.75

Personally run hotel in small Highland village. All rooms with en suite facilities.
Live entertainment on some evenings. Meals served all day.

DERVAIG
Isle of Mull, Argyll Map 1 C1

Ardbeg House Hotel
Dervaig,by Tobermory
Isle of Mull, Argyll
PA75 6QJ
Tel:(Dervaig) 06884 254

1 Single　3 En Suite fac
1 Twin　1 Pub.Bath/Show
1 Double
1 Family

B&B per person
£18.00-£20.00 Single
£18.00-£20.00 Double

Open Jan-Dec
Dinner 1900-2030
B&B + Eve.Meal
£29.00-£31.00

BELLACHROY HOTEL
DERVAIG, ISLE OF MULL, ARGYLL PA75 6QW
Tel: 06884 314

Situated in Mull's most picturesque village. Good home cooking, two
lively bars, regular live entertainment and comfortable rooms. Ideal for
touring the north of Mull. Special packages by arrangement. Fishing,
shooting, ponytrekking and wildlife tours arranged.

Phone Sue Rosier on 06884 314.

Bellachroy Hotel
Dervaig,by Tobermory
Isle of Mull, Argyll
PA75 6QW
Tel:(Dervaig) 06884 225/314
(reservations)

3 Twin　3 Pub.Bath/Show
3 Double
2 Family

B&B per person
from £21.00 Double

Open Jan-Dec
Dinner 1900-2100
B&B + Eve.Meal
from £33.00

Druimnacroish Country
House Hotel
Dervaig, by Tobermory
Isle of Mull, Argyll
PA75 6QW
Tel:(Dervaig) 06884 274/212
Fax:06884 311

COMMENDED
☗ ☗ ☗
☗

4 Twin　6 En Suite fac
2 Double

B&B per person
from £55.00 Single
from £55.00 Double

Open May-Oct
Dinner from 2000
B&B + Eve.Meal
from £73.00

An imaginatively converted steading, small and exclusive with a delightful
conservatory offering glorious views. Emphasis on good food.

Ardrioch Farm Guest House
Dervaig,by Tobermory
Isle of Mull, Argyll
PA75 6QR
Tel:(Dervaig) 06884 264

COMMENDED
☗ ☗

1 Single　1 En Suite fac
1 Twin　1 Pub.Bath/Show
2 Double

B&B per person
£17.00-£19.50 Single
£17.00-£19.50 Double

Open Apr-Oct
Dinner 1830-2000
B&B + Eve.Meal
£27.50-£30.00

Attractive cedarwood house with adjoining farm; lovely loch and hill views
Home cooking. Taste of Scotland. Sea sailing available. Activity holidays.

Details of Grading and Classification are on page vi.　　　| Key to symbols is on back flap. |　93

| DERVAIG
Isle of Mull, Argyll | Map 1
C1 | | |

Druimard Country House

Dervaig, Isle of Mull, Argyll, PA75 6QW. Tel: (06884) 345.

Beautifully restored Victorian country house offering extremely comfortable accommodation with an award winning restaurant. Widely known for excellent food, recommended in many leading Hotel and Good Food Guides. Recently awarded Red Rosette from AA. Well situated for touring, boat trips, fishing, walking and sandy beaches.

| Druimard Country House
Druimard
Dervaig, by Tobermory
Isle of Mull, Argyll
PA75 6QW
Tel:(Dervaig) 06884 345/291 | **HIGHLY
COMMENDED**
♨ ♨ ♨ | 2 Twin   4 En Suite fac
3 Double 1 Pub.Bath/Show
1 Family
Suite avail. | B&B per person
£49.00-£54.50 Single
£33.00-£42.50 Double | Open Jan-Dec
Dinner 1800-2100
B&B + Eve.Meal
£50.50-£62.00 |
| | | **Small Victorian country house hotel, with elegant restaurant, interesting cuisine using fresh ingredients. Adjacent to Mull Little Theatre.** | | |

| Glenbellart Vegetarian
Guest House
Dervaig
Isle of Mull, Argyll
PA75 6QJ
Tel:(Dervaig) 06884 282 | | 1 Twin   2 Pub.Bath/Show
2 Double | B&B per person
from £17.00 Single
from £14.00 Double | Open Mar-Oct
Dinner at 1900
B&B + Eve.Meal
£24.00-£27.00 |

| **DINGWALL
Ross-shire**
National Hotel
High Street
Dingwall
Ross-shire
IV15 9HA
Tel:(Dingwall) 0349 62166
Fax:0349 65178 | Map 4
A8 | 9 Single 54 En Suite fac
22 Twin
16 Double
7 Family | B&B per person
from £32.00 Single
from £29.50 Double | Open Jan-Dec
Dinner 1900-2130
B&B + Eve.Meal
from £46.00 |

| Tulloch Castle Hotel
Tulloch Castle Drive
Dingwall
Ross-shire
IV15 9ND
Tel:(Dingwall) 0349 61325
Fax:0349 63993 | | 2 Single 19 En Suite fac
5 Twin
4 Double
8 Family | B&B per person
£25.00-£36.50 Single
£20.00-£33.50 Double | Open Jan-Dec
Dinner 1900-2100
B&B + Eve.Meal
£35.00-£38.50 |

| **DINNET
Aberdeenshire**
Profeits Hotel
Dinnet
Aberdeenshire
AB34 5JY
Tel:(Dinnet) 03398 85229 | Map 4
E1 | 4 Single 9 En Suite fac
6 Twin   6 Pub.Bath/Show
10 Double
2 Family | B&B per person
£16.00-£27.00 Single
£16.00-£27.00 Double | Open Jan-Dec
Dinner 1700-2100
B&B + Eve.Meal
£25.00-£40.00 |

DIRLETON **East Lothian** Open Arms Hotel Dirleton East Lothian EH39 5EG Tel:(Dirleton) 062085 241 Fax:062085 570	Map 2 E4 HIGHLY COMMENDED 👑 👑 👑 👑	6 Twin 1 Double	7 En Suite fac	B&B per person £35.00-£75.00 Single £30.00-£70.00 Double	Open Jan-Dec Dinner 1900-2200 B&B + Eve.Meal £45.00-£90.00	

Personally run inn with reputation for good food, situated in picturesque village, overlooking green and castle. 20 miles (32kms) East of Edinburgh.

DOLLAR **Clackmannanshire** Castle Campbell Hotel Bridge Street Dollar Clackmannanshire FK14 7DE Tel:(Dollar) 0259 742519 Fax:0259 742519	Map 2 B4 COMMENDED 👑 👑 👑 👑	1 Single 4 Twin 1 Double 1 Family	7 En Suite fac 1 Pub.Bath/Show	B&B per person £40.00-£45.00 Single £55.00-£65.00 Double	Open Jan-Dec Dinner 1900-2130	

Completely renovated family run hotel in picturesque town. Good food in comfortable surroundings. Sky TV, fax machine.

DORNIE **by Kyle of Lochalsh** **Ross-shire** Castle Inn 8-10 Francis Street Dornie,by Kyle of Lochalsh Ross-shire IV40 8TQ Tel:(Dornie) 059985 205 Fax:059985 429	Map 3 F1 COMMENDED 👑 👑 👑	3 Single 3 Twin 7 Double	8 En Suite fac 2 Pub.Bath/Show	B&B per person £20.50-£24.50 Single £22.50-£28.50 Double	Open Jan-Dec Dinner 1900-2100	

Family run inn overlooking Loch Long and the Hills of Skye. Restaurant specialising in local seafood.

Loch Duich Hotel Ardelve Dornie,by Kyle of Lochalsh Ross-shire IV40 8DY Tel:(Dornie) 059985 213 Fax:059985 214	COMMENDED 👑 👑	5 Single 6 Twin 6 Double 1 Family	5 En Suite fac 6 Pub.Bath/Show	B&B per person £21.00-£27.50 Single £21.00-£27.50 Double	Open Mar-Nov Dinner 1900-2100	

Beautifully situated, personally run hotel with emphasis on home cooking using fresh local produce. Taste of Scotland.

DORNOCH **Sutherland**	Map 4 B6

Burghfield House Hotel

DORNOCH · SUTHERLAND IV25 3HN
Telephone: (086 2810) 212 Fax: (086 2810) 404

Turreted Baronial Mansion in beautiful gardens overlooking Dornoch.
Refurbished 1991. Same ownership 46 years.
Superb food and wines. Golf Packages for Royal Dornoch and other
courses. Fishing. Hairdressing Salon, Sauna & Solarium.
DINNER B&B FROM £48.50.

Burghfield House Hotel Dornoch Sutherland IV25 3HN Tel:(Dornoch) 0862 810212 Fax:0862 810404	COMMENDED 👑 👑 👑 👑	18 Twin 2 Double 10 Family	30 En Suite fac 4 Pub.Bath/Show	B&B per person £28.00-£48.00 Single £25.00-£42.00 Double	Open Apr-Oct Dinner from 1930	

Set in 5 acres of well maintained gardens and overlooking Dornoch and the Firth beyond. Flowers and open fires. Annexe accomodation available.

DORNOCH continued — Map 4 B6

Dornoch Castle
Castle Street
Dornoch
Sutherland
IV25 3SD
Tel:(Dornoch) 0862 810216
Fax:0862 810981

COMMENDED

3 Single
8 Twin
2 Double
4 Family

17 En Suite fac

B&B per person
£35.00-£37.00 Single
£30.50-£39.00 Double

Open Apr-Oct
Dinner 1930-2045
B&B + Eve.Meal
£47.50-£56.00

Dating in part from 16c with modern bedroom wing. Centrally situated in town square facing Dornoch Cathedral. Views of Dornoch Firth.

Royal Golf Hotel
Grange Road
Dornoch
Sutherland
IV25 3LG
Tel:(Dornoch) 0862 810283
Fax:0862 810923

COMMENDED

5 Single
17 Twin
2 Double

24 En Suite fac

B&B per person
£45.00-£57.00 Single
£39.50-£48.00 Double

Open Mar-Dec
Dinner 1900-2100

Previously a family mansion, the hotel overlooks the golf course and the Dornoch Firth. 5 minutes walk to town.

Trentham Hotel
The Poles
Dornoch
Sutherland
IV25 3HZ
Tel:(Dornoch) 0862
810391/810551

2 Twin
3 Double
1 Family

2 Pub.Bath/Show

B&B per person
£19.00-£21.00 Single
£17.00-£19.00 Double

Open Jan-Dec
Dinner 1800-2100

DOUNBY Orkney — Map 5 B1

Smithfield Hotel
Dounby
Orkney
KW17 2HT
Tel:(Harray) 085677 215

COMMENDED

2 Single
2 Twin
2 Double

2 Pub.Bath/Show

B&B per person
from £23.00 Single
from £23.00 Double

Open Apr-Sep
Dinner from 1800
B&B + Eve.Meal
from £35.00

Charming village inn recently refurbished, but retaining true Orcadian character. Friendly comfortable atmosphere and good food.

DRUMBEG Sutherland — Map 3 G4

Drumbeg Hotel
Drumbeg, Assynt
Sutherland
IV27 4NW
Tel:(Drumbeg) 05713 236
Fax:05713 333

2 Twin
4 Double

6 En Suite fac

B&B per person
£35.00-£40.00 Single
£33.00-£38.00 Double

Open Jan-Dec
Dinner 1900-2100
B&B + Eve.Meal
£50.00-£55.00

Drumbeg House
Drumbeg
Sutherland
IV27 4NW
Tel:(Drumbeg) 05713 209

COMMENDED

1 Twin
2 Double

3 En Suite fac

B&B per person
£20.00 Double

Open Jan-Dec
Dinner 1800-1900
B&B + Eve.Meal
£30.00-£32.50

In house-party style, Ron and Margaret provide a warm welcome, convivial company. Fresh veg, self indulgent puddings. Wonderfully peaceful situation.

DRUMNADROCHIT **Inverness-shire** Drumnadrochit Hotel Drumnadrochit Inverness-shire IV3 6TU Tel:(Drumnadrochit) 04562 218/0456 450218 Fax:04562 565/0456 450565	Map 4 A9	APPROVED 👑 👑 👑	3 Single 10 Twin 5 Double 2 Family	20 En Suite fac	B&B per person £22.50-£27.50 Single £22.50-£27.50 Double	Open Jan-Dec Dinner 1900-2130	
			En suite accommodation at the official Loch Ness Exhibition Centre. Lounge Bar, Restaurants and Scottish musical entertainment.				
Loch Ness Lodge Hotel Drumnadrochit Inverness-shire IV3 6TJ Tel:(Drumnadrochit) 0456 450342 Tlx:75518 Fax:0456 450429		COMMENDED 👑 👑 👑 👑	4 Single 37 Twin 10 Double 6 Family	57 En Suite fac	B&B per person £35.00-£50.00 Single £25.00-£35.00 Double	Open Mar-Nov Dinner 1900-2230 B&B + Eve.Meal £35.00-£45.00	
			Set in 8 acres of varied woodland above Loch Ness. The Lodge has 2 modern bedroom wings. Visitor Centre & organised boat cruises on Loch Ness.				
Polmaily House Drumnadrochit Inverness-shire IV3 6XT Tel:(Drumnadrochit) 0456 450343 Fax:0456 450813		COMMENDED 👑 👑 👑	2 Single 2 Twin 4 Double 1 Family	7 En Suite fac 1 Pub.Bath/Show	B&B per person £25.00-£50.00 Single £20.00-£50.00 Double	Open Jan-Dec Dinner 1930-2100 B&B + Eve.Meal £32.00-£62.00	
			A comfortable, country house hotel in extensive grounds with a restaurant using fresh local ingredients, some home grown. Fixed price menus.				
Glen Rowan Guest House West Lewiston Drumnadrochit Inverness-shire IV3 6UW Tel:(Drumnadrochit) 04562 235/0456 450235		COMMENDED 👑 👑	2 Twin 1 Double	3 En Suite fac	B&B per person £22.00-£32.00 Single £14.50-£19.50 Double	Open Jan-Dec Dinner 1830-1900 B&B + Eve.Meal £25.00-£30.00	
			Modern house with garden running down to river in a quiet village by Loch Ness between Drumnadrochit and Urquhart Castle.				
BY DRUMNADROCHIT **Inverness-shire** The Clansman Hotel Brackla, Loch Ness Side Inverness-shire IV3 6LA Tel:(Drumnadrochit) 0456 450326 Fax:0456 450845	Map 4 A9	COMMENDED 👑 👑 👑	3 Single 8 Twin 13 Double 4 Family	27 En Suite fac 1 Pub.Bath/Show	B&B per person £19.50-£28.50 Single £19.50-£28.50 Double	Open Jan-Dec Dinner 1900-2100	
			Family run hotel on the banks of Loch Ness. Bar and restaurant with panoramic views. Inverness 9 miles (14kms), Skye ferry 73 miles (117kms).				

Scotland for Golf...

Find out more about golf in Scotland. There's more to it than just the championship courses so get in touch with us now for information on the hidden gems of Scotland.

Write to: **Information Unit, Scottish Tourist Board, 23 Ravelston Terrace, Edinburgh EH4 3EU or call: 031-332 2433.**

DRYMEN Stirlingshire	Map 1 H4

Buchanan Arms Hotel

DRYMEN · By LOCH LOMOND
Stirlingshire G63 0BQ Tel: 0360 60588
Fax: 0360 60943

This traditional country house hotel sits in the picturesque village of Drymen, close by Loch Lomond and the Trossachs, and midway between Glasgow and Stirling.
All 50 bedrooms have private bathroom, telephone, colour satellite TV, trouser press, hairdryer and tea and coffee making facilities.
Tapestries Restaurant offers an excellent selection of Scottish and international cuisine and a carefully selected range of wines, while The Granary bar/Restaurant provides a tempting range of snacks and meals.
Leisure Club, with swimming pool, spa bath, saunas, solarium, gymnasium and squash courts.
Dinner, bed and breakfast rates from £49. Over 60's from £35. Free accommodation and breakfast for children under 16 sharing parents room.

Buchanan Highland Hotel
Loch Lomond
Stirlingshire
G63 0BQ
Tel:(Drymen) 0360 60588
Fax:0360 60943

COMMENDED

10 Single
32 Twin
4 Double
4 Family
Suite avail.

50 En Suite fac

B&B per person
£80.00-£96.00 Single
£64.00-£66.00 Double

Open Jan-Dec
Dinner 1900-2130
B&B + Eve.Meal
£75.00-£78.00

Recently refurbished hotel in picturesque village close to Loch Lomond andTrossachs. New leisure facilities with swimming pool and squash courts.

Winnock Hotel
The Square
Drymen
Stirlingshire
G63 0BL
Tel:(Drymen) 0360 60245

4 Single
15 Twin
15 Double

34 En Suite fac

B&B per person
to £44.00 Single
to £32.50 Double

Open Jan-Dec
Dinner 1800-2150
B&B + Eve.Meal
to £40.50

TELEPHONE DIALLING CODES

Many telephone dialling codes have changed this year. If you experience difficulty in connecting a call, please call Directory Enquiries – **192** – where someone will issue the correct number. Please note: a charge will be placed for this service when using a private telephone

---

DULNAIN BRIDGE by Grantown-on-Spey Moray	Map 4 C9

Auchendean Lodge Hotel

DULNAIN BRIDGE, by GRANTOWN-ON-SPEY PH26 3LU

Egon Ronay Telephone: (047) 985 347

More a country home than a hotel – elegantly furnished with antiques and books. We offer a friendly welcome with walks, drives, fishing, birdwatching, golf. Finest river and mountain views from any Spey Valley hotel. We cook fresh, interesting food – you relax with log fires, wines and malts from extensive cellars.

Auchendean Lodge Hotel Dulnain Bridge, by Grantown-on-Spey Moray PH26 3LU Tel:(Dulnain Bridge) 047985 347 Fax:047985 347	HIGHLY COMMENDED	1 Single 2 Twin 4 Double	5 En Suite fac 2 Pub.Bath/Show	B&B per person £22.50-£35.00 Single £21.50-£33.50 Double	Open Jan-Dec Dinner 1930-2300 B&B + Eve.Meal £45.00-£61.50	
		Edwardian former shooting lodge, retaining character and style. Friendly welcome, warm atmosphere, interesting cuisine and extensive wine list.				

Skye of Curr Hotel Dulnain Bridge, by Grantown-on-Spey Inverness-shire PH26 3PA Tel:(Dulnain Bridge) 047985 345	APPROVED	1 Single 3 Twin 3 Double 2 Family	7 En Suite fac 3 Pub.Bath/Show	B&B per person from £22.50 Single from £22.50 Double	Open Jan-Dec Dinner 1900-2030 B&B + Eve.Meal from £40.50	
		Small baronial mansion with many period features including wood panelling and feature fire places. Log fires in season.				

DUMBARTON	Map 1 H5					
Dumbuck Hotel Glasgow Road Dumbarton Dunbartonshire G82 1EG Tel:(Dumbarton) 0389 34336 Fax:0389 34336		13 Single 3 Twin 7 Double 2 Family	25 En Suite fac 3 Pub.Bath/Show	B&B per person to £44.50 Single to £29.00 Double	Open Jan-Dec Dinner 1900-2130	

WELCOME

Whenever you are in Scotland, you can be sure of a warm welcome at your nearest Tourist Information Centre.

For guide books, maps, souvenirs, our Centres provide a service second to none – many now offer bureau-de-change facilities. And, of course, Tourist Information Centres offer free, expert advice on what to see and do, route-planning and accommodation for everyone – visitors and residents alike!

| DUMFRIES | Map 2 B9 | | |

Cairndale Hotel and Leisure Club
ENGLISH STREET · DUMFRIES · DG1 2DF
Tel: 0387 54111   Fax: 0387 50555

Privately owned and managed by the Wallace family, this well established hotel offers all the comforts expected from one of the regions leading three-star hotels. Regular entertainment includes a dinner dance on Saturdays and the popular "Cairndale Ceilidh" and "Taste of Scotland" Dinner every Sunday (May-Nov incl.). Residents enjoy use of leisure facilities including heated pool, spa bath, sauna, steam room, gymnasium, health and beauty salon, sunbeds.

Golf Breaks from £55.00 per person.
Leisure Breaks from £55.00 per person DB&B.
Special Winter and Spring Breaks.
For details contact Dept. WHS.
Conferences, Scottish Ceilidh Weekends, Themed Breaks.
Please ask for further details.

| Cairndale Hotel and Leisure Club English Street Dumfries DG1 2DF Tel:(Dumfries) 0387 54111 Fax:0387 50555 | COMMENDED ♛♛♛ ♛♛ | 20 Single 34 Twin 20 Double 2 Family Suites avail. | 76 En Suite fac | B&B per person £35.00-£75.00 Single £25.00-£50.00 Double | Open Jan-Dec Dinner 1700-2200 B&B + Eve.Meal £35.00-£65.00 |
| | | Family run hotel in town centre and on Euro-route to Stranraer. Some executive rooms with jacuzzi baths. | | | |

| Edenbank Hotel Laurieknowe Dumfries DG2 Tel:(Dumfries) 0387 52759 | COMMENDED ♛♛♛ | 1 Single 4 Twin 3 Double 2 Family | 10 En Suite fac | B&B per person £35.00-£40.00 Single £22.00-£25.00 Double | Open Jan-Dec Dinner 1800-2030 B&B + Eve.Meal £27.50-£32.50 |
| | | Refurbished detached sandstone building, garden, car park. Short walk to town centre. Bowls, golf, leisure centre nearby. Weekly entertainment. | | | |

| Fulwood Hotel Lovers Walk Dumfries DG1 1LX Tel:(Dumfries) 0387 52262 | | 1 Single 1 Twin 2 Double 1 Family | 3 Pub.Bath/Show | B&B per person £15.00-£16.00 Single £13.50-£14.50 Double | Open Jan-Dec |

| Moreig Hotel 67 Annan Road Dumfries DG1 3EG Tel:(Dumfries) 0387 55524 | | 2 Twin 4 Double 2 Family | 1 Pub.Bath/Show | B&B per person from £20.00 Single from £15.00 Double | Open Jan-Dec Dinner 1700-2000 B&B + Eve.Meal £25.00-£30.00 |

DUMFRIES continued	Map 2 B9						

Queensberry Hotel
16 English Street
Dumfries
DG1 2BT
Tel:(Dumfries) 0387 53526

| 4 Single 5 Twin 5 Double 2 Family | 11 En Suite fac 3 Limited ensuite 1 Pub.Bath/Show | B&B per person £15.00-£30.00 Single £13.00-£26.00 Double | Open Jan-Dec Dinner 1600-2200 B&B + Eve.Meal £20.00-£40.00 |

Station Hotel
49 Lovers Walk
Dumfries
DG1 1LT
Tel:(Dumfries) 0387 54316
Fax:0387 50388

COMMENDED ♛ ♛ ♛ ♛

| 11 Single 12 Twin 9 Double | 32 En Suite fac | B&B per person £45.00-£68.00 Single £27.50-£45.00 Double | Open Jan-Dec Dinner 1900-2130 |

Victorian red sandstone building next to railway station and and close to the town centre. Enterprising use of local fish and game.

Comlongon Castle

CLARENCEFIELD, DUMFRIES DG1 4NA
Tel: (038787) 283 / (038787) 870283 Fax: (038787) 266 / (038787) 870266

Medieval Castle and Period Mansion set in 50 acres of park and woodland.
Secluded walks, Golf, fishing, horse-riding nearby. Spacious bedrooms, some with antique four-posters and jacuzzis. All modern amenities, period furnishings, arms, armour, etc. Excellent cuisine.
Guests are taken on a candlelit tour of Castle each evening.

Comlongon Castle
Clarencefield
Dumfries
Dumfriesshire
DG1 4NA
Tel:(Clarencefield)
038787 283/038787 870283
Fax:038787 266/038787 870266

| 2 Single 2 Twin 6 Double 1 Family | 11 En Suite fac | B&B per person from £39.00 Single from £39.00 Double | Open Feb-Dec Dinner 2015-2200 |

Dalston House
Laurieknowe
Dumfries
DG2
Tel:(Dumfries) 0387 54422
Fax:0387 54422

COMMENDED ♛ ♛ ♛ ♛

| 3 Single 3 Twin 7 Double 4 Family | 16 En Suite fac 1 Priv.NOT ensuite 1 Pub.Bath/Show | B&B per person £40.00-£50.00 Single £25.00-£30.00 Double | Open mid Jan-Nov Dinner 1800-2200 B&B + Eve.Meal £35.00-£65.00 |

Family run establishment close to town centre and all amenities.
Varied menu with accent on fresh produce. Special breaks off-season.

Glenaldor House
5 Victoria Terrace
Dumfries
DG1 1NL
Tel:(Dumfries) 0387 64248

COMMENDED Listed

| 1 Twin 1 Double 2 Family | 2 En Suite fac 1 Pub.Bath/Show | B&B per person £14.00-£19.00 Single £14.00-£19.00 Double | Open Jan-Dec Dinner from 1800 B&B + Eve.Meal £22.00-£27.00 |

Elegant Victorian terraced house within a few minutes walk of the town centre.

Laurelbank Guest House
7 Laurieknowe
Dumfries
DG2 7AH
Tel:(Dumfries) 0387 69388

COMMENDED ♛ ♛

| 2 Twin 1 Double 1 Family | 3 Limited ensuite 1 Pub.Bath/Show | B&B per person £16.00-£18.00 Double | Open Feb-Nov |

Elevated sandstone villa, a short walk to River Nith, town centre and Bus Station. New Ice Bowl 3 minutes away. Private car park at rear.

Key to symbols is on back flap.

DUMFRIES continued	Map 2 B9							
Torbay Lodge Guest House 31 Lovers Walk Dumfries Tel:(Dumfries) 0387 53922			1 Single 2 Twin 3 Family	3 Pub.Bath/Show	B&B per person £14.00 Single £14.00 Double	Open Jan-Dec Dinner 1700-1900	

BY DUMFRIES	Map 2 B9						
Hetland Hall Hotel Carrutherstown Dumfries Dumfriesshire DG1 4JX Tel:(Dumfries) 0387 84201 Tlx:776819 Fax:0387 84211		COMMENDED ♛ ♛ ♛ ♛	10 Twin 14 Double 5 Family	29 En Suite fac 2 Pub.Bath/Show	B&B per person £50.00-£70.00 Single £35.00-£55.00 Double	Open Jan-Dec Dinner 1900-2130 B&B + Eve.Meal £70.00-£90.00	
			Recently refurbished hotel, personally run, situated in 45 acre grounds and open countryside. Conference facilities, bowls, badminton, games room.				

Nith Hotel Glencaple Dumfriesshire DG1 4RE Tel:(Glencaple) 038777 213/505			3 Single 4 Twin 2 Double 1 Family	7 En Suite fac 2 Pub.Bath/Show	B&B per person £20.00-£25.00 Single £20.00-£25.00 Double	Open Jan-Dec Dinner 1800-2100 B&B + Eve.Meal £25.00-£35.00	

DUNBAR East Lothian	Map 2 E4						
Bayswell Hotel Bayswell Park Dunbar East Lothian EH42 1AE Tel:(Dunbar) 0368 62225 Fax:0368 62225		COMMENDED ♛ ♛ ♛ ♛	1 Single 4 Twin 4 Double 4 Family	13 En Suite fac	B&B per person to £42.50 Single to £35.00 Double	Open Jan-Dec Dinner 1900-2100	
			Town house by the sea, situated on the cliff top overlooking the Firth of Forth. Only half an hour by car or train to Edinburgh.				

Hillside Hotel Queens Road Dunbar East Lothian EH42 1LA Tel:(Dunbar) 0368 62071			4 Single 4 Twin 4 Double 4 Family	9 En Suite fac 1 Limited ensuite 2 Pub.Bath/Show	B&B per person £19.00-£27.00 Single £19.00-£21.50 Double	Open Jan-Dec Dinner 1730-2130 B&B + Eve.Meal £30.00-£33.00	

Lothian Hotel 52 High Street Dunbar East Lothian EH42 1JH Tel:(Dunbar) 0368 63205 Fax:0368 63205		APPROVED Listed	5 Twin 2 Double 3 Family	3 Pub.Bath/Show	B&B per person £15.00-£18.00 Single £15.00-£18.00 Double	Open Jan-Dec Dinner 1700-2130 B&B + Eve.Meal £20.00-£23.00	
			Family run hotel in town centre. All day coffee shop.				

	Map 2 E4						
DUNBAR continued							

Redheugh Hotel
Bayswell Park
Dunbar
East Lothian
EH42 1AE
Tel:(Dunbar) 0368 62793
Fax:0368 62793

COMMENDED ♔ ♔ ♔ ♔

2 Single
3 Twin
3 Double
2 Family

10 En Suite fac

B&B per person
£32.00-£36.50 Single
£25.00-£29.50 Double

Open Jan-Dec
Dinner 1900-2030
B&B + Eve.Meal
£37.50-£44.50

Red sandstone Victorian house, family owned and managed, in quiet residential area with fine views to Firth of Forth. Golfing packages available.

Royal MacKintosh Hotel
Station Road
Dunbar
East Lothian
EH42 1JY
Tel:(Dunbar) 0368 63231/63516
Fax:0368 65200

COMMENDED ♔ ♔ ♔ ♔

2 Single
6 Twin
6 Double
1 Family
Suite avail.

15 En Suite fac

B&B per person
£30.00-£34.00 Single
£23.50-£26.50 Double

Open Jan-Dec
Dinner 1900-2130
B&B + Eve.Meal
£38.50-£42.00

Family run hotel ideally situated at centre of this coastal town. Restaurant has original carved panelling from the "Mauretania" liner.

Cruachan Guest House
East Links Road
Dunbar
East Lothian
EH42 1LT
Tel:(Dunbar) 0368 63006/863006

Award Pending

1 Single
1 Twin
2 Family

1 Limited ensuite
2 Pub.Bath/Show

B&B per person
to £15.00 Single
to £15.00 Double

Open Jan-Dec
Dinner 1800-1830
B&B + Eve.Meal
£20.00-£22.00

Marine Guest House
Marine Road
Dunbar
East Lothian
EH42 1AR
Tel:(Dunbar) 0368 63315

COMMENDED ♔

2 Single
4 Twin
1 Double
3 Family

2 Pub.Bath/Show

B&B per person
£14.00-£15.00 Single
£14.00-£15.00 Double

Open Mar-Oct

Comfortable personally run Guest House with sea views from most rooms. Ideal centre for golf, diving and fishing.

Overcliffe Guest House
11 Bayswell Park
Dunbar
East Lothian
EH42 1AE
Tel:(Dunbar) 0368 64004

COMMENDED ♔ ♔

3 Double
3 Family

3 En Suite fac
3 Pub.Bath/Show

B&B per person
£18.00-£21.00 Single
£15.00-£18.50 Double

Open Jan-Dec
Dinner 1830-1930
B&B + Eve.Meal
£24.00-£27.50

Personally run, situated in pleasant residential area. Convenient for town centre and local amenities. Close to sea and cliff tops.

St Beys Guest House
Bayswell Road
Dunbar
East Lothian
EH42 1AB
Tel:(Dunbar) 0368 63571

COMMENDED ♔

2 Single
1 Twin
2 Double
2 Family

3 Limited ensuite
1 Pub.Bath/Show

B&B per person
£16.00-£17.50 Single
£16.00-£17.50 Double

Open Jan-Dec
Dinner 1830-2000
B&B + Eve.Meal
£25.00-£26.50

A warm welcome and home cooking, using fresh ingredients, at this Victorian house overlooking the seafront, a few minutes walk from town centre.

St Helen's Guest House
Queens Road
Dunbar
East Lothian
EH42 1LN
Tel:(Dunbar) 0368 863716

COMMENDED ♔ ♔

1 Single
4 Twin
1 Double
1 Family

2 En Suite fac
2 Pub.Bath/Show

B&B per person
£15.00 Single
£14.00-£16.00 Double

Open Jan-Oct

Victorian red sandstone house situated in quiet area of Dunbar. Few minutes walk from beach and golf course. Friendly welcome.

Details of Grading and Classification are on page vi.

Key to symbols is on back flap.

DUNBAR continued

	Map 2 E4						
Springfield Guest House Belhaven Road Dunbar East Lothian EH42 1NH Tel:(Dunbar) 0368 62502		COMMENDED ⌣	1 Single 1 Twin 1 Double 2 Family	2 Pub.Bath/Show	B&B per person £17.00 Single £16.00 Double	Open Jan-Nov Dinner at 1800 B&B + Eve.Meal £26.00	

An elegant 19th century villa with attractive garden and under the personal supervision of the owner.

DUNBEATH
Caithness — Map 4 D4

DUNBEATH HOTEL

Dunbeath, Caithness KW6 6EG

Tel: 05933 217/208
Fax: 05933 242

DUNBEATH HOTEL is situated with views to the sea and ideally placed for touring the North or visiting the Orkneys. Our restaurant offers salmon and venison from local estates and seafoods from northern waters. Sporting, fishing, pony-trekking, llama walking, mountain bike hire, Autumn/Spring Breaks.
For further details contact: Pat Buchanan.

Dunbeath Hotel Dunbeath Caithness KW6 6EG Tel:(Dunbeath) 05933 217/208		COMMENDED ⌣ ⌣ ⌣	3 Twin 3 Double 1 Family	7 En Suite fac	B&B per person £33.00-£38.00 Single £28.00-£32.00 Double	Open Jan-Dec Dinner 1900-2130 B&B + Eve.Meal £40.00-£50.00	

Victorian coaching inn with sound reputation for good food. Close to the sea and the Strath of Dunbeath.

DUNBLANE
Perthshire — Map 2 A3

The Chimes Hotel Cathedral Square Dunblane Perthshire FK15 0AL Tel:(Dunblane) 0786 822164		COMMENDED ⌣ ⌣	2 Twin 2 Double	2 En Suite fac 1 Priv.NOT ensuite	B&B per person £29.00 Single from £16.00 Double	Open Jan-Dec Dinner from 1700	

A warm welcome at this 18th century inn situated in the shadow of the magnificent medieval cathedral. Comfortable with a relaxing atmosphere.

Dunblane Hotel Stirling Road Dunblane Perthshire FK15 9EP Tel:(Dunblane) 0786 822178		COMMENDED ⌣ ⌣	2 Single 1 Twin 1 Family	2 En Suite fac 1 Pub.Bath/Show	B&B per person £25.00-£30.00 Single £20.00-£25.00 Double	Open Jan-Dec Dinner 1700-2000	

Located in central Dunblane, convenient for shopping and eating out. Good base for touring and sightseeing.

DUNDEE
Angus — Map 2 D2

Airlie House Hotel 40 Roseangle Dundee Angus DD1 4LY Tel:(Dundee) 0382 27496 Fax:0382 21118			3 Single 5 Twin 3 Double 1 Family	3 En Suite fac 2 Pub.Bath/Show	B&B per person from £15.00 Single	Open Jan-Dec Dinner 1700-2300	

DUNDEE continued	Map 2 D2						
The Angus Thistle Hotel 101 Marketgait Dundee Angus DD1 1QU Tel:(Dundee) 0382 26874 Tlx:76456 Fax:0382 22564	APPROVED	15 Single 32 Twin 9 Double 2 Family Suites avail.	58 En Suite fac	B&B per person £59.90-£96.50 Single £36.40-£58.75 Double	Open Jan-Dec Dinner 1900-2230 B&B + Eve.Meal £54.25-£76.60		
		Purpose built modern hotel in city centre, ideally situated for both tourist and businessman. Extensive conference facilities available.					
Barton House Hotel 2 Union Terrace Dundee Angus DD3 6JD Tel:(Dundee) 0382 23521/201802		7 Single 2 Twin 1 Double 1 Family	2 En Suite fac 4 Pub.Bath/Show	B&B per person £15.50-£25.00 Single £18.00-£22.50 Double	Open Jan-Dec Dinner 1730-2000 B&B + Eve.Meal £19.50-£29.50		
Beach House Hotel 22 Esplanade, Broughty Ferry Dundee Angus DD5 2EQ Tel:(Dundee) 0382 76614/75537 Fax:0382 480241	HIGHLY COMMENDED	2 Twin 2 Double 1 Family	5 En Suite fac	B&B per person £35.00-£38.00 Single £20.00-£22.50 Double	Open Jan-Dec Dinner 1800-2000 B&B + Eve.Meal £31.00-£33.00		
		Small, friendly tourist and commercial hotel, 4 miles (6kms) to centre, overlooking River Tay to Fife coast. Ideal base for touring, walking, golf.					
The Bruce Hotel 39 Roseangle Dundee Angus DD1 4LZ Tel:(Dundee) 0382 23021/203203 (office)		14 Single 2 Twin 1 Double 2 Family	2 Pub.Bath/Show	B&B per person from £16.50 Single from £15.50 Double	Open Jan-Dec		
Downfield Hotel 530 Strathmartine Road Dundee Angus DD3 9BR Tel:(Dundee) 0382 826633		2 Single 1 Twin 1 Double 1 Family	2 Pub.Bath/Show	B&B per person £14.00 Single £14.00 Double	Open Jan-Dec Dinner 1700-1900 B&B + Eve.Meal £19.00		
The Fort Hotel 58-60 Fort Street Broughty Ferry, Dundee Angus DD5 2AB Tel:(Dundee) 0382 737999		2 Single 4 Twin 4 Double	10 En Suite fac	B&B per person to £33.00 Single to £25.00 Double	Open Jan-Dec Dinner 1700-2300		
Invercarse Hotel 371 Perth Road Dundee Angus DD2 1PG Tel:(Dundee) 0382 69231 Fax:0382 644112	COMMENDED	17 Single 11 Twin 9 Double 1 Family	38 En Suite fac	B&B per person £30.00-£44.00 Single £27.50-£40.00 Double	Open Jan-Dec Dinner 1915-2145 B&B + Eve.Meal £36.45-£49.95		
		Situated in own grounds in quiet residential area, close to city centre. Ample car parking; conference facilities. Bar meals, a la carte restaurant.					

DUNDEE continued — Map 2 D2

Invermark Hotel
23 Monifieth Road,
Broughty Ferry
Dundee
Angus
DD5 2RN
Tel:(Dundee) 0382 739430

COMMENDED
👑 👑

3 Twin   2 En Suite fac
1 Family   1 Limited ensuite
     1 Pub.Bath/Show

B&B per person
£25.00-£30.00 Single
£17.50-£20.00 Double

Open Jan-Dec
Dinner 1930-2100
B&B + Eve.Meal
£27.50-£30.00

Privately run, in residential suburb of Dundee and within easy reach of many
championship golf courses. Non smoking.

Park Hotel
40 Coupar Angus Road
Dundee
Angus
DD2 3HY
Tel:(Dundee) 0382 610691
Fax:0382 612633

COMMENDED
👑 👑 👑
👑

1 Single   11 En Suite fac
6 Twin
3 Double
1 Family

B&B per person
£38.00-£43.00 Single
£28.50-£31.50 Double

Open Jan-Dec
Dinner 1830-2030

Situated 2 miles (4kms) from city centre with easy access from ring road.
Conference/banqueting facilities; all rooms with private bathrooms.

The Queen's Hotel
160 Nethergate
Dundee
Tayside
DD1 4DU
Tel:(Dundee) 0382 22515
Fax:0382 202668

COMMENDED
👑 👑 👑
👑

15 Single   47 En Suite fac
4 Twin
25 Double
3 Family
Suites avail.

B&B per person
£60.00-£70.00 Single
£80.00-£100.00 Double

Open Jan-Dec
Dinner 1830-2130
B&B + Eve.Meal
£70.00-£85.00

Prestigious city centre hotel, with some modern facilities offered. Yet still
retaining elegance of a bygone age.

Shaftesbury Hotel
1 Hyndford Street
Dundee
Angus
DD2 1HQ
Tel:(Dundee) 0382 69216

HIGHLY
COMMENDED
👑 👑 👑

2 Single   12 En Suite fac
3 Twin
7 Double

B&B per person
£38.00-£51.00 Single
£29.00-£35.00 Double

Open Jan-Dec
Dinner 1900-2130

Newly refurbished Victorian mansion in quiet residential area. Close to town
centre, Ninewells Hospital and University.

Stakis Dundee
Earl Grey Hotel
Earl Grey Place
Dundee
Angus
DD1 4DE
Tel:(Dundee) 0382 29271
Tlx:76569
Fax:0382 200072

COMMENDED
👑 👑 👑
👑 👑

90 Twin   104 En Suite fac
14 Double
Suites avail.

B&B per person
from £94.00 Single
from £65.00 Double

Open Jan-Dec
Dinner 1830-2200
B&B + Eve.Meal
from £82.00

Modern hotel with leisure facilities situated on the banks of the River Tay with
views of the Kingdom of Fife. Easy access by road, rail and air.

Strathdon Hotel
277 Perth Road
Dundee
Angus
DD2 1JS
Tel:(Dundee) 0382 65648

2 Single   9 En Suite fac
3 Twin   1 Priv.NOT ensuite
3 Double
2 Family

B&B per person
£25.00-£32.00 Single
from £20.00 Double

Open Jan-Dec
Dinner 1900-2030

Taychreggan Hotel
4 Ellieslea Road,
Broughty Ferry
Dundee
Angus
DD5 1JG
Tel:(Dundee) 0382 78626
Fax:0382 738177

4 Single   11 En Suite fac
3 Twin   1 Pub.Bath/Show
3 Double
1 Family

B&B per person
£28.00-£35.00 Single
£18.50-£25.00 Double

Open Jan-Dec
Dinner 1700-1900
B&B + Eve.Meal
£25.00-£40.00

DUNDEE continued	Map 2 D2					
The West End Hotel 57 Seafield Road, Roseangle Dundee Angus DD1 4NA Tel:(Dundee) 0382 25712	APPROVED ♛	12 Single 3 Twin 2 Double 1 Family	4 Pub.Bath/Show	B&B per person £16.00-£18.00 Single £15.00-£17.00 Double	Open Jan-Dec Dinner 1750-1900 B&B + Eve.Meal £23.00-£26.00	
		Family run hotel in Georgian house in quiet residential area. Close to city centre, university, Ninewells hospital, airport.				
Woodlands Hotel 13 Panmure Terrace, Barnhill Dundee Angus DD5 2QN Tel:(Dundee) 0382 480033 Fax:0382 480126	COMMENDED ♛ ♛ ♛	2 Single 10 Twin 5 Double	15 En Suite fac 2 Pub.Bath/Show	B&B per person £52.00-£65.00 Single £52.00-£65.00 Double	Open Jan-Dec Dinner 1730-2130	
		Set in 4 acres of private grounds in quiet residential area. Close to the village of Broughty Ferry. Leisure facilities, satellite TV.				
Aberlaw Guest House 230 Broughty Ferry Road Dundee Angus DD4 7JP Tel:(Dundee) 0382 456929	COMMENDED ♛ ♛	2 Single 1 Twin 1 Double 1 Family	1 En Suite fac 2 Pub.Bath/Show	B&B per person £15.00-£16.00 Single £14.00-£17.00 Double	Open Jan-Dec	
		Family run house with private parking. Close to city centre, overlooking River Tay.				
Alberta Forfar Road Guest House 51 Forfar Road Dundee Angus DD4 7BE Tel:(Dundee) 0382 461484	COMMENDED Listed	2 Single 1 Twin 2 Family	2 Pub.Bath/Show	B&B per person £11.00-£14.00 Single £12.50-£15.00 Double	Open Jan-Dec Dinner 1700-1830 B&B + Eve.Meal £16.00-£19.00	
		Comfortable centrally situated house set in gardens with private parking. On main bus route, 5 minutes from the centre.				
Alcorn Guest House 5 Hyndford Street Dundee Angus DD2 1HQ Tel:(Dundee) 0382 68433	APPROVED Listed	3 Twin	1 En Suite fac 2 Pub.Bath/Show	B&B per person £15.00-£18.00 Single £12.00-£18.00 Double	Open Jan-Dec Dinner 1800-2000 B&B + Eve.Meal £16.00-£22.00	
		Family run guest house in quiet residential area. Handy for main bus routes. Convenient for Ninewells hospital.				
Anderson's Guest House 285 Perth Road Dundee Angus DD2 1JS Tel:(Dundee) 0382 68585		1 Single 2 Twin 2 Double 2 Family	4 En Suite fac 2 Pub.Bath/Show	B&B per person £16.00-£18.00 Single from £16.00 Double	Open Jan-Dec Dinner 1730-1830 B&B + Eve.Meal from £22.00	
Ashley House 15 Monifieth Road Broughty Ferry, Dundee Angus DD5 2RN Tel:(Dundee) 0382 76109	Award Pending	1 Twin 1 Double	2 En Suite fac	B&B per person £16.00-£18.00 Single £15.00-£16.00 Double	Open Jan-Dec	

DUNDEE – BY DUNDEE

DUNDEE continued

Dawmara Guest House
54 Monifieth Road,
Broughty Ferry
Dundee
Angus
DD5 2RX
Tel:(Dundee) 0382 77951

Map 2 D2

1 Single	1 Pub.Bath/Show	B&B per person £14.00-£16.00 Single £13.00-£16.00 Double	Open Jan-Dec
1 Twin			
1 Family			

Errolbank Guest House
9 Dalgleish Road
Dundee
Angus
DD4 7JN
Tel:(Dundee) 0382 462118

COMMENDED

1 Single	2 En Suite fac	B&B per person from £16.00 Single from £15.00 Double	Open Jan-Dec
2 Twin	1 Pub.Bath/Show		
1 Double			
2 Family			

Victorian villa, quiet residential area, centrally situated for touring, golf and all local amenities.

Hillside Guest House
Hillside,
43 Constitution Street
Dundee
Angus
DD3 6JH
Tel:(Dundee) 0382 23443

HIGHLY COMMENDED

| 2 Twin | 1 En Suite fac | B&B per person £19.00-£25.00 Single £17.00-£23.00 Double | Open Jan-Dec |
| 1 Family | 2 Pub.Bath/Show | | |

Victorian family home in quiet residential area close to city centre and all amenities. Off street parking.

Stonelee Guest House
69 Monifieth Road,
Broughty Ferry
Dundee
Angus
DD5 2RW
Tel:(Dundee) 0382 737812
Fax:0382 737812

2 Twin	5 En Suite fac	B&B per person £17.50-£24.50 Double	Open Jan-Dec
1 Double	1 Priv.NOT ensuite		
2 Family	1 Pub.Bath/Show		
Suite avail.			

Northern College
(Dundee Campus)
Mayfield Hall,
169 Arbroath Road
Dundee
Angus
DD4 6LN
Tel:(Dundee) 0382 462014
Fax:0382 464900

| 181 Single | 24 Pub.Bath/Show | B&B per person £15.00 Single £15.00 Double | Open Mar-Sep Dinner from 1800 B&B + Eve.Meal £21.75 |
| 34 Twin | | | |

BY DUNDEE
Fife

Map 2 D2

The Sandford Country House Hotel
Wormit
nr Dundee
Fife
DD6 8RG
Tel:(Newport-on-Tay)
0382 541802
Fax:0382 542136

HIGHLY COMMENDED

4 Single	16 En Suite fac	B&B per person from £75.00 Single from £44.00 Double	Open Jan-Dec Dinner 1800-2130 B&B + Eve.Meal from £62.95
5 Twin			
6 Double			
1 Family			

Detached country house hotel standing in its own grounds, about 6 miles (10kms) from Dundee and 11 miles (18kms) from St Andrews.

VAT is shown at 17.5%: changes in this rate may affect prices. Prices shown are for guidance only. Please send SAE with each enquiry.

DUNDONNELL **Ross-shire** Dundonnell Hotel Dundonnell Ross-shire IV23 2QR Tel:(Dundonnell) 085483 204 Fax:085483 366	Map 3 G7	HIGHLY COMMENDED 👑 👑 👑 👑	2 Single 11 Twin 9 Double 2 Family	24 En Suite fac	B&B per person £35.00-£49.50 Single £29.50-£42.50 Double	Open Apr-Dec Dinner 1900-2030 B&B + Eve.Meal £55.00-£69.50	

Family run hotel with emphasis on personal service. Interesting cuisine with use of fresh local produce. Situated at end of Little Loch Broom.

DUNFERMLINE **Fife** Abbey Park Hotel 5 Abbey Park Place Dunfermline Fife KY12 7PT Tel:(Dunfermline) 0383 739686	Map 2 C4	COMMENDED 👑 👑	3 Single 5 Twin 2 Double 1 Family	8 En Suite fac 1 Limited ensuite 2 Pub.Bath/Show	B&B per person £27.50-£30.00 Single £18.75-£20.00 Double	Open Jan-Dec	

Built around 1870, a magnificent mansion house set in the shadow of the abbey, with its own rear gardens, yet close to the town centre.

DAVAAR HOUSE HOTEL
126 Grieve Street, Dunfermline, Fife KY12 8DW
Tel: 0383 721886/736463

Situated in a residential part of this historic town within 30 mins drive of Scotland's Capital City, Edinburgh, and various golf courses and beautiful parkland, this very comfortable family run hotel with en-suite bedrooms specialises in home cooking and offering warm hospitality and a memorable stay.

Davaar House Hotel 126 Grieve Street Dunfermline Fife KY12 8DW Tel:(Dunfermline) 0383 721886/736463	COMMENDED 👑 👑 👑	1 Single 3 Twin 4 Double	8 En Suite fac	B&B per person £32.00-£36.00 Single £24.00-£25.00 Double	Open Jan-Dec Dinner 1800-2030 B&B + Eve.Meal £44.00-£50.00	

Comfortable, tastefully furnished hotel retaining original Victorian features. Personally run with friendly individual attention.

Halfway House Hotel Main Street, Kingseat Dunfermline Fife KY12 0TJ Tel:(Dunfermline) 0383 731661 Fax:0383 621274	COMMENDED 👑 👑 👑	9 Twin 3 Double	12 En Suite fac	B&B per person £30.00-£37.00 Single £35.00-£47.00 Double	Open Jan-Dec Dinner 1830-2100	

Former coaching inn, fully modernised. Supper dances on Sundays. Trout fishing on local loch and golf packages available.

King Malcolm Thistle Hotel Queensferry Road Dunfermline Fife KY11 5DS Tel:(Dunfermline) 0383 722611 Tlx:727721 Fax:0383 730865	COMMENDED 👑 👑 👑 👑	7 Single 37 Twin 4 Double	48 En Suite fac	B&B per person £33.00-£68.00 Single £33.00-£40.00 Double	Open Jan-Dec Dinner 1900-2200 B&B + Eve.Meal £38.00-£83.00	

On outskirts of town with relaxing atmosphere, located on A823 near M90. Edinburgh 17 miles (27kms). Choice of bars.

Name & Address	Map Ref	Award	Rooms	Bath Facilities	Price	Opening
DUNFERMLINE continued St Margarets Hotel Canmore Street Dunfermline Fife KY11 7NU Tel:(Dunfermline) 0383 722501 Fax:0383 722501	Map 2 C4	Award Pending	2 Single 3 Twin 1 Double	6 En Suite fac	B&B per person £30.00-£40.00 Single £22.50-£27.50 Double	Open Jan-Dec Dinner 1900-2130 B&B + Eve.Meal £40.00-£50.00
Broomfield Guest House 1 Broomfield Drive Dunfermline Fife KY12 0PJ Tel:(Dunfermline) 0383 732498			1 Single 1 Twin 2 Double 2 Family	6 En Suite fac 1 Pub.Bath/Show	B&B per person from £18.00 Single from £16.00 Double	Open Jan-Dec
Garvock Guest House 82 Halbeath Road Dunfermline Fife KY12 7RS Tel:(Dunfermline) 0383 734689		APPROVED Listed	1 Single 2 Twin 2 Double 1 Family	3 En Suite fac 1 Pub.Bath/Show	B&B per person from £14.00 Single £14.00-£16.00 Double	Open Jan-Dec
			19C modernised and converted house situated 1 mile (2kms) from the town centre. Convenient for M90 and on main bus routes.			
Pitreavie Guest House 3 Aberdour Road Dunfermline Fife KY11 4PB Tel:(Dunfermline) 0383 724244			2 Single 2 Twin 1 Double 1 Family	2 Pub.Bath/Show	B&B per person £15.00-£17.00 Single £16.00-£17.00 Double	Open Jan-Dec
The Dunfermline Conference Centre Lauder College, Halbeath Road Dunfermline Fife KY11 5DX Tel:(Dunfermline) 0383 726201			34 Single	2 En Suite fac 8 Pub.Bath/Show	B&B per person from £11.00 Single	Open Jan-Dec Dinner from 1700 B&B + Eve.Meal from £20.00
DUNKELD Perthshire Atholl Arms Hotel Tay Terrace Dunkeld Perthshire PH8 0AQ Tel:(Dunkeld) 0350 727219	Map 2 B1		5 Single 10 Twin 4 Double 1 Family	4 En Suite fac 5 Pub.Bath/Show	B&B per person from £19.00 Single from £21.50 Double	Open Jan-Nov Dinner 1900-2030 B&B + Eve.Meal from £34.50
Birnam Hotel Perth Road Birnam,by Dunkeld Perthshire PH8 0BQ Tel:(Dunkeld) 0350 727462 Fax:0350 728979			21 Twin 6 Double 1 Family	28 En Suite fac	B&B per person £35.00-£45.00 Single £35.00-£47.50 Double	Open Jan-Dec Dinner 1800-2100

DUNKELD continued	Map 2 B1						

Hillhead of Dunkeld
Brae Street
Dunkeld
Perthshire
PH8 0BA
Tel:(Dunkeld) 0350 728996
Fax:0350 728705

HIGHLY COMMENDED

1 Single
2 Twin
1 Double
2 Family

6 En Suite fac

B&B per person
£36.00-£53.00 Single
£36.00-£53.00 Double

Open Jan-Dec
Dinner 1830-2130
B&B + Eve.Meal
£45.00-£77.50

Impressive country house situated above the town with spectacular views of the River Tay, wooded parkland and distant mountains.

Merryburn Hotel
Station Road
Birnam, by Dunkeld
Perthshire
PH8 0DS
Tel:(Dunkeld) 0350 727216
Fax:0350 727216

2 Single
2 Twin
2 Double
2 Family
Suites avail.

2 Priv.NOT ensuite
2 Pub.Bath/Show

B&B per person
£19.00-£21.00 Single
£19.00-£21.00 Double

Open Jan-Dec
Dinner 1800-2100
B&B + Eve.Meal
£32.00-£34.00

Royal Dunkeld Hotel
Atholl Street
Dunkeld
Perthshire
PH8 0AR
Tel:(Dunkeld) 0350 727322
Fax:0350 728989

APPROVED

16 Twin
11 Double
8 Family

35 En Suite fac

B&B per person
£45.00 Single
£30.00 Double

Open Jan-Dec
Dinner 1700-2130
B&B + Eve.Meal
£42.50-£55.00

Personally run, early 19th century coaching inn, situated in centre of historic town of Dunkeld. Golfing breaks and packages a speciality.

Stakis Dunkeld House
Resort Hotel
Dunkeld
Perthshire
PH8 0HX
Tel:(Dunkeld) 0350 727771
Tlx:76657
Fax:0350 728924

HIGHLY COMMENDED

3 Single
21 Twin
55 Double
13 Family

92 En Suite fac

B&B per person
£75.00-£102.50 Single
£54.00-£74.00 Double

Open Jan-Dec
Dinner 1900-2200
B&B + Eve.Meal
£95.50-£116.00

Country house hotel, set in 280 acres of private ground with conference and leisure facilities. Originally owned by the 7th Duke of Atholl.

Waterbury Guest House
Birnam, by Dunkeld
Perthshire
PH8 0BG
Tel:(Dunkeld) 0350 727324

COMMENDED

1 Single
1 Twin
1 Double
2 Family

2 Pub.Bath/Show

B&B per person
£14.50-£16.00 Single
£14.50-£15.50 Double

Open Jan-Dec

Traditional Scottish hospitality in this listed building in rural village on Grampian fringe. Ideal for walkers and bird watchers.

DUNLOP **Ayrshire**	Map 1 H6						

Struther Farm Guest House
17 Newmill Road
Dunlop
Ayrshire
KA3 4BA
Tel:(Stewarton) 0560
484946

APPROVED

1 Twin
1 Double
2 Family

2 Pub.Bath/Show

B&B per person
£15.00-£18.00 Single
£15.00-£18.00 Double

Open Jan-Dec
Dinner 1700-1930
B&B + Eve.Meal
£28.00-£32.00

Old Scottish farmhouse with large garden. Fresh seafood and meat in season. Only 17 miles (27kms) from Glasgow. Good base for touring.

DUNNET Caithness	Map 4 D2						
Northern Sands Hotel Dunnet Caithness KW14 8DX Tel:(Barrock) 084785 270		3 Twin 3 Double 3 Family	9 En Suite fac 1 Pub.Bath/Show	B&B per person £35.50-£37.50 Single £28.75-£30.75 Double	Open Jan-Dec Dinner 1900-2030	

DUNOON Argyll	Map 1 G5

Abbot's Brae

Bullwood,
West Bay,
Dunoon.
Telephone: 0369-5021
Fax: 0369-5021

Charming Victorian Country House Hotel in secluded woodland glen with breathtaking views of the sea and hills. Spacious, tastefully furnished en-suite bedrooms with TV, radio, telephone and tea/coffee facilities. Our well-appointed lounge and comfortable dining room with delicious menu and select wine list complete the perfect base to explore Argyll.

👑👑👑 Highly Commended

Abbot's Brae West Bay Dunoon Argyll PA23 7QJ Tel:(Dunoon) 0369 5021 Fax:0369 5021	HIGHLY COMMENDED 👑👑👑 👑	4 Double 3 Family	7 En Suite fac	B&B per person £27.00-£32.00 Single £20.00-£25.00 Double	Open Mar-Oct Dinner 1900-2030 B&B + Eve.Meal £32.50-£44.50	
		Privately run hotel, in a woodland setting, with magnificent sea views.				
Albany Hotel & Restaurant John Street Dunoon Argyll PA23 8BH Tel:(Dunoon) 0369 3044	COMMENDED 👑👑👑	2 Twin 6 Double 2 Family	10 En Suite fac	B&B per person £17.50-£25.00 Single £15.00-£17.50 Double	Open Jan-Dec Dinner 1830-2130 B&B + Eve.Meal from £22.50	
		Personally run by owners, conveniently situated between town centre and esplanade. Open coal fire in lounge. Some annexe accommodation.				
Ardfillayne Hotel West Bay Dunoon Argyll PA23 7QJ Tel:(Dunoon) 0369 2267 Fax:0369 2501	DELUXE 👑👑👑 👑	2 Twin 5 Double	7 En Suite fac	B&B per person £35.00 Single £25.00-£35.00 Double	Open Jan-Dec Dinner from 1830	
		150 year old mansion in 16 acres of wood and garden. Elegant Victorian restaurant; Taste of Scotland.				
The Ardtully Hotel Hunters Quay Dunoon Argyll PA23 8HN Tel:(Dunoon) 0369 2478	COMMENDED 👑👑👑	2 Twin 5 Double 2 Family	9 En Suite fac	B&B per person £20.00-£27.00 Single £20.00-£25.00 Double	Open Jan-Dec Dinner 1800-1900 B&B + Eve.Meal £30.00-£35.00	
		Personally supervised with superb views over the Firth of Clyde. Some motel bedrooms. Interesting menu using fresh produce.				
Argyll Hotel Argyll Street Dunoon Argyll PA23 7NE Tel:(Dunoon) 0369 2059	COMMENDED 👑👑👑	4 Single 13 Twin 9 Double 4 Family	21 En Suite fac 9 Limited ensuite 5 Pub.Bath/Show	B&B per person £30.00-£32.00 Single £30.00-£32.00 Double	Open Jan-Dec Dinner 1830-2130 B&B + Eve.Meal £38.00-£40.00	
		Traditional family run hotel, centrally situated near ferry terminal and all amenities.				

DUNOON continued	Map 1 G5					

Caledonian Hotel and Restaurant
Argyll Street
Dunoon
Argyll
PA23 7DA
Tel:(Dunoon) 0369 2176

COMMENDED ♛ ♛

2 Single 4 En Suite fac
1 Twin   3 Pub.Bath/Show
5 Double

B&B per person
£18.50-£25.00 Single
£15.00-£22.00 Double

Open Jan-Dec
Dinner 1630-2100

Family run hotel situated in town centre, 100 yards from ferry terminal and sea front.

Cedars Hotel
51 Alexandra Parade,
East Bay
Dunoon
Argyll
PA23 8AF
Tel:(Dunoon) 0369 2425
Fax:0369 6964

HIGHLY COMMENDED ♛ ♛ ♛

2 Single 12 En Suite fac
3 Twin
5 Double
2 Family

B&B per person
£18.00-£27.50 Single
£18.00-£24.50 Double

Open Jan-Dec
Dinner from 1830

Family run hotel in prime position on seafront. Full private facilities. Warm and friendly atmosphere.

Craigieburn Hotel
Alexandra Parade, East Bay
Dunoon
Argyll
PA23 8AN
Tel:(Dunoon) 0369 2048

2 Single 4 Pub.Bath/Show
2 Twin
3 Double
2 Family

B&B per person
£15.00-£19.00 Single
£14.00-£19.00 Double

Open Jan-Dec
Dinner 1800-1900
B&B + Eve.Meal
£21.00-£26.00

Enmore Hotel
Marine Parade
Dunoon
Argyll
PA23 8HH
Tel:(Dunoon) 0369 2230
Fax:0369 2148

HIGHLY COMMENDED ♛ ♛ ♛ ♛

2 Single 11 En Suite fac
2 Twin
6 Double
1 Family

B&B per person
£28.00-£45.00 Single
£25.00-£55.00 Double

Open Jan-Dec
Dinner 1930-2200
B&B + Eve.Meal
£50.00-£80.00

Georgian house with four poster beds. Gardens overlooking the Firth of Clyde. Squash courts and games room. Taste of Scotland.

Esplanade Hotel
West Bay
Dunoon
Argyll
PA23 7HU
Tel:(Dunoon) 0369 4070
Fax:0369 2129

COMMENDED ♛ ♛ ♛

4 Single 56 En Suite fac
30 Twin 1 Priv.NOT ensuite
17 Double 1 Pub.Bath/Show
6 Family

B&B per person
£25.00-£35.00 Single
£22.50-£30.00 Double

Open 15th Apr-15th Oct
Dinner 1830-2000
B&B + Eve.Meal
£30.00-£45.00

Run by the Togwell family, overlooking beautiful West Bay and providing comfort and relaxation for all.

Glenmorag Hotel
West Bay
Dunoon
Argyll
PA23 7QH
Tel:(Dunoon) 0369 2227

14 Single 62 En Suite fac
55 Twin   5 Pub.Bath/Show
17 Double

B&B per person
£15.00-£27.00 Single
£15.00-£27.00 Double

Open Mar-Nov
Dinner 1830-1930
B&B + Eve.Meal
£22.00-£34.00

Mayfair Hotel
Clyde Street, Kirn
Dunoon
Argyll
PA23 8DX
Tel:(Dunoon) 0369 2182
Fax:0369 2182

COMMENDED ♛ ♛ ♛

1 Single 14 En Suite fac
2 Twin
7 Double
4 Family

B&B per person
£18.00-£21.00 Single
£17.50-£20.00 Double

Open Apr-Nov
Dinner from 1830
B&B + Eve.Meal
£24.00-£29.00

Family run hotel, all rooms with en suite facilities and some with views to the Firth of Clyde. Golfing and walking packages.

DUNOON continued

Map 1 G5

Royal Marine Hotel
Hunter's Quay
Dunoon
Argyll
PA23 8HJ
Tel:(Dunoon) 0369 5810
Fax:0369 2329

COMMENDED
♕ ♕ ♕

7 Single	35 En Suite fac	B&B per person
12 Twin		£25.00-£38.00 Single
13 Double		£20.00-£35.00 Double
3 Family		

Open Jan-Dec
Dinner 1900-2130
B&B + Eve.Meal
£30.00-£45.00

Of considerable character and architectural and historical interest with friendly, informal atmosphere. Views over the Clyde.

St Ives Hotel
West Bay
Dunoon
Argyll
PA23 7HU
Tel:(Dunoon) 0369
4825/2400 (payphone)

COMMENDED
♕ ♕ ♕

2 Single	6 En Suite fac	B&B per person
2 Twin	2 Priv.NOT ensuite	£19.50-£21.50 Single
2 Double	1 Pub.Bath/Show	£19.50-£21.50 Double
2 Family		

Open Jan-Dec
Dinner from 1830
B&B + Eve.Meal
£26.50-£28.50

Family run hotel on traffic free promenade with magnificent, uninterrupted views of Firth of Clyde. Sea cruises and coach tours by arrangement.

West End Hotel
West Bay Promenade
Dunoon
Argyll
PA23 7HU
Tel:(Dunoon) 0369 2907
Fax:0369 6266

3 Single	6 En Suite fac	B&B per person
10 Double	4 Pub.Bath/Show	£18.00-£20.00 Single
2 Family		£18.00-£20.00 Double

Open Jan-Dec
Dinner 1800-1930
B&B + Eve.Meal
£23.00-£26.00

Allanton Inn
Allanton
Duns
Berwickshire
TD11 3JZ
Tel:(Chirnside) 0890
818260

1 Twin	3 En Suite fac	B&B per person
1 Double		from £20.00 Single
1 Family		from £18.00 Double

Open Jan-Dec
Dinner 1800-2100
B&B + Eve.Meal
from £23.00

DUNTOCHER
Dunbartonshire

Map 1 H5

The Duntocher Hotel
Dumbarton Road
Duntocher, Glasgow
Dunbartonshire
G81 6PO
Tel:(Duntocher) 0389 75371
Fax:0389 77373

15 Single	27 En Suite fac	B&B per person
8 Twin		£28.00-£38.00 Single
2 Double		£22.00-£27.00 Double
2 Family		
Suite avail.		

Open Jan-Dec
Dinner 1830-2115
B&B + Eve.Meal
£37.00-£45.00

DUNTULM
**Isle of Skye,
Inverness-shire**

Map 3 D7

Duntulm Castle Hotel
Duntulm
Isle of Skye, Inverness-shire
IV51
Tel:(Duntulm) 047052 213

5 Single	22 En Suite fac	B&B per person
11 Twin	6 Pub.Bath/Show	£20.00-£30.00 Single
10 Double		£20.00-£30.00 Double
2 Family		

Open Easter-Oct
Dinner from 1900
B&B + Eve.Meal
£35.00-£45.00

DUNVEGAN
Isle of Skye, Inverness-shire
Map 3 C9

Harlosh House Hotel
Harlosh
Dunvegan
Isle of Skye, Inverness-shire
IV55 8ZG
Tel:(Dunvegan) 047022 367

HIGHLY COMMENDED

1 Twin
2 Double
3 Family

5 En Suite fac
1 Priv.NOT ensuite

B&B per person
£45.00 Double

Open Easter-Oct
Dinner 1830-2100

Small friendly hotel overlooking Loch Bracadale, with superb views southwards to the Cuillins. Freshly prepared local seafoods a speciality

Tables Hotel & Restaurant
Dunvegan
Isle of Skye, Inverness-shire
IV55 8WA
Tel:(Dunvegan) 047022 404

COMMENDED

1 Single
1 Twin
1 Double
2 Family

3 En Suite fac
2 Pub.Bath/Show

B&B per person
£16.00-£28.00 Single
£18.00-£30.00 Double

Open Jan-Dec
Dinner 1900-2230
B&B + Eve.Meal
£28.00-£42.00

100 year old house in village, 0.75 mile (1km) from castle. Fine views over MacLeods Tables. Accent on relaxation, informality. Vegetarians welcomed

Roskhill Guest House
Roskhill
Dunvegan
Isle of Skye, Inverness-shire
IV55
Tel:(Dunvegan) 047022 317

COMMENDED

1 Twin
3 Double
1 Family

3 En Suite fac
1 Pub.Bath/Show

B&B per person
£14.50-£18.00 Double

Open Mar-Oct
Dinner 1900-2000
B&B + Eve.Meal
£22.50-£36.00

Personally run converted croft house offering home cooking and baking. Situated 2 miles (3kms) south of Dunvegan.

DURNESS
Sutherland
Map 3 H3

Far North Hotel
Durness
Sutherland
IV27 4PT
Tel:(Durness) 0971 511221

4 Single
1 Twin
4 Double
1 Family

4 Pub.Bath/Show

B&B per person
from £20.50 Single
from £20.50 Double

Open Jan-Dec
Dinner from 1930
B&B + Eve.Meal
from £35.00

Parkhill Hotel
Durness
Sutherland
IV27 4PN
Tel:(Durness) 0971 511209/511202
Fax:0971 511321

2 Single
4 Twin
4 Double

4 Pub.Bath/Show

B&B per person
£17.50-£20.00 Single
£17.50-£20.00 Double

Open Apr-Oct
Dinner 1900-2030
B&B + Eve.Meal
£25.00-£27.00

Port-na-Con Guest House
Loch Eriboll
Portnacon,by Altnaharra
Sutherland
IV27 4UN
Tel:(Durness) 0971 511367

COMMENDED

1 Twin
2 Double
1 Family

2 Pub.Bath/Show

B&B per person
from £16.00 Double

Open Apr-Oct
Dinner 1900-2100
B&B + Eve.Meal
from £26.00

Former customs house on the edge of Loch Eriboll. Ideal centre for touring north coast of Scotland.

EAGLESHAM
Renfrewshire
Map 1 H6

Eglinton Arms Hotel
Gilmour Street
Eaglesham
Renfrewshire
G76 0LG
Tel:(Eaglesham) 03553 2631
Fax:03553 2955

COMMENDED

7 Single
4 Twin
3 Double

14 En Suite fac

B&B per person
£57.50-£60.00 Single
£33.75-£35.00 Double

Open Jan-Dec
Dinner 1830-2130
B&B + Eve.Meal
£67.50-£70.00

Former coaching inn overlooking village green in Conservation Village. Only 20 minutes from Glasgow. All rooms ensuite.

EAST KILBRIDE **Lanarkshire**	Map 2 A6		

The Busby Hotel

Field Road, Clarkston G76 8RX Tel: 041-644 2661 Fax: 041-644 4417

A warm welcome awaits you at this family run hotel located in a tree-lined avenue by the River Cart in the southern outskirts of Glasgow. Excellent bus and rail links to city centre. All bedrooms to executive standard. Choice of bars and restaurants featuring 'Taste of Scotland'.

RAC ☆ ☆ ☆

B&B from £30

| Busby Hotel
Field Road
Clarkston
Glasgow
G76 8RX
Tel:041 644 2661
Fax:041 644 4417 | | 4 Single
22 Twin
5 Double
1 Family | 32 En Suite fac | B&B per person
£28.00-£60.00 Single
£25.00-£40.00 Double | Open Jan-Dec
Dinner 1200-2130
B&B + Eve.Meal
£35.00-£60.00 |

EDINBURGH	Map 2 D5				
The Adam Hotel 19 Lansdowne Crescent Edinburgh EH12 5EH Tel:031 337 1148		**Award Pending**	3 Single 2 Twin 2 Double 2 Family	3 Limited ensuite 2 Pub.Bath/Show	B&B per person £20.00-£22.00 Single £20.00-£21.00 Double	Open Jan-Dec

| Ailsa Craig Hotel
24 Royal Terrace
Edinburgh
EH7 5AH
Tel:031 556 1022/6055
Fax:031 556 6055 | | **COMMENDED**
👑 👑 👑 | 2 Single
5 Twin
5 Double
6 Family | 15 En Suite fac
1 Priv.NOT ensuite
1 Pub.Bath/Show | B&B per person
£25.00-£50.00 Single
£22.50-£40.00 Double | Open Jan-Dec
Dinner 1800-2000
B&B + Eve.Meal
£32.50-£50.00 |

Hotel in Georgian row overlooking a small park, in a quiet residential area. Within 10 minutes walk of St James Shopping Centre and Princes Street.

| Albany Hotel
39 Albany Street
Edinburgh
EH1 3QY
Tel:031 556 0397/0398
Tlx:727079
Fax:031 557 6633 | | **COMMENDED**
👑 👑 👑 | 5 Single
12 Twin
1 Double
2 Family | 20 En Suite fac | B&B per person
£49.00-£65.00 Single
£29.50-£46.00 Double | Open Jan-Dec
Dinner 1830-2130 |

Georgian Listed building with many original features. Close to city centre Refurbished to a high standard of comfort.

| Allison House Hotel
17 Mayfield Gardens
Edinburgh
EH9 2AX
Tel:031 667 8049
Fax:031 667 5001 | | **COMMENDED**
👑 👑 👑 | 3 Single
3 Twin
4 Double
3 Family | 11 En Suite fac
3 Pub.Bath/Show | B&B per person
£23.00-£32.00 Single
£23.00-£32.00 Double | Open Jan-Dec
Dinner 1830-2030 |

On main route into the city, convenient for all attractions, private parking and regular bus service. All rooms double glazed.

EDINBURGH continued	Map 2 D5						
Argus Hotel 14 Coates Gardens Edinburgh EH12 5LB Tel:031 337 6159		COMMENDED 👑 👑 👑	4 Single 2 Twin 3 Double 1 Family	8 En Suite fac 2 Priv.NOT ensuite	B&B per person £24.00-£32.00 Single £24.00-£32.00 Double	Open Jan-Dec Dinner 1900-2000	

Privately owned small hotel in residential area of city, close to centre and a few minutes walk from Haymarket Station. Small-sized bedrooms.

Arkle Hotel 41 Coates Gardens Edinburgh EH12 5LF Tel:031 337 1168		APPROVED 👑 👑	2 Single 2 Twin 2 Double 4 Family	6 En Suite fac 4 Limited ensuite 3 Pub.Bath/Show	B&B per person £20.00-£25.00 Single £20.00-£25.00 Double	Open Jan-Dec	

Family-run traditional stone built Victorian house in quiet street, very close to Edinburgh city centre.

Arthurs View Hotel 10 Mayfield Gardens Edinburgh EH9 2BZ Tel:031 667 3468 Fax:031 662 4232		COMMENDED 👑 👑 👑	2 Single 4 Twin 2 Double 4 Family	12 En Suite fac	B&B per person £27.50-£37.50 Single £27.50-£37.50 Double	Open Jan-Dec Dinner 1800-2130 B&B + Eve.Meal £39.50-£49.50	

Friendly hotel, personally run by owners, 1.5 miles (3kms) from Royal Mile. Own off-street parking. On main bus routes.

Avon Hotel 1-2 Spence Street Edinburgh EH16 5AG Tel:031 667 8681			1 Single 1 Twin 4 Double 4 Family	2 En Suite fac 3 Pub.Bath/Show	B&B per person £18.00-£20.00 Single £16.00-£20.00 Double	Open Jan-Dec	

EDINBURGH continued	Map 2 D5

THE BALMORAL EDINBURGH

PRINCES STREET, EDINBURGH EH2 2EQ
Telephone: 031-556 2414

The Balmoral Edinburgh (formerly the North British Hotel) re-opened in February 1991 after a 2½-year refurbishment costing £23,000,000. First opened in 1902, the hotel has been fully restored to its former glory with 167 Bedrooms and 22 Suites, 10 Function Rooms, 2 Restaurants, 2 Bars, Traditional Lounge, Cake Shop, Business Centre and Health Club including a Swimming Pool.

The Balmoral Hotel Princes Street Edinburgh EH2 2EQ Tel:031 556 2414 Tlx:727282 Fax:031 557 3747	**DELUXE** 👑👑👑 👑👑	25 Single 68 Twin 74 Double Suites avail.	189 En Suite fac	B&B per person from £132.50 Single from £97.50 Double	Open Jan-Dec Dinner 1830-2300
		Edinburgh's landmark hotel completely refurbished to international standard.			
The Barnton Thistle Hotel Queensferry Road Edinburgh EH4 6AS Tel:031 339 1144 Fax:031 339 5521	**COMMENDED** 👑👑👑 👑	2 Single 35 Twin 10 Double 3 Family	50 En Suite fac	B&B per person £75.00-£90.00 Single £50.00-£60.00 Double	Open Jan-Dec Dinner 1900-2200
		Originally a coaching inn. Conveniently situated for airport and Forth Road Bridge. Choice of restaurants.			
Beresford Hotel 32 Coates Garden Edinburgh EH12 5LE Tel:031 337 0850		4 Twin 1 Double 4 Family	3 En Suite fac 2 Pub.Bath/Show	B&B per person £20.00-£25.00 Single £17.50-£22.50 Double	Open Jan-Dec
Beverley Hotel 40 Murrayfield Avenue Edinburgh EH12 6AY Tel:031 337 1128	**COMMENDED** 👑👑	2 Single 2 Twin 2 Double 2 Family	4 En Suite fac 3 Pub.Bath/Show	B&B per person £18.00-£24.00 Single £18.00-£22.00 Double	Open Jan-Dec
		Privately owned hotel in quiet residential area close to city centre. Unrestricted car parking.			

EDINBURGH continued	Map 2 D5						

Boisdale Hotel
9 Coates Gardens
Edinburgh
EH12 5LG
Tel:031 337 1134

COMMENDED
♕ ♕ ♕

3 Single   11 En Suite fac
5 Twin
1 Double
2 Family

B&B per person
£25.00-£35.00 Single
£30.00-£35.00 Double

Open Jan-Dec
Dinner from 1830
B&B + Eve.Meal
£33.00-£43.00

Victorian terraced house, close to Haymarket station. All rooms have full private facilities.

Braid Hills Hotel
134 Braid Road
Edinburgh
EH10 6JD
Tel:031 447 8888
Tlx:72311
Fax:031 452 8477

COMMENDED
♕ ♕ ♕
♕

3 Single   68 En Suite fac
29 Twin
24 Double
12 Family

B&B per person
£45.00-£79.00 Single
£30.00-£45.00 Double

Open Jan-Dec
Dinner 1845-2130
B&B + Eve.Meal
£40.00-£55.00

Victorian baronial style in residential area, overlooking Braidburn Park, with views to Castle, Braid and Pentland hills. Ample parking.

Brunswick Hotel
7 Brunswick Street
Edinburgh
EH7 5JB
Tel:031 556 1238
Fax:031 556 1238

COMMENDED
♕ ♕

1 Single   10 En Suite fac
3 Twin
5 Double
1 Family

B&B per person
£23.00-£35.00 Single
£20.00-£35.00 Double

Open Jan-Dec

Georgian stone Listed building, convenient for bus and railway station. Street parking. All rooms with private facilities.

Bruntsfield Hotel
69-74 Bruntsfield Place
Edinburgh
EH10 4HH
Tel:031 229 1393
Tlx:727897
Fax:031 229 5634

COMMENDED
♕ ♕ ♕
♕

13 Single   50 En Suite fac
22 Twin
15 Double

B&B per person
£55.00-£90.00 Single
£35.00-£60.00 Double

Open Jan-Dec
Dinner 1800-2200

Privately owned hotel 1 mile (2kms) from city centre with interesting and tastefully furnished restaurant, incorporating a conservatory dining area.

Cairn Hotel
10-18 Windsor Street
Edinburgh
EH7 5JR
Tel:031 557 0175
Fax:031 556 8221

APPROVED
♕ ♕ ♕

15 Single   52 En Suite fac
11 Twin   12 Pub.Bath/Show
19 Double
7 Family

B&B per person
£25.00-£55.00 Single
£22.50-£40.00 Double

Open Jan-Dec
Dinner 1800-2100
B&B + Eve.Meal
£32.50-£45.00

Situated in quiet residential area, close to Princes Street, with easy access to city centre and all amenities.

Caledonian Hotel
Princes Street
Edinburgh
EH1 2AB
Tel:031 225 2433
Tlx:72179
Fax:031 225 6632

DELUXE
♕ ♕ ♕
♕ ♕

34 Single   239 En Suite fac
95 Twin
110 Double
Suites avail.

B&B per person
from £105.00 Single
from £75.00 Double

Open Jan-Dec
Dinner 1830-2230
B&B + Eve.Meal
from £95.00

Traditional hotel with friendly atmosphere; elegantly furnished. Situated on world famous Princes Street, affording spectacular views of the castle.

EDINBURGH continued Camore Hotel 7 Links Gardens, Leith Edinburgh EH6 7JH Tel:031 554 7897	**Map 2** D5	**Award Pending**	4 Single 2 Twin 2 Family	3 Pub.Bath/Show	B&B per person £16.00-£18.00 Single £15.00-£17.00 Double	Open Jan-Dec Dinner 1800-2000 B&B + Eve.Meal £22.00-£24.00	
Capital Moat House & Leisure Club Clermiston Road Edinburgh EH12 6UG Tel:031 334 3391 Tlx:728284 Fax:031 334 9712		**COMMENDED** 👑 👑 👑 👑	8 Single 43 Twin 14 Double 45 Family Suites avail.	110 En Suite fac	B&B per person £75.00-£85.50 Single £45.00-£54.50 Double	Open Jan-Dec Dinner 1800-2300 B&B + Eve.Meal £90.00-£101.00	

Situated on slopes of Corstorphine Hill, extensively refurbished hotel with leisure complex. 10 mins by car from city centre. Conference facilities.

Carlton Highland Hotel

NORTH BRIDGE · EDINBURGH EH1 1SD

Tel: 031-556 7277 Tlx: 727001 Fax: 031-556 2691

The Carlton Highland Hotel combines a traditional, elegant exterior with an interior of modern comfort. Bordering the Royal Mile, overlooking Princes Street and in close proximity to Waverley Station, the hotel has 200 bedrooms each with private bathroom, colour satellite TV, telephone, mini bar, trouser press, hairdryer, tea and coffee making facilities.

A choice of restaurants and bars is available as well as a superb health and leisure club with swimming pool, jacuzzi, saunas, steam room, solaria, gymnasium, squash courts, aerobics area, snooker room, creche and snack bar.

Dinner, bed and breakfast rates from £51. Over 60's from £36. Free accommodation and breakfast for children under 16 sharing parents room.

Carlton Highland Hotel North Bridge Edinburgh EH1 1SD Tel:031 556 7277 Tlx:727001 Fax:031 556 2691	**HIGHLY COMMENDED** 👑 👑 👑 👑 👑	41 Single 64 Twin 32 Double 60 Family	197 En Suite fac	B&B per person from £99.00 Single from £74.00 Double	Open Jan-Dec Dinner 1900-2230	

Centrally located, spacious, traditional style hotel with modern amenities. Choice of restaurant (except Sat. Lunch and all Sun).

BE SURE TO CHOOSE THE SCOTTISH TOURIST BOARD'S SIGN OF QUALITY

CHANNINGS TEL: 031 315 2226
South Learmonth Gardens, Edinburgh EH4 1EZ
Stylish Town House Hotel with traditional club atmosphere situated in peaceful garden setting, yet only minutes from the city centre. 48 rooms, tastefully and individually designed with all today's expected facilities. The brasserie and bar offer fashionable elegance with Scottish and international cuisine.

Weekends from £96 DB&B Per Person for 2 nights.

Channings South Learmonth Gardens Edinburgh EH4 1EZ Tel:031 315 2226 Fax:031 332 9631	COMMENDED ♛ ♛ ♛ ♛	8 Single 19 Twin 15 Double 6 Family	48 En Suite fac	B&B per person £78.00-£103.00 Single £50.00-£72.50 Double	Open Jan-Dec Dinner 1830-2200
		Stylish transformation of Edwardian town house into hotel of character. Ideal for small conferences, Brasserie restaurant.			
Christian Alliance (of Scotland)(Female) Francis Kinnaird House, 13-14 Coates Cr. Edinburgh EH3 7AG Tel:031 225 3608		9 Single 7 Twin 3 Double 3 Family	6 Pub.Bath/Show	B&B per person £16.00-£17.00 Single £11.00-£14.00 Double	Open Jan-Dec Dinner 1800-1830 B&B + Eve.Meal £15.00-£21.00
Christopher North House Hotel 6 Gloucester Place Edinburgh EH3 6EF Tel:031 225 2720	COMMENDED ♛ ♛ ♛	7 Twin 1 Double 3 Family	8 En Suite fac 2 Limited ensuite 1 Pub.Bath/Show	B&B per person £43.00-£63.00 Single £29.75-£40.00 Double	Open Jan-Dec Dinner 1830-2030
		Family run Georgian hotel in Edinburgh's New Town, convenient for Princes Street and all city centre amenities.			
Claremont Hotel 14a/15 Claremont Crescent Edinburgh EH7 4HX Tel:031 556 1487		4 Single 6 Twin 4 Double 6 Family	18 En Suite fac 1 Limited ensuite 1 Pub.Bath/Show	B&B per person £15.00-£25.00 Single £15.00-£25.00 Double	Open Jan-Dec Dinner from 1900 B&B + Eve.Meal £18.00-£28.00
Clarendon Hotel 18-22 Grosvenor Street Edinburgh EH12 5EG Tel:031 337 7033 Tlx:72450 Fax:031 346 7606	Award Pending	14 Single 25 Twin 6 Double 6 Family	51 En Suite fac	B&B per person £27.50-£70.00 Single £25.00-£45.00 Double	Open Jan-Dec Dinner 1800-2100 B&B + Eve.Meal £36.00-£81.00
Claymore Hotel 6 Royal Terrace Edinburgh EH7 5AB Tel:031 556 2693 Fax:031 556 2693	APPROVED ♛ ♛	2 Single 2 Twin 1 Double 3 Family	2 En Suite fac 6 Limited ensuite 2 Pub.Bath/Show	B&B per person £28.00-£35.00 Single £28.00-£38.00 Double	Open Jan-Dec
		Family run hotel conveniently placed for Playhouse Theatre and other city centre amenities.			

EDINBURGH continued	Map 2 D5						
Clifton Private Hotel 1 Clifton Terrace, Haymarket Edinburgh EH12 5DR Tel:031 337 1002		COMMENDED ♕ ♕	3 Single 4 Twin 4 Double	4 En Suite fac 2 Pub.Bath/Show	B&B per person £21.00-£25.00 Single £19.00-£23.50 Double	Open Jan-Dec	
			Personally run Victorian town house in city centre opposite Haymarket station. On main bus routes.				
Craigelachie Private Hotel 21 Murrayfield Avenue Edinburgh EH12 6AU Tel:031 337 4076/2619		COMMENDED ♕	1 Single 2 Twin 1 Double 3 Family	2 Pub.Bath/Show	B&B per person £20.50-£25.50 Single £18.00-£21.00 Double	Open Jan-Dec	
			Victorian terraced house in a quiet residential area with ample street parking. Near Murrayfield Stadium and bus services to the city centre.				
Culane House Hotel 9 Hermitage Place Edinburgh EH6 8AF Tel:031 554 7331			4 Single 3 Twin 1 Family	2 Limited ensuite 5 Pub.Bath/Show	B&B per person £13.00-£17.50 Single £13.00-£17.50 Double	Open Jan-Dec	

CUMBERLAND HOTEL

RAC Highly Acclaimed

1 West Coates, Edinburgh EH12 5JQ
Telephone: 031-337 1198

Ideally situated on main A8, Edinburgh to Glasgow Road, 5 mins from City Centre and 15 mins from Edinburgh Airport.

A warm welcome awaits you as you enter this elegant, family owned hotel.

You will find excellent accommodation, our attractive cocktail bar and residents' lounge offer comfort, together with a relaxed atmosphere.

A large, private car park is available for our guests.

Cumberland Hotel 1 West Coates Edinburgh EH12 5JQ Tel:031 337 1198/1022		COMMENDED ♕ ♕	2 Single 2 Twin 2 Double 3 Family	8 En Suite fac 1 Pub.Bath/Show	B&B per person £35.00-£45.00 Single £27.50-£42.00 Double	Open Jan-Dec	
			Personally run by resident partners, 5 minutes from city centre; car parking available. Small weddings/private functions catered for.				
Dean Hotel 10 Clarendon Crescent Edinburgh EH4 1PT Tel:031 332 0308 Fax:031 555 0482		COMMENDED ♕ ♕	2 Single 6 Twin 3 Double 1 Family	5 En Suite fac 2 Limited ensuite 2 Pub.Bath/Show	B&B per person £33.00-£45.00 Single £23.00-£30.00 Double	Open Jan-Dec	
			Personally run hotel in traditional Edinburgh terrace. Close to West End and all amenities. Comfortable and popular lounge bar.				

EDINBURGH continued	Map 2 D5						

Dorstan Private Hotel
7 Priestfield Road
Edinburgh
EH16 5HJ
Tel:031 667 6721/5138
Fax:031 668 4644

COMMENDED
♕ ♕ ♕

5 Single
1 Twin
6 Double
2 Family

9 En Suite fac
3 Limited ensuite
3 Pub.Bath/Show

B&B per person
£30.00-£31.00 Single
£25.00-£28.50 Double

Open Jan-Dec
Dinner 1800-1900
B&B + Eve.Meal
£43.00-£44.00

Victorian villa in quiet residential area. Own car parking. Near main bus route
to city centre. Most rooms en suite. Golf course adjacent.

Dunstane House Hotel
4 West Coates
Edinburgh
EH12 5JQ
Tel:031 337 5320/6169

COMMENDED
♕ ♕

3 Single
4 Twin
3 Double
5 Family

4 En Suite fac
11 Limited ensuite
4 Pub.Bath/Show

B&B per person
£26.50-£32.50 Single
£25.00-£40.00 Double

Open Jan-Dec

Victorian house standing in its own grounds. Private car park. On major bus
route to city, railway station and airport. Near Murrayfield.

EGLINTON HOTEL
29 EGLINTON CRESCENT
EDINBURGH EH12 5BY
Tel: 031 337 2641   Fax: 031-337 4495

THE EGLINTON *is a three-storey building designed
by John Chesser between 1875-1880 and displays
some of Chesser's finest architectural features. At
present the Eglinton is privately owned and
administered by Mr and Mrs Barlow who offer their
guests a warm and relaxing welcome. The lounge bar
offers a comprehensive selection of malt and blended
whiskies, wines and draught beers. The menu and
wine list will suit all occasions whether a business or
family lunch, or an intimate dinner for two. The
bedrooms are tastefully decorated and have private
baths or showers, colour TV, tea and coffee-making
facilities, direct-dial telephones, trouser press,
hairdryers, radios.*

**B&B per person: £30.00-£45.00 Single
£30.00-£40.00 Double**

Eglinton Hotel
29 Eglinton Crescent
Edinburgh
EH12 5BY
Tel:031 337 2641
Fax:031 337 4495

COMMENDED
♕ ♕ ♕

2 Single
2 Twin
4 Double
4 Family

12 En Suite fac
1 Pub.Bath/Show

B&B per person
£25.00-£39.00 Single
£27.50-£35.00 Double

Open Jan-Dec
Dinner 1200-2230
B&B + Eve.Meal
£35.00-£49.00

Family run hotel in Regency Terrace in West End of Edinburgh and within walking
distance of Princes St and Haymarket Railway Station.

Ellersly Country House Hotel
Ellersly Road, Murrayfield
Edinburgh
EH12 6HZ
Tel:031 337 6888
Tlx:727239
Fax:031 313 2543

COMMENDED
♕ ♕ ♕
♕

14 Single
29 Twin
8 Double
6 Family

57 En Suite fac

B&B per person
to £87.50 Single
to £58.00 Double

Open Jan-Dec
Dinner 1900-2130
B&B + Eve.Meal
to £74.95

Formerly an Edwardian residence. Quietly situated in own 2 acre grounds, yet
only a few minutes from city centre. Ideal for tourists/businessmen.

Ellwyn Hotel
37-39 Moira Terrace
Edinburgh
EH7 6TD
Tel:031 669 1033

APPROVED
♕ ♕

2 Single
3 Twin
5 Double
2 Family

8 En Suite fac
2 Pub.Bath/Show

B&B per person
£22.00-£32.00 Single
£14.00-£21.00 Double

Open Jan-Dec
Dinner 1930-2130
B&B + Eve.Meal
£22.95-£40.95

Personally managed, conveniently situated in residential area on main bus route.
1 mile (2kms) from city centre.

Details of Grading and Classification are on page vi. | **Key to symbols is on back flap.** |

	Map 2 D5						
EDINBURGH continued Forte Posthouse Edinburgh Corstorphine Road Edinburgh EH12 6UA Tel:031 334 0390 Tlx:1727103 PHEDIN Fax:031 334 9237		COMMENDED 👑 👑 👑	48 Single 66 Twin 86 Family	200 En Suite fac	B&B per person £49.75-£63.75 Single £28.50-£35.50 Double	Open Jan-Dec Dinner 1900-2200	
			Ideally situated on outskirts of Edinburgh, easy access to city centre and airport. 200 bedrooms. Small and medium sized conferences catered for.				
The George Hotel Inter-Continental George Street Edinburgh EH2 2PB Tel:031 225 1251 Tlx:72570 Fax:031 226 5644		COMMENDED 👑 👑 👑 👑 👑	52 Single 94 Twin 46 Double 3 Family Suites avail.	195 En Suite fac	B&B per person £137.00-£147.00 Single £87.00-£92.00 Double	Open Jan-Dec Dinner 1830-2200 B&B + Eve.Meal £154.00-£164.00	
			Located in heart of business and commercial centre of city, offering extensive Scottish and French Cuisine in classically elegant surroundings.				
Glenisla Hotel 12 Lygon Road Edinburgh EH16 5QB Tel:031 667 4098/4877 Fax:031 667 4098			1 Single 2 Twin 4 Double 1 Family	5 En Suite fac 2 Pub.Bath/Show	B&B per person £21.50-£26.00 Single £20.00-£24.50 Double	Open Jan-Dec Dinner 1830-2030 B&B + Eve.Meal £31.00-£35.00	
Glenora Hotel 14 Rosebery Crescent Edinburgh EH12 5JY Tel:031 337 1186		COMMENDED 👑 👑	3 Single 2 Twin 2 Double 3 Family	10 En Suite fac 1 Pub.Bath/Show	B&B per person £28.00-£35.00 Single £25.00-£30.00 Double	Open Jan-Dec	
			Georgian terraced house close to Haymarket station; central for shopping and all entertainment.				
Greens Hotel 24 Eglinton Crescent Edinburgh EH12 5BY Tel:031 337 1565			18 Single 44 Twin 16 Double 3 Family	18 En Suite fac 17 Pub.Bath/Show	B&B per person £27.00-£33.00 Single £23.00-£29.00 Double	Open Feb-Dec Dinner 1830-2000 B&B + Eve.Meal £33.00-£41.50	
Greenside Hotel 9 Royal Terrace Edinburgh EH7 5AB Tel:031 557 0022			4 Single 3 Twin 2 Double 3 Family	7 En Suite fac 3 Pub.Bath/Show	B&B per person £25.00-£37.00 Single £22.50-£30.00 Double	Open Mar-Dec	

SCOTTISH TOURIST BOARD
QUALITY COMMENDATIONS ARE:

Deluxe – *An EXCELLENT quality standard*
Highly Commended – *A VERY GOOD quality standard*
Commended – *A GOOD quality standard*
Approved – *An ADEQUATE quality standard*

EDINBURGH continued	Map 2 D5	APPROVED ♛					
Halcyon Hotel 8 Royal Terrace Edinburgh EH7 5AB Tel:031 556 1032/1033			4 Single 4 Twin 4 Double 4 Family	6 Limited ensuite 4 Pub.Bath/Show	B&B per person £25.00-£31.00 Single £24.00-£30.00 Double	Open Jan-Dec	

Within walking distance of Princes Street, Victorian terrace hotel in quiet area.

| Haymarket Hotel
1 Coates Gardens
Edinburgh
EH12 5LG
Tel:031 337 1775/346 8727 | | | 2 Single
2 Twin
2 Double
2 Family | 8 En Suite fac | B&B per person
£30.00-£40.00 Single
£35.00-£70.00 Double | Open Jan-Dec
Dinner 1800-2300
B&B + Eve.Meal
from £40.00 | |

Herald House Hotel

70 Grove Street, Edinburgh EH3 8AP.
Tel: 031-228 2323. Fax: 031-228 3101

Conveniently situated near West End. A friendly and welcoming 45 bedroom hotel offering individual attention. All rooms with private facilities and fully modernised. Close to main galleries and theatres, Princes Street 10 minutes walk and Haymarket Railway Station 5 minutes walk. Airport 6 miles. From £35 per person B&B. Contact: Reservations.

| Herald House Hotel
70/72 Grove Street
Edinburgh
EH3 8AP
Tel:031 228 2323
Tlx:72372
Fax:031 228 3101 | | APPROVED ♛ ♛ ♛ | 11 Single
20 Twin
11 Double
3 Family | 45 En Suite fac | B&B per person
£40.00-£55.00 Single
£35.00-£50.00 Double | Open Jan-Dec
Dinner 1830-2130
B&B + Eve.Meal
£50.00-£70.00 | |

Located within 10 minutes walk of city centre. Fully modernised but small enough to give individual attention.

| Hilton National
69 Belford Road
Edinburgh
EH4 3DG
Tel:031 332 2545
Tlx:727979
Fax:031 332 3805 | | | 62 Twin
82 Double
Suite avail. | 144 En Suite fac | B&B per person
£75.00-£108.00 Single
£40.00-£75.00 Double | Open Jan-Dec
Dinner 1830-2200
B&B + Eve.Meal
from £55.75 | |

| Holiday Inn Garden Court Edinburgh
Queensferry Road
Edinburgh
EH4 3HL
Tel:031 332 2442
Tlx:72541
Fax:031 332 3408 | | COMMENDED ♛ ♛ ♛ | 42 Single
40 Twin
36 Double | 118 En Suite fac | B&B per person
£46.00-£52.00 Single
£36.00-£42.00 Double | Open Jan-Dec
Dinner 1830-2200 | |

A modern, purpose built hotel. Convenient for the city centre.

EDINBURGH continued	Map 2 D5						
Iona Hotel 17 Strathearn Place Edinburgh EH9 2AL Tel:031 447 6264/5050 Fax:031 452 8574	APPROVED ♛ ♛	5 Single 4 Twin 10 Double 2 Family	4 En Suite fac 11 Limited ensuite 5 Pub.Bath/Show	B&B per person £23.00-£30.00 Single £23.00-£30.00 Double	Open Jan-Dec Dinner 1900-2100		
		Privately run hotel with own car park in residential area. Convenient for bus route to city centre.					
Kildonan Lodge Hotel 27 Craigmillar Park Edinburgh EH16 5PE Tel:031 667 2793	Award Pending	1 Single 6 Twin 4 Double 2 Family	8 En Suite fac 2 Pub.Bath/Show	B&B per person £18.00-£30.00 Single £16.00-£25.00 Double	Open Jan-Dec		
King James Thistle Hotel 107 Leith Street Edinburgh EH1 3SW Tel:031 556 0111 Tlx:727200 Fax:031 557 5333	HIGHLY COMMENDED ♛ ♛ ♛ ♛ ♛	14 Single 103 Twin 25 Double 5 Family	147 En Suite fac	B&B per person £90.00-£112.00 Single £53.00-£76.50 Double	Open Jan-Dec Dinner 1830-2220		
		Modern hotel in city centre location with friendly and efficient staff. Saint Jacques a la carte restaurant/brasserie, Boston Bean cocktail bar.					
Kings Manor Hotel 100 Milton Road East Edinburgh EH5 2NP Tel:031 669 0444 Tlx:727237 Fax:031 669 6650	COMMENDED ♛ ♛ ♛ ♛	14 Single 28 Twin 16 Double 11 Family	69 En Suite fac	B&B per person £49.50-£85.00 Single £35.00-£55.00 Double	Open Jan-Dec Dinner 1830-2130 ♿A		
		Family run hotel 4 miles (6kms) east of city centre but close to beach and A1 Full range of conference and banqueting facilities.					
Learmonth Hotel 18-20 Learmonth Terrace Edinburgh EH4 1PW Tel:031 343 2671 Tlx:57476 Att LEAR Fax:031 315 2232	COMMENDED ♛ ♛ ♛ ♛	16 Single 26 Twin 6 Double 14 Family	62 En Suite fac	B&B per person to £66.50 Single to £45.50 Double B&B + Eve.Meal to £51.00	Open Jan-Dec Dinner 1830-2130		
		Newly refurbished hotel in attractive Georgian terrace, only 15 minutes walk from Princes Street.					
Lodge Hotel 6 Hampton Terrace Edinburgh EH12 5JD Tel:031 337 3682	HIGHLY COMMENDED ♛ ♛ ♛	2 Single 2 Twin 6 Double	10 En Suite fac 1 Pub.Bath/Show	B&B per person £36.00-£45.00 Single £25.00-£40.00 Double	Open Jan-Dec Dinner 1800-2000 B&B + Eve.Meal £36.00-£52.00		
		Family run hotel recently extended and refurbished. Situated on main A8 Edinburgh-Glasgow road, convenient to city centre. Car parking available.					
Lygon Hotel 4 Lygon Road Edinburgh EH16 5QE Tel:031 667 1374 Fax:031 667 4098		1 Single 1 Twin 1 Double 3 Family	2 Pub.Bath/Show	B&B per person £20.00-£23.00 Single £18.00-£21.00 Double	Open Jan-Dec Dinner 1830-2030 B&B + Eve.Meal £29.50-£32.50		

EDINBURGH continued	Map 2 D5						
Lyncliff Hotel 4 Windsor Street Edinburgh EH7 5JR Tel:031 556 6972	APPROVED ≋	2 Twin 3 Double 2 Family	3 Pub.Bath/Show	B&B per person £14.00-£18.00 Single £14.00-£18.00 Double	Open Jan-Dec		
		Family run hotel with free parking nearby. Main city centre bus route. Handy for the Playhouse Theatre.					
Maitland Hotel 33 Shandwick Place Edinburgh EH2 4RG Tel:031 229 1467 Fax:031 229 7549	COMMENDED ≋ ≋ ≋	3 Single 10 Twin 6 Double 3 Family	22 En Suite fac	B&B per person £30.00-£75.00 Single £25.00-£50.00 Double	Open Jan-Dec Dinner 1200-2130 B&B + Eve.Meal £35.00-£87.50		
		City centre hotel at West End of Princes Street. Central for shopping. Limited parking nearby.					
Marchhall Hotel 14-16 Marchhall Crescent Edinburgh EH16 5HL Tel:031 667 2743	COMMENDED ≋ ≋	3 Single 3 Twin 4 Double 3 Family	6 En Suite fac 2 Limited ensuite 3 Pub.Bath/Show	B&B per person £19.50-£28.00 Single £19.50-£28.00 Double	Open Jan-Dec Dinner from 1800 B&B + Eve.Meal £29.50-£38.00		
		Family run hotel in a quiet residential area, near main bus routes. Close to City Centre and all major tourist attractions.					
Maxwell's Hotel 2 West Coates Edinburgh EH12 5JQ Tel:031 337 2173		2 Twin 3 Double 5 Family	8 En Suite fac 1 Pub.Bath/Show	B&B per person £30.00-£35.00 Double	Open Jan-Dec		
Merith House Hotel 2-3 Hermitage Place, Leith Links Edinburgh EH6 8AF Tel:031 554 5045	Award Pending	2 Single 5 Twin 3 Family	1 En Suite fac 2 Limited ensuite 3 Pub.Bath/Show	B&B per person £18.00-£22.00 Single £15.00-£20.00 Double	Open Jan-Dec Dinner 1700-1930		
Merton Hotel 23 Hope Terrace Edinburgh EH9 2AP Tel:031 447 6910	COMMENDED ≋ ≋	4 Single 5 Twin 5 Double	8 En Suite fac 4 Pub.Bath/Show	B&B per person £19.50-£21.00 Single £22.50-£24.00 Double	Open Jan-Dec		
		A family run hotel in a quiet residential area but near all facilities. Bus route nearby to city centre.					
Mount Royal Hotel 53 Princes Street Edinburgh EH2 2DG Tel:031 225 7161 Tlx:727641 Fax:031 220 4671	COMMENDED ≋ ≋ ≋ ≋	22 Single 70 Twin 55 Double 14 Family	152 En Suite fac 3 Pub.Bath/Show	B&B per person £39.00-£97.50 Single £39.00-£63.00 Double	Open Jan-Dec Dinner 1830-2130 B&B + Eve.Meal £39.50-£112.00		
		Ideally situated on Princes St, some bedrooms and public rooms have magnificent views of castle and gardens. All bedrooms refurbished 1990.					

EDINBURGH continued	Map 2 D5						
Murrayfield Hotel 18 Corstorphine Road Edinburgh EH12 6HN Tel:031 337 1844 Fax:031 346 8159		COMMENDED ♕ ♕ ♕ ♕	18 Single 7 Twin 7 Double 1 Family	33 En Suite fac	B&B per person £52.50-£57.50 Single £34.50-£36.75 Double	Open Jan-Dec Dinner 1800-2100	
			Stone built Victorian house with newly decorated rooms and garden for alfresco dining. Some annexe accommodation. On A8, airport 3 miles (5kms).				
Navaar House Hotel 12 Mayfield Gardens Edinburgh EH9 2BZ Tel:031 667 2828		COMMENDED ♕ ♕ ♕	2 Twin 3 Double 1 Family	6 En Suite fac	B&B per person £25.00-£35.00 Single £22.50-£30.00 Double	Open Jan-Dec Dinner 1830-2000	
			On main city centre bus route with private parking. Spacious rooms, all recently refurbished and with en suite facilities.				
Nirvana Hotel 9-10 Ardmillan Terrace Edinburgh EH11 2JW Tel:031 337 9588			2 Single 2 Twin 1 Double 2 Family	2 Pub.Bath/Show	B&B per person £16.00 Single £15.00 Double	Open Jan-Dec	
Northumberland Hotel 31-33 Craigmillar Park Edinburgh EH16 5PE Tel:031 667 6971 Fax:031 667 3092			2 Single 6 Twin 6 Double 4 Family	16 En Suite fac 2 Limited ensuite 1 Pub.Bath/Show	B&B per person £40.00-£50.00 Single £25.00-£35.00 Double	Open Jan-Dec Dinner 1830-2100	
Nova Hotel 5 Bruntsfield Crescent Edinburgh EH10 4EZ Tel:031 447 6437/7349 Fax:031 452 8126		COMMENDED ♕ ♕	2 Single 2 Twin 2 Double 4 Family	10 En Suite fac	B&B per person £25.00-£40.00 Single £25.00-£40.00 Double	Open Jan-Dec Dinner 1800-2000 B&B + Eve.Meal £35.00-£40.00	
			Recently refurbished hotel, to the south-west of city in quiet position overlooking putting green and park area.				

HERE'S THE DIFFERENCE

STB's scheme has two distinct elements, grading and classification.

GRADING:

measures the quality and condition of the facilities and services offered, eg, the warmth of welcome, quality of food and its presentation, condition of decor and furnishings, appearance of buildings, tidiness of grounds and gardens, condition of lighting and heating and so on.
Grading awards are: **Approved, Commended, Highly Commended, Deluxe.**

CLASSIFICATION:

measures the range of physical facilities and services offered, eg, rooms with private bath, heating, reception, lounges, telephones and so on.
Classification awards are: **Listed or from one to five crowns.**

EDINBURGH continued	Map 2 D5

Old Waverley Hotel

**43 PRINCES STREET,
EDINBURGH EH2 2BY
Tel: 031-556 4648 Fax: 031-557 6316**

This traditional, elegant hotel occupies a prime site on Princes Street, directly opposite Waverley Station, Airport Bus Terminal and the Information Bureau. The hotel has 66 comfortable bedrooms each with private bathroom, telephone, satellite TV, hairdryer, trouser press, tea and coffee making facilities. Cranston's Restaurant with its superb views across Princes Street Gardens to Edinburgh Castle offers a relaxing atmosphere, choice of carvery or à la carte menus and an excellent selection of wines.

Dinner, bed and breakfast rates from £45. Over 60's from £31. Free accommodation and breakfast for children under 16 sharing parents room.

Old Waverley Hotel 43 Princes Street Edinburgh EH2 2BY Tel:031 556 4648 Tlx:C R O 727331 Fax:031 557 6316	COMMENDED 	11 Single 66 En Suite fac 36 Twin 19 Double Suites avail.	B&B per person £76.00-£80.00 Single £61.00-£64.00 Double	Open Jan-Dec Dinner 1900-2130 B&B + Eve.Meal £90.50-£95.50	

Refurbished city centre hotel overlooking Princes Street Gardens within 100 yards of Waverley station. Views of castle and Scott Monument.

Osbourne Hotel

**53-59 York Place, Edinburgh EH1 3JD.
Tel: 031-556 5577. Fax: 031-556 1012**

This ♛♛♛ city centre hotel is ideally located within easy walking distance of Edinburgh's main tourist attractions. With en-suite rooms, restaurant, lounge bar, lift, night porter, etc., start your holiday with us. Tariff Low-Season £29. High Season £44. Allow us to book your tickets and tours. Friendly service at reasonable rates.

Osbourne Hotel 53-59 York Place Edinburgh EH1 3JD Tel:031 556 5746/2345/5577 Tlx:727972 F.A.O. OSBOURNE HOTEL Fax:031 556 1012	COMMENDED	13 Single 36 En Suite fac 11 Twin 3 Pub.Bath/Show 11 Double 5 Family	B&B per person £29.00-£46.00 Single £27.00-£42.00 Double	Open Jan-Dec Dinner 1730-2100 B&B + Eve.Meal £37.00-£52.00	

Personally run hotel close to city centre and all amenities. Short distance from Railway and Bus Stations.

Park View House Hotel 14 Hermitage Place, Leith Links Edinburgh EH6 8AF Tel:031 554 6206/6468 Fax:031 554 6206		2 Single 12 En Suite fac 4 Twin 2 Pub.Bath/Show 4 Double 2 Family	B&B per person £15.00-£19.00 Single £15.00-£17.00 Double	Open Jan-Dec Dinner 1800-2230	

	Map 2 D5					

EDINBURGH continued

Peel Hotel
1 Peel Terrace
Edinburgh
EH9 2AY
Tel:031 667 7580/2118
Fax:031 667 7580

3 Single
1 Twin
2 Double
3 Family

4 En Suite fac
3 Pub.Bath/Show

B&B per person
£17.00-£22.00 Single
£17.00-£25.00 Double

Open Jan-Dec
Dinner 1200-2300
B&B + Eve.Meal
£20.00-£26.00

Prestonfield House Hotel
Priestfield Road
Edinburgh
EH16 5UT
Tel:031 668 3346
Fax:031 668 3976

1 Twin
4 Double

2 En Suite fac
2 Pub.Bath/Show

B&B per person
£65.00-£105.00 Double

Open Jan-Dec
Dinner 1900-2130

Raeburn House Hotel
112 Raeburn Place
Edinburgh
EH4 1HG
Tel:031 332 2348
Fax:031 315 2381

Award Pending

2 Single
4 Twin
2 Double
1 Family

3 Pub.Bath/Show

B&B per person
£25.00-£35.00 Single
£19.75-£25.00 Double

Open Jan-Dec
Dinner to 2100
B&B + Eve.Meal
£29.00-£35.00

Richmond House Hotel
20 Leopold Place,
London Road
Edinburgh
EH7 5LB
Tel:031 556 3556
Fax:031 557 6669

COMMENDED

2 Single
2 Twin
2 Double
2 Family

6 En Suite fac
2 Pub.Bath/Show

B&B per person
£33.50-£40.00 Single
£30.00-£35.00 Double

Open Jan-Dec
Dinner 1700-2300
B&B + Eve.Meal
£46.00-£52.50

A-Listed Georgian house close to city centre and convenient for all travel services. Most rooms en-suite. All with colour TV, tea/coffee making facs.

Ritz Hotel
14-18 Grosvenor Street
Edinburgh
EH12 5EG
Tel:031 337 4315
Fax:031 346 0597

COMMENDED

3 Single
20 Twin
4 Double
7 Family

34 En Suite fac

B&B per person
£35.25-£52.88 Single
£30.55-£47.00 Double

Open Jan-Dec
Dinner 1800-2000

On five floors, each room of individual character, some featuring four poster beds. Within easy walking distance of Haymarket railway station.

Rosebery Hotel
13 Rosebery Crescent,
Haymarket
Edinburgh
EH12 5JY
Tel:031 337 1085

2 Single
2 Twin
3 Double
1 Family

6 En Suite fac
2 Pub.Bath/Show

B&B per person
£15.50-£25.00 Single
£13.50-£25.00 Double

Open Jan-Dec

Rosehall Hotel
101 Dalkeith Road
Edinburgh
EH16 5AJ
Tel:031 667 9372

APPROVED

2 Single
2 Twin
1 Double
4 Family

1 En Suite fac
5 Limited ensuite
2 Pub.Bath/Show

B&B per person
£15.00-£22.00 Single
£15.00-£20.00 Double

Open Jan-Dec
Dinner 1700-2100

City Hotel on busy Dalkeith Road. Nearby to Commonwealth Pool. Regular bus service to centre.

EDINBURGH continued	Map 2 D5							
Ross Hotel 2 Murrayfield Avenue Edinburgh EH12 6AX Tel:031 337 4060 Fax:031 337 4060	APPROVED Listed	1 Single 1 Twin 5 Double 2 Family	4 En Suite fac 5 Pub.Bath/Show	B&B per person £15.00-£25.00 Single £15.00-£20.00 Double	Open Jan-Dec Dinner 1800-2230 B&B + Eve.Meal £22.50-£32.50			
		Privately owned hotel conveniently situated for both city centre and airport (4 miles [6kms]). Unrestricted street parking.						
Rothesay Hotel 8 Rothesay Place Edinburgh EH3 7SL Tel:031 225 4125/4126 Tlx:727025 Fax:031 220 4350	COMMENDED 👑 👑 👑	12 Single 13 Twin 8 Double 3 Family	30 En Suite fac 4 Pub.Bath/Show	B&B per person £20.00-£50.00 Single £20.00-£40.00 Double	Open Jan-Dec Dinner 1830-2100			
		Family run Georgian terraced building in a quiet residential area, yet convenient for Princes Street.						
Roxburghe Hotel 38 Charlotte Square Edinburgh EH2 4HG Tel:031 225 3921 Tlx:727054 Fax:031 220 2518	COMMENDED 👑 👑 👑 👑	22 Single 43 Twin 8 Double 2 Family	75 En Suite fac	B&B per person £40.00-£95.00 Single £25.00-£70.00 Double	Open Jan-Dec Dinner 1800-2200 B&B + Eve.Meal £50.00-£100.00			
		Centrally situated off Princes Street. Retaining many original features. Convenient for shops and theatres.						

Royal Circus Hotel
19-21 Royal Circus, Edinburgh EH3 6TL.
Tel:031-220 5000. Fax: 031-220 2020.

This City Centre Hotel is located within ten minutes walk of Princes Street and easy walking distance of Edinburgh's other main attractions. All thirty rooms have showers and en-suite facilities. A popular restaurant and lounge bar, telephones, tea/coffee facilities, full central heating. Night porter service. Reasonable rates.

Royal Circus Hotel 19-21 Royal Circus Edinburgh EH3 6TL Tel:031 220 5000 Fax:031 220 2020	APPROVED 👑 👑	14 Twin 13 Double 3 Family	18 En Suite fac 12 Limited ensuite 3 Pub.Bath/Show	B&B per person £24.00-£44.00 Single £22.00-£37.00 Double	Open Jan-Dec Dinner 1700-2200 B&B + Eve.Meal £34.00-£54.00			
		Situated in crescent in elegant Georgian New Town area of city. Good access to centre and amenities.						
Royal Ettrick Hotel 13 Ettrick Road Edinburgh EH10 5BJ Tel:031 228 6413 Fax:031 229 7330	COMMENDED 👑 👑 👑	3 Single 3 Twin 3 Double 3 Family	9 En Suite fac 2 Limited ensuite 2 Pub.Bath/Show	B&B per person £44.00-£48.00 Single £35.00-£40.00 Double	Open Jan-Dec Dinner 1900-2100 B&B + Eve.Meal £57.00-£59.00			
		Family run hotel in residential area convenient for city centre. Bar lunches and evening meals served. Small conference facilities available.						

EDINBURGH continued	Map 2 D5					
The Royal Over-Seas League Over-Seas House, 100 Princes Street Edinburgh EH2 3AB Tel:031 225 1501 Tlx:72165 ROSL G Fax:031 226 3936		COMMENDED ♛ ♛ ♛ ♛	5 Single 8 Twin 2 Double 2 Family Suites avail.	17 En Suite fac	B&B per person from £55.00 Single from £42.50 Double	Open Jan-Dec Dinner 1930-2100
			Ideal central location on Princes Street. Public rooms and front bedrooms have spectacular views of the Castle and gardens.			
Royal Terrace Hotel 18 Royal Terrace Edinburgh EH7 5AQ Tel:031 557 3222 Tlx:727182 Fax:031 557 5334			22 Single 47 Twin 25 Double 3 Family	97 En Suite fac	B&B per person £65.00-£110.00 Single £55.00-£80.00 Double	Open Jan-Dec Dinner 1830-2115
Salisbury View Hotel 64 Dalkeith Road Edinburgh EH16 5AE Tel:031 667 1133 Fax:031 667 1133		COMMENDED ♛ ♛ ♛	3 Single 2 Twin 2 Double 1 Family	8 En Suite fac	B&B per person £26.00-£37.00 Single £22.00-£28.00 Double	Open Jan-Dec Dinner 1830-1930 B&B + Eve.Meal £34.00-£49.00
			On main bus route to city centre and with ample private parking. All rooms have private facilities. Evening meals on request.			

SCANDIC CROWN HOTEL

80 HIGH STREET, THE ROYAL MILE EDINBURGH
Tel: 031-557 9797 Fax: 031-557 9789

Edinburgh's newest international hotel has an unbeatable location, situated right on the historic Royal Mile in the city centre. Just a 5-minute walk from Waverley station and a 7-mile drive from the airport, the hotel offers 238 spacious bedrooms including family rooms, non-smoking rooms and 10 suites. This accommodation is complemented by a choice of restaurants and bars, leisure centre and the most up-to-date conference facilities in town catering for 2 to 220 Delegates. For guests travelling by car, the Scandic Crown Hotel offers on-site parking for 150 cars.

| Scandic Crown Hotel Edinburgh 80 High Street, The Royal Mile Edinburgh EH1 1TH Tel:031 557 9797 Tlx:727298 Fax:031 557 9789 | | | 26 Single 128 Twin 76 Double 8 Family Suites avail. | 238 En Suite fac | B&B per person to £103.95 Single to £77.45 Double | Open Jan-Dec Dinner 1900-2230 B&B + Eve.Meal to £92.40 |

EDINBURGH continued	Map 2 D5

Sheraton Grand
HOTEL
EDINBURGH

1 FESTIVAL SQUARE, EDINBURGH EH3 9SR
Telephone: 031-229 9131

A major refurbishment programme has transformed the hotel and created a classic, individual Scottish hotel style. Enjoy the comfort of a spacious room, many with superb views of Edinburgh Castle, featuring king or twin beds, satellite TV and tea and coffee making facilities.

Two new outstanding restaurants have been created. The Terrace, which overlooks Festival Square, and The Grill room specialising in Scottish food. A pianist provides entertainment in the evening in The Lobby Bar.

For those who wish to relax there is a leisure club and free car parking is available for guests.

Sheraton Grand Hotel
1 Festival Square
Edinburgh
EH3 9SR
Tel:031 229 9131
Tlx:72398
Fax:031 228 4510

DELUXE

113 Twin
113 Double
35 Family
Suites avail.

261 En Suite fac

B&B per person
£85.00-£142.75 Single
£60.00-£100.25 Double

Open Jan-Dec
Dinner 1800-2300

Luxury hotel refurbished to the highest standards. Dine in the elegant terrace or more formal Grill Room. Extensive meeting facilities. Leisure club

---

Suffolk Hall Hotel
10 Craigmillar Park
Edinburgh
EH16 5NE
Tel:031 668 4333
Fax:031 668 4506

APPROVED

1 Single
4 Twin
3 Double
4 Family

11 En Suite fac
1 Pub.Bath/Show

B&B per person
£45.00-£50.00 Single
£30.00-£35.00 Double

Open Jan-Dec
Dinner 1830-2100

Privately owned hotel, Victorian mansion with large secluded garden and patio. On main bus routes to city centre. Function facilities for 120.

Swallow Royal Scot Hotel
111 Glasgow Road
Edinburgh
EH12 8NF
Tel:031 334 9191
Tlx:727197
Fax:031 316 4507

COMMENDED

19 Single
134 Twin
76 Double
30 Family
Suites avail.

259 En Suite fac

B&B per person
£45.00-£95.00 Single
£30.00-£60.00 Double

Open Jan-Dec
Dinner 1830-2200
B&B + Eve.Meal
£59.00-£110.00

Modern hotel in outskirts of city and only 5 minutes drive from Edinburgh Airport.

Templehall Hotel
7 Promenade, Joppa
Edinburgh
EH15 2EL
Tel:031 669 4264

COMMENDED

1 Single
1 Twin
2 Double
3 Family

2 Pub.Bath/Show

B&B per person
£20.00-£25.00 Single
£20.00-£25.00 Double

Open Jan-Dec
Dinner 1800-1900

Victorian house retaining many original features situated on sandy beach in residential area with fine views over Firth of Forth. Beer garden.

Key to symbols is on back flap.

EDINBURGH continued	Map 2 D5					

Terrace Hotel
37 Royal Terrace
Edinburgh
EH7 5AH
Tel:031 556 3423

COMMENDED ♕ ♕

2 Single
3 Twin
2 Double
7 Family

11 En Suite fac
2 Pub.Bath/Show

B&B per person
£20.00-£30.00 Single
£18.50-£30.00 Double

Open Jan-Dec

Personally run private hotel in impressive Georgian terrace close to city centre, shopping and all amenities. Excellent views.

Teviotdale House Private Hotel
53 Grange Loan
Edinburgh
EH9 2ER
Tel:031 667 4376
Fax:031 667 4376

COMMENDED ♕ ♕ ♕

2 Twin
2 Double
3 Family

5 En Suite fac
2 Priv.NOT ensuite

B&B per person
£39.00-£42.00 Single
£22.00-£30.50 Double

Open Jan-Dec
Dinner 1830-1930
B&B + Eve.Meal
£37.00-£45.50

Pleasant Victorian house in quiet Conservation area, under 2 miles (3kms) from Princes St. Home cooking, baking and preserves. Non-smoking.

Thistle Hotel
59 Manor Place
Edinburgh
EH3 7EG
Tel:031 225 6144
Fax:031 225 5014

APPROVED ♕ ♕ ♕

1 Twin
5 Double
4 Family

10 En Suite fac

B&B per person
£30.00-£35.00 Single
£30.00-£32.50 Double

Open Jan-Dec
Dinner 1730-1930

Three storey Georgian terrace house within 10 minutes walk of Princes Street.

Thrums Private Hotel
14/15 MINTO STREET, EDINBURGH   Tel: 031-667 5545

Georgian House with gardens/locked car park. City Centre 5 minutes.
Near many tourist attractions. Bedrooms have central heating, TV,
telephone, tea/coffee, hairdrier, H&C (most with private bathrooms).
Residents' lounge and bar. À la carte restaurant. Children/special diets
catered for. Brochure and off-season packages available.
B&B FROM £35-£40   DINNER £6-£18

Thrums Private Hotel
14 Minto Street, Newington
Edinburgh
EH9 1RQ
Tel:031 667 5545

COMMENDED ♕ ♕ ♕ ♕

2 Single
2 Twin
5 Double
5 Family

13 En Suite fac
2 Pub.Bath/Show

B&B per person
£35.00-£50.00 Single
£29.00-£35.00 Double

Open Jan-Dec
Dinner 1730-2030
B&B + Eve.Meal
from £35.00

Detached Victorian house on main bus route to city centre. Ample parking. Some bedrooms in annexe of period style, retaining many original features.

Victoria Hotel
3-5 Forth Street
Edinburgh
EH1 3JX
Tel:031 556 1616

4 Single
3 Twin
7 Double
5 Family

3 En Suite fac
3 Limited ensuite
3 Pub.Bath/Show

B&B per person
£15.00-£20.00 Single
£15.00-£20.00 Double

Open Jan-Dec

Westbury Hotel
92-98 St John's Road,
Corstorphine
Edinburgh
EH12 8AT
Tel:031 316 4466
Fax:031 316 4333

17 Twin
10 Double
3 Family

30 En Suite fac

B&B per person
£35.00-£60.00 Single
£19.50-£35.00 Double

Open Jan-Dec
Dinner 1800-2130
B&B + Eve.Meal
£50.00-£75.00

53 Grange Loan
Edinburgh EH9 2ER

Telephone/Fax:
Reception 031-667 4376

Both now and in the past, the Owners have been dedicated to the restoration of all the finest features of this elegant Victorian townhouse which, today, is probably among the finest of its kind in the city.

Over the years, exceptional skills and endeavours have created and added the most comfortable of furnishings. Every room has private shower, toilet, wash basin, colour television, tea and coffee tray, hair driers, etc. All the bed linen is hand sewn which is in keeping with the finest beds, sheepskin bedmats, down duvets and pillows and freshly laundered towels each day. The highly efficient central heating system provides very hot water throughout the house.

Similarly, in the kitchen, the knowledge and selection of fresh foods have allowed the development of a menu of dishes which are prepared to order and make breakfast at Teviotdale a banquet to start each day. Home baked bread supported by fresh baked scones every morning and home made jams and marmalade ensure the perfect balanced diet. (No tins, or smokers here!)

Add to these, the most outstanding housekeeping skills and willing staff, who ensure a degree of cleanliness and care which promise the finest welcome to Scotland and its traditions.

At Teviotdale House, there exists a standard of accommodation, which is of the very best. Your Hosts, Jane & John Coville, look forward to sharing it with you.

A NON-SMOKING HOUSE

Please write early for brochure and tariff.

BREAKFAST MENU

A Choice of Fresh Fruit Juices
Orange, Pineapple, Grapefruit etc

Porridge
Old Fashioned Scottish Porridge
(made from Pin Head Oatmeal and Wholegrain Wheat)
with Fresh Cream

Fresh Fruit Muesli
À la Anton Mosimann

Teviotdale Special
A delightful mixture of Dried and Soaked Apricots,
Pineapple, Raisins, Sultanas and Prunes

Fresh Grapefruit Segments

Duke of Edinburgh's Favourite Breakfast
Lightly Scrambled Free Range Eggs with Fresh Cream
or Delicately Muddled Eggs with Scottish Smoked Salmon
and Garnished with Parsley

Loch Fyne Kippers

Poached Free Range Eggs on Slivers of Wholemeal Toast

Boiled Free Range Eggs

Omelettes
Tomatoes, Mushroom, Cheddar Cheese, Finnan Haddock,
Plain, Bacon and Mint or Chives when available

Mixed Grill

All the above individually cooked to order

Every Day Freshly Baked Scones
Old Fashioned Scottish Fadge (White & Wheaten)

Home Made Brown Bread
(From Organically Grown Allinson's 100% Organic Flour)

Home Made Marmalade & Jams

Scottish Honey

Oatcakes

A selection of Teas & Real Ground Coffee

All vegetables used are grown in our own private Organic Garden.

EDINBURGH continued	Map 2 D5		

WEST END HOTEL
35 PALMERSTON PLACE, EDINBURGH EH12 5AU
Telephone: 031-225 3656

A truly Highland Hotel in a City Centre location, only 5 minutes from Princes Street. It is a very lively hotel where the sounds of fiddles, accordion and even pipes can be heard every weekend.

Prices from £22 B&B. For brochure contact Donald Park.

West End Hotel 35 Palmerston Place Edinburgh EH12 5AU Tel:031 225 3656		2 Single 1 Twin 2 Double 3 Family	6 En Suite fac 2 Pub.Bath/Show	B&B per person £22.00-£27.00 Single £22.00-£27.00 Double B&B + Eve.Meal £28.00-£33.00	Open Jan-Dec Dinner 1800-1900

Young's Hotel 12-14 Leamington Terrace Edinburgh EH10 4JN Tel:031 229 6481		2 Single 1 Twin 2 Double 5 Family	1 En Suite fac 1 Limited ensuite 2 Pub.Bath/Show	B&B per person £15.00-£30.00 Single £15.00-£23.00 Double B&B + Eve.Meal £20.00-£30.00	Open Jan-Dec Dinner 1700-2100

Aaron Guest House 16 Hartington Gardens Edinburgh EH10 4LD Tel:031 229 6459 Fax:031 228 5807	COMMENDED Listed	2 Single 4 Twin 2 Double 2 Family	5 En Suite fac 1 Limited ensuite 2 Pub.Bath/Show	B&B per person £18.00-£19.00 Single £18.00-£25.00 Double	Open Jan-Dec

Family run, in quiet residential area, yet close to the West end of city. Private parking. Many rooms have ensuite facilities.

Abbeylodge Guest House 137 Drum Street Edinburgh EH17 8RJ Tel:031 664 9548	COMMENDED ♨ ♨ ♨	1 Single 2 Twin 1 Double 1 Family	5 En Suite fac	B&B per person £16.00-£25.00 Single £16.00-£25.00 Double B&B + Eve.Meal £26.00-£35.00	Open Jan-Dec Dinner 1800-2100

New guest house in Edinburgh all on ground level. Close to city centre. A 1 and City Bypass. All rooms ensuite, Sky TV, telephone. Private Parking.

Abcorn Guest House 4 Mayfield Gardens Edinburgh Tel:031 667 6548	COMMENDED ♨ ♨	2 Twin 2 Double 2 Family	2 En Suite fac 2 Pub.Bath/Show	B&B per person £15.00-£24.00 Double	Open Jan-Dec

Detached house with private parking on main route to city centre.

Acorn Guest House 70 Pilrig Street Edinburgh EH6 5AS Tel:031 554 2187	APPROVED ♨	1 Twin 1 Double 3 Family	2 Pub.Bath/Show	B&B per person £13.50-£15.50 Double	Open Jan-Dec

Terraced house on bus route to and from city centre.

EDINBURGH continued	Map 2 D5					
Adam Guest House 2 Hartington Gardens Edinburgh EH10 4LD Tel:031 229 8664 Fax:031 228 5807		COMMENDED Listed	1 Single 1 Twin 1 Double 2 Family	1 En Suite fac 1 Priv.NOT ensuite 2 Pub.Bath/Show	B&B per person £16.00-£20.00 Single £16.00-£25.00 Double	Open Jan-Dec

Family run Victorian terraced house in quiet cul de sac. Easy access to city centre by bus or 15 minute walk. Unrestricted parking. Non smoking.

| Afton Guest House
1 Hartington Gardens
Edinburgh
EH10 4LD
Tel:031 229 1019 | COMMENDED | 2 Single
1 Twin
1 Double
3 Family | 3 En Suite fac
1 Limited ensuite
2 Pub.Bath/Show | B&B per person
£15.00-£22.00 Single
£15.00-£22.00 Double | Open Jan-Dec
Dinner 1830-2000
B&B + Eve.Meal
£22.50-£30.00 |

Semi-detached Victorian house in quiet residential area but near main bus route to city centre.

| A-Haven in Edinburgh
180 Ferry Road
Edinburgh
EH6 4NS
Tel:031 554 6559
Fax:031 554 5252 | COMMENDED | 2 Single
2 Twin
2 Double
4 Family
Suite avail. | 7 En Suite fac
2 Pub.Bath/Show | B&B per person
£20.00-£35.00 Single
£16.00-£30.00 Double | Open Jan-Dec
Dinner 1830-1930
B&B + Eve.Meal
£30.00-£47.00 |

Family run city centre guest house with private parking and main bus routes. Scottish welcome and hospitality.

| Airlie Guest House
29 Minto Street
Edinburgh
EH9 1SB
Tel:031 667 3562
Fax:031 662 1399 | COMMENDED | 2 Single
3 Twin
5 Double
2 Family | 7 En Suite fac
1 Priv.NOT ensuite
2 Pub.Bath/Show | B&B per person
£18.00-£25.00 Single
£16.00-£25.00 Double | Open Jan-Dec |

Formerly two terraced houses, some rooms featuring plaster cornicing. On bus route with easy access to city centre.

| Akbar Guest House
25 East Hermitage Place
Edinburgh
EH6 8AD
Tel:031 554 4709 | | 1 Single
3 Twin
1 Double | 3 Pub.Bath/Show | B&B per person
£14.00-£20.00 Single
£14.00-£20.00 Double | Open Jan-Oct
Dinner 1800-2000
B&B + Eve.Meal
£18.00-£24.00 |

| Alpha Guest House
7b West Maitland Street
Edinburgh
EH12 5DS
Tel:031 228 2896 | | 2 Twin
2 Double
2 Family | 3 En Suite fac
2 Pub.Bath/Show | B&B per person
£16.50-£27.50 Double | Open Jan-Dec |

| Amaragua Guest House
10 Kilmaurs Terrace
Edinburgh
EH16 5DR
Tel:031 667 6775 | APPROVED | 2 Single
2 Twin
1 Double
1 Family | 3 En Suite fac
2 Pub.Bath/Show | B&B per person
£16.00-£18.00 Single
£17.00-£20.00 Double | Open Jan-Dec |

Victorian terraced house in residential area, close to Prestonfield Golf Course, Holyrood Park and Commonwealth Pool. Nearby bus routes to centre.

| An Fuaran Guest House
5 Seaview Terrace, Joppa
Edinburgh
EH15 2HE
Tel:031 669 8119 | COMMENDED | 2 Twin
1 Double
1 Family | 4 En Suite fac | B&B per person
£20.00-£30.00 Single
£18.00-£22.00 Double | Open Jan-Dec |

Victorian house overlooking the Firth of Forth, 4 miles (6 kms) from Edinbrgh city centre. Regular bus service. Evening meal by arrangement.

EDINBURGH continued	Map 2 D5						
Angusbeag Guest House 5 Windsor Street Edinburgh EH7 5LA Tel:031 556 1905			1 Double 3 Family	1 En Suite fac 2 Limited ensuite 1 Pub.Bath/Show	B&B per person £16.50-£20.00 Single £15.00-£19.50 Double	Open Jan-Dec	

| Appleton House 15 Leamington Terrace Edinburgh EH10 4JP Tel:031 229 3059 | | APPROVED Listed | 1 Twin 2 Family | 1 Pub.Bath/Show | B&B per person £15.00-£20.00 Double | Open Jan-Dec | |

Terraced house in quiet residential area, close to the Kings Theatre and ideal for shopping and entertainment.

| Ard Thor Guest House 10 Mentone Terrace, Newington Edinburgh EH9 2DG Tel:031 667 1647 | | COMMENDED Listed | 1 Twin 2 Double | 2 Pub.Bath/Show | B&B per person £17.00-£19.00 Single £15.00-£18.50 Double | Open Jan-Dec | |

Victorian semi-detached villa in quiet residential area. Friendly and family run. Easy access to city centre by car and public transport.

| Ardblair Guest House 1 Duddingston Crescent, Milton Road Edinburgh EH15 3AS Tel:031 669 2384 | | COMMENDED | 1 Double 2 Family | 2 Pub.Bath/Show | B&B per person £15.00-£18.00 Single £14.00-£17.00 Double | Open Jan-Dec Dinner 1800-2000 B&B + Eve.Meal £21.00-£23.00 | |

Conveniently placed on main bus route to city centre. Private parking area.

| Ardenlee Guest House 9 Eyre Place Edinburgh EH3 5ES Tel:031 556 2838 | | APPROVED Listed | 1 Single 2 Twin 2 Double 3 Family | 2 En Suite fac 2 Pub.Bath/Show | B&B per person £17.00-£21.00 Single £16.00-£20.00 Double | Open Jan-Dec | |

Terraced house on bus routes to city centre which is about 0.75 miles (1.5kms) away.

| Ardmor Guest House 74 Pilrig Street Edinburgh EH6 5AS Tel:031 554 4944 | | COMMENDED | 2 Twin 1 Double 1 Family | 2 Limited ensuite 2 Pub.Bath/Show | B&B per person £15.00-£17.00 Single £15.00-£17.00 Double | Open Jan-Dec | |

Stone built house in residential area overlooking Pilrig Park 0.5 miles (1km) from city centre, with convenient bus routes.

EDINBURGH continued	Map 2 D5					
The Armadillo Guest House 5 Upper Gilmore Place Edinburgh EH3 9NW Tel:031 229 4669		1 Twin 2 Double	2 Pub.Bath/Show	B&B per person £11.00-£20.00 Single £11.00-£16.00 Double	Open Jan-Dec	
Ascot Guest House 98 Dalkeith Road Edinburgh EH16 5AF Tel:031 667 1500	Award Pending	1 Single 2 Double 5 Family	2 En Suite fac 1 Limited ensuite 2 Priv.NOT ensuite 2 Pub.Bath/Show	B&B per person £15.00-£20.00 Single £15.00-£25.00 Double	Open Jan-Dec Dinner 1800-1930 B&B + Eve.Meal £22.00-£32.00	
Ashdene House 23 Fountainhall Road Edinburgh EH9 2LN Tel:031 667 6026	HIGHLY COMMENDED ♛ ♛	1 Twin 2 Double 2 Family	4 En Suite fac 1 Priv.NOT ensuite 1 Pub.Bath/Show	B&B per person £18.00-£22.00 Double	Open Jan-Dec	

Edwardian town house retaining many features, in quiet residential Conservation area. Convenient for bus route to city centre (10 minutes).

| Ashgrove House 12 Osborne Terrace Edinburgh EH12 5HG Tel:031 337 5014 Fax:031 313 5043 | Award Pending | 3 Single 2 Twin 2 Double 2 Family | 6 En Suite fac 2 Pub.Bath/Show | B&B per person £20.00-£25.00 Single £20.00-£28.00 Double | Open Jan-Dec Dinner 1800-2000 | |

| Ashlyn Guest House 42 Inverleith Row Edinburgh EH3 5PY Tel:031 552 2954 | COMMENDED ♛ ♛ ♛ | 2 Single 2 Twin 3 Double 1 Family | 5 En Suite fac 1 Priv.NOT ensuite 3 Pub.Bath/Show | B&B per person £20.00-£25.00 Single £18.00-£25.00 Double | Open Jan-Dec Dinner 1730-1900 B&B + Eve.Meal £36.00-£43.00 | |

Georgian listed building in residential area of city. On main bus route to centre with street parking.

AVERON GUEST HOUSE
44 Gilmore Place, Central Edinburgh EH3 9NQ

★ Excellent accommodation with traditional Scottish Breakfast.

★ All credit cards accepted.

★ Colour TV, Video, Satellite TV all rooms.

Tel: 031-229 9932   CAR PARK

| Averon Guest House 44 Gilmore Place Edinburgh EH3 9NQ Tel:031 229 9932 | Award Pending | 1 Single 4 Twin 2 Double 3 Family | 3 Pub.Bath/Show | B&B per person £16.00-£22.00 Single £12.00-£22.00 Double | Open Jan-Dec | |

	Map 2 D5						
EDINBURGH continued Avondale Guest House 10 South Gray Street Edinburgh EH9 1TE Tel:031 667 6779		**Award Pending**	1 Single 1 Twin 2 Double 1 Family	2 Pub.Bath/Show	B&B per person £14.00-£25.00 Single £18.00-£30.00 Double	Open Jan-Dec	
Balmoral Guest House 32 Pilrig Street Edinburgh EH6 5AL Tel:031 554 1857		**COMMENDED** 👑	1 Single 3 Twin 1 Double 2 Family	2 Pub.Bath/Show	B&B per person £15.00-£17.00 Single £14.50-£17.00 Double	Open Jan-Dec	

Situated in residential area of city, convenient for all amenities. On main bus route and with easy access to city centre.

BALQUHIDDER GUEST HOUSE
94 PILRIG STREET . EDINBURGH . EH6 5AY Tel: 031-554 3377

Built in 1857 as a church manse, this charming centrally situated Victorian detached house offers a high standard of accommodation at very favourable terms. Own keys with access to rooms at all times.
B&B from £15 per person per night.
For details contact Proprietor: Mrs N. Ferguson.

Balquhidder Guest House 94 Pilrig Street Edinburgh EH6 5AY Tel:031 554 3377		**COMMENDED** 👑 👑	1 Single 2 Twin 2 Double 1 Family	5 En Suite fac 1 Limited ensuite 1 Pub.Bath/Show	B&B per person £15.00-£25.00 Single £15.00-£25.00 Double	Open Jan-Dec	

Detached house in its own grounds overlooking public park and on bus routes to the city centre.

Barrosa Guest House 21 Pilrig Street Edinburgh EH6 5AN Tel:031 554 3700			1 Twin 2 Double 3 Family	4 En Suite fac 3 Pub.Bath/Show	B&B per person £16.00-£26.00 Double	Open Jan-Dec	
Beechcroft Guest House 46 Murrayfield Avenue Edinburgh EH12 6AY Tel:031 337 1081			1 Single 3 Twin 3 Double 3 Family	5 En Suite fac 2 Pub.Bath/Show	B&B per person £18.00-£25.00 Single £12.00-£20.00 Double	Open Jan-Dec	

Welcome Hosts provide a warm welcome, good service and information about their area. Look out for the people wearing the Welcome Host badge.

EDINBURGH continued	Map 2 D5

Belford Guest House
13 BLACKET AVENUE · EDINBURGH · EH9 1RR
Telephone: 031-667 2422

Small and friendly family run guest house in a quiet tree-lined avenue 1 mile from the city centre.
Buses run from either end of the avenue to all attractions in the city.
Private parking.

Belford House 13 Blacket Avenue Edinburgh EH9 1RR Tel:031 667 2422			3 Twin 4 Family	2 Pub.Bath/Show	B&B per person £20.00-£22.00 Single £17.00-£20.00 Double	Open Jan-Dec
Bellrock Guest House 105 Ferry Road Edinburgh EH6 4ET Tel:031 554 2604			1 Single 1 Twin 2 Double 3 Family	1 Limited ensuite 2 Pub.Bath/Show	B&B per person £15.00-£20.00 Single £15.00-£20.00 Double	Open Jan-Dec
Bonnington Guest House 202 Ferry Road Edinburgh EH6 4NW Tel:031 554 7610	COMMENDED 👑 👑		1 Twin 2 Double 3 Family	2 En Suite fac 2 Pub.Bath/Show	B&B per person £19.00-£26.00 Double	Open Jan-Dec

Early Victorian Listed building with private parking on the north side of the city; convenient bus routes to centre.

Brae Guest House 119 Willowbrae Road Edinburgh EH8 7HN Tel:031 661 0170			1 Single 1 Twin 2 Family	2 En Suite fac 1 Pub.Bath/Show	B&B per person £14.00-£24.00 Single £14.00-£24.00 Double	Open Jan-Dec
Brig O'Doon Guest House 262 Ferry Road Edinburgh EH5 3AN Tel:031 552 3953	COMMENDED Listed		3 Twin 1 Double 2 Family	3 Pub.Bath/Show	B&B per person £15.00-£18.00 Double	Open Jan-Dec

Stone built terraced house on North side of city centre, overlooking playing fields with fine views to castle. Bus route to city centre.

Bruntsfield Guest House 55 Leamington Terrace Edinburgh EH10 4JS Tel:031 228 6458 Fax:031 228 6458	COMMENDED Listed		2 Single 2 Twin 2 Double 1 Family	1 En Suite fac 2 Pub.Bath/Show	B&B per person £15.00-£20.00 Single £15.00-£24.00 Double	Open Jan-Dec

Situated in residential area close to main bus route to city centre. No residents lounge but TV in all bedrooms.

EDINBURGH continued	Map 2 D5					
Buchan Guest House 3 Coates Gardens Edinburgh EH12 5LG Tel:031 337 1045	COMMENDED ≋ ≋	2 Single 1 Twin 2 Double 5 Family	7 En Suite fac 1 Limited ensuite 2 Pub.Bath/Show	B&B per person £24.00-£30.00 Single £20.00-£28.00 Double	Open Jan-Dec	

Warm welcome and comfortable stay are assured at this former merchants house. Centrally situated for Princes Street and close to Haymarket Station.

| Buchanan Guest House
97 Joppa Road
Edinburgh
EH15 2HB
Tel:031 657 4117 | COMMENDED ≋ ≋ | 2 Twin
1 Double
1 Family | 1 En Suite fac
1 Pub.Bath/Show | B&B per person
£13.50-£20.00 Double | Open Jan-Dec | |

Comfortable personally run guest house, on major bus route to city centre. Unrestricted parking.

| Cameron Toll Guest House
299 Dalkeith Road
Edinburgh
EH16 5JX
Tel:031 667 2950 | COMMENDED ≋ ≋ ≋ | 2 Single
2 Twin
2 Double
2 Family | 7 En Suite fac
1 Priv.NOT ensuite | B&B per person
£20.00-£30.00 Single
£16.00-£28.00 Double | Open Jan-Dec
Dinner 1800-1900
B&B + Eve.Meal
£23.00-£37.00 | |

Family run guest house with some private parking. Conveniently located on A7 with frequent bus service to city centre. Close to Commonwealth Pool.

| Camus House
4 Seaview Terrace, Joppa
Edinburgh
EH15 2HD
Tel:031 657 2003 | COMMENDED Listed | 1 Twin
2 Double | 1 Priv.NOT ensuite
2 Pub.Bath/Show | B&B per person
£14.00-£20.00 Single
£14.00-£20.00 Double | Open Jan-Dec | |

Late Victorian terraced house with fine sea views. Relaxed and comfortable atmosphere; easy access to the city.

| Carrington Guest House
38 Pilrig Street
Edinburgh
EH6 5AN
Tel:031 554 4769 | | 3 Twin
2 Double
2 Family | 2 En Suite fac
2 Limited ensuite
3 Pub.Bath/Show | B&B per person
£15.50-£25.00 Double | Open Jan-Dec | |

| Castle Park Guest House
75 Gilmore Place
Edinburgh
EH3 9NU
Tel:031 229 1215 | Award Pending | 1 Single
2 Twin
3 Double
1 Family | 2 En Suite fac
2 Limited ensuite
2 Pub.Bath/Show | B&B per person
£13.50-£16.00 Single
£12.50-£16.00 Double | Open Jan-Dec
Dinner 1800-1900 | |

| Chalumna Guest House
5 Granville Terrace
Edinburgh
EH10 4PQ
Tel:031 229 2086 | APPROVED ≋ | 1 Single
2 Twin
2 Double
1 Family | 1 Limited ensuite
2 Pub.Bath/Show | B&B per person
£18.00-£20.00 Single
£15.00-£20.00 Double | Open Jan-Dec | |

Family run guest house in quiet residential area, close to Kings Theatre and within easy reach of Princes Street.

| Classic Guest House
50 Mayfield Road
Edinburgh
EH9 2NH
Tel:031 667 5847 | HIGHLY COMMENDED ≋ | 1 Single
1 Twin
1 Double
1 Family | 3 En Suite fac
1 Priv.NOT ensuite
1 Pub.Bath/Show | B&B per person
£15.00-£25.00 Single
£15.00-£25.00 Double | Open Jan-Dec
Dinner 1800-1900
B&B + Eve.Meal
£25.00-£35.00 | |

Friendly welcome at this family home, recently refurbished to a high standard. Short bus ride from city centre. Non smoking.

EDINBURGH continued	Map 2 D5						
Claymore Guest House 68 Pilrig Street Edinburgh EH6 5AS Tel:031 554 2500	COMMENDED 👑 👑	2 Twin 2 Double 2 Family	3 En Suite fac 1 Priv.NOT ensuite 1 Pub.Bath/Show	B&B per person £15.00-£22.50 Double	Open Jan-Dec		

Red sandstone Victorian terraced villa, a former manse, situated close to the city centre and on the main bus routes.

| Counan Guest House
6 Minto Street
Edinburgh
EH9 1RG
Tel:031 667 4454 | | 1 Twin
3 Double
2 Family | 6 En Suite fac | B&B per person
£12.00-£22.00 Double | Open Jan-Dec | | |

| Crioch Guest House
23 East Hermitage Place
Edinburgh
EH68AO
Tel:031 554 5494 | | 2 Single
3 Twin
1 Family | 2 Pub.Bath/Show | B&B per person
£13.00-£20.00 Single
£13.00-£20.00 Double | Open Jan-Dec | | |

Crion Guest House

33 MINTO STREET, EDINBURGH EH9 2BT

FAX: 031-662 1946 TEL: 031-667 2708

A warm and friendly welcome awaits you at the family-run guest house. Fully refurbished with your comfort in mind, offering outstanding Bed & Breakfast value. Recently completely refurbished, 3 en-suite rooms now available. Conveniently situated within 1½ miles of the City Centre on an excellent bus route. The ideal base to explore Edinburgh's many tourist attractions and visitors centres, i.e. the Castle, Museums and Art Galleries etc. There are also several top-class golf courses in the surrounding area. Near University and Commonwealth Pool. **For enquiries send s.a.e. or telephone.**

| Crion Guest House
33 Minto Street
Edinburgh
EH9 2BT
Tel:031 667 2708
Fax:031 662 1946 | COMMENDED
👑 👑 | 1 Single
2 Twin
2 Double
1 Family | 3 En Suite fac
3 Pub.Bath/Show | B&B per person
£17.00-£20.00 Single
£14.00-£25.00 Double | Open Jan-Dec | | |

Refurbished, friendly family run guest house, close to city centre.

| Cruachan Guest House
53 Gilmore Place
Edinburgh
EH3 9NT
Tel:031 229 6219
Fax:031 229 6219 | APPROVED
Listed | 1 Single
1 Twin
1 Double
2 Family | 1 Pub.Bath/Show | B&B per person
£16.00-£21.00 Single
£14.00-£19.00 Double | Open Jan-Dec | | |

Comfortable family run accommodation close to city centre and major bus routes.

| Daisy Park Guest House
41 Abercorn Terrace, Joppa
Edinburgh
EH15 2DG
Tel:031 669 2503 | COMMENDED
👑 👑 | 1 Single
2 Twin
1 Double
2 Family | 3 Pub.Bath/Show | B&B per person
£16.00-£21.00 Single
£15.00-£21.00 Double | Open Jan-Dec | | |

Family run small guest house with spacious rooms on bus route for city centre. 100 yards from beach. Vegetarians welcome.

EDINBURGH continued	Map 2 D5						
Dalwin Lodge Guest House & Restaurant 75 Mayfield Road Edinburgh EH9 3AA Tel:031 667 2294		COMMENDED ♕	2 Single 1 Twin 1 Double 1 Family	2 Pub.Bath/Show	B&B per person £14.00-£17.00 Single £14.00-£17.00 Double	Open Jan-Dec Dinner 1800-2000	
			Stone terraced house, c100 years old, within walking distance of Observatory and Arthur's Seat, with an inhouse licensed restaurant.				
Dargil Guest House 16 Mayfield Gardens Edinburgh EH9 2BZ Tel:031 667 6177			2 Twin 1 Double 1 Family	2 En Suite fac 2 Pub.Bath/Show	B&B per person £16.00-£22.00 Single £10.00-£22.00 Double	Open Jan-Dec	
Dene Guest House 7 Eyre Place Edinburgh EH3 5ES Tel:031 556 2700		APPROVED Listed	2 Single 3 Twin 2 Family	2 En Suite fac 2 Pub.Bath/Show	B&B per person £18.00-£22.00 Single £17.00-£23.00 Double	Open Jan-Dec	
			Family run, centrally located guest house, close to Botanic Gardens.				
Devon Guest House 2 Pittville Street, Portobello Edinburgh EH15 2BY Tel:031 669 6067		COMMENDED Listed	1 Single 1 Twin 2 Double 2 Family	1 En Suite fac 1 Pub.Bath/Show	B&B per person £15.00-£17.00 Single £15.00-£17.00 Double	Open Jan-Dec	
			Victorian villa in quiet residential cul-de-sac. 100 metres from sandy beach. 4 miles (6kms) to Princes Street. Excellent bus service.				
Dickie Guest House No. 22, East Claremont Street Edinburgh EH7 4JP Tel:031 556 4032 Fax:031 556 9739		COMMENDED ♕ ♕	1 Single 1 Twin 1 Double 1 Family	2 En Suite fac 1 Pub.Bath/Show	B&B per person £19.00-£22.00 Single £18.00-£25.00 Double	Open Jan-Dec	
			Small, friendly and family run; a Victorian town house in a cobbled street only 15 minutes walk from Princes Street. Scottish breakfasts a speciality				
Dukes of Windsor Street 17 Windsor Street Edinburgh EH7 5LA Tel:031 556 6046 Fax:031 556 6046			1 Single 3 Twin 5 Double 1 Family	10 En Suite fac	B&B per person £25.00-£45.00 Single £20.00-£35.00 Double	Open Jan-Dec	
Dunard Guest House 16 Hartington Place Edinburgh EH10 4LE Tel:031 229 6848			2 Single 2 Twin 1 Double	2 Pub.Bath/Show	B&B per person £15.00-£20.00 Single £15.00-£20.00 Double	Open Jan-Dec	
Dunedin Guest House 8 Priestfield Road Edinburgh EH16 5HH Tel:031 668 1949		Award Pending	1 Single 2 Twin 2 Double 1 Family	5 En Suite fac 1 Priv.NOT ensuite 1 Pub.Bath/Show	B&B per person £16.00-£18.00 Single £15.00-£20.00 Double	Open Jan-Dec	

EDINBURGH continued	Map 2 D5

CENTRAL EDINBURGH

Ellesmere House

ELLESMERE HOUSE
11 GLENGYLE TERRACE EDINBUrGH EH3 9LN
TEL: 031-229 4823 FAX: 031-229 5285

Central location overlooking the Meadows area within easy walking distance to most places of interest. Theatre and various good restaurants are situated nearby.
All rooms are decorated and furnished to a very high standard and are equipped with every comfort in mind.
Most rooms are en-suite.

Ellesmere Guest House
11 Glengyle Terrace
Edinburgh
EH3 9LN
Tel:031 229 4823
Fax:031 229 5285

HIGHLY COMMENDED

1 Single	4 En Suite fac
2 Twin	2 Pub.Bath/Show
1 Double	
2 Family	

B&B per person
£17.00-£20.00 Single
£17.00-£28.00 Double

Open Jan-Dec

Terraced house overlooking the Meadows. Side street location but near Kings Theatre and bus routes to city centre.

Falcon Crest Guest House
70 South Trinity Road
Edinburgh
EH5 3NX
Tel:031 552 5294

APPROVED

1 Single	2 Pub.Bath/Show
1 Twin	
1 Double	
2 Family	

B&B per person
£12.00-£20.00 Single
£11.00-£18.00 Double

Open Jan-Dec
Dinner 1730-1900
B&B + Eve.Meal
£16.00-£26.00

Victorian terraced family home in attractive residential area, near main bus route to city centre.

Fountainhall Guest House
40 Fountainhall Road
Edinburgh
EH9 2LW
Tel:031 667 2544

APPROVED

1 Single	3 Pub.Bath/Show
2 Twin	
1 Double	
3 Family	

B&B per person
£16.00-£19.00 Single
£16.00-£19.00 Double

Open Jan-Dec

Victorian house in quiet residential area, 2 miles (3 kms) from City Centre, with public transport nearby.

Four Seasons Guest House
47 Minto Street
Edinburgh
EH9 2BR
Tel:031 667 2963

1 Twin	3 En Suite fac
1 Double	2 Pub.Bath/Show
3 Family	

B&B per person
£15.00-£22.00 Double

Open Jan-Dec

Galloway Guest House
22 Dean Park Crescent
Edinburgh
EH4 1PH
Tel:031 332 3672

COMMENDED

1 Single	6 En Suite fac
3 Twin	2 Pub.Bath/Show
3 Double	
3 Family	

B&B per person
£22.00-£40.00 Single
£17.00-£25.00 Double

Open Jan-Dec

Friendly, family run guest house beautifully restored and situated in a residential area of the city centre. Free street parking.

SPECIAL INTEREST HOLIDAYS
Write for your free brochure on Short Breaks, Activity Holidays, Skiing, to:

Scottish Tourist Board, PO Box 15, Edinburgh EH1 1VY.

Details of Grading and Classification are on page vi.

Key to symbols is on back flap.

EDINBURGH continued	Map 2 D5						
Gifford Guest House 103 Dalkeith Road Edinburgh EH16 5AJ Tel:031 667 4688		COMMENDED ≝ ≝	3 Twin 1 Double 2 Family	3 En Suite fac 2 Limited ensuite 2 Pub.Bath/Show	B&B per person £13.00-£26.00 Double	Open Jan-Dec	
			Situated on one of the main routes into Edinburgh. A well appointed guest house with nearby bus service to city centre. Commonwealth pool 100 metres				
Gil Dun Guest House 9 Spence Street Edinburgh EH16 5AG Tel:031 667 1368		APPROVED ≝	1 Twin 1 Double 4 Family	2 En Suite fac 3 Pub.Bath/Show	B&B per person £15.00-£20.00 Double	Open Jan-Dec	
			Family guest house situated in cul de sac with private parking. Close to Commonwealth Pool and bus route to city centre.				
Gilmore Guest House 51 Gilmore Place Edinburgh EH3 9NT Tel:031 229 5008			1 Single 1 Twin 1 Double 3 Family	1 Limited ensuite 2 Pub.Bath/Show	B&B per person £12.00-£20.00 Single £12.00-£18.00 Double	Open Jan-Dec	
Glenalmond Guest House 25 Mayfield Gardens Edinburgh EH9 2BX Tel:031 668 2392		COMMENDED ≝ ≝	1 Twin 2 Double 2 Family	5 En Suite fac	B&B per person £17.00-£25.00 Double	Open Mar-Oct	
			Personally run guest house with private parking. On main bus route to city centre.				
Glendale House 5 Lady Road Edinburgh EH16 5PA Tel:031 667 6588			1 Single 3 Twin 3 Double 1 Family	3 En Suite fac 3 Pub.Bath/Show	B&B per person £17.00-£25.00 Single £15.00-£19.00 Double	Open Jan-Dec Dinner 1800-1900 B&B + Eve.Meal £20.00-£22.00	
Glenerne Guest House 4 Hampton Terrace Edinburgh EH12 5JD Tel:031 337 1210		COMMENDED ≝ ≝	1 Twin 2 Double	2 En Suite fac 1 Priv.NOT ensuite	B&B per person £21.00-£25.00 Double	Open Jan-Dec	
			Comfortable family home with off street parking within walking distance of city centre. All rooms with private facilities.				
Glenesk Guest House 39 Liberton Brae Edinburgh EH16 6AG Tel:031 664 1529 Fax:031 664 1529		APPROVED Listed	2 Twin 1 Double 1 Family	1 Pub.Bath/Show	B&B per person £15.00-£20.00 Single £13.00-£18.00 Double	Open Jan-Dec Dinner 1800-2000 B&B + Eve.Meal £18.50-£20.50	
			Personally run, small guest house. Convenient for bus route to city centre. Limited car parking available.				
Glenorchy 22 Glenorchy Terrace Edinburgh EH9 2DH Tel:031 667 5708		APPROVED ≝ ≝	1 Single 2 Twin 4 Double 2 Family	3 En Suite fac 6 Limited ensuite 1 Pub.Bath/Show	B&B per person £18.00-£20.00 Single £20.00-£22.00 Double	Open Jan-Dec Dinner from 1800 B&B + Eve.Meal £28.50-£30.50	
			Privately owned Victorian house situated in quiet residential area, convenient for bus routes to city centre. Unrestricted parking.				

EDINBURGH continued	Map 2 D5					
Hamilton House Guest House 12 Moston Terrace Edinburgh EH9 2DE Tel:031 667 2540	COMMENDED ♛	2 Single 1 Twin 1 Double 2 Family	1 En Suite fac 1 Limited ensuite 2 Pub.Bath/Show	B&B per person £16.00-£18.00 Single £16.00-£19.00 Double	Open Jan-Dec Dinner 1800-1830 B&B + Eve.Meal £25.00-£28.00	

Elegant Victorian villa retaining many original features, in quiet residential area convenient for city centre. One room with private facilities.

| The Havrist Guest House 33 Straiton Pl, The Promenade, Portobello Edinburgh EH15 2BH Tel:031 657 3160 Fax:031 657 3160 | Award Pending | 2 Single 1 Twin 2 Double 2 Family | 2 Pub.Bath/Show | B&B per person £12.00-£18.00 Single £10.00-£16.00 Double | Open Jan-Dec | |

| Heatherlea Guest House Mayfield Gardens Edinburgh EH9 2AX Tel:031 667 3958 | | 1 Single 3 Twin 3 Double 3 Family | 4 En Suite fac 2 Pub.Bath/Show | B&B per person £18.00-£25.00 Single £15.00-£20.00 Double | Open Jan-Dec | |

| Heriott Park Guest House 256 Ferry Road Edinburgh EH5 3AN Tel:031 552 6628 | COMMENDED ♛ ♛ | 1 Twin 2 Double 3 Family | 2 En Suite fac 2 Pub.Bath/Show | B&B per person £20.00-£25.00 Single £16.00-£22.00 Double | Open Jan-Dec | |

Panoramic views of castle and city by day and night. Regular bus route to city centre. Car parking opposite. 5 minutes walk to Botanical Gardens.

| Hermitage Guest House 16 East Hermitage Place, Leith Links Edinburgh EH6 8AB Tel:031 555 4868 | Award Pending | 2 Twin 2 Double 1 Family | 2 Pub.Bath/Show | B&B per person £14.00-£20.00 Double | Open Jan-Dec | |

| Highfield Guest House 83 Mayfield Road Edinburgh EH9 3AE Tel:031 667 8717 | COMMENDED ♛ | 1 Single 1 Twin 2 Double 1 Family | 2 Pub.Bath/Show | B&B per person £13.00-£18.00 Single £13.00-£18.00 Double | Open Jan-Dec | |

Stone built Victorian house offering friendly and comfortable accommodation for non-smokers. 10 minutes from city centre on bus routes 40 and 42.

| Highland Park Guest House 16 Kilmaurs Terrace Edinburgh EH16 5DR Tel:031 667 9204 | COMMENDED ♛ | 1 Single 2 Twin 2 Family | 2 Pub.Bath/Show | B&B per person £14.00-£18.00 Single £13.00-£17.00 Double | Open Jan-Dec | |

Victorian stone built house retaining many original features in quiet residential area 1.5 miles (3kms) from city centre. On main bus routes.

EDINBURGH continued	Map 2 D5					

Hillview
22 Hillview, Queensferry Road, Blackhall
Edinburgh
EH4 2AF
Tel:031 343 2969

HIGHLY COMMENDED
👑 👑

1 Double 1 En Suite fac B&B per person Open Jan-Dec
1 Family 1 Priv.NOT ensuite £16.00-£22.00 Double

Elegant Edwardian terraced family home with easy access to the city centre

---

Hopetoun Guest House
15 Mayfield Road
Edinburgh
EH9 2NG
Tel:031 667 7691

COMMENDED
👑

1 Double 2 Pub.Bath/Show B&B per person Open Jan-Dec
2 Family £14.00-£18.00 Double

Completely non-smoking, small, friendly guest house on the south side of the city, 1.5 miles (2.5kms) from Princes Street.

Ivy House Guest House
7 Mayfield Gardens, Newington
Edinburgh
EH9 2AX
Tel:031 667 3411

3 Twin 1 Limited ensuite B&B per person Open Jan-Dec
3 Double 3 Pub.Bath/Show £14.00-£22.00 Double
3 Family

Joppa Turrets Guest House
1 Lower Joppa
Edinburgh
EH15 2ER
Tel:031 669 5806

COMMENDED
👑 👑

1 Single 1 En Suite fac B&B per person Open Jan-Dec
1 Twin 1 Priv.NOT ensuite £13.00-£15.00 Single
3 Double 2 Pub.Bath/Show £13.00-£19.00 Double

Quiet and friendly, with fine sea views and close to sandy beach. Easy access to city centre. Unrestricted street parking.

Kariba Guest House
10 Granville Terrace
Edinburgh
EH10 4PQ
Tel:031 229 3773

COMMENDED
👑 👑

2 Twin 2 En Suite fac B&B per person Open Jan-Dec
4 Double 5 Limited ensuite £16.00-£20.00 Single
2 Family 2 Pub.Bath/Show £16.00-£20.00 Double

A Victorian house on major bus route to city centre about 10 minutes away. Easy access to country areas.

KENVIE GUEST HOUSE
16 Kilmaurs Road, Edinburgh EH16 5DA **031-668 1964**

Quiet and comfortable house situated in a residential area with easy access to City Centre on an excellent bus route. All rooms have tea and coffee-making facilities and TV's. Central heating throughout.

A warm and friendly welcome is guaranteed.

Kenvie Guest House
16 Kilmaurs Road
Edinburgh
EH16 5DA
Tel:031 668 1964

COMMENDED
👑 👑

2 Twin 2 En Suite fac B&B per person Open Jan-Dec
1 Double 2 Pub.Bath/Show £16.00-£20.00 Single
2 Family £16.00-£20.00 Double

Personally run, situated in quiet residential area close to city centre, and on main bus routes.

EDINBURGH continued	Map 2 D5						
Kew Guest House 1 Kew Terrace, Murrayfield Edinburgh EH12 5JE Tel:031 313 4407	Award Pending	1 Single 1 Twin 1 Double 2 Family	2 En Suite fac 2 Pub.Bath/Show	B&B per person £19.00-£23.00 Single £19.00-£26.00 Double	Open Jan-Dec	
Kilmaurs Guest House 9 Kilmaurs Road Edinburgh EH16 5DA Tel:031 667 8315	COMMENDED ♕ ♕	2 Twin 1 Double 2 Family	3 En Suite fac 2 Pub.Bath/Show	B&B per person £18.00-£24.00 Single £16.00-£24.00 Double	Open Jan-Dec	
		Family run guest house in quiet residential area close to Commonwealth Pool and only ten minutes by bus from city centre.				
Kingsley Guest House 30 Craigmillar Park Edinburgh EH16 5PS Tel:031 667 8439	COMMENDED ♕ ♕	2 Twin 1 Double 3 Family	4 En Suite fac 1 Priv.NOT ensuite 2 Pub.Bath/Show	B&B per person £15.00-£20.00 Double	Open Jan-Dec	
		Friendly, comfortable and family run with own off street parking. Easy access to city centre.				
Kingsview Guest House 28 Gilmore Place Edinburgh EH3 9NQ Tel:031 229 8004		1 Single 2 Twin 2 Double 4 Family	1 En Suite fac 4 Limited ensuite 1 Pub.Bath/Show	B&B per person £12.00-£18.00 Single £12.00-£18.00 Double	Open Jan-Dec	
Kirklea Guest House 11 Harrison Road Edinburgh EH11 1EG Tel:031 337 1129/346 7866 Fax:031 337 1129	COMMENDED ♕	2 Single 2 Twin 1 Double 1 Family	1 En Suite fac 2 Pub.Bath/Show	B&B per person £17.00-£21.00 Single £15.00-£21.00 Double	Open Jan-Dec	
		A family run guest house in Victorian terrace convenient for bus routes to city centre and all attractions.				
Kirtle Guest House 8 Minto Street Edinburgh EH9 1RG Tel:031 667 2813 (office) /5353 (guests)	COMMENDED ♕ ♕	3 Double 4 Family	4 En Suite fac 3 Limited ensuite	B&B per person £17.00-£22.00 Double 2 Pub.Bath/Show	Open Jan-Dec	
		On main bus routes for city centre, 1 mile (2kms). Some private car parking available. Close to Commonwealth Pool.				
Kisimul Guest House 16 Claremont Park Edinburgh EH6 7PJ Tel:031 554 4203	COMMENDED Listed	1 Single 2 Twin 3 Double	3 Pub.Bath/Show	B&B per person £13.00-£16.00 Single £13.00-£16.00 Double	Open Jan-Dec	
		Stone built house overlooking Leith Links. Convenient bus routes to city centre.				

	Map 2 D5						
EDINBURGH continued The Lairg 11 Coates Gardens Edinburgh EH12 5LG Tel:031 337 1050 Fax:031 346 2167	APPROVED ♛ ♛	2 Single 3 Twin 2 Double 3 Family	7 En Suite fac 1 Limited ensuite 2 Pub.Bath/Show	B&B per person £17.00-£25.00 Single £17.00-£25.00 Double	Open Jan-Dec Dinner from 1715		
		Personally run guest house with large lounge area. Easy access to city centre and all tourist attractions.					
Lauderville Guest House 52 Mayfield Road Edinburgh EH9 2NH Tel:031 667 7788/4005	COMMENDED ♛	1 Single 1 Twin 2 Double 1 Family	3 En Suite fac 1 Priv.NOT ensuite 1 Pub.Bath/Show	B&B per person £17.00-£25.00 Single £17.00-£25.00 Double	Open Jan-Dec Dinner 1830-1930 B&B + Eve.Meal £25.00-£33.00		
		Family run Victorian terraced guest house, on main bus route into city centre. En-suite facilities available.					
Lindsay Guest House 108 Polwarth Terrace Edinburgh EH11 1NN Tel:031 337 1580 Fax:031 337 9174	COMMENDED Listed	2 Single 3 Twin 2 Double 1 Family	3 En Suite fac 2 Pub.Bath/Show	B&B per person £19.00-£25.00 Single £20.00-£25.00 Double	Open Jan-Dec		
		Semi-detached sandstone house in residential area on bus route to city centre. Car parking; TV in all bedrooms.					
Lorne Villa Guest House 9 East Mayfield Edinburgh EH9 1SD Tel:031 667 7159	COMMENDED Listed	1 Single 2 Double 3 Family	2 En Suite fac 1 Priv.NOT ensuite 2 Pub.Bath/Show	B&B per person £12.00-£18.00 Single £15.00-£25.00 Double	Open Jan-Dec		
		Personally run guest house conveniently situated for city centre bus route with off street parking.					
McIntosh Guest House 20 Downie Terrace, Corstorphine Road Edinburgh EH12 7AU Tel:031 334 3108		1 Twin 2 Double 1 Family	2 Pub.Bath/Show	B&B per person £13.00-£16.00 Double	Open Jan-Dec		
Maple Leaf Guest House 23 Pilrig Street Edinburgh EH6 5AN Tel:031 554 7692		2 Single 2 Twin 2 Double 3 Family	3 En Suite fac 1 Limited ensuite 1 Priv.NOT ensuite 2 Pub.Bath/Show	B&B per person £16.00-£19.00 Single £13.00-£18.00 Double	Open Jan-Dec		

FOR QUALITY GO GRADED

Scottish Tourist Board
COMMENDED
Facilities

EDINBURGH continued	Map 2 D5

MARRAKECH GUEST HOUSE

Family-run hotel situated within walking distance of Botanic Gardens, Castle which overlooks PrincesStreet. Central heating. Àla carte restaurant. Colour TV, radio/clock and tea-making facilities. Children welcome - baby chair, baby cot and a baby-sitter can be arranged.

Contact: Marrakech Guest House, 30 London Street, Edinburgh EH3 6NA.
Tel: 031-556 7293/556 4444. Fax: 031-557 3615
Commended 👑 👑 👑

Marrakech Guest House
30 London Street
Edinburgh
EH3 6NA
Tel:031 556 4444/7293
Fax:031 557 3615

COMMENDED
👑 👑 👑

2 Single
3 Twin
4 Double
2 Family

9 En Suite fac
2 Pub.Bath/Show

B&B per person
£20.00-£30.00 Single
£17.00-£25.00 Double

Open Jan-Dec
Dinner 1800-2200

Family run in New Town. Close to the city centre with its own restaurant serving North African cuisine and featuring many home made specialities.

Marvin Guest House
46 Pilrig Street
Edinburgh
EH6 5AL
Tel:031 554 6605

COMMENDED
👑 👑

1 Single
2 Twin
2 Double
2 Family

2 En Suite fac
2 Pub.Bath/Show

B&B per person
£17.00-£25.00 Single
£14.00-£19.00 Double

Open Jan-Dec

Georgian town house offering personal attention. Good bus service to the city. Some off street parking.

The Mayfield Guest House
15 Mayfield Gardens
Edinburgh
EH9 2AX
Tel:031 667 8049
Fax:031 667 5001

COMMENDED
👑 👑 👑

2 Single
2 Twin
4 Double
3 Family

11 En Suite fac
1 Pub.Bath/Show

B&B per person
£23.00-£32.00 Single
£23.00-£32.00 Double

Open Jan-Dec
Dinner 1830-2030

On main route into the city, convenient for all attractions. Private parking and regular bus service. All rooms double glazed.

The Meadows Guest House

Terraced Flat in quiet location overlooking park. Spacious rooms with colour TV's. Hospitality trays. Most rooms en-suite. Guestaccom Good Room Award. Access & Visa accepted. Metered car parking by day.

Jon & Gloria Stuart, 17 Glengyle Terrace,
Edinburgh EH3 9LN. Tel: 031-229 9559. Fax: 031-229 2226
Scottish Tourist Boards 👑 👑 Commended.

The Meadows Guest House
17 Glengyle Terrace,
Bruntsfield
Edinburgh
EH3 9LN
Tel:031 229 9559
Fax:031 229 2226

COMMENDED
👑 👑

1 Single
2 Twin
1 Double
3 Family

5 En Suite fac
1 Pub.Bath/Show

B&B per person
£20.00-£38.00 Single
£20.00-£24.00 Double

Open Jan-Dec

Quietly situated terraced house overlooking Bruntsfield Links. Convenient for theatre and shops. Family run.

Details of Grading and Classification are on page vi.

Key to symbols is on back flap.

EDINBURGH continued	Map 2 D5					
Menzies Guest House 33 Leamington Terrace Edinburgh EH10 4JS Tel:031 229 4629		APPROVED ♛ ♛	2 Double 5 Family	2 En Suite fac 1 Limited ensuite 2 Pub.Bath/Show	B&B per person £12.50-£22.50 Double	Open Jan-Dec
Situated in residential area near Bruntsfield Links and close to main bus route to city centre. Private parking.						
Meriden Guest House 1 Hermitage Terrace Edinburgh EH10 4RP Tel:031 447 5152/5155			2 Twin 2 Double 1 Family	2 Pub.Bath/Show	B&B per person £14.00-£19.00 Double	Open Jan-Dec
Milton House 24 Duddingston Crescent Edinburgh EH15 3AT Tel:031 669 4072		COMMENDED ♛	1 Twin 3 Double	3 Pub.Bath/Show	B&B per person £16.00-£20.00 Single £15.00-£18.00 Double	Open Jan-Dec
Friendly family atmosphere with off street parking and easy access to the city centre. Adjacent to 9 hole golf course.						
Muffin Guest House 164 Ferry Road Edinburgh EH6 4NS Tel:031 554 4162		COMMENDED Listed	1 Single 1 Twin 2 Double 1 Family	1 En Suite fac 1 Pub.Bath/Show	B&B per person £16.00-£19.00 Single £13.00-£22.00 Double	Open Jan-Dec Dinner 1830-1930 B&B + Eve.Meal £19.00-£28.00
Personally run, situated on main bus route with easy access to town centre and all amenities.						
Newington Guest House 18 Newington Road Edinburgh EH9 1QS Tel:031 667 3356		COMMENDED ♛ ♛	1 Single 2 Twin 3 Double 2 Family	5 En Suite fac 1 Limited ensuite 1 Pub.Bath/Show	B&B per person £26.00-£30.00 Single £18.50-£28.50 Double	Open Jan-Dec
Interestingly furnished Victorian house on main road into city from South. Easy access to centre, most rooms double glazed.						
Park View Villa Guest House 254 Ferry Road Edinburgh EH5 3AN Tel:031 552 3456		COMMENDED ♛ ♛	2 Twin 2 Double 3 Family	4 En Suite fac 2 Pub.Bath/Show	B&B per person £20.00-£26.00 Single £15.00-£20.00 Double	Open Jan-Dec
Victorian villa retaining original woodwork and enjoying panoramic views of the city skyline.						
Parklands Guest House 20 Mayfield Gardens Edinburgh EH9 2BZ Tel:031 667 7184		COMMENDED ♛ ♛	2 Twin 3 Double 1 Family	5 En Suite fac 1 Priv.NOT ensuite	B&B per person £19.00-£25.00 Double	Open Jan-Dec
Look forward to a warm welcome at this late Victorian house with fine woodwork and ceilings, situated on the south side of the city.						

EDINBURGH continued	Map 2 D5						
Pearlview Guest House 2 Seaview Terrace, Joppa Edinburgh EH15 2HD Tel:031 669 8516		COMMENDED Listed	1 Single 1 Twin 1 Double 1 Family	2 En Suite fac 2 Pub.Bath/Show	B&B per person £15.00-£20.00 Single £14.00-£17.00 Double	Open Jan-Dec	
			Family run guest house on main road facing the sea front and 4 miles (7kms) from centre of Edinburgh and all amenities.				
Priestville Guest House Priestville, 10 Priestfield Road Edinburgh EH16 5HJ Tel:031 667 2435		COMMENDED ♕ ♕	1 Twin 2 Double 3 Family	4 En Suite fac 1 Pub.Bath/Show	B&B per person £18.00-£25.00 Single £15.00-£20.00 Double	Open Jan-Dec	
			Semi detached Victorian villa in quiet residential area but close to main bus routes to city centre, about 15 minutes away.				
Quendale Guest House 32 Craigmillar Park Edinburgh EH16 5PS Tel:031 667 3171			1 Single 2 Twin 2 Double 1 Family	2 Pub.Bath/Show	B&B per person from £13.50 Double	Open Jan-Dec	
Ravensdown Guest House 248 Ferry Road Edinburgh EH5 3AN Tel:031 552 5438		COMMENDED ♕	1 Twin 1 Double 5 Family	2 Pub.Bath/Show	B&B per person £15.00-£19.00 Double	Open Jan-Dec	
			Friendly family run guest house on the main bus route to centre. Panoramic view of the city, including the Castle and Arthurs Seat.				
Regis Guest House 57 Gilmore Place Edinburgh EH3 9NT Tel:031 229 4057			2 Single 1 Twin 2 Double 2 Family	1 En Suite fac 1 Limited ensuite 2 Pub.Bath/Show	B&B per person £11.00-£20.00 Single £11.00-£17.00 Double	Open Jan-Dec	
Robertson Guest House 5 Hartington Gardens Edinburgh EH10 4LD Tel:031 229 2652/3862		COMMENDED ♕	1 Single 1 Twin 1 Double 4 Family	1 En Suite fac 2 Pub.Bath/Show	B&B per person £15.00-£20.00 Single £15.00-£20.00 Double	Open Jan-Dec Dinner 1900-2100 B&B + Eve.Meal £25.00-£30.00	
			Friendly, family run guest house situated in quiet residential area of city. Easy access to centre and close to main bus routes.				
Roselea Guest House 4 Kew Terrace Edinburgh EH12 5JE Tel:031 337 8396		COMMENDED ♕ ♕	1 Single 1 Twin 1 Double 2 Family	4 En Suite fac 1 Limited ensuite	B&B per person £20.00-£24.00 Single £18.00-£24.00 Double	Open Feb-Nov	
			Friendly welcome in Listed building, convenient for Haymarket station and on city centre bus route. Spacious bedrooms, most rooms ensuite.				
Roselea House 11 Mayfield Road Edinburgh EH9 2NG Tel:031 667 6115 Fax:031 667 3556		HIGHLY COMMENDED ♕ ♕	2 Twin 1 Double 4 Family	4 En Suite fac 1 Priv.NOT ensuite 1 Pub.Bath/Show	B&B per person £20.00-£28.00 Single £18.00-£28.00 Double	Open Jan-Dec Dinner from 1800	
			Family run guest house on bus route to city centre. A short walk from the Commonwealth Pool and Pollock Halls of Residence.				

EDINBURGH continued	Map 2 D5	Award Pending	1 Twin 2 Double 4 Family	5 En Suite fac 2 Priv.NOT ensuite 2 Pub.Bath/Show	B&B per person £17.00-£20.00 Single £17.00-£20.00 Double	Open Jan-Dec
Rosevale House 15 Kilmaurs Road Edinburgh EH16 5DA Tel:031 667 4781						

Rowan Guest House 13 Glenorchy Terrace Edinburgh EH9 2DQ Tel:031 667 2463	COMMENDED ✧	2 Single 2 Twin 3 Double 2 Family	2 En Suite fac 2 Pub.Bath/Show	B&B per person £17.00-£21.00 Single £16.00-£20.00 Double	Open Jan-Dec

Victorian town house in quiet residential area with easy access to city centre and all amenities.

Rowand Guest House 7 Hermitage Terrace Edinburgh EH10 4RP Tel:031 447 4089	COMMENDED Listed	1 Twin 1 Double 3 Family	1 Limited ensuite 2 Pub.Bath/Show	B&B per person £18.00-£24.00 Single £16.00-£18.00 Double	Open Jan-Dec

Listed building in residential area convenient for city centre. Television in all rooms. Unrestricted parking.

St. Conan's Guest House
30 Minto Street, Edinburgh EH9 1SB
Telephone: 031 667 8393

Edinburgh St. Conan's is situated on the main A772 into Edinburgh. It is easily accessible to the city centre, in an area well served by buses. Accommodation, twin, double, family rooms most with en-suite. All rooms H/C, C/H, T.V, Tea, coffee facilities. Set of keys. Large private car park.

Proprietor: Mrs. M. McGilvary

St Conans Guest House 30 Minto Street Edinburgh EH9 1SB Tel:031 667 8393		2 Twin 3 Double 2 Family	5 En Suite fac 2 Pub.Bath/Show	B&B per person £16.00-£25.00 Single £16.00-£22.00 Double	Open Jan-Dec

St Hilary's House 41-43 Craigmillar Park Edinburgh EH16 5PD Tel:031 667 8005 Fax:031 662 0957		35 Twin	35 En Suite fac 5 Pub.Bath/Show	B&B per person £17.00-£20.00 Double	Open Jul-Aug

St Margaret's Guest House 18 Craigmillar Park Edinburgh EH16 5PS Tel:031 667 2202	COMMENDED ✧ ✧	2 Twin 2 Double 3 Family	1 En Suite fac 1 Limited ensuite 1 Priv.NOT ensuite 2 Pub.Bath/Show	B&B per person £20.00-£25.00 Single £15.00-£20.00 Double	Open Mar-Dec

Well appointed Victorian house with comfortable lounge and thoughtfully decorated bedrooms. Private car park.

EDINBURGH continued	Map 2 D5						
Salisbury Guest House 45 Salisbury Road Edinburgh EH16 5AA Tel:031 667 1264	COMMENDED ♛ ♛	2 Single 3 Twin 4 Double 3 Family	9 En Suite fac 3 Priv.NOT ensuite	B&B per person £20.00-£25.00 Single £18.00-£24.00 Double	Open Jan-Dec		
		Georgian Listed building in quiet conservation area, near Holyrood Park and Royal Commonwealth Pool. (1 mile (2kms) from city centre).					
San Marco Guest House 24 Mayfield Gardens Edinburgh EH9 2BZ Tel:031 667 8982 Fax:031 662 1945	COMMENDED ♛ ♛	2 Twin 2 Double 4 Family	3 En Suite fac 2 Pub.Bath/Show	B&B per person £13.00-£26.00 Double	Open Jan-Dec		
		Friendly guest house with some large spacious rooms, on main A772 route south of the city centre. Some off street parking.					
Shalimar Guest House 20 Newington Road Edinburgh EH9 1QS Tel:031 667 2827/0789		1 Single 2 Twin 2 Double 4 Family	4 En Suite fac 1 Limited ensuite 2 Pub.Bath/Show	B&B per person £20.00-£24.00 Single £16.00-£18.00 Double	Open Jan-Dec		
Sharon Guest House 1 Kilmaurs Terrace Edinburgh EH16 5BZ Tel:031 667 2002 Fax:0506 858160	COMMENDED Listed	2 Single 1 Twin 3 Double 3 Family	2 Pub.Bath/Show	B&B per person £16.00-£22.00 Single £12.00-£20.00 Double	Open Jan-Dec		
		Victorian house in residential area but near bus routes for city centre.					
Sheridan Guest House 1 Bonnington Terrace Edinburgh EH6 4BP Tel:031 554 4107	COMMENDED ♛ ♛	6 Twin 1 Family	2 En Suite fac 1 Priv.NOT ensuite 2 Pub.Bath/Show	B&B per person £16.50-£24.50 Double	Open Jan-Dec		
		Situated in residential area on bus route to city centre and its amenities. No parking restrictions.					

SIX MARY'S PLACE

Raeburn Place, Stockbridge, Edinburgh EH4 1JN

Tel: 031 332 8965   Commended ♛ ♛

A beautiful Georgian Town House in the heart of Edinburgh. Bedrooms have been individually furnished with antiques. Offering a restful, friendly atmosphere and smoke free environment. Emphasising quality wholesome/vegetarian home cooking where guests have the opportunity to eat together.

Bed and Breakfast £20   Details: Elaine Gale, Manager

| Six Mary's Place Guest House 6 Mary's Place Edinburgh EH4 1JH Tel:031 332 8965 | COMMENDED ♛ ♛ | 3 Single 2 Twin 3 Double | 2 En Suite fac 2 Pub.Bath/Show | B&B per person £22.00-£24.00 Single £23.00-£25.00 Double | Open 10 Jan-Dec Dinner 1800-2130 B&B + Eve.Meal £30.00-£32.00 | | |
| | | Restored Georgian townhouse in central location offering vegetarian cuisine and a restful homely atmosphere. | | | | | |

EDINBURGH continued	Map 2 D5						
Sonas Guest House 3 East Mayfield Edinburgh EH9 1SD Tel:031 667 2781	COMMENDED ♛ ♛	1 Single 2 Twin 4 Double 1 Family	8 En Suite fac	B&B per person £18.00-£30.00 Single £18.00-£27.00 Double	Open Jan-Dec		
		Terraced house situated on south sidw of city. With private parking. Convenient bus routes to centre and all amenities.					
Southdown Guest House 20 Craigmillar Park Edinburgh EH16 5PS Tel:031 667 2410	COMMENDED ♛ ♛	2 Twin 2 Double 2 Family	2 En Suite fac 4 Limited ensuite 2 Pub.Bath/Show	B&B per person £18.00-£30.00 Single £16.00-£22.00 Double	Open Feb-Nov		
		Victorian terraced house in residential area on main A7 (A701) road, with many bus routes to city centre. Friendly and family run. Private car park					
Strathmohr Guest House 23 Mayfield Gardens Edinburgh EH9 2BX Tel:031 667 8475	COMMENDED ♛ ♛	2 Twin 1 Double 4 Family	7 En Suite fac 2 Pub.Bath/Show	B&B per person £13.00-£25.00 Double	Open Jan-Dec		
		Built in 1867 this Victorian refurbished property retains many original features. Family run. Easy access to city cntre.					
Straven Guest House 3 Brunstane Road North Edinburgh EH15 2DL Tel:031 669 5580	COMMENDED ♛ ♛	2 Twin 2 Double 3 Family	7 En Suite fac	B&B per person £18.00-£27.00 Single £18.00-£25.00 Double	Open Jan-Dec		
		Semi detached Victorian villa in a quiet residential area just off the beach in Joppa. 5 miles (8kms) from Edinburgh city centre.					

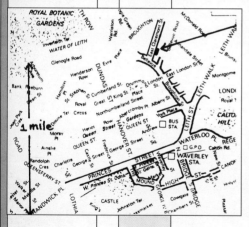

Stuart House

Gloria Stuart invites you to experience hospitality and a truly warm welcome in her traditional Old Town House in City-centre. Beautifully renovated and decorated, the 7 comfortable bedrooms, each with private bath/showerroom, are thoughtfully equipped with TV, telephone, hospitality-tray and hairdryer. Delicious breakfast in elegant Dining Room. **No Smoking throughout.**

12 East Claremont Street, Edinburgh EH7 4JP Scotland
Phone 031 557 9030   Fax 031 557 0563

| Stuart House 12 East Claremont Street Edinburgh EH7 4JP Tel:031 557 9030 Fax:031 557 0563 | HIGHLY COMMENDED ♛ ♛ | 1 Single 2 Twin 3 Double 1 Family | 6 En Suite fac 1 Priv.NOT ensuite | B&B per person £30.00-£50.00 Single £30.00-£35.00 Double | Open Jan-Dec Dinner 1700-2130 B&B + Eve.Meal £36.00-£56.00 | | |
| | | Comfortable, Georgian style house (c1860) situated in the historic New Town. Close to the city centre and Princes Street. | | | | | |

EDINBURGH continued	Map 2 D5						
Sylvern Guest House 22 West Mayfield Edinburgh EH9 1TQ Tel:031 667 1241		COMMENDED Listed	2 Twin 1 Double 3 Family	4 En Suite fac 2 Pub.Bath/Show	B&B per person £17.00-£20.00 Double	Open Jan-Dec	
			Detached Victorian House in residential area. Private parking and convenient for main bus routes. Four rooms en suite.				
Tania Guest House 19 Minto Street Edinburgh EH9 1RQ Tel:031 667 4144		Award Pending	1 Single 1 Twin 1 Double 3 Family	1 En Suite fac 1 Pub.Bath/Show	B&B per person £15.00-£24.00 Single £12.50-£20.00 Double	Open Jan-Dec	
Taylor Guest House 10 Grove Street Edinburgh EH3 8BB Tel:031 229 7739		Award Pending	2 Twin 2 Double	2 Pub.Bath/Show	B&B per person £15.00-£18.50 Single £15.00-£17.50 Double	Open Jan-Dec	
The Thirty-Nine Steps Guest House 62 South Trinity Road Edinburgh EH5 3NX Tel:031 552 1349		COMMENDED	1 Single 2 Twin 1 Double 3 Family	3 Pub.Bath/Show	B&B per person £16.50-£20.00 Single £14.50-£18.00 Double	Open Jan-Dec	
			Victorian terraced house in quiet residential area. Convenient bus route for city centre. Unrestricted parking.				
Tiree Guest House 26 Craigmillar Park Edinburgh EH16 5PS Tel:031 667 7477			1 Single 2 Twin 1 Double 1 Family	3 En Suite fac 1 Limited ensuite 2 Pub.Bath/Show	B&B per person £14.00-£18.00 Single £16.00-£24.00 Double	Open Jan-Dec	
Torivane Guest House 1 Morton Street Edinburgh EH15 2EW Tel:031 669 1648		COMMENDED Listed	1 Single 1 Double 1 Family	1 Pub.Bath/Show	B&B per person £13.00-£16.00 Single £13.00-£16.00 Double	Open Feb-Nov	
			Stone built house on main bus route to city centre. A one minute walk to beach and seafront promenade.				
The Town House 65 Gilmore Place Edinburgh EH3 9NU Tel:031 229 1985		COMMENDED	1 Single 2 Twin 1 Double 1 Family	3 En Suite fac 1 Pub.Bath/Show	B&B per person £18.00-£23.00 Single £18.00-£26.00 Double	Open Jan-Dec	
			A Victorian terraced family house built in 1876. Situated in a residential area within easy walking distance of the town centre.				
Turret Guest House 8 Kilmaurs Terrace Edinburgh EH16 5DR Tel:031 667 6704		HIGHLY COMMENDED	1 Single 2 Twin 2 Double 1 Family	3 En Suite fac 1 Limited ensuite 2 Pub.Bath/Show	B&B per person £16.00-£20.00 Single £13.00-£25.00 Double	Open Jan-Dec	
			Recently refurbished Victorian house in quiet residential area. Convenient for buses to city centre. Commonwealth Pool nearby.				

EDINBURGH continued	Map 2 D5						
Villa Nina Guest House 39 Leamington Terrace Edinburgh EH10 4JS Tel:031 229 2644		APPROVED Listed	1 Twin 2 Double 1 Family	3 Limited ensuite 2 Pub.Bath/Show	B&B per person £13.00-£16.50 Double	Open Jan-Dec	♿ V ⏷ ▢ ☕ ▥ 🖨 ⏷ ▥ ⏷ T
			Terraced house, close to bus routes to city centre, near King's Theatre and Bruntsfield Links.				
Belford Youth Hostel 6/8 Douglas Gardens Edinburgh EH4 3DA Tel:031 225 6209			2 Double 18 Family	9 Pub.Bath/Show	B&B per person £9.45-£14.00 Single	Open Jan-Dec Dinner 1800-2030	V ⏷ ▥ ▥ TV ● ♫ ▥ ⏷ 🖨 ▥ ⏷ 🔒 ⚒ 🏠 🔍
Jewel & Esk Valley College 24 Milton Road East Edinburgh EH15 2PP Tel:031 669 8461/ ext 292/222 Fax:031 657 2276			244 Single 4 Double	42 Pub.Bath/Show	B&B per person £18.50-£22.85 Single £18.50-£22.85 Double	Open Jan-Nov Dinner 1800-1930 B&B + Eve.Meal £19.45-£23.95	♿ ▥ V S C ⏷ ▥ ▥ TV ● ▥ ⏷ 🖨 ⏷ ✳ P ▥ ⏷ 🔒 ⚒ 🖼 ⏷ 🌐 🏠 🔍 �️
Melvin House 3 Rothesay Terrace Edinburgh EH3 7RY Tel:031 220 6715/ext 222 Fax:031 225 9107		Award Pending	20 Single 5 Twin 1 Family	6 Pub.Bath/Show	B&B per person £21.50-£24.00 Single £21.00 Double	Open Jan-Dec	♿ C ⏷ ☕ ▥ ⏷ TV ⏷ ● ▥ ⏷ ⏷ 🏠 ▥ ⏷ ⏷ SP 🔒 🏠
Napier University St Andrews Hall of Resid., 219 Colinton Rd Edinburgh EH14 1DJ Tel:031 444 2266/ext 4621 Fax:031 445 7209			62 Single 57 Twin	1 En Suite fac 31 Pub.Bath/Show	B&B per person £17.60-£18.70 Single £17.60-£18.70 Double	Open Apr, Jul-Sep Dinner 1800-1930 B&B + Eve.Meal £26.10-£27.70	♿ ▥ V S C ▥ ⏷ ▥ ▥ TV ⏷ ● ▥ ⏷ ⏷ ✳ P ▥ ⏷ ⏷ 🔒 ⚒ 🏠 ⏷ 🔍 🌐 �️
Patrick Geddes Hall Mound Place Edinburgh EH1 2LU Tel:031 225 8400			14 Single 29 Twin	12 Pub.Bath/Show	B&B per person £14.50-£24.00 Single £14.50-£24.00 Double	Open Jul-Sep Dinner 1830-1930 B&B + Eve.Meal £21.75-£31.25	♿ V C ⏷ ☕ M ▥ TV ▥ ⏷ 🖨 ▥ ⏷ 🔒 ⚒ ⏷ T 🏠
Pollock Halls of Residence 18 Holyrood Park Road Edinburgh EH16 5AY Tel:031 667 1971 Fax:031 668 3217			850 Single	140 Pub.Bath/Show	B&B per person £14.50-£24.00 Single £14.50-£24.00 Double	Open Mar-Apr, Jun-Sep Dinner 1800-1900 B&B + Eve.Meal £21.75-£31.25	♿ ▥ V S C ⏷ ☕ ▥ ▥ TV ⏷ ● ▥ ⏷ 🖨 ✳ P ▥ ⏷ ⏷ 🔒 ⏷ ⏷ T 🏠 🔍 �️

EDZELL **Angus** Central Hotel 18-20 Church Street Edzell Angus DD9 7TQ Tel:(Edzell) 0356 648218 Fax:0356 647480	Map 4 F1		2 Single 10 Twin 6 Double 1 Family	11 En Suite fac 3 Pub.Bath/Show	B&B per person £20.00-£30.00 Single £15.00-£21.50 Double	Open Jan-Dec Dinner 1900-2030 B&B + Eve.Meal £22.00-£34.50
Glenesk Hotel High Street Edzell Angus DD9 7TF Tel:(Edzell) 0356 648319 Fax:0356 647333		**COMMENDED** 👑 👑 👑 👑	6 Single 11 Twin 6 Double 2 Family	23 En Suite fac 1 Pub.Bath/Show	B&B per person from £44.00 Single from £38.00 Double	Open Jan-Dec Dinner from 1930
			Family run hotel with sports complex including an indoor swimming pool. **Golf course, with fishing and shooting available locally**			
ELGIN **Moray** Braelossie Hotel 2 Sheriffmill Road Elgin Moray IV30 1SB Tel:(Elgin) 0343 547181	Map 4 D8		3 Single 6 Twin 2 Double 2 Family	11 En Suite fac 2 Limited ensuite 1 Pub.Bath/Show	B&B per person £25.00-£35.00 Single £26.00-£28.00 Double	Open Jan-Dec Dinner 1700-2000 B&B + Eve.Meal £37.00-£50.00
Eight Acres Hotel Sheriffmill Elgin Moray IV30 3UN Tel:(Elgin) 0343 543077/543078 Fax:0343 540001			19 Single 25 Twin 8 Double 5 Family	55 En Suite fac 2 Limited ensuite 1 Pub.Bath/Show	B&B per person £25.00-£55.00 Single £20.00-£35.00 Double	Open Jan-Dec Dinner 1800-2100 B&B + Eve.Meal £35.00-£68.50
Laichmoray Hotel Maisondieu Road Elgin Moray IV30 1QR Tel:(Elgin) 0343 540045 Fax:0343 540055		**HIGHLY** **COMMENDED** 👑 👑 👑	16 Single 11 Twin 6 Double 1 Family	33 En Suite fac 1 Pub.Bath/Show	B&B per person £36.00-£48.00 Single £30.00-£36.00 Double	Open Jan-Dec Dinner 1700-2130 B&B + Eve.Meal £38.00-£45.00
			Listed building in town centre close to railway station. Function suite available. **New "Scotch Corner" distillery Theme Bar.**			

Scotland for Golf ...

Find out more about golf in Scotland. There's more to it than just
the championship courses so get in touch with us now for
information on the hidden gems of Scotland.

Write to: **Information Unit, Scottish Tourist Board,
23 Ravelston Terrace, Edinburgh EH4 3EU
or call: 031-332 2433.**

ELGIN continued

Map 4
D8

Mansfield House Hotel Mayne Road Elgin Moray IV30 1NY Tel:(Elgin) 0343 540883 Fax:0343 552491	**HIGHLY COMMENDED** 👑 👑 👑 👑	5 Single 4 Twin 6 Double 2 Family	17 En Suite fac	B&B per person £55.00 Single £35.00-£45.00 Double	Open Jan-Dec Dinner 1830-2200 B&B + Eve.Meal from £62.50	
		Completely refurbished home with a la carte restaurant conveniently situated near centre of Elgin.				

Mansion House Hotel
THE HAUGH, ELGIN, MORAY IV30 1AW
Telephone: 0343-548811

The charm of the past with ultimate up-to-date comfort in a peaceful setting by the riverside, surrounded by mature trees. Only minutes walk from the ancient city of Elgin, all the facilities on can imagine are available on our doorstep. The standard of cuisine matches the most demanding expectations. The Country Club, which is overlooked by the "Dip Inn" Bistro and snooker room is comprised of an indoor swimming pool, spa, sauna, turkish bath, solarium, sophisticated gymnasium. Attractive four-poster weekend and packages are available. An ideal base for Whisky, Castle and Golf Trails.

The Mansion House Hotel & Country Club The Haugh Elgin Moray IV30 1AW Tel:(Elgin) 0343 548811 Fax:0343 547916	**HIGHLY COMMENDED** 👑 👑 👑	4 Twin 16 Double	20 En Suite fac	B&B per person £75.00-£90.00 Single £55.00-£70.00 Double	Open Jan-Dec Dinner 1930-2130	
		19c Scots baronial mansion with a castellated tower. Quietly situated overlooking the River Lossie. Tastefully restored and decorated.				

Sunninghill Hotel Hay Street Elgin Moray IV30 1NH Tel:(Elgin) 0343 547799	**COMMENDED** 👑 👑 👑	3 Single 2 Twin 2 Double 3 Family	10 En Suite fac 1 Pub.Bath/Show	B&B per person £30.00-£42.00 Single £25.00-£35.00 Double	Open Jan-Dec Dinner 1700-2100	
		Victorian house, modern extension with annexe accommodation. Near centre of historic Cathedral town. Many golf courses. Sandy beaches 5 miles (8kms)				

Torr House Hotel 8 Moss Street Elgin Moray IV30 1LU Tel:(Elgin) 0343 542661		4 Twin 2 Double 1 Family	2 En Suite fac 2 Pub.Bath/Show	B&B per person from £18.50 Single £16.00-£19.00 Double	Open Jan-Dec Dinner 1800-1900 B&B + Eve.Meal £20.00-£23.00	

ELGIN continued **Moray** The Lodge Guest House 20 Duff Avenue Elgin Moray IV30 1QS Tel:(Elgin) 0343 549981	Map 4 D8	COMMENDED ≈ ≈	4 Single 2 Twin 1 Double 1 Family	8 En Suite fac	B&B per person from £15.00 Single from £15.00 Double	Open Jan-Dec Dinner 1830-2000 B&B + Eve.Meal from £25.00

Recently refurbished listed villa in extensive grounds with private parking. Quietly situated but handy for all amenities.

BY ELGIN **Moray** Ardgye House Elgin Moray IV30 3UP Tel:(Alves) 034385 618	Map 4 D8	HIGHLY COMMENDED ≈ ≈	1 Single 2 Twin 3 Double 3 Family	3 En Suite fac 3 Limited ensuite 3 Priv.NOT ensuite 2 Pub.Bath/Show	B&B per person £14.00-£16.00 Single £14.00-£16.00 Double	Open Jan-Dec

Gracious Edwardian mansion in own extensive grounds easily accessible from A96. 3 miles (5kms) from Elgin. Private facilities available.

ELIE **Fife** Golf Hotel Bank Street Elie Fife KY9 1EF Tel:(Elie) 0333 330209 Fax:0333 330381	Map 2 E3		2 Single 14 Twin 4 Double 2 Family	22 En Suite fac	B&B per person £30.00-£45.00 Single £30.00-£45.00 Double	Open Jan-Dec Dinner 1900-2130 B&B + Eve.Meal £45.00-£60.00

The Elms 14 Park Place Elie Fife KY9 1DH Tel:(Elie) 0333 330404		COMMENDED ≈ ≈ ≈	1 Single 3 Twin 1 Double 2 Family	4 En Suite fac 2 Pub.Bath/Show	B&B per person £23.50-£45.00 Single £18.00-£24.00 Double	Open Apr-Sep Dinner from 1900 B&B + Eve.Meal £28.00-£34.00

Privately owned detached Victorian house with large secluded garden, in picturesque coastal village with sandy beach, local golf courses, walks.

ELPHIN **Sutherland** Mr T Strang, Assynt Guided Holidays Birchbank Holiday Lodge, Knockan Elphin, by Lairg Sutherland IV27 Tel:(Strathkanaird) 085486 203/215 Fax:085486 215	Map 3 G5	COMMENDED ≈	1 Twin 2 Double 1 Family	2 En Suite fac 2 Pub.Bath/Show	B&B per person £15.00-£17.00 Single £15.00-£17.00 Double	Open Jan-Dec Dinner at 1930 B&B + Eve.Meal £27.00-£31.00

Peaceful rural location, modern holiday lodge 14 miles (22kms) north of Ullapool. Hosts Tom and Ray offer a wide range of activity holidays.

ETTRICK BRIDGE **by Selkirk, Selkirkshire** Ettrickshaws Hotel Ettrick Bridge,by Selkirk Selkirkshire TD7 5HW Tel:(Ettrick Bridge) 0750 2229	Map 2 D7	COMMENDED ≈ ≈ ≈ ≈	3 Twin 2 Double 1 Family	6 En Suite fac	B&B per person £45.00-£55.00 Single £33.00-£38.00 Double	Open Feb-Nov Dinner 1900-2030 B&B + Eve.Meal £47.00-£52.00

Elegantly furnished Victorian country house, overlooking Ettrick Water with private fishing. Noted for food and wines.

EVIE Orkney	Map 5 B1	COMMENDED ♔ ♔ ♔	1 Single 2 Twin 2 Double 1 Family Suites avail.	3 En Suite fac 2 Pub.Bath/Show	B&B per person £28.00-£35.00 Single £20.00-£32.00 Double	Open Jan-Dec Dinner 1900-2030 B&B + Eve.Meal £31.00-£46.00
Woodwick House Evie Orkney KW17 2PQ Tel:(Evie) 085675 330						

Peace and seclusion in idyllic surroundings. 12 acres of wooded grounds with views to the islands. Imaginative fresh food.

EYEMOUTH Berwickshire	Map 2 G5		1 Single 4 Double 2 Family	2 Pub.Bath/Show	B&B per person from £18.00 Single from £17.00 Double	Open Jan-Dec Dinner 1900-2130
Ship Hotel Harbour Road Eyemouth Berwickshire TD14 5HT Tel:(Eyemouth) 08907 50224						

FALKIRK Stirlingshire	Map 2 B4	COMMENDED ♔ ♔ ♔ ♔	9 Single 15 Twin 6 Double 3 Family	33 En Suite fac	B&B per person £61.00-£75.00 Single £35.00-£45.00 Double	Open Jan-Dec Dinner 1900-2100 B&B + Eve.Meal £70.00-£75.00
Friendly Hotel Manor Street Falkirk Stirlingshire FK1 1NT Tel:(Falkirk) 0324 24066 Fax:0324 611785						

Town centre hotel adjacent to, and with direct access to, new shopping centre. Function and conference facilities for up to 220 persons

Hotel Cladhan			2 Single 23 Twin 11 Double 1 Family Suite avail.	37 En Suite fac	B&B per person £45.00-£50.00 Single £35.00-£38.00 Double	Open Jan-Dec Dinner 1700-2200 B&B + Eve.Meal from £45.00
Kemper Avenue Falkirk Stirlingshire FK1 1UF Tel:(Falkirk) 0324 27421						

FEARNAN, by Kenmore Perthshire	Map 2 A1	COMMENDED ♔ ♔	3 Single 2 Twin 2 Double 1 Family	3 En Suite fac 2 Pub.Bath/Show	B&B per person £23.00-£18.10 Single from £23.00 Double	Open Apr-Oct Dinner 1900-2000 B&B + Eve.Meal from £35.00
Tigh-an-Loan Hotel Fearnan, Aberfeldy Perthshire PH15 2PF Tel:(Kenmore) 0887 830249						

Personally run hotel, beautifully situated on the shores of Loch Tay, with splendid views. Some rooms with private facilites.

TELEPHONE DIALLING CODES

Many telephone dialling codes have changed this year. If you experience difficulty in connecting a call, please call Directory Enquiries – **192** – where someone will issue the correct number. Please note: a charge will be placed for this service when using a private telephone

FI...
FIONNPHORT – FORRES...
FIONNPHORT
Isle of Mull, Argyll
Achaban Guest House
Fionnphort, Isle of Mull

| FENWICK
by Kilmarnock,
Ayrshire
Fenwick Hotel
A77 Ayr Road
Fenwick, by Kilmarnock
Ayrshire
KA3 6AU
Tel:(Fenwick) 0560 600478
Fax:0560 600334 | Map 1
H6 | Award
Pending | 1 Single
4 Twin
4 Double
1 Family | 10 En Suite fac | B&B per person
£29.00-£45.00 Single
£20.00-£27.50 Double | | |

| FINSTOWN
Orkney
Atlantis Lodges
Finstown
Orkney
KW17 2EH
Tel:(Finstown) 085676 581
Fax:085687 5361 | Map 5
B1 | COMMENDED
♛ ♛ ♛ | 8 Twin
2 Double

Self contained ground floor apartments. At waters edge with birds and seals watching you eat breakfast. | 10 En Suite fac | B&B per person
£19.75-£27.75 Single
£18.00-£25.00 Double | Open Jan-Dec
Dinner 1830-2100
B&B + Eve.Meal
£27.75-£38.00 | (symbols) |

| FINTRY
Stirlingshire | Map 2
A4 | | | | | | |

Culcreuch Castle Hotel
Culcreuch Castle, Fintry, Stirlingshire G63 0LW
Telephone: (036 086) 228/555

Magnificent 1600-acre parkland estate in breath-taking scenery. 700-year-old Culcreuch is a unique opportunity to sample the historic atmosphere of Central Scotland's oldest inhabited castle. Comfortable accommodation, cosy bar, licensed restaurant, free fishing and boating, adjacent squash courts, log fires, warm welcome. Central for all Scotland's attractions, including Edinburgh (55 minutes by road). For free brochures on accommodation, fishing and golf:—

Contact: Laird of Culcreuch, Culcreuch Castle, Stirlingshire G63 0LW. Tel: (036086) 555.

| Culcreuch Castle
Culcreuch Castle Country
Park
Fintry
Stirlingshire
G63 0LW
Tel:(Fintry) 036086 228/555
Fax:036086 556 | | COMMENDED
♛ ♛ ♛ | 2 Twin
5 Double
1 Family

14C castle with Dungeon Bar set in 1600 acre estate, with impressive views of Campsie Hills. Good base for touring central Scotland. | 8 En Suite fac | B&B per person
£45.00-£70.00 Single
£35.00-£60.00 Double | Open Jan-Dec
Dinner 1900-2030
B&B + Eve.Meal
£55.00-£80.00 | (symbols) |

| | Map 1 B3 | COMMENDED ♕ | 1 Single
3 Twin
2 Double
1 Family | 2 Pub.Bath/Show | B&B per person
to £18.00 Single
to £18.00 Double | Open Mar-Dec
Dinner to 1900
B&B + Eve.Meal
to £25.00 | |
| ...se
... Mull, Argyll
...A66 6BL
Tel:(Fionnphort) 06817 205 | | | | | | | |

Former manse overlooking Loch Pottie. Imaginative cooking, emphasis on fresh local produce.

FLICHITY
Inverness-shire
The Grouse & Trout Hotel
Flichity, Farr
Inverness-shire
IV1 2XE
Tel:(Farr) 08083 314

Map 4 B9 — Award Pending

8 Twin / 3 Double / 1 Family / Suites avail. 12 En Suite fac

B&B per person
£35.00-£40.00 Single
£20.00-£32.50 Double

Open Mar-Dec
Dinner 1800-2115
B&B + Eve.Meal
£40.00-£50.00

FORFAR
Angus
Royal Hotel
Castle Street
Forfar
Angus
DD8 3AE
Tel:(Forfar) 0307
62691/462691

Map 2 D1 — COMMENDED ♕ ♕ ♕

5 Single / 6 Twin / 7 Double / 1 Family 19 En Suite fac

B&B per person
£39.50 Single
£32.50 Double

Open Jan-Dec
Dinner 1900-2100
B&B + Eve.Meal
£45.00-£55.00

Privately owned hotel in town centre, with leisure facilities, function suite, hairdressing salon and two restaurants. Meals served all day.

FORRES
Moray
Carisbrooke Hotel
Drumduan Road
Forres
Moray
IV36 0QT
Tel:(Forres) 0309 672585

Map 4 C8 — APPROVED ♕ ♕

3 Single / 5 Twin / 3 Family 8 En Suite fac / 3 Pub.Bath/Show

B&B per person
£28.50-£40.00 Single
£23.00-£25.00 Double

Open Jan-Dec
Dinner from 1700
B&B + Eve.Meal
£30.00-£40.00

Privately run hotel on east side of town close to A96 and Kinloss airbase. Annexe accommodation.

Parkmount House Hotel
St Leonard's Road
Forres
Moray
IV36 0DW
Tel:(Forres) 0309 673312
Fax:0309 673312

COMMENDED ♕ ♕ ♕

4 Twin / 1 Double / 3 Family 8 En Suite fac

B&B per person
£40.00-£45.00 Single
£30.00-£40.00 Double

Open Feb-Nov
Dinner 1900-2030
B&B + Eve.Meal
£45.00-£60.00

Family run Victorian stone built house with a large garden. Emphasis on fresh food and local produce.

FORRES continued	Map 4 C8		

RAMNEE HOTEL
Victoria Road, Forres, Morayshire IV36 0BN
Tel: 0309 672410 Fax: 0309 673392
Consistently commended for quality cuisine, service and true Scottish hospitality. This charming Country House Hotel has been tastefully refurbished and retains a distinguishable ambience and character. Enjoying a delightful garden setting adjacent to magnificent Britain in Bloom floral displays. Ideally located for golfing, malt whisky, coastal and castle trails.

Ramnee Hotel Victoria Road Forres Moray IV36 0BN Tel:(Forres) 0309 672410 Fax:0309 673392	COMMENDED 👑 👑 👑 👑	2 Single 8 Twin 8 Double 2 Family 20 En Suite fac	B&B per person £45.00-£50.00 Single £34.00-£40.00 Double	Open Jan-Dec Dinner 1800-2100 B&B + Eve.Meal £51.00-£67.00

Close to the River Findhorn and golf course, imposing Victorian mansion house refurbished to high standard. Noted cuisine, hospitality and service.

BY FORRES Moray	Map 4 C8		

KNOCKOMIE HOTEL
GRANTOWN ROAD, FORRES, MORAY IV36 0SG
Telephone: (0309) 673146   Fax: (0309) 673290
Delightfully set in secluded grounds overlooking Forres. Excellent cuisine, complemented by a fine cellar. Being close to the Whisky Trail, the bar has an enviable selection of malt whiskies. Golf, fishing, stalking, shooting and riding can be arranged or just relax and enjoy the beautiful scenery of the Moray coastline.

Knockomie House Hotel Grantown Road Forres Moray IV36 0SG Tel:(Forres) 0309 673146 Fax:0309 673290	COMMENDED 👑 👑 👑 👑	8 Twin 6 Double 14 En Suite fac	B&B per person £55.00-£80.00 Single £37.50-£45.00 Double	Open Jan-Dec Dinner 1830-2100 B&B + Eve.Meal £60.50-£103.00

19c listed country house of warmth and character in extensive grounds. Enterprising menu and wine list. Taste of Scotland.

The Old Mill Inn Brodie by Forres Moray IV36 0TD Tel:(Brodie) 03094 412	APPROVED 👑	1 Twin 2 Double 1 Family 1 Pub.Bath/Show	B&B per person £15.00 Single £30.00 Double	Open Jan-Dec Dinner 1600-2200 B&B + Eve.Meal £21.00-£35.00

Historic, former granary mill, now a restaurant and bar with accommodation in two rooms. 3 miles (5kms) from to Forres.

FORSINARD **Sutherland** Forsinard Hotel Forsinard Sutherland KW13 6YT Tel:(Halladale) 06417 221 Fax:06417 259	Map 4 B4		3 Single 3 Twin 3 Double 1 Family	10 En Suite fac 1 Pub.Bath/Show	B&B per person from £25.00 Single	Open Jan-Dec Dinner 1930-2030
FORT AUGUSTUS **Inverness-shire** The Brae Hotel Fort Augustus Inverness-shire PH32 4DG Tel:(Fort Augustus) 0320 6289/366289	Map 3 H1	HIGHLY COMMENDED	2 Single 2 Twin 4 Double	5 En Suite fac 1 Pub.Bath/Show	B&B per person to £20.00 Single £23.00-£27.00 Double	Open Mar-Oct, New Year Dinner 1900-2030 B&B + Eve.Meal £34.00-£45.00
			Comfortable hotel with emphasis on good food. Panoramic views of Caledonian Canal and Great Glen. Ideal for walking and touring Highlands.			
Caledonian Hotel Fort Augustus Inverness-shire PH32 4BQ Tel:(Fort Augustus) 0320 6256/6450/366256/ 366450		APPROVED	1 Single 3 Twin 4 Double 3 Family	7 En Suite fac 2 Pub.Bath/Show	B&B per person £18.50-£30.00 Single £18.50-£26.00 Double	Open Apr-Sep Dinner 1900-2100 B&B + Eve.Meal £33.00-£40.00
			Warm welcome at this family run hotel overlooking Benedictine Abbey. 32 miles (53 kms) from Inverness and Fort William.			
Inchnacardoch Lodge Hotel Loch Ness by Fort Augustus Inverness-shire PH32 4BL Tel:(Fort Augustus) 0320 6258/366258		COMMENDED	2 Twin 6 Double 4 Family	12 En Suite fac	B&B per person £40.00-£55.00 Single £27.50-£35.00 Double	Open Mar-Nov Dinner 1900-2030 B&B + Eve.Meal £42.50-£49.50
			Country house hotel on north of Fort Augustus with fine views of Loch Ness and surrounding hills. Ideal base for touring and outdoor activities.			
Lovat Arms Hotel Fort Augustus Inverness-shire PH32 4DU Tel:(Fort Augustus) 0320 6206/6204/366206/366204 Fax:0320 6677/366677		COMMENDED	2 Single 7 Twin 8 Double 4 Family	21 En Suite fac 4 Pub.Bath/Show	B&B per person £29.50-£36.50 Single £29.50-£36.50 Double	Open Jan-Dec Dinner 1900-2030 B&B + Eve.Meal £46.00-£57.00
			Privately owned spacious hotel with many traditional features. Close to Benedictine Abbey, Loch Ness and Caledonian Canal.			
FORTINGALL **Perthshire** Fortingall Hotel Fortingall,by Aberfeldy Perthshire PH15 2NQ Tel:(Kenmore) 0887 830367	Map 2 A1	APPROVED	3 Twin 3 Double 3 Family	9 En Suite fac 3 Pub.Bath/Show	B&B per person £28.00-£32.00 Single £24.00-£28.00 Double	Open Jan-Dec Dinner 1900-2100 B&B + Eve.Meal £38.00-£45.00
			Family run country hotel situated in fine Conservation area. Located 2 miles (3kms) from Loch Tay; ideal for fishing, golf and sailing.			
FORTROSE **Ross-shire** Royal Hotel Union Street Fortrose Ross-shire IV10 8TD Tel:(Fortrose) 0381 20236/620236	Map 4 B8		2 Single 2 Twin 4 Double 2 Family	5 En Suite fac 2 Pub.Bath/Show	B&B per person £20.00-£28.00 Single £16.50-£22.00 Double	Open Jan-Dec Dinner 1715-2030

 VAT is shown at 17.5%: changes in this rate may affect prices. Prices shown are for guidance only. Please send SAE with each enquiry

| FORT WILLIAM
Inverness-shire | Map 3
G1 | | |

ALEXANDRA HOTEL
The Parade, Fort William PH33 6AZ
Tel (0397) 702241 Fax (0397) 705554

Alexandra Hotel is part of the very fabric of Fort William. Choice of restaurants, nicely furnished bedrooms with all modern gadgetry – is worthy of its AA 3-star commendation. Centrally situated off the town Parade near shops and local amenities.

MILTON HOTEL
North Road, Fort William PH33 6TG
Tel (0397) 702331 Fax (0397) 703695

Nothing is overlooked except Ben Nevis! Special care taken of shoppers: great woollens everywhere – walkers: fabulous terrain – skiiers: the Ben Nevis range is a miniature Switzerland – heritage lovers: the Battle of Inverlochy took place in 1646 where the lounge is now! Don't fancy walking? Take a cable car instead. Modern 2-star, all bedrooms with bathrooms, first-class evening entertainment

With other hotels in Oban, Inverness and Stirling, we can offer you many holiday ideas from our Scottish Holiday brochure.

Car touring programmes, centred or short breaks, rail inclusive and all-inclusive packages starting at only £119 for five days.

**Call our Central Reservations:
0397-703139**

| Alexandra Hotel
The Parade
Fort William
Inverness-shire
PH33 6AZ
Tel:(Fort William) 0397
702241
Tlx:777210
Fax:0397 705554 | COMMENDED
👑 👑 👑
👑 | 20 Single
61 Twin
8 Double
8 Family | 97 En Suite fac | B&B per person
£39.00-£59.00 Single
£29.00-£46.00 Double | Open Jan-Dec
Dinner 1800-2300
B&B + Eve.Meal
£36.00-£74.00 | |

Large modernised hotel, situated in town centre. Some rooms with views of the surrounding hills and lochside.

Clan Macduff Hotel
Achintore Road, Fort William, Inverness-shire PH33 6RW.
Tel: (0397) 702341, Fax: (0397) 706174

Situated overlooking Loch Linnhe, public rooms have outstanding views of magnificent Highland scenery. Well appointed bedrooms with colour television and hospitality tray. Large choice dinner menu and wine list. All day lounge service. This family hotel is dedicated to providing good quality economic accommodation. Dinner, bed and breakfast from £30.00.

| Clan MacDuff Hotel
Fort William
Inverness-shire
PH33 6RW
Tel:(Fort William) 0397
702341
Fax:0397 706174 | COMMENDED
👑 👑 👑 | 1 Single
12 Twin
20 Double
3 Family | 26 En Suite fac
3 Pub.Bath/Show | B&B per person
£15.00-£25.00 Single
£15.00-£24.00 Double | Open Apr-Oct
Dinner 1830-2000
B&B + Eve.Meal
£25.00-£35.00 | |

Friendly family run hotel, lochside setting but close to Fort William.

FORT WILLIAM continued	Map 3 G1

Croit Anna Hotel Fort William Inverness-shire PH33 6RR Tel:(Fort William) 0397 702268 Fax:0397 704099	COMMENDED ♚♚♚	18 Single 57 Twin 14 Double 3 Family	80 En Suite fac 12 Pub.Bath/Show	B&B per person £18.00-£36.00 Single £16.00-£33.00 Double	Open Apr-Oct Dinner 1900-2030 B&B + Eve.Meal £28.00-£51.00	
		Modern hotel on the outskirts of Fort William overlooking Loch Linnhe. Hotel shop, games room, launderette and function room.				
Grand Hotel Fort William Inverness-shire PH33 6DX Tel:(Fort William) 0397 702928 Fax:0397 705060	COMMENDED ♚♚♚	3 Single 17 Twin 6 Double 4 Family	30 En Suite fac	B&B per person from £25.00 Single from £25.00 Double	Open Jan-Dec Dinner 1730-2030 B&B + Eve.Meal from £38.00	
		Modern purpose built hotel in the centre of town. Good touring base for Lochaber.				
Highland Hotel Union Road Fort William Inverness-shire PH33 6QY Tel:(Fort William) 0397 702291		27 Single 61 Twin 23 Double 1 Family	112 En Suite fac	B&B per person £42.00-£50.00 Single £38.00-£46.00 Double	Open Mar-Nov Dinner 1830-2000 B&B + Eve.Meal £48.00-£58.50	

Imperial Hotel Fort William Inverness-shire PH33 6DW Tel:(Fort William) 0397 702040/703921 Fax:0397 706277	COMMENDED ♚♚♚	6 Single 17 Twin 10 Double 1 Family	34 En Suite fac	B&B per person £35.00-£45.00 Single £25.00-£35.00 Double	Open Jan-Dec Dinner 1845-2045 B&B + Eve.Meal £40.00-£50.00	
		Family run hotel in town centre. Easy access to all of Lochaber's wonderful attractions.				

INNSEAGAN HOUSE HOTEL
FORT WILLIAM
"The hotel for the independant guest"

Innseagan House Hotel is situated on the shores of Loch Linnhe, only 1½ miles from the centre of Fort William and has spectacular views over the loch and surrounding mountains. Our guests are accommodated in modern bedrooms with private bathrooms, tea making facilities and television. Many bedrooms have views over the loch. The cocktail lounge, main lounge and dining room all offer superlative views. We offer you the following checklist of your requirements if you are planning a holiday in the West Highlands

LOCATION		**BEDROOM FACILITIES**	
Central Location for touring	✔	Private bathrooms	✔
Superb Loch side location	✔	Teamaking facilities	✔
Spectacular views	✔	Television	✔
		Radio Alarms	✔

HOTEL FACILITIES		**MEALS**	
Relaxing and friendly atmosphere	✔	Full breakfast	✔
Large car parks	✔	Packed lunch available	✔
Cocktail lounge	✔	Choice of menu for dinner	✔
Loch views from public rooms	✔	Tour planning assistance	✔
Own grounds	✔	Value for money	✔

Scottish Tourist Board Commendation ✔

INNSEAGAN HOUSE HOTEL
offers you all this and more

DINNER, BED AND FULL BREAKFAST
from £29.95 per person

— Send now for a colour brochure —

Innseagan House Hotel
Achintore Road, Fort William, PH33 6RW
Telephone: 0397 702452 Fax: 0397 702606

	Map 3 G1						
FORT WILLIAM **continued** Innseagan House Hotel Achintore Road Fort William Inverness-shire PH33 6RW Tel:(Fort William) 0397 702452 Fax:0397 702606		COMMENDED ♛ ♛ ♛	1 Single 8 Twin 15 Double	21 En Suite fac 1 Pub.Bath/Show	B&B per person £25.00-£30.00 Single £20.00-£25.00 Double	Open Apr-Oct Dinner 1800-1900 B&B + Eve.Meal £29.00-£34.00	
Family managed and standing in its own grounds. Panoramic views of Loch Linnhe and the mountains.							
Inverlochy Castle Hotel Torlundy,by Fort William Inverness-shire PH33 68N Tel:(Fort William) 0397 702177 Fax:0397 702953		DELUXE ♛ ♛ ♛ ♛ ♛	1 Single 15 Twin	16 En Suite fac 2 Pub.Bath/Show	B&B per person £135.00-£150.00 Single £100.00-£120.00 Double	Open Mar-Nov Dinner 1930-2130	
Privately owned and personally managed Scottish Baronial home standing in 50 acres of attractive grounds. Finest produce used in period dining room.							
Mercury Hotel Achintore Road Fort William Inverness-shire PH33 6RW Tel:(Fort William) 0397 703117 Tlx:8778454 Fax:0397 700550		COMMENDED ♛ ♛ ♛ ♛	12 Single 47 Twin 14 Double 13 Family	86 En Suite fac	B&B per person £30.00-£58.00 Single £20.00-£38.00 Double	Open Jan-Dec Dinner 1830-2100 B&B + Eve.Meal £34.00-£51.00	
Modern hotel situated on the edge of the town overlooking Loch Linnhe.							
Milton Hotel North Road Fort William Inverness-shire PH33 6TG Tel:(Fort William) 0397 702331 Tlx:777210 Fax:0397 703695		COMMENDED ♛ ♛ ♛	24 Single 85 Twin 7 Double 7 Family	123 En Suite fac	B&B per person £34.00-£49.00 Single £24.50-£34.50 Double	Open Mar-Nov Dinner 1830-2030 B&B + Eve.Meal £34.00-£59.00	
Modern hotel in its own grounds beside A82 road to Inverness,about 1 mile (2kms) from the town centre.							

The Moorings Hotel

Banavie, Fort William
Inverness-shire PH33 7LY.   ♛ ♛ ♛ ♛
Tel: 0397 772 797   HIGHLY COMMENDED

Situated alongside the Caledonian Canal, THE MOORINGS HOTEL offers splendid panoramic views of Ben Nevis and surrounding Mountains. Fort William's premier 3-star AA and RAC hotel. Award-winning restaurant offering superb cuisine featuring the best in Scottish produce complemented by an outstanding selection of wines. Additionally, Mariners Cellar Wine Bar serves fireside Bistro meals. 24 bedrooms, all en-suite with telephone, satellite TV and hospitality trays. Elegant canal-side lounge and lounge bar. Ideal touring base, open all year, with excellent sporting facilities; fishing and ski-ing nearby.

The Moorings Hotel Banavie,by Fort William Inverness-shire PH33 7LY Tel:(Corpach) 0397 772797 Fax:0397 772441		HIGHLY COMMENDED ♛ ♛ ♛ ♛	1 Single 7 Twin 15 Double 1 Family	24 En Suite fac	B&B per person £35.00-£70.00 Single £25.00-£45.00 Double	Open Jan-Dec Dinner 1900-2130 B&B + Eve.Meal £49.00-£69.00	
Family run hotel, 3 miles (5kms) west of Fort William at the south end of the Caledonian Canal. Some annexe accommodation.							

FORT WILLIAM continued	Map 3 G1		

NEVIS BANK HOTEL

Belford Road, Fort William PH33 6BY
Tel: 0397-705721. Fax: 0397-706275

Nestling in the foothills of Ben Nevis yet only 10 minutes walk from the town centre.

This Best Western hotel has been tastefully modernised. All rooms having private facilities, colour TV, telephone and complimentary hospitality tray.

Both bars stock real ales and a wide range of malt whiskies with a wholesome bar lunch and supper menu.

Our Country Kitchen Restaurant provides thoughtfully prepared menus for a relaxing evening meal and traditional Scottish Breakfasts. DB&B from £34.50 per person.

For colour brochure - contact Jim Lee, Manager.

Nevis Bank Hotel Belford Road Fort William Inverness-shire PH33 6BY Tel:(Fort William) 0397 705721 Fax:0397 706275	COMMENDED ≈≈≈ ≈	6 Single 16 Twin 14 Double 3 Family	39 En Suite fac	B&B per person £42.00-£49.00 Single £29.00-£34.00 Double	Open Jan-Dec Dinner 1900-2100 B&B + Eve.Meal £34.00-£65.00
		Privately owned hotel situated on A82 at Glen Nevis access road. Ideally situated for touring and business. Some annexe accommodation.			
Stag's Head Hotel (Fort William Ltd) High Street Fort William Inverness-shire PH33 6DH Tel:(Fort William) 0397 704144 Fax:0397 705060/706279		11 Single 10 Twin 10 Double 3 Family	29 En Suite fac 3 Pub.Bath/Show	B&B per person from £25.00 Single from £25.00 Double from £38.00	Open Feb-Dec Dinner 1830-2100 B&B + Eve.Meal
West End Hotel High Street Fort William Inverness-shire PH33 Tel:(Fort William) 0397 702614 Fax:0397 706279	COMMENDED ≈≈≈ ≈	7 Single 23 Twin 18 Double 3 Family	51 En Suite fac	B&B per person £25.00-£37.50 Single £25.00-£35.00 Double	Open Jan-Dec Dinner 1900-2030 B&B + Eve.Meal £40.00-£50.00
		Family run hotel in the centre of Fort William overlooking Loch Linnhe. Ideal base for touring the West Highlands.			
Achintee Farm Guest House Glen Nevis Fort William Inverness-shire PH33 6TE Tel:(Fort William) 0397 702240/705899	COMMENDED ≈≈	1 Single 1 Twin 3 Double	2 En Suite fac 1 Pub.Bath/Show	B&B per person to £18.00 Single to £18.00 Double	Open Jan-Dec Dinner 1900-2100 B&B + Eve.Meal to £28.00
		Farmhouse in Glen Nevis, at the start of the path to Ben Nevis & the end of the West Highland Way. About 2 miles (3 kms) from town centre.			

	Map 3 G1						
FORT WILLIAM continued Ashburn House Achintore Road Fort William Inverness-shire PH33 6RQ Tel:(Fort William) 0397 706000 Fax:0397 706000		**HIGHLY COMMENDED** ⛲ ⛲	1 Single 1 Twin 3 Double 1 Family	6 En Suite fac 2 Pub.Bath/Show	B&B per person £20.00-£30.00 Single £15.00-£30.00 Double	Open Feb-Nov	
			Family run totally refurbished Victorian villa in its own grounds, with magnificent views across the Loch. Short distance from town centre.				
Ben View Guest House Belford Road Fort William Inverness-shire PH33 6ER Tel:(Fort William) 0397 702966			1 Single 2 Twin 5 Double 1 Family	8 En Suite fac 6 Pub.Bath/Show	B&B per person £15.00-£18.00 Single £15.00-£21.00 Double	Open Feb-Nov Dinner 1845-1930 B&B + Eve.Meal £23.00-£28.00	
Ceilearadh Achintore Road Fort William Inverness-shire PH33 Tel:(Fort William) 0397 703542			2 Twin 3 Double 1 Family	6 En Suite fac	B&B per person £13.00-£18.00 Double	Open Jan-Dec	
Craig Nevis Guest House Belford Road Fort William Inverness-shire PH33 6BU Tel:(Fort William) 0397 702023			1 Twin 3 Double 2 Family	2 Pub.Bath/Show	B&B per person from £14.00 Single from £13.00 Double	Open Jan-Dec	
Crolinnhe Grange Road Fort William Inverness-shire PH33 6JF Tel:(Fort William) 0397 702709		**DELUXE** ⛲ ⛲	1 Twin 3 Double 1 Family	1 En Suite fac 2 Pub.Bath/Show	B&B per person from £19.00 Double	Open Mar-Nov	
			Family run detached Victorian villa c1880, refurbished to a high standard. Friendly and welcoming atmosphere. Large colourful garden. Superb views.				
Daraich Guest House Cameron Road Fort William Inverness-shire PH33 6LQ Tel:(Fort William) 0397 702644			1 Single 2 Family	2 Pub.Bath/Show	B&B per person £14.00-£15.00 Single £14.00-£15.00 Double	Open Jan-Dec	

FORT WILLIAM continued	Map 3 G1

DISTILLERY HOUSE

Situated at the entrance to Glen Nevis, just 5 minutes from the town centre, Distillery House is set in the extensive grounds of the former Glenlochy Distillery with views over the River Nevis.

The House has been upgraded to high standards to offer the discerning visitor all modern conveniences.

Tariff for Bed and Breakfast £28.00 (per person sharing).

Contact: Mr D Claase, Distillery House, North Road, Fort William PH33 6LR. Telephone: 0397 700103.

Distillery House, Glenlochy Distillery North Road Fort William Inverness-shire PH33 6LR Tel:(Fort William) 0397 700103 Fax:0397 706277	**HIGHLY COMMENDED** ≋ ≋	1 Single 4 Twin 3 Double 1 Family	6 En Suite fac 1 Priv.NOT ensuite 1 Pub.Bath/Show	B&B per person £25.00-£35.00 Single £20.00-£32.00 Double	Open Jan-Dec

Distillery house at old Glenlochy Distillery in Fort William. Beside A82, the road to the Isles and Ben Nevis.

The Factors House Torlundy, by Fort William Inverness-shire PH33 6SN Tel:(Fort William) 0397 705767 Tlx:776229 Fax:0397 702953		1 Twin 5 Double	6 En Suite fac	B&B per person £47.00-£58.75 Single £30.00-£42.00 Double	Open mid Mar-mid Nov Dinner 1900-2130 B&B + Eve.Meal £65.00-£75.00

GLENLOCHY GUEST HOUSE
NEVIS-BRIDGE . FORT WILLIAM   (0397) 702909

This comfortable, family run guest house is set in its own spacious grounds, halfway between Town Centre and Ben Nevis, overlooking River Nevis. Eight bedrooms have en-suite facilities. All rooms have colour TV and tea/coffee facilities. Rooms serviced to a high standard daily.

Glenlochy Guest House Nevis Bridge Fort William Inverness-shire PH33 6PF Tel:(Fort William) 0397 702909	**COMMENDED** ≋ ≋	4 Twin 5 Double 1 Family	8 En Suite fac 1 Pub.Bath/Show	B&B per person £17.00-£22.00 Single £14.00-£22.00 Double	Open Jan-Dec

Detached house with garden situated at Nevis Bridge, midway between Ben Nevis and the town centre. 0.5 miles (1km) to railway station.

Glen Shiel Guest House Achintore Road Fort William Inverness-shire PH33 6RW Tel:(Fort William) 0397 702271	**COMMENDED** ≋ ≋	1 Twin 3 Double 1 Family	2 En Suite fac 1 Priv.NOT ensuite 2 Pub.Bath/Show	B&B per person from £13.50 Double	Open Apr-Oct

Modern house on the outskirts of the town with excellent views over Loch Linnhe. Good touring base.

FORT WILLIAM continued	Map 3 G1

GUISACHAN HOUSE Tel/Fax: 0397-703797
ALMA ROAD, FORT WILLIAM, INVERNESS-SHIRE PH33 6HA

Beautifully situated overlooking Loch Linnhe and Ardgour Hills, within 5 mins walking distance of town centre, rail and bus stations. Most rooms have private facilities, TV, tea-making. There is a comfortable lounge where you can enjoy a drink from our well-stocked bar.
♕♕♕ Commended

Guisachan Guest House Alma Road Fort William Inverness-shire PH33 6HA Tel:(Fort William) 0397 703797/704447	COMMENDED ♕ ♕ ♕	2 Single 5 Twin 6 Double 3 Family	15 En Suite fac 1 Pub.Bath/Show	B&B per person £16.00-£24.00 Single £17.00-£24.00 Double	Open Jan-Dec Dinner from 1830 B&B + Eve.Meal £25.00-£32.00	

Family run establishment within easy walking distance of town centre, rail and bus stations. Home cooking. Some annexe accommodation.

Hillview Guest House Achintore Road Fort William Inverness-shire PH33 6RW Tel:(Fort William) 0397 704349	COMMENDED ♕ ♕	1 Single 1 Twin 4 Double 2 Family	3 En Suite fac 2 Pub.Bath/Show	B&B per person £15.00-£16.00 Single £13.00-£16.50 Double	Open Jan-Dec	

Family run guest house over looking Loch Linnhe and about 1.5 miles (2.5kms) from Fort William.

Lochiel Villa Guest House Achintore Road Fort William Inverness-shire PH33 6RQ Tel:(Fort William) 0397 702379/703616	COMMENDED ♕ ♕	1 Twin 6 Double 1 Family	3 En Suite fac 3 Pub.Bath/Show	B&B per person £15.00-£24.00 Double	Open Feb-Nov	

Granite semi-villa with open views over Loch Linnhe. 500 yards (450 mts) from town centre.

LOCHVIEW GUEST HOUSE
Heathercroft Road, Fort William PH33 6RE
Telephone: 0397 703149

Lochview is situated on the hillside above the town in a quiet location with panoramic views over Loch Linnhe and the Ardgour Hills.
All bedrooms are tastefully decorated and have private facilities, colour TV and tea/coffee facilities. There is a large garden and private parking.

Lochview Guest House Heathercroft, off Argyll Terrace Fort William Inverness-shire PH33 6RE Tel:(Fort William) 0397 703149	COMMENDED ♕ ♕	1 Single 2 Twin 5 Double	8 En Suite fac	B&B per person £20.00-£25.00 Single £16.00-£21.00 Double	Open Apr-Oct	

Situated on a hillside above the town giving panoramic views over Loch Linnhe and the Ardgour Hills.

FORT WILLIAM continued Orchy Villa Guest House Alma Road Fort William Inverness-shire PH33 6HA Tel:(Fort William) 0397 702445	Map 3 G1		4 Family	3 Pub.Bath/Show	B&B per person £12.50-£15.50 Single £12.50-£15.50 Double	Open Jan-Dec	

Rhu Mhor Guest House Alma Road Fort William Inverness-shire PH33 6BP Tel:(Fort William) 0397 702213		**COMMENDED** Listed	3 Twin 2 Double 2 Family	2 Pub.Bath/Show	B&B per person £14.30-£15.50 Single £14.30-£15.50 Double	Open Apr-Sep Dinner from 1900 B&B + Eve.Meal £22.80-£24.50	

Large family house with extensive wild garden in quiet area above town. Short distance from town centre and all amenities.

Saray Guest House Achintore Road Fort William Inverness-shire Tel:(Fort William) 0397 704422		**Award Pending**	6 Double	6 En Suite fac	B&B per person £12.00-£30.00 Double	Open Jan-Oct	

Thistle Bank Guest House Cameron Road Fort William Inverness-shire PH33 6LQ Tel:(Fort William) 0397 702700			1 Twin 2 Double	2 Pub.Bath/Show	B&B per person £14.50-£16.00 Single £14.50-£16.00 Double	Open Dec-Oct	

BY FORT WILLIAM Inverness-shire Glen Loy Lodge Hotel Banavie,by Fort William Inverness-shire PH33 7PD Tel:(Spean Bridge) 0397712 700	Map 3 G1	**COMMENDED** ♔ ♔ ♔	2 Single 3 Twin 4 Double	5 En Suite fac 2 Pub.Bath/Show	B&B per person £14.50-£18.00 Single £14.50-£18.00 Double	Open Mar-Oct Dinner from 1900 B&B + Eve.Meal £25.00-£27.50	

Peace and quiet are assured in this secluded house 6 miles (10kms) from centre of Fort William. Magnificent views of Aonach Mor and the mountains.

Mansefield Guest House Corpach,by Fort William Inverness-shire PH33 7LT Tel:(Corpach) 0397 772262		**COMMENDED** ♔ ♔	1 Twin 2 Double 2 Family	1 En Suite fac 2 Pub.Bath/Show	B&B per person £15.00-£20.00 Single £15.00-£18.00 Double	Open Jan-Dec Dinner from 1900 B&B + Eve.Meal £25.00-£30.00	

Victorian house with its own garden. 3 miles (5kms) from Fort William, on the road to Mallaig. Home cooking and preserves, fresh produce.

FOYERS Inverness-shire The Foyers Hotel Lochness-side Inverness Inverness-shire IV1 2XT Tel:(Gorthleck) 04563 216/0456 486216	Map 4 A1	**COMMENDED** ♔ ♔	2 Single 5 Double 2 Family	2 Limited ensuite 3 Pub.Bath/Show	B&B per person £16.00-£20.00 Single £14.00-£25.00 Double	Open Jan-Dec Dinner 2000-2200 B&B + Eve.Meal £22.00-£33.00	

Situated in an elevated position in its own grounds with fine views across Loch Ness. Excellent walks to Falls and fishing available.

	Map 4 A1	Award Pending	4 Twin 5 Double 3 Family	12 En Suite fac	B&B per person £15.00-£23.50 Single £15.00-£23.50 Double	Open Jan-Dec Dinner 1900-2100 B&B + Eve.Meal £25.00-£33.50	
FOYERS continued Craigdarroch House Foyers South Loch Ness Side Inverness-shire IV1 2XU Tel:(Gorthleck) 0456 486400 Fax:0456 486444							

| Foyers Bay House Foyers Inverness-shire IV1 2YB Tel:(Gorthleck) 0456 486624 Fax:0456 486337 | | COMMENDED ♕ ♕ ♕ | 2 Twin 1 Double | 3 En Suite fac | B&B per person £20.00-£27.00 Single £18.00-£23.00 Double | Open Jan-Dec Dinner 1800-2000 B&B + Eve.Meal £24.00-£32.00 | |

Friendly welcome at modernised Victorian house overlooking Loch Ness and set in 4 acres of ground. 500 yards from Falls of Foyers.

| **FRASERBURGH** **Aberdeenshire** Saltoun Arms Hotel Saltoun Square Fraserburgh Aberdeenshire AB43 5DA Tel:(Fraserburgh) 0346 518282 Fax:0346 515882 | Map 4 H7 | Award Pending | 2 Single 9 Twin 2 Double 1 Family | 14 En Suite fac | B&B per person from £32.00 Single from £22.50 Double | Open Jan-Dec Dinner 1700-2100 B&B + Eve.Meal £32.50-£35.00 | |

| **FREUCHIE** **Fife** Lomond Hills Hotel Parliament Square Freuchie, by Falkland Fife KY7 7EY Tel:(Falkland) 0337 57329 Fax:0337 57498 | Map 2 D3 | COMMENDED ♕ ♕ ♕ ♕ | 1 Single 11 Twin 9 Double 3 Family | 24 En Suite fac 1 Pub.Bath/Show | B&B per person £44.00-£48.00 Single £31.00-£33.00 Double | Open Jan-Dec Dinner 1830-2100 B&B + Eve.Meal £57.00-£63.00 | |

Set in rolling countryside, hotel with leisure facilites, in the centre of the village which won the 1992 "Village in Bloom" award.

HERE'S THE DIFFERENCE

STB's scheme has two distinct elements, grading and classification.

GRADING:

measures the quality and condition of the facilities and services offered, eg, the warmth of welcome, quality of food and its presentation, condition of decor and furnishings, appearance of buildings, tidiness of grounds and gardens, condition of lighting and heating and so on.
Grading awards are: **Approved, Commended, Highly Commended, Deluxe.**

CLASSIFICATION:

measures the range of physical facilities and services offered, eg, rooms with private bath, heating, reception, lounges, telephones and so on.
Classification awards are: **Listed or from one to five crowns.**

GAIRLOCH Ross-shire	Map 3 F7

Creag Mor Hotel

**GAIRLOCH,
WESTER ROSS IV21 2AH
Tel: (0445) 2068 Fax: (0445) 2044**

Luxurious family run hotel, overlooking old harbour. Golf course, sandy beaches and Inverewe Gardens all nearby. Trout and salmon fishing available. Wine and dine in our superb restaurant specialising in salmon, trout, venison and locally landed seafoods. Over 100 whiskies to choose from. Exhibition of original watercolours on view and for sale.

Creag Mor Hotel Gairloch Ross-shire IV21 2AH Tel:(Gairloch) 0445 2068 Fax:0445 2044	COMMENDED ✿ ✿ ✿ ✿ ✿	1 Single 7 Twin 7 Double 2 Family Suite avail.	17 En Suite fac	B&B per person £21.00-£38.00 Single £21.00-£38.00 Double	Open Jan-Dec Dinner 1700-2200 B&B + Eve.Meal £40.00-£59.00

Family run hotel situated in landscaped gardens with trout pond and bowling green, overlooking the old harbour. Sandy beaches, golf courses nearby.

Myrtle Bank Hotel

LOW ROAD, GAIRLOCH ROSS-SHIRE IV21 2BS Tel: 0445-2004

MYRTLE BANK is a small, family-run hotel on the waterfront with panoramic views over to the Isle of Skye. Ideally situated for touring Wester Ross. Golf course, watersports, Heritage Museum all nearby with the Famous Inverewe Gardens only 10 minutes away.
All rooms have private facilities, colour TV, tea/coffee-making facilities. Come and enjoy our superb meals and excellent wine list served in our dining room overlooking the bay. Bar meals served daily.
Special rates for children. Open all year.
Colour brochure from: Myrtle Bank Hotel, Low Road, Gairloch IV21 2BS

Myrtle Bank Hotel Gairloch Ross-shire IV21 2BS Tel:(Gairloch) 0445 2004 Fax:0445 2214	COMMENDED ✿ ✿ ✿	1 Single 5 Twin 3 Double 3 Family	12 En Suite fac	B&B per person £31.00-£36.00 Single £31.00-£36.00 Double	Open Jan-Dec Dinner 1830-2100 B&B + Eve.Meal £48.00-£53.00

Family run hotel, situated on waterfront with views over Gairloch towards Isle of Skye. Restaurant and bar meals available.

The Old Inn Gairloch Ross-shire IV21 2BD Tel:(Gairloch) 0445 2006 Fax:0445 2445	COMMENDED ✿ ✿ ✿	1 Single 6 Twin 4 Double 3 Family	14 En Suite fac	B&B per person £24.50-£36.50 Single £24.50-£36.50 Double	Open Jan-Dec Dinner 1800-2100 B&B + Eve.Meal £29.50-£55.00

18C coaching inn in picturesque setting near sea-loch and hills. All rooms ensuite with colour TV. Specialities include Real Ale and Malt Whisky.

GAIRLOCH

GAIRLOCH continued	Map 3 F7						
Shieldaig Lodge Hotel Gairloch Ross-shire IV21 2AW Tel:(Badachro) 044583 250 Fax:044583 305			8 Twin 5 Double	8 En Suite fac 2 Priv.NOT ensuite 4 Pub.Bath/Show	B&B per person £32.00-£44.00 Single £27.00-£38.00 Double	Open Apr-Nov Dinner 1915-2015 B&B + Eve.Meal £49.00-£60.00	
Birchwood Guest House Gairloch Ross-shire IV21 2AH Tel:(Gairloch) 0445 2011	COMMENDED 👑 👑		2 Twin 3 Double 1 Family	6 En Suite fac 1 Pub.Bath/Show	B&B per person from £20.00 Single from £20.00 Double	Open Apr-Oct	
			Personally run, completely refurbished house in elevated position affording excellent views over harbour. All rooms with ensuite facilities.				
Charleston Guest House Gairloch Ross-shire IV21 2AH Tel:(Gairloch) 0445 2497	COMMENDED 👑		2 Single 2 Twin 2 Double 3 Family	2 Pub.Bath/Show	B&B per person from £16.00 Single from £16.00 Double	Open Apr-Oct Dinner from 1900 B&B + Eve.Meal from £21.00	
			Large 18C house, situated on sea-loch overlooking Gairloch harbour. Personally run, all home cooking. Children and pets welcome.				
Horisdale House Strath Gairloch Ross-shire IV21 2DA Tel:(Gairloch) 0445 2151	COMMENDED 👑		2 Single 2 Twin 1 Double 1 Family	1 Priv.NOT ensuite 4 Pub.Bath/Show	B&B per person £15.00-£17.00 Single £15.00-£16.00 Double	Open May-Sep Dinner from 1900 B&B + Eve.Meal £25.00-£27.00	
			Modern detached house with attractive garden and excellent views. Home cooking with emphasis on fresh produce. Regret no pets allowed.				
Kerrysdale House Gairloch Ross-shire IV21 2AL Tel:(Gairloch) 0445 2292	COMMENDED 👑 👑		1 Twin 2 Double	2 En Suite fac 1 Priv.NOT ensuite	B&B per person £18.00-£20.00 Double	Open Feb-Nov Dinner from 1900 B&B + Eve.Meal £26.50-£28.50	
			18C farmhouse recently refurbished and tastefully decorated. Modern comforts in a peaceful setting. 1 mile (2kms) south of Gairloch.				
Little Lodge North Erradale Gairloch Ross-shire IV21 2DS Tel:(North Erradale) 044585 237	HIGHLY COMMENDED 👑 👑 👑		1 Twin 2 Double	3 En Suite fac	B&B per person	Open Feb-Dec Dinner 1900-2000 B&B + Eve.Meal £30.50-£35.50	
			Peaceful crofthouse off the beaten track 7 miles (11kms) from Gairloch. Wood burning stove. Emphasis on good food using local produce.				
The Mountain Restaurant & Lodge Strath Square Gairloch Ross-shire IV21 2BX Tel:(Gairloch) 0445 2316	COMMENDED 👑 👑		1 Twin 2 Double	1 En Suite fac 2 Priv.NOT ensuite	B&B per person £19.95-£39.90 Single £19.95-£24.95 Double	Open Mar-Nov Dinner 1830-2230 B&B + Eve.Meal from £29.90	
			In Gairloch's main square, with views across the bay. Day time coffee shop dinners by candlelight in an informal atmosphere.				
Strathgair Guest House Gairloch Ross-shire IV21 2BT Tel:(Gairloch) 0445 2118			2 Twin 1 Double	3 Pub.Bath/Show	B&B per person £15.00-£16.00 Single £15.00-£16.00 Double	Open Apr-Aug Dinner from 1830 B&B + Eve.Meal £25.00-£26.00	

GAIRLOCH continued
Map 3 F7

Whindley Guest House
Auchtercairn
Gairloch
Ross-shire
IV21 2BN
Tel:(Gairloch) 0445 2340

COMMENDED ♛ ♛ ♛

1 Twin
1 Double
2 Family

4 En Suite fac

B&B per person
£14.00-£20.00 Double

Open Jan-Dec
Dinner 1850-2000
B&B + Eve.Meal
£22.75-£28.75

Modern bungalow with large garden in elevated position, with fine views overlooking Gairloch Bay. Some annexe accommodation with steep access.

GALASHIELS
Selkirkshire
Map 2 E6

Abbotsford Arms Hotel
Stirling Street
Galashiels
Selkirkshire
TD1 1BY
Tel:(Galashiels) 0896 2517

COMMENDED ♛ ♛ ♛

3 Single
5 Twin
3 Double
3 Family

10 En Suite fac
2 Pub.Bath/Show

B&B per person
£28.00-£35.00 Single
£21.00-£25.00 Double

Open Jan-Dec
Dinner 1800-2100
B&B + Eve.Meal
£38.00-£45.00

Family run hotel, recently completely refurbished. Interesting restaurant menu. Suitable base for touring the Borders, convenient for bus station.

Kings Hotel
Galashiels
Selkirkshire
TD1 3AN
Tel:(Galashiels) 0896 55497

COMMENDED ♛ ♛ ♛

1 Single
4 Twin
2 Double

7 En Suite fac

B&B per person
£34.00-£40.00 Single
£25.00-£30.00 Double

Open Jan-Dec
Dinner 1700-2200
B&B + Eve.Meal
£38.00-£44.00

Family run hotel centrally situated in the heart of market town. Restaurant offers traditional Scottish fayre with emphasis on fresh local produce.

Kingsknowes Hotel
Selkirk Road
Galashiels
Selkirkshire
TD1 3HY
Tel:(Galashiels) 0896 58375
Fax:0896 50377

COMMENDED ♛ ♛ ♛ ♛

6 Twin
2 Double
3 Family

10 En Suite fac
1 Priv.NOT ensuite
1 Pub.Bath/Show

B&B per person
£40.00-£50.00 Single
£34.00-£40.00 Double

Open Jan-Dec
Dinner 1800-2130

Overlooking River Tweed and Eildon Hills. A Listed large Baronial, former mansion house in 3 acres, with tennis court and magnificent conservatory.

Woodlands House Hotel & Restaurant
Windyknowe Road
Galashiels
Selkirkshire
TD1 1RQ
Tel:(Galashiels) 0896 4722
Fax:0896 4722

COMMENDED ♛ ♛ ♛ ♛

2 Single
2 Twin
4 Double
1 Family

9 En Suite fac

B&B per person
to £40.00 Single
to £70.00 Double

Open Jan-Dec
Dinner 1800-2130
B&B + Eve.Meal
from £50.00

Gothic style Victorian hotel in woodland setting of 2 acres on the outskirts of Galashiels. "Taste of Scotland".

Buckholmburn Guest House
Edinburgh Road
Galashiels
Selkirkshire
Tel:(Galashiels) 0896 2697

2 Twin
2 Double
3 Family

4 Limited ensuite
2 Pub.Bath/Show

B&B per person
£18.00-£20.00 Single
from £17.00 Double

Open Jan-Dec
Dinner from 1800
B&B + Eve.Meal
from £25.00

Tara Guest House
15 Abbotsford Road
Galashiels
Selkirkshire
TD1 3DR
Tel:(Galashiels) 0896 2987

1 Single
1 Twin
2 Double
2 Family

3 En Suite fac
1 Limited ensuite
3 Pub.Bath/Show

B&B per person
£18.00 Single
£18.00 Double

Open Jan-Dec
Dinner 1900-1930
B&B + Eve.Meal
from £26.50

GALASHIELS continued Scottish College of Textiles Halls of Residence, Tweed Road Galashiels Selkirkshire TD1 3HG Tel:(Galashiels) 0896 3474	Map 2 E6		200 Single	46 Pub.Bath/Show	B&B per person £15.00-£17.00 Single	Open Apr, Jul-mid Sep Dinner 1700-1900 B&B + Eve.Meal £23.00-£27.00	

GARTMORE Perthshire Black Bull Hotel Gartmore,by Stirling Perthshire FK8 3RW Tel:(Aberfoyle) 08772 225	Map 1 H4		1 Twin 1 Double	1 Pub.Bath/Show	B&B per person £18.50-£22.50 Single £15.50-£18.50 Double	Open Jan-Dec Dinner 1200-2100	

BY GARVE — Map 3 H8
Ross-shire

Inchbae Lodge Hotel
INCHBAE, by GARVE, ROSS-SHIRE IV23 2PH
Telephone: (09975) 269
This small, comfortable, unpretentious hotel has one of the finest restaurants in the North. One of only three hotels north of Inverness to hold the AA Rosette for quality food. Recommended by Egon Ronay, 'Taste of Scotland', and other leading guides.
"Taste of Scotland" • *AA Rossette for quality food*
Egon Ronay Recommended

Inchbae Lodge Inchbae,by Garve Ross-shire IV23 2PH Tel:(Aultguish) 09975 269		COMMENDED	4 Twin 6 Double 2 Family	11 En Suite fac 1 Priv.NOT ensuite	B&B per person £33.00 Single £28.00 Double	Open Jan-Dec Dinner 1930-2100 B&B + Eve.Meal £49.00-£54.00	

On River Blackwater, family run former hunting lodge; open fires. Emphasis on quality cuisine, fresh produce. Trout fishing. Annexe accommodation.

GATEHEAD by Kilmarnock, Ayrshire Old Rome Farmhouse Hotel Gatehead,by Kilmarnock Ayrshire KA2 9AJ Tel:(Drybridge) 0563 850265	Map 1 H7		1 Twin 1 Double 1 Family	1 Pub.Bath/Show	B&B per person from £15.00 Double	Open Jan-Dec Dinner 1800-2100	

GATEHOUSE-OF-FLEET Kirkcudbrightshire Bank O'Fleet Hotel 47 High Street Gatehouse-of-Fleet Kirkcudbrightshire DG7 2HR Tel:(Gatehouse) 0557 814302	Map 2 A1		2 Twin 2 Double 2 Family	4 En Suite fac 2 Pub.Bath/Show	B&B per person £18.00-£21.00 Single £18.00-£21.00 Double	Open Jan-Dec Dinner 1830-2100 B&B + Eve.Meal £26.00-£27.00	

GATEHOUSE-OF-FLEET continued

Cally Palace Hotel
Gatehouse-of-Fleet
Kirkcudbrightshire
DG7 2DL
Tel:(Gatehouse) 0557 814341
Fax:0557 814522

Map 2 A1

DELUXE

3 Single
38 Twin
6 Double
9 Family

56 En Suite fac

B&B per person
£45.00-£50.00 Single
£43.00-£52.00 Double

Open Mar-Jan
Dinner 1830-2130
B&B + Eve.Meal
£56.00-£68.00

Georgian mansion, with original moulded ceilings, in 100 acres of forest and parkland. Extensive leisure facilities.

Murray Arms Hotel
Ann Street
Gatehouse-of-Fleet
Kirkcudbrightshire
DG7 2HY
Tel:(Gatehouse) 0557 814207
Fax:0557 814370

COMMENDED

1 Single
5 Twin
5 Double
2 Family

13 En Suite fac

B&B per person
£39.50-£43.00 Single
£39.50-£43.00 Double

Open Jan-Dec
Dinner 1700-2145
B&B + Eve.Meal
£52.50-£55.00

Built c1760, an attractive old Posting Inn where Robert Burns is known to have written "Scots Wha Hae". Free golf, fishing and tennis for residents.

BY GATEHOUSE-OF-FLEET
Kirkcudbrightshire

Girthon Kirk Guest House
Sandgreen Road
by Gatehouse-of-Fleet
Kirkcudbrightshire
DG7 2DW
Tel:(Gatehouse) 0557 814352

Map 2 A1

COMMENDED

1 Twin
2 Double

3 En Suite fac

B&B per person
£19.00-£21.00 Double

Open Mar-Oct
Dinner from 1830
B&B + Eve.Meal
£28.00-£30.00

Lovely country house in idyllic rural setting. Fine home cooking. All rooms with private facilities. 0.5 miles off A75 on Sandgreen road.

GIFFORD
East Lothian

Goblin Ha' Hotel
Main Street
Gifford
East Lothian
EH41 1QH
Tel:(Gifford) 062081 244
Fax:062081 718

Map 2 E5

APPROVED

2 Single
3 Twin
2 Double

6 En Suite fac
1 Limited ensuite
1 Pub.Bath/Show

B&B per person
£22.00-£30.00 Single
£22.00-£30.00 Double

Open Jan-Dec
Dinner 1830-2130

18C family run village inn of great character. With emphasis on home cooking. Fine wines and real ale.

Tweeddale Arms Hotel
High Street
Gifford
East Lothian
EH41 4QU
Tel:(Gifford) 062081 240
Fax:062082 488

COMMENDED

2 Single
7 Twin
5 Double
3 Family

15 En Suite fac

B&B per person
from £50.00 Single
from £50.00 Double

Open Jan-Dec
Dinner 1900-2100
B&B + Eve.Meal
£60.00-£65.00

Tastefully modernised 17C inn, situated in Conservation village, only 18 miles (29kms) from Edinburgh. Ideal for touring the Borders.

GIGHA, Isle of
Argyll

Gigha Hotel
Gigha, Isle of
Argyll
PA41 7AD
Tel:(Gigha) 05835 254
Fax:05835 282

Map 1 D6

Award Pending

8 Twin
5 Double

11 En Suite fac
2 Pub.Bath/Show

B&B per person
£34.00-£40.00 Single
£32.00-£35.00 Double

Open Mar-Oct,
Xmas, New Year
Dinner 1900-2100
B&B + Eve.Meal
£48.00-£55.00

Details of Grading and Classification are on page vi.

Key to symbols is on back flap.

GIGHA, Isle of continued Post Office House Gigha, Isle of Argyll PA41 7AA Tel:(Gigha) 05835 251	Map 1 D6		1 Single 1 Twin 1 Double 1 Family	1 Pub.Bath/Show	B&B per person £16.00-£17.00 Single £16.00-£17.00 Double	Open Jan-Dec Dinner from 1800 B&B + Eve.Meal £23.00-£24.00	
GIRVAN **Ayrshire** Ailsa Craig Hotel Old Street Girvan Ayrshire KA26 9HG Tel:(Girvan) 0465 3754 Fax:0465 5474	Map 1 G9		4 Single 1 Double 4 Family	2 Pub.Bath/Show	B&B per person from £15.95 Single from £14.95 Double	Open Jan-Dec Dinner 1700-2300 B&B + Eve.Meal from £28.45	
Hamilton Arms Hotel Bridge Street Girvan Ayrshire KA26 9HH Tel:(Girvan) 0465 2182/4202			3 Single 3 Twin 3 Double 4 Family	5 En Suite fac 2 Pub.Bath/Show	B&B per person £16.00-£18.00 Single £15.00-£17.00 Double	Open Jan-Dec Dinner 1700-2000 B&B + Eve.Meal £21.00-£23.00	
Hotel Westcliffe 15 Louisa Drive Girvan Ayrshire KA26 9AH Tel:(Girvan) 0465 2128 Fax:0465 2128			3 Single 6 Twin 5 Double 7 Family	11 En Suite fac 7 Limited ensuite 3 Pub.Bath/Show	B&B per person £20.00-£27.00 Single £20.00-£24.00 Double	Open Jan-Dec Dinner from 1800 B&B + Eve.Meal £27.00-£33.00	

KINGS ARMS HOTEL
DALRYMPLE STREET, GIRVAN, AYRSHIRE KA26 9AE
Tel: (0465) 3322 Fax: (0465) 5463
Situated in the centre of this picturesque harbour town, the Kings Arms Hotel offers 25 comfortable en-suite bedrooms, and is the ideal base for touring, fishing, golfing, or simply relaxing in this beautiful corner of South-West Scotland. 2 nights DB&B from £68 per person.

Please write or telephone for brochure and further details.
Commended ♚ ♚ ♚

Kings Arms Hotel Dalrymple Street Girvan Ayrshire KA26 9AE Tel:(Girvan) 0465 3322	**COMMENDED** ♚ ♚ ♚		12 Twin 6 Double 7 Family	25 En Suite fac 2 Pub.Bath/Show	B&B per person £39.00-£42.00 Single £29.00-£32.00 Double	Open Jan-Dec Dinner 1800-2200 B&B + Eve.Meal £41.50-£44.50	
			Family run hotel in town centre with ample car parking. Close to harbour and beach. Good touring centre for Ayr and Wigtownshire.				
The Sands Private Hotel 20 Louisa Drive Girvan Ayrshire KA26 9AH Tel:(Girvan) 0465 2178			2 Twin 3 Double 4 Family	4 En Suite fac 2 Pub.Bath/Show	B&B per person £16.00-£20.00 Single £16.00-£20.00 Double	Open Jan-Dec Dinner from 1800 B&B + Eve.Meal £23.00-£27.00	

GIRVAN continued

	Map 1 G9					

Southfield Hotel
18 The Avenue
Girvan
Ayrshire
KA26 9DS
Tel:(Girvan) 0465 4222
Fax:0465 4222

COMMENDED
♛ ♛ ♛

1 Single
4 Twin
2 Double

7 En Suite fac

B&B per person
£30.00-£40.00 Single
£40.00-£50.00 Double

Open Jan-Dec
Dinner 1800-2100
B&B + Eve.Meal
£40.00-£50.00

Privately owned 19C former bank house, in quiet residential area. Town centre within 100 yards. Vegetarian meals a speciality.

Glendrissaig Guest House
Glendrissaig,
Newton Stewart Road
by Girvan
Ayrshire
KA26 0HJ
Tel:(Girvan) 0465 4631

HIGHLY
COMMENDED
♛ ♛ ♛

1 Twin
1 Double
1 Family

1 En Suite fac
1 Priv.NOT ensuite
1 Pub.Bath/Show

B&B per person
£18.00-£22.00 Single
£17.50-£21.00 Double

Open Apr-Oct
Dinner 1800-1900
B&B + Eve.Meal
£24.00-£29.00

Modern detached house in elevated position with excellent outlook towards Mull of Kintyre. Organic produce when available used in vegetarian meals.

Thistleneuk Guest House
19 Louisa Drive
Girvan
Ayrshire
KA26 9AH
Tel:(Girvan) 0465 2137

COMMENDED
♛ ♛ ♛

1 Single
2 Twin
2 Double
2 Family

6 En Suite fac
1 Pub.Bath/Show

B&B per person
£17.00-£20.00 Single
£15.00-£18.00 Double

Open Jan-Dec
Dinner from 1800
B&B + Eve.Meal
£22.00-£25.00

19C terraced house on seafront overlooking Ailsa Craig. Within easy walking distance of town centre.

GLASGOW

	Map 1 H5					

Adamson Hotel
4 Crookston Drive
Glasgow
G52 3LY
Tel:041 882 3047

APPROVED
♛

3 Single
2 Twin
1 Double
1 Family

2 Pub.Bath/Show

B&B per person
£18.00-£20.00 Single
£14.00-£15.00 Double

Open Jan-Dec

Situated on main route between Ayrshire and the Borders, convenient for the Burrell Collection, city and touring.

Albion Hotel
405-407 North Woodside
Road
Glasgow
G20 6NN
Tel:041 339 8620
Fax:041 334 8159

COMMENDED
♛ ♛ ♛

6 Single
1 Twin
4 Double
5 Family

16 En Suite fac

B&B per person
£35.00-£40.00 Single
£25.00-£27.50 Double

Open Jan-Dec
Dinner 1900-2100

Privately owned hotel in residential area close to Kelvingrove Park, University and underground station. All rooms with private facilities.

Ambassador Hotel
7 Kelvin Drive
Glasgow
G20
Tel:041 946 1018
Fax:041 945 5377

COMMENDED
♛ ♛ ♛

5 Single
3 Twin
4 Double
2 Family

14 En Suite fac

B&B per person
£35.00-£40.00 Single
£25.00-£27.50 Double

Open Jan-Dec
Dinner 1800-2100

Victorian townhouse quietly located in West End, convenient for city centre, museums, art galleries and the Botanic Gardens.

Angus Hotel
966-970 Sauchiehall Street
Glasgow
G3
Tel:041 357 5155
Fax:041 357 5155

COMMENDED
Listed

5 Single
3 Twin
5 Double
4 Family

17 En Suite fac

B&B per person
to £41.00 Single
to £26.00 Double

Open Jan-Dec

Refurbished, privately owned hotel situated on bus route to city centre. Within walking distance of Glasgow University and Kelvin Hall sports arena.

GLASGOW continued	Map 1 H5		Rooms	En Suite	B&B	Opening / Dinner	
Argyll Hotel 973 Sauchiehall Street Glasgow G3 7TQ Tel:041 337 3313 Fax:041 337 3283			7 Single 7 Twin 13 Double 7 Family	34 En Suite fac	B&B per person to £48.00 Single to £29.00 Double	Open Jan-Dec Dinner 1730-2100 B&B + Eve.Meal to £62.00	
Babbity Bowster 16-18 Blackfriars Street Glasgow G1 1PE Tel:041 552 5055			1 Single 4 Twin 1 Double	6 En Suite fac	B&B per person to £40.00 Single from £30.00 Double	Open Jan-Dec Dinner 1700-2300 B&B + Eve.Meal from £51.50	
Boswell Hotel 27 Mansionhouse Road Langside, Glasgow G41 3DN Tel:041 632 9812	APPROVED		2 Single 5 Twin 4 Double 2 Family	13 En Suite fac	B&B per person £38.50-£40.00 Single £27.50-£30.00 Double	Open Jan-Dec Dinner 1100-2145	
		Fully refurbished 'Real Ale' hotel with busy bar and meals served throughout the day. Live jazz on Tuesdays. Family suites.					
Botanic Hotel 1 Alfred Terrace, by 625 Gt Western Road G12 8RF G12 8RF Tel:041 339 6955/6802 Fax:041 339 6955			1 Single 2 Twin 5 Double 3 Family	3 En Suite fac 4 Pub.Bath/Show	B&B per person £23.00-£40.00 Single £18.00-£26.00 Double	Open Jan-Dec Dinner 1830-2100 B&B + Eve.Meal £29.00-£46.00	
The Buchanan Hotel 185 Buchanan Street Glasgow G1 2JY Tel:041 332 7284 Tlx:776320 Fax:041 333 0635			20 Single 27 Twin 10 Double	57 En Suite fac	B&B per person £39.50 Single £24.75 Double	Open Jan-Dec Dinner 1700-2200	
Burrell Hotel 30 Shawlands Square, Kilmarnock Road Glasgow G41 3NR Tel:041 632 9226 Fax:041 649 0279			6 Twin 16 Double 2 Family	22 En Suite fac	B&B per person £49.50 Single £32.50 Double	Open Jan-Dec Dinner 1830-2130	
The Carrick 377-383 Argyle Street Glasgow G2 8LL Tel:041 248 2355 Tlx:779652 CENTEL G Fax:041 221 1014			10 Single 46 Twin 65 Double	121 En Suite fac	B&B per person to £68.50 Single to £38.95 Double	Open Jan-Dec Dinner 1900-2200	
Cathedral House 28/32 Cathedral Square Glasgow G4 0XA Tel:041 552 3519	Award Pending		6 Twin 1 Double	7 En Suite fac	B&B per person £50.00-£60.00 Single £32.50-£35.00 Double	Open Jan-Dec Dinner 1200-2200	

VAT is shown at 17.5%: changes in this rate may affect prices. Prices shown are for guidance only. Please send SAE with each enquiry.

GLASGOW continued	Map 1 H5					
Central Hotel Gordon Street Glasgow G1 3SF Tel:041 221 9680 Tlx:777771 Fax:041 226 3948	COMMENDED ♔ ♔ ♔ ♔	66 Single 103 Twin 43 Double 9 Family Suites avail. **City centre hotel next to Central railway station.**	221 En Suite fac	B&B per person £63.25-£75.25 Single £42.25-£48.50 Double	Open Jan-Dec Dinner 1800-2130 B&B + Eve.Meal £76.25-£88.25	
Clifton Hotel 26/27 Buckingham Terrace Glasgow G12 8ED Tel:041 334 8080	COMMENDED ♔ ♔ ♔	9 Single 3 Twin 11 Double Suites avail. **Victorian terrace in the heart of the West End, near the Botanic Gardens, within easy reach of all amenities. Private parking.**	18 En Suite fac 4 Limited ensuite 3 Pub.Bath/Show	B&B per person £40.00-£55.00 Single £30.00-£45.00 Double	Open Jan-Dec Dinner 1800-2200	
The Coach House Hotel 14 Hyndland Road Glasgow G12 9UP Tel:041 357 2186/339 6153	COMMENDED ♔ ♔ ♔	3 Single 3 Twin 3 Double 4 Family **Personally run hotel in substantial Victorian town house in residential area of Glasgow. Convenient for city centre. Accent on food.**	7 En Suite fac 3 Pub.Bath/Show	B&B per person £30.00-£49.00 Single £22.00-£28.00 Double	Open Jan-Dec Dinner 1800-2230	
Copland House Hotel 78-80 Copland Road Glasgow G51 2RF Tel:041 445 1459		4 Single 5 Twin 5 Double 2 Family	16 En Suite fac 3 Pub.Bath/Show	B&B per person £20.00 Single £20.00 Double	Open Jan-Dec Dinner 1800-2100 B&B + Eve.Meal £26.00-£30.00	
The Copthorne Hotel George Square Glasgow G2 1DS Tel:041 332 6711 Tlx:778147 Fax:041 332 4264	COMMENDED ♔ ♔ ♔ ♔ ♔	15 Single 78 Twin 47 Double 1 Family Suites avail. **Recently refurbished landmark hotel in the heart of Scotland's commercial capital. Ideal for city centre attractions and amenities.**	141 En Suite fac	B&B per person £101.00-£120.00 Single £61.00-£72.00 Double	Open Jan-Dec Dinner 1830-2200 B&B + Eve.Meal £77.00-£89.00	
Crookston Hotel 90 Crookston Road Glasgow G52 3ND Tel:041 882 6142 Fax:041 810 3313		11 Single 2 Twin 7 Double 2 Family	10 En Suite fac 7 Limited ensuite 3 Pub.Bath/Show	B&B per person £25.00-£42.00 Single £25.00-£28.00 Double	Open Jan-Dec Dinner 1800-2000 B&B + Eve.Meal £35.00-£38.00	
Dalmeny Hotel 62 St Andrews Drive Glasgow G41 5EZ Tel:041 427 1106/6288		5 Single 2 Twin 1 Double	2 En Suite fac 1 Pub.Bath/Show	B&B per person £27.00-£45.00 Single £26.00-£26.50 Double	Open Jan-Dec Dinner 1700-2300	

GLASGOW continued	Map 1 H5						
Devonshire Hotel 5 Devonshire Gardens Glasgow G12 0UX Tel:041 339 7878 Fax:041 339 3980		DELUXE	3 Twin 9 Double 4 Family	16 En Suite fac	B&B per person £85.00-£140.00 Single £55.00-£80.00 Double	Open Jan-Dec Dinner 1930-2200 B&B + Eve.Meal £105.00-£160.00	
			Sumptuously refurbished substantial Victorian town house in West End of Glasgow. 1.5 miles (3kms) from city centre, 7 miles (11kms) from Airport.				
Drumlin Hotel 4 Kelvin Drive Glasgow G20 Tel:041 945 4877 Fax:041 945 5152		COMMENDED	2 Single 1 Twin 2 Double 2 Family	7 En Suite fac	B&B per person £45.00-£50.00 Single £40.00-£50.00 Double	Open Jan-Dec Dinner 1700-1900	
			Totally refurbished Victorian B-Listed town house close to city centre, West End and Botanic Gardens.				
Dunkeld Hotel 10-12 Queens Drive Glasgow G42 8BS Tel:041 424 0160 Fax:041 423 4437			7 Single 10 Twin 3 Double 1 Family	10 En Suite fac 3 Pub.Bath/Show	B&B per person £27.00-£36.00 Single £18.50-£25.00 Double	Open Jan-Dec Dinner 1800-2000 B&B + Eve.Meal £36.00-£45.00	
Ewington Hotel 132 Queens Drive Glasgow G42 8QW Tel:041 423 1152 Fax:041 422 2030		COMMENDED	13 Single 19 Twin 8 Double 2 Family Suites avail.	42 En Suite fac	B&B per person £50.00-£70.00 Single £35.75-£45.00 Double	Open Jan-Dec Dinner 1730-2045 B&B + Eve.Meal £62.95-£82.95	
			Privately run, close to Queens Park with ample parking. Near city centre and the Burrell Collection.				
Forte Crest Glasgow Bothwell Street Glasgow G2 7EN Tel:041 248 2656 Tlx:77440 ALBGLA G Fax:041 221 8986		HIGHLY COMMENDED	148 Single 65 Twin 38 Double Suites avail.	251 En Suite fac	B&B per person £109.00-£110.00 Single £59.00-£62.00 Double	Open Jan-Dec Dinner 1730-2300 B&B + Eve.Meal £123.00-£125.00	
			City centre location with easy access from M8. Choice of dining in Carvery or the newly opened "Jules" themed restaurant and bar. Part of Forte Crest				
Garfield House Hotel Cumbernauld Road, Stepps Glasgow G33 6HW Tel:041 779 2111 Fax:041 779 2111		COMMENDED	2 Single 19 Twin 26 Double	47 En Suite fac	B&B per person £65.00-£70.00 Single £40.00-£42.50 Double	Open Jan-Dec Dinner 1900-2130	
			Country house with refurbished modern wing close to main Glasgow-Stirling road. Large car park.				

WELCOME

Whenever you are in Scotland, you can be sure of a warm welcome at your nearest Tourist Information Centre.

For guide books, maps, souvenirs, our Centres provide a service second to none – many now offer bureau-de-change facilities. And, of course, Tourist Information Centres offer free, expert advice on what to see and do, route-planning and accommodation for everyone – visitors and residents alike!

GLASGOW continued	Map 1 H5

GLASGOW HILTON

1 William Street
Glasgow G3 8HT
Tel: 041-204 5555 Fax: 041-204 5004

Located in the city centre close to the major shopping centres and theatres. Offering 319 beautifully appointed rooms with 4 restaurants and bars. Camerons, serving the finest of Scottish produce. Minsky's, our New York style deli. Raffles Bar, conjuring up the images and splendour of years gone by and the Scotch Bar featuring over 200 malt whiskies.

The health club offers you extensive facilities including a 15m swimming pool, sauna, steam room, jacuzzi, massage, impulse shower and 2 solariums.

Glasgow Hilton William Street Glasgow G3 8HT Tel:041 204 5555 Fax:041 204 5004	DELUXE 👑👑👑 👑👑	107 Twin 108 Double 104 Family Suites avail.	319 En Suite fac	B&B per person £127.50-£137.50 Single £70.00-£75.00 Double	Open Jan-Dec Dinner 1800-2230 B&B + Eve.Meal £145.00-£155.00

Recently opened (1992) luxury hotel near city centre. Fine dining with themed restaurants and bars. Extensive conference and business facilities. ♿

Glasgow Marriott Argyle Street, Anderston Glasgow G3 8RR Tel:041 226 5577 Tlx:776355 Fax:041 221 7676		80 Twin 218 Double Suites avail.	298 En Suite fac	B&B per person £99.00-£270.00 Single £50.00-£145.00 Double	Open Jan-Dec Dinner 1830-2230 B&B + Eve.Meal £75.00-£290.00

Hampton Court Hotel 230 Renfrew Street Glasgow G3 Tel:041 332 6623/5885		2 Single 6 Twin 4 Double 3 Family	11 En Suite fac 4 Pub.Bath/Show	B&B per person £17.00-£25.00 Single £22.00-£34.00 Double	Open Jan-Dec Dinner 1900-2030 B&B + Eve.Meal £24.00-£41.00

Hillhead Hotel 32 Cecil Street Glasgow G12 Tel:041 339 7733		1 Single 4 Twin 1 Double 5 Family	10 En Suite fac 1 Priv.NOT ensuite 1 Pub.Bath/Show	B&B per person £25.00-£30.00 Single £20.00-£22.50 Double	Open Jan-Dec

GLASGOW continued — Map 1 H5

The Hospitality Inn & Convention Centre
36 Cambridge Street
Glasgow
G2
Tel:041 332 3311
Tlx:777334
Fax:041 332 4050

COMMENDED

230 Twin 307 En Suite fac
77 Double

B&B per person
£89.95-£104.95 Single
£54.96-£62.45 Double
B&B + Eve.Meal
£105.20-£120.20

Open Jan-Dec
Dinner 1700-2300

Modern hotel situated in the heart of the city. Choice of restaurants and fresh produce. Banqueting and conference facilities. Private parking.

Jurys Pond Hotel
Great Western Road
Glasgow
G12 0XP
Tel:041 334 8161
Tlx:776573
Fax:041 334 3846

COMMENDED

90 Twin 133 En Suite fac
26 Double
17 Family

B&B per person
£73.00 Single
£41.00 Double
B&B + Eve.Meal
£61.45-£88.50

Open Jan-Dec
Dinner 1800-2200

Modern hotel, convenient for Botanic Gardens and City Centre.

Kelvin Hotel
15 Buckingham Terrace
Glasgow
G12 8EB
Tel:041 339 7143
Fax:041 339 5215

COMMENDED

10 Single 9 En Suite fac
4 Twin   6 Pub.Bath/Show
2 Double
4 Family

B&B per person
£24.00-£34.00 Single
£20.00-£27.00 Double

Open Jan-Dec

Victorian terraced house in the West End. Close to BBC and Botanic Gardens. On main bus routes to city centre. Close to Underground.

Kelvin Park Lorne Hotel
923 Sauchiehall Street
Glasgow
G3 7TE
Tel:041 334 4891
Tlx:778935
Fax:041 337 1659

COMMENDED

40 Twin 99 En Suite fac
55 Double
3 Family
Suite avail.

B&B per person
£73.00-£83.00 Single
£41.00-£46.00 Double

Open Jan-Dec
Dinner 1830-2230

Modern building, recently refurbished, in city's West End.

Kelvingrove Hotel
944 Sauchiehall Street
Glasgow
G3
Tel:041 339 5011
Fax:041 337 2644

APPROVED

5 Single 5 En Suite fac
6 Twin   6 Pub.Bath/Show
5 Double
4 Family

B&B per person
£22.00-£32.00 Single
£19.00-£22.00 Double
B&B + Eve.Meal
£27.75-£30.75

Open Jan-Dec
Dinner 1800-2000

City centre hotel, some en-suite rooms, TV, tea and coffee facilities. 15 minutes walk to shopping centre. SECC nearby.

Kirklee Hotel
11 Kensington Gate
Glasgow
G12 9LG
Tel:041 334 5555
Fax:041 339 3828

HIGHLY COMMENDED

2 Twin 9 En Suite fac
4 Double
3 Family

B&B per person
£44.00-£47.00 Single
£28.00-£29.50 Double

Open Jan-Dec

Early Victorian house in quiet residential area near Glasgow University and Botanic Gardens. Breakfast in the privacy of your own bedroom.

Lomond Hotel
6 Buckingham Terrace
Glasgow
G12 8EB
Tel:041 339 2339
Fax:041 339 5215

COMMENDED

8 Single 6 En Suite fac
2 Twin   6 Pub.Bath/Show
3 Double
4 Family

B&B per person
£23.00-£35.00 Single
£20.00-£27.00 Double

Open Jan-Dec

Victorian terraced house in the West End. Close to the BBC and Botanical Gardens. On main bus routes to city centre. Near to underground.

GLASGOW continued	Map 1 H5					
Macdonald Thistle Hotel Eastwood Toll Giffnock Renfrewshire G46 6RA Tel:041 638 2225 Tlx:779138 Fax:041 638 6231	COMMENDED ♛ ♛ ♛ ♛	23 Single 22 Twin 7 Double 4 Family Modern hotel in quiet residential area and convenient for Glasgow Airport.	56 En Suite fac	B&B per person £70.00-£77.00 Single £42.50-£45.00 Double	Open Jan-Dec Dinner 1900-2200	
Manor Park Hotel 28 Balshagray Drive Glasgow G11 7DD Tel:041 339 2143 Fax:041 339 5842		2 Single 4 Twin 3 Double	9 En Suite fac	B&B per person £41.50-£45.00 Single £29.00-£38.00 Double	Open Jan-Dec Dinner 1830-2030	
Marie Stuart Hotel 46-48 Queen Mary Avenue Glasgow G42 8DT Tel:041 424 3939 Fax:041 423 9070		3 Single 20 Twin 5 Double Suite avail.	18 En Suite fac 2 Pub.Bath/Show	B&B per person £25.00-£44.50 Single £27.50 Double	Open Jan-Dec Dinner 1730-1900 B&B + Eve.Meal £32.50-£52.00	
Moat House International Hotel Congress Road Glasgow G3 8QT Tel:041 204 0733 Tlx:776244 Fax:041 221 2022	HIGHLY COMMENDED ♛ ♛ ♛ ♛ ♛	192 Twin 90 Double Suites avail. Modern hotel with full business and leisure facilities, adjacent to Conference Centre.	282 En Suite fac	B&B per person £110.00 Single £55.00-£65.00 Double	Open Jan-Dec Dinner 1700-2300	
One Devonshire Gardens 1 Devonshire Gardens, Great Western Rd Glasgow G12 0UX Tel:041 339 2001/334 9494 Fax:041 337 1663	DELUXE ♛ ♛ ♛ ♛	3 Twin 24 Double Adjoining Victorian town houses, elegantly refurbished to a high standard. Award winning restaurant; interesting cuisine complemented by fine wines.	27 En Suite fac	B&B per person £125.00-£135.00 Single £82.50-£87.50 Double	Open Jan-Dec Dinner 1900-2300	
Queens Park Hotel 10 Balvicar Drive Glasgow G42 8QT Tel:041 423 1123 Fax:041 423 4917	APPROVED ♛ ♛ ♛	5 Single 16 Twin 8 Double 6 Family Privately owned, in quiet area opposite public park. Just off main Kilmarnock road. Handy for transport to city centre.	30 En Suite fac 4 Pub.Bath/Show	B&B per person £27.00-£35.00 Single £22.00-£26.00 Double	Open Jan-Dec Dinner 1800-2030	
Rab Ha's 83 Hutcheson Street Glasgow G1 1SH Tel:041 553 1545		2 Twin 2 Double	4 En Suite fac	B&B per person £25.00-£50.00 Single £25.00-£50.00 Double	Open Jan-Dec Dinner 1800-2400 B&B + Eve.Meal £35.00-£50.00	

GLASGOW

GLASGOW continued — Map 1 H5

Sherbrooke Castle Hotel 11 Sherbrooke Avenue Glasgow G41 4PG Tel:041 427 4227 Fax:041 427 5685	COMMENDED	7 Single 5 Twin 10 Double 3 Family	25 En Suite fac	B&B per person £55.00-£95.00 Single £27.50-£62.50 Double	Open Jan-Dec Dinner 1830-2200
		Baronial style hotel, situated in an elevated position in a quiet residential area of the city. Some annexe accommodation.			
Smiths Hotel 963 Sauchiehall Street Glasgow G3 7TQ Tel:041 339 6363/7674	Award Pending	17 Single 7 Twin 7 Double 2 Family	8 Pub.Bath/Show	B&B per person £16.00-£22.00 Single £16.00-£17.00 Double	Open Jan-Dec
Stakis Glasgow Grosvenor Hotel Grosvenor Terrace, Great Western Road Glasgow G12 0TA Tel:041 339 8811 Tlx:776247 Fax:041 334 0710	COMMENDED	70 Twin 13 Double 12 Family Suites avail.	95 En Suite fac	B&B per person from £97.50 Single to £58.00 Double	Open Jan-Dec Dinner 1100-2300
		Originally a Victorian terrace, now modernised with double glazed bedrooms. Choice of restaurants.			
Stakis Glasgow Ingram Hotel Ingram Street Glasgow G1 1DQ Tel:041 248 4401 Tlx:776470 Fax:041 226 5149	COMMENDED	44 Single 35 Twin 10 Double 1 Family	90 En Suite fac	B&B per person from £62.00 Single to £35.25 Double	Open Jan-Dec Dinner 1830-2145
		Modern hotel in city centre. Double glazing in bedrooms. Car parking. Satellite TV. Conference facilities.			
The Terrace House Hotel 14 Belhaven Terrace Glasgow G12 0TG Tel:041 337 3377 Fax:041 337 3377	HIGHLY COMMENDED	2 Single 4 Twin 6 Double 3 Family	13 En Suite fac 2 Priv.NOT ensuite	B&B per person from £52.00 Single from £34.00 Double	Open Jan-Dec Dinner 1830-2100
		19th C townhouse, West End of city, within easy reach of main business centres and tourist attractions. Traditional values of comfort and service.			
Tinto Firs Thistle Hotel 470 Kilmarnock Road Glasgow G43 2BB Tel:041 637 2353 Tlx:778329 Fax:041 633 1340	COMMENDED	20 Single 2 Twin 3 Double 2 Family Suites avail.	27 En Suite fac	B&B per person £70.00-£80.00 Single £35.00-£40.00 Double	Open Jan-Dec Dinner 1830-2145 B&B + Eve.Meal £45.00-£96.50
		In a residential area, 4 miles (7kms) from Glasgow city centre and 6 miles (9kms) from the airport.			
Wickets Hotel 52 Fortrose Street Glasgow G11 5LP Tel:041 334 9334 Fax:041 334 9334		2 Single 4 Twin 3 Double 1 Family	10 En Suite fac	B&B per person £59.95-£64.95 Single £34.98-£37.48 Double	Open Jan-Dec Dinner 1830-2230 B&B + Eve.Meal £69.95-£74.95

GLASGOW continued	Map 1 H5						

Willow Hotel
228 Renfrew Street
Glasgow
G3
Tel:041 332 2332/7075

COMMENDED

5 Single 7 En Suite fac B&B per person Open Jan-Dec
4 Twin 7 Limited ensuite £22.00-£27.00 Single
2 Double 3 Pub.Bath/Show £20.00-£25.00 Double
6 Family

Privately owned hotel in quiet city centre location. Short walk from Sauchiehall Street. Convenient for railway station and Art School.

Alamo Guest House
46 Gray Street
Glasgow
G3 7SE
Tel:041 339 2395

APPROVED

2 Single 3 Pub.Bath/Show B&B per person Open Jan-Dec
1 Twin from £15.00 Single
2 Double from £13.00 Double
2 Family

Friendly family run, in quiet location overlooking park. Easy access to centre and within walking distance of SECC, galleries and Transport Museum.

Belle Vue Guest House
163 Hamilton Road,
Mount Vernon
Glasgow
G32 9QT
Tel:041 778 1077

Listed

3 Single 1 En Suite fac B&B per person Open Jan-Dec
4 Twin 1 Pub.Bath/Show £18.00-£20.00 Single
3 Double £15.00-£16.00 Double
2 Family

Brighton House
5 Brighton Place
Glasgow
G51 2RP
Tel:041 440 1782

1 Twin 1 Pub.Bath/Show B&B per person Open Jan-Dec
1 Double £15.00-£20.00 Single Dinner 1730-2100
1 Family £13.50-£15.00 Double B&B + Eve.Meal
£23.00-£28.00

Browns Guest House
2 Onslow Drive
Glasgow
G31 5LX
Tel:041 554 6797

7 Single 4 Pub.Bath/Show B&B per person Open Jan-Dec
4 Twin £14.00-£15.00 Single
1 Double £13.00-£14.00 Double
2 Family

Charing Cross House
310 Renfrew Street
Glasgow
G3 6UW
Tel:041 332 2503
Fax:041 332 2503

5 Single 10 En Suite fac B&B per person Open Jan-Dec
7 Twin 7 Pub.Bath/Show £18.00-£25.00 Single
4 Double £16.00-£21.00 Double
7 Family

Chez Nous Guest House
33 Hillhead Street
Glasgow
G12
Tel:041 334 2977

COMMENDED

13 Single 14 En Suite fac B&B per person Open Jan-Dec
4 Twin 4 Limited ensuite £18.50-£27.50 Single
8 Double 6 Pub.Bath/Show £18.50-£27.50 Double
7 Family

Situated in West End of city, close to University and Art Gallery. Within easy reach of M8 and all amenities. Private parking.

Craigielea House
35 Westercraigs
Glasgow
G31 2HY
Tel:041 554 3446

APPROVED
Listed

2 Twin 1 Limited ensuite B&B per person Open Jan-Dec
1 Double 1 Pub.Bath/Show £18.00 Single
1 Family £14.00-£14.50 Double

Victorian semi-villa in East End of city, yet close to centre and all amenities.

GLASGOW

GLASGOW continued	Map 1 H5						
Glades Guest House 142 Albert Road Glasgow G42 8UF Tel:041 423 4911	Award Pending	1 Single 3 Twin 2 Double 2 Family	2 En Suite fac 2 Pub.Bath/Show	B&B per person £16.00-£18.00 Single £17.00-£19.00 Double	Open Jan-Dec	
Hillview Guest House 18 Hillhead Street Glasgow G12 Tel:041 334 5585 Fax:041 353 3155	COMMENDED Listed	4 Single 2 Twin 2 Double 2 Family	3 Pub.Bath/Show	B&B per person £21.00-£25.00 Single £18.00-£20.00 Double	Open Jan-Dec	
		Privately owned hotel situated close to Glasgow University and the Kelvin Hall Sports Arena. Convenient for city centre.				
Iona Guest House 39 Hillhead Street Glasgow G12 8PX Tel:041 334 2346		3 Single 2 Twin 1 Double 3 Family	3 Pub.Bath/Show	B&B per person £20.00 Single £17.00 Double	Open Jan-Dec Dinner 1800-1900 B&B + Eve.Meal £27.00	
Kelvin View Guest House 411 North Woodside Road Glasgow G20 6NN Tel:041 339 8257		1 Single 4 Twin 1 Double 3 Family	3 En Suite fac 2 Pub.Bath/Show	B&B per person £16.00 Single £15.00 Double	Open Jan-Dec	
Linby Guest House 29 Carmyle Avenue Glasgow G32 Tel:041 763 0684		1 Single 2 Twin 1 Family	1 Pub.Bath/Show	B&B per person to £14.00 Single to £14.00 Double	Open Jan-Dec	
McLays Guest House 268 Renfrew Street Glasgow G3 6TT Tel:041 332 4796 Fax:041 353 0422	COMMENDED 👑👑	16 Single 17 Twin 15 Double 14 Family	39 En Suite fac 9 Pub.Bath/Show	B&B per person £17.50-£19.50 Single £17.50-£19.50 Double	Open Jan-Dec	
		Family run guest house in city centre site near Charing Cross. Close to University and Kelvingrove Park.				
Oakley Guest House 10 Oakley Terrace Glasgow G31 2HX Tel:041 554 5409	Award Pending	3 Single 3 Twin 2 Double 2 Family	3 Pub.Bath/Show	B&B per person £17.50-£18.00 Single £14.00-£15.00 Double	Open Jan-Dec	
Regent Guest House 44 Regent Park Square Glasgow G41 2AG Tel:041 422 1199/423 7531 Fax:041 423 7531	APPROVED 👑👑	3 Single 2 Double 2 Family	2 En Suite fac 2 Pub.Bath/Show	B&B per person £20.00-£26.00 Single £20.00 Double	Open Jan-Dec	
		1860 terrace house in quiet, residential area. Ideal for city centre and under 2 miles (3kms) from the Burrell Collection. Warm welcome.				

VAT is shown at 17.5%: changes in this rate may affect prices. Prices shown are for guidance only. Please send SAE with each enquiry.

GLASGOW continued	Map 1 H5						

Reidholme Guest House
36 Regent Park Square
Glasgow
G41 2AG
Tel:041 423 1855

APPROVED ≋

1 Single 1 Priv.NOT ensuite B&B per person Open Jan-Dec
3 Twin 2 Pub.Bath/Show £18.00-£20.00 Single Dinner from 1800
1 Double £18.00-£20.00 Double B&B + Eve.Meal
1 Family £25.00-£27.00

"B" Listed terraced townhouse in quiet residential area. Ideal for city centre and under 2 miles (3kms) from the Burrell Collection.

Rosewood Guest House
4 Seton Terrace
Glasgow
G31 2HU
Tel:041 550 1500/556 2478

1 Single 3 Pub.Bath/Show B&B per person Open Jan-Dec
4 Twin £14.50-£16.50 Single
1 Double £14.50 Double
2 Family

Scott's Guest House
417 North Woodside Road
Glasgow
G20 6NN
Tel:041 339 3750

1 Single 4 Pub.Bath/Show B&B per person Open Jan-Dec
4 Twin £17.00 Single
1 Double £15.00 Double
2 Family

Symington Guest House
26 Circus Drive
Glasgow
G31 2JH
Tel:041 556 1431

1 Twin 2 Pub.Bath/Show B&B per person Open Jan-Dec
1 Double £12.00-£14.00 Single Dinner 1700-1900
1 Family £12.00-£14.00 Double

The Town House
4 Hughenden Terrace
Glasgow
G12 9XR
Tel:041 357 0862
Fax:041 339 9605

HIGHLY COMMENDED ≋ ≋ ≋

3 Twin 10 En Suite fac B&B per person Open Jan-Dec
5 Double £44.00-£48.00 Single Dinner 1830-2000
2 Family £29.00-£29.50 Double

Elegantly refurbished Victorian town house in quiet conservation area in Glasgow's West End.

The Victorian House
212 Renfrew Street
Glasgow
G3
Tel:041 332 0129
Fax:041 353 3155

COMMENDED ≋ ≋

12 Single 37 En Suite fac B&B per person Open Jan-Dec
12 Twin 4 Pub.Bath/Show £21.00-£28.00 Single
12 Double £18.00-£23.00 Double
9 Family

Terraced house in quiet location close to city centre.

The Glasgow Caledonian Univ. Gibson Hall
183 Dorchester Avenue
Glasgow
G12 0DA
Tel:041 339 8481
Fax:041 337 4500

30 Single 10 Pub.Bath/Show B&B per person Open Jun-Sep
40 Twin £20.00 Single Dinner 1800-2000
£19.00 Double

Univ. of Glasgow, Dalrymple Hall
22 Belhaven Terrace West
Glasgow
G12 0UW
Tel:041 339 5271
Fax:041 337 2584

APPROVED ≋

35 Single 16 Pub.Bath/Show B&B per person Open Mar-Apr, Jul-Sep
21 Twin to £20.50 Single Dinner 1730-1830
1 Family to £20.50 Double B&B + Eve.Meal
to £28.50

Hall of residence, part of Victorian terrace in West End of Glasgow, close to Botanic Gardens.

GLASGOW

GLASGOW continued	Map 1 H5					
Univ. of Glasgow, Queen Margaret Hall 55 Bellshaugh Road Glasgow G12 0SQ Tel:041 334 2192 Fax:041 339 2833			328 Single 27 Twin	100 Pub.Bath/Show	B&B per person to £20.50 Single to £20.50 Double	Open Mar-Apr, Jul-Sep Dinner 1730-1830 B&B + Eve.Meal to £28.50
Univ. of Glasgow, Reith Hall 10-13 Botanic Crescent Glasgow G20 8QQ Tel:041 945 1636 Fax:041 945 5246	APPROVED Listed		70 Single 15 Twin	29 Pub.Bath/Show	B&B per person to £20.50 Single to £20.50 Double	Open Mar-Apr, Jul-Sep Dinner 1730-1830 B&B + Eve.Meal to £28.50
		Hall of residence part of Victorian terrace in West End of Glasgow, close to Botanic Gardens.				
Univ. of Glasgow, Wolfson Hall Garscube Estate, Maryhill Road Glasgow G20 0TH Tel:041 946 5252 Fax:041 945 2031			221 Single 19 Twin 1 Double 1 Family	43 Pub.Bath/Show	B&B per person to £20.50 Single to £20.50 Double	Open Mar-Apr, Jul-Sep Dinner 1730-1830 B&B + Eve.Meal to £28.50
Univ. of Strathclyde Chancellors Hall, Rottenrow East Glasgow G4 0QF Tel:041 553 4148 Tlx:77472 Fax:041 553 4149			217 Single	231 En Suite fac 14 Double	B&B per person to £41.13 Single to £32.32 Double	Open Jun-Sep Dinner from 1800 B&B + Eve.Meal to £50.30
Univ. of Strathclyde, Baird Hall 460 Sauchiehall Street Glasgow G2 3LN Tel:041 553 4148 Tlx:77472 Fax:041 553 4149			65 Single 115 Twin 5 Family	25 Pub.Bath/Show	B&B per person £21.15-£21.50 Single £17.33-£17.50 Double	Open Jan-Dec Dinner from 1730 B&B + Eve.Meal £26.50-£30.67
Univ. of Strathclyde Chancellors Hall, Rottenrow East Glasgow G4 0QF Tel:041 553 4148 Tlx:77472 Fax:041 553 4149			217 Single	231 En Suite fac 14 Double	B&B per person to £41.13 Single to £32.32 Double	Open Jun-Sep Dinner from 1800 B&B + Eve.Meal to £50.30
Univ. of Strathclyde, Clyde Hall 318 Clyde Street Glasgow G1 4NR Tel:041 553 4148 Fax:041 553 4149			91 Single 37 Twin	71 En Suite fac 18 Pub.Bath/Show	B&B per person £21.15-£28.50 Single £20.56-£20.75 Double	Open Jun-Sep Dinner from 1800 B&B + Eve.Meal £30.32-£37.67

GLASGOW continued	Map 1 H5				
Univ. of Strathclyde, Forbes Hall Rottenrow East Glasgow G4 0QF Tel:041 553 4148 Tlx:77472 Fax:041 553 4149			104 Single 32 Pub.Bath/Show	B&B per person £21.15-£21.50 Single	Open Jun-Sep Dinner from 1800 B&B + Eve.Meal £30.32-£30.67
Univ. of Strathclyde, Garnett Hall Cathedral Street Glasgow G4 0QG Tel:041 553 4148 Tlx:77472 Fax:041 553 4149			124 Single 38 Pub.Bath/Show	B&B per person £21.15-£21.50 Single	Open Jun-Sep Dinner from 1800 B&B + Eve.Meal £30.32-£30.67
Univ. of Strathclyde, Graduate Business School 199 Cathedral Street Glasgow G4 0QU Tel:041 553 6000 Tlx:77472 Fax:041 552 2501			74 Single 108 En Suite fac 34 Double	B&B per person £35.00-£60.00 Single £35.00-£60.00 Double	Open Jan-Dec Dinner from 1800 B&B + Eve.Meal £42.00-£76.00
Univ. of Strathclyde, Jordanhill Campus 76 Southbrae Drive Glasgow G13 1PP Tel:041 553 4148 Tlx:77472 Fax:041 553 4149		APPROVED Listed	131 Single 20 Pub.Bath/Show 50 Twin Hostels in 60 acres of parkland with bus service from college gates to city centre. Sports facilities on campus.	B&B per person £18.35-£20.00 Single £18.35-£20.00 Double	Open Jan-Dec Dinner 1730-1830
Univ. of Strathclyde, Murray Hall Collins Street Glasgow G4 0NG Tel:041 553 4148 Tlx:77472 Fax:041 553 4149			70 Single 23 Pub.Bath/Show	B&B per person £21.15-£21.50 Single	Open Mar-Apr, Jun-Sep Dinner from 1730 B&B + Eve.Meal £30.32-£30.67
Y M C A Glasgow, Aparthotel David Naismith Ct, 33 Petershill Dr Glasgow G21 4QH Tel:041 558 6166 Fax:041 557 0874			17 Single 24 Pub.Bath/Show 40 Twin 3 Double	B&B per person £10.00-£18.00 Single £10.00-£14.00 Double	Open Jan-Dec Dinner 1730-2200 B&B + Eve.Meal £12.50-£20.00

GLENCOE
Argyll
Map 1 F1

Clachaig Inn
Glencoe
Argyll
PA39 4HX
Tel:(Ballachulish)
08552 252
Fax:08552 679

APPROVED
♛ ♛ ♛

2 Single
7 Twin
5 Double
5 Family

16 En Suite fac
1 Pub.Bath/Show

B&B per person
from £22.00 Single
from £22.00 Double

Open Jan-Dec
Dinner from 1900

Historic Highland inn at the scene of the massacre. Stunning mountain scenery.
Popular with hill-walkers; open all year. Some annexe accommodation.

The Glencoe Hotel
Glencoe
Argyll
PA39 4HW
Tel:(Ballachulish) 08552
245/673/216/337
Fax:08552 492

COMMENDED
♛ ♛ ♛
♛

1 Twin
10 Double
4 Family

15 En Suite fac

B&B per person
£30.00-£42.00 Single
£20.00-£30.00 Double

Open Jan-Dec
Dinner 1900-2130

Traditional Highland hospitality in completely refurbished hotel in historic
Glen Coe.

Kings House Hotel
Glencoe
Argyll
PA39 4HY
Tel:(Kingshouse) 08556 259
Fax:08556 250

5 Single
7 Twin
8 Double
2 Family

12 En Suite fac
3 Pub.Bath/Show

B&B per person
£22.50-£26.00 Single
£36.00-£58.00 Double

Open Jan-Dec
Dinner 1900-2100
B&B + Eve.Meal
£33.00-£44.00

Dorrington Lodge
6 Tigh Phurist
Glencoe
Argyll
PA39 4HN
Tel:(Ballachulish) 08552 653

COMMENDED
♛

1 Twin
3 Double
1 Family

3 Pub.Bath/Show

B&B per person
£16.50-£17.50 Single
£13.50-£14.00 Double

Open Feb-Oct Xmas/New Year
Dinner 1845-1930
B&B + Eve.Meal
£21.50-£22.50

Comfortable, modern house just off main road, with excellent views over Loch
Leven. Home cooked meals using quality local produce.

Dunire Guest House
Glencoe
Argyll
PA39 4HS
Tel:(Ballachulish) 08552 305

2 Twin
3 Double

4 En Suite fac
2 Pub.Bath/Show

B&B per person
from £12.00 Double

Open Jan-Dec

The Glencoe Guest House
Strathlachlan
Glencoe
Argyll
PA39
Tel:(Ballachulish) 08552 244
Fax:08552 679

COMMENDED
♛ ♛

2 Twin
3 Double
1 Family

4 En Suite fac
1 Pub.Bath/Show

B&B per person
£12.00-£18.00 Double

Open Jan-Dec

Quiet peaceful riverside setting on edge of village. Magnificent views. Ideal
base for touring and for mountain sports. Family run.

Scorry Breac Guest House
Glencoe
Argyll
PA39 4HT
Tel:(Ballachulish) 08552 354

COMMENDED
♛ ♛

2 Twin
2 Double
1 Family

2 En Suite fac
2 Pub.Bath/Show

B&B per person
£14.00-£18.00 Single
£13.00-£18.00 Double

Open Jan-Dec
Dinner 1800-1830
B&B + Eve.Meal
£24.00-£28.00

Modern single storey house with large garden overlooking Loch Leven. In a
quiet secluded situation on the edge of the village with local forest walk

---

GLENCOE continued

Map 1
F1

Glencoe Outdoor Centre
Carnoch House
Glencoe
Argyll
PA39 4HS
Tel:(Ballachulish) 08552 350
Fax:08552 644

1 Twin	3 Pub.Bath/Show	B&B per person	Open Jan-Dec
6 Family		to £13.00 Single	Dinner from 1830
		to £13.00 Double	B&B + Eve.Meal
			to £16.00

GLENCRIPESDALE
Argyll

Map 1
D1

COMMENDED
👑 👑 👑

Glencripesdale House
Loch Sunart
Acharacle
Argyll
PH36 4JH
Tel:(Salen) 096785 263

2 Twin	4 En Suite fac	B&B per person	Open Mar-Oct, Xmas, New Year
2 Double	1 Pub.Bath/Show		Dinner from 1900
			B&B + Eve.Meal
			£60.00-£69.00

9 miles (13kms) of forestry track make isolation key attraction of converted 18C farmhouse. Warm hospitality, comfort and food are a close second.

GLENDEVON
Perthshire

Map 2
B3

Tormaukin Hotel & Restaurant
GLENDEVON, By DOLLAR, PERTHSHIRE FK14 7JY
Telephone: 0259 781252 Fax: 0259 781526
Egon Ronay Recommended

A friendly, ten-bedroomed Inn, ideally located in beautiful countryside between Gleneagles and Kinross, serving some of the best fresh food in Scotland. Come along and sample our extensive bar food menu or treat yourself to dinner in the restaurant.

Tormaukin Hotel
Glendevon, Dollar
Perthshire
FK14 7JY
Tel:(Muckhart) 0259 781252
Fax:0259 781526

COMMENDED
👑 👑 👑
👑

1 Single	10 En Suite fac	B&B per person	Open Feb-Dec
7 Twin		£40.00-£48.00 Single	Dinner 1830-2130
1 Double		£25.00-£35.00 Double	
1 Family			

Originally a Drovers' Inn, retaining the olde worlde warmth. Open log fires, beamed ceilings, good food. Ideal centre for the keen golfer.

GLENFARG
Perthshire

Map 2
C3

Glenfarg Hotel
Main Street
Glenfarg
Perthshire
PH2 9NU
Tel:(Glenfarg) 0577 830241
Fax:0577 830665

COMMENDED
👑 👑 👑

2 Single	13 En Suite fac	B&B per person	Open Jan-Dec
5 Twin	1 Limited ensuite	£15.00-£28.00 Single	Dinner 1830-2130
4 Double		£15.00-£26.00 Double	B&B + Eve.Meal
3 Family			£25.00-£38.00

Family run Victorian hotel, fully modernised, in picturesque Glenfarg. Many Scottish dishes using mainly fresh produce. Golf packages available.

Lomond Hotel
Main Street
Glenfarg
Perthshire
PH2 9NU
Tel:(Glenfarg) 0577 830474

3 Single	5 En Suite fac	B&B per person	Open Jan-Dec
3 Twin	2 Pub.Bath/Show	£16.00-£23.00 Single	Dinner 1900-2100
7 Double		£16.00-£23.00 Double	B&B + Eve.Meal
			£24.00-£31.00

GLENFINNAN Inverness-shire	Map 3 F1

Glenfinnan House Hotel

GLENFINNAN, FORT WILLIAM PH37 4LT 0397 722235

This pine-panelled mansion house, former seat of the Jacobite Macdonalds of Glenaladale, overlooks Loch Shiel and the monument to Prince Charlie and his men. We offer Highland hospitality, comfortable accommodation, good home cooking and Highland bagpipe music. Boating, fishing and hill-walking are also available in this idyllic location.

Glenfinnan House Hotel Glenfinnan Inverness-shire PH37 4LT Tel:(Kinlocheil) 0397722 235	APPROVED 👑 👑 👑	5 Single 6 Twin 6 Double 3 Family	10 En Suite fac 3 Priv.NOT ensuite 6 Pub.Bath/Show	B&B per person £28.00-£40.00 Single £28.00-£40.00 Double	Open Apr-Oct Dinner 1900-2030 B&B + Eve.Meal £45.00-£57.00

Victorian mansion set in its own mature grounds overlooking Loch Shiel and the Glenfinnan monument. Views of Ben Nevis in the distance.

THE PRINCE'S HOUSE

GLENFINNAN, INVERNESS-SHIRE PH37 4LT
Telephone 0397 722 246

On the romantic "Road to the Isles" in the heart of Bonnie Prince Charlie country, The Prince's House was one of the only buildings standing in 1745. All rooms are fully modernised with en-suite, while retaining their original characters. The Taste of Scotland restaurant offers superb cuisine using local gourmet produce. *Smoking restricted.*

The Prince's House, Road to the Isles Glenfinnan Inverness-shire PH37 4LT Tel:(Kinlocheil) 0397722 246 Fax:0397722 307	COMMENDED 👑 👑 👑	1 Single 3 Twin 4 Double 1 Family	9 En Suite fac	B&B per person £30.95-£40.95 Single £25.95-£35.95 Double	Open Mar-mid Dec, New Year Dinner 1930-2030 B&B + Eve.Meal £45.90-£55.90

Former coaching inn, fine mountain views. Ideal touring base: Aonach Mor and Fort William 15 miles (24kms). Taste of Scotland using local produce.

GLENLIVET Banffshire	Map 4 D9				
Old Manse Guest House The Old Manse, Craggan Glenlivet, Ballindalloch Banffshire AB37 9EB Tel:(Glenlivet) 0807 590481		HIGHLY COMMENDED 👑 👑	1 Twin 2 Double	2 Pub.Bath/Show	B&B per person £25.00-£28.00 Single £18.00-£20.00 Double	Open Jan-Dec Dinner 1830-2000 B&B + Eve.Meal £34.00-£36.00

Elegant 19C house beside B9008 on the Whisky Trail. Emphasis on good food and comfort. Panoramic views over River Avon and Cromdale Hills.

GLENLUCE Wigtownshire	Map 1 G1				
Kelvin House Hotel 53 Main Street Glenluce Wigtownshire Tel:(Glenluce) 05813 303 Fax:05813 258		COMMENDED 👑 👑 👑	2 Twin 4 Family	3 En Suite fac 3 Priv.NOT ensuite 1 Pub.Bath/Show	B&B per person £17.50-£22.50 Single £17.50-£22.50 Double	Open Jan-Dec Dinner 1800-2230

Located in tranquil village with easy access to major routes. Convenient for touring, sightseeing, golfing, fishing, shooting.

GLENLUCE continued	Map 1 G1						
Torwood House Hotel Glenluce Wigtownshire DG8 0PB Tel:(Glenluce) 05813 469 Fax:05813 258			1 Single 2 Twin 2 Double 4 Family	2 Pub.Bath/Show	B&B per person £16.50-£18.50 Single £16.50-£18.50 Double	Open Jan-Dec Dinner 1700-2200 B&B + Eve.Meal £22.50-£25.50	

| Rowantree Guest House 38 Main Street Glenluce Wigtownshire DG8 0PS Tel:(Glenluce) 05813 244 | COMMENDED ♛ | | 1 Twin 1 Double 2 Family | 2 Limited ensuite 1 Pub.Bath/Show | B&B per person £12.00-£15.00 Double | Open Jan-Dec Dinner 1830-2000 B&B + Eve.Meal £18.00-£21.00 | |

Family run house situated in centre of small village, 10 miles (16kms) from Stranraer and the Irish ferry. Car parking; large garden; home cooking.

GLENROTHES Fife	Map 2 D3						
Balgeddie House Hotel Balgeddie Way Glenrothes Fife KY6 3ET Tel:(Glenrothes) 0592 742511 Fax:0592 621702	COMMENDED ♛ ♛ ♛ ♛		4 Single 7 Twin 7 Double	17 En Suite fac 1 Priv.NOT ensuite	B&B per person £27.65-£68.00 Single £30.00-£68.00 Double	Open Jan-Dec Dinner 1900-2130 B&B + Eve.Meal £50.00-£84.50	

Under personal supervision of resident directors, 1930's country house hotel set in 6 acres of parkland. Games room and croquet lawn.

| Rescobie Hotel 6 Valley Drive Leslie Fife KY6 3BQ Tel:(Glenrothes) 0592 742143 Fax:0592 620231 | COMMENDED ♛ ♛ ♛ ♛ | | 3 Single 7 Twin | 10 En Suite fac | B&B per person £32.00-£52.00 Single £25.00-£35.00 Double | Open Jan-Dec Dinner 1900-2130 B&B + Eve.Meal £40.00-£56.00 | |

1920's former country residence, tastefully converted to a family run hotel. All fresh produce.

GLENSHEE Perthshire	Map 4 D1						
Blackwater Inn Blackwater Glenshee Perthshire PH10 7LH Tel:(Blacklunans) 0250 882234			1 Single 3 Twin 3 Double 2 Family	2 En Suite fac 3 Pub.Bath/Show	B&B per person £18.00-£22.00 Single £18.00-£22.00 Double	Open Jan-Dec Dinner 1700-2130 B&B + Eve.Meal £28.00-£32.00	

BE SURE TO CHOOSE THE SCOTTISH TOURIST BOARD'S SIGN OF QUALITY

GLENSHEE Perthshire	Map 4 D1

Dalmunzie House Hotel
Tel: 0250 885224
Fax: 0250 885225

SPITTAL OF GLENSHEE
BLAIRGOWRIE · PERTHSHIRE PH10 7QG

This family-run Country House Hotel "in the hills", situated 1½ miles off the main A93 Perth-Braemar road, offers an ideal base for touring Royal Deeside and the Highlands. A relaxed, informal atmosphere, where roaring log fires, personal service, traditional Scottish cooking and 16 bedrooms all with private bathrooms are our hallmarks.

Golf, tennis, fishing and shooting are available on our 6,000 acre estate, and in the winter months, skiing is on our doorstep - only 5 miles away.

Dalmunzie House Hotel Glenshee, Blairgowrie Perthshire PH10 7QG Tel:(Glenshee) 0250 885224/885226 Fax:0250 885225	COMMENDED 👑 👑 👑	1 Single 8 Twin 9 Double 8 Family	16 En Suite fac 1 Pub.Bath/Show	B&B per person £45.00-£51.00 Single £33.50-£41.50 Double	Open Jan-Nov Dinner 1900-2030 B&B + Eve.Meal £52.50-£60.50	
		Referred to as a "house in the hills", a warm and friendly family run hotel with log fires, games room, tennis, shooting and golfing.				
Dalrulzion Hotel Glenshee Perthshire PH10 7LJ Tel:(Blacklunans) 0250 882222		2 Single 3 Twin 4 Double 3 Family	6 En Suite fac 3 Pub.Bath/Show	B&B per person £18.00-£20.00 Single £16.00-£18.00 Double	Open Jan-Dec Dinner 1700-2100 B&B + Eve.Meal £24.00-£26.00	
Spittal of Glenshee Hotel Glenshee Perthshire PH10 7QF Tel:(Glenshee) 0250 885215 Fax:0250 885223	AWARD Pending	7 Single 23 Twin 10 Double 8 Family	45 En Suite fac 3 Priv.NOT ensuite	B&B per person £20.00-£28.00 Single £20.00-£28.00 Double	Open Jan-Dec Dinner 1830-2100 B&B + Eve.Meal £30.00-£39.00	

GLENSHIEL by Kyle of Lochalsh, Ross-shire	Map 3 F1

Kintail Lodge Hotel Glenshiel,by Kyle of Lochalsh Ross-shire IV40 8HL Tel:(Glenshiel) 059981 275 Fax:059981 226	COMMENDED 👑 👑 👑	3 Single 2 Twin 5 Double 2 Family	10 En Suite fac 1 Pub.Bath/Show	B&B per person £25.00-£36.00 Single £25.00-£36.00 Double	Open Jan-Dec Dinner 1900-2030 B&B + Eve.Meal £42.00-£53.00	
		Early Victorian former shooting lodge on shores of Loch Duich at the foot of Five Sisters of Kintail. Ideal touring and hill walking centre.				

GOLSPIE
Sutherland
Golf Links Hotel
Church Street
Golspie
Sutherland
KW10 6TT
Tel:(Golspie) 0408 633408

Map 4
B6

COMMENDED
👑 👑 👑

5 Twin
3 Double

8 En Suite fac

B&B per person
£27.00-£30.00 Single
from £27.00 Double

Open Jan-Dec
Dinner 1900-2100
B&B + Eve.Meal
from £44.00

Personally run, this former manse is well sited for golf enthusiasts and ideal for business or pleasure.

Stags Head Hotel
Main Street
Golspie
Sutherland
KW10 6TG
Tel:(Golspie) 0408 633245

Award
Pending

3 Twin
1 Double
1 Family

5 En Suite fac

B&B per person
from £27.50 Single
from £22.50 Double

Open Jan-Dec
Dinner 1800-2100

GOREBRIDGE
Midlothian
Borthwick Castle
North Middleton
Gorebridge
Midlothian
EH25 4QY
Tel:(Gorebridge) 0875 820514
Fax:0875 821702

Map 2
D5

5 Twin
5 Double

10 En Suite fac
2 Pub.Bath/Show

B&B per person
£80.00-£150.00 Single
£47.50-£82.50 Double

Open Mar-Nov
Dinner 1930-2130
B&B + Eve.Meal
£108.00-£168.00

GOTT BAY
Isle of Tiree, Argyll
Kirkapol Guest House
Gott Bay
Isle of Tiree, Argyll
PA77 6TN
Tel:(Scarinish) 08792 729

Map 1
A2

COMMENDED
👑 👑

2 Twin
4 Double
1 Family

7 En Suite fac

B&B per person
£17.50-£21.00 Single
£17.50-£21.00 Double

Open Jan-Dec
Dinner 1800-2000
B&B + Eve.Meal
£26.50-£30.00

Former church converted in a comfortable, practical style. All rooms en suite. Birds and wildflowers abound on this timeless isle. Windsurfing area.

GOUROCK
Renfrewshire
The Anchorage Hotel
1 Ashton Road
Gourock
Renfrewshire
PA19 1BY
Tel:(Gourock) 0475 32202

Map 1
G5

4 Single
5 Double
1 Family

10 En Suite fac

B&B per person
£35.00-£40.00 Single
from £30.00 Double

Open Jan-Dec
Dinner 1800-2000

GOUROCK continued *0 14756346 7)* Stakis Gourock Gantock Hotel Cloch Road Gourock Renfrewshire PA19 1AR Tel:(Gourock) 0475 34671 Tlx:778584 Fax:0475 32490	Map 1 G5	COMMENDED 👑 👑 👑 👑	46 Twin 13 Double 40 Family	99 En Suite fac	B&B per person from £80.50 Single to £49.50 Double	Open Jan-Dec Dinner 1830-2130

Modern hotel overlooking Clyde Estuary and the Hills of Argyll. Fine views from first floor restaurant.

GRANTOWN-ON-SPEY **Moray** The Ardlarig Woodlands Terrace Grantown-on-Spey Moray PH26 3JU Tel:(Grantown-on-Spey) 0479 3245	Map 4 C9	COMMENDED 👑 👑	1 Twin 5 Double 1 Family	3 En Suite fac 2 Priv.NOT ensuite 3 Pub.Bath/Show	B&B per person £17.50-£21.50 Single £17.50-£18.50 Double	Open Jan-Dec Dinner at 1900 B&B + Eve.Meal £28.00-£32.00

Comfortable Victorian home, many original features, set in 3/4 acre garden. Views of Cromdale hills and pine woodlands. Emphasis on Scottish fayre.

Coppice Hotel Grantown-on-Spey Moray PH26 3LD Tel:(Grantown-on-Spey) 0479 2688 Fax:0479 2688		COMMENDED 👑 👑 👑	4 Single 14 Twin 6 Double 2 Family	26 En Suite fac	B&B per person £22.50-£27.50 Single £22.50-£25.00 Double	Open Jan-Dec Dinner 1900-2100 B&B + Eve.Meal £35.00-£40.00

Personally supervised family hotel in 2 acres of grounds, a few minutes walk from the town centre.

Craiglynne Hotel Grantown-on-Spey Moray PH26 3JX Tel:(Grantown-on-Spey) 0479 2597			21 Single 42 Twin 18 Double 1 Family	82 En Suite fac	B&B per person £42.00-£50.00 Single £38.00-£46.00 Double	Open Mar-Nov Dinner 1830-2000 B&B + Eve.Meal £48.00-£58.50

Dunvegan Hotel Grantown-on-Spey Moray PH26 3HX Tel:(Grantown-on-Spey) 0479 2301			1 Twin 2 Double 5 Family	2 En Suite fac 2 Pub.Bath/Show	B&B per person £15.00-£19.00 Single £15.00-£19.00 Double	Open Jan-Dec Dinner from 1900 B&B + Eve.Meal £26.00-£30.00

Garth Hotel Castle Road Grantown-on-Spey Moray PH26 3HN Tel:(Grantown-on-Spey) 0479 2836 Fax:0479 2116		HIGHLY COMMENDED 👑 👑 👑 👑	8 Twin 9 Double	17 En Suite fac	B&B per person to £47.00 Single to £38.00 Double	Open Jan-Dec Dinner 1900-2030 B&B + Eve.Meal to £60.00

17C building retains Olde Worlde charm with 4 acre garden. Fishing available. Cairngorm and Lecht ski slopes equidistant from hotel.

GRANTOWN-ON-SPEY Moray	Map 4 C9

The Pines Hotel

18 WOODSIDE AVENUE, GRANTOWN-ON-SPEY PH26 3JR
TELEPHONE/FAX: (0479) 87 2092

A family-run hotel on edge of pine woods; home cooking, licensed. All bedrooms have tea/coffee facilities and colour TV. En-suite available. Large, comfortable residents' lounge. An ideal base for salmon and trout fishing and the many other activities the area provides.

DB&B from £26 per night - Reductions for children.

The Pines Hotel Woodside Avenue Grantown-on-Spey Moray PH26 3JR Tel:(Grantown-on-Spey) 0479 87 2092 Fax:0479 87 2092	COMMENDED ♨ ♨ ♨	1 Single 3 Twin 2 Double 3 Family	5 En Suite fac 2 Pub.Bath/Show	B&B per person from £17.00 Single £17.00-£21.00 Double	Open Jan-Dec Dinner from 1830 B&B + Eve.Meal £26.00-£30.00	

Family run, situated on edge of pine wood, only 0.5 miles (1km) from town centre. All home cooking. Special diets on request. Dogs welcome.

Ravenscourt House Hotel

STB ♨♨♨ DELUXE

SEAFIELD AVENUE
GRANTOWN-ON-SPEY PH26 3JG
Telephone: 0479-2286 Fax: 0479-3260

All bedrooms have luxury en-suite facilities, welcome tray, colour TV. Comfortable beds, some KINGSIZE. Two lounges (one for non-smokers). LICENSED. The 'ORANGERY' Restaurant specialises in fresh fish, game, prime Scottish beef. Vegetarian dishes. The generous portions herald a return to meals that are satisfying and not just decorative! RAC Highly Acclaimed and 'Best Small Hotel' in Scotland winner 1990. ROUTIERS regional winner 'Best Newcomer Award 1991.' Taste of Scotland Member. Privately owned and run by the proprietors. DB&B from £56 per day. Bedrooms: Total 9, 4 Twin, 3 Double, 2 Family, all with private facilities.

Ravenscourt House Hotel Seafield Avenue Grantown-on-Spey Moray PH26 3JG Tel:(Grantown-on-Spey) 0479 2286 Fax:0479 3260	DELUXE ♨ ♨ ♨	3 Twin 3 Double 3 Family	9 En Suite fac	B&B per person from £39.00 Single from £39.00 Double	Open Feb-Dec Dinner 1900-2200 B&B + Eve.Meal from £60.00	

Elegantly furnished, former manse in quiet residential area near centre. Fine conservatory restaurant using fresh produce. Fish dishes a speciality.

Seafield Lodge Hotel Woodside Avenue Grantown-on-Spey Moray PH26 3JN Tel:(Grantown-on-Spey) 0479 872152 Fax:0479 872340		2 Single 6 Twin 4 Double 2 Family Suites avail.	14 En Suite fac	B&B per person £26.50-£39.50 Single £26.50-£39.50 Double	Open Dec-Oct Dinner 1800-2100 B&B + Eve.Meal £39.00-£52.00	

GRANTOWN-ON-SPEY continued	Map 4 C9						
Spey Valley House Hotel Seafield Avenue Grantown-on-Spey Moray PH26 3EJ Tel:(Grantown-on-Spey) 0479 2942/2052			5 Single 10 Twin 2 Double	10 En Suite fac 2 Pub.Bath/Show	B&B per person £21.00-£26.50 Single £21.00-£26.50 Double	Open Jan-Dec Dinner at 1900 B&B + Eve.Meal £29.00-£34.50	
Tyree House Hotel Grantown-on-Spey Moray PH26 Tel:(Grantown-on-Spey) 0479 2615	COMMENDED		2 Single 7 Double	9 En Suite fac	B&B per person from £25.00 Single from £20.00 Double	Open Jan-Dec Dinner 1750-2300 B&B + Eve.Meal from £30.00	
		Small family run hotel in centre of Grantown-on-Spey. Within easy reach of Aviemore and the amenities of the Spey Valley.					
Ardconnel Woodlands Terrace Grantown-on-Spey Moray PH26 3JU Tel:(Grantown-on-Spey) 0479 2104	HIGHLY COMMENDED		1 Twin 4 Double 2 Family	6 En Suite fac 1 Priv.NOT ensuite	B&B per person from £25.00 Single from £20.00 Double	Open Jan-Dec Dinner from 1900 B&B + Eve.Meal from £30.00	
		Large detached Victorian house with croquet lawn pleasantly situated with open aspects to hills, forests and lochan. Comfortable lounge.					
Brooklynn Grant Road Grantown-on-Spey Moray PH26 3LA Tel:(Grantown-on-Spey) 0479 3113	COMMENDED		1 Single 1 Twin 3 Double 1 Family	2 En Suite fac 1 Pub.Bath/Show	B&B per person from £16.00 Single from £16.00 Double	Open Jan-Dec Dinner 1830-1930	
		Attractive villa and garden in quiet area within easy walking distance of town, woods and river. Many personal touches; evening meal by arrangement.					
Crann Tara Guest House High Street Grantown-on-Spey Moray PH26 3EN Tel:(Grantown-on-Spey) 0479 2197	COMMENDED		1 Single 1 Twin 3 Family	2 Pub.Bath/Show	B&B per person £14.00-£16.00 Single £14.00-£16.00 Double	Open Jan-Dec Dinner from 1830 B&B + Eve.Meal £21.00-£24.00	
		19C town house, recently modernised and personally run. Near River Spey, with rod storage and drying room. Cycles for hire. Off-street car parking.					

SCOTTISH TOURIST BOARD
QUALITY COMMENDATIONS ARE:

Deluxe – *An EXCELLENT quality standard*
Highly Commended – *A VERY GOOD quality standard*
Commended – *A GOOD quality standard*
Approved – *An ADEQUATE quality standard*

GRANTOWN-ON-SPEY continued	Map 4 C9

Culdearn House
WOODLANDS TERRACE, GRANTOWN-ON-SPEY PH26 3JU
TEL: (0479) 872106 Fax: (0479) 873641

Private Country House offering house party atmosphere and a warm welcome from the Scottish proprietors. Isobel and Alasdair Little provide freshly prepared food, malt whiskies and a moderately priced wine list. All guest rooms have en-suite private facilities with colour TV, radio and welcome tray. Log and peat fires in season.

Ideal location for birdwatching, walking, salmon and trout fishing. Several golf courses nearby. Horse-riding arranged. Historic sites and many good walks. 3-day and 7-day breaks available.

AA/RAC Highly Acclaimed
Taste of Scotland Members
Please contact Isobel and
Alasdair Little for reservations.

Culdearn House Woodlands Terrace Grantown-on-Spey Moray PH26 3JU Tel:(Grantown-on-Spey) 0479 872106 Fax:0479 873641	HIGHLY COMMENDED 👑 👑 👑	1 Single 3 Twin 5 Double	9 En Suite fac	B&B per person	Open Mar-Oct Dinner 1845-1930 B&B + Eve.Meal £38.00-£50.00	
		Elegant Victorian house, retaining many original features. Warm and friendly atmosphere. All rooms en suite facilities. Taste of Scotland member.				

Garden Park Guest House Woodside Avenue Grantown-on-Spey Moray PH26 3JN Tel:(Grantown-on-Spey) 0479 3235	COMMENDED 👑 👑 👑	3 Twin 2 Double	5 En Suite fac	B&B per person £19.30-£21.80 Single £19.30-£21.80 Double	Open Jan-Dec Dinner 1830-1900 B&B + Eve.Meal £28.70-£31.70	
		Victorian, stone built house set in own grounds. Home cooking, peat fires. No steps and ground floor accommodation.				

Kinross Guest House Woodside Avenue Grantown-on-Spey Moray PH26 3JR Tel:(Grantown-on-Spey) 0479 872042	COMMENDED 👑 👑 👑	1 Single 2 Twin 2 Double 2 Family	4 En Suite fac 2 Pub.Bath/Show	B&B per person £17.00-£21.00 Single £16.00-£23.00 Double	Open Mar-Nov Dinner from 1900 B&B + Eve.Meal £26.50-£34.00	
		Victorian villa with original features in peaceful residential area. Friendly, informal atmosphere with Scottish hosts. No smoking house.				

Parkburn Guest House High Street Grantown-on-Spey Moray PH26 3EN Tel:(Grantown-on-Spey) 0479 3116	COMMENDED 👑 👑	1 Twin 3 Double	2 En Suite fac 1 Pub.Bath/Show	B&B per person from £15.00 Single from £15.00 Double	Open Jan-Dec Dinner at 1900 B&B + Eve.Meal from £24.00	
		Semi detached Victorian villa standing back from main road with ample parking available. Fishing and fishing tuition can be arranged.				

Details of Grading and Classification are on page vi.

Key to symbols is on back flap.

GRANTOWN-ON-SPEY continued
Map 4 C9

Rossmor Guest House
Woodlands Terrace
Grantown-on-Spey
Moray
PH26 3JU
Tel:(Grantown-on-Spey)
0479 872201

COMMENDED
👑 👑 👑

1 Twin	5 En Suite fac	B&B per person
4 Double	1 Priv.NOT ensuite	£18.00-£20.00 Double
1 Family	1 Pub.Bath/Show	

Open Jan-Dec
Dinner at 1830
B&B + Eve.Meal
£28.00-£30.00

Spacious Victorian detached house with original features and large garden. Magnificent views of countryside. Home cooking; a warm welcome. Parking.

Willowbank Guest House
Grantown-on-Spey
Moray
PH26 3HN
Tel:(Grantown-on-Spey)
0479 2089

4 Twin	2 Pub.Bath/Show	B&B per person
1 Double		from £15.00 Double
4 Family		

Open Jan-Dec
Dinner from 1800
B&B + Eve.Meal
from £23.00

GRANTSHOUSE
by Duns, Berwickshire
Map 2 F5

Haggerston House Hotel
Grantshouse
Berwickshire
TD11 3RW
Tel:(Grantshouse) 03615
229

COMMENDED
👑 👑 👑

3 Twin	3 En Suite fac	B&B per person
2 Double	1 Pub.Bath/Show	£26.00-£28.75 Single
		£20.00-£21.75 Double

Open Jan-Dec
Dinner 1900-2100
B&B + Eve.Meal
£32.00-£34.75

Quietly situated just off the A1 in its own gardens. Relaxed atmosphere and good food. Ideal centre for touring Borders and Edinburgh.

GREENOCK
Renfrewshire
Map 1 G5

Tontine Hotel
6 Ardgowan Square
Greenock
Renfrewshire
PA16 8NG
Tel:(Greenock) 0475 23316
Tlx:779801

20 Twin	29 En Suite fac	B&B per person
9 Double		£40.00-£55.00 Single
		£37.50 Double

Open Jan-Dec
Dinner 1830-2130
B&B + Eve.Meal
£47.50

GRETNA
Dumfriesshire
Map 2 D1

The Gables Hotel
1 Annan Road
Gretna
Dumfriesshire
CA6 5DQ
Tel:(Gretna) 0461 338300

2 Twin	12 En Suite fac	B&B per person
8 Double		£35.00 Single
2 Family		£22.50-£32.50 Double

Open Jan-Dec
Dinner 1900-2100

The Garden House Hotel
Sarkfoot Road
Gretna
Dumfriesshire
Tel:(Gretna) 0461 337621
Fax:0461 337692

COMMENDED
👑 👑 👑

4 Twin	21 En Suite fac	B&B per person
15 Double		£39.00 Single
2 Family		£39.00 Double
Suite avail.		

Open Jan-Dec
Dinner 1900-2130
B&B + Eve.Meal
£52.00-£60.00

The hotel, opened 1992, situated close to romantic Gretna Green. Well maintained, extensive grounds including a floodlit Japanese water garden.

GRETNA continued
Map 2 D1

Hunters Lodge Hotel Annan Road Gretna Dumfriesshire CA6 5DL Tel:(Gretna) 0461 338214	**COMMENDED** 👑 👑 👑	1 Single 1 Twin 4 Double 2 Family	5 En Suite fac 1 Pub.Bath/Show	B&B per person £30.00-£35.00 Single £20.00-£30.00 Double	Open Jan-Dec Dinner 1900-2030

Modernised Listed building in centre of Gretna, close to Registry Office at the Gateway to Scotland. Wedding functions catered for.

Surrone Guest House Annan Road Gretna Dumfriesshire CA6 5DL Tel:(Gretna) 0461 338341	**COMMENDED** 👑 👑 👑	3 Twin 3 Double 1 Family	6 En Suite fac 1 Priv.NOT ensuite	B&B per person £30.00 Single £22.00 Double	Open Jan-Dec Dinner 1900-2000 B&B + Eve.Meal £29.00-£37.00

Former farmhouse modernised to a high standard, in a quiet position, yet only minutes from the A74. Friendly personal welcome.

GRETNA GREEN
Dumfriesshire
Map 2 D1

Forte Travelodge, Welcome Break, Gretna Green S/A, A(M)74 Northbound Gretna Dumfriesshire CA6 5HQ Tel:(Freephone) 0800 850950/0461 337567 Fax:0461 337752	**COMMENDED** **Lodge**	1 Twin 63 Family	64 En Suite fac	Price per room £31.95	Open Jan-Dec Dinner to 2400

Forte Travelodge offering convenient overnight en suite accommodation. Restaurant facilities on site. Reservations telephone 0800 850 950.

Gretna Hall Hotel Gretna Green Dumfriesshire CA6 5DY Tel:(Gretna) 0461 338257		28 Single 59 Twin 27 Double 4 Family	118 En Suite fac	B&B per person £35.00-£42.00 Single £31.00-£38.00 Double	Open Mar-Nov Dinner 1830-2000 B&B + Eve.Meal £41.00-£50.50

Lovers Leap Travel Lodges Gretna Green Dumfriesshire CA6 5EA Tel:(Gretna) 0461 337917 Fax:0461 338411	**APPROVED** 👑 👑	2 Single 6 Twin 11 Double 2 Family	21 En Suite fac	B&B per person £22.00-£27.50 Single £16.50-£31.00 Double	Open Jan-Dec Dinner 1700-2130 B&B + Eve.Meal £21.50-£36.50

Motel accommodation opposite Old Blacksmiths Shop in the heart of the village.

GULLANE
East Lothian
Map 2 E4

Golf Inn Hotel Main Steet Gullane East Lothian EH31 2AB Tel:(Gullane) 0620 843259 Fax:0620 842006		3 Single 12 Twin 2 Double 2 Family	11 En Suite fac 4 Pub.Bath/Show	B&B per person £30.00-£40.00 Single £30.00 Double	Open Jan-Dec Dinner 1900-2200 B&B + Eve.Meal £42.00-£52.00

Greywalls Hotel Muirfield Gullane East Lothian EH31 2EG Tel:(Gullane) 0620 842144 Fax:0620 842241	**HIGHLY** **COMMENDED** 👑 👑 👑 👑	4 Single 16 Twin 2 Double	22 En Suite fac	B&B per person £90.00-£140.00 Single £70.00-£75.00 Double	Open Apr-Nov Dinner 1930-2100

Renowned family owned Lutyens house with friendly atmosphere; gardens by Gertrude Jekyll. Adjacent to Muirfield Golf Course. Views over Forth.

GULLANE continued — Map 2 E4

Mallard Hotel
East Links Road
Gullane
East Lothian
EH31 2AF
Tel:(Gullane) 0620 843288

COMMENDED

2 Single
15 Twin
1 Family

18 En Suite fac
4 Pub.Bath/Show

B&B per person
£33.00-£43.00 Single
from £33.00 Double

Open Jan-Dec
Dinner 1900-2130
B&B + Eve.Meal
from £45.00

Family run hotel in peaceful location overlooking Gullane's famous golf courses
Close to sandy beach and Nature Reserve.

The Queen's Hotel
Main Street
Gullane
East Lothian
EH31 2AS
Tel:(Gullane) 0620
842275/842125

APPROVED

5 Single
24 Twin
3 Double
3 Family

16 En Suite fac
6 Limited ensuite
9 Pub.Bath/Show

B&B per person
to £33.00 Single
to £33.00 Double

Open Jan-Dec
Dinner 1900-2200
B&B + Eve.Meal
to £49.50

Family run hotel in picturesque village. Ideal base for golfing holiday.

HADDINGTON — Map 2 E5
East Lothian

BROWNS' HOTEL
1 WEST ROAD, HADDINGTON, EH41 3RD.
TEL: (0620) 822254. FAX: (0620) 822254.

Uninterrupted view of the Lammermuir Hills is afforded from this hotel,
within easy access to Edinburgh golf courses and many sports facilities.
The bedrooms are furnished to the standard of the Hotel. The restaurant
has an excellent reputation in the area with dinner available each evening
and lunch Sundays.

Browns' Hotel
1 West Road
Haddington
East Lothian
EH41 3RD
Tel:(Haddington) 062082
2254
Fax:062082 2254

HIGHLY
COMMENDED

1 Single
2 Twin
2 Double

5 En Suite fac

B&B per person
£59.50 Single
£39.00 Double

Open Jan-Dec
Dinner 1900-2100
B&B + Eve.Meal
£84.00

Regency town house, elegant furnishings and decor with contemporary Scottish
paintings. Restaurant noted in many guides.

Maitlandfield House Hotel
24 Sidegate
Haddington
East Lothian
EH41 4BZ
Tel:(Haddington)
062082 6513
Fax:062082 6713

COMMENDED

3 Single
16 Twin
3 Double

22 En Suite fac

B&B per person
£30.00-£37.50 Single
£30.00-£37.50 Double

Open Jan-Dec
Dinner to 2200
B&B + Eve.Meal
£40.00-£47.50

A magnificent Country House Hotel privately owned and professionally managed.
Ideally located for hill walking, shooting, fishing and golfing.

HALKIRK — Map 4 C3
Caithness

Ulbster Arms Hotel
Halkirk
Caithness
KW12 6XY
Tel:(Halkirk) 084783 206

COMMENDED

11 Single
14 Twin
3 Double

24 En Suite fac
2 Limited ensuite
5 Pub.Bath/Show

B&B per person
from £35.00 Single
from £35.00 Double

Open Jan-Dec
Dinner 1900-2100
B&B + Eve.Meal
from £50.00

Fishing and sporting hotel in centre of Halkirk and next to river. Some chalet
accommodation.

HAMILTON **Lanarkshire** Avonbridge Hotel Carlisle Road Hamilton Lanarkshire ML3 Tel:(Hamilton) 0698 420525/420529 Tlx:776838 Fax:0698 427326	Map 2 A6	COMMENDED 👑 👑 👑 👑	5 Single 17 Twin 20 Double 2 Family	44 En Suite fac	B&B per person £34.00-£53.00 Single £22.00-£33.00 Double	Open Jan-Dec Dinner 1815-2245 B&B + Eve.Meal £34.00-£45.00	

Family run hotel, 400 yards from the town centre. Convenient for motorway, Strathclyde Park and Chatelherault Country Park.

HARRAY **Orkney** Merkister Hotel Harray Orkney KW17 2LF Tel:(Harray) 085677 366/289 Fax:085677 515	Map 5 B1	COMMENDED 👑 👑 👑	2 Single 6 Twin 6 Double 1 Family Suite avail.	15 En Suite fac 3 Pub.Bath/Show	B&B per person £25.00-£29.50 Single £25.00-£35.50 Double	Open Mar-Nov Dinner 1900-2100 B&B + Eve.Meal £38.50-£48.50	

Peacefully situated on the shore of Loch Harray with distant views of the hills of Hoy. Fisherman's haven; own birdwatching hide.

HAWICK **Roxburghshire** Elm House Hotel 17 North Bridge Street Hawick Roxburghshire TD9 9BD Tel:(Hawick) 0450 72866	Map 2 E8	COMMENDED 👑 👑 👑	2 Single 6 Twin 4 Double 3 Family	15 En Suite fac	B&B per person £25.00-£28.00 Single £18.00-£20.00 Double	Open Jan-Dec Dinner 1830-2100 B&B + Eve.Meal £34.00-£37.00	

Family run, centrally situated in old town. Ideal base for touring the Borders. Fishing, bowling, golfing and shooting available. 8 annexe bedrooms.

KIRKLANDS HOTEL
HAWICK . SCOTTISH BORDERS
TEL: (0450) 72263   FAX: (0450) 370404

Charming, small hotel pleasantly situated in the beautiful Scottish Borders. Ideal base for tourist or businessman. Close to many attractions. Recommended by most leading hotel guides. Weekly terms and weekend breaks available.

Colour brochure and tariff on request.

Kirklands Hotel West Stewart Place Hawick Roxburghshire TD9 8BH Tel:(Hawick) 0450 72263/372263 Fax:0450 370404		COMMENDED 👑 👑 👑 👑	5 Twin 7 Double	12 En Suite fac 1 Pub.Bath/Show	B&B per person £48.50-£52.00 Single £37.50-£40.00 Double	Open Jan-Dec Dinner 1900-2100 B&B + Eve.Meal £55.00-£60.00	

Personally run, small hotel with some annexe accommodation quietly situated in its own grounds with fine views over town and countryside.

Mansfield House Hotel Weensland Road Hawick Roxburghshire TD9 9EL Tel:(Hawick) 0450 73988 Fax:0450 72007		COMMENDED 👑 👑 👑	4 Twin 4 Double 2 Family	10 En Suite fac	B&B per person £42.00-£52.00 Single £30.00-£40.00 Double	Open Jan-Dec Dinner 1900-2115 B&B + Eve.Meal £45.00-£67.00	

Family run hotel in extensive grounds with an outstanding reputation for excellent food and friendly atmosphere.

HAWICK continued

Map 2 E8

Whitchester Christian
Guest House
Borthaugh
Hawick
Roxburghshire
TD9 7LN
Tel:(Hawick) 0450 77477

COMMENDED
👑 👑 👑

1 Single	4 En Suite fac	B&B per person	Open Jan-Dec
5 Twin	1 Limited ensuite	£22.15-£25.00 Single	Dinner 1900-2030
2 Double	1 Pub.Bath/Show	£20.00-£22.00 Double	B&B + Eve.Meal
			£27.00-£29.00

Set in glorious countryside, early Victorian house with log fires and extensive gardens. Croquet and badminton. "Taste of Scotland" recommended.

BY HAWICK
Roxburghshire

Map 2 E8

Teviotdale Lodge
Hawick
Roxburghshire
TD9 0LB
Tel:(Teviotdale) 045085 232

COMMENDED
👑 👑 👑

1 Single	5 En Suite fac	B&B per person	Open Jan-Dec
2 Twin	1 Limited ensuite	£20.00-£25.00 Single	Dinner 1930-2030
3 Double	1 Pub.Bath/Show	£15.00-£20.00 Double	B&B + Eve.Meal
1 Family			£23.50-£28.50

Charming country house in beautiful Border hill country overlooking the River Teviot, 7 miles (11 kms) south of Hawick. 0.5 miles (1km) off the A7.

HELENSBURGH
Dunbartonshire

Map 1 G4

County Hotel
Old Luss Road
Helensburgh
Dunbartonshire
G84 7BH
Tel:(Helensburgh) 0436 72034

APPROVED
👑 👑

3 Single	4 En Suite fac	B&B per person	Open Jan-Dec
7 Twin	1 Pub.Bath/Show	£28.00-£32.00 Single	Dinner 1800-2100
1 Double		from £44.00 Double	
1 Family			

Family run hotel on edge of popular coastal town, convenient for road and rail. Scuba diving locally; compressor and boat available.

Bellfield Guest House
199 East Clyde Street
Helensburgh
Dunbartonshire
G84 7AJ
Tel:(Helensburgh) 0436 71628

1 Single	2 En Suite fac	B&B per person	Open Jan-Dec
2 Twin	2 Pub.Bath/Show	£16.00-£20.00 Single	Dinner 1800-1900
1 Double		£14.50-£16.50 Double	B&B + Eve.Meal
1 Family			£21.50-£27.00

HELMSDALE
Sutherland

Map 4 C5

Navidale House Hotel
Helmsdale
Sutherland
KW8 6JS
Tel:(Helmsdale) 04312 258

1 Single	14 En Suite fac	B&B per person	Open Feb-mid Nov
6 Twin		£30.00-£40.00 Single	Dinner 1900-2100
7 Double		£25.00-£30.00 Double	B&B + Eve.Meal
			£45.00-£50.00

Welcome Hosts provide a warm welcome, good service and information about their area. Look out for the people wearing the Welcome Host badge.

HOPEMAN **Moray** Clashach Lodge Hotel Forsyth Street Hopeman, Elgin Moray IV30 2SY Tel:(Hopeman) 0343 835077 Fax:0343 830050	Map 4 D7		2 Twin 2 Double 2 Family	1 Pub.Bath/Show	B&B per person £18.00-£20.00 Single £16.00-£18.00 Double	Open Jan-Dec Dinner 1800-2200 B&B + Eve.Meal £25.00-£27.00	
HOUSTON **Renfrewshire** The Houston Inn North Street Houston Renfrewshire PA6 7HF Tel:(Bridge of Weir) 0505 614315	Map 1 H5		2 Double 2 Family	1 Pɓb.Bath/Show	B&B per person £26.00-£28.00 Single £21.00-£22.00 Double	Open Jan-Dec	
HOWWOOD **Renfrewshire**	Map 1 H5						

Bowfield Hotel & Country Club

HOWWOOD · RENFREWSHIRE · PA9 1DB
Tel: 0505-705225. Fax: 0505-705230
Scotland's most established Country Club nestles in the peaceful
Renfrewshire countryside just 10 minutes from Glasgow Airport.
Comfortable hotel accommodation in a unique country-cottage style;
swimming, squash, fitness room, sauna, spa, health and beauty studio,
snooker and games room in addition to an excellent restaurant and lively bar,
all in a friendly Scottish atmosphere. **AA & RAC ★★★**

Bowfield Hotel & Country Club Lands of Bowfield Howwood Renfrewshire PA9 1DB Tel:(Kilbarchan) 0505 705225 Fax:0505 705230	**COMMENDED** 	6 Twin 3 Double 3 Family	12 En Suite fac	B&B per person £55.00-£65.00 Single £38.00-£45.00 Double	Open Jan-Dec Dinner 1800-2200 B&B + Eve.Meal £75.00-£85.00	
		Situated in pleasant countryside 7 miles (11kms) from Glasgow airport with full range of leisure facilities. Health and beauty salon.				
HUNTLY **Aberdeenshire** Castle Hotel Huntly Aberdeenshire AB54 4SH Tel:(Huntly) 0466 792696 Fax:0466 792641	**COMMENDED** ♛ ♛ ♛	12 Twin 5 Double 4 Family Suite avail.	20 En Suite fac	B&B per person £36.50-£42.00 Single £26.25-£29.50 Double	Open Jan-Dec Dinner 1800-2145 B&B + Eve.Meal £50.75-£56.50	
		Formerly the ancient family home of the Gordons. Standing in own grounds overlooking Huntly. Open fires in dining room and lounge. Local fishing.				

	Map 4 F9	**Award Pending**					
HUNTLY continued Huntly Hotel The Square Huntly Aberdeenshire AB54 5BR Tel:(Huntly) 0466 792703 Fax:0466 792703			3 Single 5 Twin 5 Double 1 Family	5 En Suite fac 7 Pub.Bath/Show	B&B per person £15.00-£40.00 Single £25.00-£55.00 Double	Open Jan-Dec Dinner 1700-2100 B&B + Eve.Meal £21.50-£46.50	

	Map 4 F9	**COMMENDED** 👑 👑 👑					
BY HUNTLY **Aberdeenshire** Forbes Arms Hotel Rothiemay, Huntly Aberdeenshire AB54 5LT Tel:(Rothiemay) 046681 248/328			2 Single 4 Twin 1 Family	6 En Suite fac 1 Pub.Bath/Show	B&B per person to £35.00 Single to £25.00 Double	Open Jan-Dec Dinner 1900-2100 B&B + Eve.Meal to £45.00	

Small coaching inn on banks of Deveron. Salmon and sea trout fishing. 40 miles (64kms) west of Aberdeen. Some lodge accommodation.

THE OLD MANSE OF MARNOCH

Luxury en-suite accommodation, fine food and wines in Georgian country house set in three acres of mature gardens on River Deveron. Acclaimed by major guidebooks, this small hotel is an oasis for the discerning traveller seeking quality and hospitality. Ideally situated to explore Grampian region, Whisky Trail, Castle Trail, etc. B&B from £30.00 per person. The Old Manse of Marnoch, Bridge of Marnoch, by Huntly, Aberdeenshire, AB54 5RS. Tel: (0466) 780873

Deluxe 👑 👑 👑

		DELUXE 👑 👑 👑					
The Old Manse of Marnoch Bridge of Marnoch,by Huntly Aberdeenshire AB54 5RS Tel:(Aberchirder) 0466 780873			2 Twin 3 Double	5 En Suite fac	B&B per person from £55.00 Single from £35.00 Double	Open Jan-Dec Dinner to 2000 B&B + Eve.Meal from £55.00	

Comfort and fine food in early 19th Century country house set in 5 acres of mature gardens on River Deveron.

	Map 2 C5	**HIGHLY COMMENDED** 👑 👑 👑 👑 👑					
INGLISTON **by Edinburgh,** **Midlothian** Norton House Hotel Ingliston,by Edinburgh Midlothian EH28 8LX Tel:031 333 1275 Fax:031 333 5305			30 Twin 17 Double Suites avail.	47 En Suite fac	B&B per person £50.00-£115.00 Single £25.00-£80.00 Double	Open Jan-Dec Dinner 1900-2130	

Ideally situated in wooded grounds, an elegant mansion house, 8 miles (13 kms) West of the city centre.

		COMMENDED Listed					
Royal Highland Lodge Royal Highland Centre Ingliston,by Edinburgh Midlothian Tel:031 333 4331 Fax:031 333 5236			29 Twin 7 Double	36 En Suite fac	Price per room from £16.75 room only	Open Jan-Dec Dinner 1800-2000	

Purpose built brick lodge on the Royal Highland Agricultural Show Grounds. Near airport. Ample car parking, 8 miles from city centre.

INNELLAN, by Dunoon
Argyll
Map 1 F5

Braemar Hotel Shore Road Innellan, by Dunoon Argyll PA23 7SP Tel:(Innellan) 036983 792/569	COMMENDED 👑 👑 👑	2 Single 2 Twin 5 Double 2 Family	11 En Suite fac	B&B per person £20.00-£23.50 Single £20.00-£23.50 Double	Open Jan-Dec Dinner 1930-2200 B&B + Eve.Meal £32.00-£35.50

Family run hotel situated on shore of Firth of Clyde with large south facing garden. All day bar menu available.

Ashgrove Guest House Wyndham Road Innellan, by Dunoon Argyll PA23 7SH Tel:(Innellan) 036983 306		1 Twin 1 Double 1 Family	3 En Suite fac	B&B per person £16.00-£18.00 Single £16.00-£18.00 Double	Open Jan-Dec Dinner 1830-1930 B&B + Eve.Meal £24.00-£26.00

INNERLEITHEN
Peeblesshire
Map 2 D6

Corner House Hotel 1 Chapel Street Innerleithen Peebles-shire EH44 6HN Tel:(Innerleithen) 0896 831181 Fax:0896 831182	COMMENDED 👑 👑 👑	2 Twin 2 Double 2 Family	6 En Suite fac	B&B per person £18.00-£25.00 Single £16.00-£22.00 Double	Open Jan-Dec Dinner 1700-2130 B&B + Eve.Meal £28.00-£35.00

Recently refurbished and upgraded family run hotel in centre of small village.

Traquair Arms Hotel Traquair Road Innerleithen Peeblesshire EH44 6PD Tel:(Innerleithen) 0896 830229 Fax:0896 830260	COMMENDED 👑 👑 👑	3 Single 2 Twin 3 Double 2 Family	10 En Suite fac	B&B per person to £35.00 Single to £27.00 Double	Open Jan-Dec Dinner 1830-2100 B&B + Eve.Meal £40.00-£48.00

A small family run Georgian hotel, in the village of Innerleithen but away from the main road and near the River Tweed.

Caddon View Guest House 14 Pirn Road Innerleithen Peeblesshire EH44 6HH Tel:(Innerleithen) 0896 830208	COMMENDED 👑 👑	1 Single 2 Twin 1 Double 1 Family	2 En Suite fac 1 Priv.NOT ensuite 1 Pub.Bath/Show	B&B per person £15.00-£16.00 Single £14.00-£17.00 Double	Open Jan-Dec Dinner 1830-1900 B&B + Eve.Meal £23.00-£26.00

A warm welcome and home cooking at this substantial Victorian house, with many period features. Ideal for touring the Borders.

The Ley Innerleithen Peeblesshire EH44 6NL Tel:(Innerleithen) 0896 830240 Fax:0896 830240	DELUXE 👑 👑 👑	1 Single 2 Twin 1 Double	4 En Suite fac	B&B per person £30.00 Single £33.00-£36.00 Double	Open mid Feb-mid Oct Dinner from 2000 B&B + Eve.Meal £48.50-£54.50

Personally run country house peacefully set in 30 acres of wooded grounds. Relax with interesting walks, log fires, imaginative cooking.

BY INSCH
Aberdeenshire
Map 4 F9

Leslie Castle Leslie, by Insch Aberdeenshire AB52 6NX Tel:(Insch) 0464 20869 Fax:0464 21076	HIGHLY COMMENDED 👑 👑 👑	1 Twin 3 Double	4 En Suite fac	B&B per person £80.00-£91.00 Single £55.00-£66.00 Double	Open Jan-Dec Dinner 1900-2100 B&B + Eve.Meal £85.00-£121.00

Magnificent 17C baronial fortified house with splendid views restored from a ruin by the present owners and now run by them as a small hotel.

BY INSCH
Aberdeenshire
Premnay Hotel
Auchleven, by Insch
Aberdeenshire
AB52 6QB
Tel:(Insch) 0464 20380

Map 4
F9

COMMENDED
👑 👑 👑

1 Single	4 En Suite fac	B&B per person	Open Jan-Dec
2 Twin	1 Priv.NOT ensuite	from £36.00 Single	Dinner 1800-2200
2 Double		from £27.00 Double	

Family run traditional coaching house with function room set in rural Aberdeenshire in the heart of the Castle Trail.

INVERARAY
Argyll
Fernpoint Hotel
Inveraray
Argyll
PA32 8UX
Tel:(Inveraray) 0499 2170

Map 1
F3

COMMENDED
👑

1 Single	7 En Suite fac	B&B per person	Open Jan-Dec
2 Twin		£28.00-£35.00 Single	Dinner 1800-2100
4 Family		£20.00-£35.00 Double	

Former Lord Provost's house (circa 1748) in its own grounds. Children and pets welcome. Speciality vegetarian food.

The Great Inn
Inveraray
Argyll
PA32 8XB
Tel:(Inveraray) 0499 2466
Fax:0499 2389

COMMENDED
👑 👑 👑

2 Single	19 En Suite fac	B&B per person	Open Jan-Dec
8 Twin	2 Pub.Bath/Show	£18.50-£34.00 Single	Dinner 1900-2100
8 Double		£18.50-£34.00 Double	B&B + Eve.Meal
6 Family			£28.50-£47.50

Built by 3rd Duke of Argyll in 1750 and operating as a hotel ever since.

Loch Fyne Hotel
Inveraray
Argyll
PA32 8XT
Tel:(Inveraray) 0499
2148/2109
Fax:0499 2348

COMMENDED
👑 👑 👑

3 Single	21 En Suite fac	B&B per person	Open Jan-Dec
6 Twin		£29.00-£33.00 Single	Dinner 1900-2100
7 Double		£25.00-£29.00 Double	
5 Family			

Family-run, stone built country house hotel overlooking Loch Fyne. On the outskirts of Inveraray and ideally situated for touring the west coast.

SPECIAL INTEREST HOLIDAYS

Write for your free brochure on Short Breaks, Activity Holidays, Skiing, to:

Scottish Tourist Board, PO Box 15, Edinburgh EH1 1VY.

INVERGARRY Inverness-shire	Map 3 H1

Glengarry Castle Hotel
Invergarry, Inverness-shire
Tel: (08093) 254 Fax: (08093) 207

Country House Hotel privately owned and personally run by the MacCallum family for over 35 years. Situated in the heart of the Great Glen, this is a perfect centre for touring both the West Coast and Inverness/Loch Ness area. Magnificently situated in 60 acres of wooded grounds overlooking Loch Oich.

Recently refurbished, 3 rooms with 4-post beds, all rooms have private bathrooms, TV, radio and telephone. Private tennis court, trout and pike fishing in Loch Oich. Children and dogs welcome.

For brochure please contact Mr D. MacCallum.

Glengarry Castle Hotel Invergarry Inverness-shire PH35 4HW Tel:(Invergarry) 08093 254 Fax:08093 207	COMMENDED 👑 👑 👑 👑	3 Single 10 Twin 9 Double 4 Family	25 En Suite fac 1 Priv.NOT ensuite 2 Pub.Bath/Show	B&B per person £38.00-£41.00 Single £31.50-£42.00 Double	Open Apr-Oct Dinner 1900-2030 B&B + Eve.Meal £55.00-£58.00

Privately owned country mansion, some rooms with four-poster beds. Extensive wooded grounds to loch with impressive hill and forest views.

INVERGARRY HOTEL
INVERGARRY, INVERNESS-SHIRE PH35 4HG
Tel: (08093) 206 Fax: (08093) 207

Our family owned and managed hotel is the ideal touring base. See Skye, Ben Nevis, Loch Ness and much, much more. Or just relax in front of an open fire with your favourite tipple and a good book. The choice is yours.
November-March from £34 DB&B daily.

Invergarry Hotel Invergarry Inverness-shire PH35 4HG Tel:(Invergarry) 08093 206 Fax:08093 207	COMMENDED 👑 👑 👑	1 Single 3 Twin 5 Double 1 Family	10 En Suite fac	B&B per person £27.00-£37.00 Single £21.00-£31.00 Double	Open Jan-Dec Dinner 1900-2100 B&B + Eve.Meal £34.00-£50.00

Victorian hotel now modernised, on main road to Skye and just off main Fort William/Inverness road. Excellent centre for touring Highlands.

Ardochy Lodge Invergarry Inverness-shire PH35 4HR Tel:(Tomdoun) 08092 232 Fax:08092 233	HIGHLY COMMENDED 👑 👑 👑	3 Twin 3 Double 2 Family	7 En Suite fac 1 Priv.NOT ensuite	B&B per person	Open Apr-Oct Dinner 1900-2000 B&B + Eve.Meal £27.00-£37.00

Former shooting lodge situated in 40 acre grounds with excellent views over Loch Garry and surrounding mountains. Home produce and baking.

INVERGARRY
continued

Craigard Guest House
Invergarry
Inverness-shire
PH35 4HG
Tel:(Invergarry) 08093 258

Map 3
H1

1 Single | 1 En Suite fac | B&B per person | Open Jan-Dec
3 Twin | 2 Pub.Bath/Show | from £15.00 Single | Dinner from 1900
3 Double | | from £15.00 Double | B&B + Eve.Meal
| | | from £28.00

Forest Lodge Guest House
South Laggan
Invergarry,by Spean Bridge
Inverness-shire
PH34 4EA
Tel:(Invergarry) 08093 219

COMMENDED

2 Twin | 5 En Suite fac | B&B per person | Open Jan-Dec
3 Double | 2 Priv.NOT ensuite | £15.00-£17.00 Double | Dinner from 1930
2 Family | | | B&B + Eve.Meal
| | | £23.00-£25.00

Family run guest house in the heart of the Great Glen where Caledonian Canal
joins Lochs Lochy and Oich. Ideal centre for outdoor activities.

Lundie View Guest House
Invergarry
Inverness-shire
PH35 4HN
Tel:(Invergarry) 08093 291

HIGHLY
COMMENDED

1 Single | 4 En Suite fac | B&B per person | Open Jan-Dec
1 Twin | 2 Pub.Bath/Show | £15.00-£20.00 Single | Dinner 1830-1930
2 Double | | £15.00-£20.00 Double | B&B + Eve.Meal
2 Family | | | £23.50-£28.50

Family run, with all accommodation on ground level and some private facilities
Set in open countryside. Craft shop adjacent.

INVERGOWRIE
by Dundee, Angus

Travel Inn
Gourdie Croft,
Kingsway West
Invergowrie, by Dundee
Perthshire
DD2 5JU
Tel:(Dundee) 0382 561115

Map 2
D2

21 Double | 40 En Suite fac | Price per room | Open Jan-Dec
19 Family | | from £32.50 | Dinner 1700-2200

INVERKEITHING
Fife

Boreland Lodge Private Hotel
31-33 Boreland Road
Inverkeithing
Fife
KY11 1DA
Tel:(Inverkeithing) 0383
413792
Fax:0383 413942

Map 2
C4

APPROVED

14 Single | 22 En Suite fac | B&B per person | Open Jan-Dec
2 Twin | 2 Pub.Bath/Show | from £19.00 Single | Dinner 1800-1900
4 Double | | from £14.50 Double | B&B + Eve.Meal
2 Family | | | from £25.00

Family run hotel with private parking, close to station, good rail links to
Edinburgh and the North. Satellite T.V.

Forth Craig Private Hotel
90 Hope Street
Inverkeithing
Fife
KY11 1LL
Tel:(Inverkeithing) 0383
418440

COMMENDED

2 Single | 5 En Suite fac | B&B per person | Open Jan-Dec
1 Twin | | £20.00-£21.00 Single | Dinner to 1830
2 Double | | £17.50-£18.50 Double |

Personally run, modern purpose-built private hotel overlooking the Forth.

INVERMORISTON Inverness-shire Glenmoriston Arms Hotel Glenmoriston Inverness-shire IV3 6YA Tel:(Glenmoriston) 0320 51206/351206	Map 4 A1	COMMENDED ♛ ♛ ♛ ♛	4 Twin 4 Double 8 En Suite fac	B&B per person £42.00-£45.00 Single £30.00-£33.00 Double	Open Jan-Dec Dinner 1700-2050 B&B + Eve.Meal £49.00-£61.00	
			18C inn in Highland village south west of Inverness offering a wide range of fine malt whiskies. Good base for walking; fishing at reduced rates.			

INVERNESS	Map 4 B8					

ARDMUIR HOUSE HOTEL

16 Ness Bank, Inverness IV2 4SF.
Tel: (0463) 231151

Georgian Town House, built in 1830, which has been tastefully modernised to incorporate all the facilities expected by today's discerning traveller whilst retaining its original character. Situated on the east bank of the River Ness, close to the town centre and Ness Islands, Ardmuir House is ideally placed for exploring the Highlands, and offers the perfect base for that relaxed holiday. At the end of the day enjoy home cooked and traditional fare in our non-smoking dining room.

Brochure with discounts for extended stays from the proprietors: Jean and Tony Gatcombe.

Ardmuir House Hotel 16 Ness Bank Inverness IV2 4SF Tel:(Inverness) 0463 231151	COMMENDED ♛ ♛ ♛	1 Single 2 Twin 6 Double 2 Family	11 En Suite fac	B&B per person £28.50-£32.00 Single £22.50-£26.00 Double	Open Jan-Dec Dinner 1830-1930 B&B + Eve.Meal £33.00-£44.00	
		Family run hotel on the bank of the River Ness close to town centre and Ness Islands. Conveniently situated for exploring the Highlands.				

Ballifeary House Hotel

10 BALLIFEARY ROAD, INVERNESS IV3 5PJ
Tel: (0463) 235572 Fax: (0463) 235572   ♛ ♛ ♛ Deluxe

Charming, small hotel with enviable reputation and recommended in many leading guides. Situated in own spacious grounds in a most desirable area of Inverness and just a 10 minute picturesque walk to town. Excellent home cooking. Residential Licence. All rooms ensuite bathrooms. Car Park.

NO-SMOKING THROUGHOUT.
Brochure/Reservations: Margaret Luscombe.

Ballifeary House Hotel 10 Ballifeary Road Inverness IV3 5PJ Tel:(Inverness) 0463 235572 Fax:0463 235572	DELUXE ♛ ♛ ♛	1 Single 3 Twin 4 Double	8 En Suite fac	B&B per person £28.00-£30.00 Single £28.00-£30.00 Double	Open Mar-Oct Dinner 1830-1900 B&B + Eve.Meal £42.00-£44.00	
		Attractive detached villa, situated in quiet residential area, a short walk from the river and theatre. Personal attention and home cooking.				

INVERNESS continued	Map 4 B8

BRAE NESS HOTEL

NESS BANK, INVERNESS IV2 4SF
TEL: (0463) 712266

Ideally situated beside the River Ness. We use only the best quality fresh produce in our excellent home cooking and baking, served in our non-smoking dining room with table licence. All rooms have private facilities.

John and Margaret Hill.

Brae Ness Hotel Ness Bank Inverness IV2 4SF Tel:(Inverness) 0463 712266	COMMENDED ♛ ♛ ♛	1 Single 3 Twin 4 Double 2 Family	9 En Suite fac 1 Priv.NOT ensuite 1 Pub.Bath/Show	B&B per person £26.00-£33.00 Single £21.00-£29.00 Double	Open Mar-Nov Dinner 1815-1915 B&B + Eve.Meal £34.00-£42.00

Family run hotel on River Ness close to town centre. Home cooking using fresh local produce a speciality. No smoking in dining room and bedrooms.

Bunchrew House Hotel Bunchrew Inverness IV3 6TA Tel:(Inverness) 0463 234917 Fax:0463 710620	Award Pending	4 Twin 7 Double	11 En Suite fac	B&B per person £55.00-£82.00 Single £55.00-£78.00 Double	Open Jan-Dec Dinner 1900-2100 B&B + Eve.Meal £78.00-£105.00

Chieftain Hotel 2 Millburn Road Inverness IV2 3PS Tel:(Inverness) 0463 232241	Award Pending	4 Twin 3 Double	7 En Suite fac	B&B per person £25.00-£30.00 Double	Open Jan-Dec Dinner 1830-2045

Columba Hotel Ness Walk Inverness IV3 5NE Tel:(Inverness) 0463 231391	COMMENDED ♛ ♛ ♛	18 Single 50 Twin 18 Double	86 En Suite fac	B&B per person £42.00-£50.00 Single £38.00-£46.00 Double	Open Jan-Dec Dinner 1830-2000 B&B + Eve.Meal £48.00-£58.50

Refurbished hotel on the banks of the River Ness, overlooking the Castle. Convenient for town centre and Eden Court Theatre.

Craigmonie Hotel Annfield Road Inverness IV2 3HX Tel:(Inverness) 0463 231649 Tlx:94013304 Fax:0463 233720	COMMENDED ♛ ♛ ♛ ♛	4 Single 18 Twin 10 Double 3 Family Suites avail.	35 En Suite fac	B&B per person £68.00-£75.00 Single £50.00-£60.00 Double	Open Jan-Dec Dinner 1830-2100 B&B + Eve.Meal £70.00-£80.00

Privately owned family run hotel. Originally 19C town house with modern bedroom extension.

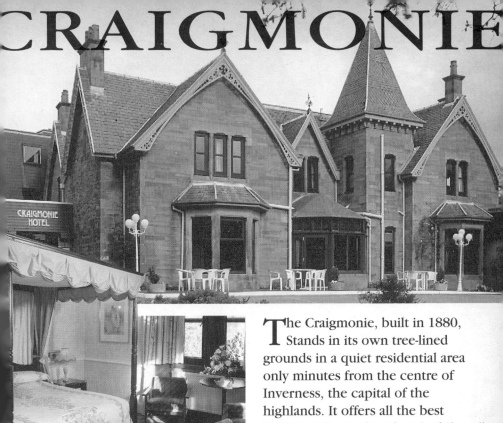

INVERNESS continued	Map 4 B8					
Cuchullin Lodge Hotel 43 Culduthel Road Inverness IV2 4HQ Tel:(Inverness) 0463 231945 Fax:0463 231613		HIGHLY COMMENDED ♛ ♛ ♛	3 Single 5 Twin 3 Double 1 Family	12 En Suite fac	B&B per person £35.00-£45.00 Single £26.50-£34.00 Double	Open Feb-Nov Dinner 1900-2100 B&B + Eve.Meal from £41.00
			Victorian house with many original features and large garden with mature trees, in residential area on south side of town centre.			

CULDUTHEL LODGE
14 Culduthel Road, Inverness IV2 4AG
Tel: (0463) 240089   Deluxe
Fax: (0463) 240089   ♛ ♛ ♛

Culduthel Lodge is a Georgian residence set in spacious colourful gardens overlooking the River Ness. Elegant public rooms are tastefully decorated and furnished providing a quiet relaxing atmosphere. Our bedrooms have private bathrooms, Telephone, Tea/Coffee making facilities, Television and Hairdryers. Each bedroom is individually decorated and furnished to a high standard. Fresh flowers, fruit and a small decanter of sherry are provided with our compliments on your arrival. A table d'hóte menu of delicious home cooking is offered at dinner complemented by our carefully selected wines and refreshments. We look forward to welcoming you.

David and Marion Bonsor.

Culduthel Lodge 14 Culduthel Road Inverness IV2 4AG Tel:(Inverness) 0463 240089		DELUXE ♛ ♛ ♛	1 Single 1 Twin 9 Double 1 Family	12 En Suite fac	B&B per person £37.50-£40.00 Single £30.00-£32.00 Double	Open Jan-Dec Dinner 1900-2000 B&B + Eve.Meal £43.00-£54.00
			Duchess mansion built c1840 set in attractive gardens on elevated site above the River Ness. Quiet location a few minutes walk from town centre.			
Culloden House Hotel Inverness IV1 2NZ Tel:(Inverness) 0463 790461 Fax:0463 792181		DELUXE ♛ ♛ ♛ ♛ ♛	2 Single 12 Twin 8 Double 1 Family	23 En Suite fac	B&B per person £120.00 Single £82.50-£105.00 Double	Open Jan-Dec Dinner 1900-2100 B&B + Eve.Meal £114.00-£136.50
			Elegant, historic Georgian mansion offering high standard of service, cuisine and ambience.			

INVERNESS continued	Map 4 B8					
Cummings Hotel Church Street Inverness IV1 1EN Tel:(Inverness) 0463 232531 Fax:0463 236541	COMMENDED ♛ ♛ ♛	6 Single 10 Twin 7 Double 3 Family	23 En Suite fac 4 Pub.Bath/Show	B&B per person £42.00-£45.00 Single £29.00-£32.00 Double	Open Jan-Dec Dinner 1800-2000 B&B + Eve.Meal £52.00-£55.00	
		Personally run, in town centre. Convenient for tourists and business people.				

Dunain Park Hotel

Inverness IV3 6JN
Tel: (0463) 230512 Fax: (0463 224532)

A82 one mile from Inverness secluded in six acres gardens and woodlands offering high standards of comfort and service. Award winning restaurant where cuisine is Scottish with a French influence. Fresh local produce according to season. Home baking. Log fires. Indoor heated swimming pool and sauna. Accommodation includes six suites with twin or double bedrooms, lounge and marble tiled bathroom with bath, shower and bidet. Four Poster and Half Tester beds available in rooms with private bathrooms. Two cottages. Ideal centre for touring golfing and walking near Inverness with its many shops and Eden Court Theatre.
Low season rates will be available.

| Dunain Park
Inverness
IV3 6JN
Tel:(Inverness) 0463 230512
Fax:0463 224532 | DELUXE
♛ ♛ ♛
♛ | 6 Twin
6 Double
2 Family
Suites avail. | 12 En Suite fac
2 Priv.NOT ensuite | B&B per person
£35.00-£50.00 Single
£35.00-£70.00 Double | Open Jan-Dec
Dinner 1900-2100
B&B + Eve.Meal
£55.00-£90.00 | |
| | | Georgian country house hotel in 6 acres of gardens and grounds including 2 acre kitchen garden. Elegant public rooms. Scottish and French cuisine. | | | | |

| Eden House Hotel
8 Ballifeary Road
Inverness
IV3 5PJ
Tel:(Inverness) 0463 230278 | HIGHLY COMMENDED
♛ ♛ ♛ | 1 Twin
2 Double
2 Family | 4 En Suite fac
1 Priv.NOT ensuite | B&B per person
£20.00-£25.00 Double | Open Jan-Dec
Dinner 1800-1900
B&B + Eve.Meal
£35.00-£40.00 | |
| | | Family run hotel in quiet residential area, close to town centre, a few minutes walk to Eden Court Theatre and River Ness. | | | | |

Scottish Tourist Board
COMMENDED
Facilities
♛ ♛ ♛

FOR QUALITY GO GRADED

INVERNESS continued	Map 4 B8		

Glendruidh House Hotel

OLD EDINBURGH ROAD, INVERNESS IV1 2AA
Telephone: Inverness (0463) 226499 Fax: (0463) 710745

Glendruidh House Hotel is situated amongst extensive grounds overlooking Inverness and the Moray Firth. After a day exploring the Highlands, enjoy traditional cuisine superbly prepared from fresh local produce, then relax in the circular drawing room or savour a dram in the sumptuous bar.
ARRIVE A GUEST - LEAVE AS A FRIEND.

Glendruidh House Old Edinburgh Road Inverness IV1 2AA Tel:(Inverness) 0463 226499 Fax:0463 710745	**COMMENDED** ♕ ♕ ♕	1 Single 1 Twin 5 Double	7 En Suite fac	B&B per person £35.00-£50.00 Single £22.00-£36.00 Double	Open Jan-Dec Dinner 1900-2000 B&B + Eve.Meal £37.00-£53.50
		19th century house in 3 acres of mature ground. Circular lounge with original Adam fireplace.			
Glen Mhor Hotel & Restaurant 10 Ness Bank Inverness IV2 4SG Tel:(Inverness) 0463 234308 Fax:0463 713170	**COMMENDED** ♕ ♕ ♕ ♕	8 Single 12 Twin 7 Double 3 Family	30 En Suite fac	B&B per person £45.00-£58.00 Single £25.00-£50.00 Double	Open Jan-Dec Dinner 1700-2230
		In quiet residential area, overlooking River Ness. Only 5 minutes walk to town centre and Eden Court Theatre. Adjacent cottage/annexe accommodation.			
Haughdale Hotel Ness Bank Inverness IV2 4SF Tel:(Inverness) 0463 233065	**COMMENDED** ♕ ♕ ♕	9 Single 11 Twin 8 Double 2 Family	22 En Suite fac 4 Pub.Bath/Show	B&B per person £22.50-£40.00 Single £22.50-£24.50 Double	Open Jan-Dec Dinner 1745-2100
		Personally run hotel on the bank of the River Ness in a quiet area within easy reach of town centre and all amenities. Ample parking.			
Heathmount Hotel Kingsmills Road Inverness IV2 3JU Tel:(Inverness) 0463 235877	**COMMENDED** ♕ ♕ ♕	3 Twin 2 Double	5 En Suite fac	B&B per person to £39.50 Single to £25.00 Double	Open Jan-Dec Dinner 1730-2115
		Personally run hotel in residential area, with busy bars and plenty of local atmosphere. Charcoal grills a speciality. All bedrooms en suite.			

INVERNESS continued	Map 4 B8

Kingsmills Hotel   Tel: 0463 237166
CULCABOCK ROAD, INVERNESS IV2 3LP

4-star hotel only one mile from town. All 79 rooms are luxuriously furnished and very spacious. Extensive leisure complex with large indoor pool. Hotel has fine restaurant, large comfortable lounge areas and a south facing conservatory.
Excellent Weekend Breaks and 5 & 7 night luxury holidays available all year.
👑👑👑👑👑 Highly Commended

Kingsmills Hotel Culcabock Road Inverness IV2 3LP Tel:(Inverness) 0463 237166 Fax:0463 225208	HIGHLY COMMENDED	31 Twin 84 En Suite fac 27 Double 26 Family Suites avail.	B&B per person £80.00-£120.00 Single £45.00-£65.00 Double	Open Jan-Dec Dinner 1900-2145 B&B + Eve.Meal £99.00-£139.00	

Set in 4 acres of woodland garden, 1 mile (2kms) from town centre. Leisure club with indoor swimming pool. Only 7 miles (11kms) from airport.

Larchfield Hotel 14/15 Ness Bank Inverness IV2 4SF Tel:(Inverness) 0463 233874 Fax:0463 711600	APPROVED	3 Single 8 En Suite fac 6 Twin 6 Limited ensuite 5 Double 3 Pub.Bath/Show 3 Family	B&B per person £20.00-£30.00 Single £20.00-£25.00 Double	Open Jan-Dec	

Personally run, on east bank of River Ness. Close to town centre. Open fire in lounge.

Lochardil House Hotel Stratherrick Road Inverness IV2 4LF Tel:(Inverness) 0463 235995 Fax:0463 713394	COMMENDED	3 Single 11 En Suite fac 2 Twin 5 Double 1 Family	B&B per person £50.00-£60.00 Single £30.00-£40.00 Double	Open Jan-Dec Dinner 1730-2100 B&B + Eve.Meal £55.00-£70.00	

18C castellated country house in 5 acres of private gardens with extensive parking. Under 2 miles (3kms) from centre. Former home of the Macdonalds.

Loch Ness House Hotel
Commended 👑👑👑👑   GLENURQUHART ROAD, INVERNESS IV3 6JL
Telephone: (0463) 231248. Fax: (0463) 239327

Cruise from our front door on a monster spotting expedition to Loch Ness. Located 1.25 miles from town centre overlooking the Caledonian Canal. Excellent restaurant and bar food. Log fires in winter. Weekend ceilidhs. Several 4-poster rooms. Special breaks. Surrounded by golf course.
Contact: A B Milroy, Loch Ness House Hotel, Glenurquhart Road, Inverness IV3 6JL. Tel: (0463) 231248. Fax: (0463) 239327.

Loch Ness House Hotel Glenurquhart Road Inverness IV3 6JL Tel:(Inverness) 0463 231248	COMMENDED	2 Single 22 En Suite fac 6 Twin 10 Double 4 Family	B&B per person £35.00-£60.00 Single £25.00-£45.00 Double	Open Jan-Dec Dinner 1800-2100 B&B + Eve.Meal £45.00-£60.00	

Privately owned, overlooking the Torvean Golf Course and Caledonian Canal and 20 minutes walk to town centre. Seasonal log fires.

INVERNESS continued	Map 4 B8					

Macdougall Clansman Hotel
Church Street
Inverness
IV1 1ES
Tel:(Inverness) 0463 713702

APPROVED
♛ ♛

2 Single	10 En Suite fac	B&B per person	Open Jan-Dec
5 Twin	1 Limited ensuite	£23.00–£27.50 Single	Dinner 1800-1930
6 Double	3 Pub.Bath/Show	£21.00–£24.00 Double	B&B + Eve.Meal
3 Family			£31.00–£34.00

Town centre hotel near to station, bus station and all shops. On street parking available & near to main Tourist Office.

Mercury Hotel
Millburn Road
Inverness
IV2 3TR
Tel:(Inverness) 0463 239666
Fax:0463 711145

COMMENDED
♛ ♛ ♛
♛

22 Single	118 En Suite fac	B&B per person	Open Jan-Dec
49 Twin		£38.00–£78.00 Single	Dinner 1830-2130
36 Double		£38.00–£47.50 Double	B&B + Eve.Meal
11 Family			£48.00–£91.75

Modern, conveniently situated to main thoroughfares of town. Lairds Table Restaurant.

Moray Park Hotel
Island Bank Road
Inverness
IV2 4SX
Tel:(Inverness) 0463 233528

COMMENDED
♛ ♛ ♛

2 Twin	6 En Suite fac	B&B per person	Open Jan-Dec
3 Double	1 Pub.Bath/Show	from £25.00 Single	Dinner 1900-2030
1 Family		£20.00–£30.00 Double	B&B + Eve.Meal
			£30.00–£40.00

Personally run and pleasantly situated with open outlook over gardens and river, yet close to town centre and all its amenities.

MOYNESS HOUSE

6 BRUCE GARDENS, INVERNESS IV3 5EN
Telephone or Fax: 0463 233836

Highest standards in a friendly, family run, 7-bedroom hotel.
All rooms with private facilities. Ample off-road parking, near to river and town centre. Breakfast and dinner menu choices with home cooking.

Brochure from Nonna or Michael Jones or book on (0463) 233836.

Moyness House
6 Bruce Gardens
Inverness
IV3 5EN
Tel:(Inverness) 0463 233836
Fax:0463 233836

DELUXE
♛ ♛ ♛

1 Single	9 En Suite fac	B&B per person	Open Jan-Dec
3 Twin		£23.00–£27.00 Single	Dinner 1815-1915
5 Double		£23.00–£27.00 Double	B&B + Eve.Meal
			£37.00–£41.00

Family run, in quiet area. Short walk to town centre, river, Eden Court Theatre and many sporting amenities. Home cooking and baking.

Palace Hotel

NESS WALK INVERNESS

Tel: (0463) 223243
Central Reservations
0397-703139

Wonderful example of Scottish Victorian grandeur; happily, with very modern plumbing. Gorgeous restaurant decor and very good local dishes. AA/RAC ★★★. Overlooks the River Ness and the Castle. Loch Ness Monster seekers exchange theories in excellent bar. Colour TV, phones, all private bathrooms etc.

Send for Scottish Holiday brochures with special prices. Also hotels in Oban, Fort William and Stirling.

Palace Hotel
Ness Walk
Inverness
IV3 5NE
Tel:(Inverness) 0463 223243
Fax:0463 236865

COMMENDED
♛ ♛ ♛
♛

14 Single	84 En Suite fac	B&B per person	Open Jan-Dec
55 Twin		£59.00–£79.00 Single	Dinner 1800-2100
6 Double		£35.00–£45.00 Double	B&B + Eve.Meal
9 Family			£50.00–£60.00

Modernised Victorian hotel on banks of the River Ness opposite the castle. Close to town centre and Eden Court theatre. Some annexe accommodation.

INVERNESS continued	Map 4 B8						
Rannoch Lodge Hotel 25 Southside Road Inverness IV2 3BQ Tel:(Inverness) 0463 234816/233114		APPROVED ♕ ♕ ♕	4 Single 5 Twin 4 Double	7 En Suite fac 3 Pub.Bath/Show	B&B per person £25.00-£35.00 Single £12.50-£17.50 Double	Open Jan-Dec Dinner 1830-2100 B&B + Eve.Meal £30.00-£45.00	
			Personally run hotel close to Inverness city and all amenities. Car parking available.				
Redcliffe Hotel 1 Gordon Terrace Inverness IV2 3HP Tel:(Inverness) 0463 232767		COMMENDED Listed	3 Single 2 Twin 3 Double 1 Family	6 En Suite fac 1 Pub.Bath/Show	B&B per person £26.00-£30.00 Single £20.00-£25.00 Double	Open Jan-Dec Dinner 1700-2200	
			Friendly, small hotel within a few minutes walk of the town centre. High tea with home-baking and dinner available. Most rooms en suite.				
Riverside House Hotel Ness Bank Inverness IV2 4SP Tel:(Inverness) 0463 231052			3 Single 2 Twin 3 Double 3 Family	6 En Suite fac 2 Pub.Bath/Show	B&B per person £24.00-£26.00 Single £24.00-£26.00 Double	Open Jan-Dec Dinner 1800-1930	
St Ann's House Hotel 37 Harrowden Road Inverness IV3 5QN Tel:(Inverness) 0463 236157		COMMENDED ♕ ♕ ♕	1 Single 2 Twin 1 Double 2 Family	5 En Suite fac 1 Priv.NOT ensuite	B&B per person £15.75-£19.50 Single £17.50-£19.50 Double	Open Jan-Dec Dinner 1830-1930 B&B + Eve.Meal £29.50-£32.00	
			19C traditional stone-built house in quiet residential area. Small comfortable family run hotel. All home cooking.				
Smithton Hotel Smithton,by Inverness Inverness-shire IV1 2NL Tel:(Inverness) 0463 791999		COMMENDED ♕ ♕ ♕	7 Twin 1 Double 2 Family	10 En Suite fac	B&B per person £28.50-£30.00 Single £26.00-£30.00 Double	Open Jan-Dec Dinner 1830-2030 B&B + Eve.Meal £34.50-£38.00	
			Modern purpose-built family run hotel. 3 miles (5kms) from Inverness and overlooking the Moray Firth.				

The Station Hotel

THE STATION HOTEL

ACADEMY STREET, INVERNESS IV1 1LG
Tel: (0463) 231926 Fax: (0463) 710705

As soon as you step through the elegant pillared entrance you are assured of the warmest of welcomes in this celebrated Highland hotel. For over a century, the Station Hotel has been at the very heart of business and social life in Inverness. Today, its Victorian grandeur is complemented by modern facilities making it ideal for conferences and functions, as well as an exceptional touring base from which to explore Loch Ness, Black Isle, Nairn's beaches and medieval Cawdor Castle. Special packages/discounts available throughout year.

| Station Hotel
Academy Street
Inverness
IV1 1LG
Tel:(Inverness) 0463 231926
Tlx:75275
Fax:0463 710705 | | Award Pending | 31 Single
23 Twin
6 Double
7 Family | 53 En Suite fac
6 Pub.Bath/Show | B&B per person
£32.00-£62.00 Single
£42.50-£47.50 Double | Open Jan-Dec
Dinner 1900-2115
B&B + Eve.Meal
£42.00-£72.00 | |

INVERNESS continued	Map 4 B8							
Stratton Lodge Hotel Culloden Inverness IV1 2NZ Tel:(Inverness) 0463 231072	APPROVED ♛	1 Single 1 Twin 1 Double 3 Family	2 Pub.Bath/Show	B&B per person £15.00-£16.00 Single £15.00-£16.00 Double	Open Jun-Oct Dinner from 1830 B&B + Eve.Meal £22.00-£24.00			
		Set in 25 acres of grounds in village of Culloden this 18C hunting lodge offers comfortable accommodation and a friendly welcome.						
Tower Hotel 4 Ardross Terrace Inverness IV3 5NQ Tel:(Inverness) 0463 232765	COMMENDED ♛ ♛ ♛	1 Single 3 Twin 4 Double 3 Family	7 En Suite fac 4 Limited ensuite	B&B per person £20.00-£35.00 Single £17.00-£30.00 Double	Open Jan-Dec Dinner 1700-2130 B&B + Eve.Meal £25.00-£38.00			
		100 year old hotel on the banks of the River Ness; short walk from town centre and all amenities.						
Whinpark Hotel 17 Ardross Street Inverness IV3 5NS Tel:(Inverness) 0463 232549	♛ ♛ ♛	3 Twin 3 Double 2 Family	4 En Suite fac 1 Pub.Bath/Show	B&B per person £15.00-£27.50 Single £16.50-£18.50 Double	Open Jan-Dec Dinner 1830-2130 B&B + Eve.Meal £30.00-£39.00			
Windsor Hotel 22 Ness Bank Inverness IV2 4SF Tel:(Inverness) 0463 715535 Fax:0463 713262	COMMENDED ♛ ♛ ♛	2 Single 2 Twin 6 Double 5 Family	15 En Suite fac	B&B per person from £29.00 Single from £29.00 Double	Open Jan-Dec Dinner 1800-1900 B&B + Eve.Meal from £39.00			
		Stone built hotel, personally run, facing River Ness, directly opposite Eden Court Theatre. Ample car parking area. Some annexe accommodation.						
Aberfeldy Lodge Guest House 11 Southside Road Inverness IV2 3BG Tel:(Inverness) 0463 231120	COMMENDED ♛ ♛ ♛	3 Twin 3 Double 3 Family	9 En Suite fac	B&B per person £19.00-£25.00 Double	Open Jan-Dec Dinner 1800-1830 B&B + Eve.Meal £31.00-£37.00			
		Substantial detached house with large garden in quiet residential area. Close to town centre and convenient for bus and railway stations.						
Abermar Guest House 25 Fairfield Road Inverness IV3 5QD Tel:(Inverness) 0463 239019	APPROVED ♛ ♛	5 Single 2 Twin 2 Double 2 Family	3 En Suite fac 2 Limited ensuite 3 Pub.Bath/Show	B&B per person £14.00-£16.00 Single £14.00-£16.00 Double	Open Jan-Dec			
		Detached house situated in a residential area. 5 minutes walk from the town centre. Convenient base for touring the Highlands. Private parking.						
Ach Aluinn Guest House 27 Fairfield Road Inverness IV3 5QD Tel:(Inverness) 0463 230127	COMMENDED ♛ ♛	2 Twin 2 Family	4 En Suite fac	B&B per person £16.00-£20.00 Double	Open Jan-Dec			
		Newly refurbished, detached, Victorian house with private parking in quiet residential road. 10 minutes walk from town centre. All rooms ensuite.						
Ardnacoille Guest House 1a Annfield Road Inverness IV2 3HP Tel:(Inverness) 0463 233451	COMMENDED ♛ ♛	1 Twin 1 Double 1 Family	1 Priv.NOT ensuite 2 Pub.Bath/Show	B&B per person £15.00-£17.00 Double	Open Mar-Oct			
		1865 red sandstone house in residential area. Spacious bedrooms. 10 minute walk from town centre. Ample parking.						

INVERNESS continued	Map 4 B8						
Atherstone Guest House Lynholme, 42 Fairfield Road Inverness IV3 5QD Tel:(Inverness) 0463 240240	COMMENDED 👑 👑	1 Single 1 Double 1 Family	3 En Suite fac	B&B per person £14.00-£17.00 Single £14.00-£17.00 Double	Open Jan-Dec		
		Attractively decorated and comfortably furnished with a homely atmosphere. Evening supper on request. All rooms en-suite.					
Atholdene House 20 Southside Road Inverness IV2 3BG Tel:(Inverness) 0463 233565	COMMENDED 👑 👑 👑	1 Single 4 Twin 2 Double 2 Family	6 En Suite fac 2 Pub.Bath/Show	B&B per person £25.00-£35.00 Single £19.00-£22.00 Double	Open Jan-Dec Dinner 1800-1900 B&B + Eve.Meal £29.00-£32.00		
		Late Victorian stone villa, modernised throughout with ample parking. Short walk from bus and railway stations.					
Balnafettack Guest House Leachkin Road Inverness IV3 6NL Tel:(Inverness) 0463 221555	COMMENDED 👑 👑	1 Twin 1 Double	2 En Suite fac	B&B per person £21.00-£24.00 Single £16.00-£19.00 Double	Open Jan-Dec		
		Detached modern house with ample parking and large garden in a residential area and on bus route to town centre.					
Braemore Guest House 1 Victoria Drive Inverness IV2 3QB Tel:(Inverness) 0463 243318	DELUXE 👑 👑	1 Twin 2 Double	1 En Suite fac 2 Priv.NOT ensuite	B&B per person £25.00-£30.00 Single £20.00-£22.00 Double	Open Jan-Dec		
		Attractive Victorian house furnished with fine antiques. Quiet location. Walking distance of town centre. No smoking.					
Cedar Villa Guest House 33 Kenneth Street Inverness IV3 5DH Tel:(Inverness) 0463 230477	COMMENDED 👑 👑	1 Twin 1 Double 3 Family	2 En Suite fac 1 Pub.Bath/Show	B&B per person from £13.00 Single from £13.00 Double	Open Jan-Dec		
		Centrally situated with easy access to theatre, bus and railway stations.					
Clisham House 43 Fairfield Road Inverness IV3 5QP Tel:(Inverness) 0463 239965	COMMENDED 👑 👑	2 Double 2 Family	4 En Suite fac	B&B per person from £18.00 Double	Open Jan-Dec		
		Large detached town house with interior woodwork of character. Ample parking. Within walking distance of town centre.					
Craigside Lodge 4 Gordon Terrace Inverness IV2 3HD Tel:(Inverness) 0463 231576 Fax:0463 713409	COMMENDED 👑 👑	3 Twin 3 Double	4 En Suite fac 1 Pub.Bath/Show	B&B per person £18.00-£20.00 Single £16.00-£18.00 Double	Open Mar-Jan		
		Detached Victorian house set in quiet elevated position. Outstanding views of Castle, river and town.					

INVERNESS continued	Map 4 B8						
Dionard Guest House 39 Old Edinburgh Road Inverness IV2 3HJ Tel:(Inverness) 0463 233557	COMMENDED 👑 👑	1 Twin 2 Double	3 En Suite fac	B&B per person £18.00-£25.00 Double	Open Jan-Dec		
Victorian house with modern extension, 1/2 mile (1 km) from town centre. Car parking available.							
Fairways Guest House 72 Telford Road Inverness IV3 6HN Tel:(Inverness) 0463 224934	COMMENDED 👑 👑	4 Twin 1 Double 1 Family	2 En Suite fac 3 Pub.Bath/Show	B&B per person £12.00-£16.00 Double	Open Jan-Dec Dinner 1800-1900 B&B + Eve.Meal £18.00-£23.00		
Personally run modernised guest house in quiet residential area. Close to town centre and all amenities.							
Felstead House 18 Ness Bank Inverness IV2 4SF Tel:(Inverness) 0463 231634	COMMENDED 👑	2 Single 2 Twin 2 Double 1 Family	4 Pub.Bath/Show	B&B per person from £16.00 Single from £16.00 Double	Open May-Sep		
Family run Georgian house overlooking River Ness; 5 minutes walk to town centre and 4 minutes walk to Eden Court Theatre.							
Heathcote Guest House 59 Glenurquhart Road Inverness IV3 5PB Tel:(Inverness) 0463 243650	APPROVED 👑	2 Single 3 Family	2 En Suite fac 2 Pub.Bath/Show	B&B per person £13.00-£15.00 Single £13.00-£18.00 Double	Open Jan-Dec		
Comfortable, stone built house with plenty of parking space. Convenient for Inverness, Loch Ness and the Highlands.							
Inverglen Guest House 7 Abertarff Road Inverness IV2 3NW Tel:(Inverness) 0463 237610	COMMENDED 👑 👑	1 Twin 2 Double 2 Family	5 En Suite fac	B&B per person £16.00-£20.00 Double	Open Apr-Oct		
Detached villa situated in quiet residential area, close to town centre. Relaxing atmosphere.							
Ivybank Guest House 28 Old Edinburgh Road Inverness IV2 3HJ Tel:(Inverness) 0463 232796	COMMENDED 👑 👑	1 Twin 2 Double	1 En Suite fac 1 Pub.Bath/Show	B&B per person £15.00-£18.00 Single £15.00-£18.00 Double	Open Jan-Dec		
Victorian villa, retaining many original features, with own large garden and ample parking, approximately half a mile walk from the town centre.							
Leinster Lodge Guest House 27 Southside Road Inverness IV2 4XA Tel:(Inverness) 0463 233311	APPROVED 👑 👑	1 Single 1 Twin 2 Double 1 Family	2 En Suite fac 2 Pub.Bath/Show	B&B per person £16.00 Single £15.00 Double	Open Jan-Dec		
19C stone built house in quiet residential area. 10 minutes walk from town centre. Centrally located for visiting Inverness and for touring.							
Oakfield Guest House 1 Darnaway Road, Kingsmills Inverness IV2 3LF Tel:(Inverness) 0463 237926	COMMENDED 👑 👑	1 Twin 3 Double 1 Family	2 En Suite fac 2 Pub.Bath/Show	B&B per person £16.00-£21.00 Single £14.00-£19.00 Double	Open Jan-Dec Dinner 1800-1900 B&B + Eve.Meal £24.00-£29.00		
Detached house with private parking in peaceful residential area within easy walking distance of town centre. Home cooking.							

INVERNESS continued	Map 4 B8						
Oak Villa 48 Harrowden Road Inverness IV3 5QN Tel:(Inverness) 0463 237182		COMMENDED Listed	4 Single 1 Twin 1 Double	2 En Suite fac 4 Limited ensuite 1 Pub.Bath/Show	B&B per person £14.00-£16.00 Single £14.00-£16.00 Double	Open Jan-Dec	

Friendly welcome at personally run guest house in residential area. 10-15 minutes walk from town centre and Eden Court Theatre.

| The Old Rectory Guest House
9 Southside Road
Inverness
IV2 3BG
Tel:(Inverness) 0463 220969 | | HIGHLY
COMMENDED
⚱ ⚱ | 1 Twin
2 Double
1 Family | 3 En Suite fac
1 Priv.NOT ensuite | B&B per person
£16.00-£19.00 Double | Open Jan-Dec | |

Privately owned former Victorian manse with large garden situated in residential area close to town centre. Good car parking. Non-smoking.

| The Old Royal Guest House
10 Union Street
Inverness
IV1 1PL
Tel:(Inverness) 0463 230551
Fax:0463 230551 | | COMMENDED
⚱ ⚱ | 2 Single
2 Twin
4 Double
2 Family | 5 En Suite fac
3 Pub.Bath/Show | B&B per person
£20.00-£24.00 Single
£17.50-£24.00 Double | Open Feb-Nov | |

Four storey terraced guest house in the heart of the town centre and a few hundred yards from the railway station.

| Pine Guest House
60 Telford Street
Inverness
IV3 5LE
Tel:(Inverness) 0463 233032 | | COMMENDED
⚱ ⚱ | 3 Single
3 Family | 2 En Suite fac
1 Limited ensuite
1 Pub.Bath/Show | B&B per person
from £16.50 Single
from £16.00 Double | Open Jan-Dec
Dinner 1800-1900
B&B + Eve.Meal
from £23.50 | |

Detached Victorian town house 1/2 a mile (800 metres) from centre of Inverness and on main bus route. Private parking available.

| Roseneath Guest House
39 Greig Street
Inverness
IV3 5PX
Tel:(Inverness) 0463 220201 | | COMMENDED
⚱ ⚱ | 1 Single
1 Twin
2 Family | 2 En Suite fac
2 Pub.Bath/Show | B&B per person
£13.00-£14.00 Single
£14.00-£15.00 Double | Open Jan-Dec | |

Family run guest house, quiet but short distance from the town centre. Off street parking; 5 minutes walk from Eden Court Theatre.

BY INVERNESS	Map 4 B8						
Inchberry House Lentran Inverness IV3 6RJ Tel:(Drumchardine) 0463 831342		HIGHLY COMMENDED ⚱ ⚱ ⚱	2 Twin 3 Double 1 Family	3 En Suite fac 1 Priv.NOT ensuite 1 Pub.Bath/Show	B&B per person £20.00-£36.00 Single £18.50-£20.00 Double	Open Jan-Dec Dinner from 1830 B&B + Eve.Meal £29.00-£37.00	

Tastefully decorated 19C country house situated off main road, with views of Beauly Firth. Home cooking. 5 miles (8kms) from Inverness.

Key to symbols is on back flap.

BY INVERNESS continued Sky House Upper Cullernie Balloch,by Inverness Inverness-shire IV1 2HU Tel:(Inverness) 0463 792582	Map 4 B8	COMMENDED 👑 👑 👑	3 Twin	2 En Suite fac 1 Priv.NOT ensuite	B&B per person £18.00-£24.00 Double	Open Jan-Dec Dinner from 1930 B&B + Eve.Meal £28.00-£34.00	

A friendly and relaxed welcome at this modern house with superb views over Moray Firth to Black Isle. 4 miles (6kms) from Inverness.

INVERURIE **Aberdeenshire** Ardennan Hotel Port Elphinstone Inverurie Aberdeenshire AB51 9XD Tel:(Inverurie) 0467 21502 Fax:0467 25818	Map 4 G9		1 Twin 2 Double 1 Family	4 En Suite fac	B&B per person £33.00-£40.00 Single £22.00-£30.00 Double	Open Jan-Dec Dinner 1700-2100 B&B + Eve.Meal £38.00-£50.00	

Gordon Arms Hotel Market Place Inverurie Aberdeenshire AB51 9SA Tel:(Inverurie) 0467 20314 Fax:0467 21792		APPROVED 👑 👑 👑	7 Single 4 Twin	6 En Suite fac 2 Pub.Bath/Show	B&B per person £29.95-£33.00 Single £19.75-£21.00 Double	Open Jan-Dec Dinner 1700-1950	

Granite building with function facilities in town centre. On main Aberdeen-Inverness road, Aberdeen 16 miles (26kms). Golf and fishing available.

Strathburn Hotel Burghmuir Drive Inverurie Aberdeenshire AB51 9GY Tel:(Inverurie) 0467 24422 Fax:0467 25133		HIGHLY COMMENDED 👑 👑 👑 👑	8 Single 5 Twin 10 Double 1 Family	24 En Suite fac	B&B per person £40.00-£55.00 Single £30.00-£40.00 Double	Open Jan-Dec Dinner 1900-2130 B&B + Eve.Meal £47.75-£55.00	

Modern, purpose built hotel and restaurant with friendly atmosphere, situated on the edge of Inverurie. Personally run.

Thainstone House Hotel & Country Club Thainstone Estate, Inverurie Road (N) Inverurie Aberdeenshire AB51 9NT Tel:(Inverurie) 0467 21643 Fax:0467 25084		HIGHLY COMMENDED 👑 👑 👑 👑 👑	19 Single 17 Twin 9 Double 3 Family Suites avail.	48 En Suite fac	B&B per person £43.00-£82.00 Single £33.50-£57.50 Double	Open Jan-Dec Dinner 1830-2130 B&B + Eve.Meal £60.50-£99.50	

Georgian A Listed mansion retaining many original features, standing in 14acres of wooded grounds. 8 miles (11kms) from Aberdeen Airport.

West High Street Guest House 7 West High Street Inverurie Aberdeenshire Tel:(Inverurie) 0467 21434		Award Pending	2 Single 2 Double	2 Pub.Bath/Show	B&B per person to £16.00 Single to £16.00 Double	Open Jan-Dec	

BY INVERURIE **Aberdeenshire** Pittodrie House Hotel Chapel of Garioch by Inverurie Aberdeenshire AB51 9HS Tel:(Pitcaple) 0467 681444 Tlx:739935 Fax:0467 681648	**Map 4** G9	**APPROVED** ≋ ≋ ≋ ≋	9 Twin 15 Double 3 Family	27 En Suite fac	B&B per person from £89.00 Single from £55.00 Double	Dinner 1930-2100 B&B + Eve.Meal from £80.00	

Country house dating from 1480 on large estate. Mixed arable, forestry and hill land with interesting walks. Open fires, billiards, squash and tennis

IONA, Isle of **Argyll**	**Map 1** B3						

ARGYLL HOTEL
ISLE OF IONA, ARGYLL PA76 6SJ Tel: 06817 334

Friendly hotel with homely lounges, open fires, plant-filled sun lounge, spacious dining room, all overlooking the Sound of Iona. Front lawn runs down to seashore. Real cooking using own vegetables. Vegetarians specially catered for using wholefoods. Residents and table licence.
From £44.00 DB&B per person.
For brochure contact Mrs Fiona Menzies.

Argyll Hotel Isle of Iona Argyll PA76 6SJ Tel.(Iona) 06817 334			10 Single 4 Twin 3 Double 2 Family	10 En Suite fac 4 Pub.Bath/Show	B&B per person £30.00-£37.50 Single £27.50-£35.00 Double	Open Apr-Oct Dinner at 1900 B&B + Eve.Meal £44.00-£54.00	

St Columba Hotel Iona, Isle of Argyll PA76 6SL Tel:(Iona) 06817 304		**COMMENDED** ≋ ≋ ≋	7 Single 16 Twin	19 En Suite fac 2 Pub.Bath/Show	B&B per person £33.00-£35.00 Single £25.00-£33.00 Double	Open Apr-Oct Dinner from 1900 B&B + Eve.Meal £35.00-£45.00	

Informal family run hotel close to the Abbey. Home cooking with fresh produce. Panoramic sea views. No T.V.

Iona Abbey Iona, Isle of Argyll PA76 6SN Tel:(Iona) 06817 404			3 Single 12 Twin 1 Double 4 Family	5 Pub.Bath/Show		Open Mar-Dec Dinner from 1730 B&B + Eve.Meal £151.00 per week	

IRVINE **Ayrshire** Irvine Hospitality Inn Annick Road Irvine Ayrshire KA11 4LD Tel:(Irvine) 0294 274272 Tlx:777097 Fax:0294 277287	**Map 1** G7	**COMMENDED** ≋ ≋ ≋ ≋ ≋	83 Twin 22 Double 22 Family Suites avail.	127 En Suite fac	B&B per person £38.00-£72.00 Single £38.00-£72.00 Double	Open Jan-Dec Dinner 1700-2400 B&B + Eve.Meal £46.00-£90.00	

Modern, convenient for Prestwick Airport with conference and banqueting facilities. Lagoon and swimming pool.

ISLE OF WHITHORN **Wigtownshire** The Steampacket Hotel Isle of Whithorn Wigtownshire DG8 Tel:(Whithorn) 0988 500334	Map 1 H1	APPROVED 👑 👑 👑	1 Twin 3 Double 1 Family	5 En Suite fac	B&B per person £22.50-£25.00 Single £22.50-£25.00 Double	Open Jan-Dec Dinner 1930-2130 B&B + Eve.Meal £28.35-£30.00

Personally run hotel situated right on the harbour front. Sea fishing available. Easy access to cliff walks and bird watching areas.

ISLEORNSAY **Isle of Skye,** **Inverness-shire** Kinloch Lodge Kinloch Isleornsay, Sleat Isle of Skye, Inverness-shire IV43 8QY Tel:(Isle Ornsay) 04713 214/333 Fax:04713 277	Map 3 E1		1 Single 6 Twin 3 Double	8 En Suite fac 2 Priv.NOT ensuite	B&B per person £40.00-£80.00 Single £40.00-£80.00 Double	Open Mar-Nov Dinner from 2000 B&B + Eve.Meal £70.00-£110.00

JEDBURGH **Roxburghshire** Glenbank Country House Hotel Castlegate Jedburgh Roxburghshire TD8 6BD Tel:(Jedburgh) 0835 862258	Map 2 E7	APPROVED 👑 👑	1 Single 3 Twin 2 Double	6 En Suite fac	B&B per person from £27.50 Single from £27.50 Double	Open Jan-Dec Dinner 1900-2030 B&B + Eve.Meal from £38.00

Set back from road in Royal Burgh rich in history. Stone built house in attractive gardens.

Glenfriars Hotel The Friars Jedburgh Roxburghshire TD8 6BN Tel:(Jedburgh) 0835 862000		COMMENDED 👑 👑 👑	2 Single 2 Twin 2 Double	6 En Suite fac	B&B per person £32.00 Single £29.00 Double	Open Jan-Dec Dinner 1900-2100 B&B + Eve.Meal £43.00-£46.00

Large Victorian house set above Jedburgh and centrally situated for touring the Borders. Sightseeing packages. Some four poster beds.

Mrs H Irvine, Froylehurst Guest House The Friars Jedburgh Roxburghshire TD8 6BN Tel:(Jedburgh) 0835 862477 Fax:0835 862477		HIGHLY COMMENDED 👑	1 Twin 2 Double 1 Family	2 Pub.Bath/Show	B&B per person £14.00-£15.00 Double	Open Mar-Oct

Detached Victorian house with large garden and private parking. Spacious rooms. Overlooking town, 2 minutes walk from the centre.

JEDBURGH continued	Map 2 E7						

KENMORE BANK HOTEL
OXNAM ROAD, JEDBURGH TD8 6JJ

A charming, family-run hotel with restricted licence. Just off the A68 above the Jed Water, it enjoys panoramic views of the Abbey and ancient town of Jedburgh. Just 5 minutes walk from the town. Excellent cuisine, choice of menu, wines and snacks. All bedrooms en-suite with colour TV.
Prices from £17.50 B&B. Proprietors: Charles and Joanne Muller.

Tel: (0835) 862369

COMMENDED 👑 👑 👑

Kenmore Bank Guest House
Oxnam Road
Jedburgh
Roxburghshire
TD8 6JJ
Tel:(Jedburgh) 0835
862369

COMMENDED 👑 👑 👑

2 Twin 6 En Suite fac
2 Double
2 Family

B&B per person
£27.00-£33.00 Single
£17.50-£21.00 Double

Open Jan-Dec
Dinner 1830-1930
B&B + Eve.Meal
£31.50-£35.50

Situated just off A68 overlooking the Abbey. Excellent base for touring the Borders.

Willow Guest House
Willow Court, The Friars
Jedburgh
Roxburghshire
TD8 6BN
Tel:(Jedburgh) 0835
863702

HIGHLY COMMENDED 👑 👑 👑

1 Twin 3 En Suite fac
2 Double 1 Priv.NOT ensuite
1 Family

B&B per person
£18.00-£25.00 Single
£15.00-£18.00 Double

Open Jan-Dec
Dinner 1800-1900
B&B + Eve.Meal
£24.00-£27.00

Set in 2 acres above the town; excellent views. Family run with home cooking, home grown produce in season. Ground floor accommodation available.

BY JEDBURGH
Roxburghshire — Map 2 E7

Spinney Guest House
The Spinney, Langlee
Jedburgh
Roxburghshire
TD8 6PB
Tel:(Jedburgh) 0835
863525
Fax:0835 863525

DELUXE 👑 👑

1 Twin 2 En Suite fac
2 Double 1 Priv.NOT ensuite
from £18.00 Double

B&B per person

Open mid Mar-Oct

A warm welcome at this attractive house recently modernised and with large pleasant garden lying just off main A68. All rooms have private facilities

---

JOHN O'GROATS
Caithness — Map 4 E2

John O'Groats House Hotel
John O'Groats
Caithness
KW1 4YR
Tel:(John O'Groats)
095581 203
Fax:095581 408

Award Pending

3 Single 3 En Suite fac
5 Twin 5 Limited ensuite
7 Double 3 Pub.Bath/Show
2 Family

B&B per person
£20.00-£30.00 Single
£20.00-£30.00 Double

Open Jan-Dec
Dinner 1930-2100
B&B + Eve.Meal
£37.50-£45.50

Seaview Hotel
John O'Groats
Caithness
KW1 4YR
Tel:(John O'Groats)
095581 220

1 Single 5 En Suite fac
2 Twin 2 Pub.Bath/Show
3 Double
3 Family

B&B per person
from £20.00 Single
from £18.00 Double

Open Jan-Dec
Dinner 1800-2100
B&B + Eve.Meal
from £21.00

JOHN O'GROATS continued

Map 4 E2

Caber-feidh Guest House
John O'Groats
Caithness
KW1 4YR
Tel:(John O'Groats)
095581 219

4 Single   3 En Suite fac
3 Twin   3 Pub.Bath/Show
2 Double
3 Family

B&B per person
£13.50-£14.50 Single
£12.50-£13.50 Double
B&B + Eve.Meal
£17.50-£18.50

Open Jan-Dec
Dinner 1830-2000

JOHNSTONE
Renfrewshire

Map 1 H5

COMMENDED

Lynnhurst Hotel
Park Road
Johnstone
Renfrewshire
PA5 8LS
Tel:(Johnstone) 0505
24331/24600
Fax:0505 24219

12 Single   23 En Suite fac
3 Twin   2 Pub.Bath/Show
5 Double
3 Family

B&B per person
£45.00-£49.95 Single
£30.00-£35.00 Double
B&B + Eve.Meal
£59.75-£64.70

Open Jan-Dec
Dinner 1830-2100

Family run hotel situated in residential area and convenient for Glasgow Airport,
5 miles (8kms). Range of function and conference facilities.

KEISS
Caithness

Map 4 D3

Award Pending

Sinclair Bay Hotel
Keiss
Caithness
KW1 4XG
Tel:(Keiss) 095583 233

1 Single   1 En Suite fac
3 Twin   2 Pub.Bath/Show
2 Double
1 Family

B&B per person
£18.00 Single
£16.50-£24.00 Double

Open Jan-Dec
Dinner 1800-2100

KEITH
Banffshire

Map 4 E8

Fife Arms Hotel
1 Regent Square
Keith
Banffshire
AB55 3DZ
Tel:(Keith) 05422 2351
Fax:05422 6310

2 Single   1 En Suite fac
3 Twin   2 Pub.Bath/Show
1 Double

B&B per person
from £12.00 Single
£12.50-£17.50 Double
B&B + Eve.Meal
£16.50-£27.50

Open Jan-Dec
Dinner 1830-2030

Royal Hotel
Church Road
Keith
Banffshire
AB55 3BR
Tel:(Keith) 05422
2528/2313/6101

6 Twin   3 En Suite fac
4 Double   2 Pub.Bath/Show
2 Family

B&B per person
£17.62-£29.38 Single
£15.00-£21.00 Double
B&B + Eve.Meal
£23.00-£28.00

Open Jan-Dec
Dinner 1830-2030

KELSO
Roxburghshire

Map 2 F6

COMMENDED

Cross Keys Hotel
36-37 The Square
Kelso
Roxburghshire
TD5 7HL
Tel:(Kelso) 0573 223303
Fax:0573 225792

6 Single   25 En Suite fac
7 Twin   1 Pub.Bath/Show
8 Double
4 Family

B&B per person
£35.00-£45.00 Single
£23.00-£29.00 Double
B&B + Eve.Meal
£33.00-£40.00

Open Jan-Dec
Dinner 1800-2130

One of Scotland's oldest coaching inns, enjoying prominent position overlooking
the cobbled Flemish style square. A la carte restaurant and Bistro.

KELSO continued	Map 2 F6						
Queen's Head Hotel 24 Bridge Street Kelso Roxburghshire TD5 7JD Tel:(Kelso) 0573 224636 Fax:0573 224459		COMMENDED 👑 👑 👑	3 Single 3 Twin 3 Double 2 Family	8 En Suite fac 2 Pub.Bath/Show	B&B per person £25.00-£27.00 Single £24.00-£25.00 Double	Open Jan-Dec Dinner 1800-2115 B&B + Eve.Meal £33.00-£37.00	

Historic coaching inn in the heart of the town centre. Good home cooking. imaginitive use of ingredients. Ideal touring centre.

BY KELSO Roxburghshire	Map 2 F6						

SUNLAWS HOUSE HOTEL

SUNLAWS · By KELSO · ROXBURGHSHIRE TD5 8JZ   0573 450 331

Sunlaws House in the heart of Scotland's Border country, in 200 acres of gardens and mature parkland along the banks of the River Teviot, 3 miles from the historic town of Kelso.
Owned by the Duke of Roxburghe, a perfect base for holidays with easy access and a range of sporting facilities.

HIGHLY COMMENDED 👑 👑 👑 👑   *Pride of Britain Member*

| Sunlaws House Hotel
Heiton
Kelso
Roxburghshire
TD5 8JZ
Tel:(Roxburgh) 0573 450331
Fax:0573 450611 | | HIGHLY
COMMENDED
👑 👑 👑
👑 | 1 Single
10 Twin
11 Double | 22 En Suite fac | B&B per person
from £85.00 Single
£64.00-£78.00 Double | Open Jan-Dec
Dinner 1930-2130
B&B + Eve.Meal
£90.00-£104.00 | |

Country house hotel owned by the Duke of Roxburgh. Set in 200 acres of woodland and park. Log fires, fresh produce. Shooting school. Fishing.

KENMORE Perthshire	Map 2 A1						
Croft-Na-Caber Hotel Kenmore Perthshire PH15 2HW Tel:(Kenmore) 0887 830236 Fax:0887 830649			1 Twin 4 Double	2 En Suite fac 3 Pub.Bath/Show	B&B per person £32.50-£39.50 Single £32.50-£39.50 Double	Open Jan-Dec Dinner 1200-2200	

| Kenmore Hotel
The Square
Kenmore
Perthshire
PH15 2NU
Tel:(Kenmore) 0887 830205
Fax:0887 830262 | | COMMENDED
👑 👑 👑
👑 | 4 Single
22 Twin
6 Double
3 Family | 35 En Suite fac
3 Pub.Bath/Show | B&B per person
£53.00-£68.00 Single
£47.00-£62.00 Double | Open Jan-Dec
Dinner 1900-2130
B&B + Eve.Meal
£61.50-£76.50 | |

The oldest inn in Scotland set in Conservation village by River Tay. 2 miles (3kms) of salmon fishing and 18 hole golf course. Some annexe bedrooms.

KENSALEYRE by Portree, Isle of Skye, Inverness-shire	Map 3 D8						
Corran Guest House Eyre Kensaleyre,by Portree Isle of Skye, Inverness-shire IV51 9XE Tel:(Skeabost Bridge) 047032 311		COMMENDED 👑 👑	1 Single 1 Double 2 Family	3 Pub.Bath/Show	B&B per person to £15.00 Single to £15.00 Double	Open Jan-Dec Dinner at 1900 B&B + Eve.Meal to £25.00	

In a small country village overlooking Loch Snizort, 6 miles (10kms) from Portree on Uig road. Extensive gardens with lovely views.

KENTALLEN, by Appin
Argyll

Ardsheal House
Kentallen, by Appin
Argyll
PA38 4BX
Tel:(Duror) 063174 227
Fax:063174 342

Map 1 F1

1 Single
5 Twin
7 Double

13 En Suite fac

B&B per person
from £85.00 Single

Open Jan-Dec
Dinner from 2000
B&B + Eve.Meal
£64.00-£90.00

Holly Tree Hotel
Kentallen, by Appin
Argyll
PA38 4BY
Tel:(Duror) 063174 292
Fax:063174 345

COMMENDED

6 Twin
5 Double

11 En Suite fac

B&B per person
to £41.50 Single
to £37.50 Double

Open Jan-Dec
Dinner 1930-2130
B&B + Eve.Meal
to £59.00

Small family run hotel built around former railway station. Excellent views of Loch Linnhe. Accent on food, using fresh produce.

KEOSE GLEBE
Lewis, Western Isles

Handa
18 Keose Glebe
Keose
Lewis, Western Isles
PA86 9JX
Tel:(Balallan) 085183 334

Map 3 C5

HIGHLY COMMENDED

1 Twin
2 Double

1 En Suite fac
1 Pub.Bath/Show

B&B per person
£16.00-£22.00 Double

Open Apr-Oct
Dinner 1900-1930
B&B + Eve.Meal
£28.00-£34.00

Detached modern house with warm friendly atmosphere in rural setting at edge of private loch. Boat and trout fishing available. Taste of Scotland.

KILCHATTAN BAY
Isle of Bute

St Blanes Hotel
Kilchattan Bay
Isle of Bute
PA20 9NW
Tel:(Kilchattan Bay)
070083 224

Map 1 F6

Award Pending

4 Single
2 Twin
4 Double
1 Family

4 En Suite fac
2 Pub.Bath/Show

B&B per person
from £18.50 Single
from £18.50 Double

Open Jan-Dec
Dinner 1800-1900
B&B + Eve.Meal
from £24.50

KILCHRENAN
Argyll

Taychreggan Hotel
Kilchrenan, by Taynuilt
Argyll
PA35 1HQ
Tel:(Kilchrenan) 08663 211
Fax:08663 244

Map 1 F2

1 Single
8 Twin
6 Double

15 En Suite fac

B&B per person

Open Jan-Dec
Dinner 1930-2100
B&B + Eve.Meal
£55.00-£72.50

KILCONQUHAR
Fife

**Kilconquhar Estate &
Country Club**
Kilconquhar
Fife
KY9 1EZ
Tel:(Colinsburgh) 033334
366
Fax:033334 239

Map 2 E3

COMMENDED

2 Twin
10 Double
3 Family

15 En Suite fac

B&B per person
to £32.00 Single
to £25.00 Double

Open Jan-Dec
Dinner 1700-2130

Renowned time share holiday complex with comprehensive leisure activities on site. Short stay breaks welcome.

| KILDRUMMY
Aberdeenshire | Map 4
E1 | | | | | | |

Kildrummy Castle Hotel
Kildrummy, By Alford, Aberdeenshire AB33 8RA
Tel: (09755) 71288 Fax: (09755) 71345

Set in the heart of the Grampian Highlands, an easy 3 hours drive from Edinburgh, Kildrummy Castle offers first-class accommodation, friendly service and our award-winning restaurant specialising in fresh local produce, game and seafood, close to Balmoral Castle, the Malt Whisky Trail, and Scotland's only Castle Trail. **Contact: Mr T. Hanna.**

DELUXE ♛♛♛♛

Kildrummy Castle Hotel Kildrummy,by Alford Aberdeenshire AB33 8RA Tel:(Kildrummy) 09755 71288 Fax:09755 71345	DELUXE	1 Single 9 Twin 3 Double 3 Family	16 En Suite fac	B&B per person £65.00 Single £52.00-£60.00 Double	Open Feb-Dec Dinner 1900-2100 B&B + Eve.Meal £57.00-£85.00
		Traditional Scottish mansion house, tastefully furnished and decorated retaining original features. A la carte restaurant using finest ingredients.			
Kildrummy Inn Kildrummy,by Alford Aberdeenshire AB33 8QS Tel:(Kildrummy) 09755 71227	Award Pending	1 Twin 1 Double 2 Family	2 Pub.Bath/Show	B&B per person £18.00-£20.00 Single £18.00 Double	Open Jan-Dec Dinner 1700-2000 B&B + Eve.Meal £23.00-£28.00
Dukeston of Brux Kildrummy Aberdeenshire AB33 8RX Tel:(Kildrummy) 09755 71344	Award Pending	1 Twin 1 Double	2 En Suite fac	B&B per person £20.00 Double	Open Feb-Oct Dinner at 1930 B&B + Eve.Meal £32.00
KILFINAN **Argyll** Kilfinan Hotel Kilfinan,by Tighnabruaich Argyll PA21 2EP Tel:(Kilfinan) 070082 201 Fax:070082 205	Map 1 E5 HIGHLY COMMENDED	7 Twin 4 Double	11 En Suite fac	B&B per person from £47.50 Single £39.00-£48.00 Double	Open Mar-Jan Dinner 1930-2130 B&B + Eve.Meal £63.00-£72.00
		Privately run coaching inn, comfortably furnished; log fires. Shooting,fishing and golf can be arranged.			
KILLEARN **Stirlingshire** Black Bull Hotel Killearn Stirlingshire G63 9NG Tel:(Killearn) 0360 50215 Fax:0360 50143	Map 1 H4 COMMENDED	1 Single 9 Double 3 Family	13 En Suite fac	B&B per person from £36.75 Single from £28.00 Double	Open Jan-Dec Dinner 1700-2100
		Situated in village centre, 17 miles (27kms) north of Glasgow at the gateway to the Trossachs, with views across the Campsie Hills.			

Details of Grading and Classification are on page vi. | Key to symbols is on back flap. |

KILLIECRANKIE Perthshire	Map 4 C1

The Killiecrankie Hotel

Killiecrankie, By Pitlochry, Perthshire PH16 5LG
Tel: (0796) 473220 Fax: (0796) 472451

Just 3 miles from Pitlochry and Blair Atholl, the Killiecrankie Hotel is beautifully situated in peaceful gardens and woodland. It offers a totally relaxed, informal haven for the discerning guest who enjoys good food and wine, as recommended by the leading guides in this sphere.

All 11 individually designed bedrooms have en-suite facilities, colour television, telephone and tea trays.

Lovely walks on the doorstep, excellent fishing, golf, shooting available by arrangement.

Special Breaks available in Low Season. Also open for Christmas and New Year. For details please contact: Colin and Carole Anderson, Resident Proprietors. Closed Jan. and Feb.

AA ★★ (71%) ✿✿ ✿✿✿✿ COMMENDED

Killiecrankie Hotel & Restaurant Killiecrankie Perthshire PH16 5LG Tel:(Pitlochry) 0796 473220 Fax:0796 472451	**COMMENDED**	3 Single 3 Twin 4 Double 1 Family	11 En Suite fac	B&B per person £39.00-£48.00 Single £39.00-£46.00 Double	Open Mar-Dec Dinner 1900-2030 B&B + Eve.Meal £64.00-£69.00

Personally run country house hotel with warm and friendly atmosphere set in 4 acres of grounds, overlooking Pass of Killiecrankie.

KILLIN Perthshire	Map 1 H2				
Bridge of Lochay Hotel Killin Perthshire FK21 8TS Tel:(Killin) 0567 820272		3 Single 10 Twin 3 Double 1 Family	7 En Suite fac 10 Limited ensuite 6 Pub.Bath/Show	B&B per person £20.00 Single £20.00 Double	Open Mar-Dec Dinner 1900-2100

Clachaig Hotel

FALLS OF DOCHART · KILLIN · PERTHSHIRE · FK21 8SL
Telephone: 0567 820270

Former Coaching House overlooking the spectacular Falls of Dochart. Enjoy Egon Ronay and Routier Recommended traditional fayre in our bar area and dining room. Ideally situated for hillwalking, golfing, shooting or fishing holidays. Private game fishing on the hotel's own beat on the River Dochart.

Clachaig Hotel Falls of Dochart Killin Perthshire FK21 8SL Tel:(Killin) 0567 820270	**APPROVED**	1 Single 1 Twin 5 Double 2 Family	8 En Suite fac 1 Pub.Bath/Show	B&B per person £19.00-£21.00 Single £19.00-£21.00 Double	Open Jan-Dec Dinner 1800-2130

Former coaching inn, now a family run hotel, beside the Falls of Dochart. Salmon fishing by arrangement.

KILLIN continued	Map 1 H2						

Dall Lodge Hotel
Killin
Perthshire
FK21 8TN
Tel:(Killin) 0567 820217
Fax:05672 726

COMMENDED
♛ ♛ ♛

1 Single
2 Twin
5 Double
2 Family

10 En Suite fac

B&B per person
to £27.50 Single
£27.50-£30.00 Double

Open Jan-Dec
Dinner 1900-2100
B&B + Eve.Meal
to £42.50

Refurbished hotel peacefully situated on the edge of the village.
Lounge conservatory.

Killin Hotel
Killin
Perthshire
FK21 8TP
Tel:(Killin) 0567 820296
Fax:0567 820647

Award
Pending

3 Single
13 Twin
13 Double
3 Family

32 En Suite fac

B&B per person
£28.00-£32.00 Single
£25.00-£35.00 Double

Open Jan-Dec
Dinner 1800-2130
B&B + Eve.Meal
£37.50-£45.00

Morenish Lodge Highland House Hotel
Morenish
Killin
Perthshire
FK21 8TX
Tel:(Killin) 0567 820258
Fax:0567 820258

COMMENDED
♛ ♛ ♛

1 Single
6 Twin
5 Double
1 Family

12 En Suite fac
1 Priv.NOT ensuite
1 Pub.Bath/Show

B&B per person
£27.00-£37.00 Single
£27.00 Double

Open Apr-Oct
Dinner 1900-2015
B&B + Eve.Meal
£36.00-£41.00

Former shooting lodge enjoying superb views over Loch Tay in an area famed for
natural history and outdoor pursuits.

Tighnabruaich Hotel
Main Street
Killin
Perthshire
FK21 8XB
Tel:(Killin) 0567 820216

Award
Pending

1 Double
4 Family

2 En Suite fac
2 Limited ensuite
1 Pub.Bath/Show

B&B per person
£15.00-£16.00 Single
£18.00 Double

Open Jan-Dec
Dinner 1830-2100
B&B + Eve.Meal
£26.00

Breadalbane House
Main Street
Killin
Perthshire
FK21 8UT
Tel:(Killin) 0567 820386
Fax:0567 820386

COMMENDED
♛ ♛ ♛

1 Twin
2 Double
2 Family

5 En Suite fac

B&B per person
£17.00-£19.00 Double

Open Jan-Dec
Dinner 1900-1945
B&B + Eve.Meal
£27.00-£29.00

Traditional stone built house in centre of small village. Ideal base for touring
central Scotland.

Fairview House
Main Street
Killin
Perthshire
FK21 8UT
Tel:(Killin) 0567 820667

COMMENDED
♛ ♛

1 Single
2 Twin
4 Double

3 En Suite fac
2 Pub.Bath/Show

B&B per person
£14.00-£16.00 Single
£14.00-£16.00 Double

Open Jan-Dec
Dinner from 1930
B&B + Eve.Meal
£22.00-£24.00

Small family run guest house specialising in home cooking. Excellent touring
centre, good walking and climbing area.

KILMARNOCK Ayrshire	Map 1 H7						
Broomhill Hotel 57A London Road Kilmarnock Ayrshire KA3 7AH Tel:(Kilmarnock) 0563 23711			2 Single 3 Twin 1 Double 2 Family	6 Limited ensuite 2 Pub.Bath/Show	B&B per person from £29.00 Single from £19.50 Double	Open Jan-Dec Dinner 1800-2100 B&B + Eve.Meal from £35.00	
Burnside Hotel 18 London Road Kilmarnock Ayrshire KA3 7AQ Tel:(Kilmarnock) 0563 22952	Award Pending		4 Single 2 Twin 2 Double 3 Family	6 En Suite fac 3 Pub.Bath/Show	B&B per person £17.00-£25.00 Single £15.00-£20.00 Double	Open Jan-Dec Dinner at 1800 B&B + Eve.Meal £27.00-£32.00	
Foxbar Hotel 62 London Road Kilmarnock Ayrshire KA3 7DD Tel:(Kilmarnock) 0563 25701 Fax:0563 20824			3 Single 12 Twin 5 Family	20 En Suite fac 1 Pub.Bath/Show	B&B per person from £30.00 Single from £40.00 Double	Open Jan-Dec Dinner from 1900	
Halfway House Hotel 27 Kilmarnock Road Symington, Kilmarnock Ayrshire KA1 5PW Tel:(Symington) 0563 830240 Fax:0563 830191	COMMENDED 👑 👑 👑 👑		2 Twin 4 Double Suite avail.	6 En Suite fac	B&B per person £39.50-£49.50 Single £33.00-£37.50 Double	Open Jan-Dec Dinner 1700-2200 B&B + Eve.Meal £51.00-£60.00	
		Family run hotel on A77 with easy access to Glasgow and Ayrshire Coast. Emphasis on good food, available all day.					
Dean Park Guest House 27 Wellington Street Kilmarnock Ayrshire KA3 1DW Tel:(Kilmarnock) 0563 72794/32061	Award Pending		1 Single 2 Twin 2 Double 1 Family	2 En Suite fac 2 Pub.Bath/Show	B&B per person £14.00-£18.00 Single £14.00-£18.00 Double	Open Jan-Dec	
Eriskay Guest House 2 Dean Terrace Kilmarnock Ayrshire KA3 1RJ Tel:(Kilmarnock) 0563 32061/72794	COMMENDED 👑 👑		2 Single 1 Twin 2 Double 1 Family	2 En Suite fac 2 Pub.Bath/Show	B&B per person £14.00-£18.00 Single £14.00-£18.00 Double	Open Jan-Dec	
		Detached villa conveniently situated on main bus route and close to Dean Park and Castle. Enclosed secure car park.					

KILMELFORD Argyll	Map 1 E3

CUILFAIL HOTEL
KILMELFORD. BY OBAN

Charming old Scottish Hotel, 14 miles south of Oban. Ideal for exploring this lovely part of the West Coast. Try our home cooked meals (Taste of Scotland member) or sample one of our many malt whiskies.
B&B from £25, with discounts for longer stays.
Catch the West Highland atmosphere!
For full details call 085 22 274

Cuilfail Hotel
Kilmelford
Argyll
PA34 4XA
Tel:(Kilmelford) 08522 274
Fax:08522 264

COMMENDED

4 Twin 12 En Suite fac
6 Double
2 Family

B&B per person
£35.00-£37.50 Single
£30.00-£32.50 Double

Open Jan-Dec
Dinner 1830-2130
B&B + Eve.Meal
£40.00-£47.50

Old coaching inn situated in small village. Emphasis on traditional Scottish fare based on local produce.

KILMORE, by Oban Argyll	Map 1 E2

Glenfeochan House
Kilmore,by Oban
Argyll
PA34 4QR
Tel:(Kilmore) 063177 273
Fax:063177 624

DELUXE

1 Twin 3 En Suite fac
2 Double

B&B per person
to £62.00 Double

Open Mar-Oct
Dinner 2000-2030
B&B + Eve.Meal
to £90.00

Turreted country house with extensive gardens and magnificent views. Homebaking and fresh produce. Fishing and shooting rights.

Braeside Guest House
Kilmore,by Oban
Argyll
PA34 4QR
Tel:(Kilmore) 063177 243

3 Twin 5 En Suite fac
2 Double 1 Limited ensuite
1 Family 1 Pub.Bath/Show

B&B per person

Open Mar-Oct
Dinner 1830-1900
B&B + Eve.Meal
£19.50-£22.50

KILNINVER, by Oban Argyll	Map 1 E3

Knipoch Hotel
Kilninver,by Oban
Argyll
PA34 4QT
Tel:(Kilninver) 08526 251
Fax:08526 249

HIGHLY COMMENDED

4 Twin 17 En Suite fac
11 Double
2 Family

B&B per person
£62.00-£82.00 Single
from £62.00 Double

Open Feb-Nov
Dinner 1930-2100
B&B + Eve.Meal
from £98.00

Family run country house hotel standing in its own grounds, overlooking Loch Feochan. 6 miles (10kms) south of Oban.

KILSYTH Stirlingshire	Map 2 A5

Coachman Hotel
Parkfoot Street
Kilsyth
Stirlingshire
G65 0SP
Tel:(Kilsyth) 0236 821649

7 Twin 11 En Suite fac
3 Double
1 Family

B&B per person
to £36.00 Single
to £23.00 Double

Open Jan-Dec
Dinner 1830-2130

Details of Grading and Classification are on page vi.

Key to symbols is on back flap.

KILWINNING – KINCRAIG

KILWINNING
Ayrshire

Montgreenan Mansion
House Hotel
Kilwinning
Ayrshire
KA13 7QZ
Tel:(Kilwinning) 0294
57733/57734
Tlx:778525
Fax:0294 85397

Map 1
G6

COMMENDED

2 Single   21 En Suite fac
8 Twin
8 Double
3 Family
Suites avail.

B&B per person
£66.00-£76.00 Single
£46.00-£73.00 Double

Open Jan-Dec
Dinner 1900-2130
B&B + Eve.Meal
£86.00-£96.00

Country house in 45 acres of garden. Family run, warm welcome, within easy reach of championship golf courses. Tennis courts and 5 hole golf course.

KINCARDINE O'NEIL
Aberdeenshire

Gordon Arms Hotel
Main Street
Kincardine O'Neil
Aberdeenshire
AB34 5AA
Tel:(Kincardine O'Neil)
03398 84236

Map 4
F1

APPROVED

1 Single   5 En Suite fac
2 Twin   2 Pub.Bath/Show
2 Double
2 Family

B&B per person
£20.00-£28.00 Single
£17.50-£22.50 Double

Open Jan-Dec
Dinner 1700-2100
B&B + Eve.Meal
£25.00-£30.00

Family run 19c coaching inn in centre of small village. Extensive menus, including vegetarian and vegan dishes, organic wines, real ales.

KINCRAIG
Inverness-shire

Ossian Hotel
Kincraig
Inverness-shire
PH21 1NA
Tel:(Kincraig) 0540 651242
Fax:0540 651633

Map 4
B1

COMMENDED

2 Single   8 En Suite fac
2 Twin   1 Priv.NOT ensuite
3 Double
2 Family

B&B per person
£17.50-£30.00 Single
£17.50-£30.00 Double

Open Feb-Nov
Dinner 1930-2100
B&B + Eve.Meal
£32.50-£45.00

Friendly, family run, in own grounds in village. A9 and Spey Valley amenities within easy reach. Tea shop with home baking.

Grampian View
Kincraig
Inverness-shire
PH21 1NA
Tel:(Kincraig) 0540 651383

COMMENDED

1 Single   4 En Suite fac
2 Twin   1 Priv.NOT ensuite
2 Double

B&B per person
£16.00-£18.00 Single
£16.00-£18.00 Double

Open Feb-Oct

Family run Victorian house, over 100 years old, with original fire places and woodwork; close to old railway station.

Insh House Guest House
Kincraig
Inverness-shire
PH21 1NU
Tel:(Kincraig) 0540 651377

COMMENDED

2 Single   2 En Suite fac
1 Twin   1 Pub.Bath/Show
1 Double
1 Family

B&B per person
from £15.00 Single
from £15.00 Double

Open Jan-Dec
Dinner from 1900
B&B + Eve.Meal
from £22.00

Fine example of a Telford House in 2 acres of secluded grounds. Close to Loch Insh, 10 minutes to Aviemore. Skiing, watersports, riding, gliding.

March House Guest House
Feshiebridge
Kincraig
Inverness-shire
PH21 1NG
Tel:(Kincraig) 0540 651388
Fax:0540 657388

COMMENDED

3 Twin   5 En Suite fac
2 Double   1 Priv.NOT ensuite
1 Family

B&B per person
from £18.00 Single
from £18.00 Double

Open Dec-Oct
Dinner from 1900
B&B + Eve.Meal
from £28.00

Situated in beautiful Glenfeshie. Excellent views of surrounding hills. Personally run relaxed atmosphere. Emphasis on fresh food.

VAT is shown at 17.5%: changes in this rate may affect prices. Prices shown are for guidance only. Please send SAE with each enquiry.

KINGHORN **Fife** The Longboat Inn 107 Pettycur Road Kinghorn Fife KY3 9RU Tel:(Kinghorn) 0592 890625	Map 2 D4	APPROVED 👑 👑 👑	2 Twin 4 Double	6 En Suite fac	B&B per person £29.95-£39.95 Single £17.50-£22.50 Double	Open Jan-Dec Dinner 1700-2130 B&B + Eve.Meal £27.50-£32.50	
			Family run hotel with seafood restaurant and Wine Bar. Panoramic views over Firth of Forth to the city of Edinburgh beyond.				
The Coach House Hitchcock, 9 Rossland Place Kinghorn Fife KY3 9SS Tel:(Kinghorn) 0592 890592			1 Twin 1 Double	1 Pub.Bath/Show	B&B per person from £12.50 Double	Open Jan-Dec Dinner 1730-1830 B&B + Eve.Meal from £17.00	
KINGUSSIE **Inverness-shire** Columba House Hotel Manse Road Kingussie Inverness-shire PH21 1JF Tel:(Kingussie) 0540 661402	Map 4 B1	COMMENDED 👑 👑 👑	3 Twin 4 Double	7 En Suite fac 1 Pub.Bath/Show	B&B per person £26.00-£39.00 Single £21.00-£29.00 Double	Open Jan-Dec Dinner 1930-2030 B&B + Eve.Meal £36.00-£47.00	
			Small, welcoming, family run hotel. Large secluded walled garden for relaxation and recreation. Croquet and putting.				
Duke of Gordon Hotel Newtonmore Road Kingussie Inverness-shire PH21 1HE Tel:(Kingussie) 0540 661302 Fax:0540 661302		APPROVED 👑 👑 👑 👑	10 Single 33 Twin 8 Double 3 Family	54 En Suite fac 2 Pub.Bath/Show	B&B per person £35.00-£44.00 Single £29.00-£38.00 Double	Open Jan-Dec Dinner 1850-2200 B&B + Eve.Meal £40.00-£47.50	
			Victorian hotel on main street with golf and fishing available locally in summer and skiing in winter. Facilities may vary depending on season.				
Homewood Lodge Kingussie Inverness-shire PH21 1HD Tel:(Kingussie) 0540 661507		COMMENDED 👑 👑	1 Double 2 Family	3 En Suite fac	B&B per person £19.50 Single £19.50 Double	Open Jan-Dec Dinner from 1900 B&B + Eve.Meal £29.00	
			Friendly guest house on edge of village. Views to Monadhliath Mountains. Ideal base for touring area.				
The Osprey Hotel Kingussie Inverness-shire PH21 1EN Tel:(Kingussie) 0540 661510		COMMENDED 👑 👑 👑	1 Single 3 Twin 4 Double	7 En Suite fac 1 Priv.NOT ensuite 1 Pub.Bath/Show	B&B per person from £22.00 Single from £22.00 Double	Open Jan-Dec Dinner from 1930 B&B + Eve.Meal from £39.00	
			Personally run hotel in centre of village, imaginative cuisine including vegetarian meals using fresh produce. Taste of Scotland restaurant.				
Royal Hotel Kingussie Inverness-shire PH21 1HX Tel:(Kingussie) 0540 661236/661898 Fax:0540 661061		APPROVED 👑 👑 👑 👑	6 Single 28 Twin 10 Double 8 Family	52 En Suite fac	B&B per person to £33.00 Single to £28.00 Double	Open Jan-Dec Dinner 1900-2130 B&B + Eve.Meal to £40.00	
			Family hotel in centre of village off main A9. Coach parties welcome. Free live entertainment nightly. Some annexe accommodation.				

KINGUSSIE continued — Map 4 B1

The Scot House Hotel
Kingussie
Inverness-shire
PH21 1HE
Tel:(Kingussie) 0540 661351
Fax:0540 661111

COMMENDED

3 Twin
4 Double
2 Family

9 En Suite fac

B&B per person
£24.50-£38.00 Single
£19.50-£29.50 Double

Open Jan-Dec
Dinner 1800-2100
B&B + Eve.Meal
£35.00-£45.00

Personally run hotel, recently refurbished throughout, situated in centre of Kingussie. Restaurant and bar meals. Ample car parking.

Star Hotel
High Street
Kingussie
Inverness-shire
PH21 1HR
Tel:(Kingussie) 0540 661431

4 Single
14 Twin
14 Double
4 Family

30 En Suite fac
2 Pub.Bath/Show

B&B per person
£19.00-£22.00 Single
£16.00-£19.00 Double

Open Jan-Dec
Dinner 1800-2100
B&B + Eve.Meal
£21.00-£24.00

Avondale Guest House
Newtonmore Road
Kingussie
Inverness-shire
PH21 1HF
Tel:(Kingussie) 0540 661731

HIGHLY COMMENDED

1 Single
3 Twin
2 Double
1 Family

3 En Suite fac
2 Pub.Bath/Show

B&B per person
£16.00-£19.00 Single
£16.00-£19.00 Double

Open Jan-Dec
Dinner from 1900
B&B + Eve.Meal
£24.00-£27.00

Stone built house with own large garden near centre of village. Friendly atmosphere, ample parking. Skiing and fishing can be arranged.

Sonnhalde Guest House
East Terrace
Kingussie
Inverness-shire
PH21 1JS
Tel:(Kingussie) 0540 661266
Fax:0540 661266

COMMENDED

1 Single
2 Twin
2 Double
3 Family

3 Pub.Bath/Show

B&B per person
from £16.00 Single
from £16.00 Double

Open Jan-Oct
Dinner from 1830
B&B + Eve.Meal
from £24.50

Warm welcome at Victorian villa overlooking Cairngorms. Home cooking with mainly fresh produce. Natural history. Photographic tours arranged.

KINLOCHBERVIE Sutherland — Map 3 G3

The Kinlochbervie Hotel
Kinlochbervie
Sutherland
IV27 4RP
Tel:(Kinlochbervie) 0971 521275
Fax:0971 521438

HIGHLY COMMENDED

4 Twin
7 Double
3 Family

14 En Suite fac

B&B per person
£52.00-£62.00 Single
£42.00-£52.00 Double

Open Mar-Nov
Dinner 1900-2030
B&B + Eve.Meal
£68.00-£78.00

Family run hotel, in elevated position with excellent views over Loch Clash and fishing harbour. Imaginative cuisine using fresh produce.

Old School Restaurant & Guest House
Inshegra
Kinlochbervie
Sutherland
IV27 4RH
Tel:(Kinlochbervie) 0971 521383

1 Single
3 Twin
1 Double
1 Family

4 En Suite fac
1 Pub.Bath/Show

B&B per person
£20.00-£25.50 Single
£18.00-£24.00 Double

Open Jan-Dec
Dinner 1800-2030

KINLOCHLEVEN
Argyll
MacDonald Hotel
Wades Road
Kinlochleven
Argyll
PA40 4QL
Tel:(Kinlochleven) 08554
539
Fax:08554 539

Map 1
F1

COMMENDED
👑 👑 👑

5 Twin	8 En Suite fac	B&B per person	Open Mar-Dec
4 Double	2 Priv.NOT ensuite	£22.00-£35.00 Single	Dinner 1900-2100
1 Family	1 Pub.Bath/Show	£22.00-£30.00 Double	B&B + Eve.Meal
			£43.00-£48.00

Modern hotel at the water's edge with spectacular views down Loch Leven.
Ideally placed for skiing, hill-walking and touring.

MAMORE LODGE HOTEL

Kinlochleven, Argyll PA40 4QN
Telephone: 0855 4213

MAMORE has in its time played host to many famous guests, not least of whom was King Edward VII in 1909. The recent modernisation of the Lodge provides walkers and holidaymakers with the opportunity to enjoy this unique Highland experience.
The Lodge sits 700 feet up on the hillside above Kinlochleven with access by a new tarmac road giving magnificent views in all directions.

Mamore Lodge Hotel
Kinlochleven
Argyll
PA40 4QN
Tel:(Kinlochleven) 08554
213

APPROVED
👑 👑 👑

2 Single	15 En Suite fac	B&B per person	Open Jan-Dec
10 Twin	1 Pub.Bath/Show	£19.50-£32.00 Single	Dinner 1900-2000
4 Double		£19.50-£32.00 Double	B&B + Eve.Meal
2 Family			£35.00-£45.00

Former Victorian hunting lodge with original wood panelling, magnificently sited
on West Highland Way. Hillwalkers welcome. Annexe accommodation.

KINLOCH RANNOCH
Perthshire
Dunalastair Hotel
Kinloch Rannoch
Perthshire
PH16 5PW
Tel:(Kinloch Rannoch)
0882 632323

Map 2
A1

3 Single	10 En Suite fac	B&B per person	Open Jan-Dec
10 Twin	12 Limited ensuite	£20.00-£35.00 Single	Dinner to 2100
7 Double	4 Pub.Bath/Show	£20.00-£35.00 Double	
4 Family			

Loch Rannoch Hotel
Kinloch Rannoch
Perthshire
PH16 5PS
Tel:(Kinloch Rannoch)
0882 632201
Fax:08822 632203

COMMENDED
👑 👑 👑
👑

8 Twin	19 En Suite fac	B&B per person	Open Jan-Dec
10 Double		from £31.00 Single	Dinner 1900-2130
1 Family		from £31.00 Double	B&B + Eve.Meal
			£35.00-£59.00

Set in 250 acres of magnificent Highland scenery overlooking Loch Rannoch.
A la carte restaurant and grill, wide range of leisure facilities.

KINNESSWOOD by Kinross, Kinross-shire	Map 2 C3

LOMOND COUNTRY INN
KINNESSWOOD, By LOCH LEVEN, KINROSS-SHIRE
Telephone: 059284 253   Fax: 059284 693
(Changing to – Telephone: 0592 840253 Fax: 0592 840693)

Enjoy real food and real ale at reasonable prices in this cosy, family run hotel overlooking Loch Leven. All rooms en-suite, colour TV and telephones. 9-hole golf course adjacent. Only 45 minutes from Edinburgh, Perth and St. Andrews.   AA ★★ ❀

Lomond Country Inn Main Street Kinnesswood, Kinross Kinross-shire KY13 7HN Tel:(Scotlandwell) 059284 253 Fax:059284 693	COMMENDED 👑 👑 👑	2 Single 5 Twin 5 Double	12 En Suite fac	B&B per person £30.00-£40.00 Single £25.00-£30.00 Double	Open Jan-Dec Dinner 1830-2030 B&B + Eve.Meal £35.00-£40.00

Recently refurbished country inn in centre of small village with superb views over Loch Leven. Speciality grill and bar menus.

KINROSS	Map 2 C3

Bridgend Hotel 257 High Street Kinross KY13 7DL Tel:(Kinross) 0577 863413 Fax:0577 864769	COMMENDED 👑 👑 👑	3 Single 8 Twin 3 Double 1 Family	15 En Suite fac 1 Pub.Bath/Show	B&B per person £34.50-£39.50 Single £24.50-£28.50 Double	Open Jan-Dec Dinner 1700-2200 B&B + Eve.Meal £44.50-£50.00

Family run hotel close to Loch Leven, famed for its trout and Mary Queen of Scots' daring escape. Some annexe accommodation. Fresh local produce.

THE GREEN HOTEL
KINROSS, SCOTLAND KY13 7AS
Tel: (0577) 863467 Fax: (0577) 863180

Independently owned holiday hotel, only 5 minutes from the M90. Well-appointed bedrooms and family suites. Restaurant, bar meals. Spacious indoor pool and leisure complex, own two 18-hole golf courses, two 'all weather' tennis courts, and world famous trout fishing. Ideal touring base, with Edinburgh, Glasgow, Perth, Stirling, St Andrews, Pitlochry and Highland Perthshire within the hour.

Green Hotel 2 The Muirs Kinross KY13 7AS Tel:(Kinross) 0577 863467 Fax:0577 863180	HIGHLY COMMENDED 👑 👑 👑 👑	30 Twin 13 Double 4 Family Suites avail.	47 En Suite fac	B&B per person £65.00-£90.00 Single £45.00-£55.00 Double	Open Jan-Dec Dinner 1900-2130 B&B + Eve.Meal £55.00-£85.00

Recently refurbished independent hotel with leisure pool, sauna, solarium and its own two 18-hole golf courses.

Kirklands Hotel 20 High Street Kinross KY13 7AN Tel:(Kinross) 0577 863313 Fax:0577 863313	COMMENDED 👑 👑 👑 👑	5 Twin 3 Double 1 Family	9 En Suite fac	B&B per person £37.50 Single £28.50 Double	Open Jan-Dec Dinner 1745-2100 B&B + Eve.Meal £42.00

Friendly service at this former Coaching Inn with extensive bar and restaurant menus. Large suite available which is ideal for groups and families.

KINROSS	Map 2 C3						
Windlestrae Hotel Kinross KY13 7AS Tel:(Kinross) 0577 863217 Fax:0577 864733		**HIGHLY COMMENDED** 👑 👑 👑 👑	1 Single 45 En Suite fac 15 Twin 10 Double 19 Family Suites avail.	B&B per person £58.50-£65.00 Single £50.00-£52.50 Double	Open Jan-Dec Dinner 1830-2130 B&B + Eve.Meal £65.00-£80.00	

Privately owned, in 4 acres next to golf course, offering comfort and good food. Ideal for businessmen and tourists; conference facilities and suites

---

Grouse & Claret

HEATHERYFORD
KINROSS
KY13 7NQ
Tel: 05778 64212

An unusually attractive restaurant with art gallery and working pottery in converted farmhouse overlooking four excellent trout fishing lochans. Only 2 mins off M90 but deep in the country. Good touring centre. Delicious home-made food, incorporating fresh herbs and wild produce. Comfortable, en-suite rooms with lovely views. Edinburgh 30 mins, Perth 20 mins, Glasgow 1 hour. St Andrews 40 mins, Gleneagles 40 mins.

| The Grouse & Claret
Heatheryford
Kinross
KY13 7NQ
Tel:(Kinross) 0577 864212
Fax:0577 864212 | **APPROVED**
👑 👑 👑 | 2 Twin 4 En Suite fac
2 Double | B&B per person
£23.50-£27.50 Single
£18.50-£22.50 Double | Open Mar-Jan
Dinner 1900-2100
B&B + Eve.Meal
£35.00-£40.00 | |

Overlooking the trout farm and situated just off the M90 motorway. Annexe accommodation.

| The Muirs Inn Kinross
49 Muirs
Kinross
KY13 7AU
Tel:(Kinross) 0577 862270 | **COMMENDED**
👑 👑 👑 | 2 Twin 5 En Suite fac
3 Double | B&B per person
to £35.00 Single
£25.00-£27.50 Double | Open Jan-Dec
Dinner 1700-2100
B&B + Eve.Meal
to £40.00 | |

Scottish country Inn. Award nominated restaurant. Simply something special.

| The Roxburghe Guest House
126 High Street
Kinross
KY13 7DA
Tel:(Kinross) 0577 862498 | **APPROVED Listed** | 1 Twin 1 Pub.Bath/Show
1 Double
2 Family | B&B per person
from £14.00 Single
from £14.00 Double | Open Jan-Dec
Dinner 1800-2000
B&B + Eve.Meal
from £25.00 | |

Personally run guest house in centre of town. Convenient for touring Perthshire. Close to Loch Leven and Castle.

BY KINROSS	Map 2 C3					
Nivingston Country Hotel & Restaurant Cleish, Kinross Kinross-shire KY13 7LS Tel:(Cleish Hills) 0577 850216 Fax:0577 850238	**HIGHLY COMMENDED** 👑 👑 👑 👑	2 Single 17 En Suite fac 4 Twin 10 Double 1 Family	B&B per person £70.00-£80.00 Single £45.00-£60.00 Double	Open Jan-Dec Dinner 1900-2100 B&B + Eve.Meal £95.00-£105.00	

Former country mansion set in 12 acres of parkland within easy motoring distance of Edinburgh. Taste of Scotland Restaurant.

KIPPFORD by Dalbeattie – KIRKCUDBRIGHT

KIPPFORD by Dalbeattie, Kirkcudbrightshire
Orchardknowes
Kippford, by Dalbeattie
DG5 4LG
Tel:(Kippford) 055662 639
Fax:055662 325

Map 2 B1

1 Single / 1 Twin / 3 Family
3 En Suite fac / 2 Pub.Bath/Show
B&B per person £13.00-£15.00 Single £17.00-£23.00 Double
Open Apr-Oct

KIRKBEAN Dumfriesshire
Cavens House Hotel
Kirkbean, by Dumfries
Dumfriesshire
DG2 8AA
Tel:(Kirkbean) 038788 234

Map 2 B1

COMMENDED

3 Twin / 2 Double / 1 Family
6 En Suite fac
B&B per person £27.00-£40.00 Single £20.00-£23.00 Double
Open Jan-Dec Dinner 1845-2000 B&B + Eve.Meal £34.00-£37.00

Comfortable accommodation in refurbished Lodge set in own grounds near Solway Firth.

KIRKCALDY Fife
Dunnikier House Hotel
Dunnikier Park
Kirkcaldy
Fife
KY1 3LP
Tel:(Kirkcaldy) 0592 268393
Fax:0592 642340

Map 2 D4

4 Single / 9 Twin / 2 Double
15 En Suite fac
B&B per person to £47.50 Single to £60.00 Double
Open Jan-Dec Dinner 1900-2145

Ollerton Hotel
48-50 Victoria Road
Kirkcaldy
Fife
KY1 1DH
Tel:(Kirkcaldy) 0592 264286
Fax:0592 265544

1 Single / 8 Twin / 3 Double / 3 Family
6 En Suite fac / 2 Pub.Bath/Show
B&B per person £15.00-£27.00 Single £30.00-£45.00 Double
Open Jan-Dec Dinner 1630-2100 B&B + Eve.Meal £17.75-£55.00

Royal Hotel
Townhead
Dysart
Fife
KY1 2XQ
Tel:(Kirkcaldy) 0592 654112/652109

5 Twin / 1 Double / 1 Family
2 Pub.Bath/Show
B&B per person from £16.50 Single from £14.00 Double
Open Jan-Dec Dinner 1700-2100 B&B + Eve.Meal from £18.50

KIRKCUDBRIGHT
Arden House Hotel
Kirkcudbright
DG6 4UU
Tel:(Kirkcudbright) 0557 330544

Map 2 A1

1 Single / 2 Twin / 3 Double / 4 Family
4 En Suite fac / 3 Pub.Bath/Show
B&B per person £22.00-£26.00 Single £22.00-£26.00 Double
Open Jan-Dec Dinner 1800-2200

Commercial Hotel
Kirkcudbright
DG6
Tel:(Kirkcudbright) 0557 330407

2 Single / 2 Double / 1 Family
1 Pub.Bath/Show
B&B per person £14.00-£15.00 Single £14.00-£15.00 Double
Open Jan-Dec Dinner 1800-2030 B&B + Eve.Meal £18.50-£25.00

KIRKCUDBRIGHT continued
Map 2 A1

Gordon House Hotel
116 High Street
Kirkcudbright
DG6 4JQ
Tel:(Kirkcudbright) 0557
330670

APPROVED

4 Single   3 Pub.Bath/Show
3 Twin
3 Double
2 Family

B&B per person
£16.00-£20.00 Single

Open Jan-Dec
Dinner 1800-2100

Early 19C building close to town centre and harbour. Scottish and Italian cooking.

Selkirk Arms Hotel
High Street
Kirkcudbright
DG6 4JG
Tel:(Kirkcudbright) 0557
330402
Fax:0557 331639

HIGHLY COMMENDED

5 Single   15 En Suite fac
3 Twin
5 Double
2 Family

B&B per person
from £44.00 Single
from £36.25 Double

Open Jan-Dec
Dinner 1900-2130

Family run 18C hotel where Burns wrote the Selkirk Grace. Regular Taste of Scotland menus.

Gladstone House
48 High Street
Kirkcudbright
DG6 4JX
Tel:(Kirkcudbright) 0557
331734

HIGHLY COMMENDED

3 Double   3 En Suite fac

B&B per person
£24.00-£27.00 Double

Open Jan-Dec

Elegance and comfort in sympathetically restored Georgian town house in a quiet corner of the old town. Secret garden.

KIRKGUNZEON by Dumfries, Dumfriesshire
Map 2 B1

Cowans Farm Guest House
Kirkgunzeon, Dumfries
Dumfriesshire
DG2 8JY
Tel:(Kirkgunzeon) 038776
284

1 Single   5 En Suite fac
2 Twin
2 Family

B&B per person
£15.00-£16.50 Single
£13.00-£13.50 Double

Open Jan-Dec
Dinner 1800-2000
B&B + Eve.Meal
£19.00-£22.50

KIRKHILL by Inverness Inverness-shire
Map 4 A8

Inchmore Hotel
Kirkhill,by Inverness
Inverness-shire
IV5 7PX
Tel:(Drumchardine) 0463
831296

COMMENDED

3 Twin   6 En Suite fac
3 Double

B&B per person
£25.00-£30.00 Single
£20.00-£25.00 Double

Open Jan-Dec
Dinner 1800-2100
B&B + Eve.Meal
£30.00-£35.00

Family run, attractive village inn situated on Beauly Firth, 7 miles (11 kms) west of Inverness on A862. Renowned for good food.

KIRKMICHAEL Perthshire
Map 2 C1

Aldchlappie Hotel
Kirkmichael
Perthshire
PH10 7NS
Tel:(Strathardle) 0250
881224
Fax:0250 881373

COMMENDED

2 Twin   7 En Suite fac
2 Double
3 Family

B&B per person
£22.00-£25.00 Single
£22.00-£25.00 Double

Open Dec-Nov
Dinner 1900-2100
B&B + Eve.Meal
£26.00-£40.00

Friendly family run hotel on outskirts of village with fine views over River Ardle and Glen of Strathardle. Conveniently situated for touring.

The Log Cabin Hotel
Glen Derby, Balnald
Kirkmichael
Perthshire
PH10 7NB
Tel:(Strathardle) 0250
881288
Fax:0250 881402

COMMENDED

2 Twin   13 En Suite fac
6 Double
5 Family

B&B per person
£22.50-£34.50 Single
£22.50-£24.50 Double

Open Jan-Dec
Dinner 1930-2045
B&B + Eve.Meal
£37.55-£39.75

Unique hotel, stunning mountain views. Emphasis on local game and fresh produce. Fishing, shooting, skiing, riding, walking and stalking.

Details of Grading and Classification are on page vi.

Key to symbols is on back flap.

KIRKMICHAEL continued
Strathlene Hotel
Kirkmichael
Perthshire
PH10 7NT
Tel:(Strathardle) 0250
881347

Map 2
C1

3 Twin
3 Double
1 Family

5 En Suite fac
2 Pub.Bath/Show

B&B per person
£17.00-£20.00 Single
£15.00-£17.00 Double

Open Jan-Dec
Dinner 1830-2030
B&B + Eve.Meal
£25.00-£27.00

KIRKNEWTON, by Ratho, Midlothian

Map 2
C5

DALMAHOY HOTEL GOLF & COUNTRY CLUB

KIRKNEWTON NEAR EDINBURGH EH27 8EB
Telephone: 031 333 1845

This recently opened resort hotel offers the ultimate in quality accommodation matched with extensive sports and leisure facilities including two 18-hole golf courses, all in a peaceful country setting only seven miles west of Edinburgh city centre.

Dalmahoy Hotel,
Golf & Country Club
Kirknewton
Midlothian
EH27 8EB
Tel:031 333 1845
Tlx:449344
Fax:031 335 3203

COMMENDED

1 Single
38 Twin
74 Double
3 Family

116 En Suite fac

B&B per person
£85.00-£115.00 Single
£60.00-£75.00 Double

Open Jan-Dec
Dinner 1900-2200
B&B + Eve.Meal
£69.00-£75.00

Centred around Georgian mansion house with full range of business and leisure facilities including two mature golf courses.

KIRKOSWALD
Ayrshire
Kirkton Jeans Hotel
47 Main Street
Kirkoswald
Ayrshire
KA19 8HY
Tel:(Kirkoswald) 06556 220

Map 1
G8

6 Twin
3 Family

9 En Suite fac
1 Pub.Bath/Show

B&B per person
£26.00-£30.00 Single
£17.50-£22.50 Double

Open Jan-Dec
Dinner 1700-2030

KIRKWALL
Orkney
Albert Hotel
Kirkwall
Orkney
KW15 1JZ
Tel:(Kirkwall) 0856 876000
Fax:0856 875397

Map 5
B1

COMMENDED

9 Single
3 Twin
5 Double
2 Family

19 En Suite fac
2 Pub.Bath/Show

B&B per person
£35.00-£48.00 Single
£27.50-£40.50 Double

Open Jan-Dec
Dinner 1800-2200
B&B + Eve.Meal
£35.00-£62.00

Traditional hotel in town centre, tastefully refurbished. Choice of bars;mainly fresh produce.

FOVERAN HOTEL

FOVERAN, ST OLA, KIRKWALL, ORKNEY ISLES KW15 1SF
Tel: 0856 872389   Fax: 0856 876430

Probably the best small hotel in Orkney, with the finest restaurant serving the very best of local produce, fish, shellfish and beef, and a full Vegetarian Menu.
Set in 34 acres of Orkney's lush green fields overlooking Scapa Flow.
All rooms have all private facilities.

Foveran Hotel
St Ola
Kirkwall
Orkney
KW15 1SF
Tel:(Kirkwall) 0856 872389

COMMENDED

3 Single
2 Twin
2 Double
1 Family

8 En Suite fac

B&B per person
£43.00-£50.00 Single
£34.00-£37.50 Double

Open Jan-Dec
Dinner 1900-2100

Family run hotel and restaurant set in 34 acres overlooking Scapa Flow. Emphasis on cuisine using fresh local produce. Kirkwall 2 miles (3kms).

KIRKWALL continued	Map 5 B1						
Lynnfield Hotel Holm Road Kirkwall Orkney Tel:(Kirkwall) 0856 872505	Award Pending	4 Twin 1 Double 3 Family	8 En Suite fac	B&B per person £30.00-£45.00 Single £18.00-£30.00 Double	Open Jan-Dec Dinner 1900-2100 B&B + Eve.Meal	
Queen's Hotel Kirkwall Orkney KW15 1LE Tel:(Kirkwall) 0856 872200	COMMENDED 🏆🏆🏆	3 Single 4 Twin 2 Family	9 En Suite fac	B&B per person from £22.00 Single from £18.00 Double	Open Jan-Dec Dinner 1800-2100 B&B + Eve.Meal £28.00-£33.00	
		Newly refurbished hotel on harbour front. Convenient for all town amenities.				
Royal Hotel Victoria Street Kirkwall Orkney KW15 1DN Tel:(Kirkwall) 0856 873477 Fax:0856 872767	APPROVED 🏆🏆🏆	12 Single 10 Twin 9 Double 1 Family	16 En Suite fac 7 Pub.Bath/Show	B&B per person £21.50-£37.00 Single £20.50-£35.00 Double	Open Jan-Dec Dinner 1830-2000 B&B + Eve.Meal £30.00-£50.00	
		Personally run hotel, parts dating from 17C, in centre of Kirkwall in narrow main street with limited vehicle access. Vegetarian specialities.				
St Ola Hotel Harbour Street Kirkwall Orkney KW15 1LE Tel:(Kirkwall) 0856 875090	COMMENDED 🏆🏆🏆	2 Single 2 Twin 1 Double 1 Family	6 En Suite fac	B&B per person from £24.00 Single from £19.00 Double	Open Jan-Dec Dinner from 1830 B&B + Eve.Meal from £29.00	
		Friendly family run harbour front hotel; most rooms have private facilities mainly en suite. Busy local bars.				
Sanderlay Guest House 2 Viewfield Drive Kirkwall Orkney Tel:(Kirkwall) 0856 872343 Fax:0856 876350	COMMENDED 🏆🏆	1 Twin 2 Double 2 Family	3 En Suite fac 1 Pub.Bath/Show	B&B per person £12.00-£18.00 Double	Open Jan-Dec	
		Comfortable modern house in quiet residential area on outskirts of town. Some ensuite and 2 self-contained family units.				
KIRRIEMUIR **Angus** Airlie Arms Hotel St Malcolm's Wynd Kirriemuir Angus DD8 4HB Tel:(Kirriemuir) 0575 72847	Map 2 D1	2 Twin 3 Double 4 Family	9 En Suite fac	B&B per person £21.50-£24.50 Single £17.50-£19.50 Double	Open Jan-Dec Dinner 1800-2100 B&B + Eve.Meal from £27.50	
KNOYDART **Inverness-shire** Pier House Guest House Inverie, Knoydart Inverness-shire PH41 4PL Tel:(Mallaig) 0687 2347	Map 3 F1	2 Twin 2 Family	1 Pub.Bath/Show	B&B per person £17.50-£20.00 Single £17.50 Double	Open Jan-Dec Dinner 1700-2230 B&B + Eve.Meal £25.00-£27.50	
KYLEAKIN **Isle of Skye,** **Inverness-shire** Dunringell Hotel Kyleakin Isle of Skye, Inverness-shire 1V41 8PR Tel:(Kyle) 0599 4180	Map 3 E1 COMMENDED 🏆🏆🏆	3 Single 2 Twin 5 Double 7 Family	10 En Suite fac 4 Pub.Bath/Show	B&B per person £16.00-£25.00 Single £16.00-£25.00 Double	Open Mar-Oct Dinner 1900-1930 B&B + Eve.Meal £26.00-£34.00	
		Country house hotel outside this attractive island village. Tranquil setting; fine mature garden. Close to ferry point. Some annexe accommodation.				

Details of Grading and Classification are on page vi.

Key to symbols is on back flap.

KYLEAKIN **Isle of Skye,** King's Arms Hotel Kyleakin Isle of Skye, Inverness-shire IV41 8PH Tel:(Kyle) 0599 4109	Map 3 E1	APPROVED 👑 👑 👑	18 Single 45 Twin 18 Double	81 En Suite fac	B&B per person £42.00-£50.00 Single £38.00-£46.00 Double	Open Apr-Oct Dinner 1830-2000 B&B + Eve.Meal £48.00-£58.50	

Modern hotel near Skye ferry. Sea views across to Kyle of Lochalsh. Entertainment some evenings.

White Heather Hotel Kyleakin Isle of Skye, Inverness-shire 1V41 8PL Tel:(Kyle) 0599 4577 Fax: 0599 4427			2 Single 8 Twin 8 Double 2 Family	10 En Suite fac 6 Pub.Bath/Show	B&B per person £20.00-£24.00 Single £17.00-£24.00 Double	Open Jan-Dec Dinner from 1900 B&B + Eve.Meal £29.00-£36.00	

KYLE OF LOCHALSH **Ross-shire** Kyle Hotel Main Street Kyle of Lochalsh Ross-shire IV40 8AB Tel:(Kyle) 0599 4204	Map 3 F1	COMMENDED 👑 👑 👑	8 Single 17 Twin 6 Double	31 En Suite fac	B&B per person £25.00-£37.00 Single £25.00-£35.00 Double	Open Jan-Dec Dinner 1830-2130 B&B + Eve.Meal £35.00-£47.00	

Recently modernised hotel, 5 minutes walk from the railway station, in the centre of the village. 8 bedrooms on the ground floor.

Tingle Creek Hotel Erbusaig Kyle of Lochalsh Ross-shire IV40 8BB Tel:(Kyle) 0599 4430		Award Pending	1 Single 6 Twin 6 Double 1 Family	12 En Suite fac 1 Pub.Bath/Show	B&B per person £20.00-£35.00 Single £20.00-£40.00 Double	Open Jan-Dec Dinner 1830-2130 B&B + Eve.Meal £30.00-£40.00	

KYLESKU **Sutherland** Newton Lodge Newton Kylesku Sutherland IV27 4HW Tel:(Scourie) 0971 502070	Map 3 G4	HIGHLY COMMENDED 👑 👑 👑	2 Single 2 Twin 4 Double	8 En Suite fac	B&B per person £20.00-£25.00 Single £20.00-£25.00 Double	Open Jan-Dec Dinner 1830-1930 B&B + Eve.Meal £32.00-£37.00	

A large, purpose-built guest house surrounded by an inspiring panorama of mountains and lochs.

TELEPHONE DIALLING CODES

Many telephone dialling codes have changed this year. If you experience difficulty in connecting a call, please call Directory Enquiries – **192** – where someone will issue the correct number. Please note: a charge will be placed for this service when using a private telephone

BY LAIRG Sutherland	Map 4 A6

Sutherland Arms Hotel

LAIRG. SUTHERLAND IV27 4AT
Telephone: 0549 2291 Fax: 0549 2261

This 25-bedroom hotel sits amidst spectacular scenery and overlooks Loch Shin. All bedrooms have private bathroom and all have colour TV, telephone, tea and coffee making facilities. Comfortable lounges and welcoming bar provide the perfect place to relax. The hotel is close to some of the finest salmon and trout fishing water in Scotland and is within easy driving distance from the seaside and golfing resorts of Golspie and Dornoch.

Dinner, Bed and Breakfast rates from £43 to £55. Over 60's from £36 to £40. Free Accommodation for children under 12 years old sharing parents room.

Sutherland Arms Hotel Lairg Sutherland IV27 4AT Tel:(Lairg) 0549 2291 Tlx:778215 Fax:0549 2261	COMMENDED 🏴 🏴 🏴	2 Single Twin 7 Double 3 Family	22 En Suite fac 4 Pub.Bath/Show	B&B per person from £49.00 Single from £45.00 Double	Open Apr-Oct Dinner 1900-2100 B&B + Eve.Meal from £49.00
		Comfortable, personally run hotel overlooking Loch Shin.			

LAMLASH Isle of Arran	Map 1 F7				
Glenisle Hotel Lamlash Isle of Arran KA27 8LS Tel:(Lamlash) 0770 600258/600559	COMMENDED 🏴 🏴 🏴 🏴	2 Single 3 Twin 5 Double 3 Family	13 En Suite fac	B&B per person £22.50-£35.00 Single £22.50-£35.00 Double	Open Feb-Dec Dinner 1900-2100 B&B + Eve.Meal £32.00-£44.50
		Situated on seafront with attractive garden and easy access to the shore. Personal attention, ample parking.			

Westfield Guest House Lamlash Isle of Arran KA27 8NN Tel:(Lamlash) 0770 600428	COMMENDED 🏴	2 Single 1 Twin 1 Double	1 Pub.Bath/Show	B&B per person £15.50-£16.00 Single £15.50-£16.00 Double	Open Feb-Nov Dinner 1830-1845 B&B + Eve.Meal £23.00
		Friendly, family guest house near to the sea front and all amenities. Private parking. Home cooking.			

LANARK	Map 2 B6				
Cartland Bridge Hotel Cartland Lanark Tel:(Lanark) 0555 664426		3 Single 3 Twin 11 Double 1 Family	18 En Suite fac	B&B per person £40.00-£55.00 Single £25.00-£35.00 Double	Open Jan-Dec Dinner 1900-2100

LANGBANK **Renfrewshire** Gleddoch House Hotel Langbank Renfrewshire PA14 6YE Tel:(Langbank) 047554 711	Map 1 H5	**HIGHLY COMMENDED** 👑 👑 👑 👑	7 Single 10 Twin 12 Double 4 Family Suites avail.	33 En Suite fac	B&B per person £90.00-£105.00 Single £65.00-£85.00 Double	Open Jan-Dec Dinner 1930-2100	

Country house hotel with golf club and extensive views of the River Clyde. Reputation for fine food using fresh produce.

LANGHOLM **Dumfriesshire** Crown Hotel Langholm Dumfriesshire DG13 0JH Tel:(Langholm) 03873 80247	Map 2 D9		2 Single 3 Twin 2 Double 1 Family	2 Pub.Bath/Show	B&B per person £18.00 Single £17.00 Double	Open Jan-Dec Dinner 1830-2100 B&B + Eve.Meal £26.00	

Eskdale Hotel Langholm Dumfriesshire DG13 0JH Tel:(Langholm) 03873 80357 Fax:03873 80357		**COMMENDED** 👑 👑 👑	5 Single 3 Twin 6 Double 2 Family	10 En Suite fac 3 Pub.Bath/Show	B&B per person £26.00-£29.00 Single £26.00-£29.00 Double	Open Jan-Dec Dinner 1800-2000 B&B + Eve.Meal £38.00-£41.00	

Family run former coaching inn in centre of small Borders town. Salmon, trout fishing and shooting available.

LARGS **Ayrshire** Brisbane House Hotel Esplanade Largs Ayrshire KA30 8NF Tel:(Largs) 0475 687200 Fax:0475 676295	Map 1 G6	**HIGHLY COMMENDED** 👑 👑 👑 👑	6 Single 7 Twin 8 Double 2 Family	23 En Suite fac	B&B per person £40.00-£70.00 Single £30.00-£50.00 Double	Open Jan-Dec Dinner 1900-2130 B&B + Eve.Meal £42.50-£65.00	

Seaside hotel with extensive front gardens and private parking, Tastefully chosen fabrics exude an aura of well being.

Springfield Hotel North Bay Largs Ayrshire KA30 8QL Tel:(Largs) 0475 673119 Fax:0475 673119			10 Single 35 Twin 10 Double 3 Family	58 En Suite fac 4 Pub.Bath/Show	B&B per person £42.50 Single £29.25 Double	Open Jan-Dec Dinner 1630-2100 B&B + Eve.Meal £40.25-£53.75	

Willow Bank Hotel 96 Greenock Road Largs Ayrshire KA30 8PG Tel:(Largs) 0475 672311/675435		**COMMENDED** 👑 👑 👑 👑	2 Single 15 Twin 9 Double 3 Family	29 En Suite fac	B&B per person £38.00-£45.00 Single £30.00-£35.00 Double	Open Jan-Dec Dinner 1900-2100 B&B + Eve.Meal £40.00-£55.00	

Modern hotel in tree-lined location on the edge of the town. Offering in-house entertainment and enjoying a local reputation for good food.

Belmont House 2 Broomfield Place Largs Ayrshire KA30 8DR Tel:(Largs) 0475 676264		**HIGHLY COMMENDED** 👑 👑	1 Twin 2 Double	1 En Suite fac 2 Priv.NOT ensuite	B&B per person £16.50-£23.00 Double	Open Easter-mid Oct	

Interesting early 19C house on the waterfront of South Largs with views of Arran, Cumbrae and Bute.

LARGS continued

Map 1 G6

Crawfordlea Guest House
12 Charles Street
Largs
Ayrshire
KA30 8HJ
Tel:(Largs) 0475 675825

COMMENDED
Listed

2 Single / 2 Limited ensuite / 1 Twin / 1 Double — 1 Pub.Bath/Show
B&B per person from £14.00 Single / from £14.00 Double
Open Apr-Sep, Nov-Feb

Family run guest house in street near sea front and town centre.

Lea-Mar Guest House
20 Douglas Street
Largs
Ayrshire
KA30 8PS
Tel:(Largs) 0475 672447

COMMENDED

2 Twin / 2 Double — 4 En Suite fac / 1 Pub.Bath/Show
B&B per person £19.00-£20.00 Double
Open Feb-Nov

Detached bungalow in quiet area, yet close to town. 100 yards from the promenade and beach. Ideal base for touring.

Lilac Holm Guest House
14 Noddleburn Road,
Off Barr Crescent
Largs
Ayrshire
KA30 8PY
Tel:(Largs) 0475 672020

COMMENDED

2 Single / 2 Twin / 3 Double / 1 Family — 2 Pub.Bath/Show
B&B per person from £15.00 Single / from £15.00 Double
Open Jan-Dec
Dinner from 1800
B&B + Eve.Meal from £23.50

Built in 1935; in quiet residential area overlooking the Noddle Burn. Evening meals available. Personal attention of owners.

Tigh-na-Ligh Guest House
104 Brisbane Road
Largs
Ayrshire
KA30 8NN
Tel:(Largs) 0475 673975

COMMENDED

2 Twin / 2 Double / 1 Family — 4 En Suite fac / 1 Priv.NOT ensuite
B&B per person £19.00-£20.00 Double
Open Jan-Dec
Dinner from 1800
B&B + Eve.Meal £27.00-£28.00

Red sandstone house in quiet residential area, close to local amenities and convenient for touring Firth of Clyde area and Burns Country.

Whin-Park Guest House
16 Douglas Street
Largs
Ayrshire
KA30 8PS
Tel:(Largs) 0475 673437

HIGHLY COMMENDED

1 Single / 1 Twin / 1 Double / 1 Family — 4 En Suite fac / 1 Pub.Bath/Show
B&B per person from £19.00 Single / from £19.00 Double
Open Jan-Dec

Warm, comfortable and relaxing atmosphere; near seafront and swimming pool.

BY LARGS
Ayrshire

Map 1 G6

Manor Park Hotel
Skelmorlie, by Largs
Ayrshire
PA17 5HE
Tel:(Wemyss Bay) 0475 520832
Fax:0475 520832

COMMENDED

4 Single / 7 Twin / 12 Double — 23 En Suite fac
B&B per person £50.00-£80.00 Single / £35.00-£55.00 Double
Open Jan-Dec
Dinner 1800-2200
B&B + Eve.Meal £50.00-£70.00

Built in 1840 and beautifully set in 15 acres of landscaped garden. Former site of Dower House of the Earls of Eglinton. Some annexe accommodation.

LARKHALL
Lanarkshire

Map 2 A6

Shawlands Roadhouse Hotel
Ayr Road, Canderside Toll
Larkhall
Lanarkshire
ML9 2TZ
Tel:(Larkhall) 0698 791111

2 Single / 1 Twin / 3 Double / 1 Family — 1 Priv.NOT ensuite / 2 Pub.Bath/Show
B&B per person £30.00 Single / £40.00 Double
Open Jan-Dec
Dinner 1100-2100

LASSWADE **Midlothian** The Laird & Dog Hotel 5 High Street Lasswade Midlothian EH18 Tel:031 663 7702	Map 2 D5		1 Single 3 Twin 2 Double 1 Family	7 En Suite fac	B&B per person £23.00-£26.00 Single £17.00-£20.00 Double	Open Jan-Dec Dinner 1800-2000 B&B + Eve.Meal £28.00-£32.00	
LAUDER **Berwickshire** Lauderdale Hotel 1 Edinburgh Road Lauder Berwickshire TD2 6TW Tel:(Lauder) 05782 231/0578 722231	Map 2 E6	COMMENDED	1 Single 7 Twin 1 Double	9 En Suite fac	B&B per person £30.00-£75.00 Single £23.00-£75.00 Double	Open Jan-Dec Dinner 1900-2100	
			Friendly hotel, conveniently situated on A68. Double glazing. Traditional char-grill and enterprising a la carte menu using fresh produce and game.				
LEACKLEE **Harris, Western Isles** Siamara 6 Leacklee Harris, Western Isles PA85 3EH Tel:(Manish) 085983 314	Map 3 C6	HIGHLY COMMENDED	2 Twin 1 Double	3 En Suite fac	B&B per person from £26.00 Single from £26.00 Double	Open Jan-Dec Dinner from 1900 B&B + Eve.Meal from £36.00	
			Recently modernised house with warm and friendly atmosphere overlooking Loch Stockinsh. All rooms with private facilities.				
LEDAIG, by Oban **Argyll** Isle of Eriska Ledaig,by Oban Argyll PA37 1SD Tel:(Ledaig) 063172 371 Tlx:777040 Fax:063172 531	Map 1 E2	DELUXE	5 Twin 10 Double 1 Family	16 En Suite fac	B&B per person £135.00-£150.00 Single £78.00-£95.00 Double	Open Feb-Nov Dinner 2000-2100 B&B + Eve.Meal £115.00-£132.00	
			Family owned and run Scottish baronial mansion on peaceful private 300 acre island reached by bridge. Accent on fresh local produce.				

HERE'S THE DIFFERENCE

STB's scheme has two distinct elements, grading and classification.

GRADING:

measures the quality and condition of the facilities and services offered, eg, the warmth of welcome, quality of food and its presentation, condition of decor and furnishings, appearance of buildings, tidiness of grounds and gardens, condition of lighting and heating and so on.
Grading awards are: **Approved, Commended, Highly Commended, Deluxe.**

CLASSIFICATION:

measures the range of physical facilities and services offered, eg, rooms with private bath, heating, reception, lounges, telephones and so on.
Classification awards are: **Listed or from one to five crowns.**

LERAGS, by Oban Argyll	Map 1 E2

Foxholes Hotel
COLOGIN, LERAGS, OBAN, ARGYLL PA34 4SE
Telephone: 0631 64982

Enjoy peace and tranquillity at Foxholes, situated in its own grounds in a quiet glen 3 miles from Oban. We have magnificent views of surrounding countryside, all bedrooms en-suite, colour TV and tea/coffee-making facilities. Enjoy our superb 6-course table d'hôte menu and large selection of wines.

Send for colour brochure and tariff to Mr G.T. Waugh, Foxholes Hotel, Cologin, Lerags, Oban PA34 4SE. Tel: 0631 64982.

Prices from £34 to £47 per person per night DB&B.

Foxholes Hotel Cologin, Lerags Oban Argyll PA34 4SE Tel:(Oban) 0631 64982	COMMENDED 👑 👑 👑	2 Twin 5 Double	7 En Suite fac	B&B per person £33.00-£35.00 Single £24.00-£26.00 Double	Open Mar-Oct Dinner 1900-2000 B&B + Eve.Meal £33.60-£47.00

Peacefully situated in a quiet glen, 3 miles (5kms) south of Oban with magnificent views. Home grown produce.

Lerags House Lerags, by Oban Argyll PA34 4SE Tel:(Oban) 0631 63381		1 Single 2 Twin 4 Double 1 Family Suites avail.	8 En Suite fac	B&B per person £18.00-£28.00 Single £18.00-£28.00 Double	Open Jan-Dec Dinner at 1900 B&B + Eve.Meal £26.00-£38.00

LERWICK **Shetland**	Map 5 G4

Grand Hotel Commercial Street Lerwick Shetland ZE1 Tel:(Lerwick) 0595 2826 Fax:0595 4048	COMMENDED 👑 👑 👑	11 Single 5 Twin 4 Double 2 Family	17 En Suite fac 3 Pub.Bath/Show	B&B per person £45.00-£60.00 Single £35.00-£45.00 Double	Open Jan-Dec Dinner 1700-2100 B&B + Eve.Meal £45.00-£55.00

Oldest purpose built hotel in Shetland, having recently undergone extensive refurbishment; situated in town centre and close to harbour front.

Kveldsro House Hotel Lerwick Shetland ZE1 Tel:(Lerwick) 0595 2195 Fax:0595 6595	HIGHLY COMMENDED 👑 👑 👑 👑	2 Single 13 Twin 2 Double	17 En Suite fac	B&B per person £82.50-£95.00 Single £48.75-£55.00 Double	Open Jan-Dec Dinner 1800-2130 B&B + Eve.Meal £58.00-£94.00

A renowned hotel with fine harbour views. Fully refurbished to the most exacting standards. Chef committed to using fresh produce when available.

LERWICK

LERWICK continued — Map 5 G4

Establishment	Award	Rooms	En Suite	B&B	Open
The Lerwick Hotel 15 South Road Lerwick Shetland ZE2 0RB Tel:(Lerwick) 0595 2166 Tlx:75128 Fax:0595 4419	COMMENDED	9 Single 20 Twin 5 Double 1 Family Suite avail.	35 En Suite fac	B&B per person to £59.50 Single to £37.50 Double	Open Jan-Dec Dinner 1830-2100 B&B + Eve.Meal £49.50-£69.50

Modern hotel in Lerwick, on sea shore overlooking Breiwick Bay and Bressay Island. Catering for holiday and business travel. Tours organised.

HOLIDAY IN SHETLAND
QUEEN'S HOTEL
Commercial Street, Lerwick ZE1 0AB
Tel: (0595) 2826 Fax: (0595) 4048

The QUEEN'S HOTEL is in the centre of Lerwick, picturesque and old fashioned in appearance but comfortably appointed within.
Many of its bedrooms face the beautiful Sound of Bressay. The restaurant offers a table d'hôte menu along with our extensive à la carte menu.
A full range of tours can be organised by the hotel reception.
B&B from £37.50 per person per night.
Fully inclusive package holidays available.
For details contact:
N.R. Wilkins, Managing Director.

Establishment	Award	Rooms	En Suite	B&B	Open
Queen's Hotel Commercial Street Lerwick Shetland ZE1 Tel:(Lerwick) 0595 2826 Fax:0595 4048	COMMENDED	7 Single 9 Twin 10 Double	26 En Suite fac	B&B per person £56.00-£65.00 Single £38.50-£40.50 Double	Open Jan-Dec Dinner 1800-2100 B&B + Eve.Meal £46.00-£76.00

Traditional stone building on the very edge of the sea. Magnificent views over Island of Bressay.

| Shetland Hotel
Holmsgarth Road
Lerwick
Shetland
ZE1 0PW
Tel:(Lerwick) 0595 5515
Fax:0595 5828 | COMMENDED | 46 Twin
15 Double
4 Family | 65 En Suite fac | B&B per person
from £68.20 Single
from £38.83 Double | Open Jan-Dec
Dinner 1900-2130 |

Modern hotel with spacious bedrooms and leisure complex. Views to busy harbour and Isle of Bressay.

| Bona Vista Guest House
26 Church Road
Lerwick
Shetland
ZE1 0AE
Tel:(Lerwick) 0595 2269 | | 5 Single
1 Twin | 1 En Suite fac
2 Limited ensuite
1 Pub.Bath/Show | B&B per person
£19.00-£22.00 Single
£17.00 Double | Open Jan-Dec |

VAT is shown at 17.5%: changes in this rate may affect prices. Prices shown are for guidance only. Please send SAE with each enquir

LERWICK continued Breiview Guest House 43 Kanterstead Road Lerwick Shetland Tel:(Lerwick) 0595 5956	**Map 5** G4	COMMENDED 👑 👑 👑	3 Twin 1 Double 1 Family	5 En Suite fac	B&B per person to £23.00 Single to £19.00 Double	Open Jan-Dec Dinner 1800-2000 B&B + Eve.Meal £26.00-£30.00	

Modern house on outskirts of town with fine views. Owner formerly chef on cross channel ferry speaks French and German. All rooms en-suite.

Glen Orchy House 20 Knab Road Lerwick Shetland ZE1 0AX Tel:(Lerwick) 0595 2031		COMMENDED 👑	2 Single 3 Twin 1 Double 1 Family	1 En Suite fac 2 Pub.Bath/Show	B&B per person £20.50 Single £19.50-£22.50 Double	Open Jan-Dec Dinner 1830-2030 B&B + Eve.Meal £29.00-£37.00	

A stone built former manse, situated in quiet residential area, yet only a few minutes walk from town centre.

Knysna Guest House 6 Burgh Road Lerwick Shetland ZE1 0LB Tel:(Lerwick) 0595 4865		COMMENDED Listed	1 Single 1 Twin 1 Family	1 Pub.Bath/Show	B&B per person £14.00-£16.00 Single £12.00-£13.00 Double	Open Jan-Dec	

Personally run guest house in quiet residential area close to town centre and all amenities. Residents' kitchen available.

LETHAM **Angus** Idvies House Letham,by Forfar Angus DD8 2QJ Tel:(Letham) 030781 787/0307 818787 Fax:030781 8933/0307 818933	**Map 2** D1	COMMENDED 👑 👑 👑 👑	1 Single 2 Twin 6 Double 1 Family	10 En Suite fac	B&B per person £40.00-£50.00 Single £30.00-£40.00 Double	Open Jan-Dec Dinner 1900-2130 B&B + Eve.Meal £40.00-£70.00	

Formerly a private Victorian country house set in own parkland. Menu specialising in local produce and game. Personally operated by resident owners.

WELCOME

Whenever you are in Scotland, you can be sure of a warm welcome at your nearest Tourist Information Centre.

For guide books, maps, souvenirs, our Centres provide a service second to none – many now offer bureau-de-change facilities. And, of course, Tourist Information Centres offer free, expert advice on what to see and do, route-planning and accommodation for everyone – visitors and residents alike!

Details of Grading and Classification are on page vi.

Key to symbols is on back flap.

LETHAM	Map 2
Fife	D3

Fernie Castle Hotel

LETHAM, CUPAR, FIFE KY7 7RU
TEL: 0337 810381 FAX: 0337 810422

With 28 acres of secluded grounds and its own small loch, 12th-century Fernie Castle is in the heart of this historic Kingdom of Fife. It has over 30 championship golf courses within a 25-mile radius and St Andrews 20 mins by car. The distinctive ambiences of the unique dungeon bar, "The Keep", the informality of "Antoinette's" and the elegance of the upstairs Dining Room complement Chef de Cuisine Christopher Sandford's creative menu. Only the best of fresh Scottish produce is used and we aim to please both palate and pocket!

For further information contact:
Norman and Zoe Smith.

Fernie Castle Hotel
Letham, by Cupar
Fife
KY7 7RU
Tel:(Letham) 0337 810381
Fax:0337 810422

COMMENDED

4 Single
5 Twin
4 Double
2 Family

15 En Suite fac

B&B per person
£38.00-£48.00 Single
£30.00-£45.00 Double

Open Jan-Dec
Dinner 1830-2130
B&B + Eve.Meal
£51.00-£61.00

14C Fernie Castle's Mature Grounds, Small Loch, Unique Dungeon and Bar make an ideal base for Golf, Business or Sightseeing.

LEUCHARS	Map 2
Fife	D2

St Michaels Inn
St Michaels
Leuchars
by St Andrews, Fife
KY16 0DU
Tel:(Leuchars) 0334 839220
Fax:0334 838299

COMMENDED

1 Single
2 Twin
3 Double
1 Family

7 En Suite fac

B&B per person
from £24.50 Single
from £24.50 Double

Open Jan-Dec
Dinner 1900-2130

200 year old former coaching inn. Ideally located for golfing, very convenient for St Andrews.

LEVEN	Map 2
Fife	D3

Hawkshill Hotel
Hawkslaw Street
Leven
Fife
KY8 4LS
Tel:(Leven) 0333 426056

1 Twin
1 Double
2 Family

1 En Suite fac
1 Pub.Bath/Show

B&B per person
£18.00-£25.00 Single
£17.50-£20.00 Double

Open Jan-Dec
Dinner 1800-2100
B&B + Eve.Meal
from £30.00

LICKISTO	Map 3
Harris, Western Isles	B7

Two Waters Guest House
Lickisto
Harris, Western Isles
PA85 3EL
Tel:(Manish) 0859530 246

HIGHLY COMMENDED

2 Twin
2 Double

3 En Suite fac
1 Priv.NOT ensuite

B&B per person
from £24.00 Double

Open May-Sep
Dinner from 1900
B&B + Eve.Meal
from £37.00

Personally run guest house, in an elevated position amidst mountain and loch scenery. Home cooking using fresh local produce, own smokehouse.

LINICLATE, Benbecula **Western Isles** Dark Island Hotel Liniclate Benbecula, Western Isles PA88 Tel:(Benbecula) 0870 603030 Fax:0870 602347	Map 3 A9	COMMENDED 👑👑👑 👑	7 Single 13 Twin 22 Double 1 Family	42 En Suite fac 4 Pub.Bath/Show	B&B per person £24.00-£60.00 Single £19.50-£42.00 Double	Open Jan-Dec Dinner 1830-2100 B&B + Eve.Meal £31.00-£75.00	

Modern hotel in centre of Benbecula, near sandy beaches, about 4 miles (7kms) from airport. Free golf and trout fishing available.

Inchyra Guest House 27 Liniclate Liniclate Benbecula, Western Isles PA88 5PY Tel:(Benbecula) 0870 2176/602176		COMMENDED 👑👑👑	1 Single 3 Twin 1 Double 1 Family	5 En Suite fac 1 Pub.Bath/Show	B&B per person £16.00-£26.00 Single £16.00-£20.00 Double	Open Jan-Dec Dinner 1800-2000 B&B + Eve.Meal £22.00-£34.00	

Family run guest house, on working croft on main Lochmaddy to Loch boisdale road, about 6 miles (10 kms) from Benbecula airport.

LINLITHGOW **West Lothian** The Star & Garter Hotel 1 High Street Linlithgow West Lothian EH49 7AB Tel:(Linlithgow) 0506 845485 Fax:0506 843015	Map 2 B5	APPROVED 👑👑👑	2 Single 6 Twin 3 Double	11 En Suite fac	B&B per person £39.00-£44.00 Single £25.00-£30.00 Double	Open Jan-Dec Dinner 1730-2130 B&B + Eve.Meal £44.00-£49.00	

Recently refurbished coaching inn in the centre of town, close to the Palace. 15 miles (24kms) West of Edinburgh.

LIVINGSTON **West Lothian** Bankton House Hotel Bankton, Murieston Livingston West Lothian EH54 9AQ Tel:(Livingston) 0506 34176/39016	Map 2 C5		1 Single 2 Twin 2 Family	5 En Suite fac	B&B per person £45.00-£49.00 Single £30.00-£35.00 Double	Open Jan-Dec Dinner 1800-2200 B&B + Eve.Meal £55.00-£65.00	

Hilton National Almondview, Almondvale East Livingston West Lothian EH54 6QB Tel:(Livingston) 0506 31222 Tlx:727680 HINLIV G Fax:0506 34666			68 Twin 34 Double 18 Family	120 En Suite fac	B&B per person £60.00-£84.00 Single £35.00-£46.00 Double	Open Jan-Dec Dinner 1800-2300 B&B + Eve.Meal £75.00-£99.00	

Livingston Inn 2 Main Street, Livingston Village Livingston West Lothian EH54 7AF Tel:(Livingston) 0506 413054 Fax:0506 461713		COMMENDED 👑👑👑	9 Single 1 Twin 2 Double	12 En Suite fac	B&B per person from £41.50 Single from £29.50 Double	Open Jan-Dec Dinner 1900-2100	

Refurbished traditional inn situated in centre of old village of Livingston.

Key to symbols is on back flap.

BY LIVINGSTON **West Lothian** Motec Training & Conference Centre Hardie Road Deans, Livingston West Lothian EH54 8AR Tel:(Livingston) 0506 414011	Map 2 C5		198 Single 2 Double	31 En Suite fac 29 Pub.Bath/Show	B&B per person £14.00-£40.00 Single	Open Jan-Dec Dinner 1800-2100 B&B + Eve.Meal £17.50-£48.50
LOCHAILORT **Inverness-shire** Lochailort Inn Lochailort Inverness-shire PH38 4LZ Tel:(Lochailort) 06877 208	Map 3 F1		1 Single 3 Twin 3 Double	3 Pub.Bath/Show	B&B per person from £18.00 Single from £18.00 Double	Open Jan-Dec Dinner 1800-2030 B&B + Eve.Meal from £30.00
LOCHALINE, Morvern **Argyll** Lochaline Hotel Lochaline, Morvern Argyll PA34 5UU Tel:(Morvern) 0967421 657	Map 1 D1		2 Twin 2 Double	1 Pub.Bath/Show	B&B per person from £20.00 Double	Open Jan-Dec Dinner 1800-2100
LOCHBOISDALE **South Uist,** **Western Isles** Lochboisdale Hotel Lochboisdale South Uist, Western Isles PA81 5TH Tel:(Lochboisdale) 08784 332 Fax:08784 367	Map 3 A1	APPROVED ≈≈≈	7 Single 6 Twin 5 Double	11 En Suite fac 5 Limited ensuite 2 Pub.Bath/Show	B&B per person £25.00-£40.00 Single £25.00-£35.00 Double	Open Apr-Oct Dinner 1800-2130 B&B + Eve.Meal £40.00-£55.00
			Stone built hotel, situated close to ferry terminal; ideally situated for fishermen. Open to non residents. Bar meals and restaurant. Dinner menu.			
LOCHCARNAN **South Uist,** **Western Isles** Orasay Inn Lochcarnan South Uist, Western Isles PA81 5PD Tel:(Carnan) 08704 298 Fax:08704 298	Map 3 A9	COMMENDED ≈≈≈	3 Single 4 Double	7 En Suite fac	B&B per person £23.00-£28.00 Single £22.00-£26.00 Double	Open Jan-Dec Dinner 1800-2230 B&B + Eve.Meal £29.00-£45.00
			Overlooking the coast and in quiet position, this newly constructed inn offers menus and many types of food.			
LOCHCARRON **Ross-shire** Lochcarron Hotel Lochcarron Ross-shire IV54 8YS Tel:(Lochcarron) 05202 226	Map 3 F9	COMMENDED ≈≈≈ ≈	2 Single 3 Twin 3 Double 2 Family Suites avail.	7 En Suite fac 1 Priv.NOT ensuite 1 Pub.Bath/Show	B&B per person £32.00-£36.00 Single £26.00-£38.00 Double	Open Jan-Dec Dinner 1900-2030 B&B + Eve.Meal £42.00-£54.00
			Friendly and family run, on shore of sea loch. Emphasis on home cooking and relaxation.			

LOCHCARRON continued Rockvilla Hotel and Restaurant Lochcarron Ross-shire IV54 8YB Tel:(Lochcarron) 05202 379	Map 3 F9	**COMMENDED** 🏆 🏆 🏆	2 Twin 2 Family	2 En Suite fac 1 Pub.Bath/Show	B&B per person £22.00-£27.00 Double	Open Jan-Dec Dinner 1800-2100
			Personally run small hotel at centre of this coastal village. Restaurant with sea views. Emphasis on fresh fish in season.			

LOCHEARNHEAD — Map 1 H2
Perthshire

This privately run hotel, situated in the Highlands, enjoys a spectacular setting on the shores of Loch Earn. The original 'Clachan' that dates back some two hundred and fifty years has been modernised and extended into a twenty-bedroom hotel.

Centrally placed for many day trips to include the scenic West coast, Trossachs, Stirling Castle, Edinburgh and Blair Atholl, to name a few. For the energetic there are twenty-six golf courses within an hour. Many scenic walks, Munros to climb, and watersports.

Taste of Scotland recommended Restaurant overlooking the Loch, alternatively a wide choice of Bar Meals.

Open fires, relaxing atmosphere and friendly service. Frequent Live Music. Three-Day, Golf, Dinner Dance and Festive Breaks.

A Warm Welcome Awaits You!
CLACHAN COTTAGE HOTEL
Dept STB. HOGU. Lochearnhead, Perthshire FK19 8PU
Please contact Andrew Low - 0567 830247

Clachan Cottage Hotel Lochside Lochearnhead Perthshire FK19 8PU Tel:(Lochearnhead) 0567 830247 Fax:0567 830300	**APPROVED** 🏆 🏆 🏆	2 Single 7 Twin 10 Double 2 Family	15 En Suite fac 2 Pub.Bath/Show	B&B per person £23.50-£33.50 Single £23.50-£26.50 Double	Open Mar-Jan Dinner 1800-2100 B&B + Eve.Meal £30.50-£52.00
		Original cottages on main road overlooking Loch Earn; now enlarged by building additional wing.			

LOCHEARNHEAD HOTEL
LOCHEARNHEAD, PERTHSHIRE FK19 8PU (0567) 830229

An ideal centre for fishing, sailing, windsurfing and water-skiing
(free mooring and launching). 7 golf courses within 14 miles.
All rooms have colour TV, tea/coffee making facilities and central heating,
and some have views over the loch.
Try our superb Scottish cooking. Families and pets welcome.

APPROVED 🏆🏆

Lochearnhead Hotel Lochside Lochearnhead Perthshire FK19 8PU Tel:(Lochearnhead) 0567 830229 Fax:0567 830364	**APPROVED** 🏆 🏆	1 Single 8 Twin 5 Double	5 En Suite fac 4 Pub.Bath/Show	B&B per person £17.50-£30.00 Single £17.50-£24.50 Double	Open Apr-Oct Dinner 1930-2100 B&B + Eve.Meal £30.50-£38.25
		Privately owned, in elevated position overlooking Loch Earn. Water sports centre and sailing facilities adjacent.			

LOCHEARNHEAD continued Mansewood Country House Lochearnhead Perthshire FK19 8NS Tel:(Lochearnhead) 0567 830213	Map 1 H2	**COMMENDED** ♕ ♕ ♕ ♕ ♕	3 Twin 4 Double	4 En Suite fac 3 Limited ensuite 2 Pub.Bath/Show	B&B per person £20.00 Single £20.00 Double	Open Mar-Nov Dinner 1930-2030 B&B + Eve.Meal £34.00-£36.00	

Former country manse of character with ground floor bedrooms. Friendly, cosy atmosphere. Water and country pursuits.

LOCHGILPHEAD **Argyll** The Argyll Hotel Lochnell Street Lochgilphead Argyll PA31 8JN Tel:(Lochgilphead) 0546 602221 Fax:0546 603576	Map 1 E4	**APPROVED** ♕ ♕ ♕	4 Single 5 Twin 2 Double 2 Family	7 En Suite fac	B&B per person £18.50-£23.50 Single £17.50-£20.00 Double	Open Jan-Dec Dinner 1700-2100 B&B + Eve.Meal £23.50-£32.50	

Traditional Highland inn in town centre. Regular live entertainment including weekly disco.

Empire Travellers Lodge Union Street Lochgilphead Argyll PA31 8JS Tel:(Lochgilphead) 0546 602381		**COMMENDED** **Lodge**	2 Twin 5 Double 2 Family	9 En Suite fac	B&B per person £18.00-£25.00 Single £18.00-£25.00 Double	Open Jan-Dec	

Originally built as Empire Cinema, now fully refurbished and situated in town centre, offering lodge style accommodation.

LOCHGOILHEAD **Argyll**	Map 1 G4

Drimsynie House Hotel

Drimsynie Estate, Reservations Office, Lochgoilhead, Argyll PA24 8AD
Tel: 03013 247/538   Fax: 03013 541

A magnificent Highland setting overlooking Loch Goil and the Argyll Forest Park. Drimsynie combines beautiful surroundings with first-class leisure facilities including 25m indoor swimming pool, sauna, ice skating rink, indoor bowling, curling (winter), 9 hole golf course. Saturday night entertainment. Choice of dinner menus. Winter dinner, B&B packages available on request. Lodges in Grounds.

Drimsynie House Hotel Lochgoilhead Argyll PA24 8AD Tel:(Lochgoilhead) 03013 247 Fax:03013 541			1 Single 6 Twin 3 Double 3 Family	13 En Suite fac	B&B per person £32.00 Single £30.00 Double	Open Jan-Dec Dinner 1900-2100 B&B + Eve.Meal £41.50	

Lochgoilhead Hotel Lochgoilhead Argyll PA24 8AA Tel:(Lochgoilhead) 03013 208/03013 247 (bookings) Fax:03013 541			4 Twin 1 Double	3 En Suite fac 1 Pub.Bath/Show	B&B per person £20.00 Single £18.00 Double	Open Jan-Dec Dinner from 1730	

LOCHGOILHEAD continued Shore House Inn Lochgoilhead Argyll Tel:(Lochgoilhead) 03013 340/580	Map 1 G4		1 Single 3 Twin 1 Double 2 Family	2 En Suite fac 1 Pub.Bath/Show	B&B per person £15.00-£16.00 Single £13.00-£18.00 Double	Open Jan-Dec Dinner 1730-2100 B&B + Eve.Meal £21.00-£26.00
LOCHINVER **Sutherland** The Albannach Hotel Baddidarroch Lochinver Sutherland IV27 4LP Tel:(Lochinver) 05714 407	Map 3 G5	COMMENDED	1 Twin 3 Double	4 En Suite fac	B&B per person £25.00-£27.00 Double	Open Jan-Dec Dinner from 1930 B&B + Eve.Meal £40.00-£42.00

19C house with great character. Spectacular views across Lochinver Bay to Suilven. Original style cooking with emphasis on fresh produce.

Culag Hotel Lochinver Sutherland IV27 4LF Tel:(Lochinver) 05714 270			3 Single 10 Twin 1 Double 8 Family	18 En Suite fac 1 Pub.Bath/Show	B&B per person from £18.00 Single from £18.00 Double	Open Jan-Dec Dinner 1730-2100
Inchnadamph Hotel Assynt Sutherland IV27 4HL Tel:(Assynt) 05712 202		COMMENDED	11 Single 8 Twin 3 Double 5 Family	10 En Suite fac 6 Pub.Bath/Show	B&B per person	Open Mar-Oct Dinner 1900-1945 B&B + Eve.Meal to £46.00

Family run hotel in remote setting overlooking Loch Assynt. Fishing free to guests and climbing available. Study area for geologists and botanists.

Inver Lodge Hotel Lochinver Sutherland IV27 4LU Tel:(Lochinver) 05714 496 Fax:05714 395		HIGHLY COMMENDED	12 Twin 8 Double	20 En Suite fac	B&B per person £60.00-£75.00 Single £50.00-£65.00 Double	Open Apr-Oct Dinner 1900-2100 B&B + Eve.Meal £65.00-£85.00

Modern hotel with accent on comfort and friendliness. Restaurant and all bedrooms can enjoy sea-scape and setting sun over Lochinver harbour.

LOCHMABEN **Dumfriesshire** Balcastle Hotel High Street Lochmaben Dumfriesshire DG11 1NG Tel:(Lochmaben) 0387 810239	Map 2 C9	APPROVED	3 Single 2 Twin 2 Double 3 Family	6 En Suite fac 1 Limited ensuite 2 Priv.NOT ensuite 3 Pub.Bath/Show	B&B per person £16.00-£19.00 Single £16.00-£19.00 Double	Open Jan-Dec Dinner 1800-2100

Private family run hotel, children welcome. Good centre for fishing, next to local golf course. Some annexe accommodation.

LOCHMADDY **North Uist,** **Western Isles** Lochmaddy Hotel Lochmaddy North Uist, Western Isles PA82 5AA Tel:(Lochmaddy) 08763 331/332 Fax:08763 428	Map 3 A8	COMMENDED	5 Single 5 Twin 5 Double	15 En Suite fac	B&B per person £25.00-£35.00 Single £23.00-£33.00 Double	Open Jan-Dec Dinner 1900-2100 B&B + Eve.Meal £40.00-£51.00

Traditional sporting hotel situated 200 yds from ferry terminal. Trout and salmon fishing available.

LOCH MAREE by Achnasheen, Ross-shire

Map 3 F7

The Old Mill Highland Lodge
Talladale
Loch Maree, by Achnasheen
Ross-shire
IV22 2HL
Tel:(Kinlochewe) 044584 271

4 Twin
2 Double

5 En Suite fac
1 Priv.NOT ensuite

B&B per person
£32.00-£37.00 Double

Open Apr-Oct
Dinner from 1930
B&B + Eve.Meal
£48.00-£55.00

LOCH RANNOCH Perthshire

Map 1 H1

Talladh-a-Bheithe Lodge
Loch Rannoch, by Pitlochry
Perthshire
PH17 2QW
Tel:(Bridge of Gaur) 0882
633203

4 Single
8 Twin
4 Double
1 Family

13 En Suite fac
1 Priv.NOT ensuite
2 Pub.Bath/Show

B&B per person
£25.00-£30.00 Single
£20.00-£40.00 Double

Open Apr-Dec
Dinner 1900-2100
B&B + Eve.Meal
£35.00-£55.00

LOCHRANZA Isle of Arran

Map 1 E6

Butt Lodge Hotel
Lochranza
Isle of Arran
KA27 8JF
Tel:(Lochranza) 077083
240/0770 830240

COMMENDED

1 Twin
3 Double
1 Family

5 En Suite fac

B&B per person
£22.00-£27.50 Double

Open Mar-Oct
Dinner from 1930
B&B + Eve.Meal
£35.00-£40.50

Country lodge set in its own grounds with a log fire in the lounge. Excellent base for wildlife, activity holiday or lazy break. Residential licence

---

Lochranza Hotel
Lochranza
Isle of Arran
KA27 8HL
Tel:(Lochranza) 077083
223/0770 830223

2 Single
4 Twin
3 Double
1 Family

3 Pub.Bath/Show

B&B per person
to £19.00 Single
to £17.00 Double

Open Jan-Dec
Dinner 1700-2200
B&B + Eve.Meal
to £24.50

Apple Lodge
Lochranza
Isle of Arran
KA27 8HJ
Tel:(Lochranza) 0770
830229

HIGHLY COMMENDED

1 Twin
2 Double

2 En Suite fac
1 Priv.NOT ensuite

B&B per person
£20.00-£25.00 Double

Open Jan-Dec
Dinner 1800-1900
B&B + Eve.Meal
£32.00-£37.00

Detached house standing in its own grounds on the edge of Lochranza village and about 0.5 miles (1km) from Lochside and Claonaig ferry terminal.

Kincardine Lodge
Guest House
Lochranza
Isle of Arran
KA27 8HL
Tel:(Lochranza) 077083
267/0770 830267

2 Twin
2 Double
2 Family

3 En Suite fac
1 Pub.Bath/Show

B&B per person
£15.00-£17.00 Single
£15.00-£17.00 Double

Open Mar-Oct
Dinner 1830-1900
B&B + Eve.Meal
£23.00-£25.00

| LOCKERBIE | Map 2 |
| Dumfriesshire | C9 |

The Dryfesdale Hotel
LOCKERBIE · DUMFRIESSHIRE   TEL: 0576 202427

Country House Hotel standing in grounds of 5 acres commanding panoramic views of the surrounding countryside. 15 beautifully furnished bedrooms, all en-suite including 6 ground floor with facilities for disabled persons. À la carte restaurant and bar meals. Situated within sight of the A74(M) but quietly peaceful, making an ideal place for overnight or longer stay.

AA and RAC ★★★

Dryfesdale Hotel
Lockerbie
Dumfriesshire
DG11 2SF
Tel:(Lockerbie) 0576 202427
Fax:0576 204187

HIGHLY COMMENDED

4 Single   15 En Suite fac
5 Twin
5 Double
1 Family

B&B per person
£48.00-£50.00 Single
£36.00-£37.00 Double
B&B + Eve.Meal
£64.00-£66.00

Open Jan-Dec
Dinner 1830-2130

Family run country house in 5 acres of ground, yet close to A74. Interesting menu serving fresh local produce. Ideal for business or pleasure.

Ravenshill House Hotel
Dumfries Road
Lockerbie
Dumfriesshire
DG11 2EF
Tel:(Lockerbie) 0576 202882
Fax:0576 202882

COMMENDED

3 Twin   7 En Suite fac
4 Double 1 Priv.NOT ensuite
1 Family 1 Pub.Bath/Show

B&B per person
£27.00-£32.00 Single
£21.00-£25.00 Double

Open Jan-Dec
Dinner 1900-2130

Small family run hotel set in 2.5 acres of gardens in quiet residential area, yet conveniently situated for the A74.

Somerton House Hotel
Carlisle Road
Lockerbie
Dumfriesshire
DG11 2DR
Tel:(Lockerbie) 0576 202583
Fax:0576 202384

COMMENDED

1 Single   7 En Suite fac
2 Twin
2 Double
2 Family

B&B per person
£41.00-£45.00 Single
£27.50-£28.50 Double

Open Jan-Dec
Dinner 1900-2100

Imposing sandstone, Victorian building standing in one acre of grounds. Comfortable accommodation and good food; Taste of Scotland member.

Rosehill Guest House
Carlisle Road
Lockerbie
Dumfriesshire
DG11
Tel:(Lockerbie) 0576 202378

COMMENDED

1 Single   1 En Suite fac
1 Twin   3 Pub.Bath/Show
1 Double
2 Family

B&B per person
£16.00-£17.00 Single
£15.00-£16.00 Double

Open Jan-Dec

Family guest house in residential area, 5 minutes walk from town centre. Ample car parking.

| LOSSIEMOUTH | Map 4 |
| Moray | D7 |

Huntly House Hotel
Stotfield Road
Lossiemouth
Moray
IV31 6QP
Tel:(Lossiemouth) 0343 812085
Fax:0599 4427

1 Single   3 Limited ensuite
6 Twin   4 Pub.Bath/Show
4 Double
1 Family

B&B per person
£23.50-£26.00 Single
£18.50-£20.50 Double

Open Jan-Dec
Dinner from 1900

LOSSIEMOUTH continued

Map 4 D7

Skerrybrae Hotel
Stotfield Road
Lossiemouth
Moray
IV31 6QS
Tel:(Lossiemouth) 0343 812040

COMMENDED

4 Single	7 En Suite fac	B&B per person	Open Jan-Dec
2 Twin	1 Priv.NOT ensuite	£18.50-£24.50 Single	Dinner 1200-2130
3 Double	2 Pub.Bath/Show	£34.00-£40.00 Double	B&B + Eve.Meal
1 Family			£28.50-£50.00

Stone built house overlooking the sea and golf course. Comfortable rooms. Popular for bar meals.

Stotfield Hotel
Stotfield Road
Lossiemouth
Moray
IV31 6QS
Tel:(Lossiemouth) 0343 812011
Fax:034381 4820

COMMENDED

17 Single	47 En Suite fac	B&B per person	Open Jan-Dec
11 Twin	2 Pub.Bath/Show	£33.00 Single	Dinner 1800-2130
17 Double		£27.00 Double	B&B + Eve.Meal
4 Family			£47.00

Family run stonebuilt Victorian hotel with fine views overlooking Moray golf courses and Moray Firth.

LOWER LARGO
Fife

Map 2 D3

Crusoe Hotel
2 Main Street
Lower Largo
Fife
KY8 6BT
Tel:(Lundin Links) 0333 320759
Fax:0333 320865

COMMENDED

1 Single	13 En Suite fac	B&B per person	Open Jan-Dec
6 Twin		£51.15 Single	Dinner 1900-2200
5 Double		£30.80 Double	B&B + Eve.Meal
1 Family			£43.80-£64.15
Suite avail.			

The Crusoe Hotel can boast its own harbour and beach front location, yet only 1 hour from Edinburgh.

LUNDIN LINKS
Fife

Map 2 D3

LUNDIN LINKS, Nr St. Andrews
Old Manor Hotel
Lundin Links, FIFE KY8 6AJ
Telephone (0333) 320368

Characterful country house hotel, mentioned in several food guides.
Overlooking Lundin golf course, Largo Bay and the River Forth.
Two Restaurants, table d'hote and à la carte menus, local seafood, game
and Aberdeen Angus Beef specialities. Outstanding wine list.
Ideal base for touring, golfing, walking, or just relaxing.

The Old Manor Hotel
Leven Road
Lundin Links
Fife
KY8 6AJ
Tel:(Lundin Links) 0333 320368
Fax:0333 320911

COMMENDED

1 Single	19 En Suite fac	B&B per person	Open Jan-Dec
10 Twin		£60.00-£66.00 Single	Dinner 1700-2200
6 Double		£35.00-£41.00 Double	B&B + Eve.Meal
2 Family			£46.50-£53.50

Late 19C house with excellent views across to Lundin Links golf course and the Firth of Forth. Function room for seminars/conferences.

LUSS, by Alexandria
Dunbartonshire

Map 1 G4

Colquhoun Arms Hotel
Luss,by Alexandria
Dunbartonshire
G83 8NY
Tel:(Luss) 043686 282

8 Single	5 En Suite fac	B&B per person	Open Jan-Dec
3 Twin	5 Pub.Bath/Show	£25.00-£30.00 Single	Dinner 1900-2130
8 Double		£22.00-£25.00 Double	
4 Family			

LUSS, continued The Lodge on Loch Lomond Rhu of Luss, Luss Loch Lomond Dunbartonshire Tel:(Luss) 043686 202	Map 1 G4		5 Twin 5 Family Suites avail.	10 En Suite fac	Price per room £35.00-£70.00	Open Feb-Dec Dinner 1900-2130
LYBSTER **Caithness** Portland Arms Hotel Lybster Caithness KW3 6BS Tel:(Lybster) 05932 208/255 Fax:05932 208	Map 4 D4	COMMENDED 👑👑👑 👑	3 Single 5 Twin 7 Double 5 Family Suites avail.	20 En Suite fac	B&B per person from £36.00 Single from £27.50 Double	Open Jan-Dec Dinner 1900-2200
Former staging inn, some beds with four poster beds or half testers. Free 9-hole golf course. Fish Rights available.						
MACDUFF **Banffshire** The Highland Haven Shore Street Macduff Banffshire AB44 1UB Tel:(Macduff) 0261 32408 Fax:0261 33652/833652	Map 4 F7	COMMENDED 👑👑👑 👑	3 Twin 11 Double 2 Family	16 En Suite fac	B&B per person £21.95-£39.95 Single £19.00-£27.00 Double	Open Jan-Dec Dinner 1900-2100 B&B + Eve.Meal £35.00-£40.00
Family run hotel overlooking fishing harbour and Deveron Bay. Duff House and Tarlair golf courses nearby. Leisure centre, sauna and solarium.						
MAIDENS **Ayrshire** Rocklea Guest House 21 Ardlochan Road Maidens Ayrshire KA26 9NS Tel:(Turnberry) 0655 31303	Map 1 G8		1 Single 2 Twin 2 Double 1 Family	3 En Suite fac 2 Pub.Bath/Show	B&B per person £18.00-£25.00 Single £17.50-£19.50 Double	Open Jan-Dec Dinner 1845-1900 B&B + Eve.Meal £26.50-£34.00
MALLAIG **Inverness-shire** Clasnacardoch Hotel Mallaig Inverness-shire PH41 Tel:(Mallaig) 0687 2184	Map 3 E1		1 Single 4 Double 4 Family	3 Pub.Bath/Show	B&B per person £12.50-£17.50 Single £12.50-£17.50 Double	Open Jan-Dec Dinner 1830-2030 B&B + Eve.Meal £21.00-£27.00

MALLAIG continued	Map 3 E1		

Marine Hotel

MALLAIG
HIGHLAND
PH41 4PY

Telephone:
0687 2217
Fax: 0687 2821

A warm welcome awaits you at our family run hotel which is conveniently situated for rail and ferry terminals. All rooms have complimentary tea/coffee, colour TV. Enjoy fresh, local seafood and our Highland cuisine.

B&B from £22-£30.

For brochure and tariff contact: Tanya Ironside.
Taste of Scotland Member

AA** RAC ** STB. ♕ ♕ ♕ Commended

Marine Hotel
Mallaig
Inverness-shire
PH41
Tel:(Mallaig) 0687 2217
Fax:0687 2821

COMMENDED
♕ ♕ ♕

1 Single
8 Twin
8 Double
2 Family

19 En Suite fac

B&B per person
from £25.00 Single
from £25.00 Double

Open Jan-Dec
Dinner 1830-2100
B&B + Eve.Meal
from £39.00

Family run hotel situated in the centre of a fishing village close to the railway station and ferry terminal. Taste of Scotland scheme member.

West Highland Hotel
Mallaig
Inverness-shire
PH41 4QZ
Tel:(Mallaig) 0687 2210
Fax:0687 2130

COMMENDED
♕ ♕ ♕

5 Single
9 Twin
11 Double
3 Family

28 En Suite fac
4 Pub.Bath/Show

B&B per person
£25.00-£32.00 Single
£25.00-£32.00 Double

Open Mar-Nov
Dinner 1845-2030
B&B + Eve.Meal
£42.00-£49.00

Hotel stands above the village of Mallaig with views over the harbour to the Isle of Skye beyond.

Springbank Guest House
East Bay
Mallaig
Inverness-shire
PH41 4QF
Tel:(Mallaig) 0687 2459

1 Single
1 Twin
1 Double
1 Family

2 Pub.Bath/Show

B&B per person
£13.00-£15.00 Single
£14.00-£15.00 Double

Open Jan-Dec
Dinner 1900-2000
B&B + Eve.Meal
£21.00-£23.00

Western Isles Guest House
East Bay
Mallaig
Inverness-shire
PH41 4QG
Tel:(Mallaig) 0687 2320

COMMENDED
♕

1 Single
1 Double
1 Family

3 Pub.Bath/Show

B&B per person
£16.00-£18.00 Single
£14.00-£16.00 Double

Open Jan-Dec
Dinner 1800-1930
B&B + Eve.Meal
£24.00-£26.00

Modern house overlooking the harbour and fishing boats, well situated for ferries to the islands. 4 miles (6kms) from renowned Morar sands.

MARKINCH
Fife
Balbirnie House Hotel
Balbirnie Park
Markinch
Fife
KY7 6NE
Tel:(Glenrothes) 0592
610066
Fax:0592 610529

Map 2
D3

DELUXE
♕ ♕ ♕
♕ ♕

2 Single
7 Twin
11 Double
10 Family

30 En Suite fac

B&B per person
£85.00-£95.00 Single
£62.50-£112.50 Double

Open Jan-Dec
Dinner 1900-2130
B&B + Eve.Meal
£107.50-£117.50

18th century Georgian country house in 416 acres of parkland. Golf and country pursuits available. Fine restaurant interesting cuisine and wine list

---

	Map 2 D3	Award Pending	3 Single 5 Twin 1 Double 2 Family	1 En Suite fac 2 Pub.Bath/Show	B&B per person £25.00-£30.00 Single £20.00-£25.00 Double	Open Jan-Dec Dinner 1700-2130 B&B + Eve.Meal £30.00-£40.00

MARKINCH continued

Laurel Bank Hotel
1 Balbirnie Street
Markinch
Leven
KY7 6DB
Tel:(Kirkcaldy) 0592 611205
Fax:0592 611104

	Map 2 C1		3 Twin 3 Double 2 Family	6 Pub.Bath/Show	B&B per person £16.50-£19.50 Single £16.50-£18.50 Double	Open Jan-Dec Dinner from 1800 B&B + Eve.Meal from £26.00

MEIGLE
Perthshire
Meigle House
Alyth Road
Meigle
Perthshire
PH12 8RP
Tel:(Meigle) 08284 270

	Map 2 E6	COMMENDED 👑 👑 👑	1 Twin 8 Double 1 Family	10 En Suite fac	B&B per person £35.00-£50.00 Single £30.00-£45.00 Double	Open Jan-Dec Dinner 1830-2100 B&B + Eve.Meal £40.00-£60.00

MELROSE
Roxburghshire
Bon Accord Hotel
Market Square
Melrose
Roxburghshire
TD6
Tel:(Melrose) 089682 2645
Fax:089682 3474

Family run hotel in the heart of small Borders town. Fishing, shooting, golfing and walking packages available.

BURTS HOTEL
MARKET SQUARE, MELROSE
AA & RAC ★★★ STB 👑 👑 👑 👑 Commended
Egon Ronay • 'Taste of Scotland' Recommended

Friendly, family run hotel, tastefully furnished with 21 en-suite bedrooms. All with telephones, colour TV, radio, tea and coffee making facilities and hair dryers. Elegant A la Carte Restaurant also Lounge Bar serving Lunches and Suppers daily. Billiard Room and Residents' Lounge. Private Car Park.

Burts Hotel is the ideal centre for touring the beautiful Border Country and enjoying Scottish hospitality at its best. Several Golf Courses are within easy reach and Salmon and Trout Fishing can be arranged. Game shooting on local estates also available with prior notice.

For brochure write to:
Graham and Anne Henderson, Proprietors
Phone (089 682) 2285 Fax (089 682) 2870

		COMMENDED 👑 👑 👑 👑	8 Single 10 Twin 3 Double	21 En Suite fac	B&B per person £40.00-£44.00 Single £36.00-£38.00 Double	Open Jan-Dec Dinner 1900-2130 B&B + Eve.Meal £50.00-£56.00

Burts Hotel
Market Square
Melrose
Roxburghshire
TD6
Tel:(Melrose) 089682 2285
Fax:089682 2870

Tastefully modernised old town house, personally run and situated in main square. Taste of Scotland and a la carte menu.

MELROSE continued
Map 2
E6

George & Abbotsford Hotel
High Street
Melrose
Roxburghshire
TD6 9PD
Tel:(Melrose) 089682 2308
Tlx:53168
Fax:089682 3363

COMMENDED
♛ ♛ ♛

8 Single	30 En Suite fac	B&B per person	Open Jan-Dec
12 Twin		£30.00-£40.00 Single	Dinner 1900-2130
7 Double		£25.00-£38.00 Double	B&B + Eve.Meal
3 Family			£32.00-£57.00

Former coaching inn in centre of town with large car park to the rear. Recently modernised and refurbished.

Kings Arms Hotel
High Street
Melrose
Roxburghshire
TD6 9PB
Tel:(Melrose) 089682 2143
Fax:089682 3812

COMMENDED
♛ ♛ ♛

1 Single	6 En Suite fac	B&B per person	Open Jan-Dec
2 Twin		£27.50-£30.00 Single	Dinner 1830-2130
2 Double		£25.00-£28.00 Double	B&B + Eve.Meal
1 Family			£32.50-£37.50

Former coaching inn dating back some 300 years, in centre of historic Border town. Cosy lounge bar with open fires.

Dunfermline House
Guest House
Buccleuch Street
Melrose
Roxburghshire
TD6 9LB
Tel:(Melrose) 089682 2148

HIGHLY
COMMENDED
♛ ♛

1 Single	4 En Suite fac	B&B per person	Open Jan-Dec
2 Twin	1 Priv.NOT ensuite	£19.00-£20.00 Single	
2 Double		£19.00-£20.00 Double	

Comfortable family home overlooking Melrose Abbey. Ideal base for touring Scott country and Edinburgh. No smoking.

BY MELROSE
Roxburghshire
Map 2
E6

Plough Inn
Lilliesleaf
Melrose
Roxburghshire
TD6 9SD
Tel:(Lilliesleaf) 08357 271

COMMENDED
♛ ♛ ♛

2 Twin	2 En Suite fac	B&B per person	Open Jan-Dec
1 Double	1 Priv.NOT ensuite	from £26.00 Single	Dinner 1800-2100
	1 Pub.Bath/Show	from £22.00 Double	B&B + Eve.Meal
			from £32.00

Friendly country inn, in small village approximately 6 miles (10 kms) south of Melrose.Comfortable lounge, home cooking and a varied bar menu.

MELVICH
Sutherland
Map 4
B3

Melvich Hotel
Melvich,by Thurso
Sutherland
KW14 7YJ
Tel:(Melvich) 06413 206
Fax:06413 347

COMMENDED
♛ ♛ ♛

5 Single	14 En Suite fac	B&B per person	Open Jan-Dec
8 Twin	6 Pub.Bath/Show	£29.00-£32.00 Single	Dinner 1900-2030
1 Double		£26.00-£30.00 Double	B&B + Eve.Meal
			£43.00-£48.00

Privately owned country hotel with views across Melvich Bay to the Orkneys. 18 miles (29kms) west of Thurso.

Shieling Guest House
Melvich
Sutherland
KW14 7YJ
Tel:(Melvich) 06413 256
Fax:06413 356

HIGHLY
COMMENDED
♛ ♛ ♛

1 Twin	2 En Suite fac	B&B per person	Open Apr-Sep
2 Double	1 Priv.NOT ensuite	£20.00-£22.00 Double	Dinner 1800-2030
	2 Pub.Bath/Show		B&B + Eve.Meal
			£32.00-£35.00

Genuine Highland hospitality, home cooked meals, choice of menu. Spectacular views over bay. Picture window in coffee lounge; separate TV lounge.

Tigh-na-Clash Guest House
Melvich
Sutherland
KW14 7YJ
Tel:(Melvich) 06413 262

COMMENDED
♛ ♛ ♛

2 Single	4 En Suite fac	B&B per person	Open Apr-Sep
2 Twin	2 Pub.Bath/Show	£15.50-£20.00 Single	Dinner 1700-2030
4 Double		£15.50-£20.00 Double	

Family run; pub and restaurant nearby. Ideal for touring north coast and overnight stop for Orkney Isles.

VAT is shown at 17.5%: changes in this rate may affect prices. Prices shown are for guidance only. Please send SAE with each enquiry.

MEY **Caithness** Castle Arms Hotel Mey, by Thurso Caithness KW14 8XH Tel:(Barrock) 084785 244	Map 4 D2	COMMENDED ♛ ♛ ♛	3 Twin 4 Double 1 Family	8 En Suite fac	B&B per person to £39.00 Single to £29.00 Double	

Privately owned, original stone built coaching inn on Thurs[...]
road, in village of Mey, 1 mile (2kms) from Castle of Mey.

MILNATHORT **by Kinross,** **Kinross-shire** Thistle Hotel 25-27 New Road Milnathort, Kinross Kinross-shire KY13 7XT Tel:(Kinross) 0577 863222	Map 2 C3		1 Single 3 Double 1 Family	2 En Suite fac 1 Pub.Bath/Show	B&B per person £26.00-£32.00 Single £25.00-£30.00 Double	Open Jan-Dec Dinner 1800-2100 B&B + Eve.Meal £35.00-£38.00

MILNGAVIE, Glasgow Black Bull Thistle Hotel Main Street Milngavie, Glasgow G62 6BH Tel:041 956 2291 Tlx:778323 Fax:041 956 1896	Map 1 H5	COMMENDED ♛ ♛ ♛	2 Single 9 Twin 14 Double 2 Family	27 En Suite fac	B&B per person £70.50-£83.50 Single £46.00-£51.00 Double	Open Jan-Dec Dinner 1900-2130 B&B + Eve.Meal £86.45-£99.45

In a quiet area of the village with easy access to Loch Lomond, the Trossachs
and Glasgow city centre.

MOFFAT **Dumfriesshire** Balmoral Hotel High Street Moffat Dumfriesshire DG10 9DL Tel:(Moffat) 0683 20288 Fax:0683 20451	Map 2 C8		3 Single 7 Twin 5 Double 1 Family	6 En Suite fac 3 Pub.Bath/Show	B&B per person £25.00-£35.00 Single £22.00-£25.00 Double	Open Jan-Dec Dinner 1800-2100

Buccleuch Arms Hotel High Street Moffat Dumfriesshire DG10 9ET *0168 5 220005* Tel:(Moffat) 0683 20003 Fax:0683 21291		COMMENDED ♛ ♛ ♛	6 Twin 5 Double	11 En Suite fac	B&B per person to £39.00 Single to £28.00 Double	Open Jan-Dec Dinner 1800-2130 B&B + Eve.Meal to £40.00

Refurbished family run 1760 coaching inn centrally situated in picturesque
village. Good touring base.

Mercury Hotel Moffat Dumfriesshire DG10 9EL Tel:(Moffat) 0683 20464 Fax:0683 20553			4 Single 22 Twin 14 Double 11 Family	48 En Suite fac 2 Pub.Bath/Show	B&B per person from £45.00 Single from £32.00 Double	Open Jan-Dec Dinner 1900-2100

Details of Grading and Classification are on page vi. | Key to symbols is on back flap. | 273

Map 2
C8

Moffat House Hotel

☕☕☕☕ HIGHLY COMMENDED AA★★★RAC
HIGH STREET, MOFFAT DUMFRIESSHIRE DG10 9HL
Telephone: (0683) 20039 Fax: (0683) 21288

MOFFAT HOUSE is a gracious 18-century Adam mansion, centrally situated in 2½ acres of our own gardens. The charming village of Moffat is just off the A74 and provides an ideal stopping-off point for breaking your journey north/south. The hotel is fully licensed and we provide a wide range of bar lunches/suppers together with an extensive dinner menu. All our rooms have private bath/shower with WC, central heating, colour TV, radio, telephone, hairdryers and tea/coffee tray. We offer a 3-day DB&B break throughout the season for only £144.00 pp (until mid-April £132.00 pp). Golfing Breaks also available.
Please send for a full-colour brochure to "The Reid Family", Moffat House Hotel, Moffat, Dumfriesshire DG10 9HL. PLEASE QUOTE MHH 8.

Moffat House Hotel High Street Moffat Dumfriesshire DG10 9HL Tel:(Moffat) 0683 20039 Fax:0683 21288	**HIGHLY COMMENDED** ☕☕☕ ☕	3 Single 7 Twin 7 Double 3 Family	20 En Suite fac	B&B per person £45.00-£49.00 Single £25.00-£35.00 Double	Open Jan-Dec Dinner 1900-2045 B&B + Eve.Meal £39.50-£49.50
		18C Adam mansion with magnificent staircase, set in own grounds with country views to rear. Some ground floor rooms.			
Star Hotel High Street Moffat Dumfriesshire DG10 9EF Tel:(Moffat) 0683 20156	**APPROVED** ☕ ☕	2 Twin 4 Double 2 Family	8 En Suite fac 1 Pub.Bath/Show	B&B per person £28.00-£32.00 Single £20.00-£24.00 Double	Open Jan-Dec Dinner 1800-2100
		A friendly welcome at this family run hotel in the centre of a popular Border town. The narrowest hotel in the United Kingdom!			
Wellview Private Hotel Ballplay Road Moffat Dumfriesshire DG10 9JU Tel:(Moffat) 0683 20184	**DELUXE** ☕ ☕ ☕	2 Twin 4 Double Suite avail.	6 En Suite fac	B&B per person £30.00-£40.00 Single £23.00-£38.00 Double	Open Jan-Dec Dinner 1900-2100 B&B + Eve.Meal £43.00-£59.00
		Victorian house with large garden, overlooking town and surrounding hills.			
The Arden House Guest House Moffat Dumfriesshire DG10 9HG Tel:(Moffat) 0683 20220		1 Single 2 Twin 2 Double 2 Family	4 En Suite fac 1 Priv.NOT ensuite 2 Pub.Bath/Show	B&B per person £16.50-£18.00 Single £14.00-£18.00 Double	Open Mar-Oct Dinner from 1845 B&B + Eve.Meal £20.50-£24.50
Barnhill Springs Country Guest House Moffat Dumfriesshire DG10 Tel:(Moffat) 0683 20580	**COMMENDED** ☕ ☕	2 Twin 2 Double 1 Family	1 Priv.NOT ensuite 2 Pub.Bath/Show	B&B per person £17.50-£19.50 Single £17.50-£19.50 Double	Open Jan-Dec Dinner from 1830 B&B + Eve.Meal £28.00-£30.00
		Early Victorian country house, ideally situated for walking the Southern Upland Way. Access from A74 via South bound slip road at Moffat junction.			

MOFFAT continued

Map 2 C8

Buchan Guest House
Beechgrove
Moffat
Dumfriesshire
DG10 9RS
Tel:(Moffat) 0683 20378

Award Pending

1 Single
2 Twin
2 Double
2 Family

4 En Suite fac
3 Pub.Bath/Show

B&B per person
£15.00-£17.00 Single
£14.00-£16.50 Double

Open Jan-Dec
Dinner from 1830
B&B + Eve.Meal
£23.00-£25.00

Failte Guest House
11 Well Road
Moffat
Dumfriesshire
DG10 9AR
Tel:(Moffat) 0683 21136

1 Single
1 Double
1 Family

1 Limited ensuite
1 Pub.Bath/Show

B&B per person
from £14.00 Single
from £14.00 Double

Open Jan-Dec
Dinner from 1830
B&B + Eve.Meal
from £24.00

Ivy Cottage Guest House
High Street
Moffat
Dumfriesshire
DG10 9HG
Tel:(Moffat) 0683 20279

2 Twin
1 Double
1 Family

1 Pub.Bath/Show

B&B per person
£14.50-£16.50 Single
from £14.50 Double

Open Jan-Dec

Rockhill Guest House
Moffat
Dumfriesshire
DG10 9RS
Tel:(Moffat) 0683 20283

COMMENDED
👑 👑

1 Twin
3 Double
4 Family

2 Pub.Bath/Show

£15.00-£18.00 Single
£15.00-£18.00 Double

Dinner from 1830
B&B + Eve.Meal
£21.50-£25.00

Victorian house overlooking bowling green and park, in quiet area close to town centre. Open outlook to hills. Own private carpark, ensuite rooms.

St Olaf Guest House
Eastgate, Dickson Street
Moffat
Dumfriesshire
DG10 9AE
Tel:(Moffat) 0683 20001

COMMENDED
👑

1 Twin
3 Double
3 Family

1 En Suite fac
2 Pub.Bath/Show

B&B per person
£16.00 Single
£14.50 Double

Open Apr-Oct

Personally run, situated in a quiet residential area, close to the town centre. Free garaging available.

MONIAIVE
Dumfriesshire

Map 2 A9

Woodlea Hotel
Moniaive
Dumfriesshire
DG3 4EN
Tel:(Moniaive) 08482
209/429

COMMENDED
👑 👑 👑

1 Single
1 Twin
2 Double
8 Family

10 En Suite fac
1 Pub.Bath/Show

B&B per person
£22.00-£42.00 Single
£22.00-£42.00 Double

Open Feb-Oct
Dinner 1930-2030
B&B + Eve.Meal
£36.00-£53.00

Family hotel with indoor swimming pool, tennis, badminton, children's play area, sauna, clay pigeon shooting, bike and pony rides.

MONIFIETH
by Dundee, Angus

Map 2 E2

Milton House Hotel
Grange Road
Monifieth
Angus
DD5 4LU
Tel:(Dundee) 0382 532016

2 Twin
2 Double

4 En Suite fac

B&B per person
from £28.00 Single
from £20.00 Double

Open Jan-Dec
Dinner 1800-2000

Details of Grading and Classification are on page vi.

Key to symbols is on back flap.

MONIFIETH continued Monifieth Hotel Albert Street Monifieth Angus DD5 4JR Tel:(Monifieth) 0382 532630	Map 2 E2	COMMENDED 👑 👑 👑	3 Twin 2 Double 1 Family	4 En Suite fac 1 Pub.Bath/Show	B&B per person £25.00-£35.00 Double	Open Jan-Dec Dinner 1700-2200 B&B + Eve.Meal £30.00-£42.00	
			Family run, elegant Victorian Hotel in extensive grounds, Friendly atmosphere.				
MONTROSE **Angus** The Carlton Hotel 139 High Street Montrose Angus DD10 8QN Tel:(Montrose) 0674 77237 Fax:0674 77237	Map 2 E1	COMMENDED 👑 👑 👑	2 Single 3 Twin 2 Double 1 Family	5 En Suite fac 1 Limited ensuite 1 Pub.Bath/Show	B&B per person £25.00-£55.00 Single £17.50-£35.00 Double	Open Jan-Dec Dinner 1800-2200	
			Personally run and totally refurbished restaurant with rooms, in the centre of town. Most rooms with private bathrooms. Interesting a la carte menu.				
Corner House Hotel 131-133 High Street Montrose Angus DD10 8QN Tel:(Montrose) 0674 73126 Fax:0674 671186		COMMENDED 👑 👑 👑	5 Single 7 Twin 3 Double	13 En Suite fac 1 Pub.Bath/Show	B&B per person £35.00-£50.00 Single £27.50-£32.50 Double	Open Jan-Dec Dinner 1800-2200	
			Privately owned hotel in town centre and close to station, sandy beaches and golf courses.				
The George Hotel 22 George Street Montrose Angus DD10 8EW Tel:(Montrose) 0674 75050 Fax:0674 671153			13 Single 5 Twin 6 Double 3 Family	27 En Suite fac	B&B per person £25.00-£40.00 Single £20.00-£35.00 Double	Open Jan-Dec Dinner 1700-2230 B&B + Eve.Meal £35.00-£50.00	
Links Hotel Mid Links Montrose Angus DD10 8RL Tel:(Montrose) 0674 72288 Fax:0674 72698		COMMENDED 👑 👑 👑 👑	3 Single 11 Twin 7 Double 2 Family	21 En Suite fac 2 Pub.Bath/Show	B&B per person £29.00-£59.00 Single £19.50-£38.00 Double	Open Jan-Dec Dinner 1830-2130 B&B + Eve.Meal £40.00-£70.00	
			Friendly hotel in quiet location yet close to town centre, golf course and beach.				
Park Hotel John Street Montrose Angus DD10 8RJ Tel:(Montrose) 0674 73415 Fax:0674 77091			1 Single 45 Twin 10 Double 4 Family	59 En Suite fac	B&B per person £45.00-£75.00 Single £30.00-£45.00 Double	Open Jan-Dec Dinner 1900-2130 B&B + Eve.Meal £61.50-£91.50	

MONTROSE
Angus

The Pipers Private Hotel & Licensed Rest 11 Union Place Montrose Angus DD10 8QB Tel:(Montrose) 0674 72298	Map 2 E1	2 Twin 1 Double 2 Family	2 Pub.Bath/Show	B&B per person from £16.00 Double	Open Jan-Dec Dinner 1900-2130 B&B + Eve.Meal from £24.00

Cranes Meadow Guest House 28 The Mall Montrose Angus DD10 8NW Tel:(Montrose) 0674 72296		1 Single 2 Twin 2 Double 2 Family	4 Limited ensuite 3 Pub.Bath/Show	B&B per person from £16.00 Single £14.00-£15.00 Double	Open Jan-Dec

The Limes Guest House 15 King Street Montrose Angus DD10 8NL Tel:(Montrose) 0674 77236 Fax:0674 77236	COMMENDED ♛ ♛	2 Single 4 Twin 4 Double 2 Family	4 En Suite fac 4 Limited ensuite 2 Priv.NOT ensuite 3 Pub.Bath/Show	B&B per person from £18.00 Single from £16.50 Double	Open Jan-Dec Dinner from 1800

Family run, centrally situated in quiet, residential part of town. A few minutes walk from the centre, railway station and beach. Private parking.

Murray Lodge 2-8 Murray Street Montrose Angus DD10 8LB Tel:(Montrose) 0674 78880 Fax:0674 78877	Award Pening	4 Single 3 Twin 5 Double	12 En Suite fac	B&B per person £23.50-£35.25 Single £20.56-£23.50 Double	Open Jan-Dec Dinner 1730-1900 B&B + Eve.Meal £27.00-£42.00

Oaklands Guest House 10 Rossie Island Road Montrose Angus DD10 9NN Tel:(Montrose) 0674 72018	COMMENDED ♛ ♛	1 Single 3 Twin 2 Double 1 Family	4 En Suite fac 1 Pub.Bath/Show	B&B per person from £15.00 Single £14.00-£17.00 Double	Open Jan-Dec

En suite facilities available at this comfortable family house within walking distance of Montrose town centre. Parking. Boat fishing available.

BY MONTROSE
Angus

Hillside Hotel Kinnaber Road, Hillside by Montrose Angus DD10 9HE Tel:(Hillside) 067483 230 Fax:067483 508	Map 2 E1 COMMENDED ♛ ♛ ♛	5 Single 2 Twin 2 Double 1 Family	10 En Suite fac	B&B per person £18.00-£22.00 Single £16.00-£20.00 Double	Open Jan-Dec Dinner 1700-2100 B&B + Eve.Meal £21.00-£27.00

Privately owned hotel in residential area on the outskirts of the town. Fishing, shooting and golf the main attractions.

MOODIESBURN
Lanarkshire

Moodiesburn House 6 Cumbernauld Road Moodiesburn Lanarkshire G69 0AA Tel:(Glenboig) 0236 873172 Fax:0236 872715	Map 2 A5	3 Single 11 Twin 43 Double 6 Family	63 En Suite fac	B&B per person £35.00-£59.00 Single £22.50-£35.00 Double	Open Jan-Dec Dinner 1800-2130 B&B + Eve.Meal £32.50-£69.00

MORAR, by Mallaig
Inverness-shire
Map 3 E1

Morar Hotel
Morar, by Mallaig
Inverness-shire
PH40 4PA
Tel:(Mallaig) 0687 2346
Fax:0687 2130

COMMENDED

6 Single
13 Twin
6 Double
4 Family

29 En Suite fac

B&B per person
£25.00-£35.00 Single
£25.00-£30.00 Double

Open Apr-Oct
Dinner 1830-2030
B&B + Eve.Meal
£40.00-£45.00

Family run hotel on "Road to the Isles" with magnificent views over Silver Sands of Morar and islands of Rhum and Eigg. Some annexe accommodation.

MOTHERWELL
Lanarkshire
Map 2 A5

Easdale Guest House
10/12 Nigel Street,
off Hamilton Road
Motherwell
Lanarkshire
ML1 3DP
Tel:(Motherwell) 0698 267312
Fax:0698 275637

2 Single
1 Twin
1 Family

1 Pub.Bath/Show

B&B per person
£13.50-£15.50 Single
£13.50-£15.50 Double

Open Jan-Dec
Dinner 1730-1930
B&B + Eve.Meal
£20.00-£21.00

Hillcrest Guest House
94 Hamilton Road
Motherwell
Lanarkshire
ML1 3DG
Tel:(Motherwell) 0698 261174
Fax:0698 265224

APPROVED Listed

2 Single
2 Twin
1 Double
3 Family

7 En Suite fac
1 Priv.NOT ensuite
3 Pub.Bath/Show

B&B per person
£20.00-£40.00 Single
£15.00-£25.00 Double

Open Jan-Dec
Dinner 1730-1900
B&B + Eve.Meal
£25.00-£40.00

Warm welcome in Victorian villa within walking distance of all amenities. Ample secure parking. Easy access M8/M74. Ground floor en suite rooms.

Strathclyde Guest House
90 Hamilton Road
Motherwell
Lanarkshire
ML1 3DG
Tel:(Motherwell) 0698 264076/263691

2 Single
2 Twin
2 Double
2 Family

1 Pub.Bath/Show

B&B per person
£14.50-£17.00 Single
£13.00 Double

Open Jan-Dec

MUIR OF ORD
Ross-shire
Map 4 A8

Ord Arms Hotel
Muir of Ord
Ross-shire
IV6 7XR
Tel:(Muir of Ord) 0463 870286
Fax:0463 870048

2 Single
3 Twin
3 Double
2 Family

6 En Suite fac
3 Pub.Bath/Show

B&B per person
£22.00-£28.00 Single
£38.00-£40.00 Double

Open Jan-Dec
Dinner 1730-2100

Ord House Hotel
Muir of Ord
Ross-shire
IV6 7UH
Tel:(Muir of Ord) 0463 870492

COMMENDED

1 Single
7 Twin
2 Double

10 En Suite fac

B&B per person
£30.00-£37.00 Single
£27.00-£37.00 Double

Open May-Oct
Dinner 1900-2200
B&B + Eve.Meal
£46.00-£56.00

Country house dating from 1637 in extensive grounds. 12 miles (19kms) from Inverness. Taste of Scotland with emphasis on fresh food.

MUIR OF ORD continued The Dower House Highfield Muir of Ord Ross-shire IV6 7XN Tel:(Muir of Ord) 0463 870090 Fax:0463 870090	Map 4 A8		3 Twin 5 En Suite fac 2 Double Suite avail.	B&B per person £35.00-£70.00 Single £35.00-£90.00 Double	Open Jan-Dec Dinner 2000-2130 B&B + Eve.Meal £60.00-£70.00	
MUSSELBURGH East Lothian Craigesk Guest House 10 Albert Terrace Musselburgh East Lothian EH21 7LR Tel:031 665 3344/3170	Map 2 D5	APPROVED 👑	1 Single 2 Pub.Bath/Show 2 Twin 2 Family	B&B per person from £14.00 Single from £14.00 Double	Open Jan-Dec	
			Victorian terraced house with private parking, overlooking golf and racecourse. Convenient bus route to city centre (20 minutes).			
NAIRN Ardgour Hotel Seafield Street Nairn IV12 4HN Tel:(Nairn) 0667 54230/ 454230	Map 4 C8	APPROVED 👑	2 Single 3 Pub.Bath/Show 2 Twin 4 Double 2 Family	B&B per person £14.00-£17.00 Double	Open Mar-Oct B&B + Eve.Meal £22.00-£25.00	
			Victorian villa with attractive garden, short walk to beach. Informal; unlicensed; large lounge with books available; children and dogs welcome.			
Braeval Hotel Crescent Road Nairn IV12 4NB Tel:(Nairn) 0667 52341/ 452341		COMMENDED 👑👑👑	2 Single 7 En Suite fac 2 Twin 1 Pub.Bath/Show 2 Double 1 Family	B&B per person from £25.00 Single from £25.00 Double	Open Jan-Dec Dinner 1830-1930 B&B + Eve.Meal from £35.00	
			Family run hotel overlooking Links with views across Moray Firth. Close to town centre, beaches and all amenities.			

Claymore House Hotel
Seabank Road, Nairn IV12 4EY Tel: 0667 53731. Fax: 0667 55290

Re-opened in 1990 after a total refurbishment, the hotel offers the highest standards and the warmest of welcomes. In luxurious surroundings you can enjoy first-class food, drink and service. The hotel is only a short distance from Nairn's beaches and famous golf courses with a further 20 within one hour. Reductions for children.
DB&B £38 per person.

Claymore House Hotel Seabank Road Nairn IV12 4EY Tel:(Nairn) 0667 53731/ 453731 Fax:0667 55290/455290	Award Pending	3 Single 12 En Suite fac 3 Twin 5 Double 1 Family	B&B per person £32.00-£38.00 Single £27.00-£32.00 Double	Open Jan-Dec Dinner 1800-2100 B&B + Eve.Meal £35.00-£45.00	

NAIRN

NAIRN continued	Map 4 C8						

Golf View Hotel
Seabank Road
Nairn
IV12 4HD
Tel:(Nairn) 0667 52301/
452301
Fax:0667 55267/455267

COMMENDED
👑 👑 👑
👑 👑

4 Single
25 Twin
15 Double
3 Family

47 En Suite fac

B&B per person
£39.50-£50.00 Single
£34.50-£59.00 Double

Open Jan-Dec
Dinner 1900-2115
B&B + Eve.Meal
£39.50-£65.00

Victorian hotel overlooking the sea and the hills of the Black Isle. Championship golf course nearby.

Invernairne Hotel
Thurlow Road
Nairn
IV12 4EZ
Tel:(Nairn) 0667 52039/
452039

COMMENDED
👑 👑 👑

1 Single
2 Twin
3 Double
3 Family

8 En Suite fac
1 Limited ensuite
1 Pub.Bath/Show

B&B per person
£27.00-£35.00 Single
£25.00-£32.00 Double

Open Jan-Dec
Dinner 1900-2000
B&B + Eve.Meal
£30.00-£38.00

Former mansion house now a family run hotel in wooded garden; private path to safe beach. Swimming pool and golf within walking distance.

Links Hotel
1 Seafield Street
Nairn
IV12 4HN
Tel:(Nairn) 0667 53321/
453321
Fax:0667 53321/453321

COMMENDED
👑 👑 👑

2 Single
3 Twin
2 Double
3 Family

10 En Suite fac

B&B per person
£25.00-£30.00 Single
£20.00-£30.00 Double

Open Jan-Dec
Dinner 1900-2100
B&B + Eve.Meal
£35.00-£45.00

Elegant Victorian hotel in quiet location with sea views. Log fires. Central for touring. Inclusive golf packages (over 30 courses).

Lothian House Hotel
Crescent Road
Nairn
IV12 4NB
Tel:(Nairn) 0667 53555/
453555

APPROVED
👑 👑

3 Single
1 Twin
1 Double
2 Family

2 En Suite fac
2 Pub.Bath/Show

B&B per person
£16.00-£19.00 Single
£13.00-£17.00 Double

Open Jan-Dec
Dinner 1800-2100
B&B + Eve.Meal
£21.00-£27.00

Stone built house, c1850 in quiet residential area of town. Personally run with easy access to beach and to town centre.

Newton Hotel
Inverness Road
Nairn
IV12 4RX
Tel:(Nairn) 0667 53144/
453144
Fax:0667 54026/454026

COMMENDED
👑 👑 👑
👑 👑

13 Single
24 Twin
4 Double
3 Family

44 En Suite fac

B&B per person
£44.00-£55.00 Single
£36.00-£47.00 Double

Open Jan-Dec
Dinner 1900-2115
B&B + Eve.Meal
£70.00-£85.00

Scottish baronial style hotel set in 27 acres of parkland. Distant views of sea and Black Isle Hills.

Sunny Brae Hotel
Marine Road
Nairn
IV12 4EA
Tel:(Nairn) 0667 52309/
452309

COMMENDED
👑 👑 👑

3 Single
2 Twin
4 Double
1 Family

8 En Suite fac
1 Pub.Bath/Show

B&B per person
£21.00-£23.00 Single
£21.00-£23.00 Double

Open Apr-Oct
Dinner from 1830
B&B + Eve.Meal
£30.00-£32.00

Purpose built guest house near town centre and facilities with beautiful views across Moray Firth to Black Isle. Games room with pool table.

NAIRN continued — Map 4 C8

Windsor Hotel
Albert Street
Nairn
IV12 4HP
Tel:(Nairn) 0667 53108/
453108
Fax:0667 56108/456108

COMMENDED
♛ ♛ ♛

9 Single
10 Twin
14 Double
7 Family

38 En Suite fac
2 Limited ensuite
4 Pub.Bath/Show

B&B per person
£29.00-£38.50 Single
£24.00-£32.75 Double

Open Jan-Dec
Dinner 1900-2130
B&B + Eve.Meal
£40.50-£55.00

Privately owned in residential area. Gourmet evenings specialising in seafood. Near sandy beach and golf course.

Bracadale House
Albert Street
Nairn
IV12
Tel:(Nairn) 0667 52547/
452547

HIGHLY
COMMENDED
♛ ♛

1 Twin
2 Double

1 En Suite fac
2 Priv.NOT ensuite

B&B per person
£15.00-£18.00 Double

Open Apr-Oct
Dinner 1800-1930
B&B + Eve.Meal
£23.00-£26.00

Elegant detached Victorian villa in quiet residential area close to beach and golf course. Warm and friendly atmosphere.

Durham House
4 Academy Street
Nairn
IV12 4RJ
Tel:(Nairn) 0667 52345/
452345

COMMENDED
♛

1 Twin
1 Double
1 Family

2 Pub.Bath/Show

B&B per person
£14.00-£16.00 Single
£14.00-£16.50 Double

Open Jan-Dec
Dinner 1800-1930
B&B + Eve.Meal
£22.00-£24.50

19th century elegant villa, set in its own grounds, with off street parking. Extensive home baking and cooking.

Rhyden House
Cumming Street
Nairn
IV12 1NQ
Tel:(Nairn) 0667 537361/
453736

COMMENDED
♛ ♛ ♛

1 Single
1 Twin
2 Double
2 Family

3 En Suite fac
1 Priv.NOT ensuite
1 Pub.Bath/Show

B&B per person
£15.00-£18.00 Single
£14.00-£17.00 Double

Open Jan-Dec
Dinner 1830-1930
B&B + Eve.Meal
£21.00-£24.00

Victorian sandstone house of character. 2 minutes level walk to beach. Secluded garden. Special diets available.

NETHY BRIDGE — Inverness-shire — Map 4 C1

Mount View Hotel
Nethy Bridge
Inverness-shire
PH25 3EB
Tel:(Nethy Bridge) 0479
821248

COMMENDED
♛ ♛ ♛

2 Single
1 Twin
4 Family

5 En Suite fac
1 Pub.Bath/Show

B&B per person
£15.00-£23.00 Single
£15.00-£23.00 Double

Open Jan-Dec
Dinner 1800-2100

Family run hotel in quiet village with views over Cairngorms. Vegetarian menu a speciality. Aviemore 10 miles (16 kms).

Nethybridge Hotel
Nethy Bridge
Inverness-shire
PH25 3DP
Tel:(Nethy Bridge) 0479
821203
Fax:0479 821686

11 Single
36 Twin
14 Double
4 Family
Suite avail.

65 En Suite fac

B&B per person
£25.00-£38.00 Single
£25.00-£38.00 Double

Open Jan-Dec
Dinner 1900-2030

NEW ABBEY by Dumfries
Dumfriesshire
Map 2
B1

Criffel Inn
2 The Square
New Abbey, by Dumfries
Dumfriesshire
DG2 8BX
Tel:(New Abbey) 038785 244

1 Single	2 En Suite fac	B&B per person	Open Jan-Dec
2 Double	1 Limited ensuite	£19.50-£22.00 Single	Dinner 1630-1930
2 Family	1 Pub.Bath/Show	£22.00 Double	B&B + Eve.Meal £28.00-£30.00

NEWCASTLETON
Roxburghshire
Map 2
E9

COMMENDED
👑 👑 👑

Liddesdale Hotel
Newcastleton
Roxburghshire
TD9
Tel:(Liddesdale) 03873 75255

2 Twin	4 En Suite fac	B&B per person	Open Jan-Dec
2 Double	1 Priv.NOT ensuite	from £30.00 Single	Dinner from 1900
1 Family		from £22.00 Double	B&B + Eve.Meal from £28.00

Family run, 18C coaching inn, situated in main square of attractive village. Central for Borders sightseeing; scenic route to Edinburgh.

NEW CUMNOCK
Ayrshire
Map 2
A8

Lochside House Hotel
New Cumnock
Ayrshire
KA18 4PN
Tel:(New Cumnock) 0290 38629
Fax:0290 38629

3 Single	11 En Suite fac	B&B per person	Open Jan-Dec
4 Twin		£32.00-£35.00 Single	Dinner 1600-2300
4 Double		£20.00-£27.50 Double	

NEW GALLOWAY
Kirkcudbrightshire
Map 2
A9

APPROVED
👑

Ken Bridge Hotel
New Galloway
Kirkcudbrightshire
DG7 3PR
Tel:(New Galloway) 06442 211

1 Single	1 En Suite fac	B&B per person	Open Jan-Dec
3 Twin	4 Pub.Bath/Show	£14.00-£15.50 Single	Dinner 1800-2030
3 Double		£14.00-£15.50 Double	B&B + Eve.Meal from £24.00
3 Family			

Victorian coach house on banks of river, situated in tourist area. Private parking & fishing rights free to residents. Privately run, home cooking.

Kenmure Arms Hotel
High Street
New Galloway
Kirkcudbrightshire
DG7 3RL
Tel:(New Galloway) 06442 240

2 Single	1 En Suite fac	B&B per person	Open Jan-Dec
6 Twin	2 Pub.Bath/Show	£13.50-£14.50 Single	Dinner 1700-2000
1 Double		£13.50-£14.50 Double	B&B + Eve.Meal
3 Family			£21.00-£22.00

Leamington Hotel
High Street
New Galloway
Kirkcudbrightshire
DG7 3RN
Tel:(New Galloway) 06442 327

COMMENDED
👑 👑 👑

2 Single	6 En Suite fac	B&B per person	Open Dec-Oct
1 Twin	2 Limited ensuite	£14.00-£22.00 Single	Dinner 1700-2030
3 Double	2 Pub.Bath/Show	£16.00-£22.00 Double	B&B + Eve.Meal
3 Family			£22.00-£30.00

Small family run hotel with warm and friendly atmosphere. Home cooking. Patio dining in Summer.

BY NEWPORT-ON-TAY **Fife** Forgan House Forgan Newport-on-Tay Fife DD6 8RB Tel:(Newport-on-Tay) 0382 542760	Map 2 D2	HIGHLY COMMENDED 👑 👑 👑	2 Twin 2 Double	3 En Suite fac 1 Priv.NOT ensuite	B&B per person £25.00-£30.00 Double	Open Jan-Dec Dinner 1900-2000 B&B + Eve.Meal £35.00-£40.00
			Georgian country house set in 5 acres of grounds and gardens located between Dundee and St Andrews.			
NEWTON **by South Queensferry,** **West Lothian** Newton Guest House Newton Village by South Queensferry West Lothian EH52 6QE Tel:031 331 3298	Map 2 C5		1 Twin 1 Double 2 Family	2 Pub.Bath/Show	B&B per person to £18.00 Single to £15.00 Double	Open Jan-Dec
NEWTONMORE **Inverness-shire** Alvey House Hotel Golf Course Road Newtonmore Inverness-shire PH20 1AT Tel:(Newtonmore) 0540 673260	Map 4 B1	COMMENDED 👑 👑	1 Single 2 Twin 3 Double 1 Family	7 En Suite fac	B&B per person from £23.00 Single from £23.00 Double	Open Dec-Oct Dinner from 1900 B&B + Eve.Meal from £33.50
			Stone built Victorian villa overlooking Spey Valley. Close to golf course and village centre. Cross country ski packages available in season.			
Balavil Sport Hotel Main Street Newtonmore Inverness-shire PH20 1DL Tel:(Newtonmore) 0540 673220 Fax:0540 673773		COMMENDED 👑 👑 👑	4 Single 28 Twin 8 Double 10 Family	50 En Suite fac	B&B per person £25.00 £45.00 Single £20.00-£40.00 Double	Open Jan-Dec Dinner 1830-2030 B&B + Eve.Meal £30.00-£50.00
			Family hotel in centre of village with many sporting facilities including indoor swimming pool and regular entertainment. All rooms en suite.			
Glen Hotel Newtonmore Inverness-shire PH20 1DD Tel:(Newtonmore) 0540 673203		APPROVED 👑 👑 👑	1 Single 3 Twin 3 Double 2 Family	5 En Suite fac 1 Priv.NOT ensuite 2 Pub.Bath/Show	B&B per person £20.00-£28.00 Single £18.00-£22.00 Double	Open Jan-Dec Dinner 1900-2100 B&B + Eve.Meal £30.00-£38.00
			Personally run, situated in centre of village. A la carte menu and bar meals featuring home-made dishes. Ample car parking.			
Pines Hotel Station Road Newtonmore Inverness-shire PH20 1AR Tel:(Newtonmore) 0540 673271		COMMENDED 👑 👑 👑	1 Single 3 Twin 2 Double	6 En Suite fac	B&B per person £23.00 Single £23.00 Double	Open Apr-Oct Dinner from 1900 B&B + Eve.Meal £33.00
			Stone built Victorian house, situated in 1.5 acres of pine wooded grounds, a few minutes from centre of village. All rooms en suite.			

Details of Grading and Classification are on page vi. | Key to symbols is on back flap.   283

NEWTON STEWART Wigtownshire	Map 1 H1					
Black Horse Hotel 62-66 Queen Street Newton Stewart Wigtownshire DG8 6JL Tel:(Newton Stewart) 0671 2054 Fax:0671 2054			2 Twin 1 Double 1 Family	1 En Suite fac 1 Pub.Bath/Show	B&B per person £17.50-£19.50 Double	Open Jan-Dec Dinner 1730-2030

| Creebridge House Hotel Newton Stewart Wigtownshire DG8 6NP Tel:(Newton Stewart) 0671 2121 | COMMENDED 👑 👑 👑 👑 | | 2 Single 8 Twin 5 Double 3 Family | 18 En Suite fac | B&B per person £40.00-£45.00 Single £30.00-£40.00 Double | Open Jan-Dec Dinner 1915-2030 B&B + Eve.Meal £50.00-£55.00 |
| | | Family run hotel in 4 acres of garden, near the centre of town. Golf and fishing by arrangement. | | | | |

| Crown Hotel 101 Queen Street Newton Stewart Wigtownshire DG8 6JW Tel:(Newton Stewart) 0671 2727 | APPROVED 👑 👑 👑 | | 2 Single 2 Twin 6 Double 1 Family | 9 En Suite fac 2 Pub.Bath/Show | B&B per person £23.00-£28.50 Single £23.00-£25.00 Double | Open Jan-Dec Dinner 1800-2100 B&B + Eve.Meal £37.00-£42.00 |
| | | Former coaching inn, now a family run hotel, situated in centre of town. Separate dining area for non smokers and service of bar meals. Fishing. | | | | |

| Kirroughtree Hotel Newton Stewart Wigtownshire DG8 6AN Tel:(Newton Stewart) 0671 2141 Fax:0671 2425 | HIGHLY COMMENDED 👑 👑 👑 👑 👑 | | 4 Single 8 Twin 8 Double 2 Family | 22 En Suite fac | B&B per person £46.00-£55.00 Single £42.00-£77.00 Double | Open Jan-Dec Dinner 1900-2130 B&B + Eve.Meal £57.00-£91.50 |
| | | Georgian mansion in 8 acres of landscaped gardens. Separate non-smoking dining room. Scottish haute cuisine. Free golf. Some annexe accommodation. | | | | |

| Flower Bank Guest House Minnigaff Newton Stewart Wigtownshire DG8 6PJ Tel:(Newton Stewart) 0671 2629 | COMMENDED 👑 | | 1 Single 1 Twin 3 Double 2 Family | 2 Pub.Bath/Show | B&B per person £15.00-£17.00 Single £15.00-£16.00 Double | Open Jan-Dec Dinner from 1830 B&B + Eve.Meal £22.50-£24.50 |
| | | Detached 18C house set in 1 acre of grounds on banks of River Cree. Quiet peaceful location 0.5 miles (1km) from town centre. | | | | |

NORTH BERWICK East Lothian	Map 2 E4					
The Belhaven Hotel 28 Westgate North Berwick East Lothian EH39 4AH Tel:(North Berwick) 0620 3009			1 Single 5 Twin 3 Family	4 En Suite fac 4 Pub.Bath/Show	B&B per person £18.50-£32.00 Single £18.00-£24.00 Double	Open Jan-Dec Dinner 1800-1830 B&B + Eve.Meal £26.00-£32.00

NORTH BERWICK continued	**Map 2** E4						
Blenheim House Hotel 14 Westgate North Berwick EH39 4AF Tel:(North Berwick) 0620 2385 Fax:0620 4010			2 Single 4 Twin 2 Double 3 Family	6 En Suite fac	B&B per person £17.00-£25.00 Single £20.00-£28.00 Double	Open Jan-Dec Dinner 1830-2100 B&B + Eve.Meal £27.00-£38.00	
The County Hotel High Street North Berwick East Lothian EH39 4HH Tel:(North Berwick) 0620 2989		COMMENDED ♛	1 Single 3 Twin 3 Double 1 Family	3 Pub.Bath/Show	B&B per person from £18.50 Single from £18.50 Double	Open Jan-Dec Dinner 1900-2200 B&B + Eve.Meal £22.00-£32.00	
			Family run hotel in town centre. Function room for 60 persons. Beer garden and childrens play area.				
Golf Hotel 34 Dirleton Avenue North Berwick East Lothian EH39 4BH Tel:(North Berwick) 0620 2202			4 Single 4 Twin 1 Double 4 Family	9 En Suite fac 2 Pub.Bath/Show	B&B per person £21.00-£30.00 Single £21.00-£27.00 Double	Open Jan-Dec Dinner 1900-2100 B&B + Eve.Meal £33.00-£39.00	
Point Garry Hotel West Bay Road North Berwick East Lothian EH39 4AW Tel:(North Berwick) 0620 2380 Fax:0620 2848			1 Single 5 Twin 3 Double 7 Family	12 En Suite fac 1 Pub.Bath/Show	B&B per person £33.00-£50.00 Single £33.00-£50.00 Double	Open Apr-Oct Dinner 1930-2100 B&B + Eve.Meal £42.00-£60.00	
Craigview Guest House 5 Beach Road North Berwick East Lothian EH39 4AB Tel:(North Berwick) 0620 2257			1 Twin 2 Double	1 En Suite fac 2 Pub.Bath/Show	B&B per person from £13.50 Double	Open Jan-Dec Dinner at 1900	
NORTH KESSOCK Ross-shire North Kessock Hotel North Kessock Ross-shire IV1 1XN Tel:(Kessock) 046373 208	**Map 4** B8	COMMENDED ♛ ♛ ♛	2 Twin 2 Double 1 Family	5 En Suite fac	B&B per person £25.00-£28.00 Double	Open Jan-Dec Dinner 1700-2100	
			Family run hotel on seafront with garden, 3 miles (5kms) north of Inverness. Panoramic views across the Beauly Firth.				
NORTH QUEENSFERRY Fife Albert Hotel Main Street North Queensferry Fife KY11 1JP Tel:(Inverkeithing) 0383 413562	**Map 2** C4		2 Single 2 Twin 4 Double 2 Family	2 En Suite fac 2 Pub.Bath/Show	B&B per person £21.00-£25.00 Single £37.00-£42.00 Double	Open Jan-Dec Dinner 1800-2130	

NORTH QUEENSFERRY continued Ferry Bridge Hotel Main Street North Queensferry Fife KY11 1JQ Tel:(Inverkeithing) 0383 416292	Map 2 C4		3 Twin 6 En Suite fac 3 Double	B&B per person to £25.00 Single to £20.00 Double	Open Jan-Dec Dinner 1900-2200	

BY NORTH QUEENSFERRY Fife Queensferry Lodge Hotel St Margarets Head North Queensferry Fife KY11 1HP Tel:(Inverkeithing) 0383 410000 Fax:0383 419708	Map 2 C4	COMMENDED 👑 👑 👑 👑	20 Twin 32 En Suite fac 12 Double	B&B per person from £55.00 Single from £27.50 Double	Open Jan-Dec Dinner 1700-2200	
			Family run hotel in own grounds with spectacular views over River Forth and famous bridges. Conference/banqueting facilities. Tourist information.			

OBAN Argyll Alexandra Hotel Corran Esplanade Oban Argyll PA34 5AA Tel:(Oban) 0631 62381 Fax:0631 64497	Map 1 E2	COMMENDED 👑 👑 👑 👑	13 Single 60 En Suite fac 25 Twin 17 Double 5 Family	B&B per person £30.00-£55.00 Single £30.00-£45.00 Double	Open Feb-Dec Dinner 1830-2100 B&B + Eve.Meal £43.00-£55.00	
			Traditional hotel with panoramic views over the Firth of Lorne. Centrally situated on Oban Esplanade. Swimming pool and leisure centre.			

Argyll Hotel Corran Esplanade Oban Argyll PA34 5PZ Tel:(Oban) 0631 62353			4 Single 27 En Suite fac 10 Twin 8 Double 5 Family Suite avail.	B&B per person £28.50-£37.50 Single £25.00-£35.00 Double	Open Jan-Dec Dinner 1700-2050 B&B + Eve.Meal £39.50-£49.50	

Balmoral Hotel Craigard Road Oban Argyll PA34 5NP Tel:(Oban) 0631 62731 Fax:0631 66810		COMMENDED 👑 👑 👑	2 Single 9 En Suite fac 2 Twin 1 Pub.Bath/Show 7 Double 1 Family	B&B per person £23.00-£25.00 Single £25.00-£27.00 Double	Open Apr-Oct, Xmas, New Year Dinner 1700-2200 B&B + Eve.Meal £35.00-£37.00	
			Personally run and centrally situated close to shops, ferry and rail terminal. Steakhouse and seafood restaurant.			

Barriemore Hotel Corran Esplanade Oban Argyll PA34 5AQ Tel:(Oban) 0631 66356		HIGHLY COMMENDED 👑 👑 👑	4 Twin 13 En Suite fac 9 Double	B&B per person £24.00-£30.00 Double	Open Mar-Jan Dinner 1900-2130 B&B + Eve.Meal £41.00-£47.00	
			Late Victorian house splendidly situated overlooking the Bay. Completely refurbished to a high standard.			

OBAN continued	Map 1 E2

Caledonian Hotel

STATION SQUARE OBAN

Tel: (0631) 63133
Fax: (0631) 62998
Central Reservations 0397-703139

Traditional by design but modern in its services and facilities, this AA/RAC 3-star hotel is superbly appointed overlooking Oban bay and its active fishing harbour.

If you want to get away, relax and absorb this area **then send off today for our Scottish Holiday brochure** – includes rail programmes, centred or touring holidays and complete packages all at special prices.

Also hotels in Fort William, Stirling and Inverness.

Caledonian Hotel Station Square Oban Argyll PA34 5RT Tel:(Oban) 0631 63133 Fax:0631 62998	COMMENDED ♛ ♛ ♛ ♛	13 Single 40 Twin 10 Double 7 Family	70 En Suite fac	B&B per person £34.00-£54.00 Single £28.00-£39.50 Double	Open Jan-Dec Dinner 1700-2300 B&B + Eve.Meal £44.00-£59.00	
		Modernised 19c building adjacent to railway station and ferry pier, overlooking the harbour and the Isles of Kerrera and Mull.				
Columba Hotel The Esplanade Oban Argyll PA34 5QD Tel:(Oban) 0631 62183 Tlx:728256 PARWAY Fax:0631 64683		5 Single 26 Twin 12 Double 6 Family	49 En Suite fac	B&B per person from £35.00 Single from £30.00 Double	Open Mar-Nov Dinner 1830-2130	
Corran House Hotel Esplanade Oban Argyll Tel:(Oban) 0631 64448		8 Twin 10 Double 4 Family	15 En Suite fac 4 Pub.Bath/Show	B&B per person £16.00-£24.00 Single £14.00-£24.00 Double	Open Jan-Dec Dinner 1800-2100	
Dungallan Country House Gallanach Road Oban Argyll Tel:(Oban) 0631 63799 Fax:0631 66711	Award Pending	2 Single 3 Twin 8 Double 1 Family Suite avail.	11 En Suite fac 2 Priv.NOT ensuite 4 Pub.Bath/Show	B&B per person £25.00-£30.00 Single £23.00-£30.00 Double	Open Jan-Dec Dinner 1900-2100 B&B + Eve.Meal £42.00-£48.00	
Glenburnie Private Hotel Esplanade Oban Argyll PA34 5AQ Tel:(Oban) 0631 62089	COMMENDED ♛ ♛	2 Single 4 Twin 6 Double 3 Family	10 En Suite fac 3 Pub.Bath/Show	B&B per person £17.50-£20.00 Single £20.00-£30.00 Double	Open Apr-Oct	
		Convenient for town centre and all amenities, this family run hotel has magnificent views of the bay and islands.				
Glenrigh Private Hotel Corran Esplanade Oban Argyll PA34 5AQ Tel:(Oban) 0631 62991	COMMENDED ♛ ♛	3 Single 4 Twin 4 Double 3 Family	14 En Suite fac	B&B per person £20.00-£28.00 Single £20.00-£28.00 Double	Open Mar-Nov	
		Refurbished Victorian hotel with excellent views across Oban Bay. Short walk from town centre and all amenities. Private car parking.				
Heatherfield Albert Road Oban Argyll PA34 5EJ Tel:(Oban) 0631 62681		2 Twin 5 Double	2 En Suite fac 2 Pub.Bath/Show	B&B per person from £17.00 Double	Open Jan-Dec Dinner 1830-2100 B&B + Eve.Meal from £32.00	

OBAN continued — Map 1 E2

Kilchrenan House Corran Esplanade Oban Argyll PA34 5AQ Tel:(Oban) 0631 62663	**HIGHLY COMMENDED** 👑 👑	1 Single 2 Twin 5 Double 2 Family	10 En Suite fac	B&B per person £23.00-£30.00 Single £22.00-£30.00 Double	Open Apr-Oct

Family run hotel in traditional Victorian house sympathetically refurbished. Short walk from town centre. Excellent sea views. Private parking.

Kings Knoll Hotel Dunollie Road Oban Argyll PA34 5JH Tel:(Oban) 0631 62536 Fax:0631 66101	**COMMENDED** 👑 👑 👑	2 Single 3 Twin 7 Double 3 Family	11 En Suite fac 3 Pub.Bath/Show	B&B per person £20.00-£26.00 Single £20.00-£26.00 Double	Open Jan-Dec Dinner 1830-2100 B&B + Eve.Meal £30.00-£38.00

Family run hotel overlooking Oban Bay and close to the town centre and seafront. Newly refurbished theme bar and dining room.

Lancaster Hotel Corran Esplanade Oban Argyll PA34 5AD Tel:(Oban) 0631 62587	**COMMENDED** 👑 👑 👑	8 Single 10 Twin 6 Double 3 Family	24 En Suite fac 3 Pub.Bath/Show	B&B per person £24.70-£30.00 Single	Open Jan-Dec Dinner 1830-2000 B&B + Eve.Meal £34.70-£40.00

On seafront with its own indoor heated swimming pool, jacuzzi, solarium and sauna. Convenient for town centre and all amenities.

The Manor House

GALLANACH ROAD · OBAN · ARGYLL · PA34 4LS

An enviable position on the foreshore of Oban Bay,
The Manor House has long held the reputation for high quality in the comfort of its accommodation and the excellence of its
Scottish and French cuisine.
All bedrooms have en-suite facilities.
Special weekends and breaks available.

For Reservations or Brochure and Tariff: Telephone 0631 62087. Fax: 0631 63053

Manor House Hotel Gallanach Road Oban Argyll PA34 4LS Tel:(Oban) 0631 62087 Fax:0631 63053	**HIGHLY COMMENDED** 👑 👑 👑 👑	5 Twin 6 Double	11 En Suite fac	B&B per person	Open Feb-Dec Dinner 1900-2030 B&B + Eve.Meal £42.00-£66.00

Family run Georgian house on the foreshore on the south side of Oban with extensive views across the Bay, close to the town centre.

Oban Bay Hotel Esplanade Oban Argyll PA34 5AE Tel:(Oban) 0631 62051	**COMMENDED** 👑 👑 👑	21 Single 48 Twin 18 Double	87 En Suite fac	B&B per person £42.00-£50.00 Single £38.00-£46.00 Double	Open Mar-Nov Dinner 1800-2100 B&B + Eve.Meal £48.00-£58.50

Refurbished holiday hotel with modern extension. Excellent views across Oban Bay. Short walk from town centre and all amenities.

Palace Hotel George Street Oban Argyll PA34 Tel:(Oban) 0631 62294		1 Single 3 Twin 2 Double 7 Family	13 En Suite fac 3 Pub.Bath/Show	B&B per person £18.00-£24.00 Single £16.00-£22.00 Double	Open Jan-Dec

OBAN continued	Map 1 E2						
Queens Hotel Esplanade Oban Argyll PA34 5AG Tel:(Oban) 0631 62505			10 Single 22 Twin 11 Double 1 Family	44 En Suite fac	B&B per person £42.00-£50.00 Single £38.00-£46.00 Double	Open Mar-Nov Dinner 1900-2100 B&B + Eve.Meal £48.00-£58.50	
Regent Hotel Esplanade Oban Argyll PA34 5PZ Tel:(Oban) 0631 62341 Fax:0631 65816		Award Pending	22 Single 36 Twin 18 Double 9 Family	85 En Suite fac	B&B per person £42.00-£50.00 Single £38.00-£46.00 Double	Open Jan-Dec Dinner 1815-2100 B&B + Eve.Meal £48.00-£58.50	
Rowantree Hotel George Street Oban Argyll PA34 5NX Tel:(Oban) 0631 62954 Fax:0631 65071		COMMENDED ⚜ ⚜ ⚜	15 Twin 9 Double	24 En Suite fac	B&B per person £31.00-£38.00 Single £26.00-£33.00 Double	Open Jan-Dec Dinner 1700-2200 B&B + Eve.Meal £37.00-£48.00	

Privately owned modern hotel situated in centre of town but close to the sea front. Specialising in fresh local seafood and steaks. Car park.

Wellpark Hotel Esplanade Oban Argyll PA34 5AQ Tel:(Oban) 0631 62948		COMMENDED ⚜ ⚜	3 Single 7 Twin 7 Double	17 En Suite fac	B&B per person £29.00-£31.00 Single £24.00-£25.00 Double	Open Apr-Oct	

Family run hotel in a quiet position on the esplanade. Magnificent views over the bay to Isles of Kerrera and Mull.

Ardblair
OBAN'S LEADING GUEST HOUSE
DALRIACH ROAD, OBAN, ARGYLL PA34 5JD
Telephone: 0631-62668

We're the third generation of this family-run business. We specialise in home-cooking and good old-fashioned friendly welcome and comfort. Our spacious sun-lounge and our garden have magnificent views over Oban Bay, and yet we're very central - only 3 minutes' walk from the town centre. Our safe car park takes 10 cars.
We're very easy to find: just turn left half way down the hill coming into Oban, up past the tennis courts, swimming pool and there we are!
We'll gladly send you a brochure, or why not phone
IAN & MONIKA SMYTH.
AA QQQ & RAC Acclaimed

Ardblair Guest House Dalriach Road Oban Argyll PA34 5JD Tel:(Oban) 0631 62668			3 Single 3 Twin 6 Double 3 Family Suite avail.	12 En Suite fac 1 Limited ensuite 2 Pub.Bath/Show	B&B per person £16.00-£20.00 Single £16.00-£20.00 Double	Open May-Sep Dinner from 1830 B&B + Eve.Meal £25.00-£29.00	

OBAN

OBAN continued — Map 1 E2

Ariogan Farmhouse
Upper Soroba
Oban
Argyll
PA34 4SD
Tel:(Oban) 0631 65257

COMMENDED ♚

1 Double	1 En Suite fac	B&B per person	Open Jan-Dec
2 Family	1 Pub.Bath/Show	£14.00-£16.00 Double	Dinner 1730-1930
			B&B + Eve.Meal
			£22.00-£24.00

Farmhouse conveniently situated 2 miles (3kms) south of Oban. Good base for touring.

Beechgrove Guest House
Croft Road
Oban
Argyll
PA34 5JL
Tel:(Oban) 0631 66111

COMMENDED ♚ ♚ ♚

1 Twin	3 En Suite fac	B&B per person	Open Mar-Oct
1 Double	1 Pub.Bath/Show	from £17.00 Double	Dinner from 1800
1 Family			B&B + Eve.Meal
			from £27.00

Family run guest house a short walk from the harbour and shops, with pleasant views of Oban Bay and the Sound of Kerrera.

Braehead Guest House
Albert Road
Oban
Argyll
PA34 5EJ
Tel:(Oban) 0631 63341

APPROVED ♚

2 Twin	1 En Suite fac	B&B per person	Open Jan-Dec
3 Double	2 Pub.Bath/Show	£15.00-£17.00 Double	
1 Family			

Attractive house convenient for town centre. Ground floor ensuite. Private parking area.

Elmbank Guest House
Croft Road
Oban
Argyll
PA34 5JN
Tel:(Oban) 0631 62545

1 Single	2 En Suite fac	B&B per person	Open Feb-Nov
2 Twin	2 Limited ensuite	from £15.00 Single	
4 Double	2 Pub.Bath/Show	from £15.00 Double	

Glenara Guest House
Rockfield Road
Oban
Argyll
PA34 5DQ
Tel:(Oban) 0631 63172

COMMENDED ♚ ♚

1 Single	3 En Suite fac	B&B per person	Open Jan-Dec
5 Double	1 Limited ensuite	£16.00-£18.00 Single	
	1 Priv.NOT ensuite	£16.00-£17.50 Double	
	1 Pub.Bath/Show		

Family run guest house close to the town centre and all amenities. Private parking.

Glenbervie Guest House
Dalriach Road
Oban
Argyll
PA34 5NL
Tel:(Oban) 0631 64770

2 Single	3 Limited ensuite	B&B per person	Open Jan-Dec
2 Twin	1 Pub.Bath/Show	£15.00-£19.00 Single	Dinner 1830-2000
2 Double		£15.00-£19.00 Double	B&B + Eve.Meal
2 Family			£22.00-£25.00

Glenroy Guest House
Rockfield Road
Oban
Argyll
PA34 5DQ
Tel:(Oban) 0631 62585

COMMENDED ♚ ♚

1 Single	3 En Suite fac	B&B per person	Open Jan-Dec
1 Twin	3 Pub.Bath/Show	to £16.00 Single	
4 Double		£15.00-£17.50 Double	
1 Family			

Family run guest house overlooking Oban Bay. Centrally situated and convenient for all amenities. Private parking.

Maridon Guest House
Dunuaran Road
Oban
Argyll
PA34 4NE
Tel:(Oban) 0631 62670

1 Single	2 En Suite fac	B&B per person	Open Jan-Dec
2 Twin	1 Pub.Bath/Show	£12.00-£18.00 Single	
5 Double		£12.00-£18.00 Double	
1 Family			

OBAN continued	Map 1 E2						
Rahoy Lodge Gallanach Road Oban Argyll PA34 4PD Tel:(Oban) 0631 62301		APPROVED ⚜	2 Twin 2 Double 2 Family	2 Pub.Bath/Show	B&B per person £15.00-£18.00 Single £12.50-£15.50 Double	Open Jan-Nov	
			Family run guest house on waterfront of Oban Bay with open views to the Sound of Kerrera and the Isle of Mull.				
Roseneath Guest House Dalriach Road Oban Argyll PA34 5EQ Tel:(Oban) 0631 62929		COMMENDED ⚜ ⚜	2 Single 3 Twin 5 Double	3 En Suite fac 4 Limited ensuite 2 Pub.Bath/Show	B&B per person £13.00-£16.00 Single £13.00-£18.00 Double	Open Jan-Dec	
			Victorian house overlooking town and bay, near seafront and shops. Private parking.				
Sand Villa Guest House Breadalbane Street Oban Argyll PA34 Tel:(Oban) 0631 62803			6 Twin 3 Double 6 Family	3 Pub.Bath/Show	B&B per person £12.00-£15.00 Double	Open Jan-Nov Dinner from 1800	
Sgeir Mhaol Guest House Soroba Road Oban Argyll PA34 4JF Tel:(Oban) 0631 62650		COMMENDED ⚜ ⚜	1 Twin 2 Double 3 Family	5 En Suite fac 1 Priv.NOT ensuite 1 Pub.Bath/Show	B&B per person £14.00-£22.00 Single £14.00-£19.00 Double	Open Jan-Dec Dinner from 1830 B&B + Eve.Meal £21.00-£27.00	
			Bungalow style, with ample private car parking and only a short walk from the town centre. All rooms and facilities on the ground floor.				
Thornloe Guest House Albert Road Oban Argyll PA34 5EJ Tel:(Oban) 0631 62879		COMMENDED ⚜ ⚜	3 Twin 4 Double 1 Family	6 En Suite fac 2 Pub.Bath/Show	B&B per person £14.00-£19.00 Double	Open Mar-Nov	
			Completely modernised Victorian semi detached house in centrally situated residential area with fine views over Oban Bay towards the Isle of Mull.				
BY OBAN **Argyll**	Map 1 E2						
Loch Etive Hotel Connel, by Oban Argyll PA37 1PH Tel:(Connel) 063171 400		COMMENDED ⚜ ⚜	2 Twin 2 Double 2 Family	4 En Suite fac 1 Pub.Bath/Show	B&B per person £23.00-£28.00 Single £20.00-£25.00 Double	Open Apr-Oct Dinner 1900-1930 B&B + Eve.Meal £32.00-£37.00	
			Fully modernised Victorian house, most rooms having private facilities, quietly situated off the main road. Home cooking and personal attention.				

BE SURE TO CHOOSE THE SCOTTISH TOURIST BOARD'S SIGN OF QUALITY

BY OBAN continued	Map 1 E2

Ards House
Connel, by Oban, Argyll, PA37 1PT. Tel: (0631 71) 255

Four miles from Oban on the shores of Loch Etive with panoramic views over the Firth of Lorn and Morvern Hills. Come and enjoy the Ards House experience of good food, wine and hospitality. Excellent base for the Central Highlands and Islands or a relaxing break any time of the year.

Ards House Connel Argyll PA37 1PT Tel:(Connel) 063171 255	COMMENDED 👑👑👑	3 Twin 4 Double	6 En Suite fac 1 Pub.Bath/Show	B&B per person £25.00-£35.00 Single £20.00-£27.00 Double	Open Mar-Nov Dinner 1900-2000 B&B + Eve.Meal £33.50-£40.50

Warm friendly atmosphere in this family run house where husband is a keen cook. Large relaxing lounge; table licence; superb sea and sunset views.

OLD DEER by Peterhead Aberdeenshire Saplinbrae House Hotel Old Deer Mintlaw,by Peterhead Aberdeenshire AB42 8LP Tel:(Mintlaw) 0771 23515 Fax:0771 22320/622320	Map 4 H8 Award Pending	2 Single 6 Twin 6 Double	14 En Suite fac 1 Pub.Bath/Show	B&B per person £47.50-£55.00 Single from £66.00 Double	Open Jan-Dec Dinner 1800-2100

OLDMELDRUM Aberdeenshire Meldrum Arms Hotel Oldmeldrum Aberdeenshire AB51 0AE Tel:(Oldmeldrum) 0651 872238 Fax:0651 872238	Map 4 G9 COMMENDED 👑👑👑	2 Single 4 Twin 1 Double	7 En Suite fac 2 Pub.Bath/Show	B&B per person £33.00 Single £22.50 Double	Open Jan-Dec Dinner 1700-2130

Privately owned, in village centre, with function suite (120) and games area in bar. On Whisky and Castle Trails; fishing and golf nearby.

OLD RAYNE Aberdeenshire The Lodge Hotel Old Rayne,by Insch Aberdeenshire AB52 6RY Tel:(Old Rayne) 04645 205	Map 4 F9 COMMENDED 👑👑👑	4 Twin 1 Double 1 Family	4 En Suite fac 1 Pub.Bath/Show	B&B per person £35.00-£38.00 Single £24.00-£27.00 Double	Open Jan-Dec Dinner 1700-2000

Family run hotel situated just of main A96 Inverurie to Huntly road. Home cooking and baking. Function suites for all occasions.

Mill Croft Guest House Old Rayne, by Inverurie Aberdeenshire AB52 6RY Tel:(Old Rayne) 04645 210	COMMENDED 👑👑	1 Twin 1 Double 1 Family	1 En Suite fac 2 Priv.NOT ensuite	B&B per person £15.00-£17.00 Single £15.00-£17.00 Double	Open Jan-Dec Dinner 1830-1930 B&B + Eve.Meal £21.00-£23.00

Friendly welcome at working croft with excellent views over Grampian countryside, on Castle Trail. Residential wood craft courses.

Allt-nan-Ros Hotel

ONICH · By FORT WILLIAM PH33 6RY
Tel: 08553-210/250   Fax: 08553 462

The Macleod family welcome you to our Highland Country House set amid landscaped gardens on the shores of Loch Linnhe midway between Glencoe and Ben Nevis.

All our beautifully furnished bedrooms overlook the loch and have private facilities, phone, colour TV, full controllable heating, hairdryers and much more.

Our dining room which overlooks the loch through ceiling-to-floor picture windows is our forté. Our cuisine is a blend of French and Highland giving you the opportunity to try the best of local game, salmon, seafood etc. A varied and interesting wine list complements our stylish table.

The Lounge and Bar also benefit from the southerly aspect of the hotel, the views are breathtaking and truly panoramic, creating a peaceful and relaxing ambience.

Malt whiskies, log fires, Highland hospitality and an all-local staff together with our spectacular situation combine to make the 'Allt-Nan-Ros' the perfect centre from which to explore the West Highlands and Islands.

Walking, touring, sailing, fishing, pony-trekking, all are on hand.

Please write or phone James, Lachlan or Fiona Macleod to book or for colour brochure, touring guides, sample menus and any other information.

● **SPRING & AUTUMN BREAKS AVAILABLE.** ●

3 DAYS DB&B £149.50 per person 7 DAYS £315 per person

STB
HIGHLY
COMMENDED

RECOMMENDED BY LEADING GUIDES INCLUDING
EGON RONAY (H&R) SIGNPOST,
ASHLEY COURTENAY

'TASTE OF SCOTLAND'

EXPERIENCE
THE LODGE ON THE LOCH

Firstly, acclimatize yourself to the panoramic mountain and loch-side setting; then relax into old world standards of comfort and service. Enjoy the gentle elegance of this Highland home, with its many special touches of distinction: award-winning lounges, log fires and beautiful designer bedrooms (each, of course, has everything including telephone, trouser press, hairdryer, tea/coffee facilities and colour television).

Delight over the renowned Highland Table. The team of Scottish Chefs select fine venison, steak, salmon and local seafoods. Naturally, there is also vegetarian fayre, wholefoods and home baking. The intimate Crofters' Bar offers a selection of real ales and very many malt whiskies.

From this idyllic centre you will discover the area of enchantment between Ben Nevis and Glencoe. Enjoy complimentary membership of the Swimming Pool and Leisure Club at our sister hotel nearby. Venture onwards for days of varied exploration in the romantic Western Highlands—leading to a world of forest trails, waterfalls and adventure. And then, at the end of each day, a welcome return to the warmth and tranquillity of this family run hotel.

Please write or telephone Norman or Jessie, Laurence or Morag Young for bookings, colour brochure and touring guide.

THE LODGE ON THE LOCH

'Creag Dhu", Onich, nr FORT WILLIAM, Inverness-shire PH33 6RY
Telephone: (08553) 237 or 238.   Fax: (08553) 463
Recommended by all Leading Guides

A   *RAC* ★★★ *AA*   *STB* 🏵🏵🏵🏵 *HIGHLY COMMENDED*   Nearby

VAT is shown at 17.5%: changes in this rate may affect prices. Prices shown are for guidance only. Please send SAE with each enquiry

	Map 1						
ONICH **Inverness-shire** Allt-Nan-Ros Hotel Onich Inverness-shire PH33 6RY Tel:(Onich) 08553 210/250/253 Fax:08553 462	F1	**HIGHLY COMMENDED** 👑👑👑 👑	3 Single 7 Twin 10 Double 1 Family	21 En Suite fac	B&B per person £37.50-£47.50 Single £37.50-£47.50 Double	Open Jan-Nov Dinner 1900-2030 B&B + Eve.Meal £55.00-£65.00	

With magnificent views over Loch Linnhe, this family run hotel offers comfortable West coast hospitality. Entries in a number of guides.

Cuilcheanna House Hotel Onich Inverness-shire PH33 6SD Tel:(Onich) 08553 226			3 Twin 3 Double 2 Family	8 En Suite fac	B&B per person £22.00-£24.00 Double	Open Apr-Oct Dinner 1900-2030 B&B + Eve.Meal £30.00-£35.00	

Loch Leven Hotel Onich, Fort William Inverness-shire PH33 6SA Tel:(Onich) 08553 236/459		**APPROVED** 👑👑👑	2 Single 2 Twin 5 Double 1 Family	10 En Suite fac	B&B per person £22.00-£32.00 Single £22.00-£32.00 Double	Open Jan-Dec Dinner 1800-2100 B&B + Eve.Meal £40.00-£50.00	

Friendly, modernised 17C coaching inn. Ideal for families. Home cooking using fresh local produce in traditional, continental and vegetarian dishes.

The Lodge On The Loch Hotel Creag Dhu Onich Inverness-shire PH33 6RY Tel:(Onich) 08553 237/238 Fax:08553 463		**HIGHLY COMMENDED** 👑👑👑 👑	3 Single 6 Twin 9 Double 2 Family	18 En Suite fac 2 Pub.Bath/Show	B&B per person £30.50-£56.00 Double	Open Feb-Nov, Xmas/New Year Dinner 1900-2200 B&B + Eve.Meal £50.00-£75.50	

Family run, with peaceful and relaxing atmosphere. Panoramic views of Loch and mountains.

Nether Lochaber Hotel Corran Onich Inverness-shire PH33 6SE Tel:(Onich) 08553 235			1 Single 1 Twin 1 Double 1 Family	2 En Suite fac 2 Pub.Bath/Show	B&B per person £18.00-£25.00 Single £18.00-£25.00 Double	Open Jan-Dec Dinner 1915-2100 B&B + Eve.Meal £28.00-£39.50	

SCOTTISH TOURIST BOARD
QUALITY COMMENDATIONS ARE:

Deluxe – *An EXCELLENT quality standard*
Highly Commended – *A VERY GOOD quality standard*
Commended – *A GOOD quality standard*
Approved – *An ADEQUATE quality standard*

ONICH continued	Map 1 F1

THE ONICH HOTEL

ONICH, Nr FORT WILLIAM
INVERNESS-SHIRE PH33 6RY
Tel: (08553) 214/266 FAX: (08553) 484

With well tended gardens extending to the lochside, this hotel occupies one of the finest situations in the Highlands. All public rooms face South and the views across Loch Linnhe to the mountains of Glencoe and Morvern are breathtaking. Recent extensive refurbishment has resulted in a high standard of comfort in both public rooms and bedrooms. The hotel is renowned for its freshly prepared restaurant cuisine with local delicacies much in evidence. The Deerstalker Bar remains open throughout the day for the service of meals and snacks and a wide choice of malt whiskies, and draught beers are always available. Surely the ideal base for touring, walking or just relaxing in the Western Highlands.

Onich Hotel Onich, nr Fort William Inverness-shire PH33 6RY Tel:(Onich) 08553 214/266 Fax:08553 484	COMMENDED 🏵 🏵 🏵 🏵	5 Single 6 Twin 9 Double 7 Family	27 En Suite fac	B&B per person £28.50-£43.50 Single £23.50-£43.50 Double	Open Jan-Dec Dinner 1900-2100 B&B + Eve.Meal £38.50-£60.00	

Personally run hotel with gardens extending to lochside. Superb all-season views across Loch Linnhe to mountains. Interesting menu; local produce.

CAMUS HOUSE LOCHSIDE LODGE

Onich, by Fort William, Inverness-shire PH33 6RY
Tel: (08553) 200

In extensive lochside gardens, midway between Ben Nevis and Glencoe. Ideal base for touring, walking, climbing and skiing. Open from January to November. Most rooms are en-suite with central heating and teasmaids. We provide excellent cooking, friendly service and licensed. DB&B £32-£40.50. Weekly £203-£266.50. Brochure. *Commended* 🏵 🏵

Camus House Lochside Lodge Onich Inverness-shire PH33 6RY Tel:(Onich) 08553 200	COMMENDED 🏵 🏵	1 Single 2 Twin 3 Double 3 Family	7 En Suite fac 1 Pub.Bath/Show	B&B per person £17.50-£28.00 Single £17.50-£28.00 Double	Open Jan-Nov Dinner to 1915 B&B + Eve.Meal £32.00-£42.50	

Large well appointed house, comfortably furnished, superb views of the sea loch and hills. Fort William 10 miles (16kms), Glen Coe 5 miles (8kms).

Glenmorven House Onich Inverness-shire PH33 6RY Tel:(Onich) 08553 247		1 Single 1 Twin 2 Double 1 Family	5 En Suite fac	B&B per person	Open May-Oct Dinner from 1900 B&B + Eve.Meal from £37.85	

ONICH continued Glendevin Inchree Onich Inverness-shire PH33 6SE Tel:(Onich) 08553 330	Map 1 F1	APPROVED 🛆 🛆	1 Twin 2 Double	1 En Suite fac 2 Pub.Bath/Show	B&B per person from £14.50 Single from £13.00 Double B&B + Eve.Meal from £21.50	Open Jan-Dec Dinner 1800-2000

Situated off main road. Convenient for Glencoe and Fort William. Ideal base for touring and activity holidays.

Tigh-an-Righ House Onich Inverness-shire PH33 6SE Tel:(Onich) 08553 255		COMMENDED 🛆 🛆	1 Single 2 Double 3 Family	2 En Suite fac 2 Pub.Bath/Show	B&B per person £12.00-£15.00 Single B&B + Eve.Meal £24.00-£25.50	Open Jan-Dec Dinner 1845-2050

Personally run guest house on the main A82 tourist route and convenient for the Corran Ferry. Emphasis on home cooking using fresh produce.

OVERSCAIG, by Lairg **Sutherland** Overscaig Hotel Overscaig,by Lairg Sutherland IV27 4NY Tel:(Merkland) 054983 203	Map 3 H5	COMMENDED 🛆 🛆 🛆	2 Single 3 Twin 2 Double 2 Family	8 En Suite fac 1 Priv.NOT ensuite	B&B per person £26.00-£35.00 Single £26.00-£35.00 Double B&B + Eve.Meal £34.00-£52.00	Open Jan-Dec Dinner 1900-2100

Birdwatchers, fishers, walkers, tourers well catered for in refurbished hotel on shores of Loch Shin. West Coast 25 miles (40 kms).

PAISLEY **Renfrewshire** Brabloch Hotel 62 Renfrew Road Paisley Renfrewshire PA3 4RB Tel:041 889 5577 Fax:041 889 5628	Map 1 H5	COMMENDED 🛆 🛆 🛆	2 Single 21 Twin 4 Double 3 Family	30 En Suite fac	B&B per person £48.00-£52.00 Single £31.00-£36.00 Double B&B + Eve.Meal £62.50-£66.50	Open Jan-Dec Dinner 1730-2200

Privately owned hotel in its own grounds close to town centre and 2 miles (3 kms) from Glasgow Airport. Conference and function rooms.

Forte Crest Glasgow Airport Glasgow Airport Abbotsinch Renfrewshire PA3 2TR Tel:041 887 1212 Tlx:777733 EXELGW G Fax:041 887 3738		COMMENDED 🛆 🛆 🛆 🛆	7 Single 95 Twin 180 Double 15 Family Suite avail.	297 En Suite fac	B&B per person to £83.95 Single to £46.45 Double	Open Jan-Dec Dinner 1830-2300

Purpose built hotel adjacent to airport; ideal for both traveller and business executive. Conference and business facilities available.

Gleniffer Hotel 9 Glenburn Road Paisley Renfrewshire Tel:041 884 2670		Award Pending	1 Single 3 Double 1 Family	5 En Suite fac	B&B per person £15.00-£20.00 Single £15.00-£20.00 Double	Open Jan-Dec Dinner 1700-2300

Rockfield Hotel 125 Renfrew Road Paisley Renfrewshire PA3 4EA Tel:041 889 6182 Fax:041 889 9526		COMMENDED 🛆 🛆 🛆	9 Single 6 Twin 4 Double 1 Family	20 En Suite fac	B&B per person from £47.50 Single from £31.50 Double	Open Jan-Dec Dinner 1830-2130

On the main road between Glasgow Airport and Paisley. Extensive car parking facilities.

PAISLEY continued
Map 1 H5

Stakis Paisley Watermill Hotel
Lonend
Paisley
Renfrewshire
PA1 1SR
Tel:041 889 3201
Tlx:778704
Fax:041 889 5938

COMMENDED

10 Single	49 En Suite fac	B&B per person
24 Twin		from £63.50 Single
13 Double		to £38.25 Double
2 Family		

Open Jan-Dec
Dinner 1700-2200

Tastefully converted former 17C flow mill situated in the town centre. Live entertainment.

Ardgowan Guest House
92 Renfrew Road
Paisley
Renfrewshire
PA3 4BJ
Tel:041 889 4763

2 Single	2 Pub.Bath/Show	B&B per person
2 Twin		£22.00-£30.00 Single
2 Double		£18.00-£20.00 Double
4 Family		

Open Jan-Dec
Dinner 1830-2030

Dryfesdale Guest House
37 Inchinnan Road
Paisley
Renfrewshire
PA3 2PR
Tel:041 889 7178/887 7751

APPROVED
Listed

1 Single	2 Pub.Bath/Show	B&B per person
3 Twin		£18.00-£20.00 Single
2 Family		£15.00-£17.00 Double

Open Jan-Dec
Dinner 1800-2000

Privately owned guest house 0.5 mile (1km) from Glasgow Airport and M8 access. Close to Paisley and all facilities.

Gleniffer House
Glenpatrick Road
Paisley
Renfrewshire
PA5 9UL
Tel:041 848 5544
Fax:0505 35898

COMMENDED

1 Twin	2 En Suite fac	B&B per person
1 Double	1 Priv.NOT ensuite	£25.00-£30.00 Single
1 Family		£18.00-£25.00 Double

Open Jan-Dec
Dinner 1800-1930
B&B + Eve.Meal
£26.00-£38.00

Quiet countryside setting, 4 miles (7kms) from Glasgow airport, 3 miles (5kms) from Paisley. Ideal touring base. 35 minutes from Loch Lomond.

Greenlaw Guest House
12 Greenlaw Drive
Paisley
Renfrewshire
PA1
Tel:041 889 5359

3 Single	3 Pub.Bath/Show	B&B per person
1 Twin		£17.00-£18.00 Single
3 Family		£16.00-£17.00 Double

Open Jan-Dec

Myfarrclan Guest House
146 Corsebar Road
Paisley
Renfrewshire
PA2 9NA
Tel:041 884 8285

DELUXE

1 Double	1 En Suite fac	B&B per person
1 Family	1 Priv.NOT ensuite	from £35.00 Single
		£22.50-£25.00 Double

Open Jan-Dec

Detached bungalow in residential area, convenient for Glasgow Airport. Non smoking house.

BY PAISLEY
Renfrewshire
Map 1 H5

Ashburn Guest House
Milliken Park Road
Kilbarchan,by Paisley
Renfrewshire
PA10 2DB
Tel:(Kilbarchan) 05057
5477/0505 705477
Fax:0505 705477

APPROVED

1 Single	2 En Suite fac	B&B per person
3 Twin	2 Pub.Bath/Show	£22.00-£31.00 Single
2 Family		£19.00-£26.50 Double

Open Jan-Dec
Dinner 1800-2000
B&B + Eve.Meal
£29.00-£41.00

19C country house in an acre of garden, 5 minutes drive to Glasgow Airport.

PAPA WESTRAY **Orkney**	Map 5 B9					
Beltane House Hotel Papa Westray Orkney KW17 2BU Tel:(Papa Westray) 08574 267		COMMENDED 👑👑	3 Twin 1 Double	4 En Suite fac	B&B per person from £25.00 Single from £22.00 Double	Open Jan-Dec Dinner 1800-1900 B&B + Eve.Meal £32.00-£35.00

Recently converted terraced cottages, modern and comfortable, with homecooking and community shop. Can collect from boat or plane.

PEEBLES	Map 2 C6					
Green Tree Hotel 41 Eastgate Peebles EH45 8AD Tel:(Peebles) 0721 720582 Fax:0721 720582		APPROVED 👑👑	3 Single 2 Twin 1 Double 2 Family	8 En Suite fac 1 Pub.Bath/Show	B&B per person £24.50-£26.50 Single £24.50-£26.50 Double	Open Jan-Dec Dinner 1900-2100 B&B + Eve.Meal £36.75-£38.75

Centrally situated, family run hotel in the centre of the town. Open fire in the lounge bar. Attractive rear garden and limited private car parking.

Kingsmuir Hotel

SPRINGHILL ROAD, PEEBLES, BORDERS EH45 9EP
Telephone: (0721) 720151

KINGSMUIR is a charming 1850's style country mansion in leafy grounds. Resident proprietors specialise in traditional Scottish cooking - Taste of Scotland Member. All bedrooms are tastefully decorated with private bathrooms, TV and telephone. Peebles is a Royal and Ancient Burgh, famous for Tweeds and Woollens, golf, fishing and mountain biking.
👑👑👑 **Commended.**

Kingsmuir Hotel Springhill Road Peebles EH45 9EP Tel:(Peebles) 0721 720151 Fax:0721 721795	COMMENDED 👑👑👑	2 Single 4 Twin 3 Double 1 Family	10 En Suite fac	B&B per person £31.00-£40.00 Single £27.00-£33.00 Double	Open Jan-Dec Dinner 1900-2130 B&B + Eve.Meal £36.00-£52.00

A small family run hotel situated in a quiet area of Peebles, overlooking parkland running down to the River Tweed.

The Park Hotel Innerleithen Road Peebles EH45 8BA Tel:(Peebles) 0721 20451/720451 Fax:0721 723510	COMMENDED 👑👑👑 👑	5 Single 11 Twin 8 Double	24 En Suite fac	B&B per person £48.40-£55.00 Single £33.95-£57.65 Double	Open Jan-Dec Dinner 1900-2130 B&B + Eve.Meal £43.95-£67.65

Quiet and comfortable, with extensive gardens and fine hill views. Ideal touring centre, and only 22 miles (35kms) from Edinburgh.

Welcome Hosts provide a warm welcome, good service and information about their area. Look out for the people wearing the Welcome Host badge.

PEEBLES continued	Map 2 C6

PEEBLES HOTEL HYDRO

INNERLEITHEN ROAD, PEEBLES EH45 8LX
Telephone: Peebles (0721) 720602 Fax: (0721) 722999

The Hydro, and its sister hotel, The Park, offer the perfect base for a Borders holiday. Excellent entertainment and leisure facilities for all ages, together with good food and traditional Scottish hospitality will ensure a perfect stay.

Peebles Hotel Hydro
Innerleithen Road
Peebles
EH45 8LX
Tel:(Peebles) 0721 720602
Fax:0721 722999

COMMENDED
♛ ♛ ♛
♛

29 Single   137 En Suite fac
62 Twin
19 Double
27 Family

B&B per person
£51.50-£59.00 Single
£37.00-£63.75 Double

Open Jan-Dec
Dinner 1930-2100
B&B + Eve.Meal
£50.50-£77.00

Set in own quiet, extensive grounds. Excellent entertainment and leisure facilities for all ages. "Taste of Scotland".

The Tontine
High Street
Peebles
EH45 8AJ
Tel:(Peebles) 0721 720892
Fax:0721 729732

APPROVED
♛ ♛ ♛

6 Single   37 En Suite fac
15 Twin
16 Double

B&B per person
£65.00-£74.00 Single
£35.00-£52.50 Double

Open Jan-Dec
Dinner 1900-2100
B&B + Eve.Meal
£49.00-£54.00

200 year old Coaching Inn, with Georgian Adam Dining room. Cosy bar, open fires, part of Forte Heritage division.

Venlaw Castle Hotel
Edinburgh Road
Peebles
EH45 8QG
Tel:(Peebles) 0721 720384

COMMENDED
♛ ♛ ♛

4 Twin   10 En Suite fac
5 Double   2 Pub.Bath/Show
4 Family

B&B per person
£25.00-£35.00 Single
£23.00-£33.00 Double

Open Apr-Oct
Dinner 1900-2000
B&B + Eve.Meal
£35.00-£50.00

Personally run, built in Scottish baronial style, with 6 acres of wooded ground overlooking the town. Vegetarian meals a speciality.

BY PEEBLES	Map 2 C6

Barony Castle Hotel
Eddleston
Peeblesshire
EH45
Tel:(Eddleston) 0721 730395
Fax:0721 730275

COMMENDED
♛ ♛ ♛
♛

1 Single   29 En Suite fac
9 Twin
12 Double
7 Family
Suites avail.

B&B per person
from £59.00 Single
from £46.00 Double

Open Jan-Dec
Dinner 1900-2130

Country house in the Scottish Baronial style, set in 65 acres 4 miles N of Peebles. Leisure facilities including pool, jacuzzi, sauna and snooker.

PENNYGHAEL Isle of Mull, Argyll	Map 1 C2

Kinloch Hotel
Pennyghael
Isle of Mull, Argyll
PA70 6HB
Tel:(Pennyghael) 06814 204
Fax:06814 204

1 Single   1 En Suite fac
2 Twin   1 Pub.Bath/Show
1 Double

B&B per person
£19.00-£29.00 Single
£23.00-£29.00 Double

Open Apr-Oct
Dinner 1900-2100
B&B + Eve.Meal
£30.00-£40.00

PENNYGHAEL continued	Map 1 C2		

PENNYGHAEL HOTEL
ISLE OF MULL, ARGYLL PA70 6HB
Tel: 068 14 288

Superbly situated on the shores of Loch Scridain with views of Ben More to Iona. Originally a 17th Century Farmhouse, this family run Hotel provides a warm welcoming atmosphere for a relaxing holiday in beautiful surroundings. Specialities: Home cooking of locally available produce; wild salmon; Dublin Bay prawns; venison.

Pennyghael Hotel Pennyghael Isle of Mull, Argyll PA70 6HB Tel:(Pennyghael) 06814 205/288	COMMENDED ♛ ♛ ♛	1 Twin 5 Double	6 En Suite fac	B&B per person £37.50-£49.50 Single £27.50-£39.50 Double B&B + Eve.Meal £37.50-£55.00	Open Mar-Oct, Xmas/New Year Dinner 1830-2030	

Informal family run hotel on the shores of Loch Scridain. Good food with emphasis on fresh local produce and seafood.

PERTH	Map 2 C2					
County Hotel 26 County Place Perth PH2 8EE Tel:(Perth) 0738 23355 Fax:0738 28969	APPROVED ♛ ♛ ♛	5 Single 11 Twin 6 Double 2 Family	24 En Suite fac	B&B per person £19.00-£33.00 Single £19.00-£27.00 Double B&B + Eve.Meal £29.00-£40.00	Open Jan-Dec Dinner 1700-2100	

Refurbished privately owned hotel conveniently situated within walking distance of city centre. Close to both bus and railway stations.

Grampian Hotel 37-41 York Place Perth PH2 8EH Tel:(Perth) 0738 21057 Fax:0738 21057		5 Twin 4 Double 5 Family	8 En Suite fac 1 Pub.Bath/Show	B&B per person £21.00-£35.00 Single £17.00-£23.00 Double B&B + Eve.Meal £24.00-£45.00	Open Jan-Dec Dinner 1700-2100
Isle of Skye Hotel Queensbridge, 18 Dundee Road Perth PH2 7AB Tel:(Perth) 0738 24471 Fax:0738 22124		6 Single 7 Twin 8 Double 30 Family Suites avail.	51 En Suite fac	B&B per person £29.95-£56.00 Single £24.92-£33.00 Double	Open Jan-Dec Dinner 1800-2200
Letham Farmhouse Hotel Old Huntingtower Road, Crieff Road Perth PH1 2SG Tel:(Perth) 0738 37188 Fax:0738 37188	Award Pending	1 Single 6 Twin 4 Double 1 Family	12 En Suite fac	B&B per person £36.00-£40.00 Single £28.50-£32.50 Double	Open Jan-Dec Dinner 1600-2130

PERTH continued	Map 2 C2					
Lovat Hotel Glasgow Road Perth PH2 0LT Tel:(Perth) 0738 36555 Tlx:76531 Fax:0738 43123	COMMENDED	4 Single 16 Twin 9 Double 1 Family	30 En Suite fac 1 Pub.Bath/Show	B&B per person £30.00-£50.00 Single £25.00-£36.00 Double	Open Jan-Dec Dinner 1700-2200 B&B + Eve.Meal £35.00-£50.00	
		Modern, privately owned. Warm, friendly atmosphere with traditional Scottish cooking and extensive bar menu. Conference facilities available.				
Parklands St Leonards Bank Perth PH2 8ER Tel:(Perth) 0738 22451 Fax:0738 22046	HIGHLY COMMENDED	2 Single 7 Twin 5 Double	14 En Suite fac	B&B per person £65.00-£100.00 Single £40.00-£60.00 Double	Open Jan-Dec Dinner 1900-2100 B&B + Eve.Meal £90.00-£125.00	
		Completely refurbished Georgian town house overlooking South Inch Park. Restaurant features the best of Scotland's larder imaginatively prepared.				
Queens Hotel Leonard Street Perth PH2 8HB Tel:(Perth) 0738 25471 Fax:0738 38496	COMMENDED	10 Single 19 Twin 16 Double 6 Family	50 En Suite fac 1 Limited ensuite	B&B per person £49.50-£59.50 Single £32.00-£37.50 Double	Open Jan-Dec Dinner 1900-2130 B&B + Eve.Meal £60.00-£70.00	
		Modernised in city centre with extensive function, conference and banqueting facilities. Leisure complex with gym, swimming pool and sauna.				
The Royal George Tay Street Perth PH1 5LD Tel:(Perth) 0738 24455 Fax:0738 30345	APPROVED	14 Single 14 Twin 14 Double	42 En Suite fac	B&B per person £70.00-£75.00 Single £40.00-£45.00 Double	Open Jan-Dec Dinner 1900-2130	
		Dating from 18C, located in centre of historic Perth overlooking River Tay. Meeting facilities. Part of Forte Heritage.				
Salutation Hotel 34 South Street Perth PH2 8PH Tel:(Perth) 0738 30066 Fax:0738 33598	APPROVED	14 Single 11 Twin 44 Double	89 En Suite fac	B&B per person £35.00-£55.00 Single £20.00-£37.00 Double	Open Jan-Dec Dinner 1900-2130	
		Town centre hotel with refurbished bedrooms conveniently situated for shops and theatre. Leisure centre within 0.5 miles (1km).				

PERTH continued	Map 2 C2				

STAKIS CITY MILLS HOTEL

WEST MILL STREET, PERTH PH1 5QP   Tel: 0738 28281
This charming hotel in centre of Perth is a conversion of an ancient mill dating back to the 15th century. Sample 'Taste of Scotland' dishes from the Laird's table or choose from the varied menu in the popular steakhouse. With 76 luxury bedrooms, this makes the ideal base for a Highland holiday.
Short Breaks available from £25 B&B pp/pn (twin accom).

Stakis Perth City Mills Hotel West Mill Street Perth PH1 5QP Tel:(Perth) 0738 28281 Fax:0738 43423	**COMMENDED** 👑 👑 👑 👑	13 Single 48 Twin 13 Double 2 Family	76 En Suite fac	B&B per person £43.00-£63.00 Single £23.00-£36.00 Double	Open Jan-Dec Dinner 1700-2200 B&B + Eve.Meal £28.00-£41.00
		Attractive stone building with millrace feature, situated in the town centre. Choice of restaurants. Excellent conference facilities available.			
Station Hotel Leonard Street Perth PH2 8HE Tel:(Perth) 0738 24141	**APPROVED** 👑 👑 👑 👑	22 Single 26 Twin 16 Double 6 Family Suites avail.	49 En Suite fac 20 Limited ensuite 1 Priv.NOT ensuite	B&B per person £25.00-£57.75 Single £25.00-£68.75 Double	Open Jan-Dec Dinner 1900-2130 B&B + Eve.Meal £37.50-£64.50
		Large, traditional hotel, next to the railway station, only a short distance from town centre. Extensive conference facilities available.			
Sunbank House Hotel 50 Dundee Road Perth PH2 7BA Tel:(Perth) 0738 24882 Fax:0738 24882	**DELUXE** 👑 👑 👑	2 Twin 5 Double 2 Family	9 En Suite fac	B&B per person £38.00-£42.00 Single £26.00-£28.00 Double	Open Jan-Dec Dinner 1830-2000 B&B + Eve.Meal £39.95-£41.95
		Elegant, stone built, early Victorian house with large garden. Access off A85 with superb views over River Tay and city.			
Two-o-Eight Hotel 208 Crieff Road Perth PH1 2PE Tel:(Perth) 0738 28936	**APPROVED** 👑 👑	6 Twin 2 Family	6 En Suite fac 2 Pub.Bath/Show	B&B per person £18.00-£24.00 Single £16.00-£21.00 Double	Open Jan-Dec Dinner 1800-2000 B&B + Eve.Meal £20.00-£32.00
		Modern detached public house with bedrooms above. On a bus route to city centre. Ample car parking. Owner a golf enthusiast : packages arranged.			
White Horse Inn 5 North William Street Perth PH1 5PT Tel:(Perth) 0738 28479		2 Single 9 Twin 2 Double 3 Family	9 En Suite fac 2 Pub.Bath/Show	B&B per person £20.00-£25.00 Single £25.00-£45.00 Double	Open Jan-Dec Dinner 1800-2100 B&B + Eve.Meal £35.00-£40.00

PERTH

Adam Guest House
6 Pitcullen Crescent
Perth
PH2 7HT
Tel:(Perth) 0738 27179

COMMENDED
♛ ♛

1 Single
1 Twin
2 Double
1 Family

2 En Suite fac
1 Priv.NOT ensuite
1 Pub.Bath/Show

B&B per person
£15.00-£17.50 Single
£15.00-£17.50 Double

Open Jan-Dec
Dinner 1830-1930
B&B + Eve.Meal
£23.00-£25.50

Small and friendly guest house beside A94, with private off road parking. Good home cooking.

Albert Villa Guest House
63 Dunkeld Road
Perth
PH1 5RP
Tel:(Perth) 0738 22730

COMMENDED
♛ ♛

3 Single
2 Twin
2 Double
2 Family

6 En Suite fac
1 Pub.Bath/Show

B&B per person
£15.00-£20.00 Single
£15.00-£16.00 Double

Open Jan-Dec

Family guest house with ample car parking, close to sports centre and swimming pool. Ground floor bedrooms each have their own entrance.

Almond Villa Guest House
51 Dunkeld Road
Perth
PH1 5RP
Tel:(Perth) 0738 29356

COMMENDED
♛ ♛

1 Single
1 Twin
1 Double
2 Family

1 En Suite fac
2 Pub.Bath/Show

B&B per person
£15.00-£18.00 Single
£15.00-£18.00 Double

Open Jan-Dec
Dinner from 1830
B&B + Eve.Meal
£22.00-£27.50

Semi detached Victorian villa, close to town centre, Bells Sports Centre, the North Inch and River Tay.

Aran Guest House
1 Pitcullen Crescent
Perth
PH2 7HT
Tel:(Perth) 0738 34216

1 Single
1 Double
2 Family

1 En Suite fac
2 Pub.Bath/Show

B&B per person
£13.00-£16.00 Single
£13.00-£17.00 Double

Open Jan-Dec
Dinner 1800-1900
B&B + Eve.Meal
£22.00-£24.00

Arisaig Guest House
4 Pitcullen Crescent
Perth
PH2 7HT
Tel:(Perth) 0738 28240

COMMENDED
♛ ♛

1 Single
1 Twin
1 Double
2 Family

4 En Suite fac
1 Priv.NOT ensuite

B&B per person
from £16.00 Single
from £16.00 Double

Open Jan-Dec

Comfortable family run guest house, with off street parking. Close to city's many facilities; local touring base. Ground floor bedroom.

Auld Manse Guest House
Pitcullen Crescent
Perth
PH2 7HT
Tel:(Perth) 0738 29187

COMMENDED
♛

2 Single
1 Twin
1 Double

1 En Suite fac
1 Pub.Bath/Show

B&B per person
£13.00-£15.00 Single
£13.00-£16.00 Double

Open Jan-Dec
Dinner from 1830
B&B + Eve.Meal
£20.00-£23.00

Former church manse, now family run guest house. On main A94, 10 minutes walk to city centre, 1 mile (2kms) from Scone Palace. Private parking.

Beechgrove Guest House
Dundee Road
Perth
PH2 7AD
Tel:(Perth) 0738 36147

HIGHLY COMMENDED
♛ ♛

1 Single
2 Twin
2 Double
1 Family

6 En Suite fac

B&B per person
from £25.00 Single
£20.00-£27.50 Double

Open Jan-Dec

Listed building and former manse set in extensive grounds. Peaceful and quiet, yet only a few minutes walk from the city centre. 1 annexe room.

PERTH continued	Map 2 C2						
Clunie Guest House 12 Pitcullen Crescent Perth PH2 7HT Tel:(Perth) 0738 23625	COMMENDED ♕ ♕ ♕	1 Single 3 Twin 2 Double 1 Family	7 En Suite fac	B&B per person from £17.00 Single from £17.00 Double	Open Jan-Dec Dinner from 1800 B&B + Eve.Meal from £25.00		
		Personally run in residential part of town. Easy access to town centre and on main bus route.					
The Darroch Guest House 9 Pitcullen Crescent Perth PH2 7HT Tel:(Perth) 0738 36893	COMMENDED ♕ ♕	2 Single 1 Twin 1 Double 2 Family	3 En Suite fac 1 Pub.Bath/Show	B&B per person £14.00-£16.50 Single £14.00-£18.50 Double	Open Jan-Dec Dinner from 1830 B&B + Eve.Meal £22.00-£26.50		
		Semi-detached, Victorian villa, easily found on main A94 tourist route. Double glazed throughout. Extensive breakfast menu. Off street parking.					
Dunallan Guest House 10 Pitcullen Crescent Perth PH2 7HT Tel:(Perth) 0738 22551	COMMENDED ♕ ♕	2 Single 3 Twin 1 Double 1 Family	3 En Suite fac 1 Pub.Bath/Show	B&B per person £16.50-£17.50 Single £16.50-£18.00 Double	Open Jan-Dec Dinner 1800-1900 B&B + Eve.Meal £23.50-£24.50		
		Family run, conveniently located on A94 tourist route, within easy reach of town centre. Most rooms with TV and ensuite bathroom. Private parking.					
The Gables Guest House 24 Dunkeld Road Perth PH1 5RW Tel:(Perth) 0738 24717	COMMENDED ♕	4 Single 1 Twin 3 Family	3 Pub.Bath/Show	B&B per person £15.00-£16.00 Single £14.00-£15.00 Double	Open Jan-Dec Dinner 1700-1830 B&B + Eve.Meal £20.00-£22.00		
		Stone built house on main road 1/2 mile (1km) north of city centre. Close to sports centre, swimming pool and local golf course. Parking.					
Hazeldene Guest House Pitcullen Crescent Perth PH2 7HT Tel:(Perth) 0738 23550	COMMENDED ♕ ♕ ♕	1 Single 1 Twin 2 Double 1 Family	5 En Suite fac	B&B per person £18.00-£20.00 Single £14.00-£18.00 Double	Open Jan-Dec		
		Family run guest house, on main tourist route to north east but near to city centre. Private car parking available.					
Iona Guest House 2 Pitcullen Crescent Perth PH2 7HT Tel:(Perth) 0738 27261	COMMENDED ♕ ♕	2 Single 1 Twin 1 Double 1 Family	2 En Suite fac 2 Pub.Bath/Show	B&B per person £15.00-£17.00 Single £15.00-£17.00 Double	Open Jan-Dec Dinner 1800-1930 B&B + Eve.Meal £23.00-£25.00		
		In residential area, 10 minutes from the town centre with private parking. Over 30 golf courses within 30 miles (48kms) radius.					
Kinnaird Guest House 5 Marshall Place Perth PH2 8AH Tel:(Perth) 0738 28021 Fax:0738 444056	COMMENDED ♕ ♕ ♕	1 Single 4 Twin 2 Double	5 En Suite fac 2 Pub.Bath/Show	B&B per person from £18.00 Single from £18.00 Double	Open Jan-Dec Dinner from 1800 B&B + Eve.Meal from £27.00		
		Georgian house, centrally situated overlooking park. Private parking. Short walk to town centre and convenient for railway and bus stations.					

PERTH continued

Map 2 C2

Kinnoull Guest House
5 Pitcullen Crescent
Perth
PH2 7HT
Tel:(Perth) 0738 34165

COMMENDED
♛ ♛ ♛

1 Twin
2 Double
1 Family

4 En Suite fac

B&B per person
£15.00-£24.00 Single
£14.00-£18.00 Double

Open Jan-Dec
Dinner 1800-1900

Family run guest house on main tourist route north (A94), within easy reach of city centre. Private facilities for all bedrooms.

Park Lane Guest House
17 Marshall Place
Perth
PH2 8AG
Tel:(Perth) 0738 37218
Fax:0738 43519

HIGHLY COMMENDED
♛ ♛

1 Single
2 Twin
2 Double
1 Family

6 En Suite fac

B&B per person
£16.50-£20.00 Single
£16.50-£20.00 Double

Open Jan-Dec

Georgian house overlooking Perth South Inch but near to city centre. All ensuite rooms, private car park. Walking distance to golf courses.

Pitcullen Guest House
17 Pitcullen Crescent
Perth
PH2 7HT
Tel:(Perth) 0738
26506/28265

COMMENDED
♛ ♛

1 Single
3 Twin
1 Double
1 Family

3 En Suite fac
2 Pub.Bath/Show

B&B per person
from £17.00 Single
from £17.00 Double

Open Jan-Dec
Dinner from 1800

Personally run and conveniently situated on A94 tourist route. Only 5 minutes from City Centre. Private parking.

Rowanbank Guest House
3 Pitcullen Crescent
Perth
PH2 7HT
Tel:(Perth) 0738 21421

HIGHLY COMMENDED
♛ ♛

1 Twin
1 Double
2 Family

2 En Suite fac
1 Limited ensuite
1 Pub.Bath/Show

B&B per person
£16.00-£25.00 Single
£16.00-£18.00 Double

Open Jan-Dec
Dinner from 1830
B&B + Eve.Meal
£24.00-£26.00

Friendly, family run guest house with off street parking in an ideal touring area. One ensuite room on ground floor.

Tigh Mhorag Guest House
69 Dunkeld Road
Perth
PH1 5RP
Tel:(Perth) 0738 22902

Award Pending

2 Single
2 Twin
2 Double

3 En Suite fac
1 Pub.Bath/Show

B&B per person
£14.00-£15.00 Single
£28.00-£30.00 Double

Open Jan-Dec
Dinner from 1800
B&B + Eve.Meal
£20.00

BY PERTH

Map 2 C2

The Anglers' Rest
Main Street
Guildtown, Perth
Perthshire
PH2 6BS
Tel:(Balbeggie) 0821 640329

Award Pending

4 Single
1 Twin
1 Double

3 En Suite fac
3 Limited ensuite
1 Pub.Bath/Show

B&B per person
£16.50-£18.00 Single
£16.50-£18.00 Double

Open Jan-Dec
Dinner 1730-2130

Ballathie House Hotel
Kinclaven, by Stanley
Perthshire
PH1 4QN
Tel:(Meikleour) 0250 883268
Fax:0250 883396

DELUXE
♛ ♛ ♛
♛

16 Single
12 Twin
8 Double
2 Family
Suite avail.

38 En Suite fac

B&B per person
£60.00-£95.00 Single
£50.00-£85.00 Double

Open Jan-Dec
Dinner 1900-2030
B&B + Eve.Meal
£75.00-£105.00

Elegantly refurbished Victorian country house within its own estate and overlooking the River Tay. Interesting cuisine using finest ingredients.

BY PERTH continued	Map 2 C2						
Glencarse Hotel Glencarse, by Perth Perthshire PH2 7LX Tel:(Glencarse) 073886 206	APPROVED Listed	3 Single 3 Twin 3 Double 1 Family	5 En Suite fac 2 Pub.Bath/Show	B&B per person £25.00-£35.00 Single £20.00-£25.00 Double	Open Jan-Dec Dinner 1830-2030	

18c coaching Inn with annexe accomodation furnished to a high standard. Traditional bar meals with emphasis on home cooking.

HUNTINGTOWER HOTEL PERTH

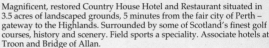

Crieff Road, Perth PH1 3JT
Tel: 0738-83771   Fax: 0738-83777

Magnificent, restored Country House Hotel and Restaurant situated in 3.5 acres of landscaped grounds, 5 minutes from the fair city of Perth – gateway to the Highlands. Surrounded by some of Scotland's finest golf courses, history and scenery. Field sports a speciality. Associate hotels at Troon and Bridge of Allan.

Please telephone 0738-83771 for a free brochure.

| Huntingtower Hotel Crieff Road Perth PH1 3JT Tel:(Perth) 0738 83771 Fax:0738 83777 | COMMENDED | 3 Single 5 Twin 6 Double 8 Family Suite avail. | 20 En Suite fac 2 Limited ensuite 1 Pub.Bath/Show | B&B per person £52.00-£62.00 Single £36.00-£40.00 Double | Open Jan-Dec Dinner 1900-2200 B&B + Eve.Meal £66.00-£80.00 |

Country house hotel with extensive conference facilities and a fine reputation for Scottish and continental cuisine. Luxury lodge suites available.

| Newton House Hotel Glencarse, nr Perth Perthshire PH2 7LX Tel:(Glencarse) 073886 250 Fax:073886 717 | HIGHLY COMMENDED | 4 Single 2 Twin 2 Double 2 Family | 10 En Suite fac | B&B per person £46.00-£50.00 Single £34.00-£37.50 Double | Open Jan-Dec Dinner 1700-2100 B&B + Eve.Meal £45.00-£58.50 |

19C former Dower House with many original features. Taste of Scotland chef uses fresh local produce. Fishing, shooting and golf. An ideal retreat.

| Waterybutts Lodge Grange Errol Perthshire PH2 7SZ Tel:(Errol) 0821 642894 Fax:0821 642523 | HIGHLY COMMENDED | 3 Twin 4 Double | 7 En Suite fac | B&B per person £30.00-£33.00 Single £25.00-£27.50 Double | Open Jan-Dec Dinner 1900-2200 B&B + Eve.Meal £40.00-£44.00 |

Beautiful Georgian Lodge with fine grounds, shrubs and trees and a unique herb garden. Set in the gentle climatic region of the Carse of Gowrie.

| Countrywide Holidays Association Kinfauns Castle Perth PH2 7JZ Tel:(Perth) 0738 20777 Fax:0738 20777 | | 6 Single 17 Twin 9 Family | 12 Pub.Bath/Show | B&B per person £15.00-£20.00 Single £15.00-£20.00 Double | Open Jan-Dec Dinner from 1900 B&B + Eve.Meal £23.00-£28.00 |

PETERHEAD
Aberdeenshire

Map 4
H8

Albert Hotel Queen Street Peterhead Aberdeenshire AB42 6TU Tel:(Peterhead) 0779 72391	**COMMENDED** 👑 👑 👑	4 Twin 6 En Suite fac 4 Double 2 Pub.Bath/Show 1 Family

4 Twin   6 En Suite fac   B&B per person   Open Jan-Dec
4 Double   2 Pub.Bath/Show   £18.50-£38.00 Single   Dinner 1730-2000
1 Family   £14.50-£45.00 Double   B&B + Eve.Meal
                                                    £20.00-£45.00

Warm and friendly welcome in family run hotel. Antique furnishings,
but modern facilities.

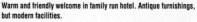

WATERSIDE INN
FRASERBURGH ROAD, PETERHEAD
ABERDEENSHIRE AB42 7BN   Telephone: 0779 71121
A nationwide reputation for cuisine and friendliness awaits you.
An over-indulgence of dishes prepared by our award-winning team
of chefs can be remedied in our Leisure Club and Swimming Pool.
Explore the Coastal, Castle and Whisky Trails, or simply play golf.
DB&B £43.00 per night (sharing)   *Children accommodated free.*

Waterside Inn Fraserburgh Road Peterhead Aberdeenshire AB42 7BN Tel:(Peterhead) 0779 71121 Tlx:739413 Fax:0779 70670	**COMMENDED** 👑 👑 👑 👑 👑	26 Twin 110 En Suite fac B&B per person Open Jan-Dec

26 Twin   110 En Suite fac   B&B per person   Open Jan-Dec
71 Double   £50.80-£82.00 Single   Dinner 1800-2200
13 Family   £30.15-£44.75 Double   B&B + Eve.Meal
                                                    from £38.00

Modern 110 bedroomed hotel with leisure club and swimming pool. All culinary
needs met by award-winning team of chefs. Reputation for hospitality.

Waverley Hotel 10 Merchant Street Peterhead Aberdeenshire AB42 6BU Tel:(Peterhead) 0779 74457	**Award Pending**	5 Twin 10 En Suite fac B&B per person Open Jan-Dec 5 Double £20.00-£25.00 Single Dinner 1700-1945 £16.00-£19.00 Double

Carrick Guest House 16 Merchant Street Peterhead Aberdeenshire AB42 6DU Tel:(Peterhead) 0779 70610 Fax:0779 70610	**COMMENDED** 👑 👑	2 Single 7 En Suite fac B&B per person Open Jan-Dec 3 Twin £15.00-£17.50 Single 2 Family £15.00-£17.50 Double

Personally run, terraced house close to town centre, harbour and beach. All
bedrooms double glazed.

Valhalla Guest House 41-43 King Street Peterhead Aberdeenshire AB42 6SL Tel:(Peterhead) 0779 76512	**Listed**	1 Single 2 Pub.Bath/Show B&B per person Open Jan-Dec 5 Twin £11.00 Single Dinner 1700-1900 1 Double B&B + Eve.Meal 1 Family £13.00

PITLOCHRY Perthshire	Map 2 B1

Acarsaid Hotel
8 ATHOLL ROAD . PITLOCHRY . PH16 5BX
Telephone: (0796) 472389

A quality, small, privately owned hotel, within strolling distance of the shops and a pleasant walk from the theatre. Stylish, comfortable lounges, attractive fully equipped bedrooms, all with bathroom, five on the ground floor. If you appreciate excellent food and high standard of service contact Howard or Mary Williams.

Acarsaid Hotel
8 Atholl Road
Pitlochry
Perthshire
PH16 5BX
Tel:(Pitlochry) 0796 472389

HIGHLY COMMENDED
🏅 🏅 🏅

2 Single 18 En Suite fac
8 Twin
7 Double
1 Family

B&B per person
£25.00-£36.00 Single
£25.00-£36.00 Double

Open Mar-Jan
Dinner 1800-2000
B&B + Eve.Meal
£35.00-£48.00

Tastefully converted Victorian villa in own grounds. Traditional cooking with mainly fresh produce.

Adderley Hotel
23 Toberargan Road
Pitlochry
Perthshire
PH16 5HG
Tel:(Pitlochry) 0796 472433

COMMENDED
🏅 🏅 🏅

1 Single 6 En Suite fac
2 Twin   1 Priv.NOT ensuite
3 Double
1 Family

B&B per person
£21.45-£25.50 Single
£21.45-£25.50 Double

Open Jan-Dec
Dinner 1800-1830
B&B + Eve.Meal
£33.00-£38.30

Privately owned hotel with ground floor bedrooms, in quiet residential area, but only a few minutes walk from town centre.

The Atholl Palace
Atholl Road
Pitlochry
Perthshire
PH16 5LY
Tel:(Pitlochry) 0796 472400
Fax:0796 473036

APPROVED
🏅 🏅 🏅

9 Single 84 En Suite fac
35 Twin
31 Double
9 Family

B&B per person
£30.00-£70.00 Single
£30.00-£50.00 Double

Open Jan-Dec
Dinner 1830-2100
B&B + Eve.Meal
£45.00-£60.00

Baronial style building with superb views over Pitlochry and hills beyond. Extensive grounds, log fires, part of Forte Heritage.

Balrobin Hotel
Higher Oakfield
Pitlochry
Perthshire
PH16 5HT
Tel:(Pitlochry) 0796 472901
Fax:0796 474200

HIGHLY COMMENDED
🏅 🏅 🏅

1 Single 15 En Suite fac
4 Twin
9 Double
1 Family

B&B per person
£20.00-£35.00 Single
£20.00-£37.00 Double

Open Mar-Oct, New Year
Dinner 1830-2000
B&B + Eve.Meal
£28.00-£47.00

Privately owned Victorian house in its own grounds in quiet area. Views of Perthshire Hills and Tummel Valley.

Scottish Tourist Board
COMMENDED
Facilities
🏅 🏅 🏅

FOR QUALITY
GO GRADED

PITLOCHRY continued	Map 2 B1

Birchwood Hotel
East Moulin Road, Pitlochry
Tel: (0796) 472477 Fax: (0796) 473951
AA ** RAC **
Ashley Courtenay Recommended
🏶🏶🏶 Highly Commended

Lovely Country House Hotel in 4 acres of gardens and woodlands, convenient for the many amenities of this popular Highland town. Ideal for walking, touring, golfing and fishing. Well known for its excellent cuisine. Varied table d'hote and full à la carte dinners served in our splendidly appointed restaurant. 'Taste of Scotland' Member.
All bedrooms have private facilities, together with colour TV, radio, direct dial telephone courtesy tray and fresh fruit. Operated by the proprietors personally, ensuring high standards of comfort, service and hospitality.
Apply for colour brochure and tariff including ● Short Breaks ● Weekly Terms ● Golfing ● Early and Late Season Bargain Breaks ● Senior Citizens Special Terms ●
OPEN MARCH to NOVEMBER.

Birchwood Hotel 2 East Moulin Road Pitlochry Perthshire PH16 5DW Tel:(Pitlochry) 0796 472477 Fax:0796 473951	HIGHLY COMMENDED 🏶 🏶 🏶	2 Single 6 Twin 5 Double 3 Family	16 En Suite fac 1 Pub.Bath/Show	B&B per person £30.00-£36.00 Single £25.00-£31.00 Double	Open Mar-Nov Dinner 1830-2015 B&B + Eve.Meal £41.00-£48.00	
		Fine Victorian country house in woodland gardens and with fine views. Personally supervised by owners. Some ground floor annexe accommodation.				
Burnside Apartment Hotel 19 West Moulin Road Pitlochry Perthshire PH16 5EA Tel:(Pitlochry) 0796 472203 Fax:0796 473586	COMMENDED 🏶 🏶 🏶 up to HIGHLY COMMENDED 🏶 🏶 🏶 🏶 🏶	13 Apartments	13 En Suite fac	B&B per person from £25.00 Double	Open Jan-Dec Dinner to 1900	
		Modern and comfortable apartments with a self catering and serviced element. Central quiet location; Taste of Scotland coffee shop open 10.00-19.00. ♿				

Scotland for Golf...

Find out more about golf in Scotland. There's more to it than just the championship courses so get in touch with us now for information on the hidden gems of Scotland.

Write to: Information Unit, Scottish Tourist Board, 23 Ravelston Terrace, Edinburgh EH4 3EU
or call: 031-332 2433.

PITLOCHRY continued	Map 2 B1

Castlebeigh House Hotel
KNOCKARD ROAD, PITLOCHRY
Telephone: (0796) 472925

An attractive Victorian building standing in 2 acres of garden with fine views over the Tummel Valley and up to Ben-y-Vrackie. The bedrooms have private bathrooms, central heating, colour TV, tea/coffee tray.

The special features of Castlebeigh are its light and sunny dining room, its "bookish" lounge and log fires. It has a relaxed and informal atmosphere with a high standard of service. Member of the Taste of Scotland Scheme. Theatre bookings arranged. Ground floor and single rooms available.

Full details from Diane and Alistair McMenemie.

Castlebeigh House 10 Knockard Road Pitlochry Perthshire PH16 5HJ Tel:(Pitlochry) 0796 472925 Fax:0796 474068	COMMENDED ♛ ♛ ♛	6 Single 8 Twin 7 Double	21 En Suite fac	B&B per person £20.00-£35.00 Single £20.00-£35.00 Double	Open Feb-Dec Dinner 1800-2000 B&B + Eve.Meal £28.00-£48.00
		Personally run hotel in own grounds. Close to the centre of Pitlochry and all attractions. Panoramic views to surrounding hills. Ground floor rooms.			
Claymore Hotel 162 Atholl Road Pitlochry Perthshire PH16 5AR Tel:(Pitlochry) 0796 472888 Fax:0796 474037	COMMENDED ♛ ♛ ♛	2 Single 4 Twin 5 Double 1 Family	10 En Suite fac 1 Pub.Bath/Show	B&B per person £22.00-£35.00 Single £22.00-£35.00 Double	Open Feb-Dec Dinner 1800-2100 B&B + Eve.Meal £29.00-£50.00
		Family run hotel, on the edge of the town with fine views of surrounding hills. Some annexe accommodation.			
Craigmhor Lodge 27 West Moulin Road Pitlochry Perthshire PH16 5EF Tel:(Pitlochry) 0796 472123 Fax:0796 472123	COMMENDED ♛ ♛ ♛	2 Single 4 Twin 3 Double 1 Family	10 En Suite fac	B&B per person £28.00-£30.00 Single £28.00-£30.00 Double	Open Jan-Dec Dinner 1830-2100 B&B + Eve.Meal £47.00-£50.00
		Family owned hotel with annexe cottage peacefully set in two acres, close to town. Restaurant with panoramic views; imaginative Scottish cuisine.			
Craigower Hotel 134-136 Atholl Road Pitlochry Perthshire PH16 5AB Tel:(Pitlochry) 0796 472590	COMMENDED ♛ ♛ ♛	2 Single 10 Twin 9 Double 5 Family	6 En Suite fac	B&B per person £25.00-£28.00 Single £25.00-£28.00 Double	Open Jan-Dec Dinner 1800-2330 B&B + Eve.Meal £37.00-£40.00
		Situated in the centre of town, a family run hotel, offering a bar, licensed restaurant and function room.			
Craig Urrard Hotel 10 Atholl Road Pitlochry Perthshire PH16 5BX Tel:(Pitlochry) 0796 472346	COMMENDED ♛ ♛ ♛	2 Single 2 Twin 6 Double 2 Family	9 En Suite fac 2 Pub.Bath/Show	B&B per person £18.00-£26.00 Single £18.00-£27.50 Double	Open Jan-Dec Dinner 1800-2000 B&B + Eve.Meal £29.00-£38.50
		Family run, with large garden. Centrally situated for station and town centre. Two family rooms in annexe.			

PITLOCHRY continued	Map 2 B1

CRAIGVRACK HOTEL

WEST MOULIN ROAD, PITLOCHRY PH16 5EQ Tel: 0796 472399

A family-run hotel in a lovely situation enjoying panoramic mountain views, yet near the town centre. Well known for its friendly atmosphere and excellent cuisine.
"Glenturret - Perthshire Tourism Award Winner"
Bed and full Scottish Breakfast from £25; including dinner from £29.50.
Brochure and full details from Proprietors and Hosts,
Rob and Janet Wallace

COMMENDED ♛♛♛

Craigvrack Hotel
West Moulin Road
Pitlochry
Perthshire
PH16 5EQ
Tel:(Pitlochry) 0796 472399
Fax:0796 473990

COMMENDED
♛ ♛ ♛

1 Single
9 Twin
6 Double
2 Family

16 En Suite fac
1 Pub.Bath/Show

B&B per person
£25.00-£36.00 Single
£25.00-£28.00 Double

Open Jan-Dec
Dinner 1830-2030
B&B + Eve.Meal
£28.00-£40.00

Family run hotel on outskirts of town in residential area and yet under 1 mile (2kms) from the centre. Glenturret tourism award winner 1992.

Dundarach Hotel
Perth Road
Pitlochry
Perthshire
PH16 5DJ
Tel:(Pitlochry) 0796 472862
Fax:0350727 462

APPROVED
♛ ♛ ♛

4 Single
13 Twin
8 Double
2 Family

27 En Suite fac

B&B per person
£35.00-£49.00 Single
£37.00 Double

Open Mar-Jan
Dinner 1830-2030
B&B + Eve.Meal
£25.00-£55.00

Country house style hotel on fringe of Pitlochry. Personally run by chef/proprietor. Two minutes walk to centre.

Dunfallandy House

Logierait Road, Dunfallandy, Pitlochry PH16 5NA
Telephone: (0796) 472648 Fax: (0796) 472017

Secluded Georgian Mansion House, ideally positioned in 3½ acres, specialising in quiet, relaxing holidays. Quality furnishings, imaginative food and fine wines. All bedrooms have panoramic views with en-suite facilities, colour TV, hairdryers, trouser press, etc. Four-poster and canopied beds available. "Johansens recommended private country houses". ½ mile from Festival Theatre and Salmon Ladder.
STB Highly Commended ♛♛♛

Dunfallandy Country House
Hotel & Rest.
Logierait Road
Pitlochry
Perthshire
PH16 5NA
Tel:(Pitlochry) 0796 472648

HIGHLY
COMMENDED
♛ ♛ ♛

1 Single
2 Twin
6 Double

8 En Suite fac
1 Priv.NOT ensuite
1 Pub.Bath/Show

B&B per person
£20.00-£37.00 Single
£20.00-£27.00 Double

Open Mar-Oct, Xmas/New Year
Dinner 1815-2000
B&B + Eve.Meal
£30.00-£48.50

Small and friendly Georgian mansion house in extensive grounds. Innovative use of fine local ingredients; "Taste of Scotland"

Fasganeoin Hotel
Perth Road
Pitlochry
Perthshire
PH16 5DJ
Tel:(Pitlochry) 0796 472387

COMMENDED
♛ ♛ ♛

2 Single
1 Twin
3 Double
3 Family

5 En Suite fac
2 Pub.Bath/Show

B&B per person
£19.00-£22.00 Single
£19.00-£28.00 Double

Open Apr-Oct
Dinner 1630-1915
B&B + Eve.Meal
£26.75-£39.50

Family run hotel, with garden, over 100 years old, situated on the edge of town, close to the theatre. Food available throughout the day.

PITLOCHRY continued	Map 2 B1						
Fishers Hotel 75-79 Atholl Road Pitlochry Perthshire PH16 5BN Tel:(Pitlochry) 0796 472000		APPROVED ♛ ♛ ♛	34 Single 65 Twin 29 Double 11 Family	139 En Suite fac	B&B per person £42.00-£50.00 Single £38.00-£46.00 Double	Open Jan-Dec Dinner 1830-2000 B&B + Eve.Meal £48.00-£58.50	

Centrally situated. Large garden with putting and bowling greens. Year round live entertainment and snooker club.

| Green Park Hotel Clunie Bridge Road Pitlochry Perthshire PH16 5JY Tel:(Pitlochry) 0796 473248 Fax:0796 473520 | | | 5 Single 13 Twin 10 Double 9 Family | 37 En Suite fac | B&B per person £30.00-£45.00 Single £30.00-£45.00 Double | Open Mar-Oct Dinner 1830-2030 B&B + Eve.Meal £45.00-£65.00 | |

| Knockendarroch House Hotel Higher Oakfield Pitlochry Perthshire PH16 5HT Tel:(Pitlochry) 0796 473473 Fax:0796 474068 | | HIGHLY COMMENDED ♛ ♛ ♛ | 6 Twin 5 Double 1 Family | 12 En Suite fac | B&B per person £25.50-£35.00 Double | Open Mar-Nov Dinner 1815-1945 B&B + Eve.Meal £40.00-£49.00 | |

Period house, personally supervised by resident proprietors. High site gives superb views of surrounding hills. Taste of Scotland.

| McKays Hotel 138 Atholl Road Pitlochry Perthshire PH16 5AG Tel:(Pitlochry) 0796 473888 | | APPROVED ♛ ♛ ♛ | 4 Single 3 Twin 4 Double 2 Family | 9 En Suite fac 4 Priv.NOT ensuite 2 Pub.Bath/Show | B&B per person £18.00-£25.00 Single £18.00-£27.00 Double | Open Jan-Dec Dinner 1800-2100 B&B + Eve.Meal £28.00-£37.00 | |

Personally run and situated on main street of town, 100 yards from the station, 10 minutes walk from theatres.

PINE TREES HOTEL

STRATHVIEW TERRACE . PITLOCHRY PH16 5QR

Tel: (0796) 472121 Fax: (0796) 472460

Family-run, Victorian Country House Hotel set in 10 acres of beautiful grounds amidst mature pine trees, with a 9-hole putting green; a peaceful and relaxing atmosphere in spacious elegant newly furnished public rooms. Well appointed bedrooms, all with private facilities, colour TV, radio, tea/coffee trays and direct-dial telephones. Spring and Autumn breaks available. Open all year. Salmon, Trout fishing, shooting and deer stalking are all available.

| The Pine Trees Hotel Strathview Terrace Pitlochry Perthshire PH16 5QR Tel:(Pitlochry) 0796 472121 Fax:0796 472460 | | HIGHLY COMMENDED ♛ ♛ ♛ ♛ | 3 Single 7 Twin 10 Double | 20 En Suite fac 3 Pub.Bath/Show | B&B per person £45.00-£51.00 Single £41.00-£47.00 Double | Open Feb-Dec Dinner 1830-2030 B&B + Eve.Meal £59.00-£65.00 | |

Stone built Victorian country house, in elevated position with 14 acres of garden and woodland, yet close to town centre and all amenities.

PITLOCHRY continued	Map 2 B1

Pitlochry Hydro Hotel

PITLOCHRY . PERTHSHIRE . PH16 5JH
Tel: 0796 472666 Fax: 0796 472238

A traditional style of hotel, standing in its own grounds, with a commanding view of Pitlochry town. The area is surrounded by trout lochs and golf courses and is the perfect base to visit some of Scotland's most historic castles - Scone Palace, Blair Castle and Balmoral Castle.

The comfortable public areas are spacious and elegant. All 62 bedrooms have en-suite bathroom, telephone, satellite T.V., tea and coffee making facilities. The leisure club features swimming pool, spa bath, solarium, sauna, exercise room and games room.

Dinner, bed and breakfast from £47.
Over 60's from £33. Free accommodation and breakfast for children under 16 sharing parents room.

Pitlochry Hydro Hotel Knockard Road Pitlochry Perthshire PH16 5JH Tel:(Pitlochry) 0796 472666 Fax:0796 472238	COMMENDED ♛ ♛ ♛ ♛	12 Single 32 Twin 14 Double 6 Family Suites avail.	64 En Suite fac	B&B per person £57.00-£60.00 Single £49.00-£52.00 Double	Open Feb-Dec Dinner 1830-2100 B&B + Eve.Meal £47.00-£61.00

Recently refurbished, the hotel and health club stand in their own grounds overlooking the town.

Poplars Hotel 27 Lower Oakfield Pitlochry Perthshire PH16 5DS Tel:(Pitlochry) 0796 472129/472554	COMMENDED ♛ ♛ ♛	2 Twin 3 Double 3 Family	7 En Suite fac 1 Limited ensuite 1 Pub.Bath/Show	B&B per person £18.00-£20.00 Single £17.00-£19.00 Double	Open Apr-Oct Dinner at 1830 B&B + Eve.Meal £26.00-£30.00

Personally run, with large garden in elevated position overlooking town. Quiet location.

Rosemount Hotel 12 Higher Oakfield Pitlochry Perthshire PH16 5HT Tel:(Pitlochry) 0796 472302/472262 Fax:0796 474216	COMMENDED ♛ ♛ ♛	2 Single 10 Twin 6 Double 4 Family	21 En Suite fac 1 Priv.NOT ensuite	B&B per person £22.00-£32.00 Single £22.00-£32.00 Double	Open Jan-Dec Dinner 1830-2100 B&B + Eve.Meal £35.00-£45.00

Personally run fully licensed hotel with friendly atmosphere, situated in elevated position overlooking Tummel Valley. Small fitness centre, sauna.

| PITLOCHRY continued | Map 2 B1 | | |

SCOTLAND'S HOTEL
BONNETHILL ROAD, PITLOCHRY, PERTHSHIRE PH16 5BT
Telephone: (0796) 472292

Central Scotland's picturesque Pitlochry is conveniently accessible to both road and rail. Our friendly family-run hotel is renowned for traditional cuisine and fine wines, beers and spirits. New Leisure Club includes an indoor swimming pool and beauty salon with massage. Nearby attractions include golf courses, fishing beats, castles and distilleries.

Scotlands Hotel
32-46 Bonnethill Road
Pitlochry
Perthshire
PH16 5BT
Tel:(Pitlochry) 0796 472292
Tlx:76392 SCOTEL G
Fax:0796 473284

COMMENDED
♛ ♛ ♛
♛

12 Single   60 En Suite fac
23 Twin   5 Pub.Bath/Show
12 Double
13 Family

B&B per person
£45.00-£60.00 Single
£39.00-£50.00 Double

Open Jan-Dec
Dinner 1830-2030
B&B + Eve.Meal
£56.00-£67.00

Traditional family run hotel with garden and views of the countryside, close to the centre of Pitlochry. Health and Leisure Club.

Tigh-Na-Cloich Hotel
Larchwood Road
Pitlochry
Perthshire
PH16 5AS
Tel:(Pitlochry) 0796 472216
Fax:0796 472216

COMMENDED
♛ ♛ ♛

2 Single   10 En Suite fac
5 Twin   1 Pub.Bath/Show
4 Double
1 Family

B&B per person
£18.00-£24.00 Single
£20.00-£28.00 Double

Open Mar-Oct
Dinner 1830-2000
B&B + Eve.Meal
£30.00-£43.00

Quiet private hotel about 5 minutes walk from town centre and with commanding views of the Tummel Valley and hills beyond. A "No Smoking" hotel.

Torrdarach Hotel
Golf Course Road
Pitlochry
Perthshire
PH16 5AU
Tel:(Pitlochry) 0796 472136

HIGHLY COMMENDED
♛ ♛ ♛

1 Single   6 En Suite fac
2 Twin   1 Priv.NOT ensuite
4 Double

B&B per person
£30.00-£33.00 Single
£25.00-£28.00 Double

Open Mar-Oct
Dinner 1830-1900
B&B + Eve.Meal
£40.00-£43.00

Personally run hotel with large wooded garden, close to golf course and enjoying an elevated position, overlooking Pitlochry.

Well House Hotel
11 Toberargan Road
Pitlochry
Perthshire
PH16 5HG
Tel:(Pitlochry) 0796 472239

COMMENDED
♛ ♛ ♛

1 Twin   6 En Suite fac
4 Double
1 Family

B&B per person
£19.00-£24.00 Double

Open Mar-Oct
Dinner 1815-1900
B&B + Eve.Meal
£31.00-£34.00

Personally run, centrally situated in residential area. Easy access to shops, amenities and theatre.

| PITLOCHRY continued | Map 2 B1 | | |

Westlands of Pitlochry

160 ATHOLL ROAD·PITLOCHRY· PH16 5AR
Telephone: (0796) 472266 ★★ RAC/AA
Beautifully situated and enjoying wonderful views, Westlands has now been carefully extended and refurbished throughout. All rooms en-suite with TV/radio, tea/coffee tray, telephone, hairdryer and central heating throughout. Outstanding restaurant. Special rates for Spring, Winter and Theatre Breaks.

For full details contact Andrew and Sue Mathieson (resident proprietors).

Westlands of Pitlochry
160 Atholl Road
Pitlochry
Perthshire
PH16 5AR
Tel:(Pitlochry) 0796 472266
Fax:0796 473994

COMMENDED 👑👑👑 👑

1 Single
6 Twin
6 Double
2 Family

15 En Suite fac

B&B per person
£23.50-£47.25 Single
£23.50-£37.25 Double

Open Jan-Dec
Dinner 1830-2130
B&B + Eve.Meal
£37.50-£56.25

Recently refurbished, the hotel is pleasantly situated on the edge of town. The new Garden Room Restaurant uses fresh produce. Taste of Scotland.

Carra Beag Guest House
16 Toberargan Road
Pitlochry
Perthshire
PH16 5HG
Tel:(Pitlochry) 0796 472835

COMMENDED 👑👑👑

2 Single
3 Twin
4 Double
2 Family

9 En Suite fac
1 Pub.Bath/Show

B&B per person
£21.45-£25.50 Single
£21.45-£25.50 Double

Open Jan-Dec
Dinner 1800-1830
B&B + Eve.Meal
£33.00-£38.30

Quiet and relaxing, centrally situated with commanding views and ample parking. Patio and putting green.

Craigroyston Guest House
2 Lower Oakfield
Pitlochry
Perthshire
PH16 5HQ
Tel:(Pitlochry) 0796 472053

COMMENDED 👑👑👑

3 Twin
3 Double
2 Family

8 En Suite fac

B&B per person
£16.00-£25.00 Double

Open Jan-Dec
Dinner 1815-1845
B&B + Eve.Meal
£29.00-£39.00

Family run Victorian villa near town centre with large garden overlooking wooded hills. 10 minutes walk from theatre.

Derrybeg Guest House
18 Lower Oakfield
Pitlochry
Perthshire
PH16 5DS
Tel:(Pitlochry) 0796 472070

COMMENDED 👑👑👑

2 Single
2 Twin
6 Double
1 Family

11 En Suite fac

B&B per person
£16.00-£21.00 Single
£16.00-£21.00 Double

Open Jan-Nov
Dinner 1815-1845
B&B + Eve.Meal
£26.50-£31.50

Privately owned detached house with large south facing garden in quiet, but central location. Elevated position overlooking Tummel Valley.

Dundarave House
Strathview Terrace
Pitlochry
Perthshire
PH16 5AT
Tel:(Pitlochry) 0796 473109

COMMENDED 👑👑👑

2 Single
2 Twin
2 Double
1 Family

5 En Suite fac
2 Pub.Bath/Show

B&B per person
£20.00-£26.00 Single
£20.00-£26.00 Double

Open Apr-Oct
Dinner 1800-1900
B&B + Eve.Meal
£35.00-£41.00

Charming Victorian house, quiet location and stunning views close to centre of Pitlochry. Ground floor room; personal, attentive service.

Duntrune Guest House
22 East Moulin Road
Pitlochry
Perthshire
PH16 5HY
Tel:(Pitlochry) 0796 472172

COMMENDED 👑👑👑

2 Single
2 Twin
2 Double
1 Family

5 En Suite fac
1 Pub.Bath/Show

B&B per person
£17.00-£18.00 Single
£17.00-£19.00 Double

Open Mar-Oct
Dinner from 1800
B&B + Eve.Meal
from £26.00

Stone built house in quiet residential area overlooking town, with warm friendly atmosphere and excellent views of surrounding area.

PITLOCHRY continued

Map 2 B1

Tir Aluinn Guest House
10 Higher Oakfield
Pitlochry
Perthshire
PH16 5HT
Tel:(Pitlochry) 0796 472231

COMMENDED
♛ ♛

1 Single	2 En Suite fac	B&B per person	Open Jan-Dec
1 Twin	2 Pub.Bath/Show	£14.50-£16.00 Single	
2 Double		£17.50-£20.50 Double	
1 Family			

Traditional Victorian villa in quiet residential area, with own large garden.
Elevated position affords excellent views over town and countryside.

BY PITLOCHRY
Perthshire

Map 2 B1

Y M C A Bonskeid House
Holiday Conference Centre
Pitlochry
Perthshire
PH16 5NP
Tel:(Pitlochry) 0796 473208
Fax:0796 473310

5 Single	12 Pub.Bath/Show	B&B per person	Open Feb-Nov
19 Twin		£13.50 Single	Dinner at 1800
6 Double		£13.50 Double	B&B + Eve.Meal
15 Family			£20.00

PLOCKTON
Ross-shire

Map 3 F9

Creag nan Darach Hotel
Innes Street
Plockton
Ross-shire
IV52 8TW
Tel:(Plockton) 059984 222

1 Single	5 En Suite fac	B&B per person	Open Jan-Dec
3 Twin	2 Pub.Bath/Show	£18.00-£20.00 Single	Dinner 1830-2030
2 Double		£20.00-£25.00 Double	B&B + Eve.Meal
2 Family			£25.00-£35.00

The Haven Hotel
Plockton
Ross-shire
IV52 8TW
Tel:(Plockton) 059984 223

HIGHLY
COMMENDED
♛ ♛
♛

2 Single	10 En Suite fac	B&B per person	Open Feb-Dec
5 Twin	3 Priv.NOT ensuite	£32.00-£35.00 Single	Dinner 1900-2030
6 Double		£32.00-£35.00 Double	B&B + Eve.Meal
			£44.00-£53.00

Originally a 19th century merchant's house, nestling in centre of NTS village.
Personally run Taste of Scotland restaurant with fresh local produce.

POLMONT, by Falkirk
Stirlingshire

Map 2 B4

Inchyra Grange Hotel
Grange Road
Polmont, Falkirk
Stirlingshire
FK2 0YB
Tel:(Polmont) 0324 711911
Tlx:777693
Fax:0324 716134

COMMENDED
♛ ♛ ♛
♛

7 Single	43 En Suite fac	B&B per person	Open Jan-Dec
21 Twin		from £77.00 Single	Dinner 1900-2130
15 Double		from £54.00 Double	

Modernised country house, retaining original features, in 8 acres of mature
grounds. Conference facilities and extensive new leisure centre.

Details of Grading and Classification are on page vi.

| Key to symbols is on back flap. |

POOLEWE
Ross-shire
Map 3 F7

Pool House Hotel
Poolewe
Ross-shire
IV22 2LE
Tel:(Poolewe) 044586 272
Fax:044586 403

COMMENDED

3 Single   11 En Suite fac
5 Twin   1 Pub.Bath/Show
4 Double
1 Family

B&B per person
£22.50-£36.50 Single
£22.50-£36.50 Double

Open Jan-Dec
Dinner 1900-2030
B&B + Eve.Meal
£41.00-£55.00

Family run, on water's edge. Walking distance to Inverewe gardens. Superb views over Loch Ewe and beyond.

PORT APPIN
Argyll
Map 1 E1

The Airds Hotel
Port Appin
Argyll
PA38 4DF
Tel:(Appin) 063173 236
Fax:063173 535

DELUXE

6 Twin   12 En Suite fac
6 Double

B&B per person
£68.00-£90.00 Single
£64.00-£95.00 Double

Open Mar-Jan
Dinner 2000-2030
B&B + Eve.Meal
£98.00-£129.00

Lochside setting, projecting all that is the best in Scottish cuisine. Extensive and fine wine list.

Linnhe House
Port Appin
Argyll
PA38 4DE
Tel:(Appin) 063173 245

COMMENDED

3 Twin   4 En Suite fac
1 Double   1 Pub.Bath/Show

B&B per person
£22.00-£25.00 Single
£22.00-£25.00 Double

Open Jan-Dec
Dinner at 1900
B&B + Eve.Meal
£30.00-£33.00

Family run detached 19th C house in own grounds overlooking Loch Linnhe and the Morven Hills. Home cooking and baking.

PORT ASKAIG
Isle of Islay, Argyll
Map 1 C5

Port Askaig Hotel
Port Askaig
Isle of Islay, Argyll
PA46 7RD
Tel:(Port Askaig) 049684 245
Fax:049684 295

COMMENDED

1 Single   4 En Suite fac
6 Twin   3 Pub.Bath/Show
3 Double
1 Family

B&B per person
£38.00-£42.00 Single
£36.00-£40.00 Double

Open Jan-Dec
Dinner 1930-2100
B&B + Eve.Meal
£52.00-£56.00

Original drovers inn overlooking Sound of Islay, with grounds to water's edge and close to ferry terminal.

PORT ELLEN
Isle of Islay, Argyll
Map 1 C6

The Trout-Fly Restaurant &
Guest House
Port Ellen
Isle of Islay, Argyll
PA42 7DF
Tel:(Port Ellen) 0496 2204

Award Pending

2 Twin   2 Limited ensuite
1 Double   2 Pub.Bath/Show

B&B per person
£15.00-£18.50 Single
£15.00-£18.50 Double

Open Jan-Dec
Dinner 1700-2100

PORTMAHOMACK
Ross-shire
Map 4 C7

Caledonian Hotel
Main Street
Portmahomack, by Tain
Ross-shire
IV20 1YS
Tel:(Portmahomack)
086287 345

Award Pending

8 Twin   18 En Suite fac
8 Double
2 Family

B&B per person
£16.00-£25.00 Single
£16.00-£25.00 Double

Open Jan-Dec
Dinner 1830-2100
B&B + Eve.Meal
£24.00-£33.00

PORTMAHOMACK **continued** Castle Hotel Portmahomack Ross-shire IV20 1YE Tel:(Portmahomack) 086287 263	Map 4 C7		2 Twin 3 Double 1 Family	4 En Suite fac 1 Pub.Bath/Show	B&B per person £18.00-£22.00 Single £18.00-£22.00 Double	Open Jan-Dec Dinner 1900-2100 B&B + Eve.Meal £26.00-£30.00	
PORT OF MENTEITH **Perthshire**	Map 1 H3						

LAKE HOTEL-TROSSACHS
PORT OF MENTEITH, PERTHSHIRE
Telephone: 0877 385258 Fax: 0877 385671

*Outstanding situation on the shore of the Lake of Menteith. Former hotel
completely refurbished under new ownership and management in 1990.
All rooms with en-suite facilities. Our cuisine emulates the restaurant with its
spectacular lakeside setting. Special weekends and breaks available.*
Reservations and brochure from above address.

Lake Hotel Port of Menteith Perthshire FK8 3RA Tel:(Port of Menteith) 0877 385258 Fax:0877 385671		**HIGHLY** **COMMENDED**	8 Twin 5 Double	13 En Suite fac	B&B per person	Open Jan-Dec Dinner 1900-2100 B&B + Eve.Meal £42.00-£85.00	

Recently fully refurbished hotel with conservatory and superb views over the
Lake of Menteith. A la carte restaurant and bistro.

PORTPATRICK **Wigtownshire** Fernhill Hotel Portpatrick Wigtownshire DG9 8TD Tel:(Portpatrick) 077681 220 Fax:077681 596	Map 1 F1	**HIGHLY** **COMMENDED**	3 Single 9 Twin 7 Double 2 Family	20 En Suite fac 1 Pub.Bath/Show	B&B per person from £50.00 Single from £35.00 Double	Open Jan-Dec Dinner 1800-2200	

Family run hotel set high above picturesque Portpatrick harbour. A la carte
restaurant. Golf Course only 400 yards from Hotel. Taste of Scotland.

Harbour House Hotel 53 Main Street Portpatrick Wigtownshire DG9 8JW Tel:(Portpatrick) 077681 456		**Award** **Pending**	2 Single 1 Twin 2 Double 4 Family Suites avail.	2 En Suite fac 4 Limited ensuite 1 Priv.NOT ensuite 2 Pub.Bath/Show	B&B per person £20.00-£25.00 Single £20.00-£25.00 Double	Open Jan-Dec Dinner 1800-2130 B&B + Eve.Meal £25.00-£30.00	

Mount Stewart Hotel Portpatrick Wigtownshire DG9 8LE Tel:(Portpatrick) 077681 291		**COMMENDED**	1 Single 2 Double 3 Family	3 En Suite fac 2 Pub.Bath/Show	B&B per person £18.00-£21.00 Single £18.00-£24.00 Double	Open Jan-Dec Dinner 1830-2200 B&B + Eve.Meal £29.50-£35.50	

Family run, detached hotel in elevated position overlooking Portpatrick harbour.
Ample parking. Interesting menu suiting both palate and pocket.

Details of Grading and Classification are on page vi.

Key to symbols is on back flap.

PORTPATRICK continued Portpatrick Hotel Portpatrick Wigtownshire DG9 8TQ Tel:(Portpatrick) 077681 333 Fax:077681 457	Map 1 F1	COMMENDED ♕ ♕ ♕	6 Single 32 Twin 13 Double 6 Family	57 En Suite fac 1 Pub.Bath/Show	B&B per person £45.00-£50.00 Single £35.00-£40.00 Double	Open Mar-Nov Dinner 1900-2100 B&B + Eve.Meal £50.00-£55.00	
			A family and golfing hotel situated above picturesque village and giving panoramic views over the harbour and beyond.				
Rickwood Private Hotel Portpatrick Wigtownshire DG9 8TD Tel:(Portpatrick) 077681 270		COMMENDED ♕ ♕ ♕	1 Twin 2 Double 2 Family	4 En Suite fac 1 Priv.NOT ensuite	B&B per person £18.95-£19.95 Single £18.95-£19.95 Double	Open Mar-mid Dec Dinner 1830-1900 B&B + Eve.Meal £27.90-£28.90	
			Detached Victorian house in mature gardens overlooking village and sea, close to golf course. Reductions for stays of 3 and 7 nights.				
Carlton Guest House South Crescent Portpatrick Wigtownshire DG9 8JR Tel:(Portpatrick) 077681 253		COMMENDED ♕ ♕ ♕	2 Twin 3 Double 2 Family	6 En Suite fac 1 Pub.Bath/Show	B&B per person £18.00-£25.00 Single £16.00-£20.00 Double	Open Jan-Dec Dinner 1800-1900 B&B + Eve.Meal £24.00-£26.00	
			Comfortable, and overlooking picturesque harbour with superb views over the Irish Sea. Fresh local produce.				
BY PORTPATRICK Wigtownshire Torrs Warren Hotel Stoneykirk,by Stranraer Wigtownshire DG9 9DH Tel:(Sandhead) 077683 204	Map 1 F1	Award Pending	3 Double 4 Family 2 Pub.Bath/Show	2 En Suite fac 1 Limited ensuite	B&B per person £19.00-£22.00 Single £19.00-£22.00 Double	Open Jan-Dec Dinner 1800-2100 B&B + Eve.Meal £25.00-£28.00	
PORTREE Isle of Skye, Inverness-shire	Map 3 D9						

Cuillin Hills Hotel
PORTREE . ISLE OF SKYE . Tel: 0478 612003

Superbly situated just outside Portree with breathtaking views over Portree Bay towards the Cuillins. This surely must be THE centre for exploring Skye. The best of food, the best of accommodation, set in the best of scenery. From £32 per person per night.
For tariff and brochure contact Mr M. McPhee.

Cuillin Hills Hotel Portree Isle of Skye, Inverness-shire IV51 9LU Tel:(Portree) 0478 612003 Fax:0478 613092	Award Pending	6 Single 8 Twin 7 Double 5 Family	26 En Suite fac	B&B per person £29.00-£55.00 Single £27.50-£42.50 Double	Open Jan-Dec Dinner 1830-2030 B&B + Eve.Meal £47.00-£73.00	

VAT is shown at 17.5%: changes in this rate may affect prices. Prices shown are for guidance only. Please send SAE with each enquiry.

PORTREE continued	Map 3 D9						

The Isles Hotel
Portree
Isle of Skye, Inverness-shire
IV51 9EX
Tel:(Portree) 0478
2129/612129

COMMENDED
♕ ♕ ♕

2 Single
3 Twin
4 Double

5 En Suite fac
1 Pub.Bath/Show

B&B per person
£22.00-£25.00 Single
£27.00-£30.00 Double

Open Apr-Oct
Dinner 1900-2030

Centrally placed on the main square at Portree. Warm and friendly, personal welcome.

Portree Hotel

SOMERLED SQUARE,
PORTREE, ISLE OF SKYE
IV51 9EH Tel: 0478-612511
Fax: 0478-613093

Centrally located in Somerled Square, Portree, the hotel offers a high standard of comfort and cuisine. All rooms en-suite with colour TV, telephone, hairdryer and hot drinks facilities. An excellent base for local amenities and touring the island. Special breaks 2 nights DB&B from £55.

Portree Hotel
Somerled Square
Portree
Isle of Skye, Inverness-shire
IV51 9EH
Tel:(Portree) 0478 612511
Fax:0478 613093

COMMENDED
♕ ♕ ♕

8 Single
7 Twin
5 Double
4 Family

24 En Suite fac
1 Pub.Bath/Show

B&B per person
£32.00-£40.00 Single
£27.00-£35.00 Double

Open Jan-Dec
Dinner 1730-2130
B&B + Eve.Meal
£41.00-£54.00

Town centre hotel overlooking the square with all amenities within short walking distance. Good centre for touring.

ROSEDALE HOTEL

PORTREE . ISLE OF SKYE. IV51 9DB
Tel: (0478) 613131 Fax: (0478) 612531

Privately owned hotel in unrivalled waterfront position. Most bedrooms with sea view and all with private facilities; radio, television, direct-dial telephone and tea-making. Cocktail bar, two residents' lounges. Restaurant overlooking harbour.

Special 3-day package available. Stay longer and we include car ferry tickets. Please write or phone for brochure. **COMMENDED**

Rosedale Hotel
Beaumont Crescent
Portree
Isle of Skye, Inverness-shire
IV51 9DB
Tel:(Portree) 0478
3131/613131
Fax:0478 2531/612531

COMMENDED
♕ ♕ ♕
♕

5 Single
14 Twin
5 Double
Suite avail.

24 En Suite fac

B&B per person
£33.00-£37.00 Single
£33.00-£37.00 Double

Open May-Sep
Dinner 1900-2030
B&B + Eve.Meal
£53.00-£58.00

Privately owned hotel, converted from former fisherman's house, situated on the waterfront overlooking the harbour.

TELEPHONE DIALLING CODES

Many telephone dialling codes have changed this year. If you experience difficulty in connecting a call, please call Directory Enquiries – **192** – where someone will issue the correct number. Please note: a charge will be placed for this service when using a private telephone

PORTREE continued	Map 3 D9		

ROYAL HOTEL
BANK STREET, PORTREE, ISLE OF SKYE IV51 9BU

Family run centrally situated hotel with commanding views over Portree Bay. All bedrooms en-suite. Hospitality tray, colour TV. Fully licensed locally renowned restaurant with extensive menu and wine list. Residents lounge. Cocktail Bar. Open all year. Accommodation from £29.50 pp B&B. *Contact Reservations, Royal Hotel, Portree. Tel: 0478 61 2525 Fax: 0478 61 3198.*

Royal Hotel Bank Street Portree Isle of Skye, Inverness-shire IV51 9BU Tel:(Portree) 0478 2525/612525	**Award Pending**	1 Single 10 Twin 7 Double 7 Family	25 En Suite fac	B&B per person £35.00-£38.00 Single £27.50-£30.00 Double	Open Jan-Dec Dinner 1700-2100 B&B + Eve.Meal £52.00-£57.00	
The Kingshaven 11 Bosville Terrace Portree Isle of Skye, Inverness-shire IV51 9DG Tel:(Portree) 0478 612290	**COMMENDED** 👑 👑	3 Twin 3 Double	6 En Suite fac	B&B per person £19.00-£26.00 Double	Open Jan-Dec	
				Tastefully converted house c1810, in elevated position near town centre, with views to the harbour. All rooms have en suite facilities.		
Springfield Guest House Portree Isle of Skye, Inverness-shire IV51 9LX Tel:(Portree) 0478 2505/612505		3 Single 4 Twin 2 Double	3 Pub.Bath/Show	B&B per person from £16.00 Single from £16.00 Double	Open Jan-Dec	

BY PORTREE Isle of Skye, Inverness-shire	Map 3 D9		

ISLE OF SKYE
👑👑👑
COMMENDED
GRESHORNISH HOUSE HOTEL IV51 9PN
Tel: (047 082) 266/326/255   Fax: (047 082) 345

Highland Mansion with 12 acres of wooded grounds and lawns, log fires, central heating. Scottish fare, piper, four-poster, private bathrooms, cocktail bar. Exceptional personal service. Situated on lochside, you may enjoy peace, bird-watching, fishing, tennis, croquet, snooker, pool. We offer 2 tasteful, attractive self catering houses in grounds for let.
Jane A. Dickson MHCIMA (HYGIENE CERTIFICATE)

Greshornish House Hotel Greshornish Isle of Skye, Inverness-shire IV51 9PN Tel:(Edinbane) 047082 266/326	**COMMENDED** 👑 👑 👑	1 Twin 2 Double 2 Family	5 En Suite fac 1 Pub.Bath/Show	B&B per person from £30.00 Single from £28.00 Double	Open Jan-Dec Dinner from 1900 B&B + Eve.Meal from £40.00	
				Georgian mansion in superb lochside situation. Hand-carved oak fireplace and log fire. Rabbits on the croquet lawn, sheep by the tennis court.		

| **BY PORTREE**
continued
The Shielings Guest House
Torvaig
Portree
Isle of Skye, Inverness-shire
IV51 9HU
Tel:(Portree) 0478
3024/613024 | Map 3
D9 | COMMENDED
♛ ♛ | 2 Double
2 Family | 1 En Suite fac
2 Pub.Bath/Show | B&B per person
£14.00-£21.00 Double | Open Jan-Dec
Dinner at 1830
B&B + Eve.Meal
£23.00-£30.00 | |
| | | | Converted croft cottage with superb views. Situated just 2 miles (3kms) outside
Portree. Home cooking and a warm homely atmosphere. | | | | |

| **PORT SETON**
East Lothian
Old Ship Inn Hotel
40 Links Road
Port Seton
East Lothian
EH32 0DZ
Tel:(Port Seton) 0875
811725 | Map 2
D5 | | 1 Single
2 Twin
1 Double
1 Family | 2 Pub.Bath/Show | B&B per person
£15.00-£20.00 Single
£15.00-£20.00 Double | Open Jan-Dec
Dinner 1700-2000
B&B + Eve.Meal
£19.00-£26.00 | |

| **PORTSOY**
Banffshire
Boyne Hotel
2 North High Street
Portsoy
Banffshire
AB45 2PA
Tel:(Portsoy) 0261 42242
Fax:0261 42242 | Map 4
F7 | COMMENDED
♛ ♛ | 4 Single
4 Twin
4 Double
1 Family | 12 En Suite fac
3 Pub.Bath/Show | B&B per person
£18.00-£22.00 Single
£18.00-£22.00 Double | Open Jan-Dec
Dinner 1900-2300
B&B + Eve.Meal
£23.00-£30.00 | |
| | | | Refurbished 18c building on square in seaside town, close to harbour and sandy
beach. Home cooking. Under personal supervision. | | | | |

| **PORT WILLIAM**
Wigtownshire
Corsemalzie House Hotel
Port William
Wigtownshire
DG8 9RL
Tel:(Mochrum) 098886 254
Fax:098886 213 | Map 1
H1 | COMMENDED
♛ ♛ ♛
♛ | 6 Twin
6 Double
2 Family | 14 En Suite fac | B&B per person
£29.50-£49.50 Single
£29.50-£39.50 Double | Open Mar-Jan
Dinner 1930-2100
B&B + Eve.Meal
from £39.50 | |
| | | | 19C country house set in 40 acres of parkland. Log fires. Pony trekking, shooting
and fishing can be arranged. | | | | |

| **POWFOOT, by Annan**
Dumfriesshire
Powfoot Golf Hotel
Links Avenue
Powfoot,by Annan
Dumfriesshire
DG12 5PN
Tel:(Cummertrees)
04617 254 | Map 2
C1 | | 1 Single
11 Twin
4 Double
2 Family | 11 En Suite fac
3 Pub.Bath/Show | B&B per person
£33.00-£44.00 Single
£25.00-£31.00 Double | Open Jan-Dec
Dinner 1830-2230
B&B + Eve.Meal
£40.00-£55.00 | |

| **PRESTWICK**
Ayrshire
The Carlton Toby Hotel
187 Ayr Road
Prestwick
Ayrshire
KA9 1TP
Tel:(Prestwick) 0292 76811
Fax:0292 74845 | Map 1
G7 | | 28 Twin
7 Double
2 Family | 37 En Suite fac | B&B per person
£30.00-£60.00 Single
£20.00-£80.00 Double | Open Jan-Dec
Dinner 1800-2130 | |

PRESTWICK continued	Map 1 G7					
The Fairways Private Hotel 19 Links Road Prestwick Ayrshire KA9 1QG Tel:(Prestwick) 0292 70396		COMMENDED 👑 👑	2 Single 2 Twin 1 Double 1 Family	5 En Suite fac 1 Priv.NOT ensuite	B&B per person £22.50 Single £21.00 Double	Open Jan-Dec
			Stone built Victorian house with private parking in quiet location overlooking Prestwick Golf Course. 100 yds from sandy beach.			
Golf View Hotel 17 Links Road Prestwick Ayrshire KA9 1QG Tel:(Prestwick) 0292 671234 Fax:0292 671244		HIGHLY COMMENDED 👑 👑	1 Single 3 Twin 1 Double 1 Family	5 En Suite fac 1 Priv.NOT ensuite	B&B per person from £22.00 Single from £22.00 Double	Open Jan-Dec
			Personally run stone built, 19C house in quiet location overlooking Prestwick Golf Course. Convenient for airport; railway station. Golf arranged.			
Kincraig Hotel 39 Ayr Road Prestwick Ayrshire KA9 1SY Tel:(Prestwick) 0292 79480			3 Single 4 Twin 1 Double	5 En Suite fac 2 Pub.Bath/Show	B&B per person £14.50-£20.00 Single £17.50-£18.50 Double	Open Jan-Dec Dinner from 1800 B&B + Eve.Meal £21.50-£24.50
Manor Park Hotel Monkton, by Prestwick Ayrshire KA9 2RJ Tel:(Prestwick) 0292 79365			1 Single 5 Twin 4 Double 1 Family	11 En Suite fac	B&B per person £30.00-£40.00 Single £22.50-£35.00 Double	Open Jan-Dec Dinner 1900-2200 B&B + Eve.Meal £40.00-£50.00
Parkstone Hotel Esplanade Prestwick Ayrshire KA9 1QN Tel:(Prestwick) 0292 77286		COMMENDED 👑 👑 👑	6 Single 4 Twin 4 Double 1 Family	15 En Suite fac	B&B per person £38.00-£40.00 Single £24.00-£26.00 Double	Open Jan-Dec Dinner 1700-2100
			On the seafront overlooking a sandy beach on the Firth of Clyde. Close to many good golf courses and local amenities.			
Prestwick Old Course Hotel 13 Links Road Prestwick Ayrshire KA9 1QG Tel:(Prestwick) 0292 77446 Fax:0292 78316			2 Single 2 Twin 3 Family	4 En Suite fac 1 Limited ensuite 1 Pub.Bath/Show	B&B per person £25.00-£30.00 Single £25.00-£30.00 Double	Open Jan-Dec Dinner 1700-2130 B&B + Eve.Meal £33.00-£38.00
St Nicholas Hotel 41 Ayr Road Prestwick Ayrshire KA9 1SY Tel:(Prestwick) 0292 79568 Fax:0292 76726		COMMENDED 👑 👑 👑	8 Single 1 Twin 5 Double 4 Family	12 En Suite fac 3 Pub.Bath/Show	B&B per person from £26.00 Single from £26.00 Double	Open Jan-Dec Dinner from 1700 B&B + Eve.Meal from £35.00
			Situated in town centre, close to beach and local golf courses. 1 mile (2kms) Prestwick Airport. Function Suite (100 persons).			

PRESTWICK continued

Map 1 G7

Towans Hotel & Motel
Powmill Road
Prestwick
Ayrshire
KA9 2NY
Tel:(Prestwick) 0292 77831
Fax:0292 671485

APPROVED

8 Single	21 En Suite fac	B&B per person
11 Twin	6 Pub.Bath/Show	£25.75-£33.50 Single
11 Double		£20.25-£23.50 Double
7 Family		

Open Jan-Dec
Dinner 1800-2030
B&B + Eve.Meal
£41.25-£49.00

Family run hotel with motel accommodation close to airport. A wide variety of amenities within a 5 mile (8kms) radius.

Fernbank Guest House
213 Main Street
Prestwick
Ayrshire
KA9 1SU
Tel:(Prestwick) 0292 75027

COMMENDED

2 Single	4 En Suite fac	B&B per person
2 Twin	1 Priv.NOT ensuite	£14.00-£16.00 Single
2 Double	3 Pub.Bath/Show	£17.00-£18.00 Double
1 Family		

Open Jan-Dec

Modernised Edwardian villa near beach and local sports. 1 mile (2kms) from airport.

RENFREW

Map 1 H5

Glynhill Leisure Hotel
PAISLEY ROAD · RENFREW · GLASGOW AIRPORT · PA4 8XB
Telephone: 041-886 5555

The Hotel of the 1990's offering businessmen and tourists alike, a quality product and service. Facilities range from Diplomat Suites, American-style bedrooms, Convention Centre, Gourmet and Carverie restaurants, all complemented by a luxurious Leisure Centre. Private, excellent value, well located hotel for the West of Scotland. Glasgow International Airport 1 mile.

Glynhill Hotel & Leisure Club
169 Paisley Road
Renfrew
PA4 8XB
Tel:041 886 5555
Tlx:779536
Fax:041 885 2838

COMMENDED

3 Single	125 En Suite fac	B&B per person
56 Twin		£69.00-£94.00 Single
32 Double		£39.50-£52.00 Double
34 Family		
Suites avail.		

Open Jan-Dec
Dinner 1800-2230
B&B + Eve.Meal
£49.00-£106.00

Set in own grounds on main Paisley-Renfrew road. Only 1 mile (2kms) from Glasgow Airport. Car park for 200 vehicles. New leisure club.

Stakis Glasgow Normandy Hotel
Inchinnan Road
Renfrew
PA4 9EJ
Tel:041 886 4100
Tlx:778897
Fax:041 885 2366

COMMENDED

43 Single	141 En Suite fac	B&B per person
32 Twin		from £74.50 Single
63 Double		to £47.50 Double
3 Family		

Open Jan-Dec
Dinner 1900-2200

Convenient for airport: courtesy coach available. Golf range nearby. Double glazing in all bedrooms.

Renfrew Guest House
4 West Avenue
Renfrew
PA4 0SZ
Tel:041 886 4350

APPROVED Listed

1 Twin	1 Pub.Bath/Show	B&B per person
1 Family		£18.00-£22.00 Single
		£14.50-£18.00 Double

Open Jan-Dec
Dinner 1800-2000
B&B + Eve.Meal
£23.00-£25.00

Family home in quiet residential street. Conveniently situated for airport, M8 and rail transport. On bus route to Glasgow.

Key to symbols is on back flap.

	Map 1 G4	COMMENDED ♛ ♛ ♛	9 Single 2 Twin 13 Double 1 Family	25 En Suite fac	B&B per person £42.00-£48.50 Single £31.75-£35.00 Double	Open Jan-Dec Dinner 1700-1900	
RHU Dunbartonshire Ardencaple Hotel Shore Road Rhu Dunbartonshire G83 8LA Tel:(Rhu) 0436 820200 Fax:0436 821099							

Coaching inn, 45 minutes drive from Glasgow, via Loch Lomond area. Choice of bars and reasonably priced food.

Rosslea Hall Hotel Rhu Dunbartonshire G84 8NF Tel:(Rhu) 0436 820684 Fax:0436 820897		COMMENDED ♛ ♛ ♛	9 Single 18 Twin 9 Double 3 Family	39 En Suite fac	B&B per person £50.00-£70.00 Single £30.00-£40.00 Double	Open Jan-Dec Dinner 1900-2130 B&B + Eve.Meal £67.50-£87.50	

Country house hotel with fine views of Gare Loch and the hills. Under an hour's drive from the centre of Glasgow. Award winning restaurant.

RHYNIE, by Huntly Aberdeenshire Richmond Arms Hotel Rhynie,by Huntly Aberdeenshire AB54 Tel:(Rhynie) 04646 226	Map 4 E9	Award Pending	2 Twin 2 Double 1 Family	2 Limited ensuite 1 Priv.NOT ensuite 2 Pub.Bath/Show	B&B per person £22.00-£25.00 Single £20.00-£25.00 Double	Open Jan-Dec Dinner 1700-2100 B&B + Eve.Meal £27.50-£32.50	

ROCKCLIFFE, by Dalbeattie, Kirkcudbrightshire	Map 2 B1						

BARON'S CRAIG HOTEL
ROCKCLIFFE, By DALBEATTIE, KIRKCUDBRIGHTSHIRE.
Telephone: 055663 225. Fax: 055663 328

Superbly situated overlooking the Solway Firth in 11 acres of grounds. Relax in the comfort of this beautifully appointed country house hotel. Log fires, cental heating, excellent bathing, golf, fishing, riding within easy reach. Children and dogs welcome. Special Breaks. Fully licensed with excellent cellar and restaurant. 27 bedrooms (20 private bathrooms), all with colour TV and direct-dial telephones. ★★★ *RAC. Egon Ronay.*

Barons Craig Hotel Rockcliffe,by Dalbeattie Kirkcudbrightshire DG5 4QF Tel:(Rockcliffe) 055663 225		COMMENDED ♛ ♛ ♛	3 Single 15 Twin 7 Double 1 Family	20 En Suite fac 5 Pub.Bath/Show	B&B per person £32.00-£45.00 Single £30.00-£40.00 Double	Open Apr-Oct Dinner 1900-2100 B&B + Eve.Meal £50.00-£60.00	

Victorian country house in 12 acres of wooded ground and garden. Elevated position overlooks Solway Firth.

Millbrae Guest House Rockcliffe,by Dalbeattie Kirkcudbrightshire DG5 4QG Tel:(Rockcliffe) 055663 217		HIGHLY COMMENDED ♛ ♛	3 Twin 2 Double	4 En Suite fac 1 Pub.Bath/Show	B&B per person £15.00-£17.00 Double	Open Jan-Dec Dinner from 1900 B&B + Eve.Meal £25.00-£27.00	

19C guest house close to beach and forest; an ideal base for walkers and nature lovers.

ROCKCLIFFE, **by Dalbeattie continued** Torbay Guest House Torbay Farmhouse Rockcliffe, by Dalbeattie Kirkcudbrightshire DG5 4QE Tel:(Rockcliffe) 055663 403	Map 2 B1	**HIGHLY** **COMMENDED** 👑 👑 👑	1 Twin 2 Double	2 En Suite fac 1 Priv.NOT ensuite	B&B per person £22.00-£24.00 Single £15.00-£18.00 Double	Open Easter-Oct Dinner 1830-1930 B&B + Eve.Meal £22.00-£25.00
			Family house in former farmhouse peacefully situated 0.5 miles (1km) from picturesque village of Rockcliffe. French and German spoken. Pets welcome.			
ROGART **Sutherland** Rovie Farm Guest House Rogart Sutherland 1V28 3YZ Tel:(Rogart) 0408 641209	Map 4 B6		1 Twin 2 Double	1 Pub.Bath/Show	B&B per person £14.00-£16.00 Single £14.00-£16.00 Double	Open Apr-Oct Dinner from 1830 B&B + Eve.Meal £28.00-£29.00
ROSEBANK **Lanarkshire** Popinjay Hotel Rosebank Lanarkshire ML8 5QB Tel:(Crossford) 0555 860441 Fax:0555 860204	Map 2 B6	**HIGHLY** **COMMENDED** 👑 👑 👑 👑	17 Single 10 Twin 14 Double 2 Family Suite avail.	43 En Suite fac	B&B per person £49.00-£55.00 Single £29.00-£34.00 Double	Open Jan-Dec Dinner 1800-2200 B&B + Eve.Meal £63.50-£69.50
			Built in Tudor style in 1882 with 8 acres of grounds extending to River Clyde. Fishing rights and free golfing facilities. Some annexe accom. On A74			
ROSEMARKIE **Ross-shire** Marine Hotel Rosemarkie Ross-shire IV10 8UL Tel:(Fortrose) 0381 20253/620253	Map 4 B8		11 Single 30 Twin 4 Double 4 Family	23 En Suite fac 7 Pub.Bath/Show	B&B per person £22.00-£26.50 Single £22.00-£30.00 Double	Open Apr-Oct Dinner 1915-2030 B&B + Eve.Meal £36.50-£44.50
ROSYTH **Fife** Gladyer Inn Heath Road/Ridley Drive Rosyth Fife KY11 2BT Tel:(Inverkeithing) 0383 419977	Map 2 C4		18 Twin 2 Double 1 Family	21 En Suite fac	B&B per person from £32.00 Single from £32.00 Double	Open Jan-Dec Dinner 1830-2100
ROTHES **Moray** East Bank Hotel 15 High Street Rothes, Aberlour Banffshire AB38 7AU Tel:(Rothes) 03403 564	Map 4 D8	**APPROVED** 👑 👑	1 Single 6 Twin 1 Double 2 Family	2 En Suite fac 1 Limited ensuite 4 Pub.Bath/Show	B&B per person £15.50-£24.00 Single £14.00-£21.00 Double	Open Jan-Dec Dinner 1700-2230
			Privately owned hotel in centre of town on Whisky Trail and Speyside Walk.			

ROTHES continued

Map 4 D8

Seafield Arms Hotel
75 New Street
Rothes
Moray
AB38 7BJ
Tel:(Rothes) 03403 587

Award Pending

1 Single
2 Twin
1 Family

1 En Suite fac
1 Pub.Bath/Show

B&B per person
£18.00-£25.00 Single
£18.00-£25.00 Double

Open Jan-Dec
Dinner 1700-2000
B&B + Eve.Meal
£22.00-£30.00

ROTHESAY
Isle of Bute

Map 1 F5

Ardmory House Hotel
Ardmory Road, Ardbeg
Rothesay
Isle of Bute
PA20 0PG
Tel:(Rothesay) 0700 502346

COMMENDED

2 Twin
2 Double
1 Family

5 En Suite fac

B&B per person
£24.00-£28.00 Double

Open Jan-Dec
Dinner 1800-2200
B&B + Eve.Meal
£32.00-£36.00

Privately owned hotel, with large established garden, situated in quiet residential area overlooking Rothesay Bay and Loch Striven.

Ardyne Private Hotel
38 Mountstuart Road
Rothesay
Isle of Bute
PA20 9EB
Tel:(Rothesay) 0700 502052
Fax:0700 505129

COMMENDED

2 Single
3 Twin
3 Double
2 Family

10 En Suite fac

B&B per person
from £22.00 Single
from £20.00 Double

Open Jan-Dec
Dinner 1800-1830
B&B + Eve.Meal
£28.00-£30.00

Personally run hotel on seafront with impressive views of the Kyles of Bute and Loch Striven. Ferry terminal 3/4 mile (1 km).

Bayview Hotel
21-22 Mountstuart Road
Rothesay
Isle of Bute
PA20 9EB
Tel:(Rothesay) 0700 502339
Fax:0700 502339

COMMENDED

2 Single
7 Twin
3 Double

12 En Suite fac

B&B per person
from £25.00 Single
from £23.00 Double

Open Jan-Dec
Dinner from 1800
B&B + Eve.Meal
from £32.00

Family run hotel with panoramic views across Rothesay Bay to Loch Striven and Kyles of Bute. Close to town centre. Some annexe accommodation.

Craigmore Hotel
Crichton Road
Rothesay
Isle of Bute
PA20
Tel:(Rothesay) 0700 503533

APPROVED

4 Single
4 Twin
4 Double
4 Family

16 En Suite fac

B&B per person
£24.00-£26.50 Single
£20.00-£22.50 Double

Open Jan-Dec
Dinner 1900-2100
B&B + Eve.Meal
£29.50-£31.75

Privately owned personally run hotel in quiet residential area with panoramic views of the Kyles of Bute and Loch Striven. Health and fitness studio

Glenburn Hotel
Glenburn Road
Rothesay
Isle of Bute
PA20 9JP
Tel:(Rothesay) 0700 502500
Fax:0700 503774

12 Single
93 Twin
26 Double
4 Family
Suite avail.

135 En Suite fac

B&B per person
£28.35-£36.75 Single
£23.10-£42.00 Double

Open Mar-Nov, Xmas/New Year
Dinner 1830-2000
B&B + Eve.Meal
£30.45-£47.25

Palmyra Private Hotel
12 Ardbeg Road
Rothesay
Isle of Bute
PA20 0NJ
Tel:(Rothesay) 0700 502929

COMMENDED

1 Single
2 Twin
2 Double

5 En Suite fac

B&B per person
from £20.00 Single
from £20.00 Double

Open Jan-Dec
Dinner from 1800
B&B + Eve.Meal
from £28.00

19C stone built house by the sea shore with views of Rothesay Bay and Firth of Clyde. Fresh seafood a speciality.

ROTHESAY continued	Map 1 F5				
Rothesay Victoria 55 Victoria Street Rothesay Isle of Bute PA20 0AP Tel:(Rothesay) 0700 503553 Fax:0700 502426	COMMENDED 👑 👑 👑 👑	6 Single 9 Twin 5 Double	20 En Suite fac	B&B per person to £27.50 Single to £27.50 Double	Open Jan-Dec Dinner 1800-2200 B&B + Eve.Meal from £27.50

Refurbished Victorian hotel in town centre. Situated on Esplanade with panoramic views across Rothesay Bay and Loch Striven.

ROWARDENNAN by Drymen. Stirlingshire	Map 1 G4				

ROWARDENNAN · LOCH LOMOND

Rowardennan, By Drymen G63 0AR
Tel: 036 087 273   Fax: 036 087 251

This family run hotel with the accent on good food, comfort and service. Situated on the loch shore in the lee of Ben Lomond. Children are welcome. This is an ideal stopover for those walking the West Highland Way – or if you are not energetic, just relaxing.

Phone for brochure.

| Rowardennan Hotel
Loch Lomond
Rowardennan,by Drymen
Stirlingshire
G63 0AR
Tel:(Balmaha) 036087 273
Fax:036087 251 | APPROVED
👑 | 2 Single
6 Twin
2 Double
1 Family | 1 En Suite fac
3 Pub.Bath/Show | B&B per person
£22.00-£27.00 Single
£18.00-£23.00 Double | Open Apr-Oct
Dinner 1830-2100 |

Family run hotel on Loch shore and in lee of the Ben. Situated on West Highland Way; ideal stopover. Fishing can be arranged.

ROY BRIDGE Inverness-shire	Map 3 H1				

Glenspean Lodge Hotel

Roybridge, Inverness-shire PH31 4AW.
Tel: (0397) 712223. Fax: (0397) 712660   👑 👑 👑 👑 **Highly Commended**

Set in own wooded grounds this completely refurbished turreted Highland Lodge offers a high standard of cuisine and comfort including 4-Poster beds and Honeymoon Suite. Wine and dine in our restaurant overlooking Ben Nevis Range. "Hunt with a Camera" and other activities available.
Contact Neal & Isabel Smith. B&B from £35.00 per person.   AA ★★★

| Glenspean Lodge Hotel
Roy Bridge
Inverness-shire
PH31 4AW
Tel:(Spean Bridge)
0397 712223
Fax:0397 712660 | HIGHLY
COMMENDED
👑 👑 👑
👑 | 1 Single
4 Twin
6 Double
4 Family
Suites avail. | 15 En Suite fac | B&B per person
£35.00-£45.00 Single
£35.00-£45.00 Double | Open Jan-Dec
Dinner 1900-2130
B&B + Eve.Meal
£53.75-£63.75 |

An imposing turreted former hunting lodge with close views of Ben Nevis range. Fishing, stalking, skiing and photographic safaris.

ST ABBS – ST ANDREWS

ST ABBS
Berwickshire

Map 2
G5

Castle Rock Guest House
Murrayfield
St Abbs
Berwickshire
TD14 5PP
Tel:(Coldingham) 08907
71715
Fax:08907 71520

COMMENDED
♛ ♛ ♛

1 Single
1 Twin
1 Double
1 Family

4 En Suite fac
1 Pub.Bath/Show

B&B per person
from £21.00 Single
from £21.00 Double

Open Easter-Oct
Dinner 1900-1930
B&B + Eve.Meal
from £34.00

Good food and comfort plus sea views from all rooms are features of this
attractive house. Close to nature reserve and 3 miles (5kms) from A1.

ST ANDREWS
Fife

Map 2
E3

Argyle House Private Hotel
127 North Street
St Andrews
Fife
KY16 9AG
Tel:(St Andrews) 0334 73387
Fax:0334 74664

2 Single
8 Twin
4 Double
5 Family

19 En Suite fac

B&B per person
£20.00-£29.00 Single
£20.00-£29.00 Double

Open Jan-Dec

Ashleigh House Hotel
37 St Mary's Street
St Andrews
Fife
KY16 8AZ
Tel:(St Andrews) 0334 75429
Fax:0334 74383

COMMENDED
♛ ♛ ♛

3 Twin
3 Double
2 Family

6 En Suite fac
2 Limited ensuite
2 Pub.Bath/Show

B&B per person
£18.00-£26.00 Double

Open Jan-Dec
Dinner 1830-2000
B&B + Eve.Meal
£28.00-£36.00

Small personally run hotel, on the outskirts of the town, with putting green,
sauna and solarium. Wall located for town and golf courses.

Hazelbank Hotel
28 The Scores
St Andrews
Fife
KY16 9AS
Tel:(St Andrews) 0334 72466

COMMENDED
♛ ♛ ♛

1 Single
3 Twin
3 Double
3 Family

10 En Suite fac

B&B per person
£20.00-£55.00 Single
£20.00-£38.00 Double

Open Jan-Dec
Dinner 1700-1900
B&B + Eve.Meal
£30.00-£65.00

Family owned hotel, only yards from the 1st tee of the Old Course and
overlooking St Andrews Bay. Street parking.

The Parkland Hotel
& Restaurant
Kinburn Castle
St Andrews
Fife
KY16 9QS
Tel:(St Andrews) 0334 73620

COMMENDED
♛ ♛ ♛

7 Single
5 Twin
1 Double
2 Family

9 En Suite fac
3 Pub.Bath/Show

B&B per person
£28.50-£42.50 Single
£26.00-£35.00 Double

Open Jan-Dec
Dinner 1830-2030
B&B + Eve.Meal
£41.00-£57.50

Late Victorian listed building with large garden, in quiet residential area. Close
to town centre and golf courses.

WELCOME

Whenever you are in Scotland, you can be sure of a warm welcome at your
nearest Tourist Information Centre.

For guide books, maps, souvenirs, our Centres provide a service second to
none – many now offer bureau-de-change facilities. And, of course, Tourist
Information Centres offer free, expert advice on what to see and do, route-
planning and accommodation for everyone – visitors and residents alike!

VAT is shown at 17.5%: changes in this rate may affect prices. Prices shown are for guidance only. Please send SAE with each enquiry

ST ANDREWS continued	Map 2 E3

Rufflets Country House

Outstanding country house in 10 acres of award winning gardens 1.5 miles from St Andrews and the "Home of Golf". All rooms en-suite, excellent cooking with fresh Scottish produce. Many visitor attractions or quiet relaxation.

Contact: Peter Aretz, Rufflets Country House, Strathkinness Low Road, St Andrews, Fife KY16 9TX. Tel: 0334 72594 Fax: 0334 78703
    Highly Commended

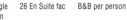

Rufflets Country House & Garden Restaurant Strathkinness Low Road St Andrews Fife KY16 9TX Tel:(St Andrews) 0334 72594 Fax:0334 78703	HIGHLY COMMENDED	6 Single 8 Twin 2 Double 10 Family	26 En Suite fac	B&B per person	Open Jan-Dec Dinner 1900-2130 B&B + Eve.Meal £54.00-£88.00	

Country house set in 10 acres of beautiful gardens providing the fresh produce served in restaurant. 1.5 miles (3kms) from golf courses and beach.

Rusacks Hotel Pilmour Links St Andrews Fife KY16 9JQ Tel:(St Andrews) 0334 74321 Fax:0334 77896	COMMENDED	7 Single 34 Twin 9 Double	50 En Suite fac	B&B per person £55.00-£95.00 Single £65.00-£95.00 Double	Open Jan-Dec B&B + Eve.Meal from £79.00	

A traditional hotel c1887, overlooking the 18th hole of the famous Old Course. Close to town centre and university. Conference facilities.

The Russell Hotel 26 The Scores St Andrews Fife KY16 9AS Tel:(St Andrews) 0334 73447 Fax:0334 78279	COMMENDED	7 Twin 1 Double 2 Family	10 En Suite fac	B&B per person £27.50-£60.00 Single £30.00-£37.50 Double	Open Jan-Dec Dinner 1900-2130 B&B + Eve.Meal £38.50-£50.00	

Family run hotel with friendly atmosphere, overlooking St Andrews Bay and convenient for golf and town centre. A la carte restaurant.

BE SURE TO CHOOSE THE SCOTTISH TOURIST BOARD'S SIGN OF QUALITY

ST ANDREWS continued	Map 2 E3

ST ANDREWS GOLF HOTEL

40 The Scores, St Andrews KY16 9AS
Tel: 0334 72611 Fax: 0334 72188

Superbly situated on the cliffs overlooking St Andrews Bay and Golf Links, 200 metres from the 1st tee of the Old Course. The Victorian listed building has been tastefully and sympathetically refurbished. There are luxurious individually styled en-suite bedrooms and elegant but comfortable lounges and bars.

The oak-panelled restaurant has earned a rosette for the excellence of its cuisine featuring the best of local produce. This is complemented by a superb list of more than 100 carefully selected wines. The hotel is family owned and run and we specialise in arranging golf in and around St Andrews or anywhere in Scotland.

St Andrews Golf Hotel 40 The Scores St Andrews Fife KY16 9AS Tel:(St Andrews) 0334 72611 Fax:0334 72188	HIGHLY COMMENDED ♛♛♛ ♛	2 Single 6 Twin 5 Double 10 Family	23 En Suite fac	B&B per person £66.00-£76.00 Single £52.50-£69.50 Double	Open Jan-Dec Dinner 1900-2130 B&B + Eve.Meal £80.00-£92.00

Privately owned hotel, situated 200 yards from the Old Course, overlooking St Andrews Bay. Taste of Scotland. Imaginative use of local ingredients.

Scores Hotel
ST ANDREWS, FIFE KY16 9BB

TEL: (0334) 72451
FAX: (0334) 73947

Only yards from the 1st tee of the Old Course and a few minutes walk from the historic town centre, this famous independently owned 3-star hotel commands magnificent views of St Andrews Bay. Facilities include an all-day coffee shop, cocktail and lounge bars, a well respected restaurant, a small private garden and car parking. Golf arrangements on request.

The Scores Hotel The Scores St Andrews Fife KY16 9BB Tel:(St Andrews) 0334 72451 Fax:0334 73947	COMMENDED ♛♛♛ ♛	7 Single 15 Twin 5 Double 3 Family	30 En Suite fac	B&B per person £45.00-£72.00 Single £38.00-£58.00 Double	Open Jan-Dec Dinner 1900-2130

Modernised, Victorian hotel, overlooking West Sands and near 1st tee of Old Course. Ballroom and conference facilities.

The Sporting Laird Hotel 5 Playfair Terrace, North Street St Andrews Fife KY16 9HX Tel:(St Andrews) 0334 75906 Fax:0334 73881	COMMENDED ♛♛♛	1 Single 3 Twin 3 Double 2 Family	9 En Suite fac	B&B per person £26.00-£30.00 Single £26.00-£30.00 Double	Open Mar-Jan Dinner 1930-2030 B&B + Eve.Meal £38.00-£42.00

Personally run small hotel offering traditional Scottish high tea. Located between shops and golf courses. Assistance with golfing holidays.

ST ANDREWS continued	Map 2 E3					

Yorkston Hotel
68-70 Argyle Street
St Andrews
Fife
KY16 9BU
Tel:(St Andrews) 0334 72019

COMMENDED ♕♕♕

2 Single
4 Twin
2 Double
2 Family

6 En Suite fac
2 Pub.Bath/Show

B&B per person
£20.00-£26.00 Single
£19.00-£28.00 Double

Open Jan-Dec
Dinner 1830-1900
B&B + Eve.Meal
£31.50-£40.50

Privately owned hotel, situated in residential area of town with easy access to golf course, shops and other amenities.

The Albany
56 North Street
St Andrews
Fife
KY16 9AH
Tel:(St Andrews) 0334 77737
Fax:0334 77737

APPROVED ♕♕♕

2 Single
3 Twin
4 Double
3 Family

6 En Suite fac
2 Pub.Bath/Show
£20.00-£25.00 Double

B&B per person
£22.00-£32.00 Single

Open Jan-Dec
Dinner 1800-1930
B&B + Eve.Meal
£30.00-£42.00

Quietly located, private hotel offering Scotrail inclusive holidays, overlooking University. Close to St.Leonards school, theatres, cinema and golf.

Arran House Guest House
5 Murray Park
St Andrews
Fife
Tel:(St Andrews) 0334 74724
Fax:0334 72072

1 Twin
1 Double
2 Family

3 En Suite fac
1 Priv.NOT ensuite £17.00-£21.00 Single
1 Pub.Bath/Show

B&B per person
£17.00-£21.00 Double

Open Feb-Nov

Aslar Guest House
120 North Street
St Andrews
Fife
KY16 9AF
Tel:(St Andrews) 0334 73460
Fax:0334 73460

HIGHLY COMMENDED ♕♕

1 Single
1 Twin
2 Double
1 Family

5 En Suite fac

B&B per person
£20.00-£25.00 Single
£20.00-£25.00 Double

Open Jan-Dec

Victorian, family run terraced house centrally situated for shops, golf courses, restaurants and cultural pursuits. All rooms en suite.

Cadzow Guest House
58 North Street
St Andrews
Fife
KY16 9AH
Tel:(St Andrews) 0334 76933

COMMENDED ♕♕

1 Single
2 Twin
4 Double
1 Family

6 En Suite fac
1 Pub.Bath/Show

B&B per person
£22.00-£27.00 Single
£14.00-£22.00 Double

Open Feb-Nov

Privately owned Victorian terraced house. Close to castle, cathedral and sea front and within walking distance of shops. Good parking available.

Cleveden Guest House
3 Murray Place
St Andrews
Fife
KY16 9AP
Tel:(St Andrews) 0334 74212

COMMENDED ♕♕

2 Single
2 Twin
1 Double
1 Family

4 En Suite fac
1 Priv.NOT ensuite £16.00-£22.00 Single
2 Pub.Bath/Show £16.00-£22.00 Double

B&B per person

Open Jan-Dec

Personally run guest house, five minutes walk from the Old Course, beach and town centre.

Craigmore Guest House
3 Murray Park
St Andrews
Fife
KY16 9AW
Tel:(St Andrews) 0334 72142/77963

2 Twin
1 Double
2 Family

5 En Suite fac

B&B per person
£18.00-£35.00 Single
£16.00-£24.00 Double

Open Feb-Nov

ST ANDREWS continued — Map 2 E3

Edenside House
Edenside
St Andrews
Fife
KY16 9SQ
Tel:(Leuchars) 0334 838108
Fax:0334 838493

COMMENDED ♛ ♛ ♛

6 Twin
3 Double

9 En Suite fac

B&B per person
£20.00-£25.00 Double

Open Jan-Dec
Dinner at 1900
B&B + Eve.Meal
£36.00-£41.00

Visible from A91 on approach to St Andrews 2.5 miles (4 kms) in superb setting on Eden estuary shore. All rooms ensuite and own parking. Non smoking

---

Glenderran Guest House
9 Murray Park
St Andrews
Fife
KY16 9AW
Tel:(St Andrews) 0334 77951
Fax:0334 77908

COMMENDED ♛ ♛

2 Single
1 Twin
2 Double

3 En Suite fac
2 Priv.NOT ensuite

B&B per person
£18.00-£25.00 Single
£18.00-£25.00 Double

Open Jan-Dec

Victorian town house retaining some original features. Warm and comfortable. Close to all amenities. Non-smoking.

Number Ten Guest House
10 Hope Street
St Andrews
Fife
KY16 9HJ
Tel:(St Andrews) 0334 74601

COMMENDED ♛ ♛

3 Single
3 Twin
3 Double
1 Family

6 En Suite fac

B&B per person
£20.00-£25.00 Single
£20.00-£23.00 Double

Open Feb-Nov

Elegant Georgian terrace house quietly situated but only minutes from the town centre and beach. All rooms with private facilities.

Riverview Guest House
Edenside
St Andrews
Fife
KY16 9ST
Tel:(Leuchars) 0334 838009
Fax:0334 838009

3 Twin
4 Family

7 En Suite fac

B&B per person
£20.50-£22.50 Double

Open Jan-Dec
Dinner 1800-2000
B&B + Eve.Meal
£32.50-£34.50

Shandon Guest House
10 Murray Place
St Andrews
Fife
KY16 9AP
Tel:(St Andrews) 0334 72412
Fax:0334 78126

COMMENDED ♛ ♛

1 Single
1 Double
2 Family

3 En Suite fac
1 Pub.Bath/Show

B&B per person
£16.00-£25.00 Single
£16.00-£27.00 Double

Open Jan-Dec

Victorian terraced house off main street, convenient for local amenities. Most rooms with en suite facilities. Golf packages arranged.

Shorecrest Guest House
23 Murray Park
St Andrews
Fife
KY16 9AW
Tel:(St Andrews) 0334 75310
Fax:0334 75310

2 Single
3 Twin
3 Double
4 Family

12 En Suite fac
1 Pub.Bath/Show

B&B per person
£17.00-£28.00 Single
£17.00-£28.00 Double

Open Jan-Dec
Dinner from 1800
B&B + Eve.Meal
£28.00-£39.00

West Park Guest House
5 St Marys Place,
Market Street
St Andrews
Fife
KY16 9VY
Tel:(St Andrews) 0334 75933

COMMENDED ♛ ♛

1 Twin
2 Double
1 Family

3 En Suite fac
1 Limited ensuite
2 Pub.Bath/Show

B&B per person
£16.50-£21.00 Double

Open Jan-Nov

Beautiful, listed Georgian house C1830 in heart of historic town. Close to Old Course and all amenities.

	Map 2						
ST ANDREWS **continued** David Russell Hall, Univ. of St Andrews Buchanan Gardens St Andrews Fife KY16 9LY Tel:(St Andrews) 0334 72281 Fax:0334 78701	E3	**Award Pending**	464 Single	112 Pub.Bath/Show	B&B per person £18.95 Single £18.95 Double	Open Mar-Apr, Jun-Sep Dinner 1800-1900 B&B + Eve.Meal £26.55	
Hamilton Hall, Univ. of St Andrews Golf Place St Andrews Fife KY16 9BD Tel:(St Andrews) 0334 62000 Fax:0334 62500		**Award Pending**	52 Single 25 Twin	17 Pub.Bath/Show	B&B per person £18.95 Single £18.95 Double	Open Jun-Sep Dinner 1800-1900 B&B + Eve.Meal £26.55	
North Haugh St Andrews Fife KY16 9SU Tel:(St Andrews) 0334 62000 Fax:0334 62500		**Award Pending**	48 Double 16 Family	64 En Suite fac	B&B per person £25.90 Single £20.75 Double	Open Jun-Sep Dinner 1800-1900 B&B + Eve.Meal £33.20	
BY ST ANDREWS **Fife** Lathones Hotel by Largoward, St Andrews Fife KY9 1JE Tel:(Peat Inn) 033484 494 Fax:033484 494	Map 2 E3	**COMMENDED**	1 Single 9 Twin 4 Double 6 miles (10kms) west of St Andrews, in rural village, an old coaching inn with open fires and timbered ceilings.	14 En Suite fac	B&B per person from £28.00 Single from £25.00 Double	Open Jan-Dec Dinner 1800-2030	
Romar Guest House 45 Main Street Strathkinness Fife KY16 9RZ Tel:(Strathkinness) 0334 85308 Fax:0334 85308		**COMMENDED**	2 Single 1 Twin 1 Double Spacious modern house in pleasant rural surroundings, 3 miles (5kms) from St Andrews.	1 En Suite fac 2 Pub.Bath/Show	B&B per person £15.00-£20.00 Single £14.00-£18.00 Double	Open Jan-Dec	

SCOTTISH TOURIST BOARD
QUALITY COMMENDATIONS ARE:

Deluxe – *An EXCELLENT quality standard*
Highly Commended – *A VERY GOOD quality standard*
Commended – *A GOOD quality standard*
Approved – *An ADEQUATE quality standard*

ST BOSWELLS Roxburghshire	Map 2 E7

Buccleuch Arms Hotel

THE GREEN, ST BOSWELLS TD6 0EW
Tel: 0835 22243 Fax: 0835 23965

The BUCCLEUCH ARMS HOTEL. Situated in the picturesque village of St Boswells, this former Coaching Inn has 17 en-suite bedrooms, also the Garden Room Restaurant with a wide choice of menus, plus lounge bar with log fires in winter offers bar food daily, or relax in our elegant lounge with an after-dinner drink. The Borders can boast of fourteen golf courses, all within a twelve-mile radius of the hotel including the 9-hole course in St Boswells itself, also shooting on some of the best Border Estates. B&B from £38 per night.
Please contact Sue Dodds on 0835 22243.

The Buccleuch Arms Hotel The Green St Boswells Roxburghshire TD6 0EW Tel:(St Boswells) 0835 22243 Fax:0835 23965	APPROVED ♛ ♛ ♛ ♛	5 Single 8 Twin 6 Double	17 En Suite fac 1 Pub.Bath/Show	B&B per person £30.00-£38.00 Single £30.00-£34.00 Double	Open Jan-Dec Dinner 1800-2100 B&B + Eve.Meal £32.00-£42.00
		A former 17C coaching inn, situated on the main A68. Ideally situated for business or pleasure, with function facilities for up to 100 guests.			
Dryburgh Abbey Hotel St Boswells Roxburghshire TD6 0RQ Tel:(St Boswells) 0835 22261 Tlx:727972 Fax:0835 23945	HIGHLY COMMENDED ♛ ♛ ♛ ♛ ♛	9 Twin 17 Double Suites avail.	26 En Suite fac	B&B per person £40.00-£100.00 Single £40.00-£100.00 Double	Open Jan-Dec Dinner 1930-2115 B&B + Eve.Meal £45.00-£110.00
		Country house hotel on banks of River Tweed and overlooked by 12C Dryburgh Abbey. Ideal base for fishing, shooting or exploring this historic area.			
ST CATHERINE'S by Dunoon, Argyll Arnish Cottage Guest House Poll Bay St Catherines Argyll PA25 8BA Tel:(Inveraray) 0499 2405	Map 1 F3 HIGHLY COMMENDED ♛ ♛ ♛	1 Twin 2 Double	3 En Suite fac	B&B per person from £23.00 Single from £18.00 Double	Open Jan-Dec Dinner from 1900 B&B + Eve.Meal from £30.00
		Family run lochside cottage in quiet conservation area. Freshly cooked local produce and seafood from the loch.			
ST COMBS by Fraserburgh, Aberdeenshire Tufted Duck Hotel St Combs,by Fraserburgh Aberdeenshire Tel:(Inverallochy) 0346 582481 Fax:0346 582475	Map 4 H7 COMMENDED ♛ ♛ ♛ ♛	4 Single 6 Twin 3 Double 5 Family	18 En Suite fac	B&B per person £20.00-£46.50 Single £20.00-£37.50 Double	Open Jan-Dec Dinner 1800-2130
		Family run hotel overlooking sand dunes and sea. Extensively modernised and refurbished. Wide menus with accent on local seafood. Taste of Scotland.			

ST FILLANS Perthshire	Map 2 A2

Achray House Hotel

LOCH EARN . ST FILLANS . PERTHSHIRE . PH6 2NF
Tel: (0764) 685231 Fax: (0764) 685320

Stunning Lochside position in St Fillans - an area of outstanding natural beauty. Well established, family run hotel, known for its wide selection of good food, service and a caring attitude that brings people back year after year. The perfect base for sightseeing, golf, walking, field and watersports. **AA** ★★ ⊛ *Egon Ronay* ♨ ♨ ♨ Highly Commended

Achray House Hotel Lochearn St Fillans Perthshire PH6 2NF Tel:(St Fillans) 0764 685231 Fax:0764 685320	**HIGHLY COMMENDED** ♨ ♨ ♨	3 Twin 6 Double 1 Family	7 En Suite fac 1 Pub.Bath/Show	B&B per person £30.00-£38.00 Single £22.00-£28.00 Double	Open Mar-Oct Dinner 1830-2130 B&B + Eve.Meal £36.00-£42.00
		Small, personally run hotel with extensive bar and restaurant menu. Picturesque village with magnificent views over Loch Earn.			
Drummond Arms Hotel St Fillans Perthshire PH6 2NF Tel:(St Fillans) 0764 685212 Fax:0764 685212		6 Single 11 Twin 10 Double 2 Family	29 En Suite fac	B&B per person from £30.00 Single from £25.00 Double	Open Apr-Oct Dinner 1900-2130
Four Seasons Hotel St Fillans Perthshire PH6 2NF Tel:(St Fillans) 0764 685333 Fax:0764 685333	**Award Pending**	6 Twin 6 Double 6 Family	18 En Suite fac	B&B per person £32.00-£40.00 Single £30.00-£38.00 Double	Open Mar-Dec Dinner 1900-2130 B&B + Eve.Meal £49.00-£57.00

ST MARGARET'S HOPE Orkney The Creel Restaurant & Rooms Front Road St Margaret's Hope Orkney KW17 2SL Tel:(St Margaret's Hope) 085683 311	Map 5 B1 **COMMENDED** ♨ ♨ ♨	1 Twin 1 Double Suites avail.	2 En Suite fac	B&B per person £20.00-£25.00 Single £20.00-£23.00 Double	Open Feb-Dec Dinner 1900-2130
		A restaurant of some renown with rooms available in this charming shore side village. Situated right on the sea front.			

ST MARY'S HOLM Orkney Commodore Motel St Mary's Holm Orkney KW17 2RU Tel:(St Mary's Holm) 085678 319 Fax:085678 219	Map 5 C12 **COMMENDED Lodge**	6 Twin	6 En Suite fac	B&B per person £20.00-£25.00 Single £15.00-£17.50 Double	Open Jan-Dec Dinner 1830-2200
		Motel rooms with bar and restaurant adjacent. Splendid views over St Marys Bay and the Churchill Barriers. 6 miles (10kms) from Kirkwall.			

ST MARY'S LOCH
Selkirkshire
Tibbie Shiels Inn
St Mary's Loch
Selkirkshire
TD7 5LH
Tel:(Selkirk) 0750 42231

Map 2
D7

APPROVED
♛ ♛

1 Twin	2 Pub.Bath/Show	B&B per person	Open Jan-Dec
3 Double		to £17.50 Double	Dinner 1830-2030
1 Family			

Country inn, full of character, on Southern Upland Way. Scenic beauty, walking, birdwatching. Restaurant and bar meals with vegetarian dishes.

ST MONANS
Fife
Mayview Hotel
Station Road
St Monans
Fife
KY10 2BN
Tel:(St Monans) 0333730 564

Map 2
E3

1 Single	1 Pub.Bath/Show	B&B per person	Open Jan-Dec
3 Double		£20.00-£24.00 Single	Dinner 1800-2130
1 Family		£20.00-£24.00 Double	

SALEN
Isle of Mull, Argyll
Salen Hotel
Salen
Isle of Mull, Argyll
PA72 6JE
Tel:(Aros) 0680 300324

Map 1
D2

4 Single	4 En Suite fac	B&B per person	Open Jan-Dec
4 Twin	3 Pub.Bath/Show	£19.00-£23.00 Single	Dinner 1900-2100
2 Double		£19.00-£23.00 Double	B&B + Eve.Meal
2 Family			£32.00-£36.00

BY SALEN
Isle of Mull, Argyll
Glenforsa Hotel
by Salen, Aros
Isle of Mull, Argyll
PA72 6JW
Tel:(Aros) 0680
300377/300379

Map 1
D2

APPROVED
♛ ♛

10 Twin	16 En Suite fac	B&B per person	Open Jan-Dec
6 Double		£39.50-£41.50 Single	Dinner 1900-2200
		£39.50-£41.50 Double	B&B + Eve.Meal
			£53.50-£55.50

Log cabin hotel on the shores of The Sound of Mull. With spectacular hill and sea views. Landing strip close by.

SALINE
by Dunfermline, Fife
The Saline Hotel
West Road
Saline,by Dunfermline
Fife
KY12 9UN
Tel:(New Oakley) 0383
852798

Map 2
B4

3 Twin	3 En Suite fac	B&B per person	Open Jan-Dec
		£20.00-£23.00 Single	Dinner 1700-2100
		£20.00-£23.00 Double	

SANDAY
Orkney
Belsair Hotel
Sanday
Orkney
KW17 2BJ
Tel:(Sanday) 08575 206
Fax:08575 488

Map 5
C1

COMMENDED
♛ ♛ ♛

3 Single	3 En Suite fac	B&B per person	Open Jan-Dec
1 Twin	1 Pub.Bath/Show	£18.00-£25.00 Single	Dinner 1700-1930
1 Double		£18.00-£25.00 Double	B&B + Eve.Meal
1 Family			£24.00-£31.00

Relax in this peaceful and comfortable island hotel. Warm welcome and home cooking. Beautiful beaches and ideal for walking.

SANDYHILLS **by Dalbeattie** **Kirkcudbrightshire** Cairngill House Hotel Sandyhills,by Dalbeattie Kirkcudbrightshire DG5 4NZ Tel:(Southwick) 038778 681	Map 2 B1	COMMENDED ♕ ♕ ♕	4 Twin 4 Double	6 En Suite fac 2 Priv.NOT ensuite	B&B per person £30.00-£32.00 Single £25.00-£27.00 Double	Open Jan-Dec Dinner at 1900 B&B + Eve.Meal £39.00-£41.00

Late Victorian house in 3 acres of garden and grounds with own tennis court. Superb views over sandy beach and sea beyond.

Craigbittern House Sandyhills, by Dalbeattie Kirkcudbrightshire DG5 4NZ Tel:(Southwick) 038778 247		HIGHLY COMMENDED ♕ ♕	1 Twin 4 Double	2 En Suite fac 2 Pub.Bath/Show	B&B per person £16.50 Single £18.50-£20.00 Double	Open Jan-Dec Dinner 1830-1900 B&B + Eve.Meal £26.00-£29.50

Granite built Victorian house with large garden and superb views over Solway Firth. Home cooking using fresh local ingredients.

SANQUHAR **Dumfriesshire** Blackaddie House Hotel Blackaddie Road Sanquhar Dumfriesshire DG4 6JJ Tel:(Sanquhar) 0659 50270	Map 2 A8	COMMENDED ♕ ♕ ♕	2 Single 3 Twin 3 Double 2 Family	10 En Suite fac	B&B per person £32.00-£35.00 Single £27.00-£29.00 Double	Open Jan-Dec Dinner 1830-2100

Personally run traditional stone farmhouse dating from 16C. Specialising in locally grown organic produce.

Nithsdale Guest House Glasgow Road Sanquhar Dumfriesshire DG4 6BZ Tel:(Sanquhar) 0659 50288		COMMENDED ♕	1 Single 2 Double 3 Family	2 Pub.Bath/Show	B&B per person to £14.00 Single to £14.00 Double	Open Jan-Dec Dinner from 1800 B&B + Eve.Meal to £20.50

Detached stone built villa on A76 but with lovely hill views. Ample car parking to rear. On Southern Upland Way, ideal for walkers.

SCARINISH **Isle of Tiree, Argyll** Scarinish Hotel Scarinish Isle of Tiree, Argyll PA77 6UH Tel:(Scarinish) 08792 308 Fax:08792 410	Map 1 A2		4 Single 1 Twin 1 Double 2 Family.	2 En Suite fac 2 Pub.Bath/Show	B&B per person £17.00-£21.00 Single £14.00-£18.00 Double	Open Jan-Dec Dinner 1830-2130 B&B + Eve.Meal £26.00-£30.00

Welcome Hosts provide a warm welcome, good service and information about their area. Look out for the people wearing the Welcome Host badge.

SCONE, by Perth **Perthshire**	Map 2 C2		

Murrayshall Country House Hotel and Golf Course
SCONE, PERTHSHIRE PH2 7PH
Tel (0738) 51171   Fax: (0738) 52595

Murrayshall is set in 300 acres of undulating parkland. The house is furnished in traditional style and combined with our 18-hole golf course provides an excellent country retreat. A range of golfing breaks and other packages are available and with Perthshire to explore our guests will never be idle.

| Murrayshall House Hotel
Scone
Perth
PH2 7PH
Tel:(Scone) 0738 51171
Fax:0738 52595 | **HIGHLY
COMMENDED**
👑 👑 👑
👑 👑 | 12 Twin   19 En Suite fac
4 Double
3 Family | B&B per person
£62.50-£80.00 Single
£55.00-£65.00 Double | Open Jan-Dec
Dinner 1900-2130
B&B + Eve.Meal
£82.50-£92.50 |

Edwardian country house with own golf course set amidst 300 acres of parkland. Winner of Taste of Scotland Restaurant of the Year Award 1988.

SCOURIE **Sutherland**	Map 3 G4		

EDDRACHILLES HOTEL
Badcall Bay   Scourie   Sutherland

| Eddrachilles Hotel
Badcall Bay
Scourie
Sutherland
IV27 4TH
Tel:(Scourie) 0971 502080
Fax:0971 502477 | **COMMENDED**
👑 👑 👑 | 7 Twin   11 En Suite fac
3 Double
1 Family | B&B per person
£35.00-£45.00 Single
£31.00-£36.00 Double | Open Mar-Oct
Dinner 1830-2030
B&B + Eve.Meal
£42.00-£47.00 |

Family run with superb views over Eddrachilles Bay and standing in 320 acres of private moorland.

SCOURIE continued	**Map 3** G4					
Scourie Hotel Scourie Sutherland IV27 4SX Tel:(Scourie) 0971 502396 Fax:0971 502423		**COMMENDED** 👑 👑 👑	5 Single 7 Twin 7 Double 2 Family	19 En Suite fac 1 Pub.Bath/Show	B&B per person £29.00-£40.00 Single £26.00-£35.00 Double	Open Mar-Oct Dinner 1930-2030 B&B + Eve.Meal £39.00-£52.00
			Personally run; ideally situated for touring this rugged area of North West Scotland. Hotel specialises in fishing for salmon, sea trout, brown trout			
SEAMILL **Ayrshire**	**Map 1** G6					
Seamill Hydro 39 Ardrossan Road Seamill Ayrshire KA23 9ND Tel:(West Kilbride) 0294 822217 Fax:0294 823939			17 Single 25 Twin 18 Double 10 Family Suites avail.	70 En Suite fac	B&B per person £50.00-£80.00 Single £37.50-£55.00 Double	Open Jan-Dec Dinner 1800-2100 B&B + Eve.Meal £55.00-£85.00
Spottiswood Guest House 3 Sandy Road Seamill Ayrshire KA23 9NN Tel:(Seamill) 0294 823131		**DELUXE** 👑 👑	1 Twin 2 Double	1 En Suite fac 1 Pub.Bath/Show	B&B per person from £16.00 Double	Open Jan-Dec Dinner at 1900 B&B + Eve.Meal from £26.00
			Victorian shore-side home. Tea in garden, island views, imaginative menus, flowers, music, books. Base for golf, Ayrshire coast, being pampered.			
SELKIRK	**Map 2** E7					
County Hotel 35 High Street Selkirk TD7 4BZ Tel:(Selkirk) 0750 21233		**COMMENDED** 👑 👑 👑	1 Single 2 Twin 2 Double 1 Family	6 En Suite fac	B&B per person £20.00-£25.00 Single £25.00-£27.50 Double	Open Jan-Dec Dinner 1800-2130 B&B + Eve.Meal £29.50-£35.00
			Small, family run hotel in centre of this historic Borders town. Popular function room.			
Glen Hotel Yarrow Terrace Selkirk TD7 5AS Tel:(Selkirk) 0750 20259		**COMMENDED** 👑 👑 👑	2 Single 1 Twin 3 Double 3 Family	7 En Suite fac 1 Pub.Bath/Show	B&B per person £25.00-£29.00 Single £22.50-£25.00 Double	Open Jan-Dec Dinner 1830-2030 B&B + Eve.Meal £30.00-£40.00
			Spacious Victorian house in pleasant gardens, set high above the A707, with views over the River Ettrick. Family run.			
Heatherlie House Hotel Heatherlie Park Selkirk TD7 5AL Tel:(Selkirk) 0750 21200		**COMMENDED** 👑 👑 👑	1 Single 2 Twin 2 Double 2 Family	6 En Suite fac 1 Pub.Bath/Show	B&B per person £21.00-£27.00 Single £23.00-£25.00 Double	Open Jan-Dec Dinner 1830-2100 B&B + Eve.Meal £32.00-£38.00
			Elegant Victorian mansion quietly situated in wooded grounds. Emphasis on original home cooking.			

SELKIRK continued	Map 2 E7

Philipburn House Hotel
SELKIRK, SCOTTISH BORDERS TD7 5LS
Tel: 0750 20747   Fax: 0750 21690

Award-winning Philipburn is one of Scotland's most popular country house hotels and restaurants. Run by the Hill family, the hotel's charm, the charming accommodation, romantic poolside and Zum Zee restaurants and a superb range of facilities make it a supremely attractive hotel for any occasion all year round. Many activities: from golf to orienteering on offer and an interesting range of speciality weekends and live folk and jazz regularly held.

DB&B from £59 a night.

Philipburn House Hotel Selkirk TD7 5LS Tel:(Selkirk) 0750 20747 Fax:0750 21690	HIGHLY COMMENDED 👑 👑 👑 👑	4 Twin 2 Double 11 Family	17 En Suite fac	B&B per person £38.50-£59.50 Single £38.50-£49.50 Double	Open Jan-Dec Dinner 1930-2130 B&B + Eve.Meal £52.00-£69.50

Personally run, former Dower house of unique style and character. Innovative and interesting cuisine. Garden suites. Outdoor heated pool. Annexe.

SHAPINSAY **Orkney** Balfour Castle Balfour Village Shapinsay Orkney KW17 2DY Tel:(Balfour) 085671 282 Fax:085671 235	Map 5 C1	1 Twin 2 Double 1 Family	3 En Suite fac 1 Pub.Bath/Show	B&B per person	Open Mar-Nov Dinner 1930-2100 B&B + Eve.Meal to £58.75

SHIELDAIG **Ross-shire** Tigh an Eilean Hotel Shieldaig by Strathcarron Ross-shire IV54 8XN Tel:(Shieldaig) 05205 251 Fax:05205 321	Map 3 F8 HIGHLY COMMENDED 👑 👑	3 Single 4 Twin 3 Double 1 Family	11 En Suite fac	B&B per person from £39.30 Single from £43.70 Double	Open Easter-Oct Dinner 1900-2030 B&B + Eve.Meal from £58.60

Personally run, recently refurbished hotel in small village. Overlooking sea loch. All rooms with private facilities. Fresh produce, local seafood.

SKEABOST **Isle of Skye,** **Inverness-shire** Skeabost House Hotel Skeabost,by Portree Isle of Skye, Inverness-shire IV51 9NR Tel:(Skeabost Bridge) 047032 202 Fax:047032 454	Map 3 D9 COMMENDED 👑 👑 👑 👑	6 Single 9 Twin 7 Double 4 Family	24 En Suite fac 3 Pub.Bath/Show	B&B per person £36.00-£44.00 Single £46.00-£54.00 Double	Open Apr-Oct Dinner 1900-2030 B&B + Eve.Meal £59.00-£67.00

Personally run country house with 9 hole golf course (par 31) and 8 miles (13 kms) of salmon fishing on River Snizort. Some annexe accommodation.

| SKELMORLIE
Ayrshire
Heywood Hotel
Shore Road
Skelmorlie
Ayrshire
PA17
Tel:(Wemyss Bay) 0475
520258
Fax:0475 520258 | Map 1
G5 | Award
Pending | 2 Single
1 Twin
4 Double
1 Family | 8 En Suite fac
1 Pub.Bath/Show | B&B per person
£35.00-£45.00 Single
£25.00-£30.00 Double | Open Jan-Dec
Dinner 1700-2200 | |

| SLEAT
Isle of Skye,
Inverness-shire | Map 3
E1 | | | | | | |

Isleornsay·DUISDALE HOTEL
Isleornsay, Sleat, Isle of Skye IV43 8QW
Telephone: (04713) 202

Set in 25 acres of garden and woodland with spectacular views over the Sound of Sleat, the DUISDALE provides good food, good wine and a warm welcome; the ideal spot to relax and unwind.
Open March to November.
For details: contact Mrs Margaret Colpus.

| Duisdale Hotel
Sleat
Isle of Skye, Inverness-shire
IV43 8QW
Tel:(Isle Ornsay) 04713 202
Fax:04713 363 | | COMMENDED
ᨌ ᨌ ᨌ | 5 Single
8 Twin
2 Double
4 Family

Family run hotel in 25 acres of wooded grounds with own yacht moorings and breathtaking views across the Sound of Sleat. | 14 En Suite fac
2 Pub.Bath/Show | B&B per person
£36.75-£42.00 Single
£31.50-£43.00 Double | Open Mar-Dec
Dinner 1930-2030
B&B + Eve.Meal
£47.80-£62.50 | |

| SOUTH GALSON
Lewis, Western Isles
Galson Farm Guest House
South Galson
Lewis, Western Isles
Tel:(Borve) 0851 850492 | Map 3
D3 | HIGHLY
COMMENDED
ᨌ ᨌ ᨌ | 2 Twin
1 Family

18th century, restored, working croft close to shore with views to Butt of Lewis.
Home cooking and licensed. | 3 En Suite fac
1 Pub.Bath/Show | B&B per person
£23.00 Double | Open Jan-Dec
Dinner 1800-2000
B&B + Eve.Meal
£39.00 | |

| SOUTH QUEENSFERRY
West Lothian
Forth Bridges Moat House
South Queensferry
West Lothian
EH30 9SF
Tel:031 331 1199
Tlx:727430
Fax:031 319 1733 | Map 2
C4 | | 15 Single
61 Twin
5 Double
27 Family | 108 En Suite fac | B&B per person
£75.00-£85.00 Single
£55.00-£62.00 Double | Open Jan-Dec
Dinner 1845-2145
B&B + Eve.Meal
£70.00-£100.00 | |

SOUTH QUEENSFERRY continued Hawes Inn Newhalls Road South Queensferry West Lothian EH30 9TA Tel:031 331 1990 Fax:031 319 1120	Map 2 C4	COMMENDED	1 Single 2 Twin 5 Double	3 Pub.Bath/Show	B&B per person from £35.70 Single from £27.00 Double	Open Jan-Dec Dinner 1800-2200	

Adjacent to magnificent Forth Railway Bridge, this historic inn (R L Stevenson, Sir Walter Scott) has the most dramatic waterside situation.

Queensferry Arms Hotel 17 High Street South South Queensferry West Lothian EH30 9PP Tel:031 331 1298 Fax:031 331 4731		COMMENDED	4 Twin 3 Double 1 Family	6 En Suite fac 2 Pub.Bath/Show	B&B per person £38.00-£55.00 Single £27.00-£40.00 Double	Open Jan-Dec Dinner 1900-2130	

Old tavern dating from 1664 in main street, now totally refurbished. Rooms to the rear and dining room overlook Firth of Forth and the Bridges.

SPEAN BRIDGE Inverness-shire Letterfinlay Lodge Hotel Spean Bridge Inverness-shire PH34 4DZ Tel:(Spean Bridge) 0397 712622	Map 3 H1	Award Pending	1 Single 7 Twin 4 Double 1 Family	9 En Suite fac 4 Pub.Bath/Show	B&B per person £20.00-£36.00 Single £20.00-£36.00 Double	Open Mar-Nov Dinner 1900-2030 B&B + Eve.Meal £37.00-£53.00	

Spean Bridge Hotel Spean Bridge Inverness-shire PH34 4ES Tel:(Spean Bridge) 039781 250		COMMENDED	6 Single 20 Twin 2 Double 4 Family	29 En Suite fac 1 Pub.Bath/Show	B&B per person £29.00-£43.00 Single £28.00-£42.00 Double	Open Jan-Dec Dinner 1900-2100 B&B + Eve.Meal £36.00-£50.00	

Family run hotel situated in the centre of Spean Bridge about 9 miles (14kms) from Fort William. Adjacent to Aonach Mhor.

Barbagianni Guest House Tirindrish Spean Bridge Inverness-shire PH34 4EU Tel:(Spean Bridge) 0397 712437		HIGHLY COMMENDED	1 Single 1 Twin 5 Double	4 En Suite fac 2 Pub.Bath/Show	B&B per person £15.50 Single £15.50-£17.50 Double	Open Easter-20 Oct Dinner from 1930 B&B + Eve.Meal £25.50-£27.50	

Detached modern house of interesting design, in its own grounds with excellent views over Ben Nevis and beyond. Friendly atmosphere, home baking.

Coire Glas Guest House Spean Bridge Inverness-shire PH34 4EU Tel:(Spean Bridge) 0397 712272		COMMENDED	2 Single 4 Twin 6 Double 2 Family	8 En Suite fac 3 Pub.Bath/Show	B&B per person £14.00-£16.00 Single £13.00-£18.00 Double	Open Jan-Oct Dinner 1900-2000 B&B + Eve.Meal £23.00-£28.00	

Family run guest house set back from A86 tourist route, only 8 miles (13kms) from Aonach Mor gondola station. Views of the Ben Nevis mountain range.

Distant Hills Guest House Spean Bridge Inverness-shire PH34 4EU Tel:(Spean Bridge) 039781 452		HIGHLY COMMENDED	4 Twin 3 Double	7 En Suite fac 1 Pub.Bath/Show	B&B per person from £15.00 Double	Open Jan-Dec Dinner 1700-2030	

Modern bungalow at edge of quiet village. Friendly and personal attention. Excellent views of Aonach Mhor; ideally situated for touring and skiing.

	Map 3						
SPEAN BRIDGE **Inverness-shire** Druimandarroch House Spean Bridge,by Fort William Inverness-shire PH34 4EU Tel:(Spean Bridge) 039781 335	H1 APPROVED ♥♥ ♥♥	2 Twin 3 Double 2 Family	2 En Suite fac 2 Pub.Bath/Show	B&B per person from £16.00 Single from £15.00 Double	Open Mar-Nov Dinner 1900-2000 B&B + Eve.Meal from £25.00	

House at the centre of this small but busy Highlands village. Ideal for touring; Fort William 10 miles (16kms), Aonach Mor Gondola 8 miles (11kms).

Grey Corries Guest House Spean Bridge Inverness-shire PH34 Tel:(Spean Bridge) 0397712 579	COMMENDED ♥♥ ♥♥	1 Twin 2 Double 3 Family	4 En Suite fac 2 Priv.NOT ensuite 2 Pub.Bath/Show	B&B per person £10.50-£16.50 Single £10.50-£16.50 Double	Open Jan-Dec Dinner 1700-2100 B&B + Eve.Meal £19.50-£24.50

Modern house on A82 Fort William to Inverness Road. Family run; home cooking with wild game and fish. Open all the year round.

Inverour Guest House Spean Bridge Inverness-shire PH34 Tel:(Spean Bridge) 039781 218	Award Pending	2 Single 2 Twin 3 Double	3 En Suite fac 2 Pub.Bath/Show	B&B per person from £14.00 Single from £13.00 Double	Open Jan-Dec Dinner 1900-2000 B&B + Eve.Meal from £25.00

Old Pines

Gairlochy Road, Spean Bridge, Inverness-shire PH34 4EG
Telephone: 0397 712324. Fax: 0397 712433.
Quiet situation. Breathtaking views of Aonach Mor and Ben Nevis. Ideal base for touring the West Highlands. Happy family home with a relaxing, informal atmosphere, pretty en-suite bedrooms, flowers, books and log fires. Imaginative fresh food carefully prepared and presented.
Contact: Niall or Sukie Scott   *"A Very Special Place"*

Niall & Sukie Scott, Old Pines Gairlochy Road Spean Bridge Inverness-shire PH34 4EG Tel:(Spean Bridge) 0397 712324 Fax:0397 712433	HIGHLY COMMENDED ♥♥ ♥♥ ♥♥	2 Single 2 Twin 2 Double 2 Family	7 En Suite fac 1 Priv.NOT ensuite 1 Pub.Bath/Show	B&B per person £20.00-£25.00 Single £20.00-£25.00 Double	Open Jan-Dec Dinner from 2000 B&B + Eve.Meal £35.00-£40.00

Scandinavian log cabin set among pine trees with panoramic views of Aonach Mor. Friendly family home. A flair for imaginative fresh food.

Details of Grading and Classification are on page vi. | Key to symbols is on back flap. |

BY SPEAN BRIDGE continued	Map 3 H1		

Corriegour Lodge Hotel

LOCH LOCHY, By SPEAN BRIDGE
Telephone: (0397712) 685 Fax: (0397712) 696

Relax in the finest setting in the "Great Glen" with warm, comfortable en-suite accommodation and antique furnishings. Dine in our Loch View Conservatory or Bistro, and enjoy friendly personal service and good company. Recommended by 'Taste of Scotland', Johansens, Signpost and Ashley Courtenay.
Colour brochure available. Proprietors: Rod and Lorna Bunney.

Corriegour Lodge Hotel Loch Lochy by Spean Bridge Inverness-shire PH34 4EB Tel:(Spean Bridge) 0397 712685 Fax:0397 712696		**HIGHLY COMMENDED**	2 Single 8 En Suite fac 3 Twin 3 Double	B&B per person £28.00-£38.00 Single £28.00-£38.00 Double	Open Mar-Oct Dinner 1800-2200 B&B + Eve.Meal £38.00-£54.00	
			100 year old former shooting/fishing lodge in commanding position overlooking Loch Lochy. Taste of Scotland member.			

SPEY BAY **Moray** Spey Bay Hotel Spey Bay Fochabers Moray IV32 7PY Tel:(Fochabers) 0343 820424	Map 4 E7	**APPROVED**	2 Single 10 En Suite fac 2 Twin 3 Double 3 Family	B&B per person £25.00 Single £22.00 Double	Open Jan-Dec Dinner 1700-2030 B&B + Eve.Meal £32.00-£33.00	
			Ideally situated adjacent to golf club with panoramic sea views. Fochabers 5 miles (8kms). Live entertainment every Saturday.			

STAFFIN **Isle of Skye,** **Inverness-shire**	Map 3 D8			

FLODIGARRY COUNTRY HOUSE HOTEL

STAFFIN, ISLE OF SKYE IV51 9HZ   Tel: (047 052) 203 Fax: (047 052) 301
One of Skye's most beautifully located hotels. Historic mansion house, set in 5 acres of woodland, beneath Quiraing Mountains. Stunning sea views, cosy bedrooms, most en-suite, log fires and old world atmosphere. Acclaimed restaurant ("Good Food Guide"/"Taste of Scotland"). Bar/Conservatory meals available all day.
Open all year: Bed and breakfast £21.00 to £43.00. Dinner from £17.00.
Contact: Andrew or Pam Butler.

Flodigarry Country House Hotel Flodigarry Staffin Isle of Skye, Inverness-shire IV51 9HZ Tel:(Duntulm) 047052 203 Fax:047052 301		**Award Pending**	4 Single 16 En Suite fac 7 Twin 3 Limited ensuite 11 Double 1 Pub.Bath/Show 2 Family	B&B per person £25.00-£36.00 Single £20.00-£45.00 Double	Open Jan-Dec Dinner 1900-2200 B&B + Eve.Meal £38.00-£63.00	

STANLEY **Perthshire** Tayside Hotel 51-53 Mill Street Stanley, Perth Perthshire PH1 4NL Tel:(Stanley) 0738 828249 Fax:0738 827216	Map 2 C2	**COMMENDED**	3 Single 12 En Suite fac 8 Twin 2 Limited ensuite 4 Double 2 Pub.Bath/Show 2 Family	B&B per person £19.50-£39.50 Single £19.50-£29.50 Double	Open Jan-Dec Dinner 1900-2100 B&B + Eve.Meal £34.50-£54.00	
			In residential area of small village, 5 miles (8kms) north of the city of Perth. Ideal touring centre; fishing, shooting and golfing packages.			

STENNESS **Orkney** Standing Stones Hotel Stenness Orkney KW16 3JX Tel:(Stromness) 0856 850449 Fax:0856 851262	Map 5 B1 **HIGHLY** **COMMENDED**	3 Single 6 Twin 5 Double 3 Family	17 En Suite fac	B&B per person £25.00-£31.50 Single £25.00-£33.00 Double	Open Jan-Dec Dinner 1830-2100 B&B + Eve.Meal £36.50-£45.00	

Recently built, on loch shore, retaining island character and warmth. Ideal for fishing, business and family holidays.

STEWARTON **Ayrshire** Chapeltoun House Hotel Stewarton Ayrshire KA3 3ED Tel:(Stewarton) 0560 482696 Fax:0560 485100	Map 1 H6 **HIGHLY** **COMMENDED**	2 Twin 6 Double	8 En Suite fac	B&B per person £65.00-£84.00 Single £45.00-£64.50 Double	Open Jan-Dec Dinner 1900-2100	

Country house, retaining all its original features, in own grounds. Interesting menu using fresh fish, game and vegetables.

Lochridge House Stewarton Ayrshire KA3 5LH Tel:(Stewarton) 0560 484334	**COMMENDED**	1 Twin 1 Family	1 En Suite fac 2 Pub.Bath/Show	B&B per person £15.00-£17.50 Single £15.00-£17.50 Double	Open Jan-Dec	

Large family house, dating back to C1635, set in wooded grounds with own tennis court. Warm welcome and friendly atmosphere.

STIRLING Garfield Hotel 12 Victoria Square Stirling FK8 2QU Tel:(Stirling) 0786 473730	Map 2 A4 **APPROVED**	2 Single 3 Twin 2 Double 1 Family	5 En Suite fac 2 Pub.Bath/Show	B&B per person £27.00-£35.00 Single £24.00-£30.00 Double	Open Jan-Dec Dinner 1800-2100	

Family run hotel in large Victorian house overlooking quiet square. Close to centre of Stirling, Castle and all amenities. Nearby golf course.

Golden Lion Hotel
KING STREET STIRLING
Tel: (0786) 475351
Fax: (0786) 472755
Central Reservations
0397-703139

Beautifully positioned in the centre of Stirling and just down the road from the Castle, this 3-star hotel provides excellent facilities throughout. Many of its 70 bedrooms have been refurbished with the addition of our Superior and Executive rooms.

Special holiday rates available in our Scottish Holiday brochure, with other hotels in Oban, Fort William and Inverness.

Golden Lion Hotel 8 King Street Stirling FK8 1BD Tel:(Stirling) 0786 475351 Fax:0786 472755	**APPROVED**	19 Single 36 Twin 14 Double 2 Family	71 En Suite fac	B&B per person £59.00-£64.00 Single £34.50-£39.50 Double	Open Jan-Dec Dinner 1830-2100 B&B + Eve.Meal £73.00-£79.00	

In the town centre with car park at the rear of the hotel. Stirling Castle Bannockburn and Wallace monument a short distance away.

STIRLING continued	Map 2 A4

Stirling Highland Hotel

SPITTAL STREET . STIRLING FK1 8DU
Tel: 0786 475444 Fax: 0786 462929

Extensive refurbishment and upgrading of this magnificent listed building has created a 76 bedroom, 4 star hotel, with a unique character and style.

All bedrooms have private bathroom, colour satellite television, telephone, hairdryer, trouser press and tea and coffee making facilities.

There are two excellent restaurants and first-class health club with swimming pool, spa bath, saunas, steam rooms, solaria, gymnasium, squash courts, and snooker room.

The hotel is 500 yards from the town's Castle and close to the Wallace Monument and the site of the Battle of Bannockburn.

Dinner, bed and breakfast rates from £52.
Over 60's from £36. Free accommodation and breakfast for children under 16 sharing parents room.

Stirling Highland Hotel
Spittal Street
Stirling
Tel:(Stirling) 0786 475444
Fax:0786 462929

HIGHLY COMMENDED

56 Twin / 76 En Suite fac
20 Double
Suites avail.

B&B per person
£80.00-£96.00 Single
£55.00-£63.00 Double

Open Jan-Dec
Dinner 1800-2230
B&B + Eve.Meal
£100.00-£116.00

Restored, listed, former high school, converted into very comfortable hotel with full leisure and conference facilities. Friendly, attentive service

---

Stirling Management Centre
University of Stirling
Stirling
FK9 4LA
Tel:(Stirling) 0786 451666
Tlx:777557 STUNIVG
Fax:0786 450472

COMMENDED

46 Single / 74 En Suite fac
4 Twin
24 Double

B&B per person
to £49.00 Single
to £31.00 Double

Open Jan-Dec
Dinner 1900-2100
B&B + Eve.Meal
from £59.00

Purpose built conference centre/hotel in peaceful setting on picturesque campus. University leisure facilities available. Ideal touring base.

Terraces Hotel
4 Melville Terrace
Stirling
FK8 2ND
Tel:(Stirling) 0786 472268
Fax:0786 450314

COMMENDED

3 Single / 18 En Suite fac
3 Twin
8 Double
4 Family

B&B per person
£55.00-£60.00 Single
£35.00-£40.00 Double

Open Jan-Dec
Dinner 1830-2100

Centrally situated and close to town centre with ample parking. Personally run with a friendly, caring staff. Function and conference facilities.

Bannockburn Guest House
24/32 Main Street
Bannockburn, Stirling
Stirlingshire
FK7 8LY
Tel:(Bannockburn) 0786 812121/816501
Fax:0786 817628

COMMENDED Lodge

3 Twin / 6 En Suite fac
2 Double
1 Family

B&B per person
£22.00-£24.00 Single
£17.00-£19.00 Double

Open Jan-Dec
Dinner at 1800
B&B + Eve.Meal
£23.00-£28.00

Purpose built 1990's facilities in a 1760's building! Ideal touring centre1 mile (2kms) from motorway.

STIRLING continued	Map 2 A4						
Castlecroft Ballengeich Road Stirling FK8 1TN Tel:(Stirling) 0786 474933		HIGHLY COMMENDED ♕ ♕	2 Twin 3 Double 1 Family	6 En Suite fac 1 Pub.Bath/Show	B&B per person £25.00-£30.00 Single £16.00-£19.00 Double	Open Jan-Dec	
			Nestling on elevated site under Stirling Castle, this comfortable, modern house offers warm welcome. Private facilities, some suitable for disabled.				
Firgrove Guest House 13 Clifford Road Stirling FK8 2AQ Tel:(Stirling) 0786 475805		COMMENDED ♕ ♕	1 Twin 2 Double	2 En Suite fac 2 Pub.Bath/Show	B&B per person £18.00-£25.00 Single £14.00-£18.00 Double	Open Apr-Oct	
			Spacious house with large comfortable rooms. Excellent parking within grounds. 5 minutes walk to town centre.				
Forth Guest House 23 Forth Place, Riverside Stirling FK8 1UD Tel:(Stirling) 0786 471020 Fax:0786 447220		HIGHLY COMMENDED ♕ ♕ ♕	1 Twin 2 Double	3 En Suite fac	B&B per person £20.00-£30.00 Single £17.50-£19.00 Double	Open Jan-Dec Dinner 1730-1830 B&B + Eve.Meal £24.50-£26.00	
			Terraced house close to railway station and town centre. Good location for touring.				
Mia-Roo Guest House 37 Snowdon Place Stirling FK8 2JP Tel:(Stirling) 0786 473979			2 Single 2 Twin 2 Double 2 Family	1 Pub.Bath/Show	B&B per person £16.50-£18.00 Single £16.50-£18.00 Double	Open Jan-Dec	
Woodside Guest House 4 Back Walk Stirling FK8 2QA Tel:(Stirling) 0786 475470		APPROVED ♕ ♕	1 Single 1 Twin 2 Double 1 Family	2 En Suite fac 3 Limited ensuite 1 Pub.Bath/Show	B&B per person £16.00-£18.00 Single £16.00-£17.00 Double	Open Jan-Dec	
			Character building on historic wall of Stirling. A warm welcome assured. Centrally located.				
Stirling Holiday Campus University of Stirling Stirling FK9 4LA Tel:(Stirling) 0786 467146 Fax:0786 467143			1030 Single 50 Twin	105 Pub.Bath/Show	B&B per person £18.35 Single £18.35 Double	Open Jan-Feb, Jun-Sep Dinner 1730-1900	

STONEHAVEN
Kincardineshire

Map 4
G1

County Hotel
Arduthie Road
Stonehaven
Kincardineshire
AB3 2EH
Tel:(Stonehaven) 0569
64386
Fax:0569 64386

1 Single
5 Twin
7 Double
1 Family

14 En Suite fac
5 Pub.Bath/Show

B&B per person
£40.00-£60.00 Single
£40.00-£60.00 Double

Open Jan-Dec
Dinner 1830-2130

Heugh Hotel
Westfield Road
Stonehaven
Kincardineshire
AB3 2EH
Tel:(Stonehaven) 0569
62379
Fax:0569 66637

COMMENDED
👑 👑 👑
👑

3 Single
2 Double

5 En Suite fac

B&B per person
from £48.00 Single
from £37.50 Double

Open Jan-Dec
Dinner 1800-2130

Granite baronial mansion with extensive oak panelling, standing in its
own grounds.

St Leonards Hotel
Stonehaven
Kincardineshire
AB3
Tel:(Stonehaven) 0569
62044
Fax:0569 66222

2 Single
3 Twin
4 Double
3 Family

11 En Suite fac
1 Pub.Bath/Show

B&B per person
£40.00-£45.00 Single
£25.00-£30.00 Double

Open Jan-Dec
Dinner 1900-2200
B&B + Eve.Meal
£35.00-£45.00

Arduthie House
Ann Street
Stonehaven
Kincardineshire
AB3 2DA
Tel:(Stonehaven) 0569
762381

COMMENDED
👑 👑

1 Twin
1 Double
2 Family

3 En Suite fac
1 Pub.Bath/Show

B&B per person
£17.00-£19.00 Single
£15.00-£17.00 Double

Open Jan-Dec
Dinner at 1830
B&B + Eve.Meal
£23.00-£27.00

Detached guest house with large attractive garden situated in the centre of
Stonehaven. Bowling green and golf course nearby.

STORNOWAY
Lewis, Western Isles

Map 3
D4

Caberfeidh Hotel

Manor Park, Stornoway, Isle of Lewis PA87 2EU
Ref WTS   Tel: 0851 702604   Fax: 0851 705572
The Caberfeidh is known as the island's finest hotel. All its merit awarded
bedrooms offer the highest standards of comfort and luxury. Our Manor
Restaurant offers you a choice of menus. Many dishes, perhaps our specialities
include fresh fish and shellfish drawn straight from local waters.
The Caberfeidh Hotel: luxury with that special touch.
Prices from: £65.00 Single; £43.00 per person Double/Twin B&B.
Dinner from £17.50.

Cabarfeidh Hotel
Manor Park
Stornoway
Lewis, Western Isles
PA87 2EU
Tel:(Stornoway) 0851 702604
Fax:0851 705572

HIGHLY
COMMENDED
👑 👑 👑
👑 👑

10 Single
27 Twin
9 Double

46 En Suite fac

B&B per person
from £68.00 Single
from £45.00 Double

Open Jan-Dec
Dinner 1900-2130
B&B + Eve.Meal
from £87.00

Recently refurbished hotel with a la carte restaurant offering interesting choice
of dishes with emphasis on local produce.

	Map 3						
STORNOWAY **continued** Caledonian Hotel 4/6 South Beach Street Stornoway Lewis, Western Isles PA87 2XY Tel:(Stornoway) 0851 702411	D4	APPROVED Listed	3 Single 2 Twin 5 Double	10 En Suite fac	B&B per person £36.00 Single £27.50 Double	Open Jan-Dec Dinner 1730-2100	

Recently refurbished, situated on harbour front, within a few minutes walk of ferry terminal. Restaurant and bar meals.

County Hotel 14 Francis Street Stornoway Lewis, Western Isles PA87 Tel:(Stornoway) 0851 703250 Fax:0851 706008			8 Single 5 Twin 4 Double	16 En Suite fac 2 Pub.Bath/Show	B&B per person £38.00-£45.00 Single £19.00-£23.00 Double	Open Jan-Dec Dinner 1900-2200	

Hebridean Guest House Bayhead Stornoway Lewis, Western Isles PA87 2DZ Tel:(Stornoway) 0851 702268		Award Pending	5 Single 3 Twin 2 Double 2 Family	7 En Suite fac 2 Pub.Bath/Show	B&B per person £18.00-£24.00 Single	Open Jan-Dec Dinner 1830-2030 B&B + Eve.Meal £26.00-£30.00	

Roddy & Catherine Afrin, Park Guest House 30 James Street Stornoway Lewis, Western Isles PA87 2QN Tel:(Stornoway) 0851 702485		COMMENDED	1 Single 2 Twin 2 Double	1 En Suite fac 3 Pub.Bath/Show	B&B per person from £20.00 Single from £19.00 Double	Open Jan-Dec Dinner 1800-2030 B&B + Eve.Meal from £32.00	

Victorian house, sympathetically refurbished to retain its character. Convenient for ferry and airport. Taste of Scotland.

	Map 1						
STRACHUR **Argyll** The Creggans Inn Strachur Argyll PA27 8BX Tel:(Strachur) 036986 279 Fax:036986 637	F4	COMMENDED	4 Single 8 Twin 9 Double	17 En Suite fac 1 Pub.Bath/Show	B&B per person £49.00-£54.00 Single £49.00-£54.00 Double	Open Jan-Dec Dinner 1930-2100 B&B + Eve.Meal £65.00-£70.00	

7C Coaching Inn, tastefully furnished, with magnificent views of Loch Fyne. An excellent reputation for seafood.

	Map 1						
STRANRAER **Wigtownshire** Arkhouse Inn 17-21 Church Street Stranraer Wigtownshire DG9 7JG Tel:(Stranraer) 0776 3161/2616	F1		3 Single 3 Twin 3 Double 1 Family	2 Limited ensuite 2 Pub.Bath/Show	B&B per person £22.00-£24.00 Single £22.00-£24.00 Double	Open Jan-Dec Dinner 1800-2200 B&B + Eve.Meal to £28.00	

Details of Grading and Classification are on page vi. | Key to symbols is on back flap.

STRANRAER Wigtownshire	Map 1 F1

NORTH WEST CASTLE

SEAFRONT, STRANRAER SOUTH-WEST SCOTLAND
Tel: (0776) 4413 Fax: (0776) 2646

AA **** RAC

1990 RAC Credit to the Industry Award
1989 'Taste of Scotland' Hotel of the Year
STB ✤✤✤✤✤ **Highly Commended**

Scottish Tourist Board Best Hotel for Food, Welcome and Hospitality.

Facilities include indoor swimming pool, jacuzzi, sauna, solarium, multi-gym, snooker, table tennis, darts and bowling.

Ask about our rates which include golf and Over 60's rates.

North West Castle Hotel Stranraer Wigtownshire DG9 8EH Tel:(Stranraer) 0776 4413 Fax:0776 2646	**HIGHLY COMMENDED** ✤✤✤ ✤✤	2 Single 39 Twin 29 Double 2 Family Suites avail.	72 En Suite fac	B&B per person £56.00-£86.00 Single £38.00-£48.00 Double	Open Jan-Dec Dinner 1900-2100 B&B + Eve.Meal £52.00-£90.00	
		Former home of Sir John Ross, Arctic explorer. On seafront, swimming pool, games room and curling. A warm Scottish welcome.				
Fernlea Guest House Fernlea, Lewis Street Stranraer Wigtownshire DG9 7AQ Tel:(Stranraer) 0776 3037	**COMMENDED** ✤✤✤	1 Twin 2 Double	2 En Suite fac 1 Pub.Bath/Show	B&B per person £13.00-£18.00 Double	Open Jan-Dec Dinner 1800-1900 B&B + Eve.Meal £20.00-£25.00	
		Personally run, with friendly atmosphere. Close to town centre, Stranraer and Cairnryan ferries. En suite facilities and ample parking. Non-smoking.				
Harbour Guest House Market Street Stranraer Wigtownshire DG9 7RF Tel:(Stranraer) 0776 4626	**COMMENDED** ✤	2 Single 1 Double 2 Family	2 Pub.Bath/Show	B&B per person £15.00-£16.00 Single £15.00-£16.00 Double	Open Jan-Dec Dinner 1700-1800 B&B + Eve.Meal £20.00-£22.00	
		Ideally situated on harbour front in the centre of Stranraer. House is fully double glazed; convenient for Stranraer and Cairnryan ferries.				
Harbour Lights Guest House 7 Agnew Crescent Stranraer Wigtownshire DG9 7JY Tel:(Stranraer) 0776 6261		3 Twin 1 Double 1 Family	2 Pub.Bath/Show	B&B per person £15.00-£18.00 Single £14.00-£16.00 Double	Open Jan-Dec	

STRANRAER Wigtownshire Jan-da-Mar Guest House 1 Ivy Place, London Road Stranraer Wigtownshire DG9 8ER Tel:(Stranraer) 0776 6194	Map 1 F1	COMMENDED 👑 👑	2 Single 3 Twin 3 Family	2 En Suite fac 2 Pub.Bath/Show	B&B per person £15.00 Single £13.00-£17.50 Double	Open Jan-Dec	
			Early 19C townhouse, modernised yet retaining some original features. Conveniently situated for town centre and ferry terminal.				
STRATHAIRD, by Broadford Isle of Skye, Inverness-shire Strathaird House Strathaird,by Broadford Isle of Skye, Inverness-shire IV49 9AX Tel:(Loch Scavaig) 04716 269/(0444 452990 off season)	Map 3 D1	APPROVED Listed	2 Single 1 Double 4 Family	4 Pub.Bath/Show	B&B per person £15.30-£24.00 Single £13.50-£22.00 Double	Open Apr-Sep Dinner 1900-2000 B&B + Eve.Meal £23.50-£34.00	
			Family run guest house in own extensive grounds with views of sea and Cuillins. 10 miles (16 kms) west of Broadford.				
STRATHAVEN Lanarkshire Springvale Hotel 18 Lethame Road Strathaven Lanarkshire ML10 6AD Tel:(Strathaven) 0357 21131	Map 2 A6	COMMENDED 👑 👑 👑	5 Single 2 Twin 4 Double 2 Family	11 En Suite fac 2 Pub.Bath/Show	B&B per person £25.00-£28.00 Single £18.00-£20.00 Double	Open Jan-Dec Dinner 1630-1845 B&B + Eve.Meal £25.00-£32.00	
			Family hotel in quiet residential area close to town centre, with park at rear. Home cooking, baking and high teas a speciality.				
Strathaven Hotel Hamilton Road Strathaven Lanarkshire ML10 6SZ Tel:(Strathaven) 0357 21778 Fax:0357 20789		HIGHLY COMMENDED 👑 👑 👑 👑	4 Single 3 Twin 3 Double	10 En Suite fac	B&B per person £30.00-£59.00 Single £30.00-£37.00 Double	Open Jan-Dec Dinner 1800-2200 B&B + Eve.Meal £45.00-£64.00	
			Recently refurbished stone built hotel (C1800) featuring Adam fireplace and stairway. Standing in own gardens. 20 miles (32kms) south of Glasgow.				
STRATHBLANE Stirlingshire	Map 1 H5						

KIRKHOUSE INN
STRATHBLANE, GLASGOW G63 9AA Tel: (0360) 770621
The **KIRKHOUSE INN** is a comfortable country inn with an excellent
cuisine supplying bar meals or restaurant. Ideally situated for touring
either Glasgow or the Highlands. 15 en-suite bedrooms.
B&B from £72.00 Double. Special Weekend Breaks available.

STB 👑👑👑👑 COMMENDED

Kirkhouse Inn Strathblane Stirlingshire G63 9AA Tel:(Blanefield) 0360 770621 Fax:0360 770896		COMMENDED 👑 👑 👑 👑 👑	2 Single 6 Twin 5 Double 2 Family	15 En Suite fac	B&B per person from £55.25 Single from £36.00 Double	Open Jan-Dec Dinner 1900-2200 B&B + Eve.Meal from £40.50	
			Comfortable country hotel at foot of Campsie Hills. Offers a wide variety of modern cuisine. Convenient for Glasgow.				

Details of Grading and Classification are on page vi. | Key to symbols is on back flap. |

STRATHCARRON
Ross-shire
Strathcarron Hotel
Strathcarron
Ross-shire
IV54 8YR
Tel:(Lochcarron) 05202 227

Map 3
F9

4 Twin
5 Double
1 Family

10 En Suite fac

B&B per person
£19.50-£26.50 Single
£17.50-£22.50 Double

Open Jan-Dec
Dinner 1800-2030
B&B + Eve.Meal
£27.50-£32.50

STRATHPEFFER
Ross-shire
Ben Wyvis Hotel
Strathpeffer
Ross-shire
IV14 9DN
Tel:(Strathpeffer) 0997
421323
Tlx:75160
Fax:0997 421228

Map 4
A8

25 Single
58 Twin
20 Double
3 Family

106 En Suite fac

B&B per person
£25.00-£31.00 Single
£25.00-£31.00 Double

Open Mar-Nov
Dinner 1830-2030
B&B + Eve.Meal
£32.00-£38.00

Brunstane Lodge Hotel
Strathpeffer
Ross-shire
IV14 9AT
Tel:(Strathpeffer) 0997
421261

COMMENDED

1 Single
2 Twin
2 Double
2 Family

6 En Suite fac
1 Pub.Bath/Show

B&B per person
£23.00-£25.00 Single
£25.00-£30.00 Double

Open Jan-Dec
Dinner 1830-2030
B&B + Eve.Meal
£38.00-£42.00

Family run hotel set in its own mature garden in residential area and close to golf course. All rooms with private facilities.

Highland Hotel
Strathpeffer
Ross-shire
IV14 9AN
Tel:(Strathpeffer) 0997
421457
Fax:0997 421228

36 Single
71 Twin
25 Double
6 Family

138 En Suite fac

B&B per person
£25.00-£31.00 Single
£25.00-£31.00 Double

Open Mar-Nov,
Xmas/New Year
Dinner 1830-2030
B&B + Eve.Meal
£32.00-£38.00

Holly Lodge Hotel
Strathpeffer
Ross-shire
IV14 9AR
Tel:(Strathpeffer) 0997
421254

COMMENDED

2 Single
3 Twin
1 Double
1 Family

7 En Suite fac
1 Pub.Bath/Show

B&B per person
from £27.50 Single
from £40.00 Double

Open Dec-Oct
Dinner 1830-2200
B&B + Eve.Meal
from £41.00

Beautifully situated Victorian house, family run, full of character, with open fires.

Strathpeffer Hotel
Strathpeffer
Ross-shire
IV14 9DF
Tel:(Strathpeffer) 0997
421200
Fax:0997 421110

7 Single
15 Twin
10 Double
2 Family

34 En Suite fac

B&B per person
£17.50-£20.00 Single
£17.50-£20.00 Double

Open Mar-Nov
Dinner 1700-2030
B&B + Eve.Meal
£29.00-£31.50

Gardenside Guest House
Strathpeffer
Ross-shire
IV14 9BJ
Tel:(Strathpeffer) 0997
421242

COMMENDED

3 Twin
4 Double

4 En Suite fac
1 Pub.Bath/Show

B&B per person
£14.00-£17.00 Double

Open Mar-Dec
Dinner 1830-2000
B&B + Eve.Meal
£26.00-£30.00

Friendly welcome at family run guest house in Spa village. Good walking country and touring base. 18 miles (27kms) from Inverness.

STRATHTAY **Perthshire** Bendarroch Guest House Strathtay Perthshire PH9 9PG Tel:(Strathtay) 0887 840420 Fax:0887 840438	Map 2 B1		1 Single 4 Twin	5 En Suite fac	B&B per person from £25.00 Single from £25.00 Double	Open Jan-Dec Dinner 1900-2000 B&B + Eve.Meal from £40.00	
STRATHY **Sutherland** Strathy Inn Strathy Sutherland KW14 7RY Tel:(Strathy) 06414 205	Map 4 B3		2 Single 1 Double 1 Family	1 En Suite fac 1 Pub.Bath/Show	B&B per person £16.00-£18.00 Single £16.00-£18.00 Double	Open Jan-Dec Dinner to 2130 B&B + Eve.Meal £24.00-£30.00	
STRATHYRE **Perthshire** Creagan House Restaurant Strathyre Perthshire FK18 8ND Tel:(Strathyre) 08774 638	Map 1 H3	HIGHLY COMMENDED	1 Twin 3 Double 1 Family	3 En Suite fac 1 Pub.Bath/Show	B&B per person £34.25-£42.50 Single £24.50-£30.50 Double	Open Mar-Jan Dinner 1930-2030 B&B + Eve.Meal £40.00-£51.50	
Our tastefully refurbished, intimate home with magnificent Baronial Dining Hall and an excellent reputation for fine dining and caring service.							
The Inn Strathyre Perthshire FK18 8NA Tel:(Strathyre) 08774 224		APPROVED	3 Twin 4 Double	5 En Suite fac 2 Priv.NOT ensuite	B&B per person £20.00-£25.00 Single £18.00-£20.00 Double	Open Jan-Dec Dinner 1900-2100	
Friendly, privately owned 18C inn with coal fire in bar, walkers welcome. Varied and interesting menu.							
Ardoch Lodge Strathyre Perthshire FK18 8NF Tel:(Strathyre) 08774 666		HIGHLY COMMENDED	1 Twin 2 Double	2 En Suite fac 1 Priv.NOT ensuite	B&B per person £24.50-£38.50 Single £20.00-£25.00 Double	Open Jan-Dec Dinner 1915-1945 B&B + Eve.Meal £34.00-£52.50	
Country house accommodation in elegantly appointed 150 year old house. Comfortable spacious rooms. Ideal for walking; bird watching. Pets welcome.							
STROMNESS **Orkney** Braes Hotel Stromness Orkney KW16 Tel:(Stromness) 0856 850495	Map 5 A1	APPROVED	2 Twin 3 Double 1 Family	3 En Suite fac 3 Limited ensuite 2 Pub.Bath/Show	B&B per person £18.00-£20.00 Single £16.00-£20.00 Double	Open Jan-Dec Dinner 1830-2100	
Personally run, with panoramic views of Hoy and Scapa Flow. All rooms with showers. Live entertainment at weekends.							

STROMNESS continued
Map 5 A1

Ferry Inn
John Street
Stromness
Orkney
KW16 3AD
Tel:(Stromness) 0856 850280
Fax:0856 851332

COMMENDED ≋≋≋

2 Single, 5 Twin, 4 Double, 6 Family
12 En Suite fac, 4 Limited ensuite, 1 Pub.Bath/Show

B&B per person
£16.00-£25.00 Single
£16.00-£22.00 Double

Open Jan-Dec
Dinner from 1830

Inn with friendly atmosphere, lively bar and a la carte restaurant, situated at harbour front close to ferry terminal.

Royal Hotel
Stromness
Orkney
KW16 3BS
Tel:(Stromness) 0856 850342

APPROVED ≋≋

2 Single, 6 Twin, 1 Double, 2 Family
11 En Suite fac

B&B per person
£15.00-£21.00 Single
£15.00-£25.00 Double

Open Jan-Dec
Dinner 1800-2000

Centrally located on main street close to the shops, ferry and golf course. All rooms ensuite.

Mrs Alison M Clouston
Thira, Innertown
Stromness
Orkney
KW16 3JP
Tel:(Stromness) 0856 851181

COMMENDED ≋≋≋

2 Single, 2 Double
4 En Suite fac

B&B per person
to £22.00 Single
to £22.00 Double

Open Jan-Nov
Dinner 1900-2000
B&B + Eve.Meal
to £30.00

Custom built guest house in a quiet location with unrivalled views of Hoy Sound. Home cooking with fresh produce.

STROND
Harris, Western Isles
Map 3 B7

Carminish House
1A Strond
An T-Ob, Leverburgh
Harris, Western Isles
Tel:(Leverburgh) 085982 400/307

3 Twin
3 En Suite fac

B&B per person
from £22.00 Double

Open Apr-Dec
Dinner 1900-1930
B&B + Eve.Meal
from £31.00

STRONTIAN
Argyll
Map 1 E1

Ben View Hotel
Strontian
Argyll
PH36 4HY
Tel:(Strontian) 0967 2333

COMMENDED ≋≋

6 Twin, 2 Double, 1 Family
4 En Suite fac, 3 Pub.Bath/Show

B&B per person
£21.50-£23.50 Single
£21.50-£23.50 Double

Open Mar-Oct
Dinner from 1930
B&B + Eve.Meal
£33.50-£35.50

A small family run hotel, situated close to the shores of Loch Sunart, in unspoilt rugged scenery.

Kilcamb Lodge Hotel
Strontian
Argyll
PH36 4HY
Tel:(Strontian) 0967 2257
Fax:0967 2041

HIGHLY COMMENDED ≋≋≋

2 Single, 4 Twin, 4 Double
10 En Suite fac

B&B per person
to £40.00 Single
to £40.00 Double

Open Easter-Oct
Dinner 1930-2030
B&B + Eve.Meal
£58.00-£65.00

Stone built Georgian house, situated in 30 acres of own grounds, facing South across Loch Sunart, with half a mile of private shoreline.

Loch Sunart Hotel
Strontian
Argyll
PH36 4HZ
Tel:(Strontian) 0967 2471

COMMENDED ≋≋≋

1 Single, 2 Twin, 7 Double, 1 Family
11 En Suite fac

B&B per person
£25.00 Single
£25.00 Double

Open Apr-Oct
Dinner 1900-1930
B&B + Eve.Meal
£43.00

18C building, some parts 16C, 40 yards from Loch Sunart. Bird watching and wildlife nearby. Taste of Scotland, emphasis on Scottish produce.

STRUAN Isle of Skye, Inverness-shire	Map 3 C9				
Ullinish Lodge Hotel & Restaurant Struan,by Portree Isle of Skye, Inverness-shire IV56 8FD Tel:(Struan) 047072 214		COMMENDED 👑 👑 👑	2 Twin 4 Double 2 Family	7 En Suite fac 1 Priv.NOT ensuite	B&B per person £30.00-£40.00 Single £30.00-£35.00 Double	Open Easter-Oct Dinner 1900-2100 B&B + Eve.Meal £48.00-£58.00

18C house, in superb situation, with fine views across the loch to the Cuillins. Walking, climbing, ornithology. Own fishing and shooting rights.

STRUY, by Beauly Inverness-shire	Map 3 H9				
Cnoc Hotel Struy,by Beauly Inverness-shire IV4 7JU Tel:(Struy) 046376 264 Fax:046376 264		COMMENDED 👑 👑 👑	3 Twin 3 Double 2 Family	8 En Suite fac	B&B per person £25.00-£37.50 Single £22.50-£32.50 Double	Open Jan-Dec Dinner 1900-2100 B&B + Eve.Meal £37.50-£52.50

Stone building in 2 acres of ground in beautiful Strathglass. Fishing, walking and climbing nearby.

SUMBURGH Shetland	Map 5 G6				
Sumburgh Hotel Sumburgh Shetland ZE3 Tel:(Sumburgh) 0950 60201 Fax:0950 60394		COMMENDED 👑 👑 👑	1 Single 19 Twin 3 Double 1 Family	24 En Suite fac	B&B per person £25.00-£45.00 Single £20.00-£30.00 Double	Open Jan-Dec Dinner 1830-2130 B&B + Eve.Meal £39.00-£59.00

Recently refurbished former Lairds house overlooking sea, next to Jarlshof ancient Viking Settlement, and close to Sumburgh Airport.

SYMINGTON Ayrshire	Map 1 H7				
Danepark House 1 Kilmarnock Road Symington Ayrshire KA1 5PT Tel:(Kilmarnock) 0563 830246 Fax:0563 830246		HIGHLY COMMENDED 👑 👑 👑	2 Twin 1 Double	3 En Suite fac	B&B per person £35.00-£40.00 Single £22.50-£28.50 Double	Open Jan-Dec Dinner 1900-2000 B&B + Eve.Meal £37.50-£43.50

Country residence set in 2.5 acres of grounds. Very convenient for Prestwick Airport, golf courses and Ayr racecourse.

TAIN Ross-shire	Map 4 B7				
Ardmore Lodge Hotel Edderton,by Tain Ross-shire IV19 Tel:(Edderton) 086282 266		COMMENDED 👑	2 Twin 2 Double	1 En Suite fac 2 Pub.Bath/Show	B&B per person £18.00-£21.00 Single £17.00-£19.00 Double	Open Jan-Dec Dinner 1800-2100 B&B + Eve.Meal £27.50-£30.50

Family run hotel in countryside location, 4 miles (6kms) north of Tain. Ideally placed for outdoor activities. Regular live music at weekends.

| Morangie House Hotel
Morangie Road
Tain
Ross-shire
IV19 1PY
Tel:(Tain) 0862 892281
Fax:0862 892872 | | COMMENDED
👑 👑 👑
👑 | 2 Single
2 Twin
6 Double
1 Family | 11 En Suite fac | B&B per person
£45.00-£50.00 Single
£33.00-£38.00 Double | Open Jan-Dec
Dinner 1730-2200
B&B + Eve.Meal
£48.00-£53.00 |

Family run, former Victorian mansion, in own grounds on northern edge of Tain. A la carte restaurant, extensive bar meal menu. Taste of Scotland.

Key to symbols is on back flap.

TAIN continued

Map 4 B7

Golf View Guest House
13 Knockbreck Road
Tain
Ross-shire
Tel:(Tain) 0862 892856

HIGHLY COMMENDED
👑 👑

3 Twin	1 En Suite fac	B&B per person	Open Jan-Dec
1 Double	2 Pub.Bath/Show	£15.00-£20.00 Single	
1 Family		£13.00-£15.00 Double	

Secluded Victorian house with panoramic views over Golf Course and across the Dornoch Firth. Centrally situated in Scotland's oldest Royal Burgh.

TARBERT
Harris, Western Isles

Map 3 C6

Harris Hotel

HARRIS ISLE OF HARRIS
WESTERN ISLES
PA85 3DL

A warm welcome and personal attention is assured with excesses of food and comfort to ensure a happy holiday in this family owned hotel. Glorious beaches, extensive hill walks, climbing, bird-watching and peace. Watch weaving of Harris Tweed. Come and enjoy the experience.
Special 5-day rate.
Tel: Harris (0859) 2154. Fax: (0859) 2281

Harris Hotel
Tarbert
Harris, Western Isles
PA85
Tel:(Harris) 0859 2154
Fax:0859 2281

COMMENDED
👑 👑 👑

4 Single	15 En Suite fac	B&B per person	Open Jan-Dec
10 Twin	4 Pub.Bath/Show	£28.85-£32.55 Single	Dinner from 1930
7 Double		£27.50-£31.20 Double	B&B + Eve.Meal
3 Family			£41.75-£48.00

Ideal centre for touring Lewis and Harris. Old, established family hotel where you will find friendliness, peace and tranquility. Adjacent to ferry.

MacLeod Motel
Tarbert
Harris, Western Isles
PA85
Tel:(Harris) 0859 2364

4 Single	4 Pub.Bath/Show	B&B per person	Open May-Sep
10 Twin		£16.00-£18.00 Single	
1 Double		£30.00-£35.00 Double	
1 Family			

Allan Cottage Guest House
Tarbert
Harris, Western Isles
PA85 3DJ
Tel:(Harris) 0859 2146

HIGHLY COMMENDED
👑 👑 👑

1 Twin	1 En Suite fac	B&B per person	Open Apr-Oct
2 Double	1 Pub.Bath/Show	£17.50-£19.50 Double	Dinner 1900-2050
			B&B + Eve.Meal
			£31.00-£33.00

Recently converted Old Harris Telephone Exchange, offering very high standard of comfort and cuisine.

TARBERT, Loch Fyne
Argyll

Map 1 E5

The Columba Hotel
Tarbert, Loch Fyne
Argyll
PA29 6UF
Tel:(Tarbert) 0880 820808

COMMENDED
👑 👑 👑

1 Single	9 En Suite fac	B&B per person	Open Jan-Dec
3 Twin	2 Pub.Bath/Show	£21.50-£30.95 Single	Dinner 1900-2100
5 Double		£18.50-£27.95 Double	B&B + Eve.Meal
2 Family			£30.95-£42.95

Tranquilly situated overlooking Loch Fyne within walking distance of Tarbert. Warm welcome, open fires, good food.

TARBERT, Loch Fyne continued	Map 1 E5		

Stonefield Castle Hotel

COMMENDED
👑👑👑👑

Tarbert, Argyll PA29 6YJ
Tel: (0880) 820836   Fax: (0880) 820929

This 19th century castle commanding spectacular views over Loch Fyne stands in 60 acres of beautiful wooded grounds two miles from the attractive fishing village of Tarbert. The hotel offers guests every comfort whilst retaining its dignity and historic charm. The traditional Scottish menu features local produce.

AA ★★★   RAC ★★★

Stonefield Castle Hotel Loch Fyne Tarbert, Loch Fyne Argyll PA29 6YJ Tel:(Tarbert) 0880 820836 Fax:0880 820929	**COMMENDED** 👑👑👑 👑	7 Single 19 Twin 3 Double 4 Family	32 En Suite fac 2 Pub.Bath/Show	B&B per person £45.00-£65.00	Open Jan-Dec Dinner 1900-2100 B&B + Eve.Meal

Set in 50 acres of wooded ground overlooking Loch Fyne, the castle has been renovated to combine original dignity with modern comfort.

Tarbert Hotel Harbour Street Tarbert, Loch Fyne Argyll PA29 6UB Tel:(Tarbert) 0880 820264 Fax:0880 820847		3 Single 9 Twin 5 Double 3 Family	14 En Suite fac 4 Pub.Bath/Show	B&B per person £17.50-£28.50 Single £17.00-£23.00 Double	Open Jan-Dec Dinner 1700-2130 B&B + Eve.Meal £25.00-£32.00

WEST LOCH HOTEL

BY TARBERT, LOCH FYNE, ARGYLL PA29 6YF
Tel: 0880 820283

Recently refurbished by new owners. This traditional Coaching Inn is situated on the shores of West Loch Tarbert. Conveniently situated for ferries sailing to Arran, Islay, Jura and Gigha. This family run hotel offers comfortable accommodation, peaceful surroundings, open log fires and good food.

Special Low Season Rates.

West Loch Hotel by Tarbert, Loch Fyne Argyll PA29 6YF Tel:(Tarbert) 0880 820283	**Award Pending**	1 Single 2 Twin 3 Double 1 Family	5 En Suite fac 2 Priv.NOT ensuite	B&B per person from £20.00 Single from £20.00 Double	Open Feb-Dec Dinner 1900-2130 B&B + Eve.Meal from £32.50

TAYNUILT
Argyll

Map 1 F2

Brander Lodge Hotel
& Restaurant
Bridge of Awe
Taynuilt
Argyll
PA35 1HT
Tel:(Taynuilt) 08662 243/225
Fax:08662 273

COMMENDED

3 Single
8 Twin
7 Double
2 Family

20 En Suite fac

B&B per person
£32.00-£38.00 Single
£32.00-£38.00 Double

Open Jan-Dec
Dinner 1900-2100
B&B + Eve.Meal
£48.00-£51.00

Set back from main Oban A85 road in extensive grounds amidst scenic
splendour near Loch Awe. Only 15 miles (24kms) from Oban.

Polfearn Hotel
Taynuilt
Argyll
PA35 1JQ
Tel:(Taynuilt) 08662 251

3 Single
6 Twin
4 Double
2 Family

14 En Suite fac
1 Pub.Bath/Show

B&B per person
£22.00-£33.00 Single
£19.00-£30.00 Double

Open Jan-Dec
Dinner 1900-2100
B&B + Eve.Meal
£33.00-£47.00

THORNHILL
Dumfriesshire

Map 2 B8

George Hotel
103-106 Drumlanrig Street
Thornhill
Dumfriesshire
DG3 5LU
Tel:(Thornhill) 0848 330326

APPROVED

1 Single
4 Twin
2 Double
1 Family

8 En Suite fac

B&B per person
£25.00-£28.00 Single
£30.00-£37.50 Double

Open Jan-Dec
Dinner 1800-2100
B&B + Eve.Meal
£35.00-£42.00

Personally run former coaching inn with friendly atmosphere. Situated in centre
of Thornhill village, amidst scenic Nithsdale.

Gill Bank Private Hotel
8 East Morton Street
Thornhill
Dumfriesshire
DG3 5LZ
Tel:(Thornhill) 0848 330597

2 Single
1 Double
3 Family

2 En Suite fac
3 Pub.Bath/Show

B&B per person
£16.00-£22.00 Single
£16.00-£18.00 Double

Open Feb-Nov
Dinner 1700-1800
B&B + Eve.Meal
£24.00-£26.00

Trigony House Hotel
Closeburn
Thornhill
Dumfriesshire
DG3 5EZ
Tel:(Thornhill) 0848 331211

COMMENDED

2 Single
4 Twin
3 Double

9 En Suite fac

B&B per person
£33.50-£37.00 Single
£28.50-£32.00 Double

Open Jan-Dec
Dinner 1900-2030
B&B + Eve.Meal
£44.50-£48.00

Victorian country house full of character, in extensive grounds. Taste of Scotland.
Set in unspoilt countryside.

THORNTON
Fife

Map 2 D3

The Crown Hotel
7 Main Street
Thornton
Fife
KY1 4AF
Tel:(Glenrothes) 0592 774416

APPROVED

2 Single
7 Twin
2 Double

3 En Suite fac
8 Limited ensuite
2 Pub.Bath/Show

B&B per person
from £21.00 Single
from £20.00 Double

Open Jan-Dec
Dinner 1930-2230
B&B + Eve.Meal
from £28.00

Traditional inn conveniently situated on the main street, well known for high teas.

THURSO
Caithness

Ormlie House Hotel
Ormlie Road
Thurso
Caithness
KW14 7EB
Tel:(Thurso) 0847 62733

Map 4
C3

2 Single	6 En Suite fac	B&B per person
2 Twin	1 Pub.Bath/Show	£17.00-£20.00 Single
3 Double		£17.00-£20.00 Double
1 Family		

Open Jan-Dec
Dinner 1700-2100

Park Hotel
Thurso
Caithness
KW14 8RE
Tel:(Thurso) 0847 63251

Award Pending

1 Single	11 En Suite fac	B&B per person
5 Twin	3 Pub.Bath/Show	£18.00-£27.00 Single
5 Double		£16.50-£25.00 Double

Open Jan-Dec
Dinner 1700-2100
B&B + Eve.Meal
£24.00-£39.00

Pentland Hotel
Princes Street
Thurso
Caithness
KW14 7AA
Tel:(Thurso) 0847 63202
Fax:0847 62761

COMMENDED
👑 👑 👑

24 Single	39 En Suite fac	B&B per person
13 Twin	7 Pub.Bath/Show	from £22.00 Single
14 Double		from £21.00 Double
2 Family		

Open Jan-Dec
Dinner 1830-2030

Recently renovated hotel in centre of town.

Royal Hotel (Caithness) Ltd
Traill Street
Thurso
Caithness
KW14 8EH
Tel:(Thurso) 0847 63191
Fax:0847 65338

APPROVED
👑 👑 👑

26 Single	106 En Suite fac	B&B per person
54 Twin		£18.00-£32.00 Single
18 Double		£16.00-£30.00 Double
8 Family		

Open Jan-Dec
Dinner 1900-2100
B&B + Eve.Meal
£23.00-£40.00

Former coaching inn, family run, in town centre. Ideally situated for business or pleasure.

TIGHNABRUAICH
Argyll

Ardeneden
Tighnabruaich
Argyll
PA21 2BD
Tel:(Tighnabruaich) 0700
811354

Map 1
F5

4 Twin	3 Pub.Bath/Show	B&B per person
2 Double		from £15.00 Single
1 Family		from £13.00 Double

Open Jan-Dec
Dinner 1900-2100
B&B + Eve.Meal
£20.00-£22.00

KAMES HOTEL

KAMES, near TIGHNABRUAICH ARGYLL PA21 2AF
Tel: 0700 811 489   Fax: 0700 811 283

Beautiful sea views, comfort and a warm welcome. Garden with children's play equipment. Safe beach. Water sports and boat hire. Good food in the restaurant or from the bar menu. Real ales and live music. Moorings and hot showers for visiting yachts. Golf, walking and touring. Dogs permitted.

Special off season breaks.

Kames Hotel
Tighnabruaich
Argyll
PA21 2AF
Tel:(Tighnabruaich) 0700
811489
Fax:0700 811283

COMMENDED
👑 👑 👑

2 Single	10 En Suite fac	B&B per person
3 Twin		from £33.00 Single
3 Double		from £28.00 Double
2 Family		

Open Jan-Dec
Dinner 1200-2100
B&B + Eve.Meal
from £45.00

A warm welcome, good food and service and stunning views all await you at the Kames Hotel. Water sports, golf, shooting or peace and tranquility.

TOBERMORY Isle of Mull, Argyll	Map 1 C1

The Tobermory Hotel

TOBERMORY, ISLE OF MULL, ARGYLL PA75 6NT TEL: (0688) 2091

Situated on Tobermory's waterfront - a haven of comfort and charm from which to explore Mull. Most rooms overlook the bay, majority with en-suite facilities, all with heating and tea/coffee facilities. Caring hospitality, good food and wine to complete your stay. 2 ground floor bedrooms suitable for disabled. Dogs at owner's discretion.

2-day Summer Break from £90 DB&B. B&B from £28 per person. Winter 2-day from £80 DB&B. B&B from £25.

| The Tobermory Hotel
53 Main Street
Tobermory
Isle of Mull, Argyll
PA75 6NT
Tel:(Tobermory) 0688 2091
Fax:0688 2140 | COMMENDED ♛ ♛ ♛ | 4 Single
4 Twin
6 Double
3 Family | 8 En Suite fac
1 Priv.NOT ensuite
3 Pub.Bath/Show | B&B per person
£25.00-£40.00 Single
£25.00-£40.00 Double | Open Jan-Dec
Dinner 1900-2000
B&B + Eve.Meal
£41.00-£57.00 |
| | | **Superbly sited on waterfront overlooking the bay. Warm welcome, friendly service, good food and comfortable bedrooms.** | | | |

| Ulva House Hotel
Strongarbh
Tobermory
Isle of Mull, Argyll
PA75 6PR
Tel:(Tobermory) 0688 2044 | Award
Pending | 1 Twin
3 Double
2 Family | 3 En Suite fac
3 Pub.Bath/Show | B&B per person
£25.95-£40.95 Single
£25.95-£33.45 Double | Open Mar-Nov
Dinner 1900-2030
B&B + Eve.Meal
£39.50-£47.00 |

| Baliscate Guest House
Tobermory
Isle of Mull, Argyll
PA75 6QA
Tel:(Tobermory) 0688 2048 | COMMENDED ♛ ♛ | 1 Twin
3 Double
1 Family | 2 En Suite fac
2 Pub.Bath/Show | B&B per person
£16.00-£20.00 Double | Open Jan-Dec |
| | | **Set in 1.5 acres of garden and woodland with magnificent views over The Sound of Mull.** | | | |

| Carnaburg
55 Main Street
Tobermory
Isle of Mull, Argyll
PA75 6NT
Tel:(Tobermory) 0688 2479 | | 2 Twin
3 Double
1 Family | 2 Pub.Bath/Show | B&B per person
£16.00-£17.50 Double | Open Jan-Dec |

| Failte Guest House
Main Street
Tobermory
Isle of Mull, Argyll
PA75 6NU
Tel:(Tobermory) 0688 2495
Fax:0688 2232 | Award
Pending | 3 Twin
3 Double
1 Family | 7 En Suite fac
2 Pub.Bath/Show | B&B per person
£25.00-£30.00 Single
£20.00-£25.00 Double | Open Mar-Oct |

TOBERMORY **continued** Staffa Cottages Guest House Tobermory Isle of Mull, Argyll PA75 6PL Tel:(Tobermory) 0688 2464 Fax:0688 2464	Map 1 C1	COMMENDED 👑 👑	2 Twin 3 Double	3 En Suite fac 2 Priv.NOT ensuite	B&B per person £16.00-£18.00 Double	Open Jan-Dec Dinner from 1900 B&B + Eve.Meal £28.00-£30.00

In quiet residential area on slopes above Tobermory with large garden. Fine views over bay to Sound of Mull and Morvern Hills.

Strongarbh House Tobermory Isle of Mull, Argyll PA75 6PR Tel:(Tobermory) 0688 2328 Fax:0688 2142		HIGHLY COMMENDED 👑 👑 👑	2 Twin 2 Double	4 En Suite fac	B&B per person £32.00-£36.00 Double	Open Jan-Dec Dinner 1900-2230 B&B + Eve.Meal £52.00-£56.00

Stone built Victorian country house, recently refurbished throughout. All rooms ensuite; a la carte menu; superb views over bay. Taste of Scotland.

TOMATIN **Inverness-shire** Strathiolaire Findhorn Bridge Tomatin Inverness-shire IV13 7YA Tel:(Tomatin) 08082 359	Map 4 B9	DELUXE 👑 👑 👑	1 Single 1 Twin 1 Double	3 En Suite fac	B&B per person £19.00-£20.00 Single £19.00-£20.00 Double	Open Apr-Oct Dinner at 1900 B&B + Eve.Meal £29.00-£32.00

Modern bungalow in secluded rural setting, ideal for birdwatching and wildlife. Tasty home cooking. Easy access from A9.

TOMICH, by Cannich **Inverness-shire** Tomich Hotel Tomich Strathglass,by Beauly Inverness-shire IV4 7LY Tel:(Cannich) 0456 415399 Fax:0456 415499	Map 3 H9	Award Pending	3 Twin 1 Double 3 Family	7 En Suite fac	B&B per person £26.00-£32.00 Single £26.00 Double	Open Jan-Dec Dinner 1900 2100 B&B + Eve.Meal £42.00

TOMINTOUL **Banffshire** Glenavon Hotel The Square Tomintoul, Ballindalloch Banffshire AB37 9ET Tel:(Tomintoul) 0807 580218	Map 4 D1	APPROVED 👑 👑	2 Single 1 Twin 2 Double 1 Family	4 En Suite fac 1 Pub.Bath/Show	B&B per person £18.00-£22.00 Single £18.00-£22.00 Double	Open Jan-Dec Dinner 1700-2100 B&B + Eve.Meal £25.00-£32.00

Small friendly family run hotel with relaxed atmosphere. Home cooking, open fire. Families and pets always welcome.

etails of Grading and Classification are on page vi. | Key to symbols is on back flap. |

| TONGUE
Sutherland | Map 4
A3 | | |

Ben Loyal Hotel

TONGUE · SUTHERLAND IV27 4XE
Telephone (0847 55) 216

"A Sanctuary from the Stress of Urban Living".
Discover the clear sea and golden sand of this
Highland oasis. Overlook the Kyle and the "Queen of
Scottish Mountains", and enjoy the magnificent
northern Scottish sunsets over dinner. The Ben is
owned and run by Mel and Pauline Cook and is
becoming renowned for its warm, personal welcome,
friendly staff and its high quality Highland cooking
using local produce of venison, salmon, beef, lamb
and shellfish, and our own garden produce. Brown
trout, sea trout and salmon fishing can all be
arranged, even individual tuition.
£32-£48.50 for DB&B or £224-£308 per week.
♛ ♛ ♛ **Highly Commended**

Ben Loyal Hotel Tongue Sutherland IV27 4XE Tel:(Tongue) 084755 216	**HIGHLY COMMENDED** ♛ ♛ ♛	3 Single 7 Twin 8 Double	9 En Suite fac 2 Pub.Bath/Show	B&B per person £22.50-£47.00 Single £18.00-£32.00 Double	Open mid Feb-Dec Dinner 1800-2030 B&B + Eve.Meal £29.00-£47.00
		Stone built hotel with fine views of Ben Loyal and Kyle of Tongue. Friendly atmosphere. Fishing and real ale available. Annexe outwith scheme.			
Tongue Hotel Tongue Sutherland IV27 4XD Tel:(Tongue) 084755 206/207 Tlx:778215 Fax:084755 345		1 Single 3 Twin 12 Double 1 Family	14 En Suite fac 3 Priv.NOT ensuite 4 Pub.Bath/Show	B&B per person £25.00-£37.50 Single £25.00-£37.50 Double	Open Jan-Dec Dinner 1900-2030 B&B + Eve.Meal £35.00-£51.00

TORRIDON Ross-shire	Map 3 F8				
Loch Torridon Hotel Torridon, Achnasheen Ross-shire IV22 2EY Tel:(Torridon) 0445 791242 Fax:0445 791296	**HIGHLY COMMENDED** ♛ ♛ ♛ ♛	1 Single 6 Twin 6 Double 6 Family Suite avail.	19 En Suite fac	B&B per person from £35.00 Single from £35.00 Double	Open Mar-Dec Dinner 1930-2130 B&B + Eve.Meal from £50.00
		Victorian shooting lodge, set amidst 60 acres of mature trees and parkland on the shores of Loch Torridon. Superb mountain scenery. Fishing avail.			
Ben Damph Lodge Torridon Ross-shire Tel:(Torridon) 0445 791242 Fax:0445 791296		14 Family	14 En Suite fac	Price per room from £25.00	Open Jan-Dec Dinner 1830-2030

TROON Ayrshire	Map 1 G7						
Ardneil Hotel St Meddans Street Troon Ayrshire KA10 6NU Tel:(Troon) 0292 311611		APPROVED Listed	3 Single 1 Twin 3 Double 2 Family	3 En Suite fac 3 Pub.Bath/Show	B&B per person from £25.00 Single from £22.50 Double	Open Jan-Dec Dinner 1700-2100	🅥 🆂 🅒 ...
			Family owned friendly hotel with extensive restaurant and bar facilities. Close to railway station and 5 minutes walk from the town centre.				
Craiglea Hotel South Beach Troon Ayrshire KA10 6EG Tel:(Troon) 0292 311366 Fax:0292 311366		APPROVED 👑 👑 👑	5 Single 10 Twin 4 Double 1 Family	10 En Suite fac 4 Pub.Bath/Show	B&B per person £30.00-£45.00 Single £22.50-£32.50 Double	Open Jan-Dec Dinner 1900-2100	🅥 🆂 🅒 ...
			Family run Hotel overlooking Troon's South Beach and only 0.5 miles (1km) from both championship golf course and town centre.				
Glenside Hotel 2 Darley Place Troon Ayrshire KA10 6JQ Tel:(Troon) 0292 313677		HIGHLY COMMENDED 👑 👑 👑	4 Twin 1 Family	5 En Suite fac	B&B per person £25.00-£27.50 Single £20.00-£22.50 Double	Open Jan-Dec Dinner 1900-2000 B&B + Eve.Meal £30.00-£32.50	...
			Victorian stone built house with accent on warm hospitality and comfort. Ideal touring centre - Glasgow 32 miles (51kms). Royal Troon close by.				

Marine Highland Hotel

TROON · AYRSHIRE KA10 6HE
Telephone: 0292 314444 Fax: 0292 316922

This traditional, luxury hotel in the heart of Burns Country overlooks the 18th fairway of Royal Troon Golf Course. The elegant Fairways Restaurant offers the best in fresh Scottish produce and an award-winning wine list, while Crosbies Brasserie is a more informal eating place with a lively, continental atmosphere.

The 72 bedrooms have private bathroom, colour satellite TV, telephone, hairdryer, trouser press, tea and coffee making facilities.

The Marine Club has a superb swimming pool, jacuzzi, saunas, steam room, solaria, gymnasium, squash courts, beauty room and games room.

Dinner, bed and breakfast from £55. Over 60's from £38. Free accommodation and breakfast for children under 16 sharing parents room.

| Marine Highland Hotel
Crosbie Road
Troon
Ayrshire
KA10 6HE
Tel:(Troon) 0292 314444
Fax:0292 316922 | | HIGHLY
COMMENDED
👑 👑 👑
👑 👑 | 16 Single
31 Twin
18 Double
7 Family | 72 En Suite fac | B&B per person
£88.00-£110.00 Single
£69.00-£72.00 Double | Open Jan-Dec
Dinner 1900-2200
B&B + Eve.Meal
from £53.00 | 🅥 🆂 🅒 ... |
| | | | Overlooking championship golf course; beaches. Leisure facilities include swimming pool, sauna, gymnasium, snooker tables, squash courts, solarium. | | | | |

TROON continued	Map 1 G7

PIERSLAND HOUSE HOTEL

Craig End Road, Troon, Ayrshire KA10 6HD
Telephone: 0292-314747   Fax: 0292-315613
Unique and historic house, built in 19th century for Sir Alexander Walker, Grandson of Scotch Whisky firm founder, Johnny Walker. Set in 3.5 acres of landscaped grounds. Unforgettable ambience. Situated Southwest coast, haven for golfers, many historic attractions, including Burns House, Culzean Castle. Associate hotels at Bridge of Allan and Perth. *Please telephone 0292-314747 for a free brochure.*

Piersland House Hotel
Craigend Road
Troon
Ayrshire
KA10 6HD
Tel:(Troon) 0292 314747
Fax:0292 315613

HIGHLY COMMENDED
👑 👑 👑
👑

1 Single	19 En Suite fac
12 Twin	
6 Double	

B&B per person
£56.00-£87.00 Single
£44.75-£57.50 Double

Open Jan-Dec
Dinner 1900-2130

Built for Sir Alexander Walker, of whisky fame; set in 4 acres of grounds. Hotel features original wood panels and open fires in main public rooms.

South Beach Hotel
Troon
Ayrshire
KA10 6EG
Tel:(Troon) 0292 312033
Fax:0292 318438

COMMENDED
👑 👑 👑
👑

1 Single	27 En Suite fac
11 Twin	
7 Double	
8 Family	
Suites avail.	

B&B per person
£35.00-£55.00 Single
£25.00-£45.00 Double

Open Jan-Dec
Dinner 1800-2200
B&B + Eve.Meal
£45.00-£60.00

Family run hotel near the sea on main road and about 0.5 miles (1km) from town centre. Convenient for Troon championship golf course.

Lochgreen House
Monktonhill Road
Troon
Ayrshire
KA10 7EN
Tel:(Troon) 0292 313343
Fax:0292 318661

2 Twin	7 En Suite fac
5 Double	
Suite avail.	

B&B per person
£69.00-£99.00 Single
£50.00-£60.00 Double

Open Jan-Dec
Dinner 1900-2130
B&B + Eve.Meal
£92.50-£122.50

TROSSACHS by Callander, Perthshire	Map 1 H3

Dundarroch Country House
Brig O'Turk
Trossachs,by Callander
Perthshire
FK17 8HT
Tel:(Trossachs) 0877 376200
Fax:0877 376200

HIGHLY COMMENDED
👑 👑 👑
👑

1 Twin	3 En Suite fac
2 Double	

B&B per person
£39.75 Single
£25.50-£29.50 Double

Open Mar-Oct
Dinner 1900-2100

A friendly welcome in this restored Victorian house, peacefully set in 14 acres, with spectacular mountain views. Own fishing available.

| TURNBERRY
Ayrshire | Map 1
G8 | | |

Malin Court
TURNBERRY, AYRSHIRE KA26 9PB
Telephone: (0655) 31457

Malin Court overlooks the famous Turnberry Open Championship links and has beautiful views of the mystical Isle of Arran and the Firth of Clyde. All our bedrooms have en-suite bathrooms and exquisite sea views. Our restaurant uses only the finest local produce. For full details contact W.R. Kerr.

Highly Commended

| Malin Court
Turnberry
Ayrshire
KA26 9PB
Tel:(Turnberry) 0655 31457
Fax:0655 31072 | HIGHLY
COMMENDED
♕ ♕ ♕
♕ | 7 Twin   17 En Suite fac
3 Double
7 Family | B&B per person
£55.00-£85.00 Single
£50.00-£70.00 Double | Open Jan-Dec
Dinner 1730-2130
B&B + Eve.Meal
£75.00-£95.00 | |
| | | Totally refurbished modern hotel with views over Turnberry Golf Course and Ailsa Craig; near Culzean Castle. Patio garden. A la carte restaurant. | | | |

| Turnberry Hotel &
Golf Courses
Turnberry
Ayrshire
KA26 9LT
Tel:(Turnberry) 0655 31000
Tlx:777779
Fax:0655 31706 | | 109 Twin   132 En Suite fac
23 Double
Suites avail. | B&B per person
£130.00-£195.00 Single
£72.50-£115.00 Double | Open Jan-Dec
Dinner 1830-2200
B&B + Eve.Meal
£165.00-£232.50 | |

| **TURRIFF**
Aberdeenshire
Union Hotel
Main Street
Turriff
Aberdeenshire
AB53 7AA
Tel:(Turriff) 0888 63704 | Map 4
F8 | 5 Twin   9 En Suite fac
3 Double
1 Family | B&B per person
£24.50-£30.00 Single
£24.50-£30.00 Double | Open Jan-Dec
Dinner 1700-2100
B&B + Eve.Meal
from £35.00 | |

TELEPHONE DIALLING CODES

Many telephone dialling codes have changed this year. If you experience difficulty in connecting a call, please call Directory Enquiries – **192** – where someone will issue the correct number. Please note: a charge will be placed for this service when using a private telephone

TYNDRUM by Crianlarich, Perthshire	Map 1 G2

INVERVEY HOTEL
TYNDRUM, by CRIANLARICH, PERTHSHIRE
FK20 8RY   Tel: 083-84-219 or 289 Fax: 083-84-280

Family-run Hotel/Free House. Set in beautiful Highland scenery (West Highland Way) at the junction of the A82/A85 to Fort William and Oban. Prime area for walking, skiing etc. Packed lunches, drying facilities, central heating, colour TV/video. Children and dogs welcome.
Special terms: parties/functions.

Invervey Hotel
Tyndrum,by Crianlarich
Perthshire
FK20 8RY
Tel:(Tyndrum) 08384
219/289
Fax:08384 280

APPROVED ♛ ♛

5 Single   18 En Suite fac
7 Twin   1 Pub.Bath/Show
5 Double
4 Family

B&B per person
£22.00-£25.00 Single
£22.00-£25.00 Double

Open Jan-Dec
Dinner 1700-2100
B&B + Eve.Meal
£30.00-£33.00

Family hotel on main tourist route, surrounded on all sides by mountain scenery. Fishing, shooting and guided walks arranged.

UDDINGSTON
Lanarkshire | Map 2
A5

Redstones Hotel
8/10 Glasgow Road
Uddingston
Lanarkshire
G71 6AS
Tel:(Uddingston) 0698
813774/814843
Fax:0698 815319

COMMENDED ♛ ♛ ♛ ♛

7 Single   16 En Suite fac
4 Twin   2 Pub.Bath/Show
7 Double

B&B per person
£55.00-£60.00 Single
£30.00-£37.50 Double

Open Jan-Dec
Dinner 1830-2130
B&B + Eve.Meal
£36.00-£57.50

Linked Victorian sandstone villas retaining original cornices and stained glass windows. Situated at north end of M74 before Glasgow Zoo Park.

Northcote Guest House
2 Holmbrae Avenue
Uddingston, Glasgow
Lanarkshire
G71 6AL
Tel:(Uddingston) 0698
813319

1 Single   1 Pub.Bath/Show
1 Double
1 Family

B&B per person
£13.00-£13.50 Single
£13.00-£13.50 Double

Open Jan-Dec

UIG
Isle of Skye,
Inverness-shire | Map 3
D8

Ferry Inn Hotel
Uig
Isle of Skye, Inverness-shire
IV51 9XP
Tel:(Uig) 047042 242

COMMENDED ♛ ♛ ♛

1 Single   6 En Suite fac
2 Twin
3 Double

B&B per person
£28.00-£30.00 Single
£26.00-£28.00 Double

Open Jan-Dec
Dinner 1900-2100
B&B + Eve.Meal
£38.00-£40.00

Family run inn overlooking bay and Loch Snizort. Handy for Uig ferry. 16 miles (26 kms) from Portree.

UIG continued	Map 3 D8

UIG HOTEL
UIG, ISLE OF SKYE IV51 9YE Tel: 047 042 205 Fax: 047 042 308

An old Coaching inn with a Country House atmosphere overlooking Uig Bay -Loch Snizort. Comfortable, well-equipped bedrooms - private facilities. TV, central heating and direct-dial telephones. Fully licensed. The hotel is 1 mile from the Outer Isles ferry terminal.
Own pony-trekking and Self-catering apartments.

Uig Hotel
Uig
Isle of Skye, Inverness-shire
1V51 9YE
Tel:(Uig) 047042 205/367
Fax:047042 308

COMMENDED
♛ ♛ ♛
♛

5 Single	17 En Suite fac	B&B per person	Open Apr-Oct
6 Twin		£28.00-£45.00 Single	Dinner 1915-2015
5 Double		£28.00-£45.00 Double	
1 Family			

Old coaching inn overlooking Uig Bay and Loch Snizort. Additional rooms in fully modernised farm steading. Pony trekking available at the hotel.

Woodbine Guest House
Uig
Isle of Skye, Inverness-shire
IV51 9XP
Tel:(Uig) 047042 243

COMMENDED
♛ ♛

1 Twin	4 En Suite fac	B&B per person	Open Jan-Dec
2 Double	1 Pub.Bath/Show	£16.50-£18.00 Double	Dinner 1830-1900
1 Family			B&B + Eve.Meal £27.00-£28.50

Traditional Island hospitality in stone-built cottage overlooking Uig Bay.

ULLAPOOL Ross-shire	Map 3 G6

Arch Inn
11 West Shore Street
Ullapool
Ross-shire
IV26 2UR
Tel:(Ullapool) 0854 612454

1 Single	3 En Suite fac	B&B per person	Open Jan-Dec
3 Twin	2 Limited ensuite	£19.00-£20.00 Single	Dinner 1830-2015
5 Double	2 Pub.Bath/Show	£19.00-£28.00 Double	
1 Family			

Argyll Hotel
Argyle Street
Ullapool
Ross-shire
IV26 2UB
Tel:(Ullapool) 0854 612422

2 Twin	6 En Suite fac	B&B per person	Open Jan-Dec
7 Double	2 Pub.Bath/Show	from £15.00 Single	Dinner 1800-2130
3 Family		from £15.00 Double	

Caledonian Hotel
Ullapool
Ross-shire
IV26 2UG
Tel:(Ullapool) 0854 612306

21 Single	88 En Suite fac	B&B per person	Open Mar-Oct
47 Twin		£42.00-£50.00 Single	Dinner 1830-2000
18 Double		£38.00-£46.00 Double	B&B + Eve.Meal £48.00-£58.50
2 Family			

ULLAPOOL

ULLAPOOL continued	Map 3 G6						
The Ceilidh Place West Argyle Street Ullapool Ross-shire IV26 2TY Tel:(Ullapool) 0854 612103 Fax:0854 612886			7 Single 4 Twin 6 Double 7 Family	10 En Suite fac 11 Pub.Bath/Show	B&B per person £18.25-£49.50 Single £18.25-£49.50 Double	Open Jan-Dec Dinner 1900-2100 B&B + Eve.Meal £30.00-£76.00	
Ferry Boat Inn Shore Street Ullapool Ross-shire IV26 2UJ Tel:(Ullapool) 0854 612366 Fax:0854 612366			2 Single 4 Twin 4 Double 1 Family	4 En Suite fac 3 Pub.Bath/Show	B&B per person £20.50-£34.00 Single £19.00-£29.00 Double	Open Feb-Dec Dinner 1900-2130	
Four Seasons Hotel Garve Road Ullapool Ross-shire IV26 2SX Tel:(Ullapool) 0854 612905		COMMENDED 👑 👑 👑	1 Single 7 Twin 7 Double 1 Family	16 En Suite fac	B&B per person £25.00-£34.00 Single £25.00-£34.00 Double	Open Mar-Oct Dinner 1900-2030 B&B + Eve.Meal £42.00-£48.00	
			Modern family run hotel overlooking Loch Broom. Under 1 mile (2kms) from Ullapool and the ferry terminal.				
Harbour Lights Hotel Ullapool Ross-shire IV26 2SX Tel:(Ullapool) 0854 612222			3 Single 10 Twin 9 Double	19 En Suite fac 1 Pub.Bath/Show	B&B per person £30.00-£36.00 Single £25.00-£35.00 Double	Open Jan-Dec Dinner 1900-2130 B&B + Eve.Meal £44.00-£53.00	
Mercury Hotel North Road Ullapool Ross-shire IV26 2UD Tel:(Ullapool) 0854 612314 Fax:0854 612158		Award Pending	15 Single 19 Twin 26 Family	60 En Suite fac	B&B per person £46.00-£55.00 Single £35.00-£40.00 Double	Open Apr-Oct Dinner 1830-2030 B&B + Eve.Meal £44.00-£50.00	
Riverside Hotel Quay Street Ullapool Ross-shire IV26 2UE Tel:(Ullapool) 0854 612239			2 Single 4 Twin 7 Double 1 Family	8 En Suite fac 2 Pub.Bath/Show	B&B per person £15.00-£18.00 Single £15.00-£24.00 Double	Open Jan-Dec Dinner 1900-2000 B&B + Eve.Meal £28.00-£36.00	
Tir Aluinn Hotel Leckmelm Lochbroom, Ullapool Ross-shire IV23 2RJ Tel:(Ullapool) 0854 612074			2 Single 7 Twin 3 Double 3 Family	3 En Suite fac 5 Pub.Bath/Show	B&B per person £21.50-£25.00 Single £21.50-£25.00 Double	Open May-Sep Dinner 1900-2000 B&B + Eve.Meal £34.50-£38.00	

ULLAPOOL continued	Map 3 G6						
Ardvreck Guest House Morefield Brae Ullapool Ross-shire IV26 2TH Tel:(Ullapool) 0854 612028/612561 Fax:0854 612028	HIGHLY COMMENDED 👑 👑	2 Single 2 Twin 4 Double 2 Family	10 En Suite fac	B&B per person £20.00-£25.00 Single £20.00-£24.00 Double	Open Jan-Dec Dinner 1830-1930 B&B + Eve.Meal from £32.50		
		Quiet secluded guest house with spectacular views over Loch Broom. All rooms ensuite. Ullapool 1.5 miles (2.5 kms).					
Brae Guest House Shore Street Ullapool Ross-shire IV26 2UJ Tel:(Ullapool) 0854 612421		1 Single 3 Twin 4 Double 3 Family	10 En Suite fac 3 Pub.Bath/Show	B&B per person from £18.00 Single from £18.00 Double	Open May-Oct Dinner 1730-2100 B&B + Eve.Meal from £24.00		
Dromnan Guest House Garve Road Ullapool Ross-shire IV26 2SX Tel:(Ullapool) 0854 612333	Award Pending	2 Twin 3 Double 2 Family	7 En Suite fac	B&B per person £17.00-£20.00 Double	Open Jan-Dec		
Essex Cottage Ullapool Ross-shire IV26 Tel:(Ullapool) 0854 612663		2 Twin 3 Double	1 En Suite fac 1 Priv.NOT ensuite 2 Pub.Bath/Show	B&B per person from £14.00 Single from £13.50 Double	Open Jan-Dec Dinner from 1900 B&B + Eve.Meal from £21.00		
The Sheiling Guest House Garve Road Ullapool Ross-shire IV26 2SX Tel:(Ullapool) 0854 612947		3 Twin 4 Double	7 En Suite fac	B&B per person £16.00-£20.00 Double	Open Jan-Dec		
Strathmore Guest House & The Highlander Restaurant Morefield Ullapool Ross-shire IV26 2TH Tel:(Ullapool) 0854 612423	COMMENDED 👑 👑	1 Single 1 Twin 4 Double	4 En Suite fac 1 Pub.Bath/Show	B&B per person £14.00-£18.00 Single £14.00-£20.00 Double	Open Apr-Oct Dinner 1800-2100		
		Guest house enjoying panoramic views over Loch Broom and Ullapool. Local game and seafood is a speciality in the Highlander Restaurant.					

WELCOME

Whenever you are in Scotland, you can be sure of a warm welcome at your nearest Tourist Information Centre.

For guide books, maps, souvenirs, our Centres provide a service second to none – many now offer bureau-de-change facilities. And, of course, Tourist Information Centres offer free, expert advice on what to see and do, route-planning and accommodation for everyone – visitors and residents alike!

BY ULLAPOOL Ross-shire Tigh na Mara Veg Guest House The Shore, Ardindrean,l Lochbroom,by Ullapool Ross-shire IV23 2SE Tel:(Lochbroom) 085485 282 Fax:085485 282	Map 3 G6		1 Twin 2 Double	1 En Suite fac 1 Pub.Bath/Show	B&B per person	Open Feb-Dec Dinner at 2000 B&B + Eve.Meal £29.00-£37.00	
UNST, Island of Shetland Baltasound Hotel Baltasound, Unst Shetland ZE2 9DS Tel:(Baltasound) 095781 334	Map 5 G1	Award Pending	27 Twin	20 En Suite fac 4 Pub.Bath/Show	B&B per person £36.00-£45.00 Single £25.00-£29.00 Double	Open Jan-Dec Dinner 1900-2030 B&B + Eve.Meal £46.50-£55.50	
UPHALL West Lothian Houstoun House Uphall West Lothian EH52 6JS Tel:(Broxburn) 0506 853831 Fax:0506 854220	Map 2 C5	COMMENDED	5 Single 14 Twin 11 Double	30 En Suite fac	B&B per person £79.00-£92.00 Single £52.00-£60.00 Double	Open Jan-Dec Dinner 1930-2130 B&B + Eve.Meal £95.00-£120.00	
			A 16C Tower House in parkland setting. Four-poster beds in many of the bedrooms. 10 minutes from Edinburgh Airport.				
UPLAWMOOR Renfrewshire Uplawmoor Hotel Neilston Road Uplawmoor Renfrewshire G78 4AF Tel:(Uplawmoor) 0505 850565	Map 1 H6	APPROVED	1 Twin 13 Double	14 En Suite fac	B&B per person £35.00 Single £20.00 Double	Open Jan-Dec Dinner 1700-2130 B&B + Eve.Meal from £47.00	
			Traditional hospitality in 18th century inn. Easy access to the Ayrshire coast and Glasgow.				
WEMYSS BAY Renfrewshire Wemyss Bay Hotel Greenock Road Wemyss Bay Renfrewshire PA18 6AY Tel:(Wemyss Bay) 0475 520285	Map 1 G5		2 Single 2 Twin 5 Double 2 Family	3 Pub.Bath/Show	B&B per person £22.00-£24.00 Single £20.00-£22.00 Double	Open Jan-Dec Dinner 1700-2200 B&B + Eve.Meal £28.00-£30.00	
WEST LINTON Peeblesshire The Gordon Arms Hotel Dolphinton Road West Linton Peeblesshire EH46 7DR Tel:(West Linton) 0968 60208	Map 2 C6	APPROVED Listed	1 Single 1 Twin 3 Double	1 Pub.Bath/Show	B&B per person from £15.00 Single from £14.00 Double	Open Jan-Dec Dinner 1800-2130	
			Former Drover's Inn on A702 only 16 miles (26km) from Edinburgh. Attractive conservation village. Good beer guide.				

WHALSAY, Isle of **Shetland** Lingaveg Guest House Marrister Symbister, Whalsay Shetland ZE2 9AE Tel:(Symbister) 08066 489	Map 5 G3		2 Twin 1 Family	1 Pub.Bath/Show	B&B per person £16.00 Single £16.00 Double	Open Jan-Dec Dinner 1800-1900 B&B + Eve.Meal £25.00
WHITEBRIDGE **Inverness-shire** Knockie Lodge Hotel Whitebridge Inverness-shire IV1 2UP Tel:(Gorthleck) 0456 486276 Fax:0456 486389	Map 4 A1	**DELUXE**	2 Single 4 Twin 4 Double	10 En Suite fac	B&B per person from £75.00 Single £65.00-£95.00 Double	Open May-Oct Dinner 2000-2030
			The ideal hideaway; refreshingly simple in style yet with a genuine warmth of hospitality and comfort amidst superb scenery.			
Whitebridge Hotel Whitebridge Inverness-shire IV1 2UN Tel:(Gorthleck) 0456 486226 Fax:0456 486413		**COMMENDED**	3 Twin 6 Double 3 Family	10 En Suite fac 1 Pub.Bath/Show	B&B per person £20.00-£30.00 Single £20.00-£26.00 Double	Open Mar-Dec Dinner 1900-2130 B&B + Eve.Meal £33.00-£43.00
			Personally run hotel, nestling in foothills of Monadhliath Mountains, beside B862 on East side of Loch Ness, 24 miles (38kms) South of Inverness.			
WHITENESS **Shetland** Westings Hotel Wormadale Whiteness Shetland ZE2 9LJ Tel:(Gott) 059584 242 Fax:059584 500	Map 5 F4	**Award Pending**	7 Double	7 En Suite fac	B&B per person £36.00-£40.00 Single £45.00-£50.00 Double	Open Jan-Dec Dinner 1900-2100 B&B + Eve.Meal £41.00-£56.00
WHITING BAY **Isle of Arran** Argentine House Hotel Shore Road Whiting Bay Isle of Arran KA27 8PZ Tel:(Whiting Bay) 0770 700662	Map 1 F7	**Award Pending**	1 Single 1 Twin 2 Double 1 Family	5 En Suite fac	B&B per person from £19.00 Single from £18.00 Double	Open Mar-Dec Dinner from 1800 B&B + Eve.Meal from £28.00
Cameronia Hotel Whiting Bay Isle of Arran KA27 8PZ Tel:(Whiting Bay) 07707 254/0770 700254		**COMMENDED**	1 Single 1 Twin 1 Double 2 Family	4 En Suite fac 1 Pub.Bath/Show	B&B per person £18.00-£20.00 Single £21.00-£23.50 Double	Open Jan-Dec Dinner 1815-2100 B&B + Eve.Meal £31.00-£33.50
			Friendly, family run hotel on sea-front overlooking the bay, in a small village on the east side of the island.			
Grange House Hotel Whiting Bay Isle of Arran KA27 8QH Tel:(Whiting Bay) 0770 700263		**HIGHLY COMMENDED**	1 Single 3 Twin 3 Double 2 Family	6 En Suite fac 1 Priv.NOT ensuite 1 Pub.Bath/Show	B&B per person £22.00-£30.00 Single £22.00-£30.00 Double	Open Mar-Oct Dinner 1845-1945 B&B + Eve.Meal £35.00-£43.00
			Victorian hotel overlooking Whiting Bay. Emphasis on use of local produce, freshly cooked. Totally non-smoking.			

WHITING BAY continued

Map 1 F7

Royal Hotel
Shore Road
Whiting Bay
Isle of Arran
KA27 8PZ
Tel:(Whiting Bay) 07707
286/0770 700286

COMMENDED
🏵 🏵 🏵

1 Single	6 En Suite fac	B&B per person	Open Mar-Dec
2 Twin	2 Pub.Bath/Show	from £20.00 Single	Dinner from 1900
3 Double		from £20.00 Double	B&B + Eve.Meal
			from £31.00

Personally run hotel with friendly atmosphere and excellent views over Whiting Bay. Home cooking and baking using fresh local produce.

View Bank
Whiting Bay
Isle of Arran
KA27 8QT
Tel:(Whiting Bay) 07707
326/0770 700326

COMMENDED
🏵 🏵

1 Single	4 En Suite fac	B&B per person	Open Jan-Nov
1 Twin	2 Pub.Bath/Show	£15.00-£18.00 Single	Dinner from 1800
3 Double		£15.00-£18.00 Double	B&B + Eve.Meal
2 Family			£22.25-£24.75

Converted farmhouse with warm, friendly welcome and home cooking. Lovely sea views and a large lawned garden. Private parking.

WICK
Caithness

Map 4 E3

Mackays Hotel
Wick
Caithness
KW1 5ED
Tel:(Wick) 0955 2323
Fax:0955 5930

APPROVED
🏵 🏵 🏵

9 Single	25 En Suite fac	B&B per person	Open Jan-Dec
5 Twin		from £39.00 Single	Dinner 1800-2100
9 Double			
2 Family			

Family run hotel in centre of Wick, overlooking the harbour and near to railway station. Free golf for residents on two courses.

Nethercliffe Hotel
Louisburgh Street
Wick
Caithness
KW1 4NS
Tel:(Wick) 0955 2044
Fax:0955 5691

COMMENDED
🏵 🏵 🏵

3 Twin	6 En Suite fac	B&B per person	Open Jan-Dec
2 Double		from £22.00 Double	Dinner 1800-2100
1 Family			

Family run hotel in easy walking distance of town centre. Convenient for Wick Airport. Good touring centre.

Queen's Hotel
16 Francis Street
Wick
Caithness
KW1 5PZ
Tel:(Wick) 0955 2992

APPROVED
🏵 🏵

3 Single	6 En Suite fac	B&B per person	Open Jan-Dec
2 Twin	2 Limited ensuite	£19.00-£27.00 Single	Dinner 1700-2100
3 Double	1 Pub.Bath/Show	£19.00-£22.00 Double	
2 Family			

Family run hotel within walking distance of town centre.

County Guest House
101 High Street
Wick
Caithness
KW1 4LR
Tel:(Wick) 0955 2911

4 Family	1 Pub.Bath/Show	B&B per person	Open Jan-Dec
		£13.00-£14.00 Double	

Harbour Guest House
6 Rose Street
Wick
Caithness
KW1 5EX
Tel:(Wick) 0955 3276

APPROVED
🏵

1 Single	2 Pub.Bath/Show	B&B per person	Open Jan-Dec
2 Twin		from £15.00 Single	
5 Double		from £13.00 Double	

Traditional stone terraced house (Listed building) on street leading to harbour. Close to Heritage centre, 5 minutes walk from station.

WICK continued	Map 4 E3						
Wellington Guest House 41-43 High Street Wick Caithness KW1 4BS Tel:(Wick) 0955 3287 Fax:0955 2237		COMMENDED Listed	6 Twin	6 En Suite fac	B&B per person to £24.00 Single to £19.00 Double	Open Mar-Oct	
			Conveniently situated in the town centre next to the Tourist Office. Private off street parking.				

WIGTOWN	Map 1 H1						
Wigtown House Hotel 19 Bank Street Wigtown DG8 9HR Tel:(Wigtown) 09884 2391		APPROVED	2 Double 1 Family	3 En Suite fac	B&B per person £20.00-£26.00 Single £18.00-£24.00 Double	Open Jan-Dec Dinner 1800-2100	
			Former bank house perched above Wigtown Bay. Residential craft courses available.				

YELL, Island of Shetland	Map 5 G2						
Pinewood Guest House South Aywick, East Yell Shetland ZE2 9AX Tel:(Mid Yell) 0957 2077 Fax:0957 2410		COMMENDED	2 Twin 1 Double	2 En Suite fac 1 Limited ensuite 1 Pub.Bath/Show	B&B per person £25.00-£30.00 Single £20.00-£25.00 Double	Open Jan-Dec Dinner from 1900 B&B + Eve.Meal £25.00-£30.00	
			Modernised crofthouse with large garden, enjoying fine views eastwards over the sea to islands of Fetlar, Unst and Skerries.				

ALPHABETICAL INDEX OF HOTELS

376

ALPHABETICAL INDEX OF HOTELS

ALPHABETICAL INDEX OF HOTELS

378

ALPHABETICAL INDEX OF HOTELS

INFORMATION FOR PEOPLE
WITH DISABILITIES

Establishments in the accommodation guides displaying one of the four wheelchair access symbols are now inspected under the Scottish Tourist Board's Grading and Classification Scheme. The four symbols indicate:

   Access for wheelchair users without assistance
Adequate parking or letting down area for visitor in wheelchair.

Clear, safe approach and entrance in wheelchair.

Access to reception and social area in wheelchair.

Public toilets fully suitable for all disabled use.

At least one bedroom on ground floor, or accessible by lift, with appropriate dimensions and facilities with suitable private bathroom for unattended visitor in wheelchair.

A Access for wheelchair users with assistance
Parking, letting down and approach and entrance possible for the visitor in wheelchair with attendant help.

Access by permanent or portable ramps, or by lift, to reception and social areas.

Public toilets suitable for wheelchair use with attendant help.

At least one bedroom with appropriate dimensions and bathroom facilities, accessible by wheelchair user, or other disabled person, with attendant help.

P Access for ambulant disabled visitors (other than wheelchair users)
Parking, letting down, approach and entrance with safe steps or ramps, not too steep and preferably with hand rails.

Access to reception and social areas all accessible on same level, by lift or safe steps.

Public toilets suitable for walking, disabled visitor.

At least one bedroom suitable for visitor with walking disability with bathroom and toilet facility nearby.

R Access for disabled residents only
At least one bedroom suitable for disabled residents, equipped to & or & A or & P standard. Bathroom and toilet facilities also equipped to the appropriate standard.

Please use your discretion and telephone the establishments in advance if you require further information.

INDEX OF ACCOMMODATION PROVIDING DISABLED FACILITIES

The following establishments have been inspected under the Scottish Tourist Board's Grading and Classification Scheme and have attained one of four possible awards for access facilities for their disabled visitors.

Accommodation for Ambulant Disabled Visitors (other than wheelchair users)
Aberlady, Kilspindie House Hotel
Arbroath, Scurdy Guest House
Ballater, Gairnshiel Lodge
Boness, Richmond Park Hotel
Contin, Coul House Hotel
Dundee, Stakis Dundee Earl Grey Hotel
Edinburgh, Abbeylodge Guest House
Elphin, Mr T Strang, Assynt Guided Holidays
Glasgow, Univ. of Strathclyde, Jordanhill Campus
Grantown-on-Spey, Kinross Guest House
Inverurie, Strathburn Hotel
Kinnesswood, by Kinross, Lomond Country Inn
Lerwick, Shetland Hotel
Lockerbie, Dryfesdale Hotel
Montrose, Links Hotel
Perth, Sunbank House Hotel
Pitlochry, Pitlochry Hydro Hotel
Rhu, Ardencaple Hotel
Rockcliffe, by Dalbeattie, Barons Craig Hotel

Accommodation for Wheelchair Users with Assistance
Colvend, Clonyard House Hotel
Crieff, Crieff Hydro
Edinburgh, Caledonian Hotel
Edinburgh, Holiday Inn Garden Court
Edinburgh, Kings Manor Hotel
Glasgow, The Hospitality Inn & Convention Centre
Hawick, Whitchester Christian Guest House
Kentallen, by Appin, Holly Tree Hotel
Killin, Dall Lodge Hotel
Kinross, Windlestrae Hotel
LochGilphead, Empire Travellers Lodge
Markinch, Balbirnie House Hotel
Mey, Castle Arms Hotel
Old Rayne, Mill Croft Guest House
Onich, The Lodge On The Loch Hotel
Perth, Ballathie House Hotel
Perth, Glencarse Hotel
Pitlochry, Craigvrack Hotel
Spean Bridge, Niall & Sukie Scott, Old Pines

Accommodation for Wheelchair Users without Assistance
Aberdeen, Altens Skean Dhu Hotel
Clydebank, Glasgow, The Patio Hotel
Edinburgh, Sheraton Grand Hotel
Glasgow, Glasgow Hilton
Gretna Green, Forte Travelodge , Welcome Break
Irvine, Irvine Hospitality Inn
Rhu, Rosslea Hall Hotel
Stirling, Stirling Management Centre
Whiting Bay, Grange House Hotel

Accommodation for Disabled Resident Guests only
Aberdeen, Gordon Hotel
Callander, Roman Camp Hotel
Dalbeattie, Auchenskeoch Lodge
Dumfries, Hetland Hall House
Inverness, Glen Mhor Hotel & Restaurant

Le secret de très

Lorsque vous choisissez vos vacances par correspondance, la qualité et le confort sont trop importants pour être laissés au hasard.

C'est pourquoi, depuis 1985, le STB inspecte systématiquement les hìtels, pensions de famille et "bed & breakfasts", déterminant la qualité à laquelle nos visiteurs s'attendent et aidant les propriétaires et les organisateurs à offrir cette qualité. Les établissements dans tout le pays, du plus simple au plus sophistiqué, sont NOTES en fonction de leur qualité et CLASSES en fonction des aménagements offerts.

Voici comment le système fonctionne.

Repérez des plaques ovales bleues arborées par les établissements adhérant au système de NOTATION et de CLASSEMENT.

Le centre de la plaque vous indique si l'établissement est noté APPROVED (qualité raisonnable), COMMENDED (bonne qualité), HIGHLY COMMENDED (très bonne qualité) ou DELUXE (excellente qualité).

Ces NOTES sont attribuées par les inspecteurs du STB une fois qu'ils ont vérifié tous les facteurs importants contribuant à la qualité d'un établissement. Comme vous le feriez, ils recherchent un cadre propre et agréable, bien meublé et bien chauffé. Ils goûtent aux repas, dorment dans les lits et parlent au personnel. Comme vous, ils apprécient une ambiance et un cadre agréable et un sourire accueillant.

bonnes vacances!

Scottish Tourist Board

COMMENDED

Facilities

Le bas de la plaque indique le classement par COURONNES, en fonction de la gamme d'aménagements et de services proposés - le classement va de LISTED à 5 COURONNES. Les critères se cumulent et tous les critères doivent être satisfaits pour chaque niveau jusqu'au nombre de COURONNES affiché.

Le tableau ci-dessous vous donnera une idée de certains des aménagements auxquels vous pouvez vous attendre à chaque niveau. Pour recevoir une liste complète de tous les critères de classement par COURONNES, contactez le STB, 23 Ravelston Terrace, Edinburgh EH4 3EU Tél.: (0)31 332 2433

	1	2	3	4	5
Etablissement propre et confortable	•	•	•	•	•
Moyens de chauffage adéquats sans supplément de prix petit déjeuner	•	•	•	•	•
Lavabo dans la chambre ou dans une salle de bains attenante	•	•	•	•	•
Clef de chambre fournie		•	•	•	•
Coin salon commun		•	•	•	•
TV couleur dans les chambres ou dans le salon 20% des chambres ont une salle de bains attenante		•	•	•	•
Possibilité de se faire servir thé/café dans la chambre le matins			•	•	•
Repas chaud le soir jusqu'à 19H			•	•	•
50% des chambres ont une salle de bains attenante			•	•	•
Accès 24 heures sur 24 pour les clients inscrits			•	•	•
Radio, TV couleur et téléphone dans toutes les chambres				•	•
Boissons et en-cas servis dans la chambre entre 7H et 23H				•	•
Salle de bains attenante avec baignoire et douche dans toutes les chambres				•	•
Au moins 1 suite et diverses possibilités de service dans la chambre					•
Restaurant ouvert pour le petit déjeuner, le déjeuner et le dâner					•

En 1993 le STB a introduit un classement pour les bungalows. Ce mode d'hébergement vous propose une salle de bains attenante dans toutes les chambres, des possibilités de restauration sur place ou non loin, mais des services supplémentaires restreints.

Plus de 3300 établissements avec service - 38000 chambres - partout en Ecosse, sont membres du système de notation et de classement.

RESERVATIONS DIRECTES? RESERVATIONS PAR LE BIAIS DU TOURIST INFORMATION CENTRE? N'OUBLIEZ PAS DE VERIFIER LA NOTATION ET LE CLASSEMENT PAR COURONNES DE L'ETABLISSEMENT CHOISI.

Ihr Schlüssel zu einem

Bei der Auswahl Ihrer Urlaubsunterkunft sollten Sie Qualität und Komfort nicht dem Zufall überlassen.

Daher unterzieht der STB seit 1985 alljährlich Hotels, Pensionen und "Bed & Breakfast"-Unterkünfte einer Prüfung. Wir definieren die Standards, die unsere Gäste von uns erwarten, und helfen Eigentümern und Veranstaltern dabei, diese Standards einzuhalten. Von Bedienungspersonal versorgte Unterkünfte in ganz Schottland – von den einfachsten bis zu den anspruchsvollsten – werden mit einer GRADIERUNG als Qualitätsauszeichnung sowie einer KLASSIFIKATION je nach Zahl der vorhandenen Einrichtungen versehen.

Und so funktioniert es:
Achten Sie auf die ovalen blauen Plaketten, die von Mitgliedern des GRADIERUNGS- und KLASSIFIKATIONS-Schemas ausgehängt werden.
Auf dem Mittelteil der Plakette wird die jeweilige Unterkunft folgendermaßen eingestuft:
APPROVED (angemessener Standard), COMMENDED (guter Standard), HIGHLY COMMENDED (sehr guter Standard) oder DELUXE (ausgezeichneter Standard).
Diese GRADIERUNGEN werden von Prüfern des STB vergeben, nachdem diese alle wichtigen Faktoren untersucht haben, auf die es bei der Qualität einer Unterkunft ankommt. Wie auch Sie achten die Prüfer auf saubere, attraktive Unterkünfte, gut eingerichtet und beheizt. Sie essen und übernachten in den Unterkünften und unterhalten sich mit dem Personal. Wie auch Sie legen die Prüfer Wert auf Atmosphäre und ein freundliches Lächeln zur Begrüßung.

Der untere Teil der Plakette zeigt die KRONEN-Klassifikation, welche den Umfang der vorhandenen Einrichtungen angibt. Die niedrigste Klassifikation ist LISTED, der bis zu 5 KRONEN hinzugefügt werden können. Höhere Klassifikationen bauen auf jeweils niedrigeren auf, und die Gesamtzahl der KRONEN gewährleistet die volle Zahl an Einrichtungen für diese Klassifikationsstufe.

Scottish Tourist Board

COMMENDED

Facilities

Die folgende Tabelle gibt Ihnen eine Vorstellung von einigen der Einrichtungen, die Sie für jede der Stufen erwarten können. Ein vollständiges Verzeichnis aller Kriterien des KRONEN-Klassifikationssystems erhalten Sie von: STB, 23 Ravelston Terrace, Edinburgh EH4 3EU Tel.: (0)31 332 2433.

	1	2	3	4	5
Saubere, komfortable Unterkunft	•	•	•	•	•
Angemessene Beheizung ohne Aufpreis	•	•	•	•	•
Waschbecken im Zimmer oder in eigenem Bad	•	•	•	•	•
Eigener Zimmerschlüssel		•	•	•	•
Gemeinschaftsbercich (Lounge)		•	•	•	•
Farbfernsehen im Zimmer oder in Gäste-Lounge		•	•	•	•
Tee/Kaffee frühmorgens			•	•	•
Warme Küche bis 19.00 Uhr			•	•	•
50% aller Zimmer mit eigenem Bad			•	•	•
24 Stunden Zugang für eingetragene Gäste			•	•	•
Radio, Farbfernsehen und Telefon in allen Zimmern				•	•
Zimmerservice mit Getränken und Snacks von 19.00-23.00 Uhr				•	•
Alle Zimmer mit eigenem Bad und Dusche				•	•
Mindestens 1 Suite und ausgedehnter Zimmerservice					•
Restaurant für Frühstück, Mittag- und Abendessen					•

1993 hat der STB auch eine Klassifikation für Ferienwohnungen eingeführt. Hier sind alle Unterkünfte mit eigenem Bad, und Abendmahlzeiten sind entweder auf dem Gelände oder in der Nähe verfügbar; zusätzliche Einrichtungen sind jedoch nur beschränkt vorhanden.

Über 3.300 von Bedienungspersonal versorgte Unterkünfte in allen Landesteilen Schottlands, mit insgesamt über 38,000 Zimmern, sind Mitglieder des Gradierungs- und Klassifikationsschemas.

DIREKTBUCHUNG? BUCHUNG ÜBER EIN TOURIST INFORMATION CENTRE? ACHTEN SIE STETS AUF DIE GRADIERUNG UND KRONEN-KLASSIFIKATION DER UNTERKUNFT IHRER WAHL.

GROUP HOTELS

Alloa Hotels in Scotland
Anderston House
389 Argyle Street
Glasgow G2 8LQ
Tel: 041 226 4271
Fax: 041 221 7932
Price per person occupying a single room B&B
from £34 to £52.
Price per person sharing a double/twin room B&B
from £27.50 to £37.50.
Price per one person dinner/B&B on application.
Special packages and reduced rates available.
Hotels located from Helensburgh across to Loch
Lomond and the Trossachs, across the central belt,
Glasgow to Edinburgh, and from the east coast to
Dundee and Aberdeen.

Best Western Hotels
Vine House
143 London Road
Kingston Upon Thames
Surrey KT2 6NA
Tel: 081 541 0033
Fax: 081 546 1638
Telex: 8814912 BW HOTL G
Price per person sharing a double/twin room B&B
from £29.
Price per one person dinner/B&B from £38 (min 2
nights).
Commission paid to travel agents by arrangement.
Special packages and reduced rates available.
Over 20 hotels located from the Lowlands to the
Highlands.

Cairn Hotels
c/o The Golden Circle Hotel
Blackburn Road
Bathgate EH48 2EL
Tel: 0506 636696
Fax: 0506 52540
Price per one person occupying a single room B&B
from £27.
Price per one person sharing a double/twin room
from £35.
Price per one person dinner/B&B from £29.50.
Commission paid to travel agents by arrangement.
Special packages and reduced rates available.
Hotels located throughout Scotland.

Croft Hotels Ltd
Ryedale Building
Piccadilly
York YO1 1PN
Tel: 0904 450 455
Fax: 0904 612 725
Telex: 57476
Price per person occupying a single room B&B
from £60.
Price per person sharing a double/twin room B&B
from £75.
Price per one person dinner/B&B from £48.
Commission paid to travel agents by arrangement.
Special packages and reduced rates available.
2 centrally located hotels in Edinburgh and one in
the heart of Fife's golfing country.

Milton Hotels
Central Reservations
North Road
Fort William PH33 6TG
Tel: 0397 703139
Fax: 0397 703695
Price per person occupying a single room B&B
from £39.
Price per person sharing a double/twin room B&B
from £29.
Price per one person dinner/B&B from £34.50.
Commission paid to travel agents by arrangement.
Special packages and reduced rates available.
Hotels located throughout Scotland, in the main
centres of Oban, Fort William, Stirling and
Inverness.

North British Trust Hotels
1 Queen Charlotte Lane
Edinburgh EH6 6BL
Tel: 031 554 7173
Fax: 031 554 8213
Price per person occupying a single room B&B by
negotiation.
Price per person sharing a double/twin room B&B
by negotiation.
Commission paid to travel agents by arrangement.
Special packages and reduced rates available.
Hotels located throughout Scotland, including 17
in Edinburgh, and others situated in Callander,
Gretna Green, Arrochar, Oban, Mull, Fort William,
Skye, Ullapool, Inverness, Grantown-on-Spey,
Ballater and Pitlochry.

GROUP HOTELS

Scotland's Commended
19 Dixon Street
Glasgow G1 4AJ
Tel: 041 221 2300
Fax: 041 221 5443
Price per person occupying a single room B&B on application.
Price per person sharing a double/twin room B&B on application.
Price per person dinner/B&B on application.
Commission paid to travel agents by arrangement.
Special packages and reduced rates available.
Hotels located throughout Scotland.

Scotland's Heritage Hotels
Suite 2D, Churchill Way
Bishopbriggs
Glasgow G64 2RH
Tel: 041 772 6911
Fax: 041 772 6917
Telex: 777205 INSCOT G
Price per person occupying a single room B&B from £50.
Price per person sharing a double/twin room B&B from £40.
Price per one person dinner/B&B from £57.
Commission paid to travel agents by arrangement.
Special packages and reduced rates available.
Hotels located throughout Scotland.

WALKERBURN, Peeblesshire

TWEED VALLEY
HOTEL *by PEEBLES* 🏵🏵🏵🏵 Commended
WALKERBURN, PEEBLESSHIRE
Tel: (089 687) 636 Fax: (089 687) 639

Escape from cares of the world to a warm country house, en-suite rooms in scenic hill country overlooking River Tweed.

À la carte menus with fresh food and herbs from our own garden. Bars and lounge log fires. Salmon and trout fishing with tuition and tackle, golf on quiet courses. Birdwatching, walking, sightseeing and shopping with wool, cashmere and tartan mill discounts for guests. Art and photography courses. Sauna and solarium. Edinburgh 40 minutes. DB&B from £48.50.

For full details contact Charles Miller, Tweed Valley Hotel and Restaurant, Walkerburn EH43 6AA. Tel: (089 687) 636. Fax: (089 687) 639.

BY KYLE OF LOCHALSH, Westr Ross

THE BALMACARA HOTEL
by KYLE OF LOCHALSH, WESTER ROSS IV40 8DH
Telephone: 059 986 283 Fax: 059 986 329

On the shores of Loch Alsh stands the Balmacara Hotel. Set amongst the glorious hills of Wester Ross overlooking Skye, the hotel aims to make your stay as memorable as the views. A 2 star hotel, fully en-suite, satellite TV, sea facing rooms and restaurant with gastronomic delights specially prepared.

ISLE OF JURA, Argyll

JURA HOTEL
Tel: 049 682243
Fax: 049 682249
ISLE OF JURA · ARGYLL · PA60 7XU

Comfortable, family-run hotel providing an ideal base for exploring this unspoilt island. Climb the Paps, see the Corryvreckan Whirlpool, watch the plentiful wildlife, deer, eagles, otters, etc and come back to warmth, comfort and good food based on local produce.

For details contact: Steve and Fiona Walton, Managers.

BE SURE TO CHOOSE THE SCOTTISH TOURIST BOARD'S SIGN OF QUALITY

Discover the Stakis Tradition

To stay at a Stakis hotel is to experience a tradition of quality and service — a reputation we've been building for 50 years.  From restored country houses to modern city centre hotels and from the Highlands of Scotland to the Garden of England, we offer a memorable variety of styles and convenient locations. A commitment to the satisfaction of our guests however is common throughout. Whichever hotel you choose, you'll remember value for money, fine cuisine and efficient service from friendly, professional staff. And whatever your reason for travelling, you'll find a warm welcome at all our hotels. So discover the Stakis Tradition soon — you'll remember the difference.

STAKIS HOTELS
Central Reservations
0800 26 26 26

Aberdeen · Aviemore · Birmingham-Bromsgrove · Bracknell-Wokingham · Bradford · Bristol · Cardiff-Newport · Dartford Bridge · Dundee · Dunkeld · Edinburgh · Falkirk · Glasgow · Glasgow Airport · Gourock · Keswick · Leeds · Leicester · London · Maidstone · Newbury · Northampton · Nottingham · Paisley · Perth · Stirling-Dunblane · Stoke-on-Trent

390

COXSTOOL, WEST WEMYSS, Fife

The Belvedere
Coxstool, West Wemyss, Fife KY1 4SL
Tel: (0592) 654167   Fax: (0592) 655279

The Belvedere is situated on the waterfront at the heart of the beautiful Fife coastline.
The twenty one en-suite bedrooms all enjoy an excellent view of the Forth and are equipped with the sort of facilities expected of a quality establishment.
Two bars, and The Waterside dining room with outstanding views provide a first class setting for enjoying the best of the fresh local produce accompanied by a range of quality wines from all over the globe.
As a centre for exploring historic Fife, seeing the sights of Edinburgh, playing Golf in the district, or just for relaxing, the Belvedere is the perfect venue.

For reservations, contact Guy Berger on the above number.

BRIDGE OF ALLAN, Stirlingshire

THE ROYAL HOTEL
55 Henderson Road. Bridge of Allan, Stirlingshire, FK9 4HG.
Tel: (0786) 832284 Fax: (0786) 834377
Built in 1842 and situated in the university town of Bridge of Allan this impressive hotel has been recently extensively refurbished. Close to Edinburgh, Glasgow and major tourist centres. Scotland's history and rich heritage virtually on the doorstep makes the Royal an excellent choice for the visitor. Associate hotels at Troon and Perth.
★★★ AA & RAC   Commended

ROY BRIDGE, Inverness-shire

Stronlossit Hotel & Restaurant
ROY BRIDGE · INVERNESS-SHIRE PH31 4AG
Telephone: 0397 712 253
Centrally situated for touring the Scottish Highlands, offering en-suite bedrooms with colour TV, tea/coffee facilities and full central heating. Lounge bar with log fire.
Excellent bar meals and restaurant.
Also 3-bedroomed apartment available.
B&B 3 nights £72.00. All major credit cards accepted.

SCOTTISH TOURIST BOARD
QUALITY COMMENDATIONS ARE:
Deluxe – *An EXCELLENT quality standard*
Highly Commended – *A VERY GOOD quality standard*
Commended – *A GOOD quality standard*
Approved – *An ADEQUATE quality standard*

NOTES